STUDIES IN BAPTIST HISTORY AND THOUGHT
VOLUME 23

Paradox and Perseverance

Hanserd Knollys, Particular Baptist Pioneer in
Seventeenth-Century England

STUDIES IN BAPTIST HISTORY AND THOUGHT
VOLUME 23

A full listing of titles in this series
appears at the end of this book

Hanserd Knollys c. 1674

Used by permission of the Principal and
Fellows of Regent's Park College, Oxford

STUDIES IN BAPTIST HISTORY AND THOUGHT
VOLUME 23

Paradox and Perseverance

Hanserd Knollys, Particular Baptist Pioneer in Seventeenth-Century England

Dennis C. Bustin

Foreword by Ian Gentles

PUBLISHERS
Eugene, Oregon

Wipf and Stock Publishers
199 W 8th Ave, Suite 3
Eugene, OR 97401

Paradox and Perseverance
Hanserd Knollys, Particular Baptist Pioneer in Seventeenth–Century England
By Bustin, Dennis C.
Copyright©2006 Paternoster
ISBN 13: 978-1-59752-874-0
ISBN 10: 1-59752-874-9
Publication date 8/11/2006
Previously published by Paternoster, 2006

This Edition Published by Wipf and Stock Publishers by arrangement with Paternoster

Paternoster
9 Holdom Avenue
Bletchley
Milton Keyes, MK1 1QR
Great Britain

STUDIES IN BAPTIST HISTORY AND THOUGHT

Series Preface

Baptists form one of the largest Christian communities in the world, and while they hold the historic faith in common with other mainstream Christian traditions, they nevertheless have important insights which they can offer to the worldwide church. *Studies in Baptist History and Thought* will be one means towards this end. It is an international series of academic studies which includes original monographs, revised dissertations, collections of essays and conference papers, and aims to cover any aspect of Baptist history and thought. While not all the authors are themselves Baptists, they nevertheless share an interest in relating Baptist history and thought to the other branches of the Christian church and to the wider life of the world.

The series includes studies in various aspects of Baptist history from the seventeenth century down to the present day, including biographical works, and Baptist thought is understood as covering the subject-matter of theology (including interdisciplinary studies embracing biblical studies, philosophy, sociology, practical theology, liturgy and women's studies). The diverse streams of Baptist life throughout the world are all within the scope of these volumes.

The series editors and consultants believe that the academic disciplines of history and theology are of vital importance to the spiritual vitality of the churches of the Baptist faith and order. The series sets out to discuss, examine and explore the many dimensions of their tradition and so to contribute to their on-going intellectual vigour.

A brief word of explanation is due for the series identifier on the front cover. The fountains, taken from heraldry, represent the Baptist distinctive of believer's baptism and, at the same time, the source of the water of life. There are three of them because they symbolize the Trinitarian basis of Baptist life and faith. Those who are redeemed by the Lamb, the book of Revelation reminds us, will be led to 'fountains of living waters' (Rev. 7.17).

Series Editors

Anthony R. Cross, Fellow of the Centre for Baptist History and Heritage, Regent's Park College, Oxford, UK

Curtis W. Freeman, Research Professor of Theology and Director of the Baptist House of Studies, Duke University, North Carolina, USA

Stephen R. Holmes, Lecturer in Theology, University of St Andrews, Scotland, UK

Elizabeth Newman, Professor of Theology and Ethics, Baptist Theological Seminary at Richmond, Virginia, USA

Philip E. Thompson, Assistant Professor of Systematic Theology and Christian Heritage, North American Baptist Seminary, Sioux Falls, South Dakota, USA

Series Consultant Editors

David Bebbington, Professor of History, University of Stirling, Scotland, UK

Paul S. Fiddes, Professor of Systematic Theology, University of Oxford, and Principal of Regent's Park College, Oxford, UK

† Stanley J. Grenz, Pioneer McDonald Professor of Theology, Carey Theological College, Vancouver, British Columbia, Canada

Ken R. Manley, Distinguished Professor of Church History, Whitley College, The University of Melbourne, Australia

Stanley E. Porter, President and Professor of New Testament, McMaster Divinity College, Hamilton, Ontario, Canada

Diane, Jay, and Abby: I thank God for you daily. To you, I dedicate this work for your love and untiring strength.
This is our accomplishment.
Jay and Abby, you are the best children a man could have. You have patiently waited, as Dad's elusive deadline always seemed just about there – first the dissertation, then the book! Thanks for your endurance and encouragement.

Diane, you have been my faithful partner through this, a true companion and support through my many years of study and research. Your love and confidence in me have made this possible. I am thankful to God for a wife and partner such as you. I could ask for no better.

Contents

Foreword by Ian Gentles	xiii
Acknowledgements	xv
Introduction	1
Chapter 1 – Hanserd Knollys: Seventeenth-Century Radical Conservative. An Introduction and Historiographical Overview	1
Introduction	1
Historiographical Overview	7
Works on Radical Religion and Dissent	7
Baptist Histories	16
Biographies of Knollys	22
Chapter 2 – The Early Years: From Lincoln to New England	27
Introduction	27
Lincolnshire Years	29
Cambridge and Ordination	35
Ministry and Marriage	38
New England	48
Conclusion	65
Chapter 3 – Hanserd Knollys and the Particular Baptists' Struggle for Legitimacy in the 1640s	68
Introduction	68
Back in London	73
The Presbyterians and the Independents	83
Knollys and the Baptist Cause – Confessions and Debates	93
Knollys' Publications and the Struggle for Legitimacy	100

A Moderate Answer Unto Dr. Bastwicks Book	103
The Shining of a Flaming Fire In Zion	108
Conclusion	114

Chapter 4 – Hanserd Knollys and the Struggle for Legitimacy: Levellers, Quakers, and the Fifth Monarch Movement — 117

Introduction	117
The Levellers	120
Knollys' Activities during the Commonwealth Period	128
Knollys' Writings during the Commonwealth Period	136
The Quakers	141
The Fifth Monarchy Movement	155
Conclusion	169

Chapter 5 – Testings, Trials, and Tribulations: Knollys' Life during the Restoration — 171

Introduction	171
Restoration and Renewed Persecution	172
Personal Tragedy	180
Financial Troubles	183
Pastoral Ministry, Peace, and Popish Plots	185
Renewed Persecution and the Glorious Revolution	188
Conclusion	191

Chapter 6 – "The World That Now Is And the World That Is To Come": Knollys' Use and Interpretation of Apocalyptic Literature — 192

Introduction	192
Overview of Knollys' Eschatological Works	198
Themes in Knollys' Eschatological Works	207
Antichrist	208
The Second Coming of Christ	214
The Millennium	223
The Eschaton	228
Conclusion	230

Chapter 7 – A Sect No More: Hanserd Knollys' Role in Particular Baptist Formalisation   235

Introduction   235
Polity – Independence and Interdependence   239
Theology – Puritan and Orthodox?   249
   Reformed Doctrine   251
   Evangelical Emphasis   259
Of Ministers and the Ministry   263
The Sacraments/Ordinances   275
   Baptism   277
   The Lord's Supper   282
Corporate Worship   290
   Seventh-Day Sabbath   291
   Singing in Public Worship   293
   Women and their Role   300
Conclusion   305

Epilogue – The Twilight Years: "An Inheritance among them which are Sanctified"   310

Conclusion   318

Appendices   324
Appendix 1: Hanserd Knollys' Date of Birth   324
Appendix 2: The Will of Christobel Lacon, Grandmother of Hanserd Knollys   329
Appendix 3: Hanserd Knollys' Continuing Ministry in Lincolnshire   330
Appendix 4: Children of Hanserd and Anne (Cheney) Knollys   335
   Sons   336
   Daughters   341
Appendix 5: Maps   342
   Figure 1: Lincolnshire   342
   Figure 2: New England in the 1630s   343
   Figure 3: New Hampshire in the 1630s   344

Bibliography   345
Works by Hanserd Knollys   345

Publications and Treatises	345
Prefaces in Works of Others	346
Written with Others	346
Primary Sources	347
Publications and Treatises	347
Manuscripts	350
Records	351
Diaries and Journals	352
Published Collections	353
Secondary Sources	353

Indices — **366**

Index of Names	366
Index of Places	370
General Index	372

Foreword

The seventeenth century was a significant period in English history. During this time, the people of England experienced unprecedented change and tumult in the political, social, and religious spheres of life. At the same time, the importance of order and the traditional institutions of society were being reinforced. Hanserd Knollys was born during this pivotal period and personified in his life the ambiguity, tension, and paradox of it, openly seeking change while at the same time, cautiously embracing order. As a founder and leader of the Particular Baptists in London, he played a critical role in helping shape their identity externally in society and internally, as they moved toward becoming more formalised. Yet Knollys has received little scholarly attention.

This work is an original and worthwhile contribution to knowledge. Dennis C. Bustin has an excellent command of the secondary material in his field, and has carried out exhaustive primary research. The result is a well-rounded, judicious, and accurate biography of one of the key founders of the Baptist Denomination in England. More than merely a biography of Hanserd Knollys, this work places Knollys within the turbulent social context of seventeenth-century England, while at the same time providing a careful analysis of his thought.

Paradox and Perseverance provides a fascinating account of Knollys' life, following him from his early years, through the periods of the Civil War, the Interregnum, and the Restoration. Throughout the book, Dr. Bustin emphasises that graciousness and humility were the leading characteristics that Knollys demonstrated in his personal life and in his dealings with others. He also examines the Particular Baptists' struggle for legitimacy in the 1640s and 1650s, highlighting the role played by Knollys. Through his writings and participation in disputations, he sought to align the Particular Baptists with the Independents and the Presbyterians, while at the same time distancing them from the more radical groups – the Levellers, Quakers and Fifth Monarchists. Dr. Bustin vividly recreates the suffering that Knollys and other religious separatists underwent with the revival of religious persecution after 1660. Knollys' struggles and personal tragedy shaped his eschatology and informed his apocalyptic understanding of current events through to the Glorious

Revolution of 1688. Bustin's final achievement is to underscore the role Hanserd Knollys played in the institutional emergence of the Particular Baptist denomination. The appendices are useful and welcome in clearing up the confusion surrounding Knollys' birth date, and in establishing that he was indeed a clergyman of the parish church in his role as rector of Scartho, Lincs. during the 1640s and 1650s.

Dr. Bustin has written an admirable book that carefully works through significant primary and secondary material. Overall, *Paradox and Perseverance* attains a high scholarly standard, and also enriches our understanding of the religious history of the English Revolution.

Ian Gentles
York University
December 2005

Acknowledgements

I am overwhelmed as I begin to ponder the many people who have contributed to this work. First, I wish to acknowledge the many workers in the numerous libraries and archives, both in North America and in Great Britain, who have assisted me in finding and copying important books and records for my work. Special thanks to Ivan Douthwright and the staff of the George A. Rawlyk Library at Atlantic Baptist University and to the staff (especially interlibrary loans) of the Stauffer Library at Queen's University. Also thanks to Susan Mills, archivist of the Angus Library at Regent's Park College, Oxford University for her assistance early in my research. I also want to thank Angeline Quek for creating the maps for me. These will certainly help those of my readers who tend to learn 'visually'. To my colleagues at Atlantic Baptist University, for your support, encouragement, stimulating discussion, and friendship, I thank you. Special thanks to Dan Goodwin, my fellow historian, and to Seth Crowell, friend as well as V. P. Academic. Together you have spurred me on, all the while understanding the restraints of the academic year.

Every scholarly pursuit follows a trail of inspirations. I acknowledge all those who have taught me at some post-secondary level. However, a few stand apart as inspiring me in special ways. Dr. Steve Dempster, once my teacher, now my colleague; thank-you for teaching me to love academia without ever abandoning my first love. The late Dr. William Nigel Kerr, whose love of history was infectious, even though at the time I was pursuing New Testament studies. Dr. Gary Pratico, 'the velvet hammer'; you taught me many lessons about being a scholar *and* a teacher. Dr. Paul Christianson, my Ph.D. supervisor; you took a New Testament scholar and gave me a passion for Stuart England as well. Thanks for helping me 'shift gears', so to speak. Your scrupulous editing and thoughtful comments have been invaluable, second only to your encouraging spirit. Also, thanks to Anthony Cross at Paternoster, who allowed me the opportunity to share this fruit of my research with a wider audience and who has prepared the text for publication. Any errors or oversights in this work are my own.

Enough can never be said about family. My 'faith' family has been very important to me and has served as a wonderful support. My friends at Bay Park Baptist Church in Kingston played an especially vital role during my Ph.D.

studies at Queen's and during those many times I returned to write and do research. Thanks for allowing us to be part of your 'family'. Special thanks to Ken and Brenda Bartlett, our 'family away from family'. Thank-you for your friendship during the years we lived in Kingston and for the futon, food, and deeper friendship during my research and writing trips to Kingston. In giving me a home for so many weeks, you have played a crucial part in this work. To my brothers and sisters at Hillside Baptist Church in Moncton, especially those in my small group: You have been an unending source of joy and encouragement through this process. I count many of you as precious friends. Thank-you.

I find it difficult to know how to express my gratitude to my family. Words seem trite. To all my family, thanks. Don and Peggy Bustin, my parents: For the years of love and sacrifice, for always believing in me, for showing me what love is and for introducing me to the Love that will never let me go, I thank you with all my heart. You are the best! Brad and Annie Ripley, my parents through marriage: For all you have done for us, the support, encouragement, and all the little things you do, I thank you. I could not have done this without your faithful expressions of love. Diane, Jay, and Abby: Your support and encouragement have been a source of constant joy. I could never express my appreciation adequately.

Finally, yet pre-eminently, I give thanks to my heavenly Father, Who has blessed me beyond my wildest dreams, and to Christ Jesus, Who daily gives me hope (Ephesians 1:3-8) and strength (Philippians 3:14). May I faithfully press forward as did "that Old Disciple of Jesus Christ", Hanserd Knollys.

Atlantic Baptist University
August 2005

CHAPTER 1

Hanserd Knollys: Seventeenth-Century Radical Conservative

Introduction and Historiographical Overview

Introduction

It was the best of times, it was the worst of times, it was the age of wisdom, it was the age of foolishness, it was the epoch of belief, it was the epoch of incredulity, it was the season of Light, it was the season of Darkness, it was the spring of hope, it was the winter of despair, we had everything before us, we had nothing before us, we were all going direct to Heaven, we were all going direct the other way....[1]

Although Charles Dickens penned these words concerning the eve of the French Revolution, more than a century beyond the events and times considered in this present work, in some ways, these words appropriately describe England in the seventeenth century. If could choose two words that effectively illustrate the overall tenor of English society in the seventeenth century, those words would be paradox and change. Although each century and generation has experienced periods of change and uncertainty, the shifting tides of early-modern Britain served as the seedbed to an entirely new understanding of life and society. Traditional assumptions regarding authority and order began to be questioned and in some instances discarded, even though many contemporaries remained highly suspect about innovation. Education and literacy had shown significant expansion as the printed word became more readily available and affordable. For some, this new medium presented a genuine danger, for others, a great opportunity. The decline of disease and warfare and advancements in agriculture had created a growing, yet stable population. Expansion in trade and commerce was redefining society, as the new middling group became a more significant force in society, challenging the

---

[1] Charles Dickens, *A Tale of Two Cities*, (New York: Penguin Books, 1985), p. 35.

role of the aristocracy and agrarian society. In the previous century, the Reformation on the Continent and in England had thrown open the floodgates of religion, creating a diversity and openness never before known, challenging the order and hegemony of the institutional churches. Although scepticism and disbelief would come to a fuller fruition in a later generation, incredulity regarding traditionally established religion flourished. Overall, the role of the individual was becoming progressively significant. In the midst of this shifting, changing world, paradox came to be evident in all aspects of life.

People and their lives are reflections of their contexts and times. This becomes increasingly clear as one immerses oneself in the life of another. Biographical research has fallen out of fashion in recent years, particularly with the demise of 'the great man' approach to history, except, perhaps, in the case of individuals who were members of minorities or of social groups now considered to be politically and socially in vogue. However, the historian can glean much about a period by exploring and, to a certain degree, experiencing the life and context of a person who lived during that period. The life of Hanserd Knollys provides a microcosm of many of the changes and paradoxes of seventeenth-century England and is therefore significant for several reasons. First, his life spanned nearly the entire century; he lived under the rule of all but one of the Stuart monarchs.[2] Second, his religious experience was a collage, which included ordination in the Church of England, nonconformity, persecution and exile, involvement in theological debates, and participation in the struggle for the establishment of a limited toleration in England. Third, Knollys was a man of diverse geographical experience. His experiences took him from Lincoln, through university at Cambridge, to London and the heart of English society. Although he spent a number of formative years in New England and had brief stays in Holland and the German states, Knollys preached, taught, and traded for most of his life in London.

The activities with which Knollys involved himself are also a testimony to the diverse milieu of his life and times. He spent much of his life in pastoral ministry, first within the Established Church of England, but mostly in a Baptist congregation he gathered in London in the mid-1640s and continued to pastor until his death. However, he did much more beyond pastoral ministry. An educated man, Knollys' love of learning never dimmed as evidenced by his writing and teaching activities, which continued throughout his life. He also became involved in government employment (in the custom and excise offices) and in overseas trade and merchandising, the latter most likely in conjunction with his close friend and fellow Particular Baptist, William Kiffin.

A broad and diverse group of people interacted with Knollys at various points in his life – men and women from all walks and stations of life – including people such as John Wheelwright, the Puritan minister who fled to

---

[2] In fact, if one accepts the traditional date of his birth, his life began in the twilight of the reign of Elizabeth I. For more on this, see Appendix 1.

New England only to become embroiled in the Antinomian controversy; John Winthrop, many times the governor of Massachusetts and perhaps one of the most influential men in Massachusetts during the early years of the colony; Christian Ravis, a prominent scholar of languages; John Williams, one time chaplain and Lord Keeper of James I, who became Bishop of Lincoln, Archbishop of York, and arch-rival of William Laud, Archbishop of Canterbury; Lord and Lady Willoughby, 5th Baron and Baroness of Parham; Dr. John Bastwick, physician, prominent Presbyterian, and staunch opponent of Archbishop Laud during the 1630s and of diverse religious sects in England during the 1640s; Henry Jessey, pastor of the famous Independent church in London known as the Jacob/Lathrop/Jessey Church[3]; William Kiffin and Benjamin Cox, two prominent Particular Baptist leaders; and Bulstrode Whitelock, Commissioner of the Great Seal and member of the Long Parliament, a governor of the Charterhouse School, and the author of one of the most complete accounts of the reign of Charles I, the English Civil War, and the Interregnum.

Born in 1609 and living until 1691, Knollys was involved as one of the founders of the Particular Baptist denomination. He served as a major participant in its struggle for recognition and tolerance, and as a partaker of its success during the 1640s and 1650s and of the persecution of the 1660s, 1670s, and 1680s. His old age allowed him to witness the limited fulfilment of the quest for toleration shortly after the accession of William of Orange and his wife Mary Stuart to the throne of England. It also permitted him the opportunity of having a significant role in the development of the Particular Baptists as they evolved from a new, and often abused, sect in the 1640s into a more organised and orthodox denomination by the end of the century. For much of his life, Knollys played a key role as the Particular Baptists sought to establish themselves in the religious milieu of the time as legitimate, orderly, and orthodox, while at the same time attempting to distance themselves from what they perceived as illegitimate, disorderly, and heretical sects, such as the Quakers, Levellers, and Fifth Monarchists. Through his published treatises, preaching, and his participation in various public disputations, Knollys played a leading role in this process. Not only did Knollys' play an important part in the Particular Baptists' establishment of relationships within society at large, but he also had significant influence as they developed their own ecclesiology. In terms of helping shape Particular Baptist doctrinal positions, Knollys participated in the formulation of Particular Baptist Confessions of Faith and was involved in internal disputes on polity. Knollys' evangelistic fervour led

---

[3] In reality, this was not purely an Independent church, but a gathered church of mixed believers, some of whom held to the practice adult baptism and some of whom were paedobaptists, but who nevertheless determined to continue to gather together. See Murray Tolmie, *The Triumph of the Saints: The separate churches of London 1616-1649*, (London: Cambridge University Press, 1977), pp. 7-27.

him to be involved in planting new Particular Baptist churches, both within London and in the rural regions of England and Wales. He was also instrumental in organising the first General Assembly of the Particular Baptists "from divers parts of England and Wales" in London in September 1689.[4]

Despite this obvious leadership role, Knollys has received relatively little scholarly attention. Although recognised and respected for his leadership in his own day and in the generation following, his contributions were gradually lost on subsequent generations. Several journal articles and shorter works have been undertaken on Hanserd Knollys, but apart from one Ph.D. thesis, no significant scholarly work has resulted.[5] Many of the works about Knollys tend to be Baptist publications and serve as an apologetic for Knollys or an elucidation of his theological position. Others, due to their brevity, tend to be more general in their treatment of his life in the context of seventeenth-century England.[6] Since Knollys played such a seminal role, not only in the development of the Baptist denomination, but also in the development of English dissent, a work such as this one is long overdue. Therefore, it is the intent of this work to provide a solid biographical overview of Hanserd Knollys, not only as a Particular Baptist, but as a seventeenth-century radical reformer and Englishman as well. This work will address aspects of his thought within the social, religious, and political context of his day. It will contend that Hanserd Knollys was influenced and shaped by two diametrically opposed aspects of seventeenth-century society, the religious and social order represented by the Established Church and the attraction of Apostolic purity promised by more radical Protestant religious groups, and that he struggled to reconcile these seemingly opposite

---

[4] *A Narrative of the Proceedings of the General Assembly Of divers Pastors, Messengers, and Ministering Brethren of the Baptized Churches, met together in London from Septemb. 3. to 12. 1689 from divers parts of England and Wales : Owning the Doctrine of Personal Election, and final Perseverance*, (London: 1689), Title page.

[5] Knollys has received mention in many of the Baptist histories that have been published to date, but even in these, his life and contributions are often not adequately recognised.

[6] The following works on Knollys will be dealt with more fully below: James Culross, *Hanserd Knollys* in *Baptist Manuals: Historical and Biographical*, George P. Gould, ed., (London: Alexander & Shepherd, 1895); Pope A. Duncan, *Hanserd Knollys: Seventeenth-Century Baptist*, (Nashville: Broadman Press, 1965); B.R. White, *Hanserd Knollys and Radical Dissent in the 17th Century*, (London: Dr. Williams's Trust, 1977); Michael Haykin, *Kiffin, Knollys, and Keach – Rediscovering our English Baptist heritage*, (Leeds: Reformation Today Trust, 1996); Muriel James, *Religious Liberty on Trial: Hanserd Knollys – Early Baptist Hero*, (Franklin, TN: Providence House Publishers, 1997); Barry Howson, "The Question of Orthodoxy in the theology of Hanserd Knollys (c. 1599-1691): a Seventeenth Century English Calvinistic Baptist", (Unpublished Ph.D. Dissertation, McGill University, 1999).

positions.[7] Raised in a moderately Puritan, middling-gentry household and the son of a minister in the Church of England, Knollys was impacted by an understanding of life and society, which strongly encouraged order. Like his father, he was an ordained minister in the Church of England. Although he would eventually take theological issue with many of the Church's practices, he would always be very conscious of being orderly.

Hanserd Knollys was influenced by a more radical mindset as well. Raised in Lincolnshire, he experienced Puritanism at a young age in a community ripe with radical ideas, some of which Knollys would eventually embrace openly, and which would shape his thought and actions. His Puritanism would itself be shaped by more radical ideas such as congregational church government, adult believer's baptism, and liberty of conscience. While very mindful of the importance of order – religious, social, and political – Knollys also grappled with his acceptance of positions often viewed by his contemporaries as disorderly and even heretical, in some instances. Thus, throughout his life, Knollys trod the fine line between these two influences, constantly seeking to maintain a balance.

Chapter 2, "The Early Years: From Lincoln to New England", will examine Knollys' early life, giving specific attention to his family history, his education, his early ministry in the Church of England his separation from the Established Church, and his brief stay in New England where he settled to avoid religious persecution, only to find it, ironically, to be present more acutely. Knollys encountered some of the most decisive influences of his life during these formative years. Although Knollys would still not have embraced the Baptist position upon his return from New England, he had become a confirmed separatist who accepted the ideas of congregationalism and the gathered church. Certainly these early 'seeking' years provided Knollys with a measure of radical influences.

Chapter 3, "Hanserd Knollys and the Particular Baptists' Struggle for Legitimacy in the 1640s", will discuss his encounter with further radical influences and his search for stability during this tumultuous period of civil war and challenge to existing institutions. The atmosphere of uncertainty and upheaval in England during the 1640s did much to augment the tension within Knollys' own life, as he struggled to balance his own radical positions with a desire to be considered by others as holding legitimate theological positions. During this period, Knollys embraced the Baptist position and founded a Particular Baptist Church in London.

The continuing struggle for legitimacy by Knollys and the Particular Baptists into the next decade is the topic of Chapter 4, "Hanserd Knollys and the Struggle for Legitimacy: Levellers, Quakers, and the Fifth Monarchy

---

[7] Mark R. Bell argued for a similar tension for the Particular Baptists in general. Mark R. Bell, *Apocalypse How? Baptist Movements During the English Revolution*, (Macon, GA: Mercer University Press, 2000), pp. 79-80.

Movement". Here the focus shifts. Whereas Chapter 3 examines the attempts of Knollys and the Particular Baptists to emphasise their similarities with other Puritans, particularly the Independents, Chapter 4 considers their attempts to distance themselves from the more radical elements of English society in the 1650s. A commitment to orderliness became increasingly important to Knollys, as he and the Particular Baptists became public critics of the more radical sects and political movements, even as they found themselves being grouped with these by their opponents. During the 1640s and 1650s, Knollys unmistakably allied himself with the Parliamentarians during the civil wars and later with the Republic and Protectorate under Cromwell.

In the 1660s, the backward swing of the pendulum returned England to monarchy and a state church. Chapter 5, "Testing, Trials, and Tribulations: Knollys' life during the Restoration" and Chapter 6, "'The World That Now Is and the World That Is To Come': Knollys' Use and Interpretation of Apocalyptic Literature", focus on the tumultuous decades of the 1660s through the 1680s. During these years, the return of the Stuart Kings and a conservative Parliament meant a renewed struggle for Knollys and the Particular Baptists. Periodic encounters with hostility and persecution as well as the constant 'spectre' of a revival of Roman Catholicism in England created an environment of apocalyptic proportions for Knollys and the Particular Baptists. Utterly convinced that the end of world history was near and that Christ would return imminently to establish his Kingdom on Earth, Knollys displayed a fascination with the Biblical apocalyptic books and a desire to apply a contemporary interpretation to them. However, even in this context of turmoil and of such apparently radical activities and publications, Knollys' commitment to order remained evident.

As James II's grip on the Throne of England very suddenly disintegrated in the late 1680s, some Englishmen saw the potential return to the chaotic years of the mid-century. However, the flight of James and the accession of William and Mary created a much more orderly atmosphere than that experienced during the 1640s. With the limited toleration extended by King William III, Hanserd Knollys and the Particular Baptists finally realised the liberty of conscience for which they had been champions for such a long time. By this point, the one-time sect had grown considerably. As this group attempted to establish its respectability, Knollys played a significant role. Just as he had crusaded with such competency throughout his life for acceptance of the Particular Baptists as a legitimate expression of Christianity, so too in his later life, he was equally valiant in his efforts to establish the Particular Baptists more formally. As a highly respected leader, Knollys was instrumental in the formulation of polity and doctrine, which would define Particular Baptists into the next century. At the heart of Knollys' efforts to organise Particular Baptists into a more formal institution, was a commitment to the importance of order under the direction of the Spirit and the Scriptures. This process of formalisation and Knollys' role in it is dealt with in Chapter 7, "A Sect No More: Hanserd Knollys' Role in

Particular Baptist Formalisation" as well as in the Epilogue, "The Twilight Years: 'An Inheritance among them which are Sanctified'", which summarise Knollys' activities and influence over the final few years of his life.

Historiographical Overview

In 1993, John Morrill suggested that the most significant event of the seventeenth century in England, the Civil Wars and Revolution of the 1640s, did not represent "the first European revolution" but were rather "the last of the Wars of Religion".[8] Although there were "localist" and "legal-constitutionalist" perceptions of misgovernment" during this crisis, it was "the force of religion that drove minorities to fight, and forced majorities to make reluctant choices".[9] Numerous historical studies focussing on religion have appeared in the last three decades. However, historians have considered and interpreted the role of religion in Stuart England in a wide variety of ways, including a concentration upon the rise of religious diversity following the Reformation. Not only can one talk of Catholic versus Protestant during this period, but also of sharp distinctions and factions within Protestantism. The historiographical section of this work is broken down into three sections covering recent works on radical religion and dissent in seventeenth-century Britain, histories of the Baptists, and studies on Hanserd Knollys.

Works on Radical Religion and Dissent

Various designations have been used to describe those who were outside of the bounds of the Church of England during this time: dissenters, separatists, and religious radicals. Since Hanserd Knollys and the Particular Baptists obviously fit into this category, a survey of the historiography of this topic is in order. Since the works on radical religion in the Stuart age are numerous, this historiographical treatment will be selective. Certainly one of the questions facing the historian, which even Knollys faced during his lifetime, is exactly where did the Particular Baptists fit into the variety of religious expression in Stuart England?

Foundational for the study of those Protestants who left the Church of England to gather their own separate congregations during the reigns of Elizabeth I and James I is B.R. White's *The English Separatist Tradition*.[10] Published in 1971, it sought to give an overview of English separatism primarily from a theological framework and traced its origins from the sixteenth century forward. Under the persecution that resulted from Queen

---

[8] John Morrill, *The Nature of the English Revolution*, (London: Longman, 1993), p. 68.
[9] Morrill, *Nature of the English Revolution*, p. 47.
[10] B.R. White, *The English Separatist Tradition*, (London: Oxford University Press, 1971).

Mary's attempts to return England to the Roman Catholic Church, a new standard of 'purity' arose. The Marian martyrs became the standard for Protestants within the Church of England, who abhorred the return to the Roman fold, and the standard for the separatists as well, who saw the church of Edward VI as the purest expression of the English Reformation.[11] With the Elizabethan settlement, expectations of a more radical reform were disappointed, leading to division among Protestants and the rise of a more distinctive separatist tradition. At the heart of this separatist tradition was the belief that the visible Church must be a pure Church, a decision that led to separation from the Established Church and the founding of congregations of gathered saints. White gave significant attention then, to separatists such as Robert Browne, Henry Barrow, Francis Johnson, and John Smythe who played a key role in the founding of the Congregationalist and Baptist traditions. He clearly traced the London congregation of Henry Jacob to earlier separatists who did not migrate to Holland.[12] This was the church of which Hanserd Knollys became a member in the early 1640s.

While White interacted with earlier historians (especially the path-breaking work of Champlin Burrage), he also made wide use of primary sources, specifically the publications of separatist leaders. Although his work served as an important building block in the study of radical reformers in early-modern England, it concentrated too sharply on theological issues. Due to the fact that White focused on the early separatist tradition, his emphasis tended to be on reformation and not revolution. Some of the more radical sects, which evolved later, such as Seekers, Ranters, Diggers, or Levellers, obviously did not receive any attention from White. However, the foundation laid by the separatists, dealt with in White's work, was vital to later developments of radical religion. As a Baptist historian, White gave some exclusive attention to the Baptist element of separatism, although this period of fluidity clearly predated denominational formation.[13] Incidentally, the issue of social change received little attention, as did the question of the calibre or intentions of those who joined separatist movements. White clearly perceived an element of continuity in the English separatist tradition, and the greatest contribution of his work, as it relates to the present study, involved his linking of the early English separatist tradition to the influential Jacob/Lathrop/Jessey church in London, which he linked to developing congregationalism in England and New England and to the Calvinistic Baptists.

Focusing on the 1640s and 1650s, Christopher Hill's work attempted to understand the religious diversity and radicalism in the seventeenth century as expressions of social discontent and responses to the social inequity of the

---

[11] White, *English Separatist Tradition*, chapter 1.

[12] White, *English Separatist Tradition*, pp. 164-7.

[13] White, *English Separatist Tradition*, chs. 6-8.

time.[14] In failing to connect later radical expressions to the earlier separatist tradition, Hill emphasised discontinuity. Where White embraced a clearly theological approach, Hill's Marxist interpretation led to more of a social approach, seeking "the worm's eye view".[15] Hill examined a broad spectrum of religious groups and expressions, such as Fifth Monarchists, Levellers, Quakers, Baptists, Diggers, Ranters, and others, lumping them all together as part of "the revolt within the Revolution".[16] Since he saw religious radicalism as more of a social phenomenon, he believed that one could not clearly differentiate among politics, religion, scepticism, and social unrest. The fluidity with which people passed from one group to another was evidence for Hill that the lines of division were "much more blurred" than would later be the case as the groups hardened into denominations.[17] For Hill, many of those who became involved in radical religion were merely using religion or religious expression as a vehicle to accomplish economic, political, and social goals – liberation and social parity.[18] However, these "revolutions", like the greater English Revolution, failed to attain their admirable social aspirations.[19]

Although examining the interconnections among the political, social, and religious aspects of seventeenth-century English society, Hill tended to reduce religious expressions to social or political concerns. His focus on erratic and revolutionary behaviour and teachings tended to portray the most extreme positions as almost normative. His understanding of religion as simply being a tool of the upper or middle classes to manipulate and control the lower classes or as an expression of lower class protest reduced it to a narrow sphere. However, two significant strengths in Hill's work have made it another seminal work. The plethora of primary sources used certainly give significant credibility to his interpretations of the significance of the role played by those in the lower ranks of Stuart society. As well, his focus on the grass-roots of society and on the less fortunate certainly have drawn attention to a segment of society that had previously received minimal attention in historical research.

Building upon White and reacting against Hill, Murray Tolmie in *The Triumph of the Saints: The separate churches of London 1616-1649*, deliberately attempted to restore a measure of balance to the study of religious radicals.[20] The period examined by Tolmie bridged those periods dealt with by the two previous works, with the first half examining the growth of separatism in the early Stuart era and the second half looking at the political ramifications

---

[14] Christopher Hill, *The World Turned Upside Down*, (London: Maurice Temple Smith, 1972; reprint ed., Penguin Books, 1991).
[15] Hill, *World*, p.11.
[16] Hill, *World*, p. 11.
[17] Hill, *World*, pp. 11-12.
[18] Hill, *World*, pp. 48-9, 88-9, 224-5.
[19] Hill, *World*, pp. 306-12.
[20] Tolmie, *Triumph*.

of religious radicalism in the Civil War and Revolution. Tolmie took issue with Hill's approach, attempting to show that growth of independent religious groups was more than religious revolution fuelled by radical social and political ideology.[21] As well, he disagreed with earlier American historians who implied that "English dissent as a movement" was "breaking apart and losing momentum by 1640".[22] Like White, Tolmie traced the development of the separatist congregations forward toward the denominations that would develop in the late seventeenth and eighteenth centuries. Ultimately, he argued, "nonconformity was part of the puritan revolution in England and not the product of its failure."[23] Tolmie's definition of separatism emphasised the importance of "non-parochial protestant congregations" that preceded denominationalism. However, while the earlier separatists in White's work assumed a single unified "true and universally binding model of a Christian church" which led to their ultimate undoing, and which separated them from Puritanism as well as the Established Church, the later separatists in Tolmie's work sought to "work out an ecclesiastical polity which avoided the isolation" of the earlier separatists.[24] Indeed, Tolmie's separatists certainly included many of the radical expressions emphasised by Hill.[25]

While Tolmie gave significant attention to religious and theological issues, he understood these as being much more than merely vehicles of a political ideology or social agenda. Tolmie approached the topic from a contextual perspective, clearly portraying the religious, social, and political concerns of the separatists. Arguing that most of the religious radicals of the 1640s had some earlier connection with the Jacob Church, he examined the London Separatists, the Baptists, the Independents, the Presbyterians, and the Levellers, and discussed the impact of political, social, and theological elements of each on the overall Revolution.[26] While showing how the political and social agendas of religious radicals often coincided and blended with ecclesiastical issues, Tolmie clearly understood the focus of the separatist groups as being primarily religious and theological.[27]

Tolmie's treatment of religious radicals during the 1640s has the advantage, like White's approach, of treating religious issues as having their own logic and, like Hill's, of recognising the importance of the social and political

---

[21] Tolmie, *Triumph*, p. ix-x.
[22] Tolmie, *Triumph*, p. x.
[23] Tolmie, *Triumph*, p. 6.
[24] Tolmie, *Triumph*, pp. 1-3.
[25] Tolmie, *Triumph*, p. x.
[26] Tolmie, *Triumph*, pp. 7ff.
[27] Tolmie, *Triumph*, pp. 8-10, 34-44, 85-8. Tolmie, pp. 144-48, 169-72, did concede that in certain instances, such as the Levellers, the political agenda took precedence, causing them to become more of a radical political group than a radical religious group. It was at this point that the Baptists and Independents, with their focus on religious reform, began to distance themselves from the Levellers..

contexts. However, Tolmie's examination of such groups as the Diggers, Ranters, Seekers, and Quakers was very limited, in part because he did not really examine the 1650s, creating somewhat of a gap in his work. In addition, he concentrated on the more respectable separatist groups, excluding many of the more radical individuals and groups examined by Hill.

In *Radical Religion in the English Revolution* Barry Reay and J.F. McGregor edited a collection of essays by a number of historians, which examined the role of radical religion during the 1640s and 1650s, arguing that radical religion was popular during this time. Intended to build on the work of Hill, most of the authors drew upon their own previous, more detailed research. All tended to accept the premise that religious changes came as a result of social opposition against the ruling classes and provided "outlets for class or social protest".[28] On the whole, they attempted to give religious elements more significance than did Hill, who viewed religious expressions as vehicles for political or social agendas. Like John Morrill nearly a decade later, Barry Reay argued that religion played a key role in the slide into Civil War and like Hill, he saw religion as part of a larger social whole.[29]

> We should not think of religion in any narrow sense. Our own neat division between religion, politics, and society would have made little sense to the majority of the women and men of the seventeenth century and it is better to think in terms of overlap and interaction.... The economic, the cultural, the moral, the theological: they all meshed in antipathy towards the regime of Charles I.[30]

Although a loose tradition of nonconformity had existed in England for some time, Reay argued that "it was only with the start of Civil War that separatism became a substantial movement."[31] Concentrating on the 1640s and 1650s, the essays in this book addressed a variety of expressions of radical religion well beyond the bounds of Tolmie's "respectable nonconformity", including Baptists, Levellers, Diggers, Seekers, Ranters, Quakers, Fifth Monarchists, and even atheists and irreligionists. Although Tolmie had sought to align the Baptists with the more respectable Independents, McGregor and Reay (like the Anglicans and Presbyterians of the 1630s and 1640s) sought to identify them with the more radical religious groups.

---

[28] B. Reay, "Radicalism and Religion in the English Revolution: An Introduction", in J.F. McGregor and B. Reay, eds., *Radical Religion in the English Revolution*, (London: Oxford University Press, 1984), pp. 4-8; J.F. McGregor and B. Reay, eds., *Radical Religion in the English Revolution*, (London: Oxford University Press, 1984), pp. v-vi.

[29] Reay, "Introduction", p. 1.

[30] Reay, "Introduction", p. 3. His use of the word "interaction" here is more in line with Tolmie's approach, which emphasised the integration rather than the blurring.

[31] Reay, "Introduction", pp. 11-12.

McGregor's essay on the Baptists examined many of the same topics as White[32] – their origins, distinctive doctrinal positions, and leaders. In addition, he studied Baptists at the grass-roots level, portraying them as a sect, which gathered many of the "victims of economic and social change into a mass evangelical movement".[33] His essay also provided insights into the relationship between the Baptists and the more radical groups of the day. At first glance, Brian Manning's chapter on the Levellers appeared to take a similar perspective to that of Tolmie, understanding the Leveller movement as having sprung from religious roots, but becoming a primarily political movement later on. However, his portrayal of their religious perceptions actually took a subtly different position. According to Manning, the Levellers' religious understanding was rooted in an emphasis on the oppressive role of organised religion and the egalitarian, anti-authoritarian aspects of popular religion. Unlike Tolmie, who seemed to understand the Levellers as a religious group who politicised, Manning saw the religion and politics of this movement as blurred.[34] Overall, this collection of essays manages to maintain a careful balance between the social and ecclesiastical aspects of radical religion during the period. What is especially significant about this work and those of Hill and Tolmie is that combined they delve into the social, political, and religious context of the formative years of Knollys' early separatism, years which were fundamental for Knollys and the Particular Baptists.

Shortly after Tolmie published his work on separatists in London, an even more comprehensive volume on dissent was going to press, the first volume of Michael Watts', *The Dissenters*.[35] Taking a wide-ranging look at English and Welsh dissent, it included questions of church and state, and sought to recover what could be of the "lives, beliefs, and religious practice of the ordinary lay men and women who constituted the overwhelming majority of English and Welsh Dissenters".[36] Watts believed that this was "the formative period of Dissenting history".[37] Although dissenters in English history have never held "the centre of the national stage", Watts contended that they played a very

---

[32] White, *English Separatist Tradition*, but more specifically, B.R. White, *The English Baptists of the Seventeenth Century*, rev. ed., (London: The Baptist Historical Society, 1997).

[33] J.F. McGregor, "The Baptists: Fount of All Heresy", in J.F. McGregor and B. Reay, eds., *Radical Religion in the English Revolution*, (London: Oxford University Press, 1984), p. 49.

[34] Brian Manning, "The Levellers and Religion", in J.F. McGregor and B. Reay, eds., *Radical Religion in the English Revolution*, (London: Oxford University Press, 1984), pp. 65-90.

[35] Watts' definition of dissent was very broad, taking in anyone given a number of tags: separatists, Brownists, sectaries, nonconformists, Anabaptists, dissenters.

[36] Michael Watts, *The Dissenters: From the Reformation to the French Revolution*, vol. 1, (Oxford: Clarendon Press, 1978), p. viii.

[37] Watts, *The Dissenters*, vol. 1, p. viii.

important and significant "supporting role in the development of the English, and still more of the Welsh, nations".[38] He saw dissenters as pioneers of many of the formative ideals of Western civilisation – liberty and freedom, social contract and democratic community, and religious tolerance and plurality.[39] "Dissent taught the value of devotion, discipline, personal probity, and responsibility", which would shape not only dissenters' own piety and religion, but would also form the foundation of English and Welsh moral and ethical development.[40] So important was dissent, Watts maintained, that the "popular forces" and "anti-Christian" emphasis, which created such revolutionary sentiment in Europe during the eighteenth and nineteenth centuries, did not take strong hold in England. In fact, he held that the relationship between religious dissent and political radicalism "contributed to the stability of English society".[41]

Chapters one and two of this work deal with the period from 1532-1662, while the third chapter continues the story through to the Glorious Revolution of 1689 and the final two chapters deal with the eighteenth century and emerging nonconformity and Methodism. Ranging widely, Watts tackled the question of the beginnings of English dissent, suggesting a two-stream origin – radical dissent and Puritan dissent – and clearly adopting a position of a continuous separatist tradition. Without 'secularising' religious and theological expressions of the period, Watts gave dissenting religion a significant place in early-modern England and examined the broad array of groups, including the Presbyterians, Baptists, Independents, Levellers, Fifth Monarchists, Ranters, Antinomians, Seekers, and Quakers. Paying careful attention to political, social, and religious issues, Watts took an integrated approach to understanding the period. His use of a wide array of both secondary and primary sources added credibility to his work. In doing so, he explored denominational histories, as well as the writings of those he discussed. The bibliographic appendix was especially valuable in indicating important sources and catalogues of sources. Due to its vast breadth combined with its intricate detail, *The Dissenters* has certainly established itself as an invaluable tome. However, at the same time, the breadth and detail often result in the work becoming somewhat mired down and Watts' thesis of the centrality of dissent to developing English politics and society obscured. His work is exhaustive, at times, to a fault.

Richard Greaves' trilogy on late seventeenth-century radicalism, published in the late 1980s and early 1990s is the final set of works to be examined in this portion of this brief historiographical overview. These three monographs carried the study of seventeenth-century religious and political radicalism during the period from the Restoration to the Glorious Revolution. Previous to

---

[38] Watts, *The Dissenters*, vol. 1, p. 3.
[39] Watts, *The Dissenters*, vol. 1, p. 4.
[40] Watts, *The Dissenters*, vol. 1, p. 5.
[41] Watts, *The Dissenters*, vol. 1, p. 4.

Greaves' research, it was quite widely held, due in part to Christopher Hill, that 1660 marked the end of the radical impulse in England. However, Greaves argued that the Restoration forced radicalism underground and caused the radicals to refocus, giving less attention to those points of division, which had led to the failure of "the Good Old Cause" in 1660, and more attention to the common points of animosity – monarchy, popery, and prelacy.[42] The underground efforts of the radicals, though they led to much plotting and many more rumours of plotting, never achieved the unity necessary for success. What they did achieve, however, was to create a "sense of unease in the government".[43] These three books examined in detail the activities and role of radicals through the reigns of Charles II and James II, analysing not only actual failed or foiled plots but also the rumours of plots as well.

In his trilogy, Greaves very clearly differentiated between radicals and Protestant nonconformists. He held that the main difference between radicals and reformers was that the radicals desired to delegitimise and replace the existing structures, while the reformers sought to better them.[44] Greaves did not "equate radicals with all Protestant nonconformists" but limited the use of the word radicals to those who practiced and encouraged active disobedience of the law, especially as it related to violent crimes. "Although virtually all radicals were Protestant nonconformists, not all nonconformists were radical."[45]

In the first of his works, *Deliver Us From Evil*, Greaves looked at the residual radicalism that remained following the return of Charles II. He focused specifically on the "insurrections, abortive plots, treasonable scheming, and baseless allegations" in a collective context. The paranoia and persecution of this period served to fuel both the radicals' activities and the government's responses to them. Greaves examined a number of plots and uprisings in a variety of geographical locations, as well as the Great Ejection of Protestant clergy who refused to conform to the reconstituted Episcopal Church of England and its affect on the dissident community. The Ejection, Conventicles Act, and the paranoia regarding exiles abroad all derived from the "skittishness" of the government in relation to nonconformity.[46] Of course these particular responses, as well as Venner's Uprising, clearly interrelated with Hanserd Knollys' life.[47]

In *Enemies Under His Feet*, the second book in the trilogy, Greaves focused his attention on radicalism during the period from 1664, when persecution

---

[42] Richard L. Greaves, *Deliver Us From Evil: The Radical Underground in Britain, 1660-1663*, (New York: Oxford University Press, 1986).
[43] Greaves, *Deliver Us From Evil*, p. 4.
[44] Greaves, *Deliver Us From Evil*, p. 5.
[45] Richard L. Greaves, *Enemies Under His Feet: Radicals and Nonconformists in Britain, 1664-1677*, (Stanford, California: Stanford University Press, 1990), p. viii.
[46] Greaves, *Deliver Us from Evil*, pp. 87-95.
[47] Greaves, *Deliver Us From Evil*, pp. 49-65.

began to subside temporarily, through the Declaration of Indulgence in 1672, until 1677, the eve of the Popish Plot. This work looked more closely at the relationship between radical political activity and nonconformist dissent, specifically, "the radicals in the wider context of nonconformity". Giving special attention to the radical press, the Indulgence controversy, and the increasing anti-Catholicism, Greaves postulated that Charles II's program of indulgence and amnesty was nearly successful in disarming nonconformity, but for the reaction against his pro-Catholic, pro-French policies. The lull in radical activity that had resulted from the brief attempt at toleration, eventually ended with a renewed, "more vigorous policy of repression".[48] This, in turn, created the context in which radical plotting would gain new life in the wake of the Popish Plot and the Exclusion crisis. Throughout this period, although "the percentage of militants was probably higher among Congregationalists and Baptists than other nonconformists, the majority of these groups were not committed to violent action against the regime."[49] The limited toleration, the unique interests of each of the three kingdoms, and the "divisions within the dissident community" in England resulted in the government's surviving the relatively weak radical challenge of the period.[50]

Greaves' final work, *Secrets of the Kingdom*, surveyed the activities of and responses to radicals through the tenuous years of the Popish Plot and the Exclusion Crisis to the remarkable events of the Glorious Revolution. *Secrets of the Kingdom* gave special attention to the Popish Plot and Exclusion Crisis, as well as to the Rye House Plot, and their contribution to future plotting and unrest, which climaxed in the Argyll and Monmouth rebellions. From abroad, the radicals continued to publish and work toward change, while the king's spies continued to monitor their activities. One extremely fascinating portion of this book detailed the alliance between Prince William of Orange and British radicals in exile in the Netherlands.[51] What is so striking about this account is that it provides a point of view, which is quite different from the usual one in which Parliament, frightened by James' overt Catholicism and the birth of a Catholic heir, invited William to become king. Greaves, on the other hand, built a very credible case for a strong radical involvement in the Glorious Revolution. Although Greaves clearly focused primarily on military and political radicals in his third book, the role of religion is never in doubt.

> Religious issues were fundamental to the radical cause. Toleration for Protestant nonconformists was the most crucial single issue; a policy that permanently granted such freedom would have substantially reduced the

---

[48] Greaves, *Enemies Under His Feet*, pp. 226-27.
[49] Greaves, *Enemies Under His Feet*, p. 245.
[50] Greaves, *Enemies Under His Feet*, pp. 245-47.
[51] Richard L. Greaves, *Secrets of the Kingdom: British Radicals from the Popish Plot to the Revolution of 1688-1689*, (Stanford, California: Stanford University Press, 1992), pp. 319-30.

radical threat to the government. Fears of religious repression were intensified by a growing paranoia toward Catholicism, especially from the late 1670s onward.[52]

Without a doubt, Richard Greaves' trilogy on radicals in post-Restoration Britain has provided a broad and exhaustive account in which the immense amount of detail can almost distract the reader from the argument. These books drew upon a vast array of primary source material and make a key distinction between radicals and nonconformists. In the end, however, these works concentrated more on political and ideological issues such as attempts to overthrow the monarchy than on religious or theological ones. What makes this trilogy so important to the work of this thesis is that it builds a very cogent depiction of a continuous tradition of radicalism in the period following the Restoration. Within this tradition of political radicalism, strands of religious radicalism continued to be interwoven. Throughout this period, Hanserd Knollys and the Particular Baptists constantly struggled to free themselves of the taint of the political radicals and yet continued to hold some beliefs and aims common to them.

Baptist Histories

Early in their history, British Baptists, both General and Particular, embraced the idea that charting their history was of importance. Within three generations of the founding of the initial Particular Baptist churches, Thomas Crosby had written the first Baptist history. It was the first of many Baptist histories, which have appeared in each passing generation, some taking a broad perspective and others, a more specific one based on things such as locale or theological persuasion. In most cases, Baptist historians have written about their roots for two interlocking reasons: to preserve their past and to provide an apology for their denomination. They desired to provide a record of the people and events that shaped the Baptist identity and to illustrate continuity in the midst of significant Baptist diversity. They also wished to have their church seen as legitimate and socially acceptable. These general histories of the English Baptists provide internal interpretations of Hanserd Knollys.

Almost from their inception, the Baptists in England, whether the General Baptists, who favoured an Arminian position on freedom of the will, or the Calvinistic Particular Baptists, faced significant opposition, and were labelled 'Anabaptists' and grouped with the more radical elements of Continental Anabaptism of the previous century. During the first generation, English Baptists were often accused of being disorderly and dangerous. The Presbyterian Thomas Edwards, writing a compendium of newly arising "heresies" in the 1640s, claimed, "Whereas they [the Baptists] plead a

---

[52] Greaves, *Secrets of the Kingdom*, pp. 332-3.

peaceable and quiet carriage, I can prove a tumultuous disorderly managing their opinions, as in Mr. Knols, and Paul Hobson, besides of many other Anabaptists in the Kingdom."[53]

Throughout the first and second generations, Baptists themselves answered many of the attacks against them. By the early eighteenth century, although the Baptists were no longer held in the same degree of contempt, Thomas Crosby (1685?-1752), son-in-law of the prominent Particular Baptist, Benjamin Keach, felt that enough "prejudice, censure, or displeasure, and occasion objections and offence" existed that it was "needful, as well as just, to have these things set in a clear open light... to remove, or prevent, or allay, scandal, or censure, for time to come".[54] Keach's other son-in-law, Benjamin Stinton, who succeeded him as minister at Horslydown church in Southwark, had collected a considerable amount of historical material in order to write a history of the Baptists. However, when he died unexpectedly, that material fell into Crosby's care. After a time, Crosby himself determined to write the history.[55] Beyond its narrative, Crosby's work contained specific emphases. He sought first to deal with doctrinal issues, arguing for the validity of believer's baptism and emphasising the differences between the Particular and General Baptists. At the same time, he sought to dispel the reputed relationship between the English Baptists and the radical Anabaptists of the Continental Reformation. Due to the apologetic nature of his history, and his concentration on detailing the lives of many of the early English Baptist forefathers, it often took on a hagiographical tone. A partial, denominational work, neither systematic nor analytical, Crosby's history, in the words of W.T. Whitley, "needs to be read with much care".[56] However, due to his prosopographical approach, Crosby gave considerable attention to Knollys, portraying him as "among the sufferers for Antipaedobaptism" and a "pious and learned" leader.[57]

Joseph Ivimey (1773-1834) was the next Baptist to write a denominational history. His four-volume history appeared over a period of years (1811-1830). Although Ivimey built upon the work of Crosby, he also sought and used the records of some of London's oldest Baptist congregations and covered the period to 1820. Giving substantial consideration to issues of doctrine, Ivimey contended that infant baptism was not Biblical and that the English Baptists pursued Reformed principles to their legitimate conclusions. Probably his most

---

[53] Thomas Edwards, *Gangraena: Or a Catalogue and Discovery of many of the Errours, Heresies, Blasphemies and pernicious Practices of the Sectaries of this time...*, (London: 1646), Part I, p. 109, hereafter designated *Gangraena*.

[54] Thomas Crosby, *The History of the English Baptists*, vol. I, (London: 1738), "To the Reader".

[55] White, *English Baptists of the Seventeenth Century*, pp. 164-5.

[56] W.T. Whitley, *A History of the British Baptists*, (London: Charles Griffin & Co., 1923; rev. 1932), pp. 180-81.

[57] Crosby, *History*, vol. 1, p. 226.

significant interpretation was an insistence that English Baptists were the first to understand the doctrine of Christian liberty and to oppose religious persecution. Ivimey also provided an apologetic account of the Baptists, which approached history in a didactic manner, addressing issues of interest to the Baptist churches in his own era. He included significant information on Knollys, sketching a brief biographical account in his second volume that used considerable primary documentation, and portrayed Knollys in a very favourable light, referring to him as "pious and venerable" an "eminent servant of the Lord Jesus Christ", and as "zealous to defend civil and religious liberty".[58]

Other nineteenth-century Baptist historians, such as B. Evans[59] and Thomas Armitage,[60] also tended to write denominational histories characterised by a long rambling narrative style and apologetic interpretations. They added little new information or interpretation and afforded Hanserd Knollys an increasingly smaller place in the record. Only in the early twentieth century did Baptist historians begin to approach their history in a more systematic way, making use of modern historical method. W.T. Whitley (1861-1947), a Baptist minister with a great interest in history, played a leading role in forming the Baptist Historical Society. The Society's *Transactions* and its successor, *The Baptist Quarterly* became key to an analytical approach to Baptist history. His works, *The Baptists in London*[61] and *History of the British Baptists*[62] provided "the first substantial modern account" of Baptist history.[63] Though Whitley shifted the focus back to the British Baptists, he devoted relatively little attention to Knollys. Very much a denominational historian, he catalogued the minutia of events and people in the evolving Baptist denomination with little contextualisation. Still, Whitley attempted to take a more systematic and objective approach than his predecessors.

The later twentieth century saw the publication of three new Baptist histories. In 1950, American Baptist Robert Torbet published *A History of the Baptists*.[64] The work would be revised twice and republished numerous times. Concentrating upon the "Baptists in the United States",[65] Torbet devoted 180

---

[58] Joseph Ivimey, *A History of the English Baptists*, vol. II, (London: 1814), pp. 261, 347-59.

[59] B. Evans, *The Early English Baptists*, (London: J. Heaton & Son, 1864).

[60] Thomas Armitage, *A History of the Baptists: traced by their principles and practices from the time of our Lord and Saviour Jesus Christ to the year 1886*, (New York: Bryan, Taylor, & Co., 1890). Armitage traced Baptist lineage back to the New Testament era and also paid significant attention to Baptists in America. Only a small percentage of his work dealt with the British Baptists.

[61] W.T. Whitley, *Baptists in London, 1612-1928*, (London: Kingsgate Press, 1928).

[62] Whitley, *British Baptists*.

[63] White, *English Baptists of the Seventeenth Century*, p. 169.

[64] Robert G. Torbet, *A History of the Baptists*, (Valley Forge: Judson Press, 1950).

[65] Torbet, *History of the Baptists*, p. 11.

pages to Baptist origins and polity in Europe and Britain, and twice as many pages to the Baptists in America, with a significant emphasis on missions, evangelism, and ecumenism. In this denominational history, Hanserd Knollys barely merited a mention.[66]

The most comprehensive Baptist history to date was published by Leon MacBeth, a Southern Baptist historian.[67] While he wrote of the Baptist people, events, and beliefs, MacBeth also attempted to deal with the context in which the Baptists developed, clearly and deliberately approaching the history chronologically and placing Baptists in all regions within the timeline. MacBeth's voluminous study relied heavily on secondary works written from a denominational perspective and analysed only a few primary sources. Although still somewhat denominational and doctrinal, this textbook for Baptists incorporated a good deal of the contemporary context. One of the strengths of the book was the section on Baptist origins, which had a very comprehensive historiography.[68] However, Knollys received minimal consideration, and was characterised as "another Fifth Monarchy Baptist", with no evidence or reason given for this interpretation.[69]

B.R. White's work, *The English Baptists of the Seventeenth Century*, published in 1983 and revised in 1996, provided the first detailed account of the first century of Baptist history based upon a professional examination of primary sources. It appeared in a multi-volume history published by the Baptist Historical Society of Britain. White's work is significant in that it served as a bridge between the denominational and the professional approaches to writing history. White had chapters on the General Baptists until 1660, the Particular Baptists until 1660, all English Baptists during the period of 1660 to 1688, Baptist women, and the Baptists under James II, looking at Baptist doctrine, leaders, and events, within the social and political context of seventeenth-century Britain.

Although dealing with theological and doctrinal aspects of Baptist development, White tended to downplay or discount the relationship between Baptists and such groups as the Levellers and Fifth Monarchists that were emphasised by earlier writers such as Tolmie and Duncan and later authors such as McGregor.[70] White's work provided a reliable context for the Baptists

---

[66] One exception to this would be the section on the issue of slavery and the American Civil War. Torbet, *History of the Baptists*, pp. 282-97.
[67] H. Leon MacBeth, *The Baptist Heritage: Four Centuries of Baptist Witness*, (Nashville, TN: Broadman Press, 1987).
[68] MacBeth, *The Baptist Heritage*, pp. 49-63.
[69] MacBeth, *The Baptist Heritage*, p. 94.
[70] The works by McGregor and Duncan will be addressed below.

of Knollys' lifetime and dealt with Knollys at several points, without attempting to assess his career.[71]

The author had, for all intents and purposes, completed this present work when, at the last moment, he discovered yet another important Baptist history. Published in 2000, Mark R. Bell's work, *Apocalypse How? Baptist Movements During the English Revolution*, is significant in that it examines all the different Baptist groups and movements that were emerging during the tumultuous years of the seventeenth century in England. What is particularly fascinating about this book is that the Baptists are analysed specifically through the lens of eschatology. Bell works under the presupposition that as a whole, the Baptists, whatever the type or movement, were very much shaped and driven by their eschatological worldview.[72] This coincides very nicely with what is being argued in the final chapters of this book, for Knollys clearly embraced a millenarian worldview which viewed his day as the last days.

Bell categorized the English Baptist into three groups. While he recognised the General Baptists and Particular Baptists, the two groups historians typically assign to early English Baptists, he also held there was yet another group – the Independent Baptists – citing Henry Jessey, Vavasor Powell, and John Bunyan as the prototypical leaders of this group. Bell understood this branch of the sect as being congregations who embraced the concept of believers' baptism, but did not accept the idea of its necessity for church membership.[73] Bell also recognised the presence of other "movements" within these groups, such as Seventh-Day Baptists and Fifth Monarchists. The framing of the Baptists in seventeenth-century England in this way is very helpful, for clearly, they were in process, moving from 'sect' to a more institutionalise form – not yet a denomination in the modern sense of the word. However, Bell himself may be too rigid in his categorisations of the "movements", for as will be shown below, Hanserd Knollys kept a fairly open perspective and free fellowship with many who embraced the different perspectives of these "movements". These

---

[71] He had given Knollys significant attention in a previously published biographical work, which will be discussed below.

[72] Bell, *Apocalypse How?*, p. 5.

[73] Bell, *Apocalypse How?*, pp. 4, 67-8. Although this is an interesting categorisation, it seems to be pushing the issue a bit. These 'mixed' congregations, the typical phrase used to describe them by historians, were not truly Baptist, for those within them who refused believer's baptism would in no way have understood themselves as being part of a Baptist congregation. Rather, these are better understood as being Independent churches whose leaders and some, perhaps many, members had also embraced a new understanding of baptism. If Bell were to use the phrase "Independent Baptists" solely about individuals, such a position would be more acceptable, for people like Knollys himself clearly embraced both Independency and believer's baptism. However, to speak of "Independent Baptist congregations", eg. Broadmead, is truly an unnecessary categorisation and a misinterpretation of the seventeenth-century Baptists. All Baptist congregations were Independent, gathered churches by their very nature.

positions were typical of the various 'journeys' of many who called themselves Baptists. And while Knollys was always careful to keep within the bounds of orthodoxy, at times, he himself 'skirted the edges' of some of these positions.

One of the strengths of Bell's book is that, like this work, it seeks to place the Baptists into the social, political context of the seventeenth century. It examines very well the relationship between the Levellers and Baptists in the 1640s and the Fifth Monarchists and the Baptists in the 1650s, stating that is was shared eschatological ideals that brought the groups together.[74] As well, like this work, Bell's book emphasises the conflict and struggle between embracing change and maintaining traditional order, which was being experienced specifically by the leaders of the Particular Baptists. He emphasised that it was this conflict that both brought the Particular Baptists close to these groups and at the same time caused them to distance themselves from the groups. And finally, like this book, Bell's work gives valuable attention to the attempts of the English Baptists in the mid to late seventeenth century at self-identity, through the issuing of Confessions and through differentiating themselves from other radical groups.[75]

A significant weakness of the book is that, like so many other Baptist histories, it emphasises the role of William Kiffin (an unschooled tradesman) to the exclusion of many others, including Hanserd Knollys.[76] Bell at several points referred to "the Kiffin circle" as being instrumental and indeed as controlling in the development of the Baptists.[77] In fact, Bell emphasised that often, Kiffin's wealth and position not only placed him in a place of influence, but informed the decisions and affiliations of the London Baptists, as they simultaneously appeased governments and associated with members of radical groups, seeking to better their own situation.[78] Thus, the Particular Baptists' struggle between radicalism and order, for Bell, could be understood as little more that pragmatism in maintaining their middling economic position and respectability in Stuart society.

One of few works about Baptists written by a secular historian is J.F. McGregor's "The Baptists: Fount of All Heresy" in *Radical Religion in the English Revolution*.[79] In this work, McGregor attempted to understand the Baptists from a social rather than a strictly theological or religious perspective. This provided some balance to a historiography otherwise dominated by denominational historians. In places, however, McGregor overemphasised the

---

[74] Bell, *Apocalypse How?*, chaps. 4 and 9.

[75] Bell, *Apocalypse How?*, chap. 5.

[76] In fact, Hanserd Knollys receives little more than a passing mention as having benefited from his association with Kiffin, or else he is ignored altogether. Bell, *Apocalypse How?*, pp. 127-28, 131.

[77] Bell, *Apocalypse How?*, pp. 127-29, 153-54, 156.

[78] Bell, *Apocalypse How?*, pp. 130, 134-35, 153-54.

[79] McGregor, "The Baptists: Fount of All Heresy", pp. 23-63.

sociological and economic aspects at the expense of theological ones. Although giving a brief outline of Baptist origins and doctrine, he approached his study of the Baptists from a Marxist point of view.[80] Grouping the Baptists with the more radical sects, McGregor still recognised their distinctive conservatism. As well, he acknowledged their unique place as "a church of the 'middling sort'" who had a measure of connection with the lower gentry and a handful of wealthy, London merchants.[81] This helped to capture the tension between religious radicalism and social respectability that characterised many mid-seventeenth-century Particular Baptists. Of course, the single greatest limitation of this article is its breadth and scope. While the other histories examined tended to chronicle the history of the Baptists over a long stretch of time, McGregor concentrated on a very brief period, the 1630s through the 1650s.

Biographies of Knollys

"I Hanserd Knollys was Born at Calkwell near Loweth in Lincoln-shire, and was removed thence with my Parents to Schartho near Market Grymsby in the same County."[82] With these words began the first biography of Hanserd Knollys, written by his own hand. It did not include the final twenty years of his life and was unfinished at the time of his death, when his good friend William Kiffin edited and published it as a legacy.[83] The next biographical sketch of Knollys, written in the 1730s, appeared in Crosby's *Baptist History*. However, it was brief, hagiographical, and based primarily upon the autobiography, as was Ivimey's sketch a century later.

In the late nineteenth century, Baptist historian James Culross wrote the first fairly full biography of Knollys in an attempt to illustrate Baptist principles at work in the world. Culross attempted to write useable, inspirational history, noting that Hanserd Knollys' life

> practically covers the seventeenth century; and is in a sense, the history of English religious life in that period – one of the most eventful periods in "our rough island-story". We see the struggle of great principles asserting themselves against enormous odds. If these principles are the commonplaces of to-day, our fathers had to fight and suffer for their triumph.[84]

---

[80] McGregor, "The Baptists: Fount of All Heresy", pp 48-49.
[81] McGregor, "The Baptists: Fount of All Heresy", pp. 35-38.
[82] Hanserd Knollys, *The Life and Death of That Old Disciple of Jesus Christ, and Eminent Minister of the Gospel, Mr. Hanserd Knollys*, edited by William Kiffin, (London: 1692), hereafter cited as *Life*, p. 1.
[83] Knollys, *Life*, pp. ii, 42.
[84] Culross, *Hanserd Knollys*, p. i.

Culross went on to expound upon how "truth and patient suffering meekness" were mightier than the power so often exhibited by the world.[85] For his sources, he relied heavily upon the autobiography and denominational histories, but did not include clear footnote references to the sources. His study did not move much beyond the autobiography, although he did broaden the story a bit beyond the brief accounts of Crosby and Ivimey.

No further attempt would be made to write on Hanserd Knollys' life until the late twentieth century. In 1965, American Baptist historian Pope A. Duncan published a brief biographical sketch of Knollys' life and thought. He emphasised the individualism of Knollys and drew out modern applications from it, for "in this day of the mass mind and of the organization man, it is imperative that Baptists again lead in insisting upon individual worth."[86]

Starting with a brief biographical and contextual overview of six pages, which again relied heavily on the autobiography and earlier Baptist histories, he went on to examine "Aspects of Baptist Thought Illustrated in Knollys' Life", in a detailed, analytical chapter of twenty-five pages. Although clearly denominational in its focus, this was the first systematic attempt to examine and analyse Knollys' own publications. A final section sought to place Knollys into the religious context of the seventeenth century, evaluating him and the Baptists in general in comparison to other radical sects of the day. This section explored aspects of Knollys' life and writings in a new way and with a fresh focus. The radical groups which received Duncan's primary attention were the Levellers, the Quakers, and the Fifth Monarchists, with two-thirds of the section being devoted to Fifth Monarchism and the charge that Knollys was a Fifth Monarchy man. These final two sections of Duncan's work dealt with the writings of Knollys, rather than reiterating the same biographical data found in the autobiography and later Baptist histories. As well, they sought to connect Knollys with his context.

In examining Knollys' writings, Duncan highlighted his Calvinistic doctrine of redemption. He emphasised Knollys' ecclesiology of a gathered church and devoted several pages to Knollys' understanding of believer's baptism, examining primarily the work written in response to Saltmarsh. Duncan argued that Knollys held to a high view of the ministry, seeking "to make the Baptist ministry more responsible and respectable".[87] Duncan mistakenly contended that Knollys and the Baptists "declared themselves supporters of the concept of full religious liberty for all".[88] In addition, Duncan appended at the end of his work a list of primary and secondary sources by and about Hanserd Knollys. This was the first such compilation. Although working within a denominational perspective, Duncan undoubtedly approached Knollys critically, based on his

---

[85] Culross, *Hanserd Knollys*, p. x.
[86] Duncan, *Hanserd Knollys*, p. 7.
[87] Duncan, *Hanserd Knollys*, p. 29.
[88] Duncan, *Hanserd Knollys*, p. 35.

study of primary sources, and provided an introduction to the works published by Knollys, all within the context of the debates and events of seventeenth-century Britain.

The second critical examination of Hanserd Knollys appeared a decade later in a brief study by B.R. White.[89] This biography integrated the thought of Knollys with the political, social, and religious context of the times. As well as the autobiography and Knollys' published works, White also examined various public and church records that revealed new information. While not providing as comprehensive, systematic, or analytical account of Knollys' thought as Duncan, White did give a more contextual and complete overview, placing Knollys' life and ideas in the context of radical dissent. He understood Knollys as playing an important role in radical dissent and argued that he warranted closer study.[90] All subsequent works on Knollys, including this thesis, have built upon the essays of Duncan and White.

In the late 1990s, a flurry of interest in Hanserd Knollys was awakened. In 1996, the historical theologian Michael Haykin published a study of the three main Particular Baptist forefathers William Kiffin, Hanserd Knollys, and Benjamin Keach.[91] The chapter on Knollys explored aspects of his theology, particularly those related to charismatic expressions and gifts of the Holy Spirit in the believer.[92]

In the subsequent year there appeared a biography of Knollys by Muriel James, a marriage and family therapist.[93] In the process of assisting her niece in some genealogical research, James encountered Hanserd Knollys and ended up writing a biographical genealogy of him. In places, the historical background provided was too broad and tended to become somewhat convoluted. Unfamiliar with the historical context of the seventeenth century, James described it as a time of "totalitarian rule" when "people began to demand religious and political freedom".[94] She viewed Hanserd Knollys as a "hero" of religious liberty and tended to portray him more as a post-Enlightenment American who was "a man ahead of his time" than as an early modern Englishman who struggled between ideals of change and tradition, diversity and order. While Knollys certainly strove toward the ideal of Christian liberty within the bounds of Protestantism, he nevertheless did not believe in carte blanche religious liberty, and would not have desired Roman Catholics or Muslims be granted freedom of worship in England. Knollys' antagonistic

---

[89] White, *Hanserd Knollys*.
[90] White, *Hanserd Knollys*, p. 24.
[91] Haykin, *Kiffin, Knollys, and Keach*.
[92] This chapter was a revision of an article Haykin had published earlier. Michael Haykin, "Hanserd Knollys (ca. 1599-1691) On the Gifts of the Spirit", *Westminster Theological Journal* 54 (Spring 1992)) : 99-113.
[93] James, *Knollys*.
[94] James, *Knollys*, p. xvi-xvii.

sentiments toward these religious groups were clearly expressed in his apocalyptic works.

One area of significant weakness in this work was that James, like earlier writers prior to Duncan, gave little attention to Knollys' writings. Throughout her work, James made claims presumably based on primary sources such as public records or church records, but provided no reference or citation.[95] Sometimes she also gave wrong information[96] or made broad generalisations that were mistaken, again with no point of reference.[97] However, she was the first to examine Knollys' pre-Baptist life in any measure. In each of the works concerning Knollys written prior to 1980, very little was written about his childhood or his experiences in New England. Her genealogical research, albeit poorly referenced, has provided a foundation for future research on Knollys' family and early life. Like White, James introduced new areas of study in regard to Knollys' life.

In 1999, Barry Howson completed a Ph.D. thesis on "The Question of Orthodoxy in the Theology of Hanserd Knollys (c. 1599-1691): A Seventeenth-Century English Calvinistic Baptist". Building upon the earlier work of Duncan and Haykin,[98] in many ways Howson wrote an apology, which sought to exonerate Knollys from charges of heresy or disorder, by undertaking to "elucidate Knollys [sic.] theology, particularly his soteriology, ecclesiology and eschatology",[99] Like earlier Baptist historians, Howson tried to dispel four specific charges that historical opponents levelled against Knollys. Three of these were criticisms made by Knollys' contemporaries: Antinomianism, Anabaptism, and Fifth Monarchism.[100] The fourth came from those in future generations who claimed that Knollys was "the grandfather of eighteenth-century hyper-Calvinism".[101] As indicated by the title of his study, Howson was concerned to establish Knollys' orthodoxy.

The first chapter examined briefly the religious and political history of seventeenth-century England and, more extensively, the emergence of the Particular Baptists. Significant attention was given to establishing a standard of

---

[95] For an example of this, see James, *Knollys*, pp. 62-64, 106, 136 in relation to Cheney Knowles' installation as rector at the church in Scartho.

[96] See James, *Knollys*, p. 93.

[97] See her discussion on Charles I, Cromwell, and the Civil Wars in James, *Knollys*, pp. 116-20.

[98] Howson claimed that his work was "a synthesis of the historical and the theological". It would be fair to state that his work is historical theology, very much in the tradition of his mentor, Michael Haykin. Howson, "Question of Orthodoxy", p. 10. Howson has since published this thesis. Barry Howson, *Erroneous and Schismatical Opinions: The Question of Orthodoxy Regarding the Theology of Hanserd Knollys (C. 1599 – 1691)*, in Studies in the History of Christian Thought, (Leiden: Brill Academic Publishers, 2001).

[99] Howson, "Question of Orthodoxy", p. v.

[100] Howson, "Question of Orthodoxy", p. 1.

[101] Howson, "Question of Orthodoxy", p. 2.

theological orthodoxy within that context. The second chapter provided a brief biography of Knollys, drawn largely from the studies of Duncan, White, and James. The remaining chapters examined the validity of each specific charge, concluding in the end that "one would be going beyond the evidence to say that he was an Antinomian, Fifth Monarchist, or even an Anabaptist according to seventeenth-century Reformed orthodoxy. And the same could be said for the charge of hyper-Calvinism made against him."[102]

Howson has scrutinized the theology of Hanserd Knollys more extensively than any other historian, but his format mitigated against a perception of changes in Knollys' thought. Indeed, Howson made the claim that "during the forty-five years in which he published his works, his theology changed very little".[103] Arguing that Knollys came to his Puritan, Independent, and Baptist convictions late in life, Howson based this interpretation on the traditional date of Knollys' birth and other traditionally held beliefs about Knollys' life. This meant that even his careful analysis of Knollys' theology overlooked the development of his ideas over time in reaction to those of his contemporaries, including subtle shifts in both his thought and his relationships with other English Protestants who held more conservative or radical positions.

While historians and theologians have shown substantial interest in seventeenth-century English Baptists and Hanserd Knollys during the past forty years, a strong need remains for a comprehensive historical biography that examines the life, work, and thought of Knollys within the context of developments in seventeenth-century England. Hanserd Knollys was a clergyman and a theologian. He was a reformer, and perhaps in some instances, a radical. He stood at the forefront of a gathering wave of dissent, which would significantly alter and shape the English nation. An Englishman, Puritan, and Baptist, who lived during a century of intense change and turmoil, Knollys encountered a paradoxical reality of coexisting change and convention, and himself became an expression and personification of that paradox. The radical Particular Baptists, so alarmingly feared and misunderstood by many in the early seventeenth century, would become a more institutionalised denomination by century's end due in part to his direction and influence. Because of Hanserd Knollys' lifelong perseverance, even in the face of persecution and tribulation, the Particular Baptists would achieve toleration and a measure of acceptance by other dissenting denominations. As well as his more direct impact upon his many students and the members of the congregations to which he ministered, this was one of Hanserd Knollys' lasting contributions.

---

[102] Howson, "Question of Orthodoxy", p. 360.
[103] Howson, "Question of Orthodoxy", p. 359.

CHAPTER 2

The Early Years: From Lincoln to New England

Introduction

In 1682, Bulstrode Whitelock, looking back over half a century of upheaval in English life, wrote: "It is not every period of time, not every king's or Caesar's reign, that furnishes matter sufficient for an history."[1] Whitelock went on to emphasize that history tends to be a series of extremely diverse events, some worthy of note and others barely so. Therefore, "there are intervals, there are flats where fortune drives swimmingly without rattle or disturbance as well as ups and downs and precipices, where she jolts and tumbles, and overturns every thing in the way."[2] The latter phrase aptly describes much of the seventeenth century in English history.

Certainly during the late Tudor and early Stuart eras, religion in England had experienced its share of "jolts and tumbles". Within the Church of England itself, several different streams of reform combined to create a moderate Calvinism, which could be said to include a majority of churchmen. The more radical among this group, many of whom were repatriated exiles of the Marian persecution, desired a further and fuller reform and would eventually come to be known as Puritans.[3] Many of these "whether by choice, or of necessity,

---

[1] Bulstrode Whitelock, *Memorials of the English Affairs from the Beginning of the Reign of Charles the First to the Happy Restoration of King Charles the Second*, vol. 1, (Oxford: At the University Press, 1853), p. iii. This edition is a reprint of the edition published in 1732. The original work was published in 1682, while this new edition appeared in 1732 with some additions to the first edition.
[2] Whitelock, *Memorials*, p. vi.
[3] For a fuller discussion of this, see Patrick Collinson, *The Elizabethan Puritan Movement*, (London: Jonathan Cape, 1967), pp.24-55; see also William Haller, *The Rise of Puritanism*, (New York: Columbia University Press, 1938, reprint ed. Philadelphia: University of Pennsylvania Press, 1984), pp. 6-10. It should be noted here that there continues to be wide debate over the definition of the term 'puritan'. Peter Lake stated "the definition of Puritanism is an issue which has been both addressed and avoided to great profit by many great scholars." See "Defining Puritanism – again?" in Francis J. Bremer, ed., *Puritanism: Transatlantic Perspectives on a Seventeenth-Century Anglo-American Faith*, (Boston: Massachusetts Historical Society, 1993), p. 3. For various perspectives, see Patrick Collinson, *The Religion of the Protestants*, (New York: Oxford

remained on the periphery, devoting themselves to the pursuit of an ideal which differed materially from the official policy of the Church".[4] From this group there emerged a more radical position, which began to pursue a separatist agenda, desiring not so much the reformation of the Church of England, but the freedom to worship and believe according to conscience.[5] It was during Hanserd Knollys' early life that he first encountered this position, which would significantly shape his life.

This chapter deals with the early years of Hanserd Knollys' life leading up to the tumultuous decade of the 1640s, and attempts to place him in the social, religious, and political context of early seventeenth-century England and New England. It will examine his family background and the region of Lincolnshire, in particular, the communities where Knollys spent his early years. As well, it will explore Knollys' education and experience at Cambridge University, his ordination and early ministry, the Puritan influences upon his life and his move into nonconformity, and finally, his New England experiences. Indeed, as will be seen, the many experiences and influences of Knollys' life and environment during these early years proved to be extremely formative ones.

University Press, 1982); Nicholas Tyacke, "Puritanism, Arminianism and Counterrevolution" in C. Russell, ed. *The Origins of the English Civil War*, (London: MacMillan, 1973); Michael Finlayson, "Puritanism and Puritans: Labels or Libels?" *Canadian Journal of History* 8 (Dec. 1973) : 207; Richard L. Greaves, "The Puritan-Nonconformist Tradition in England, 1560-1700", *Albion*, 17 (Winter, 1985) : 449-86.

[4] Collinson, *Elizabethan Puritan*, p. 45.

[5] According to Barrington White, this separatist tradition actually had its roots during the Marian period. B.R. White, *The English Separatist Tradition*, (London: Oxford University Press, 1971), chs. 1-2. See also C.J. Clement, *Religious Radicalism in England, 1535-1565*, (Edinburgh: Rutherford House, 1997), pp. 315-20. This movement is that which Michael Watts referred to as English Dissent. Watts divided the source of this dissent into two distinct currents: the radical current of dissent, traced back to Lollardy and mixed with Dutch Anabaptist influences, and the Calvinist current of dissent, the mainstream of English separatist activity. *The Dissenters*, vol. 1, (Oxford: Clarendon Press, 1978), pp. 7-26. Initially, the more popular element of this dissent, the radical current, continued underground, carried on due to the rise of the conventicle, particularly important for the Lollards. In this secret context, the exposition of the Bible and the activity of instruction took place, something which had personal ramifications, but also which preserved and nurtured the reform and separatist ideal until a later time. J.W. Martin, *Religious Radicals in Tudor England*, (London: The Hambledon Press, 1989), pp. 13-39. G.M. Trevelyan pointed out the important role of the laity in the Lollard tradition, a key element in separatist tradition that developed in the Stuart church. *England in the Age of Wycliffe*, (London: Longmans, Green and Co., 1948 ed.), pp. 351-52.

Lincolnshire Years

Hanserd Knollys was born in the autumn of 1609[6] in Cawkwell, Lincolnshire, near the town of Louth.[7] Cawkwell was a rather inconsequential village on the road from Lincoln to Horncastle.[8] Of more significance was the nearby town of Louth, approximately six miles to the northeast. Louth had been the seat of a major uprising in 1536.[9] Although the Louth rebellion resulted in the execution of several members of the gentry, many of those involved drifted back into ordinary life, albeit the feelings and resentment likely remained for some time.[10] In all, thirty-four leaders were condemned to death, including men from Louth, Scartho, and Biscathorpe, villages where some of Hanserd Knollys' ancestors lived and where he spent his childhood.[11]

His father, Richard Knowles, a graduate of Cambridge, served as vicar at Cawkwell from 1608-14.[12] The family soon moved to Scartho and Grimsby where Hanserd lived his younger years.[13] Agriculture was the primary mainstay

---

[6] This differs from the date traditionally held for Knollys' birth. The argument supporting this difference is dealt with in detail in Appendix 1.

[7] Hanserd Knollys, *The Life and Death of That Old Disciple of Jesus Christ, and Eminent Minister of the Gospel, Mr. Hanserd Knollys*, edited by William Kiffin, (London: 1692), hereafter cited as *Life*, p. 1. Pope A. Duncan, *Hanserd Knollys: Seventeenth-Century Baptist*, (Nashville: Broadman Press, 1965), p. 8. See Appendix 5 for maps of the places mentioned in this chapter.

[8] According to the Diocesan return taken in 1563, during this period Cawkwell was a farming area with only three houses and it doubled in size over the next three centuries. The church there evidently served the surrounding farmers and their tenants. Muriel James, *Religious Liberty on Trial: Hanserd Knollys – Early Baptist Hero*, (Franklin, TN: Providence House Publishers, 1997), pp. 46-47.

[9] G.R. Elton, *England Under the Tudors*, (London: Methuen & Co. Ltd., 1955), pp.140-46; J.F. Hill, *Tudor and Stuart Lincoln*, (Cambridge: At the University Press, 1956), pp. 44-45.

[10] Hill, *Lincoln*, pp. 47-48.

[11] James, *Knollys*, p. 24.

[12] Records in the Lincolnshire archives contain the approval of the original presentation deed of Richard Knowles to Cawkwell on 5 August 1608, document PD, 1608/3. Other records show he served in this church until 1614. John Venn and J.A. Venn, *Alumni Cantabrigienses*, Part I to 1751, vol. III Kaile to Ryves, (Cambridge: University Press, 1924), p. 32.

[13] Knollys, *Life*, p. 1. It would seem that Richard Knowles was installed as vicar of Grimsby as early as 1593. C.W. Foster, ed., *The State of the Church in the Reigns of Elizabeth I and James I*, vol. 1, in *The Publications of the Lincoln Record Society*, vol. 23, (Horncastle: W. K. Morton & Sons Ltd., 1926), pp. 89, 390, 407, 422. Then, according to the Bishop's Certificates of Canterbury, he was presented and instituted to the St. Giles rectory at Scartho on December 2, 1613. Thus, the most likely scenario is that as Vicar of Grimsby, Knowles held a second living in Cawkwell until 1614. At that time, he resigned from the church in Cawkwell and took a new second living in Scartho, a town much closer to Grimsby. Lambeth Palace Library, Abbot Register, part 1, f. 310.

in Lincolnshire during this period, as it was in many other parts of England. The best agricultural regions tended to be the vales and the wolds, where the people practiced mixed husbandry. In Lincolnshire, the vale lands were held within a strong manorial framework, often centred on a village or villages. Wheat, barley, and peas were the main crops, with a mix of cattle, sheep, and horses, which grazed on the leys, meadows or the common fields.[14] On the wolds, sheep-barley farming took place with sheep raised to provide both meat and wool. The chief crops consisted of barley and wheat. In these regions, less communal attitudes prevailed so that often a large farmer could dominate.[15] This became much easier with the increase of the practise of enclosure in the early seventeenth century.[16]

The marshlands were the lowlands that had been drained and converted for agrarian use. Mixed husbandry was also the custom in this region with an emphasis on cattle and sheep fattening and wheat and corn growing. In this region, villages formed the centre of society, often affording a congenial environment for a country gentleman. Well populated and prosperous, the marshlands boasted many rich squires and yeomen.[17] The last regions were the fens and forests, often settled by the poorest of society. Both of these regions served as important dairy centres due to the abundant grazing and meagre arable land. Since Royal forest law inhibited the freedom of inhabitants to improve their land, pasture farming and the raising of grazing stock tended to be the primary focus of the forest farms.[18] The fens presented a different sort of problem. The soil in these coastal regions was a combination of silt and peat and often very wet. These "drowned lands" as Eric Kerridge called them, were unsuitable for significant farming or settlement. At best, they might be used for grazing in the winter, if they were dry, or during the summer, the dryer strips of land might be cut for winter fodder. It could be said that the best 'crop' of the fens was the fish and eels that inhabited the region, which remained almost constantly under water. Although attempts were made at draining the fens, most in this period failed and would not succeed for at least another century.[19]

For Hanserd Knollys, growing up in northeastern Lincolnshire, many of these regions served as a basic backdrop to his life experience. He knew well the rolling hills of the wolds and the fertile pasturelands of the marsh because

---

[14] Joan Thirsk, ed., *The Agrarian History of England and Wales*, vol. IV 1500-1640, H. P. R. Finberg, gen. ed., (Cambridge: University Press, 1967), pp. 32-33.

[15] Thirsk, *Agrarian History*, pp. 33-34.

[16] Joan Thirsk, *English Peasant Farming – The Agrarian History of Lincolnshire from Tudor to Recent Times*, (London: Routledge & Kegan Paul, 1957), pp. 159-69.

[17] Thirsk, *Agrarian History*, pp. 35-36; Thirsk, *English Peasant Farming in Lincolnshire*, pp. 95-107.

[18] Thirsk, *Agrarian History*, pp. 36-37.

[19] Eric Kerridge, *The Agricultural Revolution*, (London: Allen & Unwin, 1967), pp. 138-44; Thirsk, *Agrarian History*, pp. 38-40; Thirsk, *English Peasant Farming in Lincolnshire*, pp. 108-12.

of the time he spent at Gayton-Le-Wold on his uncle William's manor and at Gayton-Le-Marsh, the farmland left to his father by his grandmother, Christobel Lacon.[20] Likewise, he probably experienced the floods and wetlands of the fens, for Grimsby and Scartho, where his father served as rector and where he spent the majority of his early years, lay in the midst of the salt marshes in north-east Lincolnshire.

Lincolnshire was the most north-easterly county directly governed by London. A vast and isolated county, everything north of the Humber River, Lincolnshire's northern border, came under the jurisdiction of the Council of the North at York or the Bishop of Durham. Many in the south of England perceived Lincolnshire as being backward, uncivilised, and uncultured.[21] Although the county of Lincolnshire appeared overwhelmingly to support the Elizabethan settlement, a growing spirit of nonconformity emerged there in the last quarter of the sixteenth century.[22] However, it was not until the 1640s that an "explosion of religious experimentation" occurred. Prior to this the majority of those dubbed Puritans had not formally broken ties with the national church.[23]

Grimsby, Hanserd's childhood home, was located on a peninsula at the mouth of the Humber River, an obvious site for a harbour.[24] A relatively prosperous port during the Middle Ages,[25] Grimsby was a market town in decline by the early seventeenth century, when Knollys was a youth, primarily due to the silting of the harbour.[26]

Hanserd Knollys' family had connections with the lesser Lincolnshire gentry, particularly on his mother's side. In his work, *Lincolnshire Wills*, A.R. Maddison focused on families in Lincolnshire who, according to his reckoning,

---

[20] See below and see Appendix 2.

[21] Henry VIII once referred to it as "one of the most brute and beastly" places in the kingdom. Hill, *Lincoln*, pp. 6-7.

[22] Gerald A.J. Hodgett, *Tudor Lincolnshire*, (Lincoln: History of Lincolnshire Committee, 1975), pp. 169, 184-85.

[23] Clive Holmes, *Seventeenth Century Lincolnshire*, (Lincoln: History of Lincolnshire Committee, 1980), pp. 41-44.

[24] It is most likely that the first settlement on the site was a Viking one, perhaps as early as 866. In fact, the name Grimsby is of Norwegian origin. Edward Gillett, *A History of Grimsby*, (London: Oxford University Press, 1970), pp. 6-7.

[25] In fact, without its waterborne trade, the town would likely not have survived. By the fourteenth century, trade had gone beyond towns along the Humber to include foreign ports in the Baltic region, Prussia, and Holland. Much of Grimsby's trade was with its English coastal neighbours such as Hull and Newcastle. This trade primarily involved fish, turf, coal, and wool. By the sixteenth century, the coal and corn trade became primary. Gillett, *Grimsby*, pp. 19-26, 31-44, 98-99.

[26] Gillett, *Grimsby*, p. 120.

"were of undoubted gentle birth and good standing in the County".[27] This work included wills of many of Knollys' relatives. Hanserd Knollys' maternal grandmother was connected with several gentry families. Christobel Lacon was born a Sutcliffe, an influential family in the market town of Grimsby. Her grandfather, John, had been a prominent urban gentleman. Her father, Matthew, the eldest son, had served as the Dean of Exeter in 1588 and after that was the founder of Chelsea College. Solomon, her uncle, served several terms as the mayor of Grimsby (1598, 1599, 1603, 1608), and his eldest son was an Esquire of the Body to James I.[28] Hanserd Knollys' grandfather was Richard Hanserd Jr. of Biscathorpe.[29] Richard Hanserd Jr., Christobel's first husband, came from a prominent family as well. His father, Richard Hanserd Sr., served as the mayor of Grimsby in 1569.[30] Richard and Christobel had two daughters and one son.[31] One of these daughters, Rachel, married Richard Knowles, vicar of Grimsby and Scartho.[32] In 1597, Richard Hanserd died and Christobel remarried. Her second husband, Harbert Lacon of Humberstone, solidified her

---

[27] A.R. Maddison, *Lincolnshire Wills, 1500-1600*, vol. 1, (Lincoln: James Williamson, 1888), p. xv. Much light is shed on Knollys' family history and genealogy through examination of the wills and pedigrees of the period compiled by A.R. Maddison. *Lincolnshire Wills 1500-1617*, vols. 1 and 2 (Lincoln: James Williamson, 1888, 1891); *Lincolnshire Pedigrees*, vols. 1-3 in *Publications of the Harleian Society*, vols. 50-51, (London: 1902-1904). Invaluable as well to the task of this research is the above-mentioned work by Muriel James, which does much valuable 'genealogical excavation', although, as already stated, her citation and notation is very haphazard and therefore not always of assistance. Sorting out these names and relationships is not without its problems. The lack of a consistent spelling of names (eg. Knollys/Knowles/Knollis), the interchangeable use of relational names (eg. son could mean son, stepson, or son-in-law), and the constant repetition of given names, sometimes within the same generation are three of the most challenging ones. In the fourteenth century, for instance, 64 per cent of all men in England had one of five given names: Henry, John, Richard, Robert, and William. David Hey, *The Oxford Guide to Family History*, (Oxford: Oxford University Press, 1993), 15-61. The situation had not changed greatly by the seventeenth century. For example, in the Hanserds of Biscathorpe, Hanserd Knollys' maternal grandfather's family, in the period between 1545 and 1630, there were at least five Richards and seven Williams. Maddison, *Pedigrees*, vol. 3, pp. 451-53.

[28] Maddison, *Pedigrees*, vol. 3, p. 937; Gillett, *Grimsby*, pp. 93-4.

[29] In March 1578, Richard and Christobel purchased a manor in Gayton, which would have been a rather profitable venture (see above section on the regions in Lincolnshire). Eventually the farm at Gayton-Le-Wold went to the eldest son, Sir William Hanserd and the farm at Gayton-Le-Marsh to Richard Knowles, Christobel's son-in-law and Hanserd's father. Maddison, *Pedigrees*, vol. 2, p. 451. See Appendix 2.

[30] Maddison, *Pedigrees*, vol. 2, p. 451.

[31] This is discussed in more detail in Appendix 1.

[32] Lincolnshire Archives, document Calkwell BT, 1608/9. See discussion in Appendix 1.

The Early Years: From Lincoln to New England 33

financial position considerably. In his will, proven 8 March 1607, he left her a sizeable inheritance.[33]

Christobel Lacon died in Jan. 1611/1612 and her will, which provides much information about Knollys' family (See Appendix 2), mentioned Hanserd Knollys by name. Hanserd and his brother Zacharie, along with their stepbrother, William Pagett, each received a sum of money.[34] Knollys' parents received a more generous and valuable legacy:

> To my dawghter Knowles my cloth gowne, my burrato kirtle, my pillyon seate, and pillion clothe, my truncke, and some of my lynnen which I used to weare. My will is that my sonne Knowles shall have all my arable land and leas belonging to my farme at Gayton this yeare, to sowe or otherwyse to dispose of as he shall thinke best.[35]

Although the farm at Gayton-Le-Wold was left to Christobel's oldest son William, Gayton-Le-Marsh, Chrisobel left the marshland that had been drained for farming to her daughter and son-in-law.[36]

A cleric in the Church of England, Richard Knowles was well-educated and placed high importance on education.[37] In 1585-86, he received his B.A. from

---

[33] "To Cristabell my wife al snch somes of monie and goods as I with my brother Blundeston stand bounde to leave her at the hower of my death. The Inventorie whereof as she herself did praise them doth remaine in this box with this my last will. Moreover I give unto her fiftie pounds with the chesse bedd wherein she lieth with all the furniture thereunto belonging." Later in the will, he stated, "To my sonne Hansert... a duble ducket" likely referring to Christobel's son Sir William Hansard of Gayton-le-Wold, Hanserd Knollys' uncle. Maddison, *Wills*, vol. 2, pp. 24-25.

[34] For more on this, see below (Appendix 1) in the discussion of Knollys' birthdate. Maddison, *Wills*, vol. 2, p. 59. For the entire will, see Appendix 2.

[35] Maddison, *Wills*, vol. 2, p. 59.

[36] Likely this daughter was her oldest daughter thereby dividing up the land between the two elder children. By willing the land to Richard, her husband, Christobel could legally leave the land to her daughter. The "goulde" jewellery went to the other daughter.

[37] He was not the only clergyman in the family. In fact, it could be stated that Hanserd Knollys came from a line of clergy. The church in Scartho, it would seem, was under the patronage of his grandfather, Richard Hanserd. Following the death of the rector, Francis Tompson, Hamond Hanserd (variously spelled – Hamon Hansard, Hamon Hanshert) was appointed rector on 20 September 1580. Hamond was Richard's brother and Hanserd Knollys' great uncle. C.W. Foster, ed., *Lincoln Episcopal Records in the Time of Thomas Cooper, A.D. 1571 to A.D. 1584*, in *The Publications of the Lincoln Record Society*, vol. 2, (Lincoln: W. K. Morton & Sons Ltd., 1912), pp. 27, 177-78. The *Liber Cleri* of 1594 referred to him as Sir Hamon Hansharte. His will was proved on 25 March 1595. The same *Liber Cleri* showed Richard Knowles as vicar of St. James Church in Grimsby and the curate and schoolmaster in Tattershall in the region of Horncastle. In this record, he was listed as Sir Richard Knowlles. Foster, *State of Church*, pp. 89, 390, 407, 422. Muriel James speculated that this indicated that these members of Knollys' family had been knighted (*Knollys*, pp. 62-64). However, in the

Cambridge University, after which he held several church postings in Lincolnshire.[38] Obviously, Richard played a formative role in the life of his son, both in terms of religion and education. It seems fairly certain that the Knowles home was a devout one in which religious observance was taken very seriously.[39] In his autobiography, Knollys recounted several events from his childhood, which would give evidence of this fact. The first event took place at age six, when he nearly drowned in a pond but "was preserved from being drowned by the water bearing up my Coats, till my Father came, leaped in, and pulled me out". He also recalled how his father attempted "to disswade me from the love and use of strong Drink" whereupon Hanserd made a vow to such an end. In a third instance, when he and his brother Zacharie had had a disagreement, Hanserd's conscience was so stricken that he said: "Brother, we have sinned, come let us be Friends, and pray God to pardon this, and other our sins; whereupon we both kneeled down upon the plowed Land, and I prayed, wept and made Supplication to God, as well as I could."[40] In an effort to see that his sons received instruction in both book knowledge and religious piety, Richard hired a tutor who

> was a godly and conscientious Young Man; He gave us good Instructions for our Souls, and convinced us of the Sin of *Sabbath-breaking*, and of Disobedience to our Parents.[41]

From an early age, Richard Knowles sought to have his sons educated, and by age ten, Hanserd could already read the Latin Bible. This mastery of Latin as well as Greek and Hebrew served him well throughout his life.[42] In between tutors, Hanserd and his brother also attended Grimsby Grammar School, whose

---

sixteenth century, it was not uncommon for "Sir" to be used as a title for clergy and non-graduate priests. See Eamon Duffy, *The Voices of Morebath: Reformation and Rebellion in an English Village*, (New Haven, Connecticut: Yale University Press, 2001), p. 14.

[38] He initially matriculated at Trinity College in 1581, but moved to Peterhouse in 1582. The church positions held following his graduation included Vicar of Grimsby (1593-1637), Vicar of Mentmore, Buckinghamshire (1597), Vicar of Cawkwell (1608-14). Venn and Venn, *Alumni Cantabrigienses*, p. 32.

[39] Such was also the case in his grandmother's home. See the statement in the will of Christobel Lacon: "First and principallie I comend and betake my soule into the hands of our Lord, the eternal and almightie God, through the passion and deathe of whose onely sonne Jesus Christ our saviour and Redeemer I beleeve cleare remission of all my sinnes." Maddison, *Wills*, vol. 2, p. 58.

[40] Maddison, *Wills*, vol. 2, pp. 1-3.

[41] Maddison, *Wills*, vol. 2, p. 2.

[42] Maddison, *Wills*, vol. 2, p. 1. Eventually, Knollys would write grammars and lexicons on the Greek and Hebrew languages and these works would themselves be written in the language of the learned – Latin. See Chapter 5 and 7 below for more on this. See also Foster Watson, *The English Grammar Schools to 1660*, (New York: Augustus M. Kelley, 1970), pp. 4-5.

pupils numbered boys from various ranks of the gentry, including members of the prominent Holles family.[43]

Cambridge and Ordination

Having received a good foundation through his tutors and his time at grammar school, Knollys continued his education at St. Catherine's Hall, Cambridge, matriculating as a pensioner at age 18, on Michaelmas of 1627.[44] This indicated a reasonably high social standing, for he had to pay for his own room and board.[45]

In 1627, when Hanserd Knollys matriculated at St. Catherine's Hall, Cambridge University was at its peak as a Puritan stronghold.[46] St. Catherine's, during this period, had as some of its students the strong Puritans, John Bradford, William Strong, and Thomas Goodwin and according to James Culross, Knollys himself studied under the well known Puritan, Richard Sibbes.[47]

Most biographers of Knollys have claimed that during his study at Cambridge, he embraced Puritanism, and "became strict in his religious views".[48] Knollys himself wrote of these years:

---

[43] Robert Lincoln, *The Rise of Grimsby*, vol. 1, (London: Farnol, Eades, Irvine and Co., 1913), p. 104; Gillett, *Grimsby*, pp. 124-25.

[44] Knollys, *Life*, p. 3; James, *Knollys*, p. 55. According to *Alumni Cantabrigienses*, Knollys matriculated on Easter, 1629. James, however, cited the college's annual audit accounts for the date 1627. It would seem that 1627 would be the better option since *Alumni Cantabrigienses* also stated that he was ordained in June 1629, meaning his a stay at Cambridge would have been too brief to be of any significance. Venn and Venn, p. 31.

[45] Henry Martyn Dexter and Morton Dexter, *The England and Holland of the Pilgrims*, (Boston: Houghton, Mifflin and co., 1905), p. 257.

[46] The great Puritan divines from Cambridge included William Perkins, Thomas Cartwright, William Ames, Richard Sibbes, and Thomas Hooker. Many of the Puritans from Cambridge became influential leaders in New England as well, people such as John Winthrop, John Cotton, John Harvard, and Simon Bradstreet. Other well-known separatists of Cambridge pedigree were Robert Browne, the 'father of English congregationalism', John Robinson and William Brewster, the leaders of the group that would come to be known as the Plimouth Pilgrims, and Roger Williams, the great champion of toleration and democratic ideals, a Baptist, later a seeker, and the founder of Rhode Island. H.C. Porter, *Reformation and Reaction in Tudor Cambridge*, (Cambridge: University Press, 1958), pp. 207-60.

[47] James Culross, *Hanserd Knollys*, (London: Alexander & Shepherd, 1895), p. 13. Sibbs was made Master of St. Catherine's in 1626. Haller, *Puritanism*, p. 66.

[48] B.R. White, *Hanserd Knollys and Radical Dissent in the 17th Century*, (London: Dr. Williams's Trust, 1977), p. 5. Pope A. Duncan made an even stronger statement in his biography of Knollys, where he claimed "Knollys became acquainted with Puritan ideas as a student at Cambridge." p. 9. Culross stated: "There is no direct evidence that

I prayed daily, heard all the godly ministers I could, read and searched the Holy Scriptures, read good Books, got acquaintance with gracious Christians, then called Puritans, kept several days of Fasting and Prayer alone, wherein I did humble my Soul for my Sins, and begg'd Pardon and Grace of God for Christs sake; grew strict in performing Holy Duties and in Reformation of my own Life, examining my self every night, confessing my Sins, and mourning for them, and had a great Zeal for God, and an Indignation against Actual Sins, both committed by my self and others.[49]

He did not state that his Cambridge experience provided him with his first contact with Puritanism, however. In fact, it would not be unreasonable at all to assume that his father Richard could have had strong Puritan leanings himself. Having attended Cambridge in the 1580s and come under the influence of some of the Puritan divines, Richard also would have experienced Puritanism as a student.[50] As the work of Patrick Collinson shows, the majority of Bishops and clergy in the Church of England in the early part of the seventeenth century embraced a sort of Calvinism.[51] Richard Knowles very likely was of that majority. Certainly those things, which he emphasised while bringing up his sons, would indicate a Puritan bent.[52] According to the *Calendar of State Papers*, in 1636, Richard Knowles, rector of Scartho, Lincolnshire, had come under enough suspicion by Archbishop Laud to undergo an examination, which lasted from October 15 to November 12 and beyond. This experience may well have been due to his Puritan leanings.[53]

After two years of study at Cambridge,[54] Knollys was ordained on June 29, 1629 as a deacon and then on June 30 as priest by the bishop of Peterborough.[55]

Knollys was born into a Puritan home; but it was a God-fearing one, and the atmosphere he breathed was Puritan." *Knollys*, p. 9.

[49] Knollys, *Life*, p. 4.

[50] As mentioned above, Richard matriculated to Trinity and received his degree from Peterhouse, both colleges with an abundance of puritans on their faculties. Porter, *Tudor Cambridge*, pp. 207-60.

[51] Collinson, *The Religion of the Protestants*, pp. 81ff. See also Tyacke, "Puritanism, Arminianism and Counter-revolution".

[52] Richard's upbringing included warning Hanserd of the dangers of strong drink and of the importance of keeping one's vows. Knollys, *Life*, pp. 1-2.

[53] *Calendar of State Papers Domestic, Charles I*, 1635-36, pp. 90, 95, 102, 110.

[54] There is no record in *Alumni Cantabrigienses* that Knollys completed his degree at Cambridge. John Tombes did refer to Knollys as a "graduate in schools" along with Henry Jessey and Benjamin Cox. John Tombes, *An Addition to the Apology For the two Treatises concerning Infant-Baptisme Published December 15. 1645*, (London: 1652), p. 21. However, this would seem to be an error on the part of Tombes.

[55] Venn and Venn, *Alumni Cantabrigienses*, p. 31. It is interesting to note that in his autobiography, Knollys' reference to his ordination claims that he was first ordained

The Early Years: From Lincoln to New England

Unable to secure a living, Knollys spent the next couple of years teaching in the Gainsborough Free School.[56] A seedbed for separatist thought, this area produced John Smythe and Thomas Helwys, the earliest founders of what would become the General Baptists, as well as the Pilgrim Fathers.

John Smythe was ordained by the Bishop of Lincoln in 1594 at the time of his appointment as a Fellow of Christ's College, Cambridge. Four years later he left to become a city-lecturer in Lincoln, but failed to obtain a license to preach. In 1600, he was appointed Lecturer to the City of Lincoln, a position that he held for two years before being forced out due to his teachings.[57] Finally, in 1606, Smythe separated from the Church of England and founded a Separatist Congregation in the town of Gainsborough.[58] Within a year, he was joined in leading that congregation by Thomas Helwys, a well-to-do member of the gentry, "descended from a family recognizable since 1243 in the borders of Lincoln and Nottingham".[59] In 1608, having come to the attention of the

---

deacon "and the next day, June 30th, I was ordained Presbyter", possibly a reflection of his anti-episcopalianism. Knollys, *Life*, p. 4.

[56] According to his autobiography, before going to his first charge he spent time in "Gainsburgh" where he taught in the Free-School. It is clear by his autobiography that it took place prior to his going to Humberstone. Knollys, *Life*, p. 5; James, *Knollys*, p. 57.

[57] He supposedly came into conflict with the next mayor who held differing views from Smythe and therefore accused him of "preaching against men of good place in the city" and of failing to be licensed to preach. Archbishop Whitgift had already previously charged him with preaching illegally in St. Peter at Arches and other Lincoln churches prior to his dismissal. Hill, *Lincoln*, pp. 110-12. A.C. Underwood, *A History of the English Baptists*, (London: The Baptist Union of Great Britain and Ireland, 1947), pp. 33-34.

[58] According to Baptist historian Thomas Armitage, Smythe served as a vicar in Gainsborough during which time he was a "determined foe of the Separatists". After examining separatist claims, he "renounced episcopacy as unscriptural and was cast into Marshalsea Prison in Southwark". Upon his release, Smythe became a separatist pastor in Gainsborough in 1609. *A History of the Baptists*, (New York: Bryan Taylor, & Co., 1890), p. 453. It has been held that Smythe contributed to the founding of a Baptist congregation in Lincoln as well, one of five such congregations in the kingdom in 1626. The correspondence between this congregation and Anabaptists in Amsterdam would perhaps give evidence to this. B. Evans, *The Early English Baptists*, vol. II, (London: J. Heaton & Son, 1864), pp. 26, 41-44. See the actual letter transcribed in both Dutch and English in *Transactions of the Baptist Historical Society*, IV, 4, (Oct. 1915) : 248-54. R.R. Kershaw argued that while Smythe may have had some indirect influence in the formation of the Baptist church in Lincoln, "some obvious evidence is to the contrary". "Lincoln: Gentlemen, musicians, and bakers", *The Baptist Quarterly*, XXXVII, 2, (Apr. 1997) : 87-89.

[59] W.T. Whitley, *A History of British Baptists*, (London: Charles Griffin & Co., Ltd., 1923), p. 30.

authorities, this congregation emigrated to Holland, a move most believe was funded by Helwys.[60]

Another significant separatist presence in the region was that of the Scrooby congregation about 20 miles to the west in Nottinghamshire. Founded by William Brewster, formerly of Gainsborough, John Robinson, a friend and associate of John Smythe, and Richard Clyfton, this congregation also emigrated to Holland in 1608 and eventually made up the nucleus of the group of puritans who would found Plimouth Plantation in New England.[61]

Even though these separatist movements had left around the time of Knollys' birth, he likely experienced their influence through a "godly old Widow... who told me of one called a Brownist, who used to pray and expound Scriptures in his Family, whom I went sometimes to hear, and with whom I had Conference, and very good Counsel."[62] This displayed an openness to separatists that few Puritan clergy would have shown at the time.

His tenure in Gainsborough also began his career as a teacher. Throughout his life, Knollys would combine his love for ministry with his love for academics. Indeed, he would own and administer private schools and tutor individuals at various times throughout his life.

Ministry and Marriage

In 1631, Knollys was appointed Vicar of Humberstone,[63] a town not far from the towns of Scartho and Grimsby where he had spent his childhood.[64] Knollys served his duties as minister very diligently, in a manner "strict and laborious".[65] He preached not only on Sundays, but also on all Church festivals and holy days, and at every funeral of his parishoners, whether the deceased was rich or poor. Usually, he spent his mornings in study and his afternoons visiting parishioners or family members. On Sundays, he always preached twice and often three or four times: "at Holton [Holton-le-Clay] at 7 in the Morning, at Humberston at 9, at Scartho [where his father was Vicar] at 11, at Humberston at 3 a Clock".[66]

---

[60] Underwood, *History*, p. 34.

[61] Armitage, *History*, p. 453; John Adair, *The Founding Fathers*, (Grand Rapids, MI: Baker Book House, 1982), pp. 116-17; William Bradford, *Of Plimouth Plantation 1620-1647*, Samuel Eliot Morison, ed., (New York: Knopf, 1953), p. 10.

[62] Knollys, *Life*, p. 5.

[63] Venn and Venn, *Alumni Cantabrigienses*, p. 31. According to this source, Knollys served in this post from 1631-34. According to Culross, Knollys was presented with this living on August 24, 1631; p. 13.

[64] Humberstone, the home of Hanserd's grandmother, Christobel Suttcliffe, when Hanserd was still a boy, was only about 4 miles from Grimsby and Scartho, the churches of which fell under his father's charge until 1637.

[65] Knollys, *Life*, p. 4.

[66] Knollys, *Life*, p. 30. Culross, *Hanserd Knollys*, p. 14.

During the following year, Knollys married Anne Cheney, who would be his wife for the next 39 years.[67] They were married on 22 May 1632, at Wyberton, Lincolnshire, not far from Boston and near her childhood home.[68] Like Knollys, she also descended from Lincolnshire gentry. Anne Cheney's great-grandfather, Sir Thomas Cheney was the Lord Warden of the Cinque Ports. As well, Anne's grandmother, Frances Cheney, married William Cheney of Boston, also of a gentry family.[69] Frances and William Cheney had four daughters and three sons. The youngest of these sons, John Cheney, was the father of Anne, who was born in 1608.[70] According to Knollys, Anne "was a Holy, Discreet Woman, and a meet Help for me, in the ways of her Houshold, and also in the way of Holiness; who was my companion in all my Sufferings, Travels, and Hardships that we endured for the Gospel".[71] Anne not only fulfilled her expected 'wifely' domestic duties, but she also played a more broadly defined role and a more important role as a "companion". Intensely spiritual, this "Holy, Discreet Woman" who contributed "in the way of Holiness" actively participated in Knollys' ministry and in his own spiritual development throughout his life.[72] Together, they had ten children, seven sons and three daughters.[73] In early 1633, Hanserd and Anne Knollys had their first son, Cheney, whom Knollys baptised in Humberstone, Lincolnshire on 13

---

[67] According to Culross, they were married in 1631, Culross, *Hanserd Knollys*, p. 14.

[68] Lincolnshire Archives, document Wyberton Parish 1/1, 1632.

[69] Maddison, *Pedigrees*, vol. 1, p. 242. William Cheney's grandfather was a knight, Sir John Cheney and his great-great-grandfather was Sir John Cheney, also a knight and married to Katherine, daughter and co-heir of Sir Laurence Pabenham, knight (her mother was also a daughter and co-heir of a knight, Sir John Engaine).

[70] Maddison, *Pedigrees*, vol. 1, p.242. According to Maddison, John Cheney of Benington had six sons (William, John of Wyberton, Edward, Thomas, John of Coningsby, and Richard) and four daughters (Frances, Jane, Agnes, Elizabeth). There is no mention of Anne. However, Agnes was baptised on October 16, 1608 (Lincolnshire Archives, document Benington in Holland Parish 1/2, 1608). It would seem that this Agnes was, in fact, Anne. Maddison, the editor of the *Pedigrees*, merely organised the notes of the compiler, Arthur Larkin. Larkin himself had enlisted others to help him prior to this, which had resulted in a variety of handwriting. Some of the entries were nearly impossible to decipher, making Maddison's editorial job difficult. Thus, it is not unlikely that the names Anne and Agnes could have been confused in this process. This is supported further by the fact that upon Anne's tombstone is stated that she died in her 63rd year in 1671. Culross, *Knollys*, p. 95.

[71] Knollys, *Life*, p. 8.

[72] This will be elaborated upon further below when, particularly in relation to the issue of Knollys' views on baptism.

[73] Knollys, *Life*, p. 8. Muriel James has done extensive work researching the genealogy of Hanserd Knollys. However, her treatment becomes convoluted and unclear in places and is very driven by her desire to connect Hanserd Knollys with her genealogical research for her neice. See *Knollys*, pp. 104-9. This author's detailed summary of Hanserd Knollys' children is developed in Appendix 4.

March 1633.[74] One year later, their second son, John, was born and was baptised by Knollys in Goulceby, Lincolnshire on 11 March 1634.[75]

From Knollys' autobiography, it would seem that he tackled his pastoral ministry with all diligence and realised a measure of success.[76] However, shortly after his marriage, he began to question several practices within the established Church of England, namely "the Surplice, the Cross in Baptism, and admitting wicked persons to the Lords Supper".[77] These issues had a history of Puritan resistance in the early seventeenth century. They were offensive due to their "ceremonial" nature. These doubts led Knollys to resign his living to the Bishop of Lincoln, John Williams, who himself held a number of Puritan positions and disagreed strongly with Laud about the placement of the communion table. He straightway attempted to convince Knollys to reconsider by offering him a better living, further evidence of Knollys' competence as a minister. However, Knollys felt at this point that he could conform to the Church of England no longer. A short time later, he also renounced his ordination, which he felt "was not right".[78] At this point, he began even to question his "Call and Commission from Christ to preach the Gospel" on the basis that, although his preaching had moved many to reform themselves, it had not, to the best of his knowledge, converted any to God.[79] For a time, he struggled with this question of his call to ministry. During this period of struggle, he came into contact with John Wheelwright, a silenced Puritan preacher who "had been Instrumental to convert many souls".[80] Wheelwright advised Knollys that he had been building his ministry upon a

---

[74] Lincolnshire Archives, document Humberstone BT, 1632/33.

[75] Lincolnshire Archives, document BT Goulceby, 1633/4.

[76] Knollys even told the rather dramatic account of one parishioner who experienced physical healing on her deathbed due to his prayers. Knollys, *Life*, pp. 5-8.

[77] Knollys, *Life*, p. 9.

[78] Knollys, *Life*, p. 9. Knollys did not give the exact year of his separation from the Church of England. According to Benjamin Stinton, writing shortly after Knollys' death, Knollys left the Church of England in 1636. *An Account of Some of the Most Eminent & Leading Men among the English Antipaedobaptists*, p. 43. The Stinton Manuscripts are housed at the Angus Library, Regent's Park College, Oxford University.

[79] Knollys, *Life*, p. 9. Culross stated, "It is a mistake to assert that Knollys attributed his want of success in his earlier ministry to his connection with the State Church. He does not say so – though his ministry *was* fruitless while he was connected. The fruitlessness is to be accounted for rather by the fact that his views of the Gospel were still confused (though his heart was right with God) – that he understood so imperfectly that standing of grace which believers enjoy." *Hanserd Knollys*, p. 14-15. However, it seems that Knollys himself did not separate the two. His association with (and ordination in) the Church of England and his misunderstanding of grace were intimately connected. See below.

[80] Knollys, *Life*, p. 11.

covenant of works and not upon a covenant of grace.[81] Both this advice and Knollys' association with Wheelwright would eventually cause Knollys to be branded an antinomian.[82] For the next several days, Knollys agonised over his spiritual condition:

> I left him at that time, and went home exceeding sorrowful about my Souls Condition, but I gave my self to Prayer, and begged of God to teach me the Covenant of Grace, and to that end I searched the Scriptures, and I heard one Mr. How preach upon Gal. 2.20. *I live by the Faith of the Son of God;* whereby I saw that I had lived a Life of Works, and not of Faith. Then I began to see a necessity of believing in Christ for pardon and Salvation.... I prayed that Night, and next Morning, and in the night season, that God would give me such a promise. The next day I locked my self in the Church, and in the Chancel, or Quire so called, I prayed very earnestly, mourning and bemoaning my self and my Souls Condition, fearing, and with great brokenness of Spirit, and many tears expressed my fears, that God would leave me and forsake me, and then I should utterly perish for ever.... And I brake forth into this kind of Expostulation with God, saying, Lord who am I! I am a vile sinful Sinner, the chief of Sinners, most unworthy of Pardon and Salvation! How, Lord! never leave me nor forsake me? O infinite Mercy! Oh Free Grace! who am I? I have bin a graceless Soul, a formal Professor, a legal performer of Holy Duties, and have gone about to establish mine own Righteousness, which I now see is but filthy Rags, &c.[83]

This conversion experience was significant for four reasons. First, it was rooted in and indeed established the theological position that would, from this point, define Knollys' ministry and experience, namely a Calvinism rooted in ideals of individual responsibility and conscience. [84] Second, it strongly

---

[81] Knollys, *Life*, pp. 11-12.

[82] Antinomianism in England in the seventeenth century "stressed the complete freedom of the regenerate – restrained by no law". According to one author, the elect were God's specially chosen and He saw no sin in their lives, even when, according to the human perspective, sin had been committed. "The antinomian godly knew their eternal reward was secure. Some drew libertine conclusions from this.... Other antinomians, conscious of the enormous love God had shown in choosing them, wished to reciprocate by living on earth as God would wish them to live." Christopher Hill, "Antinomianism in 17th-century England", in *The Collected Essays of Christopher Hill*, Vol. 2, (Sussex: The Harvester Press, 1986), pp. 162-84. Knollys and Wheelwright would have been the latter, expecting godly behaviour. For a treatment of Knollys and antinomianism, see Barry Howson, "The Question of Orthodoxy in the theology of Hanserd Knollys (c. 1599-1691): a Seventeenth Century English Calvinistic Baptist", (Unpublished Ph.D. Dissertation, McGill University, 1999), ch. 3.

[83] Knollys, *Life*, pp. 12-14.

[84] This is especially evident in the preaching tours upon which Knollys embarked throughout his ministry and in the content of his sermons, as evidenced in *Christ*

connected with and was instrumental in his move into nonconformity. At the heart of this event was the admission that he was a "graceless Soul, a formal Professor, a legal performer of Holy Duties". Thus, his conversion involved more than an awareness of his personal sin, but it included an evaluation of the state and structure of the established Church of England. This statement contained a clear condemnation of formalism and legalism, as it existed in the Established Church, something that he would continue to denounce throughout his life, particularly in his apocalyptic writings.[85] Knollys had not become a Baptist or Independent or even a separatist in any organised manner at this point. He had merely become disenchanted with the Church of England and, in a day of few or no choices, was attempting to find his way. It would take a decade for him finally to settle into a denominational position. Third, his conversion was clearly connected to his call to ministry and to preach, a call that he now saw as based not on the formal recognition of a priest, bishop, or church, but upon the inner urging of the Holy Spirit.[86] As further evidence of this spiritual call, his autobiography mentioned the empowerment of his preaching through revelations on the Scriptures, which came in his sleep.[87] Fourth, his conversion experience associated him with a particular religious expression that was essential within congregationalism – the identification of the true church as a "voluntary association" of "visible saints" whereby individuals entered into a covenant relationship.[88] Within congregationalism, the conversion experience not only had important spiritual ramifications, but it had important social implications as well.[89]

Each of these elements contained reflections of seventeenth-century Puritan theology. Although a conversionist theology of the magnitude of that of Knollys may not have been typical of all Puritans, a self-abasing introspection

---

Exalted: A Lost Sinner Sought, and Saved by Christ: Gods People are an Holy people... the summe of divers Sermons Preached in Suffolk, 2nd ed., (London: 1646). See below, Chapter 7.

[85] See below, Chapter 6.

[86] After this 'conversion' experience, while in prayer seeking guidance as to his call, Knollys related that "whereupon those words were spoken by his Spirit to my Heart, *Act. 26.16. I have appeared unto thee for this purpose, to make thee a Minister, and a Witness both of those things which thou hast seen, and of those things in which I will appear unto thee;* whence I believed that now I had received a Call and Commission from my Lord Jesus Christ to preach the Gospel of his Free Grace." Knollys, *Life*, pp. 14-15. He reiterated this point later when being questioned by the Committee for Plundered Ministers. Knollys, *Life*, p. 21.

[87] Knollys, *Life*, p. 15.

[88] Knollys, *Life*, pp. 1, 3-5; Edmund S. Morgan, *Visible Saints: The History of a Puritan Idea*, (Ithaca, NY: Cornell University Press, 1963), pp. 26, 31-32.

[89] Joy Ann Young, "The Language of Conversion in Early America: Social Identity and the Ineffable, 1630-1850", (UMI Dissertation Services: University of California, Berkeley, 1999), ch. 2.

for the purpose of bringing about personal holiness was certainly not uncommon. Both Norman Pettit and R.T. Kendall have given insight into aspects of English Calvinism, which would distinguish Puritan theology from Continental Calvinism.[90] Pettit clarified what he termed the "preparationist" position of Richard Rogers (1550?-1618), which emphasised the cooperation between the individuals who prepared themselves and the Holy Spirit who drew the individual into the process of conversion. Throughout the preparation, the individual participated through seeking after humility and godly sorrow. At that point the Holy Spirit equipped the natural man with the supernatural ability to turn to God and receive salvation.[91] Kendall emphasised the aspect of assurance in Puritan soteriology, arguing that the thought of William Perkins (1558-1602) represented the Puritans' soteriological struggle, which dealt with the questions of how they could know they were truly in a state of grace and how conversion signalled a state of assured election. Out of this developed the "experiential predestinarian tradition" within which Kendall placed Richard Rogers and other "preparationists".[92] It would appear that Pettit and Kendall were, in fact, emphasising two sides of the same issue – the experience of preparation leading up to conversion and the experience of assurance following conversion.

The writings of Richard Baxter (1615-91), particularly *A Treatise of Conversion* and *Directions and Persuasions to a Sound Conversion*, give evidence of these aspects of Puritan conversionist theology.[93] Baxter argued that: "It is a weight so unconceiveable that depends on the soundness of conversion and sanctification, that our care and diligence cannot be too great to make it sure."[94] The "care and diligence" included an elaborate series of steps and fruits. The process outlined by Baxter coincided with the morphology of conversion set forth by William Perkins and embraced by other "preparationists" or "experiential predestinarians". Conversion came as the result of a process of stages involving both the diligence of the individual and the "Works" of the Spirit.[95] In this process, "man is neither wrenched from sin to grace nor violently constrained by divine coercion but is 'secretly drawn, he cannot tell how, by the unspeakable work of the Spirit'."[96] It would consequently follow then that

---

[90] Norman Pettit, *The Heart Prepared: Grace and Conversion in Puritan Spiritual Life*, (New Haven: Yale University Press, 1966); R.T. Kendall, *Calvin and English Calvinism to 1649*, (Oxford: Oxford University Press, 1981).

[91] Pettit, *The Heart Prepared*, pp. 51-61.

[92] Kendall, *English Calvinism*, pp. 67-93.

[93] Richard Baxter, *The Practical Works of Richard Baxter: Select Treatises*, (Grand Rapids: Baker Book House, 1981), pp. 286-428; 527-642.

[94] "Directions to a Sound Conversion", in *Practical Works*, p. 530.

[95] Morgan, *Visible Saints*, pp. 68-73; Pettit, *The Heart Prepared*, pp. 52-55.

[96] Pettit, *The Heart Prepared*, p. 52.

a man seeking admission to the company of the faithful demonstrate his worthiness not merely by a formal profession, by covenant, by good behavior, but also by showing that he had received true saving faith according to the established pattern by which faith had been shown to come.[97]

In the same line, one could be assured of one's own election by very similar evidence.

While the "preparationist" or "experiential" approach appeared to place great importance on the "work" of conversion, there was no guarantee that the "work" would produce conversion.[98] Comparing one's own life with the lives of visible saints revealed several steps taken by the elect, which led up to their conversion. Puritan preachers urged their parishioners to follow this pattern. While Knollys emphasised the aspect of God's grace in both his earlier sermons and his later treatises, he also stressed the individual's attitude and volitional response:

> But albeit some of you see it is **that which you ought to do, and that you had neede to do**, to wit, **to seeke the Lord; assenting to what you heard** in the first use of the doctrine, that there is much worth, beauty and excellency in Christ, and that poor lost undone sinners stand in neede of him: Notwithstanding how to obtain Christ, you know not as yet. Let me tell you, God offers you Christ upon Gospel-termes, which are these three.... First, God in the dispensation of the Gospell propounds Christ to lost sinners, as the only necessary, and and [sic] all sufficient meanes of Salvation.... Secondly, God doth offer Christ to lost sinners without respect to price or person. And **any one, that will, are invited to take Christ freely**.... Thirdly, God requires, that **those, who do receive him, shall depart from iniquity**,... Live soberly, righteously, and Godly in this present world... And that they shall sell all, lose all, and hate all for the sake of Christ, and take up the Crosse and follow him.[99]

> Any one, **every one that is willing to come** to Christ, and **receive** Christ, and **have Christ freely**; for HE is the **free Gift of God** to Sinners, who are without Christ in the World. **Be but willing to take Christ, and the**

---

[97] Morgan, *Visible Saints*, p. 73.

[98] Baxter urged his readers to "look therefore to this great, important business, and 'give all diligence to make your calling and election sure,' and trust not your hearts too easily, or too confidently". He went on to say, "Consider also, that if you do not go through with the work when you are upon it, you may perhaps make it more difficult that it was before ever you meddled with it, and make it a very doubtful case whether ever it will be done.... Consider, if you take up short of a thorough conversion, you lose all your labour, sufferings, and hopes, as to the matter of your salvation." "Directions to a Sound Conversion", in *Practical Works*, pp. 531-32, 536.

[99] Knollys, *Christ Exalted*, p. 17 (emphasis added).

> **work is done... suffer the LORD Jesus Christ to come** by his Spirit and Word into your hearts, and set up the Kingdom of his Grace in your souls... **Open your hearts** to Christ, when he knocks at the Door of your Souls, and calls you to come to him, to receive him, and **let him come** into your hearts, and dwell in your hearts by his holy Spirit, and sanctifying Grace... **Let the LORD Jesus Christ have the Throne, and be exalted** above ALL in your Souls.[100]

In the account of his conversion in his autobiography, Knollys' placed great emphasis on his preparation and self-abasement during the process.[101] The "preparationist" or "experiential" approach would become extremely important for Knollys and the Particular Baptists as they embraced a Reformed doctrinal position on election while at the same time accepted a congregational ecclesiology that required believer's baptism.[102]

Knollys shared with many contemporary Puritans a dissatisfaction with the formality of the Laudian Church of England. The range of this dissatisfaction and the varied responses of many clerics to forced conformity during the Laudian years have been well documented by Tom Webster.[103] Clearly, there was indeed a "collective insecurity" amongst the godly ministers in the 1630s.[104] Ralph Josselin noted in his diary entry for 10 January 1644: "The Archbishop that grand enemy of the power of godlynes. That great stickler for all outward pompe in the service of god lost his head at Tower hill London, by ordinance of Parliament."[105] Writing nearly a decade later, Josselin showed the depth of the contempt and suspicion that surrounded Laudian formalism. For most, the hostility to Laudian 'innovation' was closely related to strong sentiments of anti-Catholicism. To many, "Laudianism was a step on the road to Catholicism, an instalment of corruption; it manifested a willingness to compromise with the world which if not checked, would eventually lead to Catholicism."[106]

---

[100] Hanserd Knollys, *The World That Now Is and the World That Is to Come*, (London: 1681, Book II, pp. 34-36 (emphasis added).

[101] Knollys, *Life*, pp. 12-14.

[102] More on this in Chapter 7 below.

[103] Tom Webster, *Godly Clergy in Early Stuart England: The Caroline Puritan Movement c. 1620-1643*, (Cambridge: Cambridge University Press, 1997), parts III and IV.

[104] Webster, *Godly Clergy*, p. 334.

[105] Alan MacFarlane, ed., *The Diary of Ralph Josselin*, (London: Oxford University Press, 1976), p. 31.

[106] Robin Clifton, "Fear of Popery", in *The Origins of the English Civil War*, Conrad Russell, ed., (London: MacMillan, 1973), pp. 151-52. See also Anthony Milton, "The Church of England, Rome, and the True Church: The Demise of a Jacobean Consensus", and Peter Lake, "The Laudian Style: Order, Uniformity, and the Pursuit of the Beauty of Holiness in the 1630s", in *The Early Stuart Church, 1603-1642*, Kenneth Fincham, ed.,

The understanding of his call as not dependent on the formal structures and offices of the Church, which Knollys now came to embrace, started to mark his shift toward separatism and an acceptance of the concept of the "gathered" church. Although more radical than that of some contemporary Puritans, this position was clearly within the tradition of quasi-separatism and Puritan lecturers whose activities often supplemented the parochial ministry.[107] In fact, the response of the Bishop of Lincoln, John Williams, himself a Calvinist, "by whom puritans were 'not imperiously commanded to be silent' but dealt with humanely and reasonably", belied a certain acceptance of this practice.[108] When Knollys resigned his living and told him he "would do nothing but preach", Williams, according to Knollys, "connived at [this] for two or three years".[109]

For the next three or four years, Knollys preached as an itinerant in the Lincolnshire villages of Wood Enderby, Fulletby, and Wainfleet. His preaching was not without effect. According to his autobiography, it now began to have a positive effect: "very many Sinners were Converted, and many Believers were established in the Faith."[110] However, it also served to stir up opposition. In Wainfleet, he was "silenced" and at some point in 1636, the Court of High Commission issued a warrant against him.[111] By 1636, this court was being widely used by Archbishop Laud to seek out and destroy nonconformity. Under Laud, a high episcopal view was adopted along with a "deeper sacramental awareness". Laud considered this more formal and sacramental approach to be "of divine right" leaving no room for dissent. It was this "concept of divine right episcopacy in its more aggressive Laudian mould" which led to an intense increase in Episcopal court activity during this period.[112] During the mid-1630s,

---

(Stanford, CA: Stanford University Press, 1993), pp. 161-85. Lake gave a fairly detailed positive description of the "Laudian Style" in this essay.

[107] Tolmie, *Triumph*, pp. 28-34. See also Collinson, *The Religion of the Protestants*, ch. 6.

[108] Collinson, *The Religion of the Protestants*, p. 90.

[109] Knollys, *Life*, p. 9. Culross stated that "the bishop practically sanctioned his continuance in the Church as a 'lecturer', with no local charge, but free to preach as opportunity offered". *Hanserd Knollys*, p. 18.

[110] Knollys, *Life*, p. 16.

[111] Knollys, *Life*, p. 16.

[112] Julian Davies, *The Caroline Captivity of the Church: Charles I and the Remoulding of Anglicanism, 1625-1641*, (Oxford: Clarendon Press, 1992), pp. 50-57. Davies examined the Caroline church, concluding that Puritanism grew more militantly opposed to the Church of England, not because of "its attempt to reinvest the catholicity of Anglicanism" but because of its close relationship with Charles I and his "obsessive drive to eradicate 'profanity', 'popularity', and disorder". He argued that the "politicisation of religious belief" created a church, which was "a weird aberration from the first hundred years of the early reformed Church of England". This "unsettled" the careful consensus that had characterised the Church of England since the time of Elizabeth. Undoubtedly Laud had a significant role in this innovation. p. 3.

the High Commission and the Star Chamber had repeatedly punished William Prynne, John Bastwick, and Henry Burton.[113] Many others fled its jurisdiction to the Continent or America.

Shortly after the issue of the warrant, Knollys was apprehended and held in Boston.[114] Knollys successfully convinced his captor to let him go and from there he and his family made their way to London, perhaps with the intent of following his mentor, John Wheelwright, to New England.[115] Upon arriving in London, they were unable to secure passage to New England right away, though they spent a significant amount of time waiting. During that time, Knollys spent nearly all of their money.[116] They may have been delayed by a lack of openings on ships because of the massive migrations, which were taking place at the time.[117] Finally, Knollys found passage on a ship to New England and on 26 April 1638, he and his family set sail from Gravesend.[118] Any hopes

---

[113] Paul Christianson, *Reformers and Babylon*, (Toronto: University of Toronto Press, 1978), pp. 156-59. See also Webster, *Godly Clergy*, Parts III and IV.

[114] How it was that Knollys ended up in Boston in the south of Lincolnshire is not mentioned. However, Anne's grandmother, Frances Cheney was from Boston and her father, John Cheney was from Benington just 7 miles from Boston. Perhaps they were staying with her family there.

[115] Knollys, *Life*, p. 16.

[116] Knollys, *Life*, pp. 16-17.

[117] One reason for this was due to the intensity of Laud's persecutions. Christianson, *Reformers and Babylon*, pp. 132-36; H.R. Trevor-Roper, *Archbishop Laud*, 2nd ed., (New York: MacMillan, 1965), pp. 258-61. See *Winthrop's Journal*, James Kendall Hosmer, ed., (New York: Scribner's, 1908), vol. 1, pp. 181, 199, 222. This period, often called 'the Great Migration' saw many relocate from England to the Colonies. Between 1630 and 1640, over 13,000 men, women, and children came from England to Massachusetts on crowded ships. Many saw this migration as "great'" because of its religious mission. Although social, economic, and political factors played a role, religious factors seemed most significant. Virginia DeJohn Anderson, *New England's Generation: The Great Migration and the formation of society and culture in the seventeenth century*, (Cambridge: Cambridge University Press, 1991), pp. 12-86. See also David Cressy, *Coming Over: Migration and communication between England and New England in the seventeenth century*, (Cambridge: Cambridge University Press, 1987), ch. 3; Cressy took a more obviously inclusive approach to the question stating, "Emigration was often the result of a bundle of motives, a cluster of considerations that funnelled into a specific decision." p. 74. An even broader and more detailed attempt to define "mobility" of the period was presented by Roger Thompson, *Mobility and Migration: East Anglian Founders of New England, 1629-1640*, (Amherst: University of Massachusetts Press, 1994). According to Thompson, "Monocausal explanations of motivation are simplistic and unhistorical." p. 235.

[118] James, *Knollys*, p. 93. The *Calendar of State Papers* contains a note on 23 February 1639, regarding the seizure of books from the house of a Mr. Knowles, including *Sir Walter Raleigh to his Son* and *A brief relation of certain special and most material passages and speeches in the Star Chamber, at the censure of the three worthy*

he had of escaping the heat of persecution by fleeing to Massachusetts soon evaporated, however. He would land in Boston in the midst of the Antinomian controversy, which had just broken out and involved his friend John Wheelwright.[119]

New England

Knollys wrote very little about his New England experience in his autobiography. Although he only lived there about three years, it certainly was anything but uneventful. Controversy seemed to swirl constantly about him for the entire time. The twelve-week voyage to New England was not a pleasant one. Knollys related in his autobiography that "our Beer and Water stank, our Bisket was green, yellow and blew, moulded and rotten, and our Cheese also, so that we suffered much hardship."[120] The poor food probably caused illness and may have contributed to the greatest tragedy of the voyage: "By the way my little Child dyed with Convulsion fits."[121] When their ship finally docked in mid-July 1638 in Boston, Massachusetts, Knollys learned that a friend had gone from Boston to Rhode Island and that he and his family could stay in the house in the meantime.[122] Because Knollys had very little money (five pounds, six farthings), he hired himself out "to work daily with my Howe" for the next three weeks.[123] Boston had recently been experiencing considerable religious controversy and shortly after his arrival, Knollys was served notice to leave the jurisdiction because, "the Magistrates were told by the Ministers that I was an Antinomian, and desired that they would not suffer me to abide in their Patent."[124] This probably stemmed from his close association with Wheelwright, who had earlier suffered exile at the hands of the Massachusetts magistracy.

---

gentlemen, Bastwick, Burton, and Prynne." *Calendar of State Papers Domestic, Charles I*, 1638-39, p. 499. Both James Culross (*Knollys*, p. 28) and Muriel James (*Knollys*, p. 31) claimed that this was Hanserd Knollys. However, they failed to notice the entry under the same date but two pages earlier, of an order to seize "all books and manuscripts of Tobias Knowles, messenger of the Chamber". *Calendar of State Papers Domestic, Charles I*, 1638-39, p. 497. This was most likely the Mr. Knowles in the second entry.

[119] *Winthrop*, vol.1, pp. 195-220.
[120] Knollys, *Life*, p. 17.
[121] Knollys, *Life*, p. 17. In spite of this hardship, Knollys recorded "but God was gracious to us, and lead us safe thro' those great Deeps".
[122] Knollys, *Life*, p. 17. Who this friend was is not specified. One might surmise that it could have been one of those who had been banished as a result of the Antinomian controversy.
[123] Knollys, *Life*, p. 17.
[124] Knollys, *Life*, p. 17.

The Early Years: From Lincoln to New England 49

In 1636, a religious dispute had broken out in the fledgling Massachusetts Bay Colony, which was to cause great division and strife. The Antinomian controversy began as a theological issue and grew into a political matter of significant proportions.[125] In its brief seven-year existence, the Colony of Massachusetts had already been forced to deal with one significant threat in the person of Roger Williams.[126] Now on the heels of that, it faced an even more divisive situation. Anne Marbury Hutchinson, a sister-in-law of John Wheelwright, had come to New England in 1634. From Alford, near Boston, Lincolnshire, Hutchinson and her husband had followed John Cotton to New England. Apparently while on board the ship, Hutchinson began to alienate people by her unique theological ideas and her "pretensions to direct revelation".[127] John Winthrop's first mention of her came two years after her arrival when he stated,

> One Mrs. Hutchinson, a member of the church of Boston, a woman of ready wit and bold spirit, brought over with her two dangerous errors: 1. That the person of the Holy Ghost dwells in a justified person. 2. That no sanctification can help to evidence to us our justification. – From these two grew many branches; as, 1. Our union with the Holy Ghost, so as a Christian remains dead to every spiritual action, and hath no gifts nor

---

[125] David Hall pointed out that the term itself is a pejorative one implying licentiousness and heterodoxy. It was clearly intended to alienate. *The Antinomian Controversy, 1636-38: A Documentary History*, (Connecticut: Wesleyan University Press, 1968), p. 3. In his introduction, Hall gave a brief history and analysis of the event. For an overview of the subject from the perspective of the 'winners', see *A Short Story of the Rise, reign, and ruine of the Antinomians, Familists, and Libertines that Infected the Churches of New England*, (London: 1644).

[126] An outspoken Puritan and separatist and one time employee of Sir Edward Coke, Williams had troubled the leadership of the Commonwealth almost since the time of his arrival in 1631. Upon his arrival, he was invited to become minister at the church in Boston, which he refused since "the congregation had not explicitly 'separated' from the Church of England". Perry Miller, *Roger Williams: His Contribution to the American Tradition*, (New York: Athenum, 1962), p. 19. By 1634, it became clear to the magistrates of Massachusetts "that Williams threatened to unravel the social tapestry they were so busily weaving and that he had laid an axe to the foundations of the New Jerusalem the Puritans sought to plant in the New England wilderness". In 1635, he was banned from the Colony, at which point he made his way to Rhode Island where he eventually embraced the position of the Seekers. Timothy L. Hall, *Separating Church and State: Roger Williams and Religious Liberty*, (Urbana and Chicago: University of Illinois Press, 1998), pp. 18-39. See also Edmund S. Morgan, *Roger Williams: The Church and the State*, (New York: Harcourt, Brace, & World, Inc., 1967).

[127] John Gorham Palfrey, *History of New England*, vol. 1, (Boston: Little, Brown, & Company, 1858), pp. 472-73.

graces, other than such as are in hypocrites, nor any other sanctification but the Holy Ghost himself.[128]

Winthrop went on to state that John Wheelwright held the same opinions. In response to these teachings, several ministers in the region surrounding Boston had expressed their concerns to the general court.

What had precipitated a feeling that action was necessary was that Hutchinson had begun to host meetings of women in her home for the purpose of discussing the sermons of the ministers of the Colony. While such a practice was not uncommon for the men of the Colony, to have nearly one hundred females involved in this activity, including many of the leading matrons of the town, was highly irregular. However, Anne Hutchinson seemed to enjoy overwhelming support from the members of the Boston church (except for the pastor, John Wilson, and the former governor, John Winthrop), though strongly opposed by the "country towns and churches".[129] Initially caught in the crossfire, John Cotton eventually came over to the side of her opponents.

Seventeen days after John Wheelwright's arrival in 1636, an attempt was made by those of the pro-Hutchinson party to have him installed as teacher in the Boston Church along with John Cotton. However, one influential member of the congregation questioned the doctrine preached by Wheelwright.[130] As well, Cotton did not support Wheelwright, arguing "though he thought reverendly of his godliness and abilities, so as he could be content to live under such a ministry; yet, seeing he was apt to raise doubtful disputations, he could not consent to choose him to that place". As a result, Wheelwright gathered a new church in Mount Wollaston (Braintree).[131] From this point, discussion and dissension continued to permeate the church in Boston and those in the surrounding region. What began as a theological controversy "soon spilt over into politics".[132] Henry Vane, the young governor of the Colony, took the side of Hutchinson in clear opposition to John Winthrop, the patriarch and former governor.[133] According to Winthrop, there was "inevitable danger of separation,

---

[128] *Winthrop*, vol. 1, pp. 195-96.

[129] Palfrey, *History*, vol. 1, pp. 473-74; *Winthrop*, vol. 1, p. 240.

[130] Likely this influential individual was John Winthrop himself. See *Winthrop*, vol.1, p. 197, note 1.

[131] *Winthrop*, vol. 1, pp. 196-97.

[132] John Adair, *Founding Fathers*, p. 173.

[133] *Winthrop*, vol. 1, p. 201. However, on December 10, 1636, Vane received letters from friends back in England requesting his return. Winthrop's journal implies that he was planning to return, but it also seems that on May 17, 1637, Vane was again running for office of governor, an election which he lost. By the end of the summer, Vane had set sail for England to make a name for himself in politics there. *Winthrop*, vol. 1, pp. 215, 229. Although Vane and Winthrop had taken opposing positions in this matter, they remained cordial and continued contact, as can be seen in a letter from Vane to Winthrop on June 10, 1645. Even from across the ocean, Vane continued to urge in

if these differences and alienations among the brethren were not speedily remedied".¹³⁴ As one reads the written record, two things become apparent – the chaotic response to the controversy and the frantic efforts of the leaders and the General Court to gain control and establish unity.

Into the beginning of 1637, "the differences in the said points of religion increased more and more" and the various ministers increasingly took the controversy into the public forum so that "all men's mouths were full of them".¹³⁵ In March, a general court convened at which John Wheelwright was questioned regarding a sermon in which he "inveighed against all that walked in a covenant of works".¹³⁶ Given Wheelwright's earlier discussion with Knollys on this topic, the charge sounds plausible. After much debate, the court found Wheelwright guilty of sedition, which eventually led to his banishment.¹³⁷ Probably within a fortnight, Wheelwright had left with a few of his followers to settle on the Piscataqua River.¹³⁸

Anne Hutchinson was not out of the picture yet. On 30 August 1637, a synod or church assembly had begun to examine doctrinal and practical differences and errors present in the colonies. Two of the resolutions of this synod obviously related to Anne Hutchinson. First, it was determined

> that though women might meet (some few together) to pray and edify one another; yet such a set assembly, (as was then in practice in Boston,)

---

support of liberty of conscience. He wrote about the situation in England in which was exercised "patience and forbearance one with another in some measure, though there be difference in our opinions, which makes me hope that, from the experience here, it may also be derived to yourselves, least whilst the congregationall way amongst you is in its freedom, and is backed with power". Thomas Hutchinson, *The Hutchinson Papers*, vol. 1, (Boston: The Prince Society, 1865, reprinted 1967), pp. 152-53. See also J. Max Patrick, "The Idea of Liberty in the Theological Writings of Sir Henry Vane the Younger", in *The Dissenting Tradition*, C. Robert Cole and Michael E. Moody, eds., (Athens: Ohio University Press, 1975), pp. 100-22.

[134] *Winthrop*, vol. 1, p. 204.
[135] *Winthrop*, vol. 1, p. 208.
[136] *Winthrop*, vol. 1, p. 211.
[137] *Winthrop*, vol. 1, pp. 211, 239-40. Wheelwright further aggravated his accusers by appealing to the King.
[138] Shortly after arriving in the region, in April 1638, Wheelwright made his way inland a short distance where he, along with some others, purchased land, about thirty square miles, from Wehanownowit, the Sagamore of Piscataqua. Here they founded the settlement of Exeter, where Wheelwright served as minister. This led to a dispute between the government of Massachusetts Bay and the settlers in Piscataqua, since many of those involved had been banished from the Bay. *Winthrop*, vol. 1, pp. 284-85, 294-96. Transcriptions of the original agreements are in Nathaniel Boulton, *Documents and Records of the Province of New Hampshire: 1623-1686*, vol. 1, (Concord: George Jenks, State Printer, 1867), pp. 131-37. Thomas Leckford, *Plaine Dealing or News From New England*, (London, 1642), p. 99.

> where sixty or more did meet every week, and one woman (in a prophetical way, by resolving questions of doctrine, and expounding scripture) took upon her the whole exercise, was agreed to be disorderly, and without rule.[139]

This upheld seventeenth-century notions of patriarchy defining spiritual initiatives by women as 'disorderly'. Beyond this, it was held that

> though a private member might ask a question publicly, after sermon, for information; yet this ought to be very wisely and sparingly done, and that with the leave of the elders: but questions of reference, (then in use,) whereby the doctrines delivered were reproved, and the elders reproached, and that with bitterness, etc., was utterly condemned.[140]

This upheld the hierarchical rule of the clergy and elders in congregations.

Following Wheelwright's banishment, in March 1638, the leaders of the colony called Anne Hutchinson to trial, after which they banished her as well. Since it was winter, they had her placed under house arrest until spring, at which time, she and her followers, rather than following Wheelwright, decided instead to go to Rhode Island, where she eventually was killed in an Indian raid.[141]

Of course, the question as to the actual nature of the Antinomian controversy remains of great interest to scholars. It certainly caused upheaval in the young colony for over two years and encompassed many, like Hanserd Knollys, in its wake. Some historians, such as Amy Schrager Lang and Selma Williams, have postulated that issues of gender drove the controversy.[142] It represented a case of women and especially a particular woman, stepping "out of her appointed place".[143] The Puritan fathers claimed the two monstrous births (one to Hutchinson and one to Mary Dyer, a committed follower of the Hutchinsonians) were God's judgment. The male leaders of the colony turned the "femaleness of the women against them", thus proving the error of the women.[144] Just as these women were usurping authority, an unnatural action for them, so the births of their children also exhibited an unnatural quality. While autonomy of the individual was a concern to the Puritan leaders in

---

[139] *Winthrop*, vol. 1, p. 234.

[140] *Winthrop*, vol. 1, p. 234.

[141] *Winthrop*, vol. 1, pp. 240-41, 264. *Winthrop*, vol. 2, pp. 137-38.

[142] Amy Schrager Lang, *Prophetic Woman: Anne Hutchinson and the problem of dissent in the literature of New England*, (Berkeley: University of California Press, 1987); Selma Williams, *Divine Rebel: The Life of Anne Marbury Hutchinson*, (New York: Holt, Rinehart and Winston, 1981). Palfrey, writing in 1858, implied likewise. *History*, vol. 1, pp. 473-74. See also Marilyn J. Westerkamp, "Anne Hutchinson, Sectarian Mysticism, and the Puritan Order", *Church History*, 59 (Dec. 1990) : 482-96.

[143] Lang, *Prophetic Woman*, p. 2.

[144] Lang, *Prophetic Woman*, pp. 56-59; see *Winthrop*, vol. 1, pp. 266-68, 277.

Massachusetts, "the problem of individual autonomy is especially problematic when the individual is female."[145] The first resolution of the synod mentioned above provided some merit to this conclusion. Winthrop made a not too subtle reference to the threat to patriarchy when he referred to Hutchinson's husband, William, as "a man of a very mild temper and weak parts, and wholly guided by his wife, who had been the beginner of all the former troubles in the country".[146] Writing about the antinomian affair half a century later Cotton Mather also concluded:

> They began usually to seduce *women* into their notions, and by these women, like their first mother, they soon hook'd in the *husbands* also. Having wrought themselves any where into a good esteem, they set themselves with a manifold subtilty to undermine the esteem of the ministers, and intimate that their *teachers* themselves, never having been 'taught of God,' had mis-taught and mis-led the people.[147]

Clearly, gender issues played a significant role in this tempest.

On the other hand, Ronald Cohen has argued that the controversy was politically motivated, that the Hutchinsonians were a threat to the civil order of the colony. Unity within the community was sought for the purpose of civil stability.[148] This was particularly important following the Roger Williams incident, when "fearing religious anarchy... the Bay colony's congregations attempted to close ranks in order to prevent their own shattering".[149] Thus, the leaders of the colony acted upon the belief that their great experiment to build a

---

[145] Lang, *Prophetic Woman*, p. 3; Ben Barker-Benfield took a slightly different approach, arguing that early Puritan mysticism had provided a sort of divine union to male Puritans. However, as time passed the metaphor of union took on sexual overtones, making the female a more natural partner for God, so that Puritan men pulled back from the mystical experience and began emphasizing education. "Anne Hutchinson and the Puritan Attitude Toward Women", *Feminist Studies* 1 (Fall,1972) : 83-84. For another interesting twist to the gender issues involved, see Emery Battis, "A Diagnosis of Mrs. Hutchinson's Behaviour in Terms of Menopausal Symptoms", in *Saints and Sectaries: Anne Hutchinson and the Antinomian Controversy in the Massachusetts Bay Colony*, (Chapel Hill: University of North Carolina Press, 1962), p. 346. In this appendix, Battis argued for a physiological source for some of Hutchinson's behaviour.

[146] *Winthrop*, vol. 1, p. 299.

[147] Cotton Mather, *Magnalia Christi Americana*, Vol. 2, (London: 1702), p. 509. Mather, p. 517, in a later chapter, addressed Hutchinson herself in a section entitled *Dux Faemina Facta* (Women made leaders). Here he referred to the meetings led by Hutchinson as "gossipings".

[148] Ronald D. Cohen, "Church and State In Seventeenth Century Massachusetts: Another Look at the Antinomian Controversy", in *Puritan New England: Essays on Religion, Society, and Culture*, Alden T. Vaughan and Francis J. Bremer, eds., (New York: St. Martin's Press, 1977), pp. 174-86.

[149] Cohen, "Church and State In Seventeenth Century Massachusetts", p. 176.

godly society "would crumble about them if the activities of the Hutchinsonians were not stemmed".[150] A lack of cohesiveness would have made the colony particularly vulnerable to native attacks. Also of concern to the colonists was the threat of England's intervention in an attempt to limit the colony's independence.[151] In the midst of explanations of a social and political nature, however, one must not lose sight of the theological issues involved. David Hall also argued that the controversy was "a struggle for control of Massachusetts". According to Hall, however, theological issues played a large role in this struggle. The relationship between justification and sanctification and the question of assurance lay at the heart of this theological debate.[152] Sanctification had become for the Puritan preachers of Massachusetts an "objective measure of grace, some outward sign of holiness".[153] Thus sanctification became the sign of justification. Initially, this emphasis touched off a small revival, which when finished gave way to a "spiritual depression" in 1635-36. This drought and the anxiety that accompanied it led to a re-examination of the emphasis on works that had become so prevalent. The renewed emphasis on grace, which had been initiated through the sermons of John Cotton, was continued by Anne Hutchinson and turned against the "legall preachers" who were preaching a "Covenant of Works".[154] Hutchinson's teaching in turn fuelled anxiety among the colonists and anger against the ministers of Boston, who were, for the most part, preparationists, holding that the individual must prepare his or her heart to receive God's grace.[155] The difference of opinion was threatening the unity of the colony. For those of the Puritan mindset, congregational and community purity was of great importance. For the leaders of the colony, unity was as, if not more, important than moral uprightness.[156]

---

[150] Cohen, "Church and State In Seventeenth Century Massachusetts", p. 175. Simultaneous to the Antinomian controversy was a continual effort by some to implement a more democratic society in Massachusetts. Many of the people of Boston seemed to support the Hutchinsonians. In fact, at the trial of Wheelwright, the church of Boston submitted a petition on his behalf, protesting against his treatment. *Winthrop*, vol. 1, p. 211. The text of this petition can be found in *The Hutchinson Papers*, vol. 1, pp. 71-74.

[151] Cohen, "Church and State In Seventeenth Century Massachusetts", pp. 177-80. Palfrey again, also raised these same points in his *History of New England*, vol. 1, pp. 489-505.

[152] Hall, *Antinomian Controversy*, pp. 3, 10-20.

[153] Hall, *Antinomian Controversy*, p. 13.

[154] Hall, *Antinomian Controversy*, pp. 13-17.

[155] Hall, *Antinomian Controversy*, pp. 18-19; see also Pettit, *The Heart Prepared* and Morgan, *Visible Saints*.

[156] See Battis, *Saints and Sectaries*; Edmund Morgan, *The Puritan Dilemma: The Story of John Winthrop*, (Boston: Little, Brown, and Co., 1958).

Undoubtedly, Hanserd Knollys was astonished by the quick attack upon him and his family by the court and church of Massachusetts. However, like a handful of others, the Knollys family was finding out that "in crossing the Atlantic they had not journeyed far enough to find liberty of conscience".[157] Having received three weeks to leave the jurisdiction, Knollys accepted a call to preach offered to him by two strangers from the Piscataqua plantation, who had heard of him by accident.[158] Knollys and his family then moved from Boston to Piscataqua, where he began to preach and immediately encountered opposition. The governor and preacher there, Mr. Burdett, inhibited him from continuing. The period between 1637 and 1640 was one of intense confusion and strife for the plantation of Piscataqua, both in civil and ecclesiastical matters (and often the two were intimately intertwined). This was due primarily to two things – self-serving ministers/governors seeking personal influence and uncertain and confused settlers with conflicting allegiances. David E. Van Deventer showed how this was evident in the five different pastors chosen by the church at Dover between 1634 and 1642: [1] a pro-Massachusetts Puritan (William Leveridge), [2] an Anglican (George Burdett), [3] an anti-Massachusetts Puritan and accused antinomian (Knollys), [4] an Anglican (Thomas Larkham), and [5] a pro-Massachusetts Puritan (Daniel Maud).[159] Eventually, Burdett left rather suddenly to go to Acomenticus (York, Maine).[160]

---

[157] Anderson, *New England's Generation*, p. 118. Thompson made a similar point stating, "within New England itself, some migration was involuntary". Most would have preferred the comfort of the established colony, but were forced to move, sometimes several times like John Wheelwright whose "problems were less itchy feet than bruised buttocks". *Mobility*, p. 211.

[158] Knollys, *Life*, p. 17. The period of time which would have been given Knollys to withdraw from the Colony was established in 1637 when, following Vane's defeat in the elections for governor, the opponents of the Hutchinsonians passed an order "to keep out all such persons as might be dangerous to the commonwealth, by imposing a penalty upon all such as should retain any etc., above three weeks, which should not be allowed by some of the magistrates". *Winthrop*, vol. 1, p. 219. Perhaps these two strangers had known of Knollys through Wheelwright.

[159] David E. Van Deventer, *The Emergence of Provincial New Hampshire, 1623-1741*, (Baltimore: The John's Hopkins University Press, 1976), p. 273, n. 1. See also ch. 1.

[160] *Winthrop*, vol. 1, p. 328. According to the court records of Saco, Maine, Burdett found himself in controversy there, being "a man of ill name and fame, infamous for incontinency, a publisher and broacher of divers dangerous speeches the better to seduce that weake sex of women to his incontinent practises". The rumours concerning his lifestyle initially resulted in several slander cases in which the court found in favour of Burdett. However, the situation reversed on September 8, 1640, when he was charged and indicted for "deflowering Ruth, the wife of John Gouch". He was also accused of "entertaining Mary, the wife of George Puddington in his house" and this "privately in his bed chamber". Because of these acts of adultery, one resulting in the impregnating of Ruth Gouch, Burdett was fined and censured and there was a report that John Gouch

Meanwhile, Captain John Underhill, another exile from Boston due to the Antinomian controversy, also settled in Piscataqua and soon became governor. Establishing himself in Dover, Underhill "gathered" a church and appointed Knollys the pastor.[161]

Once settled in Dover, Knollys, angry at his treatment in Boston, proceeded to write a letter of protest to friends back in London. In this letter, Knollys vented his feelings, claiming that the ministers and magistrates of Massachusetts Bay Colony were more oppressive than the high-handed Court of High Commission back in England and stating "that here was nothing but oppression, etc., and not so much as a face of religion".[162] For Knollys, the comparison was quite understandable. Having fled England because of his experience of persecution by the Court of High Commission, he resented the unjust treatment received upon his arrival in New England. Unfortunately for Knollys, a copy of his letter was forwarded to John Winthrop, who believed that he "had most falsely slandered this government".[163] Winthrop notified Knollys and John Underhill, governor of Dover, of his knowledge of the letter, which immediately caused Knollys anxiety.

In an effort to avoid further trouble with the Massachusetts authorities, Knollys requested safe passage to come before the authorities in Boston and apologize for his letter.[164] In support, Hugh Peter, an influential member of the

---

threatened to shoot Burdett. *Province and Court Records of Maine*, vol. 1, (Portland: Maine Historical Society, 1928), pp. 70-71, 73-75, 80.

[161] Winthrop stated that Knollys "gathered some of the best minded into a church body, and became their pastor". Vol. 1, p. 328, 295. Nathaniel Boulton, citing Belknap, stated "Underhill also procured a church to be gathered who chose Hanserd Knollys for their minister. He had come over from England the year before; but being an Anabaptist, of the Antinomian cast, he was not well received in Massachusetts, and came here while Burdet was in office, who forbade his preaching. But Underhill, agreeing better with him, prevailed to have him chosen minister." *Documents and Records*, vol. 1, p. 120.
It is questionable that Knollys was indeed "an Anabaptist" at this point. Cotton Mather in his *Magnalia* made the following statement: "I confess, there were some of those persons whose names deserve to live in our book for their *piety*, although their particular *opinions* were such as to be disserviceable unto the declared and supposed *interests* of our churches. Of these there were some godly Anabaptists; as namely, Mr. Hanserd Knollys, (whom his adversaries called *Absurd Knowless*,) of Dover." Vol. 1, p. 243. Perhaps Mather, in looking back and knowing of Knollys being a Baptist in later life, was collapsing events somewhat. However, it could be that by this point, Knollys was beginning to explore the question of baptism. Thomas Leckford in *Plaine dealing*, p. 98, wrote about Knollys' friction with Thomas Larkham, another minister in New England over "baptizing children".

[162] *Winthrop*, vol. 1, p. 309.

[163] *Winthrop*, vol. 1, p. 309. Again, the constant threat of intervention by the Motherland was not likely far from Winthrop's mind in this case and Knollys' letter would be seen as a potential catalyst.

[164] *Winthrop*, vol. 1, p. 328.

Massachusetts colony, who would later become a famous Puritan in Cromwell's army and a regicide, wrote to John Winthrop on 6 September 1639, "I would in his behalfe desire your wonted lawfull tendernes to which wee are inuited by all the 3 parables in Luke 15... I need not cast my drop into your ocean, who knowe how to deale in these matters, only I tender the man etc."[165] Meanwhile, Underhill proceeded to have Knollys arrested and the matter was brought before the Court in Dover, which was satisfied with Knollys' repentance. Knollys, however, was eager to be heard and exonerated by the Court of Massachusetts.[166] Having already sent several letters seeking an opportunity to address Winthrop and the court of Massachusetts, on 21 January 1640, Knollys wrote an exceedingly contrite letter of apology. He opened in great humility:

> Honoured Sir, Duty bindes mee to returne humble thankes to your wor[ship] for your vndeserved love manifested to mee in your letter I lately received; wherein also you againe certify mee, that for your owne parte you are fully satisfyed in my repentence and acknowledgment. I would the Lord (in mercy to my poore afflicted soule) were pleased, to give mee soe much fauour in the eyes of all, who are offended by that my letter, that my eares might heare, or mine eyes may see from them, as I doe from your Wor[shi]p, to witt, That they were fully satisfyed: Till then I am not, (nay I cannot be) satisfyed. By these delayes, I thinke god would haue mee more humbled for my sinne. The Lord of his rich mercy give mee what he requires of mee, and what I see not teach mee, that wherein I haue done Iniquity, I may doe noe more.[167]

---

[165] "Hugh Peter to John Winthrop" in *The Winthrop Papers*, vol. IV, 1638-1644, (Boston: Massachusetts Historical Society, 1944), p. 140. The governor, John Underhill, himself at the time out of favour with the Massachusetts governor, also wrote seeking assurances "that cuch percons as we shall send to tret with youer state maye hafe free egres and regres with out mollestachon: youer letter sent to Mr. Knolse we hafe sene, and both of vs labrod to advanc the work which we hope will redound to the glori of god and the soresing the wicked among vs, but we are prifat in oure prosedingse tel a conkluchon: and so desier you: for we ar threttend". "John Underhill to John Winthrop and Thomas Dudley" in *The Winthrop Papers*, vol. IV, p. 144.
[166] "Hanserd Knollys to John Winthrop", in *The Winthrop Papers*, vol. IV, pp. 177-78. Underhill sent letters to Winthrop as well. One of these survives in fragments and has been transcribed in the Introduction to *Suffolk Deeds*, Liber I, (Boston: 1880). It was originally written in cipher and William Upham who deciphered it, believed it was probably written by Underhill. In it Underhill indicated his satisfaction as to Knollys' innocence in the matter. In another letter of 22 January 1640, Underhill restated his satisfaction, but, according to Knollys' wishes, sought to have the matter dealt with in Massachusetts. "John Underhill to John Winthrop" in *The Winthrop Papers*, vol. IV, p. 179.
[167] "Hanserd Knollys to John Winthrop", in *The Winthrop Papers*, vol. IV, pp. 176-77.

The rest of the letter continued this self-effacing tone. Knollys indicated that he regarded the writing of the letter of criticism as yielding to his human nature and falling in sin. He compared this to the temptation experience of Christ, but acknowledged his own failure: "that I was called out of my Natiue Country etc: and led into the wildernesse to be tempted is not my sorrow, but that I haue sinned in the wilderness, and tempted my god in the desart is the greife of my heart".[168] Knollys further bemoaned his shame, that he who "professe[d] loue to Christ and to the brethren, should pearce him, and his members by that my sinne" thus indicating the seriousness with which he considered the matter.[169] In the remainder of the letter, he again asked for safe passage to offer contrition before the court of Boston and for Winthrop "to compassionate and commiserate my afflicted Condition".[170] He signed the letter, "Your poore afflicted and vnworthy friend in the Lo[rd], Hnsrd Knollys."

Shortly after this, on 29 January, Winthrop sent a response to Knollys assuring him of "peace & saftye wthin this Jurisdiction duringe the time of his cominge stayinge, and returninge free from any arrest ore othere molestation by ore from any Awthy. Here he demeaninge himselfe well according to the order of such Publ Assu pvided that he shall not staye wthin this Jurisdiction aboue tenn dayes."[171] With this assurance, Knollys proceeded to Boston, where on 19 February 1640 he made a "very free and full confession of his offence" on a lecture day to "most of the magistrates and elders" so that the assembly was satisfied. He also agreed to write a letter of retraction and apology to the friends in England to whom he had written in the first place. This he did, leaving it with Winthrop for posting.[172]

While this second letter of apology was not as self-abasing as the one Knollys wrote to Winthrop, it clearly indicated four areas in which he had erred. The first two had to do with the state. First, Knollys admitted that he had been "mistaken" as to their manner of government of both Church and state. He confessed that his own experiences had clouded his understanding and judgment, "For then," he wrote, "I apprehended that they dealt not Christianwise with me in not suffering me to set down within their pattent, because I differed from them in my judgement."[173] He went on to admit that he

---

[168] *Winthrop*, vol. IV, p. 177.
[169] *Winthrop*, vol. IV, p. 177.
[170] *Winthrop*, vol. IV, p. 178.
[171] *Suffolk Deeds*, Liber I., 3.
[172] *Winthrop*, vol. 1, p. 328. Winthrop's journal entry is dated 20 February, while Knollys' letter is dated 19 February. The latter seems the most likely date since Winthrop sometimes tended to collapse several days together in his journal entries.
This letter, like that of John Underhill mentioned above, was originally written in cipher and survives in fragments. However, enough survives that one can easily ascertain the contents and substance of it. *Suffolk Deeds*, Liber I., 1, Introduction, pp. 18-20.
[173] *Suffolk Deeds*, Liber I., 1, Introduction, p. 19.

"should have prayed for them and even blessed them for their favors" rather than taking a critical stance.[174]

His second error lay in the statement "that the Court is more censorious about the faith as a witness of Christianity than the High Commission in England". In hindsight, he regretted that he had allowed himself to be "misinformed by such as favored those who, for their sinful miscarriage and dangerous errors, were censured", that is the Hutchinsonians. Experience had since taught him otherwise and he felt that he had "sinned in speaking false of the Rulers", especially Winthrop.[175]

The last two errors had to do with the religious faith and practice of the colony. Third, he confessed for having "cast so much doubt upon the [faith] and [practice] of Mr. Cotton; 'that he hath no creed.'" He had acted too hastily in this judgment. Here Knollys seemed to imply his concurrence with the position of the Colony leaders with respect to the Antinomian controversy.[176]

Fourth, Knollys expressed regret for his statement "that there is hardly so much as a face of Religion in New England unless upon Saboth", an affront not only to the leaders, but also to all the inhabitants of Massachusetts. Here, he seemed to be more concerned with having made such a general statement, claiming, "I did very sinfully to accuse all." This statement might have applied to "some poor persons who have lost their faith living in the woods and famishing", to "others who have been exercised in Covitous practices oppressing their brethren in bargaining", and to some who profane the Sabbath with "[fans] hoops and costly apparel". However, clear evidences of godliness also presented themselves in the Colony, both in public and in private.[177] Although this apology officially ended the incident, Winthrop in his journal continued to portray Knollys as someone of flawed character and seemed to take great pleasure in his misfortune.[178]

The years of continual upheaval in Piscataqua had left the inhabitants in a state of uneasiness and apprehension. By 1638, when Hanserd Knollys made his way to the area, this conflict had reached a state of near crisis. The region had been placed under the control of Sir Fernando Gorges and Captain John Mason and their merchant-based Council for New England in 1619, but it was only in 1629 that settlements began to be established. Those who came were

---

[174] *Suffolk Deeds*, Liber I., 1, Introduction, p. 19.

[175] *Suffolk Deeds*, Liber I., 1, Introduction, p. 19.

[176] *Suffolk Deeds*, Liber I., 1, Introduction, p. 19. Here the transcription of the letter is sketchy. However, there is a mention of "women" and that "many began to follow their pernishious waye".

[177] *Suffolk Deeds*, Liber I., 1, Introduction, pp. 19-20.

[178] This is nowhere more clearly seen than in Winthrop's account of the trouble, which arose between Knollys and Thomas Larkham, a newly arrived minister in Dover in 1640. This incident will be addressed further below.

primarily merchants, farmers, and fishermen.[179] Even though some of the discontent in the region sprang from mixed religious motives and loyalties, another source of strife came from disagreements between those with interests in fishing and the fish trade and those who had established an agricultural farming community. These issues soon became embedded in political issues as well, the one party desiring union with Puritan Massachusetts and the other seeking to maintain a closer connection with England. This struggle became most intense in the settlement of Dover.[180]

As early as 1631, the governor, Thomas Wiggan, and some residents friendly to Winthrop had urged the Massachusetts colony to extend its jurisdiction northward to include New Hampshire, an invitation that Winthrop cautiously put off.[181] In 1635, John Mason died and the Council for New England was dissolved. In Dover, chaos and anarchy threatened as the opposing factions poised for conflict. The minister George Burdett, an Anglican, overthrew Wiggin and made himself governor. He then appealed to Archbishop Laud to bring the region under royal jurisdiction. By October, Burdett had removed himself to Maine and the people of Dover had chosen John Underhill as governor, understanding that he was a Puritan who was nonetheless hostile to Winthrop and the Massachusetts colony.[182] The new governor became embroiled in the midst of this controversy, as did Hanserd Knollys.

The inhabitants of Dover were not absolutely certain themselves as to where their loyalties lay. These ambiguities emerged in a letter dated 4 March 1640, which a number of them sent to Winthrop following rumours that Underhill was secretly negotiating to bring Piscataqua under the jurisdiction of Massachusetts.

> Honored Sir: We the Inhabitants of Northam [Dover] make bould to trouble you with these few lynes, certifyinge you that whereas wee suppose Captaine Underhill hath informed you and the rest of your brethren of the Matechuseth baye, that wee are all willinge, voluntarily to submit ourselves to your Government upon fformer articles propounded; truth it is wee doe very well approve of your judicious wayes, and shall be very joyful, yu please God to enlarge us, that wee may be free from other ingagements and promises whc some of us are obliged in to the owners or patentees, from whom under his Mat's Letter Patents we enjoy our free liberty, wch causeth us not for present to submit to any other

---

[179] Van Deventer, *Provincial New Hampshire*, pp. 3-6, 9-11; Elizabeth Forbes Morison and Elting E. Morison, *New Hampshire: A Bicentennial History*, (New York: Norton, 1976), pp. 21-27.
[180] Van Deventer, *Provincial New Hampshire*, pp. 3-13.
[181] Van Deventer, *Provincial New Hampshire*, pp. 12-13. Boulton, *Documents and Records*, vol. 1, pp. 118-19.
[182] Van Deventer, *Provincial New Hampshire*, pp. 13, 232 n. 66; Palfrey, *History*, vol. 1, pp. 518-19. *Winthrop*, vol. 1, pp. 279-81; 285; 294-96; 300.

government than that wch wee have already entered into combination to observe according to the King's Mat's lawes.... But for the proceedings of Captain Underhill seeking to undermyne us, and contrary to his oath and fidellyty as we suppose intrusted to him, hath went from house to house, and for his own ends by flattery and threatening gotten some hands to a note of their willingness to submit themselves under your government, and some that have no habitation to bring his purposes to pass.... he hath raysed such a mutinie amongst us wch if we take not course for the stoping thereof, it may cause the effusion of blood, by reason he hath by his designes privately rent the combination as much as in him lyeth...[183]

In this letter, the people of Dover accused Underhill of seeking to bring them under the authority of Massachusetts against their will, "contrary to his oath". And yet, one of those signing this letter, Edward Starbuck, had previously written Winthrop in February, claiming that Underhill was the cause of the delay of Piscataqua coming under Massachusetts' control.[184] Clearly, the region had become paralysed by political indecisiveness and turmoil. Finally, on 22 October 1640, the inhabitants of Dover drew up a covenant organising themselves into

a Body Politique that wee may the more comfortably enjoy the benefit of his Maties Lawes And do hereby actually engage our Selves to Submit to his Royal Maties Lawes together with all such Orders as shalbee concluded by a Major part of the Freemen of our Society, in case they bee not repugnant to the Lawes of England and administered in the behalfe of his Majesty.[185]

Hanserd Knollys and forty-one others signed The Dover Combination, as it was called. It indicated a clear attempt on the part of the citizens of Dover to establish a measure of social and political stability and independence. The purpose given for having drawn up the compact was the "sundry Mischeifes and inconveniences" which had plagued the inhabitants of the region.[186]

---

[183] Boulton, *Documents and Records*, vol. 1, pp. 126-27. Prior to this in September 1639, a group had written to Winthrop "to offer themselves to come under our government". Again, this shows the lack of unity on the subject. *Winthrop*, vol. 1, pp. 320-21.
[184] "Edward Starbuck to John Winthrop" in *The Winthrop Papers*, vol. IV, pp. 185-88.
[185] Nathaniel Boulton, *New Hampshire Provincial Papers*, vol. 10, (Concord, NH: Edward Jenkes, 1877), pp. 700-701.
[186] Boulton, *New Hampshire Provincial Papers*, vol. 10, p. 700. In June of 1639, the nearby settlement of Exeter, under the leadership of Wheelwright, had established a similar compact, the Exeter Combination. Whether or not this document had an influence on the people of Dover is not certain. However, from the correspondence on 4

As well, this document pledged an undisputed loyalty to the King and his laws. This was not an attempt to separate from or defy the government of England, but a clear proclamation of loyalty "till his Excellent Matie shall give other Order concerning us".[187] Not only did the people who signed agree to live by the laws of the King, but they also established their own self-government, holding up as equally essential, laws formed "by a Major part of the Freemen of our Society".[188] In essence, this compact was a political reflection of the ecclesiastical system characteristic of the 'New England way' – non-separating Congregationalism.[189] Whether Hanserd Knollys had a part in the writing of this combination or not, the very fact that he signed his name to it indicated his agreement with it.[190]

Any political harmony established in Dover by the Combination soon came undone due to a religious discord, which had simmered beneath the surface for most of the year. At some time during 1640, Thomas Larkham, a minister who had come over from Northam in England, settled in Dover.[191] The people of Dover "were much taken with his public preaching, he being of good parts and

---

March to Winthrop, it seems that the inhabitants at Dover had already reached an informal agreement. Boulton, *Documents and Records*, vol. 1, pp. 131-33.

[187] Boulton, *New Hampshire Provincial Papers*, vol. 10, p. 701.

[188] Boulton, *New Hampshire Provincial Papers*, vol. 10, p. 701. In light of these two stated positions, it is also quite clear that the people of Dover were indicating here that they not moving toward amalgamation with the Massachusetts Bay Colony.

[189] "The essence of the Congregational idea was the autonomous church, limited to visible saints and founded on a covenant of their profession, which meant deliberate exclusion of the townsfolk." Perry Miller, *The New England Mind: From Colony to Province*, (Cambridge, MA: Harvard University Press, 1953), p. 68. The Puritans of New England prided themselves as being the most successful of reformers – they were non-separating Congregationalists. The New England churches had succeeded in maintaining ties with the Church of England, asserting that it was the true church of God, while at the same time, they had been successful in establishing a church of 'visible saints', a congregation of the 'godly'. This was something the Puritans in England could not do because of the presence of parochial religion and the pressures of Laudian conformity, although eventually the gathered churches of the 1640s would do a similar thing. Thus, the New England Puritans found themselves battling both separatism and corruption. Perry Miller, *Orthodoxy in Massachusetts, 1630-1650*, (Boston: Beacon Press, 1933), especially chs. 3, 6; Morgan, *Visible Saints*, chs. 1, 3; Francis Bremer, *The Puritan Experiment: New England Society from Bradford to Edwards*, (New York: St. Martin's Press, 1976), especially ch. 8.

[190] Of those who signed the Dover Combination, twenty-three had signed the earlier letter to Winthrop. Interestingly, Knollys was not one of them.

[191] Culross stated that he came in 1641. However, Larkham was most definitely in Dover in 1640, for he signed the both the letter to Winthrop of 4 March 1640 and the Dover Combination of 22 October 1640. Culross, *Knollys*, p. 29. Boulton, *Documents and Records*, vol. 1, pp. 126-27. Boulton, *New Hampshire Provincial Papers*, vol. 10, pp. 700-701.

well gifted".[192] Not able to maintain two ministers, the majority determined to call Larkham and "cast off Mr. Knolles, their pastor".[193] While this further rejection must have caused difficulty for Knollys, he adhered to the wishes of the congregation.[194]

In early 1641, Knollys and Larkham began to experience open disagreement over issues of theology, mostly centred on church polity. According to Culross, they disagreed about baptism (the legitimacy of infant baptism) and membership where Knollys claimed that Larkham "received all – 'even immoral persons'". As well, it seems that Larkham followed the service of the Book of Common Prayer at funerals.[195] This disagreement between pastor and former pastor soon erupted into open division with "the more religious" following Knollys, which resulted in the formation of two churches.[196] Knollys and his followers then excommunicated Larkham and his followers. At this point, the tension escalated from a war of words to physical confrontation. Larkham "laid violent hands on Mr. Knolles" and then, with some of the magistrates, gathered a force at his house for protection. Meanwhile, Underhill had gathered an armed force and with Knollys, made his way to Larkham's house.[197] The show of force frightened Larkham, who called for help from the governor of Strawbery Banke, Francis Williams. Williams promptly responded with troops and arrested the participants of the tumult. A trial ensued, followed by an enquiry by the government of Massachusetts.[198] All were found guilty of riot and censured. Knollys and Underhill were each assessed a fine of 100 pounds. Eventually, however, the participants were released from the punishments and all was brought to a peaceable end.[199]

Not long after this incident, the Massachusetts colony successfully extended its jurisdiction to include the New Hampshire settlements. The preoccupation of King Charles I with Parliament lessened the possibility of royal interference. In October 1641, one year after the drafting of the Dover Combination, the

---

[192] Boulton, *Documents and Records*, vol. 1, p. 122. According to Winthrop, Larkham's personal wealth also had an influence on the people's decision. *Winthrop*, vol. 2, p. 27.
[193] *Winthrop*, vol. 2, p. 27.
[194] *Winthrop*, vol. 2, p. 27; Jeremy Belknap, *The History of New Hampshire*, vol. 1, 2nd ed., (Boston: Bradford and Read, 1813), p. 43.
[195] *Knollys*, pp. 29. See also Leckford, *Plaine dealing*, p. 98 and *Winthrop*, vol. 2, p. 27.
[196] *Winthrop*, vol. 2, p. 27.
[197] There are two contemporary accounts of this disturbance. One is by Winthrop in his journal, (vol. 2, pp. 27-8). The other is in Leckford's *Plaine dealing*, pp. 98-9. The one most favourable to Knollys is that of Leckford, who claimed that Knollys went before the troop with a Bible on a pole. Winthrop portrayed him as being more violent, stating that Knollys was armed with a pistol.
[198] Belknap, *History of New Hampshire*, vol. 1, p. 44.
[199] Belknap, *History of New Hampshire*, vol. 1, p. 44; See also related letters, "Hugh Peter to John Winthrop", and "Thomas Larkham to John Winthrop", in *The Winthrop Papers*, vol. IV, pp. 316-19.

Piscataqua region came under the domination of the Massachusetts Bay Colony.[200] Any inhabitants formerly banished from Massachusetts had to leave. Shortly before this change in government occurred, Knollys once more pulled up stakes, left Piscataqua,[201] and, with his family and some others, attempted to relocate to Long Island.[202] Once again, however, trouble seemed to follow.

The territory of Long Island was part of a rather large parcel of land which King Charles I had bestowed on Sir William Alexander, later to be Earl of Stirling, for the purpose of colonisation.[203] The encroachment of uninvited parties, such as Knollys, was not well received. According to an entry in the Suffolk Deeds, Knollys, Edward Tomlins, Timothy Tomlins and some others had "latly entered and taken possession of some parte of the longe Iland in New England". On 28 September 1641, a protest was lodged with Winthrop and the

---

[200] This was accomplished through a combination of means: the purchasing of the Patents for the region, the convincing of the inhabitants to join, and the embracing of a rather loose interpretation of the Massachusetts Charter. Van Deventer, *Provincial New Hampshire*, p. 14.

[201] There is a record reported by Boulton of a Mr. Knowles purchasing land at Strawbery Banke in September 1643 and of land belonging to a Mr. Knowles in Kettery being given as payment of service to a Captain William Hawthorne in October 1651. *Documents and Records*, vol. 1, pp. 172, 197. Muriel James assumed that this Mr. Knowles was Hanserd Knollys. There is no evidence to substantiate this. By 1643, Knollys was settled back in England and there is no indication of further association with New England. James, *Knollys*, p. 101.

[202] Leckford, *Plaine dealing*, p. 98; Winthrop claimed, "Mr. Knolles was discovered to be an unclean person, and to have solicited the chastity of two maids, his servants, and to have used filthy dalliance with them, which he acknowledged before the church there, and so was dismissed, and removed from Pascataquack." *Winthrop*, vol. 2, p. 27. As was evident in the case of Burdett above, such claims were certainly not uncommon at that place and time (similar charges later surfaced against Larkham). However, no official records, neither church nor court, exist to verify this story about Knollys. In fact, Cotton Mather, a second generation Massachusetts Puritan, described Knollys as a person of piety. *Magnalia*, vol. 1, p. 243. Certainly, no incident prior to or after this in Knollys' life coincided with this allegation. Thus, in light of the lack of evidence and of Winthrop's obvious hostility to Knollys, the veracity of this claim by Winthrop should be received sceptically.

[203] William Alexander was, like James, a Scotsman. He was a poet who moved to London in 1603, upon James' accession to the Throne of England. After holding several positions in the King's Household, under Charles I he was made a Privy Councillor and Secretary of State for Scotland and was created a Peer, first the Viscount and then the Earl of Stirling. In 1621 he began to express to James I his interest in the American colonies. His first grant in 1621 included the regions in eastern Canada of the Gaspe, New Brunswick, and Nova Scotia. This was later expanded in 1629 and 1635 to include most of Canada, northern New England (from Atlantic to Pacific Oceans), and many of the Islands along the eastern seaboard. See Edmund Slafter, *Sir William Alexander and American Colonization*, (Boston: The Prince Society, 1873, reprinted, 1966).

government of Massachusetts against "the said indruders" by James Farrett, the agent of Sir William Alexander who was in charge of overseeing the sale and settling of the lands and of establishing several plantations.[204] Any further actions to be taken against these settlers were not mentioned. However, at this time, word had reached Knollys that his aging father needed him back in England.[205] As well, the winds of change were sweeping England. The invasion of England by Scottish troops in August 1640, the calling of the Long Parliament in November 1640, the abolition of the Star Chamber and the Court of High Commission in July 1641 – all of these events indicated that new opportunities were opening up back home. Without question, life had not been easy for Knollys in New England and in the words of Culross, he "made up his mind that he might as well be knocked about in *Old* England".[206]

Conclusion

Hanserd Knollys' early life and environment had a vital role in shaping his later career. Knollys did not publish anything during these early years, and, indeed, his thought had not yet taken any coherent shape. However, the emphasis placed on education by his father, Richard, had a very practical effect on young Hanserd. Not only did Richard provide for and encourage the education of his sons, but he also created in them, at least in Hanserd, a love of learning. This is evident in Knollys' continued participation in learning even after leaving Cambridge. For Hanserd Knollys, life was a constant process of learning,

---

[204] Liber I., 21. Of especial interest to Alexander was the settling of Long Island. It seems that shortly after Alexander's death in February 1641, Farrett's agency came to an end. In all likelihood, this was an attempt on the part of Farrett to keep things in order during an interim period. Slafter, *Alexander*, pp. 88-90.

[205] According to the *Protestation Returns of 1640/41 for Lincolnshire*, both Richard Knollys and Zachary Knollis signed their names, Richard on 15 March, Zachary on 18 March 1641. Both were still in Scartho, Richard being the clerk. This vow and protestation bound the one who took it "to maintain and defend... the true Reformed Protestant Religion, expressed in the Doctrine of the Church of England, against all Popery and Popish Innovations,... and according to the duty of my Allegiance, His Majesty's Royal Person, Honour, and Estate, as also the Power and Privileges of Parliaments, the lawful Rights and Liberties of the Subjects." The escalating tension in England at this time could likely be the reason that Richard Knollys, now about seventy-five years old, desired his eldest son to return home. *Protestation Returns of 1640/41 for Lincolnshire*, transcribed by W.F. Webster, (Nottingham: 1984), p. 55.

[206] *Knollys*, p. 30. David Cressy assessed that people like Knollys and Larkham were "failures in New England, misfits in the godly commonwealth, who departed America in a cloud of scandal and recrimination. The revolution in England afforded them an opportunity to make something of their lives, after making only blunders and enemies in New England." *Coming Over*, p. 199. However, such an assessment seems to have unfairly embraced and accepted Winthrop's biased position.

particularly in the study of the Scriptures and theology. This love of learning not only would make itself known in his personal study, but in his desire that others learn as well. At least one of his children would go on to graduate from university and another would study for a time at Charterhouse.[207] As well, Knollys was nearly as committed throughout his life to teaching as he was to ministry.

Undoubtedly the 'puritan' environment of his childhood, the clear Puritan influences of Cambridge, the incidental separatist elements encountered at Gainsborough, and the impact of John Wheelwright helped to form the 'scruples of conscience', which later drove him to give up his charge, renounce his ordination, and embrace separatist tendencies. These experiences started Knollys down the road of questioning nonconformity. Long before Knollys became a 'Puritan', he had begun to embrace the theological principles and practices that characterised many Puritans. Prior to his becoming a separatist and a Baptist, Knollys had begun to exhibit an inclination to 'come apart'; like many Puritans, he questioned the ceremony and practices of the Laudian Church of England. In New England, he may have raised questions about infant baptism. Even before departing for New England, John Wheelwright had a great impact on young Knollys. A key influence on his piety and theology, Wheelwright contributed to Knollys' own conversion experience, and shaped his theology in very practical ways, causing him to be gracious and tempered with gentleness, even in the heat of debate, when most of his contemporaries were more often characterised by a harsh intolerance.[208] The conversion experience facilitated by Wheelwright was instrumental in instilling within Knollys a determination to preach in order that others be "Converted, and... established in the Faith".[209]

The time Knollys spent in New England, though fraught with trial and tribulation, helped him to mature socially and spiritually. For one who had withdrawn from the Church of England, but had not yet reached a clear understanding of his new ecclesiastical position, having an extended exposure to the Congregational way provided experience unavailable elsewhere. Upon his return to England, Knollys naturally joined in fellowship with the

---

[207] Cheney would graduate from Cambridge University. Venn and Venn, *Alumni Cantabrigienses*, p. 31. Knollys' son John would enrol briefly at Charterhouse. Bower Marsh and Frederic Crisp, eds., *Alumni Carthusiani: A Record of the Foundation Scholars of Charterhouse, 1614-1872*, (1913), pp. 22-23. It is a reasonable assumption that two more of Knollys' sons, Hanserd and Samuel, were educated as well. See Appendix 4.

[208] Perhaps his experiences in Dover, both with respect to the severe letter he wrote against the Boston leaders and to the confrontation he had with Larkham, served as practical lessons in grace as well.

[209] Knollys, *Life*, p. 16.

Independent Jessey Church.[210] This acceptance by Knollys of the congregational style of church government also eased the transition to becoming a Baptist. Without question, Knollys' experience of Laudian persecution and New England oppression helped to form of his views on tolerance and liberty of conscience. Having felt the bite of intolerance and the sting of injustice, Knollys became perhaps more sensitive to those holding opinions divergent from his. While throughout his life and in his writings he would hold tenaciously to his theological positions and stubbornly take a stand on them, he always seemed to do so with a measure of humility.

---

[210] W.T. Whitley, "The Jacob-Jessey Church, 1616-1678", *Transactions of the Baptist Historical Society*, I, 4, (Jan. 1910) : 246-56; W.T. Whitley, "Debate on Infant Baptism, 1643", *Transactions of the Baptist Historical Society*, I, 4, (Jan. 1910) : 237-45.

CHAPTER 3

Hanserd Knollys and the Particular Baptists' Struggle for Legitimacy in the 1640s

Introduction

In a society where much of life is based upon convention and tradition and where stability is perceived as being present in a clearly established order, changes, whether small or great, can trigger a chain of events, which seem to disrupt the very foundation of that society. Such was the situation in England during the decade of the 1640s, when established social, political, and religious values and norms suddenly came into a state of flux. In the words of Christopher Hill, "anything seemed possible; not only were the values of the old hierarchical society called in question, but also the new values". In a manner of speaking, the world was turned upside down![1] This period witnessed the overthrow of established religion, two civil wars, the execution of the Archbishop of Canterbury and of the King, and the establishment of a republican government. Barry Reay wrote that in the early 1640s, religion was the primary factor. "For it was religion," he claimed, "which in a real sense stimulated and fired revolution."[2] He went on to justify his position by pointing out that religion was central to life in the seventeenth century, "the legitimising ideology of the rulers" as well as "the revolutionary idiom of the ruled".[3] John Morrill further concurred with this assessment. He claimed that the civil war "was an *aggressive* religious operation, a challenge to the whole of the existing structure and practice". He went on to argue that the English Civil Wars were,

---

[1] Christopher Hill, *The World Turned Upside Down*, (London: Maurice Temple Smith, 1972; reprint ed., Penguin Books, 1991), pp. 14-15.
[2] Barry Reay, "Radicalism and Religion in the English Revolution: an Introduction", in *Radical Religion in the English Revolution*, ed. B. Reay and J.F. McGregor, (New York: Oxford University Press, 1984), p. 1.
[3] Reay, "Introduction", p. 3. William Haller wrote, "The church was one with the living whole which was the nation. Rulers were responsible to God for their subjects' welfare, a responsibility to be exercised vigorously and in the fear of the Lord." *The Rise of Puritanism*, (New York: Columbia University Press, 1938, reprint ed. Philadelphia: University of Pennsylvania Press, 1984), p. 228.

in fact, "England's Wars of Religion", the last series of European wars of religion springing out of the Reformation of the sixteenth century.[4]

Following the tension of the 1630s when Laudian censorship and persecution aimed at creating uniformity in both Church and State, the people of England were poised for change. With the opening of the Long Parliament in the fall of 1640, a parliament which very quickly made clear its desires for reform, and with the execution of the Earl of Strafford in 1641, it was unmistakable that a new political order was replacing the old. That first year of the Long Parliament witnessed a "year of expectation" when many believed God would establish reformation, both religious and secular.[5] This expectation was heightened even more by the return of Prynne, Burton, and Bastwick from exile and the breakdown of religious censorship of the press.[6] In the words of Paul Christianson, "the land, the time, and the people all seemed ripe for this culmination of holy history."[7] In the midst of this expectation, many others, who had been in exile on the continent or in the colonies, returned to England, including Hanserd Knollys.

Although, no freedom of the press or religious toleration was enacted, considerable freedom of expression existed in England, especially in comparison to the previous decade. The actual situation seemed like a religious vacuum, which would quickly to be filled by a variety of religious opinions and systems ranging from Presbyterianism to scepticism. This was a period of questioning and re-evaluating. The only area of consensus among the reformers (whether conservative or radical) involved an attack upon the Arminian, papist edifices of the Episcopalians. Like the altars of Baal in ancient Israel, the idolatrous and blasphemous practices instituted and propagated by Laud were demolished through popular reaction and official initiatives. In everything else though, division and confusion reigned. The situation was perhaps best summed up in the comment of Sir Henry Vane, Sr. "We all tended to one end, that was reformation, only we differed in the way."[8] Hill pointed out the diversity of the time by showing how some of the various groups that arose had political aims, some religious aims, and some social aims. He also indicated that there existed much elasticity, much movement from one ideology or group

---

[4] John Morrill, *The Nature of the English Revolution*, (New York: Longman, 1993), pp. 14, 33-175.

[5] Paul Christianson, *Reformers and Babylon*, (Toronto: University of Toronto Press, 1978), p. 180, ch. 5. In many instances, this expectation was expressed in apocalyptic or millenarian terms, interpreting the events taking place in eschatological ways. More on this below in Chapter 6.

[6] Christianson, *Reformers and Babylon*, pp. 181-82. Joseph Ivimey, *A History of the English Baptists*, vol. I, (London: 1811), pp. 146-47.

[7] Christianson, *Reformers and Babylon*, p. 208.

[8] Cited by J.P. Kenyon, ed., *The Stuart Constitution*, 2nd ed., (Cambridge: Cambridge University Press, 1986), p. 229.

to another.[9] Often sectaries began their lives within the Church of England, some even as clergy, and moved through Presbyterian or Independent circles to the even more radical positions of the Baptists, Levellers, or Ranters. This was in fact the route that Hanserd Knollys pursued. Perhaps one of the best examples of this 'fluidity' was Lawrence Clarkson who went from the Church of England to Presbyterianism to Independency to Antinomianism. From this point he became a Baptist, a Seeker, a Ranter who dabbled in astrology and magic, and finally a Muggletonian.[10] Other religious radicals often changed groups, for example, from Baptist to Leveller or Ranter to Quaker, or held sympathies for more than one group at any given time (e.g. Baptists who were also Levellers or Fifth Monarchists). Within this atmosphere of openness, diversity, turmoil and confusion, the fledgling Baptist churches defined their doctrines and practices. A relatively new religious group in England, many of its eventual members had experienced persecution during the 1630s. The Baptists now faced a new struggle – the struggle for acceptance and religious liberty.

The predominantly Puritan[11] Long Parliament for the first year of its existence had managed to avoid legislation on the issue of religion, seeking

---

[9] Hill, *World*, p. 14. He highlighted the 'fluidity' of the period. "One of the aims of this book will be to suggest that in this period things were much more blurred. From, say, 1645 to 1653, there was a great overturning, questioning, revaluing, of everything in England. Old institutions, old beliefs, old values came in question. Men moved easily from one critical group to another."

[10] Lawrence Claxton, *The Lost Sheep Found or The Prodigal returned to his Fathers house, after many sad and weary Journey through many Religious Countreys*, (London: 1660); A.L. Morton, *The World of the Ranters: Religious Radicalism in the English Revolution*, (London: Lawrence & Wishart, 1970), pp. 115-42; "Claxton or Clarkson, Laurence", *Dictionary of National Biography*, vol. IV, pp. 461-63.

[11] When using different 'tags' or designations such as puritan or radical, one must be aware of the differences in meanings present in the 17th century. An Episcopalian would see Presbyterians, or Independents, as being radicals. The word Puritan was a slanderous one, and came to be used primarily for one who desired reform to bring about a stricter, more zealous spirituality in religion. It must not be overlooked that there existed Puritans who wished to remain Episcopalian. Many times, those in the Presbyterian party grouped Independents with such sects as the Baptists, Seekers, Quakers, and Ranters. At the same time, Baptists did not consider themselves to be radically different from the Independents or Presbyterians. In fact, they viewed themselves as being equally legitimate as these two groups. With regard to other religious groups, some Baptists moved freely among the Seekers and Levellers and other sects, while others disdained them and sought to distance themselves from such 'radicals'. Ultimately how one defined oneself and others very much depended on one's perspective. It is also important to keep in mind that the same difficulty arises in the way modern historians group people from the seventeenth century, again, depending on one's own perspective (Baptist, Anglican, Presbyterian or secular). Haller, p. 3-5. Christopher Hill, *Society and Puritanism in Pre-Revolutionary England*, (London: Secker & Wartburg, 1964), ch. 1.

instead to deal with political issues related to the limiting of the power of the king, the righting of wrongs done through the abuse of royal power, and the prosecution of those royal servants, such as the Earl of Strafford and Archbishop Laud, whom they felt had misled the King. Following this, however, the Parliament had to deal with the reformation of England's religion. Two dominant groups emerged among the Parliamentarians: 1] the more conservative Presbyterians, who advocated a reformed state Church and 2] the more radical Independents, who advocated religious accommodation for independent, gathered congregations.[12] As these two groups grappled with the issue of the nature of England's religious future, as well as the political issues which eventually led to the first Civil War, smaller groups, such as the Baptists, struggled for legitimacy, calling for toleration and recognition as orthodox expressions of faith within the church. In many ways, the situation in England mirrored many of the debates within the Reformation in Europe of the previous century.

Although the 1640s brought reprieve from physical persecution, much opposition to the Baptists still existed, mostly in the form of pamphlets. One of the charges laid against this unfamiliar new group held that their leaders were unschooled and ignorant. Ephraim Pagett, a harsh opponent of the Baptists wrote: "For their learning: they have none at all... many of them scarcely read; yea... many of their Preachers never saw a Bible."[13] In light of these criticisms, it was noteworthy when an educated theologian did join their ranks. Hanserd

---

Murray Tolmie, *The Triumph of the Saints*, (London: Cambridge University Press, 1977), p. 130. Even fellow Puritans, William Prynne and Henry Burton who had together faced persecution under Laud, squared off against each other in the 1640s. Burton wrote in the preface of his work on Independent Churches: "To Mr. William Prinne, etc. My Deare Brother and late companion in tribulation..." *A Vindication of Churches Commonly Called Independent*, (London: 1644). Prynne's attitude toward the Independents was not nearly so conciliatory. For a brief discussion on the disagreement among modern historians as to the meaning of the tag Puritan, see above, Chapter 2, note 4.

[12] In a religious sense, the major distinguishable difference between Presbyterians and Independants was liberty of conscience. However, these two terms also delineated political groupings in the Long Parliament. The Presbyterians favoured a negotiated settlement with the king, were pro-Scots, and feared social revolution. The Independents favoured defeating the king militarily, were anti-Scots and exhibited much less apprehension about social revolution. They had no objection to lay preaching, for example, something that the Presbyterians regarded with horror since it smacked of disorder and presented an affront to religious hierarchy, which Presbyterians continued to embrace. See See Ian Gentles, *The New Model Army in England, Ireland, and Scotland, 1645-1653*, (Cambridge, MA: Blackwell, 1992) and Ernest Sirluck, "Introduction", in Don M. Wolfe, Gen. Ed., *The Complete Prose Works of John Milton*, vol. 2, (New Haven: Yale University Press, 1959), chapters 1 and 2.

[13] Ephraim Pagett, *Heresiography: Or, A Description of the Heretickes and Sectaries of These Latter Times*, (London: 1645), p. 37. Hereafter designated *Heresiography*.

Knollys was such a person. A former Episcopalian minister who had become a separatist, Knollys continued grappling with his own beliefs even as the Long Parliament began to sit. In 1643, when the Parliament appointed the Westminster Assembly of Divines with the task of charting England's religious direction, Knollys had started to shift his own direction. Sometime in 1644 or 1645, Knollys became convinced that believer's baptism was the biblical model becoming instrumental in the early Particular Baptist movement.[14] By 1645, he had become actively involved in the Baptist struggle for recognition as a legitimate church, with its own doctrines and polity. Knollys and other Baptists attempted to gain this recognition through the publication of a Baptist Confession and through participation in public debates, both oral and written. In his response to John Bastwick and John Saltmarsh, for example, Knollys focused on the two most distinctive aspects of the doctrine and polity of the Particular Baptists – gathered congregational church government and believer's baptism.[15]

This chapter attempts to examine and analyse the Baptist struggle[16] for tolerance and recognition in the 1640s within the context of the reformation taking place in the English Church. At the heart of the issue of toleration were the questions of the nature of church membership and of the nature of truth. Should church membership be compulsory, based on the place of one's birth, as in the parochial systems of the Episcopalians and Presbyterians? According to John Bastwick, the New Testament ordained such a model. Or, should church membership be voluntary, based on the individual believer's choice and beliefs, as in the 'gathered church' system of the Independents and the Baptists? Was Truth unified? Could a particular group or denomination legitimately monopolise the Truth? Was a particular doctrinal system the total embodiment of Truth? Or did all groups have a portion of the Truth, as John Saltmarsh contended, so that no one system embodied it? These were some of the questions with which the Baptists and their contemporaries wrestled in the tumultuous 1640s.

This chapter examines Knollys' involvement in and contribution to this Baptist struggle and the overall debate to determine the religious future of England. Focusing primarily on his two treatises of 1645-46, in which Knollys engaged Bastwick and Saltmarsh as leading spokesmen for the Presbyterians

---

[14] See the document known as the Knollys Memorandum, in W.T. Whitley, "Debate on Infant Baptism", *Transactions of the Baptist Historical Society* I, 4, (Jan. 1910) : 237-45.

[15] His response to these men is found in Knollys, *A Moderate Answer unto Dr. Bastwicks Book Called "Independency not God's Ordinance"*, (London: 1645) and *The Shining of a Flaming Fire In Zion Or, A clear Answer unto 13 Exceptions, against the Grounds of New Baptism; (so called) in Mr. Saltmarsh his Book; Intituled, "The Smoke in the Temple"*, p. 15, etc., (London: 1645).

[16] The focus will be specifically on the Particular Baptists.

and Independents, it will also examine the role of the Baptist Confessions of Faith and the participation of Baptists, specifically Knollys, in conferences and public debates. In these activities, Knollys attempted to defend the Baptist positions on independent gathered churches and believer's baptism, and also to gain respectability for the Baptist cause. Through his use of logic and rhetoric, and other academic and exegetical skills, Knollys entered the arena of debate on equal footing with his university-educated opponents.

Back in London

In the autumn of 1641, Hanserd Knollys with his wife, Anne, who was at this point "great with another Child", and their son Cheney, boarded a ship bound for London. They docked in London on 24 December 1641.[17] King Charles I had just returned from his rather dubious trip to Scotland. In Ireland, rebellion had broken out in October, fanning the fires of fear of 'popery'. And in Westminster, a growing distrust of the King had led to the introduction of a bill which would take the command of the army out of the hands of the King, so that Parliament alone would appoint the commanders. The House of Lords stalled the Militia Bill, but the attempt to pass such a bill served as an indication of the mounting tension in the capital.[18]

As these momentous events were transpiring, Hanserd Knollys had more pressing concerns at hand – earning a living and finding a home for his family:

> I was still poor, and sojourned in a Lodging till I had but sixpence left, and knew not how to provide for my Wife and Child…. having paid for my Lodging, I went out not knowing whither Gods good hand of Providence would lead me to receive something towards my present subsistence.[19]

Having experienced so much difficulty in New England, Knollys must have wondered when his fortunes would shift. In the midst of this crisis, a woman

---

[17] Hanserd Knollys, *The Life and Death of That Old Disciple of Jesus Christ, and Eminent Minister of the Gospel, Mr. Hanserd Knollys*, edited by William Kiffin, (London: 1692), p. 18. According to Knollys, his son "was about three years old". It would seem that Knollys, writing nearly three decades later, was mistaken here in his remembrance of Cheney's age. In the Lincolnshire Archives is the baptismal record for Cheney Knowles dated 13 March 1633. Lincolnshire Archives, document Humberstone BT, 1632/3. According to *Alumni Cantabrigienses*, Cheney Knowles matriculated at Queen's at Cambridge on July 21, 1647. If he had been three in 1641 when they returned to London, he would have entered university at age nine. Venn and Venn, p. 31.
[18] Barry Coward, *The Stuart Age – England 1603-1714*, 2nd ed., (London: Longman, 1994), pp. 198-200.
[19] Knollys, *Life*, p. 18.

who had sought him out met him in the street. She informed him that "some Christian Friends" had provided a house for him for the next fifteen weeks, and she gave him 20s., which Dr. John Bastwick had left for him. Knollys and his wife were extremely grateful for "this Mercy and Divine Providence, being so suitable and seasonable a supply".[20] Indeed it was, for his wife Anne, battered and aching from their voyage "had sore Labour", which laid her up for about the next ten weeks. Once again, Providence smiled upon them as two doctors, a surgeon, and an apothecary cared for her on a daily basis free of charge.[21]

At the end of the fifteen weeks, some other friends gave them seven pounds. Knollys, thankful of the charity, but eager to gain some employment, asked these friends if they might acquire some students for him while he arranged for a place to open a school. Soon after, a schoolmaster on great Tower-hill died suddenly, and Knollys obtained some of his scholars and began teaching.[22] A short time later, he was selected to be the master of the Mary-Axe Free School, to which he took sixty scholars. Within a year at Mary-Axe Free School, he had gathered under his tutelage one hundred and forty scholars and sixteen boarders.[23] Knollys was quite fortunate in this regard. According to David Cressy, records of the period indicate that in the early 1640s, throughout the Civil War period and afterward, England experienced "a catastrophic collapse of elementary education".[24] Despite this trend, Knollys seemed able to develop and expand a school in the early 1640s. During the next year and a half or two years, Knollys improved his economic situation through his teaching activities. In comparison to the difficult years in New England, these years must have seemed something of a respite. However, as stable as this time may have been for Knollys personally, for the nation it was quite the opposite. England stood poised on the brink of civil war.

The early 1640s witnessed increased restlessness due to a depression of trade, unemployment and the presence of a Scottish army on English soil in the

---

[20] Knollys, *Life*, pp. 18-19. This is a most curious event. John Bastwick was a staunch Presbyterian who had suffered greatly under Laud. He would later become one of Knollys' literary opponents. It seems that somehow he had been made aware of Knollys' plight or had been awaiting his return. For more on this, see below.
Anne Knollys' own 'Puritan devotion' can be seen in this instance in her response to these acts of kindness: "Oh dear Husband, how sweet is it to live by Faith, and trust God upon his bare Word: Let us rely upon him whilst we live and trust him in all Straits; with many such like expressions." Knollys, *Life*, p. 19.

[21] Knollys, *Life*, p. 19. It causes one to wonder if once again, John Bastwick, himself a medical doctor, played a role in her care.

[22] Knollys, *Life*, p. 20. The text seems to imply that Knollys actually continued to teach at great Tower-hill for a time. By scholars, what is meant is students who would come to study under him for the day, as opposed to boarders.

[23] Knollys, *Life*, p. 20.

[24] David Cressy, *Literacy and the Social Order*, (New York: Cambridge University Press, 1980), pp. 171-72.

North. A growing distrust of Charles' government had created an uncertain political situation. Although the members of the House of Commons disagreed on individual issues, a large majority agreed that the King had been led astray by his 'evil counsellors'.[25] In 1640 and 1641, though there were allegations aplenty of royal tyranny, the word 'tyrant' itself was used sparingly and even less so as the possibility of civil war loomed.[26] However, "in the perception of most of his subjects, the king was misusing his emergency powers. The consequence was widespread distrust."[27] Suspicions, which had taken root and grown during the period of Charles' personal rule, broke out into full bloom during the opening years of the 1640s. In January 1642, Charles' attempt at regaining control of Parliament by impeaching five members of the Commons and one Lord for treason had failed. He withdrew from London and began to prepare for conflict. In response, in the early months of 1642, the Parliament began a concerted attack on the powers of the bishops in the House of Lords and the military powers of the King.[28] This only served to heighten tensions further. On 22 August 1642, Charles I, King of England, raised his standard at Nottingham. Although people had expected war for some time, when it finally became a reality, it met with little initial enthusiasm.[29]

The first few months of war witnessed widespread neutrality as many Englishmen declined to declare for King or Parliament. As well, the initial battles, such as Edgehill, proved indecisive. In fact, by November 1642 through April 1643, it looked as if peace might be negotiated.[30] However, while moderates and conservatives in Parliament negotiated with Charles I in an attempt to end the war, the royalist forces pressed forward and by the summer it appeared they might be victorious. With the collapse of potential peace came a

---

[25] Maurice Ashley, *The English Civil War: A Concise History*, (London: Thames and Hudson, 1974), p. 47.
[26] Morrill, *Nature of the English Revolution*, p. 286.
[27] Morrill, *Nature of the English Revolution*, pp. 291-92.
[28] The act excluding clergy from holding secular offices, prevented bishops from sitting in the House of Lords and was clearly a reaction to Laudianism and a fear of popishness. The petitioning movement that had overtaken London and the counties openly demonstrated support for this measure. The Militia Ordinance, passed a month later without the king's approval, was perceived by many as Parliament claiming the power to legislate without the king and to appropriate the King's control over the militia. Coward, *Stuart Age*, pp. 202-203.
[29] Coward, *Stuart Age*, p. 204.
[30] Coward, *Stuart Age*, pp. 204-207; Anthony Fletcher, "The Coming of War", in *Reactions to the English Civil War*, edited by John Morrill, (New York: St. Martins, 1982), pp. 29-35; Conrad Russell, *The Crisis of Parliaments: English History, 1509-1660*, (Oxford: Oxford University Press, 1971), pp. 342-43.

rise in enthusiasm for the cause of Parliament, particularly among those who held to more radical political and religious positions.[31]

During this period, Knollys continued teaching but also engaged in some preaching. According to Thomas Edwards, Knollys preached at "Christophers Church behinde the Exchange, a little after his coming over".[32] Whether this was a regular occurrence or a sporadic one, Edwards did not say. As well, Edwards opened an old chapter of Knollys' life by claiming that Knollys was an Antinomian and that he and a Mr. Simpson, wrote a treatise concerning the moral law and the Ten Commandments.[33] In 1643, shortly after the outbreak of war, Knollys decided to give up his teaching and he entered the service of the Parliamentary Army as a chaplain.[34] This was not uncommon as many ministers found themselves drawn to support the parliamentary cause through this means. The individual Colonels appointed them for the purposes of keeping up the spirits of and creating a unified resolve among the soldiers. The primary task of these chaplains appears to have been that of reading prayers to the soldiers daily and of exhorting them, primarily on Sundays and holy days, but often before and after military engagements as well. In the early stages of the war, a plentiful number of chaplains volunteered, most of them Presbyterians, who had benefices or lectureships.[35] However, following the Battle of Edgehill, many chaplains left the army, creating considerable demand for replacements. Because of this shortage, preachers and lay preachers from various religious groups were appointed as chaplains, though the vast majority continued to be Presbyterians.[36] In 1643, Knollys served in the army of the

---

[31] F.D. Dow, *Radicalism in the English Revolution*, (Oxford: Basil Blackwell, 1985), pp. 58-60; Coward, *Stuart Age*, pp. 207-209, 213-14. It was at this point that Parliament, in an attempt to strengthen its position, negotiated an alliance with the Scots, a move which introduced a whole new element to the situation – negotiated Presbyterianism. Russell, *Parliaments*, pp. 355-56. At the same time, the gathering of congregations began on a large scale in London. Murray Tolmie, *Triumph of the Saints*, (Cambridge: Cambridge University Press, 1977), p. 94.

[32] Thomas Edwards, *Gangraena: Or a Catalogue and Discovery of many of the Errours, Heresies, Blasphemies and pernicious Practices of the Sectaries of this time...*, (London: 1646), Part I, p. 39, hereafter designated *Gangraena*.

[33] *Gangraena*, Part I, p. 39. If this statement of Edwards is true, this treatise is no longer extant.

[34] Knollys, *Life*, p. 20.

[35] The main criterion used in the early stages of the war included one's credentials as a conspicuous opponent of Laudian innovations. Anne Laurence, *Parliamentary Army Chaplains, 1642-1651*, (Suffolk: Boydell Press, 1990), pp. 2, 6-7, 10.

[36] Laurence, *Chaplains*, pp. 7, 78-79. Thomas Edwards bemoaned this fact in his *Gangraena*, highlighting how it had resulted in the spread of sectarian errors among the soldiers. Part 1, p. 14. In this thesis, the word 'sects' applies to those Protestants who were not satisfied with or participants in the Church of England, which by this time was mostly controlled by Presbyterians. Thus, for people like Edwards or Richard Baxter,

Eastern Association under the Earl of Manchester. At that time, Knollys probably would have counted himself an Independent, since he had not yet embraced Baptist doctrines.[37] His stay in the army was short-lived, however. Knollys became disillusioned with the commanders, believing that they were more dedicated to self-serving purposes than to the cause of "God and his People".[38] Late in 1643, Knollys left the army and returned to London.

The exact details of Knollys' life and activities during the remainder of the 1640s remain somewhat less clear. Following his brief experience with the Parliamentary army, he belonged to the separatist Independent church of Henry Jessey in London. In early 1644, Knollys and his friend and future fellow Baptist, William Kiffin, initiated a discussion on baptism in the Jessey church.[39] In March 1644, Kiffin withdrew and formed his own church. In October 1644, several Baptist churches joined together in signing a Confession of Faith. Knollys was not among the signatories. At this juncture, Knollys had not yet completely embraced believer's baptism.[40] During the summer of 1644, however, Knollys was becoming more and more convinced against infant baptism and in favour of believer's baptism, proclaiming it openly at the church

---

most so-called Independents were sectaries who had a proliferation of other radical beliefs in addition to a congregational polity. See *Gangraena*, Part 1, pp. 12-14.

According to Laurence, in Essex's army, over half of the chaplains were Presbyterians, while the ecclesiastical leanings of about a third are unknown, the remainder being Independents. In Waller's army, both chaplains were Presbyterians and in the Eastern Association army, again half were Presbyterians and the rest, Independents or of unknown affiliation. *Chaplains*, pp. 32-34.

[37] Laurence, *Chaplains*, p. 34; Knollys, *Life*, p. 20; Edwards, *Gangraena*, Part 1, p. 39. Laurence claimed Knollys was a Baptist. However, his conversion to Baptist beliefs did not occur until 1644 or later. W.T. Whitley, "Debate on Infant Baptism, 1643" in *Transactions of the Baptist Historical Society*, I, 4, (Jan. 1910) : 237-45. Tolmie made the statement that Knollys joined the Jessey church after his return in 1641. This could have been true, but the only evidence available concerning his membership comes from 1643/44. *Triumph*, p. 44; W.T. Whitley, "The Jacob-Jessey Church, 1616-1678", in *Transactions of the Baptist Historical Society*, I, 4, (Jan. 1910) : 254.

[38] Knollys, *Life*, p. 20. This would not end Knollys' career as a chaplain. He would later serve in the New Model Army in 1649 under Whalley. Ironically, all three of the ministers who were involved in the dispute in Dover, New Hampshire in the 1630s ended up as chaplains in the New Model Army. Thomas Larkham served from 1647-1649, Hanserd Knollys in 1649, and George Burdett in 1650. Laurence, *Chaplains*, pp. 52, 55, 194, 197.

[39] This debate would eventually help him formulate his own position on the issue. This will be dealt with in detail below in chapter 7. See Whitley, "Debate" and Whitley, "Jacob-Jessey Church", p. 254; Tolmie, *Triumph*, pp. 44, 55-56.

[40] Within less than a year, however, he would change his mind, separate from the Jessey congregation, and gather his own Baptist church. Whitley, "Debate", pp. 244-45. He had withdrawn from the Jessey church by June 1645 when he returned to baptise Henry Jessey.

of St. Mary le Bow Cheapside.[41] This led to the lodging of complaints against him in the Westminster Assembly.[42] In response, as well, the Committee for Plundered Ministers of the House of Commons issued a warrant against him and he was subsequently arrested and held without bail for several days at Ely House until such time when he could appear before the Committee.[43]

The Committee for Plundered Ministers arose out of the desire of the Long Parliament to purify the ministry of the Church and out of the religious politics of the Civil War. Almost immediately, upon the opening of the Long Parliament, the Committee for Scandalous Ministers was established with the purpose of removing persecuting, innovating or scandalous ministers from office. While this committee stumbled along from action to inaction, with the outbreak of war, a new problem presented itself. In Royalist held territories, Puritan incumbents were deprived of their pulpits. In an effort to provide these ministers with new livings, Parliament proceeded to expel ministers with Royalist sympathies in London and to replace them with "plundered" Puritan ministers. The Committee for Plundered Ministers, for all intents and purposes took over the tasks of the earlier established Committee for Scandalous Ministers. In 1643, this Committee enjoyed a widening influence and authority so that it became a vital instrument in London and the surrounding counties for dealing with complaints related to ministry even beyond scandalous or 'popish' ministers. The Committee had the authority to gather evidence and record the answer of the accused, but the Westminster Assembly retained the power to examine and hear those laying charges, the accused, and any witnesses before passing final judgment.[44]

Why Knollys came to the attention of this Committee remains unclear. Perhaps he preached in a pulpit made vacant by the dismissal of a Royalist clergyman. Or perhaps some perceived his preaching as scandalous. When Knollys finally came before the Committee for questioning, he answered their inquiries directly. When the chairman of the Committee, John White, questioned him on the issue of his ordination and authority to preach, Knollys stated clearly his belief that ordination at the hands of a bishop or church had

---

[41] *Gangraena*, Part 1, p. 39.

[42] For a description of the Westminster Assembly of Divines, see below, note 90.

[43] Knollys, *Life*, p. 20. *Gangraena*, Part 1, p. 39. John Lightfoot, *The Whole Works of the Rev. John Lightfoot, D.D. Master of Catherine Hall, Cambridge*, vol. XIII: *The Journal of the Proceedings of the Assembly of Divines*, edited by J.R. Putnam, (London: J.F. Dove, 1825), p. 302. One of the results of these types of public proclamations was that a controversy was ignited in London over the issue of baptism. Stephen Marshall attempted to counter Knollys and other Baptist ministers in his sermon to the Assembly of Divines at Westminster Abbey on August 28, 1644. *A Sermon of the Baptizing of Infants. Preached In the Abbey-Church at Westminster, at the Morning Lecture, appointed by the Honorable House of Commons*, (London: 1644).

[44] Clive Holmes, ed., *The Suffolk Committee for Scandalous Ministers 1644-46*, "Introduction", (Suffolk: Suffolk Records Society, 1970), pp. 9-13.

no intrinsic authority. The source of authority for his own ordination, Knollys claimed, was Jesus Christ, not the Bishop of Peterborough. To further emphasise this, Knollys once again renounced his Episcopal ordination before the Committee.[45]

The Committee then pressed him further, asking by whose authority he had filled the pulpit at Bow Church. He answered that the Churchwardens had invited him repeatedly until he finally obliged them. At this point, he began recapping his sermon for the members of the Committee, thirty of whom were from the Westminster Assembly. Knollys' answers and sermon seemed so satisfactory to the Committee members that not only was he sent away "without any blame, or paying of any Fees", but the jailor, who had kept Knollys illegally for a long time without bail, was rebuked and threatened with discipline for this action.[46]

The years 1645 and 1646 were especially significant for Knollys. As previously mentioned, throughout 1644, additional discussions were held on the issue of baptism.[47] Sometime in late 1644 or early 1645, Knollys finally embraced the doctrine of believer's baptism.[48] Leaving the Jessey church[49], he gathered his own Baptist church in 1645 "in the heart of London" at Great St. Helens, next door to an established parish church. According to Edwards, Knollys held his meetings simultaneously to those of the parish church, attracting over a thousand listeners, and no doubt detracting from the worship of the parish church.[50] Eventually, Knollys' landlord refused to renew his lease

---

[45] Knollys, *Life*, pp. 20-21.

[46] Knollys, *Life*, p. 20.

[47] Whitley, "Debate", pp. 242-43.

[48] It is quite fascinating that Knollys, who felt so strongly about baptism and who played such a major role in the formulation of the Particular Baptists doctrine regarding it, never mentioned the time of his conversion to Baptist principles nor of his own baptism in his autobiography.

[49] Knollys continued to remain on good terms with the Mother church, returning on 29 June 1645 to baptise Henry Jessey, who himself came to embrace believer's baptism but in terms of ecclesiology maintained an understanding of a 'mixed fellowship'. Whitley, "Debate", p. 245.

[50] Most likely, the meetings were held in a private dwelling. Therefore, the report of the neighbours whom Edwards quoted as seeing over "1000" in attendance would be dubious at best. Edwards himself must have realised the impossibility of fitting 1000 people for worship into a private dwelling. Perhaps his "1000" was a misprint for "100" people. *Gangraena*, Part 1, p. 39; Knollys, *Life*, p. 23. Tolmie felt the number of attendees could be explained by the fact that his meetings were open to the general public and people "would be less disturbed by the ministry of a former clergyman than by a lay pastor or preacher". *Triumph*, p. 60.

and he had to move his church to Finsbury Fields, where he enlarged the meeting room by knocking down the wall between two rooms.[51]

In February 1645, at the height of the conservative Presbyterian print war against the Independents, Knollys faced violence during a preaching tour of Suffolk. During his sermon, "Christ Exalted", which was "begun to be preached at Debenham", Knollys was dragged from the pulpit and stoned by "a company of rude fellowes, and poor women of that Town; who were sent for, called together, and set on by a Malignant High-Constable".[52] It seems that this was not Knollys' first trouble on this particular preaching tour. Just a month prior, in early January, Knollys had been listed on the same arrest warrant from Parliament as Laurence Clarkson, who was at that point in his spiritual pilgrimage a Baptist as well. Knollys was at the time preaching in Ipswich, where he was arrested and jailed. How long he was imprisoned and how he got out of prison is not known.[53] Knollys eventually published the sermons from this preaching tour.[54]

In one sermon entitled "Christ is all, and in all", based on Colossians 3:11, Knollys appealed to his listeners to place Jesus Christ and His love above any differences that might exist between Christians. This called for a sort of equality in Christ founded upon humility. In his opening statements, Knollys proclaimed

---

[51] Edwards, *Gangraena*, Part 1, p. 39. This mobile existence would continue to be the norm for Knollys' church, as it was for most gathered congregations. Knollys' church would during his lifetime meet in Wapping, Piccadilly, the Old Artillery Ground, Tower Street, Artichoke Lane, Booby Lane, Coleman Street, the George Yard, and finally at Broken Wharf. Because of the nomadic nature of many of these Baptist congregations, who often took on the name of where they were meeting at a particular time, tracing the histories of these early churches is difficult at best. Some kept church books with records, but often the moving about or persecution by authorities made even this a difficult task. W.T. Whitley, *The Baptists of London, 1612-1928*, (London: Kingsgate Press, n.d.), pp. 13-15, 107; "Baptist Meetings in the City of London", in *Transactions of the Baptist Historical Society*, V, (June 1916) : 81.

It appears from the signatures on the "1646 Confession" that ministering with Knollys during this period was one Thomas Holms. Preface to the 2nd edition. Throughout Knollys' life, he would continue to minister at this church, usually with an assistant. Other assistants included Watson, Perry, and Steed, who eventually succeeded Knollys at his death. "Baptist Meetings", p. 81.

[52] Hanserd Knollys, *Christ Exalted*, 1st ed., (London: 1645), title page; Knollys, *Life*, pp. 21-22; Edwards, *Gangraena*, Part 1, p. 39. Muriel James claimed at one place that this stoning took place in 1646 and yet claimed elsewhere that it took place in 1645. Whether this is merely a typographical error or whether she was confused, thinking that it was two separate events is not clear. *Knollys*, pp. 141, 143.

[53] Claxton, *Lost Sheep*, pp. 11-19; Morton, *Ranters*, pp. 117-30.

[54] Hanserd Knollys, *Christ Exalted: A Lost Sinner Sought, and Saved by Christ: Gods People are an Holy people... the summe of divers Sermons Preached in Suffolk*, 2nd ed., (London: 1646).

that the advantage of a Jew above a Gentile, the dignity of a Scythian above a Barbarian, or the Immunities of a Freeman above a Bondslave, however esteemed amongst men, are nothing without Christ; *Who is all, and in all*. These words have their dependence upon the exhortation unto Mortification.[55]

According to Knollys, this equality came from the nature of Christ and the gifts that He bestowed upon believers, especially "the glorious liberties of his Spirit: For where the Spirit of the Lord is, there is liberty, 2 Cor. 3.17. Not any carnall liberty to sin,... but Spirituall liberty, and freedome from sin", that is the guilt, pollution, power, and punishment of sin.[56] Clearly, his position was not antinomian. Though the exegetical emphasis of this sermon was on spiritual equality between believers and spiritual liberty, the practical aspect of that equality and liberty found expression in toleration and liberty for all Christ's people.[57] At the core of his sermon, however, was an appeal to his listeners to embrace Christ and His call on their lives.[58] He concluded this sermon with the admonition to "prize Christ far above all his owne gifts and graces, for he is the life of them all" and to "let Christ be all, in all your affections, words & actions.... Love every one and every thing that God hath put the name of Christ upon, for his sake."[59] Ironically, Knollys was stoned after preaching this sermon.

"The chief Publicans Conversion", the second sermon in the collection, presented a strongly evangelistic message based on Luke 19:10, "For the Son of Man is come to seek and to save that which was lost." It issued a call to the "lost sinner" to be "saved by Christ".[60] However, this call came through the

---

[55] Knollys, *Christ Exalted*, p. 1.
[56] Knollys, *Christ Exalted*, pp. 2-6.
[57] Knollys, *Christ Exalted*, p. 11.
[58] This evangelistic thrust would be central throughout Knollys' entire ministry.
[59] Knollys, *Christ Exalted*, pp. 10-11.
[60] Knollys, *Christ Exalted*, p. 15. In fact, both of the first two sermons have a strong evangelistic appeal. This conversionist tendency hearkened back to Knollys' own conversion experience and would continue to characterise his preaching throughout his life. This was highlighted in the sermon preached at his funeral when it was stated, "When he had, as it were, *one foot in the Grave,* he was *Instrumental to the Resurrection of many Dead Souls to a Spiritual Life."* Thomas Harrison, A SERMON On the Decease of Mr. Hanserd Knollis, Minister of the Gospel. Preached at Pinners Hall, Octob. 4. 1691, (London: 1694), p. 39. This conversionism, explicit in this second sermon as well as in his next one, is something which is somewhat paradoxical, considering the strongly Reformed bent of his theology. However, there were Puritans who embraced a "preparationist" understanding of conversion. These ones placed significant emphasis on the role of the individual in preparing his or her soul for the drawing of God. Norman Pettit, *The Heart Prepared: Grace and Conversion in Puritan Spiritual Life*, (New Haven: Yale University Press, 1966), pp. 52-55. See Chapter 2 above and Chapter 7 below.

language of high Puritan theology, which would have given Knollys' Presbyterian opponents very little to criticise. After an excursus on the person of Christ, Knollys launched into a lengthy exposition of the "powerfull drawing" without which "no sinner can come to Christ". This "drawing" happens through the Spirit and the Word of God.[61] Near the end, Knollys focused on the element of grace in salvation, clearly contrasting it to legalistic "Ceremonies or Elements of the Law", perhaps a reference to the ceremonialism of the established church.[62]

The third sermon, "That we should be holy", dealt with sanctification from sin. Taken from Ephesians 1:4, the compelling basis of this sermon was the doctrine of election. Strongly Puritan in its theology, this sermon entreated listeners to exhibit their election through lives of holiness.[63] He went on to describe the different sorts of "professors" of holiness – the "legall professors" who seek to establish their own righteousness, the "formall professors" who take comfort in religious form, the "carnall professors" who "take liberty to live in sin and walk after the flesh".[64] This theme of false versus true professors would continue as a prominent one throughout his ministry and he wrote at length on it in his eschatological writings.[65] The first kind of professor, the "legall professors" may have been duly convinced by the Word and Spirit of their sin, "sorely wounded in their consciences", and may have even reformed their behaviour, but theirs was a "legall reformation" with no change of heart. In the end, they trusted in their own righteousness.[66] The "formall professors", though they claim not to "rest on duties", they follow a joyless religiosity.[67] Finally, the "carnall professors" claim to be people of God, but "are the servants of corruption". Their lives show neither evidence of spiritual hunger

---

[61] Knollys, *Christ Exalted*, pp. 16-22.

[62] Knollys, *Christ Exalted*, pp. 23-25. This attack on the "Covenant of the Law" would have given fuel to those who so quickly accused Knollys of antinomianism. An entry in the *Minutes of the Sessions of the Assembly of Divines* on 20 May 1645 gives evidence that the charge of antinomianism continued to plague Knollys even after returning from Massachusetts. "Upon information against Mr. Knowles, his preaching in private, and venting his Antinomian opinions... a Committee to consider of this complaint, and of all other disorders formerly complained of, or fit to be complained of, to be of like nature." Alex F. Mitchell and John Struthers, eds., (London: William Blackwood and Sons, 1874), p. 96.

[63] Knollys, *Christ Exalted*, pp. 30-33. This clearly shows that Knollys was not in reality an antinomian in the sense of being one who taught or encouraged licentious, lawless living.

[64] Knollys, *Christ Exalted*, pp. 33-34.

[65] Hanserd Knollys, *The Parable of the Kingdom of Heaven Expounded. Or, An Exposition of the first thirteen Verses of the twenty fifth Chapter of Matthew*, (London: 1674).

[66] Knollys, *Christ Exalted*, p. 33.

[67] Knollys, *Christ Exalted*, pp. 33-34.

nor of the work of the Spirit.[68] Knollys concluded this sermon with a call to a true life of holiness.[69] This sermon provided clear evidence that Knollys doctrine of grace did not embrace libertine or antinomian beliefs. While he undoubtedly placed great importance upon free grace in Christ, he saw the responsibility of the believer to live a life of holiness as being equally important.

None of these sermons contained a word about baptism nor did they preach doctrines worthy of criticism from Puritan contemporaries. As a result, when Knollys was called before the House Committee of Examinations to explain the disturbance in Suffolk occasioned by these sermons, he was not only found innocent of wrongdoing but "Ordered That I might preach in any part of Suffolk when the Minister of that place did not preach".[70] Edwards noted that during the closing months of 1645, Knollys continued to preach "up and down in severall Churches in London and Southwarke, and that with all fiercenesse against Childrens Baptism, and against our Ministers, as being Antichristian, and having no call to baptize".[71]

The Presbyterians and the Independents

During this period, religious commitments and beliefs often intertwined closely with political commitments and goals. The initial unity of the Long Parliament during its first year allowed for it to accomplish such political and religious goals as limiting the power of the King and his advisors (including the bishops), and of halting and reversing what were perceived as Laud's attempts to return the Church to popishness.[72] However, the political atmosphere became more volatile by late 1641. Suddenly, as Parliament and King drifted toward war, the political issues and considerations affected the progress of religious reform. The outbreak of the Irish rebellion, the situation in Scotland, where Charles recognised the abolition of the episcopacy, the constitutional crisis in England and legal difficulties presented by Parliament's attempts to limit Charles' power and gain new power for itself, and the movement of Peers and

---

[68] Knollys, *Christ Exalted*, p. 34.

[69] Knollys, *Christ Exalted*, pp. 33-38.

[70] Knollys, *Life*, p. 22. *Christ Exalted*, 2nd ed., title page. The legal cost of this incident for Knollys was 60 pounds. However, it appears that some of this was recovered, for according to an entry in the proceedings of the Committee of Examinations for 21 June 1645, the church at Dallinghoo was to pay Hanserd Knowles for his services. Cited in James, *Knollys*, p. 144. Of course, Edwards' account of this did not see Knollys as being vindicated, for, he noted, "the Sectaries finde too many friends in Committees". *Gangraena*, Part 1, p. 39.

[71] *Gangraena*, Part 3, p. 241. Knollys' activities during the last half of the 1640s will be addressed in the next chapter.

[72] Kenyon, *Stuart Constitution*, pp. 175-80. Christianson, *Reformers and Babylon*, pp. 180-88.

Members of the House of Commons to a Royalist or Parliamentarian position; these all affected the religious landscape.[73] Matters became further complicated by the raising of a Parliamentary Army, the outbreak of the first Civil War, the passing of the "Solemn League and Covenant", the creation of the New Model Army, and the passing of the "Self Denying Ordinance".[74] Ernest Sirluck has argued that from 1642 to the early part of 1643, the primary focus of the Parliament was on the issue of supremacy of state. The issue of religious reform, which had dominated in late 1641, was moved to the background. However, in 1643-44 Parliament once again turned its attention to religion. By then, however, the issue of reform was further compounded by the addition of the issue of religious toleration.[75]

Two major religious groups arose in Parliament and in the Westminster Assembly, which Parliament had appointed to recommend on religious reform: the Presbyterians and the Independents.[76] Both took a strongly Calvinist theological stance and both opposed the Episcopalian form of church government.[77] As well, both emphasised the importance of preaching and personal purity as forms of religious expression and both placed less emphasis on traditional forms of religious worship and ritual. During the 1630s, both groups had stood together against intolerance and persecution, some of their members conforming, others suffering, all desiring reformation. In 1640, these Puritans found themselves with the opportunity to usher in this reformation, but seemed suddenly paralysed by indecision and differences over the question of toleration.[78]

---

[73] See Anthony Fletcher, *The Outbreak of the English Civil War*, (London: Edward Arnold Publishers Ltd., 1981) and Conrad Russell, *The Fall of the British Monarchies, 1637-1642*, (Oxford: Clarendon Press, 1991). Also Kenyon, *Stuart Constitution*, pp. 229-31. Austin Woolrych, "The English Revolution: an introduction", in *The English Revolution, 1600 to 1660*, ed. by E.W. Ives (London: Edward Arnold Ltd., 1968), pp. 16-23.

[74] See Gentles, *New Model Army*, pp. 1-10, 24-5. Sirluck, *John Milton*, vol. 2, chapters 1 and 2. Kenyon, *Stuart Constitution*, pp. 231-39, 243-47. Woolrych, "The English Revolution", pp. 19-24.

[75] Sirluck, *John Milton*, pp. 57-58.

[76] Ian Gentles held that these two factions actually formed as a result of their war views: "During the ensuing months [while the New Model Army was being established] the war faction would come to be known as the Independents, while the peace party would acquire the label 'presbyterian'. It should be borne in mind that most MPs did not identify themselves with any political grouping." *New Model Army*, p. 5.

[77] Morrill, *Nature of the English Revolution*, pp. 69-91.

[78] Russell, *Parliaments*, pp. 348-50; Haller, *Rise*, pp. 16-17. Again, one must understand the flexibility of these designations, as noted by Christopher Hill in *A Century of Revolution, 1603-1714*, (Edinburgh: Thomas Nelson and Sons Ltd., 1961), p. 165: "many 'Independent' members became elders when Presbyterianism was the established Church; many who voted for a Presbyterian establishment in 1646 were moderate Episcopalians or conservative Erastians, choosing the lesser evil."

Working within more traditional understandings of uniformity, social hierarchy, and parochial boundaries, the Presbyterians sought a reformed national Church. They wished to do away with the Episcopacy so that the leadership of the Church came not under the control of the Bishops, but of local councils or presbyteries comprised of lay and clerical presbyters (elders) from the parish churches.[79] Many of the Presbyterians had suffered under Laudian uniformity during the 1630s, including Prynne, Bastwick, and numerous Puritan clergymen and preachers.[80] For these, the toleration afforded by the disintegration of Charles' personal rule came as a welcome relief. However, they themselves did not favour religious toleration as a principle. In fact, as Haller made clear, "they were very far from approving in principle the tolerance by which they profited."[81] Instead, they sought an established church that would enforce a unity of religious truth. Such a position was somewhat ironic because they had themselves preached in favour of Christian liberty during the period of Laudian uniformity, enforced by the bishops. Although Presbyterians had held that in areas of religious ambiguity, in which Scripture neither prescribed nor prohibited, conformity remained at the discretion of the individual's conscience, when they found themselves in the majority the degree of latitude allowed to others suddenly contracted and their goal of 'godly rule' came to the fore.[82] They opposed toleration, desiring a "united national church with no dissent permitted".[83] The good of society demanded the suppression of heresy and schism and the enforcement of religious uniformity "based upon the will of a godly people and maintained with the support of a godly civil state".[84]

The Independents also sought to reform the national Church but they had a more relaxed perception of the powers of such a church. Where the Presbyterians worked within the more traditional understanding of an Established Church to which all belonged by birth, the Independents envisaged 'gathered churches' based not on a geographic parish, but on a spiritual commitment. Their vision of the church took into account differences, included toleration, and stressed the need for independent authority of each congregation in matters of doctrine, worship, and discipline. Kenyon described them as "decentralised Calvinists" who favoured a national Church that operated on a broad basis to define doctrine and heresy and to help the magistrate to regulate true and false doctrine, and immorality.[85] The Kingship of Christ was the basis

---

[79] Tolmie, *Triumph*, pp. 100-101. Haller, *Rise*, p. 173.
[80] Haller, *Rise*, pp. 230-32.
[81] Haller, *Rise*, p. 173.
[82] Sirluck, *John Milton*, pp. 92-94.
[83] Russell, *Parliaments*, p. 349.
[84] Haller, *Rise*, p. 173.
[85] Kenyon, *Stuart Constitution*, p. 233. Hill concurred with this view of the Independents as favouring a more loosely defined national Church. However, he claimed that religious toleration was not part of their program, but "was forced upon the 'Independent'

of the Independents' belief in the 'gathered churches'. Each individual congregation of visible, gathered saints was a literal manifestation of Christ's kingdom on earth. By transferring headship and authority from human institutions, whether king, pope, episcopacy, or presbytery, intermediaries between the individual or the individual congregations and King Jesus were eliminated.[86] On most issues, the Baptists were at one with the Independents, as Tolmie pointed out, differing primarily on adult versus infant baptism.[87] Ernest Sirluck saw the issue of liberty of conscience as the "only... distinguishable difference" between the preaching of the Independents and the Presbyterians.[88] Initially, he contended, outright religious toleration was not the aim of the Independents. Rather, they sought religious "accommodation" of orthodox (Calvinist) non-separatist gathered churches outside of the jurisdiction of the established Presbyterian system. Only later, when attempts to establish accommodation had failed, did the Independents call for toleration.[89]

Whether because of the vacillation of the Parliament and the Westminster Assembly, the disunity among the Puritans, or the constantly shifting political scene, "progress towards Presbyterianism was slow and halting."[90] Initially, military uncertainties had stymied the primarily Presbyterian Parliament.[91] The price of an alliance with the Scots was the abolition of episcopacy and

---

members of Parliament by political necessity". He cited the intolerance of the New England Congregationalists as evidence of this. *Century of Revolution*, p. 166.

[86] One must be careful not to confuse this with millenarianism. Although the spiritual presence of Christ's kingdom on earth was considered an historic reality, the future return of Christ was to be anticipated. "They were not advocating the immediate rule of the saints but rather the immediate gathering of saints into churches, quite a different matter." Tolmie, *Triumph*, pp. 85-88.
Neither did the Independents reject the Church of England (although some were accused of exclusivism, and indeed were exclusive) as a false church. They merely wished to gather the visible church "into a higher church form that transcended the parish churches because it incorporated the voluntary principle into its very essence". *Triumph*, p. 94.

[87] Tolmie saw divisions along denominational lines as being "rough and ready" at this particular period in time. Even the dispute over baptism "extended beyond Baptist congregations to influence people who remained in the parish congregations". *Triumph*, p. 50. See also pp. 50-55; 85-87; 120-24. Watts also pointed out the close ties between the Independents and the Separatists. *The Dissenters*, vol. 1, (Oxford: Clarendon Press, 1978), pp. 94-99. Perhaps Edwards was not off the mark when he later stated that anabaptism was "the highest form of Independency". *Antapologia*, (London: 1644), p. 201.

[88] Sirluck, *John Milton*, p. 65.

[89] Sirluck, *John Milton*, p. 66. See also Tolmie, *Triumph*, pp. 128-29.

[90] Kenyon, *Stuart Constitution*, p.232. Christopher Hill pointedly argued that: "the Presbyterian establishment was virtually stillborn. By the time it reached the statute book (1646) power was passing to the 'Independent' Army." *Century of Revolution*, p. 165.

[91] Sirluck, *John Milton*, p. 56.

establishment of a church based upon "the Word of God and the example of the best reformed churches" in all three kingdoms. In the interest of not sabotaging the negotiations with the Scots, the internal religious divisions of the Puritans were kept quiet.[92] The establishment of the Westminster Assembly in July 1643, which contained a Presbyterian majority, gave further advantage to the Presbyterian party. Summoned by the Long Parliament, "a general synod of the most grave, pious, learned, and judicious divines of this island", the intent was that the Assembly draw up proposals for reform that would establish a Presbyterian system in the Church of England.[93] However, the Independent minority was able to create a sort of gridlock. Once the negotiation of the Scottish alliance was completed, the Independents presented their proposal of accommodation. They desired an "accommodation" or allowance from the Assembly and Parliament for Calvinist Congregationalists to form "gathered churches" beyond the boundaries of the established Church system.[94] The Presbyterians assumed that accommodation meant that the gathered churches of the Independents could in some sense be incorporated into the existing parochial schema, thereby isolating the sectarian churches and making it easier to root them out. When they realised that this assumption was false, they disbanded the Parliamentary accommodation committee and abandoned further attempts at accommodation.[95] However, these debates took up much of 1643 and 1644, giving the London separate churches opportunity to further establish themselves. As long as Parliament did not institute an effective, coercive established church, both the Independents and the sects could go on gathering

---

[92] Sirluck, *John Milton*, pp. 57-66; Russell, *Parliaments*, pp. 355-56.

[93] Watts, *Dissenters*, vol. 1, pp. 83-84. Haller, *Rise*, pp. 5, 11, 16, 173-74. The Assembly consisted of ninety divines, ten peers, and twenty members of the House of Commons. Of these 120, about twenty favoured episcopacy, about ten favoured congregationalism, and over two dozen favoured Presbyterianism. The remainder had no firm commitment and were eager for order to be restored. This lack of commitment among the majority, combined with the poor attendance of the Assembly, allowed the small Presbyterian majority to control the proceedings. Watts, *Dissenters*, vol. 1, p. 93.

[94] Sirluck, *John Milton*, p. 66.

[95] Tolmie, *Triumph*, pp. 124-28. At issue was the debate over whether or not the gathering of churches outside of parochial boundaries was schismatic. According to the most conservative Presbyterians, such was the case. However, some of the more moderate Presbyterians, led by Stephen Marshall, and the Independents held that it was merely "unseasonable". This became the basis for the accommodation order introduced into the Commons. In effect, by accepting this, the Assembly and the Parliament "threw away the one ground, separation from parish churches, which would have permitted a decisive and simple definition of the sectarian offence against the national church". *Triumph*, p. 124.

congregations without opposition or fear of persecution.[96] By the middle of 1644, a further military concern had presented itself, which would shift the advantage to the side of the Independents.

In July 1644, at the battle of Marston Moor, the Royalist forces suffered a significant defeat, much of the credit going to the cavalry commanded by Oliver Cromwell. Cromwell wrote: "It had all the evidence of an absolute victory obtained by the Lord's blessing upon the godly party principally. We never charged but we routed the enemy,... God made them as stubble to our swords."[97] However, on the heels of this victory, came a comparable defeat for the Parliamentarians. In September, the Royalist forces defeated the Earl of Essex in Cornwall and Cromwell, who happened to be in Parliament at the time, used the opportunity to push for the Accommodation Ordinance, which instructed those responsible for the reformation of the Church

> to indeavour the finding out some way how farre tender consciences, who cannot in all things submit to the Common Rule which shall be established, may be borne with according to the Word, and as may stand with the public peace; that so the proceedings of the Assembly may not be so much retarded.[98]

Then, in October, at the second battle of Newbury, when it seemed that the Parliamentarians might win the war, Manchester's refusal to attack as agreed, allowed Charles to escape.[99] Ultimately, this failure on the part of the Parliamentarian forces led to the passing of the Self-Denying Ordinance in April 1645. This required members of both Houses to resign their commands, both military and civil.[100] The army was placed under the command of Sir Thomas Fairfax, with Cromwell later named as his Lieutenant-General of Horse. As well, an Ordinance for the reorganisation of the army was passed, creating the New Model Army. The New Model gradually became a receptive and safe setting for sectaries and Independents.[101] Initially, most of the soldiers

---

[96] Sirluck, *John Milton*, pp. 56, 66-71. Nicholas Tyacke, "The 'Rise of Puritanism' and the Legalizing of Dissent, 1571-1719", in *From Persecution to Toleration*, ed. O.P. Grell, J.I. Israel, and N. Tyacke, (Oxford: Clarendon Press, 1991), p. 28.

[97] Cited by J.R. Tanner, *English Constitutional Conflicts of the Seventeenth Century, 1603-1689*, (Cambridge: University of Cambridge Press, 1928, reprinted 1961), p. 130.

[98] *The Papers and Answers of the Dissenting Brethren and Committee of the Assembly of Divines... for Accomodation 1645*, (London: 1648), p. 12.

[99] Gentles, *New Model Army*, pp. 3-6. The question was posed as to whether or not Manchester was wholeheartedly committed to the cause of winning the Civil War and capturing King Charles.

[100] Gentles, *New Model Army*, pp. 6-10, 24-25. Gentles gave a detailed account of the struggle in Parliament between the 'peace party' and the 'war party' and between the Commons and Lords over this ordinance.

[101] C.H. Firth contended that the Parliamentarian armies were fairly evenly divided between Independents and Presbyterians, and that even after the formation of the New

were "pressed men" or enlisted merely for pay during a time of high unemployment. This recruiting activity was ongoing "labour-intensive business" due to constant desertions, particularly among the foot soldiers. "Two were pressed for every one who eventually arrived at the front. Few of them had any political opinions."[102] However, for some, the relative freedom in the Army from interference by the magistrates, clergy, and even parliament created a "freedom of preaching and theological speculation" and a favourable atmosphere of *de facto* toleration.[103] The move to reconstruct the army proved decisive, for in July 1645, at the battle of Naseby, the New Model Army defeated the Royalist forces, effectively ending the First Civil War.

In November 1645, the Parliamentary accommodation committee was re-established and the Presbyterians now offered accommodation to Calvinist Independents to form gathered churches beyond parochial boundaries. However, this time the Independents would not agree. Instead, they demanded toleration, not merely for Puritans of the gathered churches, but for other Trinitarians as well.[104] This clearly indicated that the Independents had moved to a position whereby they closely associated themselves in public with other separatist groups, including the Particular Baptists. This change of mind by the Parliament may have represented an attempt to alienate the Independents from

---

Model Army and battle at Naseby, the Independents were in the minority. *Cromwell's Army* (London: Methuen & Co. Ltd., 1902; reprint ed., University Paperbacks, 1962), pp. 315-17. Mark Kishlansky in his *The Rise of the New Model Army*, disputed the idea that the New Model army was a radical army, heavily infiltrated by extremists and Levellers prior to 1647. (Cambridge: Cambridge University Press, 1979), pp. xi-xii, 4-10. Ian Gentles, on the other hand, has argued in favour of the radicalism of the army in spite of attempts by the Lords and those in the 'peace party' to maintain a conservative Presbyterian leadership in the army. *New Model Army*, pp.7-24, 88-103, 140-41.

[102] Gentles, *New Model Army*, pp. 31-40; Sirluck, *John Milton*, pp. 54-55.

[103] Kenyon, *Stuart Constitution*, p. 246-47. White held that due to this atmosphere of toleration, "the soldiers of the Parliamentary army played a part in the spread of Baptist convictions and of Baptist churches across the British countryside during the period of the Great Rebellion". "The English Particular Baptists and the Great Rebellion". *Baptist History and Heritage* 9 (1) (Jan. 1974) : 29.

[104] Tolmie, *Triumph*, p. 128. They desired liberty for Christians to act, worship, etc. "according to the principles of their own consciences" so that tolerance was extended to those who were "children of truth in the main". Thus, the result would not be religious pluralism, but diversity of Christian worship (Protestant pluralism) in a Christian commonwealth. Tolmie, *Triumph*, p. 121. This was precisely the same intention expressed by Knollys and Saltmarsh. See below. In fact, at one point in January 1646, when it appeared that the Presbyterians would successfully establish Presbyterianism with no toleration of other polities, Knollys wrote to one John Dutton of Norwich of his concerns about the Presbyterians' "further contrivings against Gods poor Innocent ones". *Gangraena*, Part 3, pp. 48-9.

the separatists.[105] Through the alliance of the sects with the Independents and their involvement in the army, and due to the fact that their numbers had grown and they had become more established during the period of relative tolerance, the Presbyterians rightly perceived that the sectarians were becoming more powerful. The offer of accommodation was merely an attempt to divide the "tolerationist coalition". It should also be noted that throughout this debate, especially during the mid-1640s, the Baptists began to become actively involved, as was evidenced by their writing of Confessions, partaking in debates, and publishing apologetic works such as those penned by Knollys.

The demand for toleration had three significant results. First, the refusal by the Presbyterian Parliament to grant toleration caused the Independents to turn to Cromwell and the Army, as the means to reach their end.[106] The second significant result was that the Presbyterians embarked upon a conservative attack against the Independents, labelling them as schismatic sectaries. Thomas Edwards was one of the primary opponents, writing against them in his *Gangraena* as much as against the sects.[107] In one section entitled *Some Passages in the Prayers of the Sectaries* he wrote "This last moneth in December, one of the Independent Ministers in his prayers at a Lecture, two or three severall Lectures, prayed to God that the Parliament might give libertie to tender consciences."[108] This, Edwards saw as spiritually and socially destructive. Edwards also published an early work attacking Independent church government. Note the attack of Edwards against toleration in his 1641 work: "And in the meanewhile till Church Government be setled, whether it be not necessary to provide by some meanes against the spreading of this **sect** and

---

[105] Sirluck, *John Milton*, pp. 116-18. Tolmie has taken the position that historians have created a "false dichotomy between Independents and the 'sects'" with a false emphasis on the rise of an "alliance" between them due to a shared dread of Presbyterianism. He contended that "there was no division" between them, that the Independent churches were always "semi-separatist" in their approach. *Triumph*, pp. 120-21. Michael Watts in his work, *The Dissenters*, provided a very concise, yet clear summary of the historiographical discussion of the relationship between the Separatists and the Independents. He concluded that due to the often-ambiguous use of terms in the seventeenth century, one could legitimately hold that Independents included "both Separatists and Congregationalists in the 1640s, the spiritual heirs of Robert Browne and of Henry Jacob alike". Vol. 1, pp. 94-99.

[106] Sirluck, *John Milton*, p.118. Tyacke, "The 'Rise of Puritanism'", p. 29. Tyacke also cited a speech of Cromwell when dissolving his first Parliament in January 1655. Looking back over ten years, which had resulted in slow religious reform, he succinctly summarised the hypocritical stance of the Presbyterians. "Is it ingenuous to ask liberty and not to give it? What greater hypocrisy than for those who were oppressed by the bishops to become the greatest oppressors themselves, as soon as their yoke was removed?" "The 'Rise of Puritanism'", p. 31.

[107] Tolmie, *Triumph*, pp. 131-33.

[108] *Gangraena*, Part I, p. 35.

the meetings of these separated Assemblies, I leave it to your great wisedomes to consider, lest otherwise wee be overgrowne with Anabaptisme, Brownisme and such like."[109] Lastly, the Independents and the separatist churches, including the Baptists, became even more closely associated in their attempts to win legal toleration, and as a result became even stronger as the decade progressed.

By the end of 1646, in and around London there was a move to restore a more conservative atmosphere, specifically on the part of the Presbyterian element in Parliament. In December 1646, a petition from the citizens of the City of London demanded that the New Model Army should be disbanded because of the great expense of maintaining it. As well, it called for an active suppression of lay preaching and separate congregations.[110] This began a campaign against lay preachers, culminating on 31 December with the passing of an ordinance against lay preaching. A parliamentary committee for examinations was established, chaired by Colonel Leigh, with its primary target as the Particular Baptists.[111] During the first week of February, Hanserd Knollys and William Kiffin were brought before this committee, which ordered Knollys to refrain from preaching. He responded: "I would preach the Gospel both publickly and from house to house; for it was more equal to obey Christ, who had commanded me, than them who forbid me, and so I went away, and ceased not to teach and preach Jesus Christ and him crucified."[112]

---

[109] Thomas Edwards, *Reasons Against the Independent Government of Particular Congregations: As Also Against the Toleration of Such Churches to be Erected in this Kingdom*, (London: 1641), Epistle Dedicatory. A shift took place in the focus of the literature of the period. In 1643, Ministers of London expressed concerns in *The Clergyes Bill of Complaint*, written to the Parliament, emphasising in the subtitle that it was written "Against Brownists, Anabaptists, and other Schismaticks". (Oxford: 1643). Two years later there appeared *A Letter of the Ministers of the City of London Presented the first of Jan. 1645. to the Reverend Assembly of Divines Sitting at Westminster by the Authority of Parliament Against **Toleration*** (emphasis added). (London: 1645). Though the two attacks were similar, the latter was diverted against the ideal of toleration.

[110] This citizens' petition was followed by a petition from the City government calling for the disbanding of the Army, not because of cost, but because it was a stronghold for heretics. The City petition also called for the re-establishment of the London Militia to police the city. Coward, *Stuart Age*, p. 229; Tolmie, *Triumph*, p. 136; Bulstrode Whitlocke, *Memorials of the English Affairs from the Beginning of the Reign of Charles the First to the Happy Restoration of King Charles the Second*, vol. 2, repr. ed., (Oxford: At the University Press, 1853), pp. 91-92.

[111] Tolmie, *Triumph*, pp. 136-37.

[112] Knollys, *Life*, pp. 22-23. According to other contemporary accounts, Knollys did just as he said in his autobiography. *The Clarke Papers*, vol. 1, ed. by C.H. Firth, (The Camden Society, 1891), p. 4. Evidently, Knollys continued his preaching, for on 31 May, 1647, the Assembly of Divines ordered Knollys along with two others to be examined. *Minutes... of the Assembly of Divines*, p. 374. The boldness of the Baptists by this point was evident in other ways as well. In 1647, Hanserd Knollys and fellow

In February 1647, the joint effort of the City and Parliament to pay off the Scots resulted in their handing over of Charles to parliament and withdrawal from England.[113] At this point, the Presbyterians began a systematic attempt to purge and disband the New Model.[114] On 25 May, the House of Commons forced through a motion to disband the Army's foot with only eight weeks of back wages, instead of the weeks owed to them. This was not well received by the Army. As the presbyterian parliament sought to raise its own army to counter the New Model, it also attempted to divide the New Model by splitting the horse from the foot and the officers from the soldiers. This attempt failed due to the New Model Army's "tenacity in sticking together against presbyterian enticements".[115]

By 2 June, in what was the "most decisive of all the army's moves to avoid extinction" under the leadership of Cromwell, the Army had taken the King captive, and through the publication of *A Solemn Engagement* and *A Representation of the Army*[116] had announced its presence as a political force.[117] This was further established on 2 August with the publication of *The Heads of the Proposals*.[118] At this point, even further radicalisation of the New Model Army began to take place. The political breakdown in Parliament, the alliance of Parliament with the City, the vacillation of the King to come to a meaningful settlement, and the move to disband the Army – all of these contributed. Obviously, religious radicals in the Army were to a certain extent the primary target of the Presbyterians, but by moving beyond that objective to the decision to move against the Army generally, they forced the New Model Army into a unified position.[119] The time for establishing accommodation had passed.

Baptist Richard Wollaston presented proposals to Parliament calling for the abolition of church tithes. "Jottings by John Lewis of Margate, 1742", in *Transactions of the Baptist Historical Society*, IV, (Oct. 1915) : 206.

[113] Gentles, *New Model Army*, pp. 144-45.
[114] Gentles, *New Model Army*, pp. 145-69.
[115] Gentles, *New Model Army*, pp. 166-67.
[116] Both of these are in A.S.P. Woodhouse, ed., *Puritanism and Liberty, Being the Army Debates, 1647-9*, 2nd edition, (Chicago: University of Chicago Press, 1951), pp. 401-409.
[117] Gentles, *New Model Army*, pp.169-73. According to Gentles, Fairfax was too moderate or ill to have engendered such a plot. The plan for Joyce to seize the king was laid in Cromwell's house and received his approval.
[118] Russell, *Parliaments*, pp. 380-81. Select portions of this document are published in Woodhouse, *Puritanism and Liberty*, pp. 422-26 and Kenyon, *Stuart Constitution*, pp. 302-308.
[119] See Gentles, *New Model Army*, chs. 6-7 and Kishlansky, *Rise of the New Model Army*, chs. 7-8.

Knollys and the Baptist Cause – Confessions and Debates

Of the many different radical religious groups, which came into being during the 17th century, the Quakers and the Baptists eventually became lasting denominations. In the 1640s, however, the Quaker movement had not yet started.[120] The Baptists started to define their position and to grow during that decade. A General Baptist congregation may have existed in London during the 1620s and 1630s while the Particular Baptists came into existence during the uncertain years of the late 1630s or early 1640s and played a fairly significant role in the struggle of Parliament to establish a reformed Church.[121] In the context of the early 1640s, though, the General Baptists and Particular Baptists are best understood as "two autonomous elements of an amorphous movement of radical Puritanism".[122]

The General Baptists, who held an Arminian theology, had sprung from the 16th century English separatist tradition, with later influences from the Dutch Mennonites. Their beginnings in England can be established as being in the early 17th century (c. 1612).[123] Their belief in general atonement and their connections with Dutch Anabaptism were well known, and used against them, and their extreme separatist tendencies kept them from becoming involved in public life.[124]

The Calvinistic branch of the Baptists, the Particular Baptists, though they may have had a remote connection with the English separatists of the late 16th century,[125] seem rather to have come from a more established independent

---

[120] B. Reay, "Quakerism and Society", ed. B. Reay and J.F. McGregor, (New York: Oxford University Press, 1984), p. 141. One major difference (of many) between the Baptists and the Quakers was that "from the start, the Quaker movement was a movement of political and social as well as religious protest".

[121] B.R. White, *The English Baptists of the Seventeenth Century*, rev. ed., (London: The Baptist Historical Society, 1997), p. 29. White believed that the Bell Alley congregation was directly descended from the Baptists who returned from Holland with Thomas Helwys in 1612. The reason he gave for the lack of evidence regarding this was the success of the church in "keeping out [sic] the hands of the authorities".

[122] J.F. McGregor, "The Baptists: Fount of All Heresy", in *Radical Religion in the English Revolution*, ed. B. Reay and J.F. McGregor, (New York: Oxford University Press, 1984), p. 28.

[123] McGregor, "The Baptists: Fount of All Heresy", pp. 21-29. Tolmie, *Triumph*, pp. 69-71. For a detailed overview of the General Baptists' emergence from early English separatism and Dutch Anabaptism see B.R. White, *The English Separatist Tradition*, (London: Oxford University Press, 1971), particularly chs. 6 through 8.

[124] Tolmie, *Triumph*, pp. 69, 72-74.

[125] Barrie White, "The Origins and Convictions of the First Calvinistic Baptists", *Baptist History and Heritage* 25 (Oct. 1990) : 40. See William R. Estep, Jr., "On the Origins of English Baptists", *Baptist History and Heritage* 22 (Apr. 1987).

tradition with Puritan roots.[126] The Particular Baptists seem to have split from the Independent Jacob Church over the issue of baptism.[127] Until recent years, it was generally held that this took place in 1633 with the separation of Samuel Eaton and some others who desired rebaptism. Ivimey, White and Carlile all viewed this as being a disagreement regarding proper baptism, i.e. infant baptism versus believer's baptism. Tolmie, however, saw these baptisms as being rebaptisms of those who believed in infant baptism, but held that theirs was invalid since it was administered by a false church. It appears that the basis of this split, however, was the repudiation by these members of the Church of England, claiming it to be a false church.[128] With its more open understanding of fellowship, the Jacob Church would not have held a strict enough view of membership for those who left. Tolmie went on to argue that the split, which gave birth to the Particular Baptists, took place in 1640 with the formation of two separate Independent congregations from the Jacob Church. Henry Jessey and half of the members comprised a new fellowship, which allowed rebaptised members and the other half became the church headed by Praise-God Barbone, which was not tolerant of rebaptised members.[129] This was followed by subsequent splits in 1641 and 1643, leading to the formation of the first Particular Baptist Fellowship under the leadership of William Kiffin.[130] The relationship of the newly established Particular Baptists with the Independents

---

[126] Tolmie, *Triumph*, pp. 7-8, 25-27. See also Kenneth Ross Manley, "Origins of the Baptists: the Case for Development from Puritanism - Separatism", *Baptist History and Heritage* 22 (Oct. 1987).

[127] Tolmie described the Jacob Church as "the model for the Independent gathered churches of the future... the mother church of a variety of congregations formed by secession, both amicable and contentious". Of the churches which sprang from it, many became Baptist. The separations which took place were mostly the result of friendly conference, and arose from the rapid growth of the Church or from differences on the issue of baptism. *Triumph*, pp. 12-27.

[128] John Carlile, *The Story of the English Baptists*, (London: James Clarke & Co., 1905), pp. 82-85. White, "Origins and Convictions", pp. 41-43. White, *English Baptists of the Seventeenth Century*, p. 59. Ivimey, *History*, I, pp. 138-39. *Triumph*, pp. 192-95.

[129] Tolmie, *Triumph*, pp. 24-26. See also B.R. White, "The Doctrine of the Church in the Particular Baptist Confession of 1644", *Journal of Theological Studies*, N. S., vol. XIX, (Oct. 1968) : 575.

[130] This would be Tolmie's perspective. He argued convincingly that the issue of believer's baptism was not the cause of the earlier splits, and did not come to the fore until 1643 when Knollys refused to have his child baptised. Although White would see this as "far less certain" ("Origins and Convictions", p. 43) it seems to this writer to be the more plausible possibility, born out by the so-called Knollys memorandum. See *Triumph*, pp. 192-95. See also W.T. Whitley, "The Jacob-Jessey Church". For the account of the 1643 debate, see W.T. Whitley, "Debate". This will be dealt with in more detail below in Chapter 7.

during the 1640s clearly remained an amicable one. The connections with the mother Jessey Church remained very close.[131]

While the Parliament struggled to determine the religious direction of the nation (1643/44) and debated about accommodation, the Particular Baptists also sought to find their own religious direction. Not only did they search to find their identity, but they also scrambled to inform the public concerning it.[132] *The Confession of Faith, Of those Churches which are commonly (though falsly) called Anabaptists*,[133] of 1644, contributed toward both of these ends. The fact that seven churches signed this document provides evidence of the rapid growth of the Particular Baptist fellowship. It also shows the desire of these churches to establish themselves into some form of defined association. The *1644 Confession* clearly arose as an apologetic document, the "Calvinistic Baptists' first public attempt at a corporate defense."[134] Significantly, Hanserd Knollys' signature did not appear on this Confession. Although Knollys was seriously questioning the validity of infant baptism when the Confession was written in October 1644, he still remained a member of the Jessey church.

Gordon Kingsley's survey of the vast collection of propaganda written against the Baptists in the first half of the 1640s showed that they came under heavy attack, mainly from Presbyterians.[135] For the Particular Baptists, not only did the slanderous claim of their being related to the Anabaptists of the Münster rebellion in early 16th century Germany constantly dog them, but so also did the attempts to associate them with the freewill General Baptists.[136] Their intent to disprove charges of "holding to free will, falling away from grace, denying original sin, disclaiming of magistracy, denying to assist them either in persons or purse, in any of their lawful commands, doing acts unseemly in the dispensing the ordinance of baptism" clearly appeared in the preface.[137] Relying

---

[131] Tolmie, *Triumph*, pp. 59-60.

[132] The Baptist formation and development of a self-identity and Knollys' role in that process will be explored in Chapter 7 below.

[133] *The Confession of Faith, Of those Churches which are commonly (though falsly) called Anabaptists*, (London: 1644), in *Baptist Confessions of Faith*, ed. William L. Lumpkin, (Philadelphia: The Judson Press, 1959), pp. 144-45; hereafter designated *1644 Confession* [with original page numbers in brackets].

[134] White, "Origins and Convictions", p. 42.

[135] In his article "Opposition to Early Baptists (1638-1645)", Gordon Kingsley pointed out that not all of the criticism came from the Presbyterians, but also from Independents. *Baptist History and Heritage* 4, (Jan. 1969) : 18-21.

[136] J.F. McGregor, "The Baptists: Fount of All Heresy", p. 27. William L. Lumpkin, *Baptist Confessions of Faith*, (Philadelphia: The Judson Press, 1959), pp. 144-45. Tolmie, *Triumph*, p. 69, 72-73; during this period, the Particular Baptists had more in common and more fellowship with the Independents than with the General Baptists.

[137] *1644 Confession*, Preface.

heavily on the 1596 Separatist Confession,[138] the *1644 Confession* combined a moderate form of High-Calvinism (balancing election with an emphasis on evangelism -Articles XXI-XXXII), with statements emphasising the tenets of Baptist belief (believer's baptism - Articles XXXIX-XLI; congregationalism - Articles XXXVI-XXXVIII, XLII-XLVI; church-state relations - Articles XLVIII-LIII).

Perhaps the two most radical aspects of this confession came in the statements affirming baptism by immersion of believers only and in the statements related to the ministry.[139] Articles XXXIX-XLI dealt with the ordinance of baptism, stating that it was to be administered only "upon profession of faith", and only by "dipping or plunging the whole body under water" representing the death, burial, and resurrection of Christ. With respect to the ministry, B.R. White has contended, "there can be little doubt that among these early Particular Baptists the position accorded the ministry was measurably less significant than it had been among the Separatists."[140] On the one hand, the Baptists attempted to limit it with statements that subordinated the authority of the ministry to that of the congregation. "Christ has likewise given power to his whole Church to receive in and cast out, by way of Excommunication, any member; and this power is given to every particular Congregation, and not to one particular person, either member or Officer, but the whole." On the other hand, though, they attempted to broaden the ministry with a greater emphasis on lay ministry. For example, "The persons designed by Christ to dispense this Ordinance, the Scriptures hold forth to be a preaching Disciple, it being no where tyed to a particular Church Officer, or person extraordinarily sent." These concerns were addressed in Articles XLI - XLV. Also, in response to accusations that Baptists posed a political threat, the *1644 Confession* combined clear statements affirming the "supreme Magistracie of this Kingdome... The King and Parliament freely chosen by the Kingdome" as established by God[141] with statements, which asserted passive resistance when civil and spiritual authority conflicted (Articles XLIX-LI).[142]

---

[138] Lumpkin, *Baptist Confessions of Faith*, p. 145; White, *English Baptists of the Seventeenth Century*, p. 61.

[139] White, *English Baptists of the Seventeenth Century*, pp. 62-63.

[140] White, "The Doctrine of the Church in the Particular Baptist Confession of 1644", p. 581.

[141] Article XLIX. This phrase was omitted in editions after 1647.

[142] Mark R. Bell argued in *Apocalypse How? Baptist Movements During the English Revolution*, (Macon, GA: Mercer University Press, 2000), that four primary reasons existed for the publication of the *1644 Confession*. First to "define themselves in contrast to the Continental Anabaptists;" second, to differentiate themselves from the English General Baptists; third, "trying to define themselves for themselves" for the purpose of internal unity & gaining converts; fourth, to convince the political authorities they were not a threat, p. 74. This argument is not far from what is being argued in this work.

The publication of the *1644 Confession* did little to ease the volume or intensity of the opposition.[143] Almost immediately, Presbyterian academic Daniel Featley responded with his famous work *The Dippers Dipt. Or, The Anabaptists Duck'd and Plung'd Over Head and Eares*. In it, he not only systematically attacked the 1644 Confession, but the life and practices of the "Anabaptists" themselves, claiming that "of all Heretiques and Schismatiques the Anabaptist in three regards ought to be most carefully looked unto, and severely punished, if not utterly exterminated and banished out of the church and Kingdome". In essence, he likened them to nearly every major heresy in Church history, stating that "in one Anabaptist you have many Heretiques, and in this one Sect . . . many erroneous and schismaticall positions and practices."[144] The charges he brought against them varied from ones of theological heresy to political danger to immoral behaviour. He accused them of sexual promiscuity, "plurality of wives, and adulterous and incestuous copulations" and compared their baptismal ceremonies with orgies: "They strip themselves stark naked, not onely when they flocke in great multitudes, men and women together, to their Jordans to be dipt; but also upon other occasions, when the season permits."[145] Another major attack against Baptists came from the pen of Ephraim Pagett. This work made similar albeit much more slanderous claims about their moral behaviour:

> those women sinne grievously that lye with their husbands that are not rebaptized, because they are Gentiles; but it to be no sin at all for them to lye with any man that hath been rebaptized, because the heavenly Father hath so commanded.... Thus they [baptists] deceive the poore people, they perswade simple women under pretence of Gods commandement, that they cannot be saved except they prostitute their bodies to their brethren, and play the harlots.[146]

These vicious attacks upon Baptists, plus the more general religious debates of the time, prompted a revision of their confession, which appeared in 1646. [147]By this point, Hanserd Knollys had joined their ranks as a university-

---

[143] However, with respect to this renewed hostility, Lumpkin noted "outside the Baptist fellowship the Confession was received with unequalled surprise. People generally were amazed at the moderation and sanity of its articles." Perhaps it was this public acceptance, which motivated the harsh response from the Presbyterians. *Baptist Confessions of Faith*, p. 147.

[144] Daniel Featley, *The Dippers Dipt. Or, The Anabaptists Duck'd and Plung'd Over Head and Eares*, (London, 1645), Epistle Dedicatory.

[145] Featley, *The Dippers Dipt.*, pp. 202-203.

[146] *Heresiography*, pp. 36-37.

[147] Bell argued that, in fact, things had begun to change for the better with the publication of the *1644 Confession*. He held that "persecution was comparatively light and that they 'had some breathing time'". Due to this new "liberal atmosphere", the Particular Baptists had allowed the confession to be "crafted to give the illusion that the

educated clergyman, and very likely played a major role in the composition of this revised statement.[148] This *1646 Confession* softened some of the distinctly Baptist emphasis of the previous one[149] and strengthened the emphasis on Calvinistic theology, perhaps in hope of finding wider acceptance.[150] Once again, the apologetic nature of the Confession was clearly stated in the Preface, highlighting how the Baptists had received unjust treatment, in spite of their seeking after the Truth and comparing themselves to Christ, who "was accused to be a seditious and mutinous fellow" and Paul, who "was called a pestilent fellow, and a mover of sedition."[151] The Particular Baptists published this Confession "to free ourselves and the truth we profess from such unjust aspersions."[152] In this revision, they attempted to counter several accusations: [1] that they held to free-will and falling from grace; [2] that they denied election, original sin, children's salvation, the Old Testament, men's propriety in

---

Baptists were prepared to jettison their critiques of society in exchange for liberty of conscience". Bell, *Apocalypse How?*, pp. 79-80.

[148] Lumpkin, *Baptist Confessions of Faith*, pp. 147-48. *A Confession of Faith of Seven Congregations or Churches of Christ in London, Which are Commonly (But Unjustly) called Anabaptists*, (London: 1646), in *Confessions of Faith and Other Public Documents, Illustrative of the History of the Baptist Churches of England in the 17th Century*, edited by Edward Bean Underhill, (London: Hanserd Knollys Society, 1854); hereafter designated *1646 Confession*. The apologetic intent of this document was clearly announced on the title page: "For the vindication of the Truth, and information of the ignorant; likewise for the taking off of those aspersions which are frequently both in pulpit and print unjustly cast upon them."

[149] Changes to the entries on baptism included: Article XXIX stated that baptism is "to be dispensed upon persons professing faith" whereas in the "1644 Confession", it stated that it was "to be dispensed **onely** upon persons professing faith" (emphasis added). This omission was in response to Featley's criticism that this entry would be acceptable if the word onely were omitted. Article XL stated that the manner of baptism is "dipping or plunging the body under water" signifying the "interest the saints have in the death, burial, and resurrection of Christ". In the "1644 Confession" it was stated that the manner "*the Scripture holds out to be* dipping or plunging the *whole* body under water" signifying "*first, the washing the whole soule in the bloud of Christ: Secondly,* that interest the Saints have in the death, buriall, and resurrection; *thirdly, together with a confirmation of our faith*" (words in italics removed from the *1646 Confession*). This was again softened in response to Featley's criticism. The argument about immersion turned on the translation of the Greek word βαπτίζω meaning 'to dip'. Featley countered that the Scriptures did not clearly define baptism as immersion. See Lumpkin, *Baptist Confessions of Faith*, p. 167, notes (a), (c).

[150] Shortly after the publication of this confession, on 30 November 1646, Benjamin Cox, the other exclergyman who in all likelihood assisted Knollys in rewriting the *1646 Confession*, published an elaboration to it containing twenty-two articles, which were even stronger in their Calvinistic flavour. Lumpkin, *Baptist Confessions of Faith*, p. 150.

[151] *1646 Confession* in Underhill, *Confessions of Faith*, p. 19.

[152] *1646 Confession* in Underhill, *Confessions of Faith*, p. 22.

their estates; and [3] that they denounced all who did not practice or believe as they did.[153] The *1646 Confession* then, contained stronger statements on election (Articles III, V-VI, XXI-XXII), original sin (Article IV), perseverance of the saints (Article XXIII), and against free-will (Article XXIV). As well, it included strong affirmation of the propriety of men's different estates, emphasising the responsibilities of those of higher and wealthier status to care for those beneath them (Article XXXV), and a statement on liberty of conscience, clearly in response to the Presbyterian attempts in 1645 for uniformity (Article XLVIII).

The publication of these Confessions was not the only way in which the Baptists attempted to clear themselves in the public arena. Another important avenue open to them during the leniency of the civil war years was that of public conferences and debates. Murray Tolmie pointed out the importance of meetings or conferences, which took place, involving Baptists, Independents, and even moderate Presbyterians. These included the conference gathered to discuss the response of the Jessey church to the withdrawal of Kiffin and the others following the baptism debate of 1644.[154] Another conference to which Knollys was invited (along with Jeremiah Burroughes, Henry Burton, and John Saltmarsh) took place in 1645 or 1646. It gathered at the request of the Duppa church to "consider the objections of this church to the attendance of Christians in the 'high places' (the parish church building)."[155]

Public debates also provided a popular venue, one such dispute having been arranged for December 1645 between Cox, Kiffin, and Knollys on the one side, and Edmund Calamy and other Presbyterians on the other. Following accepted practices of academic debate, they agreed to address, for six hours, the question 'Should the children of believing parents be baptised?'.[156] Citing the threat of rumoured violence by the Baptists, however, the Lord Mayor of London "thought fit upon serious consideration, for prevention of the inconveniencies that might happen thereby, to forbid the same Meeting and Disputation, upon

---

[153] *1646 Confession* in Underhill, *Confessions of Faith*, p. 21.

[154] This conference included such prominent Independents as Praise-God Barbone, William Erbury, Thomas Goodwin, Sidrach Simpson, Philip Nye, and Jeremiah Burroughs, to name a few. Whitley, "Debate", p. 243; *Triumph*, p. 122.

[155] *Triumph*, p. 123. David Brown, *Two Conferences Between Some of Those That Are Called Separatists and Independents*, (London: 1650). This document reports on that conference which discussed, beyond the parish church building, many other aspects of worship and polity.

[156] Benjamin Cox, Hanserd Knollys, William Kiffin, *A Declaration Concerning the Publike Dispute Which Should have been in the Publike Meeting-House of Alderman-Bury, the 3d of this instant Moneth of December; Concerning Infants-Baptisme. Together, with some of the Arguments which should then have been propounded and urged by some of those that are falsly called Anabaptists, which should then have disputed*, (London: 1645), pp. 2-3.

that day, or at any other time in a publike way".[157] Somewhat frustrated that the Mayor had cancelled the dispute on sudden notice, the Baptists published arguments as a sort of doctrinal statement or declaration on baptism. After discounting the so-called threat of violence, Knollys, Cox, and Kiffin went on to specify not only who should be baptised (believers), but also how baptism should take place,[158] arguing that baptism must be by immersion and without set form (i.e. set prayers, the sign of the cross).[159] Although this dispute never happened, a year later in 1646, a similar debate took place at Trinity Church, Coventry between Knollys and Kiffin, and Rev. John Bryan, D.D., Vicar of Trinity Church and Rev. Obediah Grew, M.A., D.D., Vicar of St. Michael's Coventry. It is significant that both of their opponents were well-educated ministers within the Established Church.[160]

Not only did these conferences and debates provide opportunities for the Baptists to defend or explain their beliefs, but they also helped them in building stronger ties with Independents and moderate Presbyterians, ties that would prove valuable during the era of persecution, which would follow the restoration of the monarchy and the episcopacy.

Knollys' Publications and the Struggle for Legitimacy

In the opening pages of his autobiographical memoirs, Hanserd Knollys portrayed himself as a man with a tender conscience who was compelled to abide by the leading of that conscience. His struggle with sin and guilt, even as a child, led him to a deep piety and ultimately into ministry. During his early years as a clergyman, Knollys became convinced of the importance of Scripture as Truth.[161] These two convictions - the necessity of adhering to the leading of conscience, and the authority of the Bible as the source of Truth - became the hallmarks of his life and work.

The years from 1644 to 1646 served significantly in the development of Knollys from a Puritan pastor to a Baptist spokesman. During this time, he became strongly involved in the propaganda wars that raged in London and in the ongoing dialogue regarding toleration. Knollys and fellow pastor Benjamin Cox were two of very few Particular Baptists who had any advanced education

---

[157] Cox, Knollys, Kiffin, *A Declaration Concerning the Publike Dispute*, p. 3.

[158] Cox, Knollys, Kiffin, *A Declaration Concerning the Publike Dispute*, pp. 7-9.

[159] Cox, Knollys, Kiffin, *A Declaration Concerning the Publike Dispute*, pp. 10-13. Knollys et al. took this opportunity to rail against formalism in a variety of forms, a bit outside of the topic of debate.

[160] Arthur S. Langley, "Seventeenth Century Baptist Disputations", in *Transactions of the Baptist Historical Society*, VI, (July, 1919) : 224. Of course, these disputes must have been instrumental in the appearance of the revised "1646 Confession", which many have held to have been formulated primarily by Cox and Knollys. Lumpkin, *Baptist Confessions of Faith*, p. 148.

[161] Knollys, *Life*, pp. 5-6.

and theological training. They became the 'big voices' for the Baptists in the debates of the 1640s. Knollys' involvement not only included his polemical writings, which will be examined below, but also his participation in conferences and public disputations, and his participation in the formulation of doctrinal or confessional statements. These activities played a vital part in the attempts of the Particular Baptists to gain acceptance from the public.

Knollys' polemical writings, *A Moderate Answer unto Dr. Bastwicks Book Called "Independency not God's Ordinance"* and *The Shining of a Flaming Fire In Zion*, produced the clearest presentation of his position on the two major issues which distinguished the Particular Baptists from the Presbyterians – independent, congregational church government and believer's baptism – and the single major aspect in which they diverged from the Independents – believer's baptism. Underlying both of these writings was Knollys' commitment to the authority of conscience informed by the authoritative Scriptures.

This section will examine these writings within a series of contexts – specifically Knollys' life experiences, the emerging Particular Baptist identity, the ongoing upheaval and religious turmoil in England in the 1640s, and the debate between the Presbyterians and Independents over uniformity and accommodation – and note that the context holds as much significance as the content. Neither of the two treatises was written in response to a direct attack from an opponent.[162] In fact, if Knollys' works were not so gentle in spirit, one might think he sought to instigate a confrontation.

A Moderate Answer was written from the perspective of an outsider, an interested third party. John Bastwick, a staunch Presbyterian, had clearly written his attack against the Independents within the context of the ongoing discussion between the Presbyterians and Independents in Parliament and in the Assembly of Divines on the proper system of church polity. Bastwick did not address the Baptists, nor show much concern with the issue of accommodation. Instead, he concentrated on the issue of the gathering of churches and the authority of those individual gathered congregations. Knollys responded, realising that this attack against the Independents contained an implicit attack against the congregational polity of the Particular Baptists. The second treatise, *The Shining of a Flaming Fire* responded to John Saltmarsh's book *The Smoke In the Temple*, a work ironically written as a plea for tolerance. Saltmarsh proposed to replace National Church with a National Covenant based on liberty of conscience with a view towards unity, not uniformity. Uniformity involved a forced union of Christians under the authority and structure of a national,

---

[162] In light of the plethora of literature being written against the Baptists at this time, such as the slanderous accusations made by Featley in *The Dippers Dipt* or by Pagett in *Heresiography* it may seem strange that Knollys made no just reply. Perhaps it was the approach of these two scurrilous works, reminiscent of a gossip or bully, which caused Knollys to ignore them as beneath consideration.

established church. In this way, doctrine and practices could be controlled and uniform. Unity, however, was more Saltmarsh's aim. Rather than creating union through the enforcement of uniform doctrine and polity, Saltmarsh's approach called for an end to polemics and attacks among differing perspectives and for fellow Christians to attempt to coexist with one another in spite of doctrinal differences. Many of Saltmarsh's contemporaries would not have understood unity in this sense. In the process of setting forth this plan for reconciliation, Saltmarsh critiqued each religious group and its beliefs. With regard to the Baptists, this involved primarily a criticism of their views on and practices of baptism, specifically as to mode (immersion), subjects (believers only), and administrators (any common disciple). Knollys responded to Saltmarsh's statements regarding baptism. Thus, in both instances, Knollys dealt with only a portion of the works to which he responded.

The tribute delivered at Knollys' funeral by Thomas Harrison summarised the mild and gentle spirit of the man.

> He loved the Image of God wheresoever he saw it. He was not a man of a narro and private, but of a large and publick spirit. The difference of his fellow Christians Opinions from his did not alienate his affections from them. He lov'd all his fellow Travellers, tho they did not walk in the same particular path with himself. He embrac'd those in the Arms of his Love upon Earth with whom he thought he should joyn in singing the Song of the Lamb in Heaven. It would be well if not only private Christians, but also Ministers did imitate him therein; there would not then be that sourness of Spirit which is too often (with grief be it spoken) found among them.... He was not of a proud and lofty Temper, but like that Master whom he profess'd to serve, meek and lowly. He was willing to bear with and forbear others. To stoop and condescend to others, and to pass by those injuries which he received from them.[163]

This attitude of forbearance and respect, albeit in the context of disagreement, appeared in both of these writings. Because of this, Knollys' works could best be described as a type of mild polemic. In his *A Moderate Answer*, he set the tone in the very title, and the opening letter to *The Shining of a Flaming Fire* took a congenial tone addressing "My Reverend Friend, and Brother, Mr. Saltmarsh."[164] Considering that Knollys had experienced much hardship and persecution at the hands of other Christians, both Presbyterians and Congregationalists, and had experienced poverty, ridicule, exile, physical abuse, and imprisonment, his irenic tone was truly remarkable. Overall, his writings took the 'high road' in the debate.

---

[163] Harrison, *SERMON*, pp. 57-8.
[164] Knollys, *A Moderate Answer*, title page; Knollys, *The Shining of a Flaming Fire*, The Epistle. It is clear, however, that Knollys was much more gracious and consonant with John Saltmarsh.

A Moderate Answer Unto Dr. Bastwicks Book

John Bastwick, a medical doctor of Presbyterian persuasion was far from mild or gentle in his writings. An experienced pamphleteer, he was no stranger to harsh and bitter dispute. Like Knollys, he had suffered under the oppressive measures of Laudian uniformity and his struggle with the Episcopacy had served only to make him a sharper, more merciless opponent.[165] His previous relationship with Knollys had been friendly.[166] When Knollys, his expectant wife, and their young child arrived destitute in London from New England, Bastwick had helped provide them with temporary shelter and financial assistance.[167] This expression of brotherly kindness only four years earlier perhaps remained in Knollys' mind as he fashioned his firm yet respectful reply to Bastwick's work.

Bastwick's *Independency Not Gods Ordinance Or a Treatise concerning Church Government, occasioned by the Distractions of these times* (London: 1645), a voluminous tome of two parts totalled 242 pages and contained long and often repetitious arguments. Knollys penned a brief, purposeful response, on the other hand, totalling a mere 20 pages. Bastwick's major point was that Presbyterian Government dependent upon a common council of Presbyters fulfilled God's ordinance. To prove this, he argued four propositions: [1] there were many congregations of believers in the Church of Jerusalem; [2] these all made but one church; [3] the Apostles and Elders ruled this church by a council or Presbytery; and [4] the Jerusalem church and its government provided the pattern for all churches, that every city was to comprise one church and the various officers of that church would comprise a ruling body or council (Presbytery).[168] Knollys maintained that Bastwick's examination of Scripture did prove that each city had a Presbytery and could ordain elders, that every known New Testament church had elders for officers, that several churches

---

[165] Knollys referred to him as a "late Sufferer" in his memoirs, perhaps betraying a sort of felt kinship. Knollys, *Life*, p. 18. Bastwick's writings against the Papacy, and later Episcopacy and the Bishops, brought him excommunication, fines, imprisonment, and eventually the loss of his ears and a sentence of exile for life. Yet even in the face of his harsh sentence, his defence was "bitter and slashing". J.C. Brauer, "Bastwick, John (1593-1654)", in *Biographical Dictionary of British Radicals in the Seventeenth Century*, ed. by R. L. Greaves and R. Zaller, (Brighton, Sussex: Harvester, 1983) : 1.47-48. Haller, *Rise*, pp. 252-56.

[166] B.R. White assumed that Knollys and Bastwick may even have been friends. *Hanserd Knollys and Radical Dissent in the 17th Century*, (London: Dr. Williams's Trust, 1977), p. 10.

[167] See ch. 3 above. Knollys also made mention that "two Doctors, an Apothecary and a Chyrurgeon" provided their services for his wife at no charge until the baby was delivered. With John Bastwick being a medical doctor, he may have had a role in this act of kindness as well. Knollys, *Life*, pp. 18-19.

[168] John Bastwick, *Independency Not Gods Ordinance Or a Treatise concerning Church Government, occasioned by the Distractions of these times* (London: 1645), pp. 12-29.

came under the rule of their several elders or Presbyters, and that Presbyterian government was ordained by God. However, he maintained that Bastwick failed to prove the kingpin of his whole argument – that such a government depended on a "Common-counsell, colledge, and court of classicall, or Synodall Presbyters."[169]

In countering these arguments, Knollys showed his training and education, particularly in dealing with the Scriptures. His mature grasp of the original biblical languages would be demonstrated firmly in 1664 and 1665, when he published grammars of Greek, Latin, and Hebrew.[170] However, evidence of this ability in the original languages also appeared at several points in this pamphlet when he questioned Bastwick's exegesis of the text in relation to his arguments for a council or Presbytery. In the first instance, Bastwick claimed that in 3 John 9, Diotrephes' sin was "to assume unto himself, and his particular congregation, that power that belonged unto the colledge or councell of Presbyters" thus creating a congregation which was Independent, not ruled by the Presbytery. Bastwick claimed that when John said, "I wrote something to the church", he was referring to a particular church of which Diotrephes was an Elder. Thus, the elder of a particular church went against the council in Jerusalem, which Bastwick saw as a presbytery. Through a simple rendering of the Greek and examination of Beza's commentary on that verse, Knollys, concluded that "no mention is made of any perticular Congregation" in this verse, but that the command addressed the whole Church, and Diotrephes' sin was taking pre-eminence to himself.[171]

The second instance had to do with the meaning of the simple Greek word μνείας. Bastwick attempted to claim that prior to the Diaspora, the Jerusalem Church was the most glorious Church in the whole of the Mediterranean world and that through the preaching of John the Baptist and Jesus, all of Jerusalem, save the Pharisees and the priesthood, believed in and followed Christ. Bastwick argued that the Greek word μνείας (which was used to describe the Jerusalem Church) meant ten thousands, thus showing that there were many churches in Jerusalem, all under the authority of the Council (Presbytery) of Jerusalem, since "certainly one place could not have contained them all".[172]

---

[169] Knollys, *A Moderate Answer*, pp. 5-6.
[170] *Grammaticae Graecae compendium* (1664); Grammaticae *Latinae compendium*, (1664); *Linguae Hebricae delineation*, (1664); *Grammaticae Latinae, Graecae, & Hebricae*, (1665). He began his publication of language aids as early as 1648 when he published *The Rudiments of Hebrew Grammar in English*.
[171] Bastwick, *Independency Not Gods Ordinance*, p. 15. Knollys, *A Moderate Answer*, pp. 5-6. The use of Beza was brilliant, for Beza, Calvin's successor in Geneva, carried great weight among the Presbyterians.
[172] Bastwick, *Independency Not Gods Ordinance*, pp. 37-40. Bastwick, citing Acts 2:46, which declared that the believers of Jerusalem "continued daily with one accord in the Temple, and that they brake bread from house to house: and that daily in the Temple,

Knollys, however, argued (again with the support of Beza) that μνείας usually meant thousands or a multitude. Thus, the Church at Jerusalem was not ten thousand in number, but perhaps one thousand. In fact, Knollys argued, the Scriptures, especially that passage cited by Bastwick himself in Acts 2:46, expressly stated that they did meet all together in one place - the Temple.[173]

One of the key passages Bastwick used to support his arguments was Acts 15 – the account of the Council of Jerusalem and its determination of the issue regarding the Gentiles. Knollys pointed out, again using rather simple exegesis, that not only were the Apostles and Presbyters of Jerusalem present and involved in the decision-making process, but so also were "the Brethren, even the whole church, the multitude (how many soever the D. can make of them)".[174] His use of this passage clearly emphasised the role of all members in church government, a central element in the congregational polity of both Baptists and Independents. Knollys' main point of contention, however, with Bastwick's Presbyterian model of church government, had to do with his understanding of the role and office of the Apostles. Knollys held that the Apostles, though called Presbyters, were not the pattern for all Presbyters. In other words, the authority held by the Apostles in the New Testament Church did not necessarily transfer to presbyters. He gave two reasons for this. First, because of their unique call by Christ, the Apostles had direct care and oversight over all of the early churches. The local elders or Presbyters, on the other hand, only had care over their local churches. The second reason he gave was that if,[175] as Bastwick asserted, the Apostles formed a pattern for all Presbyters, then all Presbyters would be independent, for the Apostles depended only upon Christ by the Holy Spirit.[176] Knollys' point was that they did not rely on earthly councils or governing ecclesiastical bodies. Instead, it was the leading of the Holy Spirit that guided their decisions. In the same way, independent elders should lead local congregations as the Holy Spirit guided them, through their New Testament Scriptures (which were written by the Apostles).

In *A Moderate Answer*, Knollys displayed a keen mind and ability to debate by clearly summarising Bastwick's own arguments and then very craftily turning them around to prove Independent polity or disprove

---

and in every house, they ceased not to teach and preach Jesus Christ", argued that the Church in Jerusalem met in many smaller 'house congregations'.

[173] Knollys, *A Moderate Answer*, p. 9.

[174] Knollys, *A Moderate Answer*, pp. 13-14. Every so often, Knollys slipped in a sarcastic barb such as his jab at Bastwick's poor exegesis in relation to the "multitude" in the Jerusalem church. However, this is as harsh a response as Knollys gave.

[175] Knollys' hypothetical use of "if" in this instance did not necessarily indicate that he accepted it as true.

[176] Knollys, *A Moderate Answer*, p. 13.

Presbyterianism.[177] One example of this can be seen in his dealing with Bastwick's treatment of the gathered churches. Knollys summed up Bastwick's observations regarding the gathering of churches in the New Testament: [1] that the Apostles should teach nothing except what Christ had commanded; [2] that the condition for admission into the Church "was Faith, Repentance, and Baptisme"; and [3] that this commission was delivered "onely to the Apostles and Ministers of the Gospel".[178] He then turned this argument against Bastwick by arguing that those who were gathering churches in England had fulfilled these conditions:

> Some godly and learned men of approved guifts and abilities for the Ministrie, being driven out of the Countries, where they lived by the persecution of the Prelates, came to sojourn in this great City, and preached the Word of God both publikely, and from house to house, and daily in the Temples and in every house they ceased not to teach and preach Jesus Christ.... And the condition which those Preachers both publikely and privately prepounded to the people, unto whom they Preached, upon which they were to be admitted into the Church was Faith, Repentance, and Baptisme; and none other.[179]

Another example of turning Bastwick's arguments against himself appeared in the section in which Knollys dealt with the question of who had the authority to make the decision about admitting or excommunicating members. He quoted Bastwick as stating that in the case of Paul in Acts 9, the congregation of Disciples (not just the Presbyters and the Apostles, but the "Brethren") had a say in whether or not he was to be admitted into membership. In that particular situation, since Paul had formerly been a persecutor of the Church, "for a time the Disciples feared" and refused Paul membership "till they had better information and proofe that he now preached the faith that he had once persecuted". Thus, the members of the Church and not the Presbyters alone determined Paul's status. Since this took place in Jerusalem, and since, as "the Doctor confesseth, yea affirmeth... 'that the Mother Church must give an

---

[177] Knollys' familiarity with the conventions of scholarly syllogistic debate was clearly evident in this work. In fact, Knollys was critical of what he believed to be Bastwick's poor debating skills: "For if the Dr. please to review his Argument, He shall finde, First; that the subject of his Major proposition is left out both in his Minor, and in his Conclusion: The first part of the Doctors Minor should have been this, to witt, But the Apostles in the holy Scripture are called Presbyters, and who ever denyed this; Also the first part of the Doctors conclusion should have been this, from these two premises, to witt; *Ergo*, The Apostles acted as Presbyters which Conclusion is not the thing in Question." Knollys, *A Moderate Answer*, p. 13. Clearly, Knollys was a living refutation of the common criticism of the Baptists that they were uneducated and unskilled in debating according to accepted academic rules. See Featley, *The Dippers Dipt*, pp. 1-13.
[178] Knollys, *A Moderate Answer*, p. 15.
[179] Knollys, *A Moderate Answer*, pp. 19 (marked 13)-20.

example of government to all the Daughter churches'", then this established a precedent for congregational decisions on membership.[180]

Although "moderate" in tone, Knollys' answer to Dr. Bastwick's book took a rigid stand against *jure divino* presbyterianism. At this point (May through July, 1645[181]), the official position of the Independent party still inclined toward accommodation, while the Presbyterians resisted such compromise. In contrast, Knollys' firm response to Bastwick took the line that the New Testament did not leave room for compromise, that it contained only one right model, a congregational one. In the New Testament, admission into a church was based upon

> Faith, Repentance, and Baptisme; *and none other*. And whosoever (poor as well as rich, bond as well as free, servants as well as Masters) did make a profession of their Faith in Christ Jesus, and would be baptized with water into the Name of the Father, Sonne, and Holy Spirit, were admitted Members of the Church; but such as did not beleeve, and would not be baptized they would not admit into Church communion. This hath been the practice of some Churches of God in this City.[182]

At this point, Knollys had departed from the position of his Independent Brethren and had moved to a Baptist perspective, emphasising believer's baptism as a prerequisite for church membership. Within a very few months of Knollys' debate with Bastwick, the Independents would demand toleration for "other tender consciences... that they may with the peace of their consciences enjoy".[183] As dogmatic as Knollys might have appeared, in essence, all that he desired was the liberty to follow his conscience and to expound the word of Scripture that others might also have their consciences awakened.[184] That Hanserd Knollys' "moderate answer" did not have its desired effect became obvious when Bastwick published his next book: *The Utter Routing of the whole Army of all the Independents & Sectaries... And all the Forces of the three Generals and Commanders of the Sectaries, Hanserdo Knollys, J. S., &*

---

[180] Bastwick, *Independency Not Gods Ordinance*, pp. 97, 101-102. Knollys, *Moderate Answer*, p. 16.

[181] Thomason transcribed the date on this particular pamphlet of Knollys as July 17th. The dates he gave to Bastwick's work were May 21 and June 10. Bastwick, *Independency Not Gods Ordinance*, Title page. Knollys, *Moderate Answer*, Title page.

[182] Knollys, *Moderate Answer*, p. 20, (emphasis added).

[183] Independent minority's proposal to the Westminster Assembly of Divines on 6 November 1645 in *The Papers and Answers of the Dissenting Brethren*.

[184] In *Christ Exalted*, Knollys wrote about the glorious liberties of Christ's Spirit: "For where the Spirit of the Lord is, there is liberty, 2 Cor. 3.17. Not any carnall liberty to sin, and so fulfill the lusts of the Flesh, Gal. 5.13. but Spirituall liberty, and freedome from sin." p. 6.

Henry Burton are all dissipated, with all their whibbling Reserves (London: 1646).[185]

The Shining of a Flaming Fire In Zion

In 1646, the seven London Particular Baptist Churches issued a revision of their Confession of Faith. Hanserd Knollys likely had a major role in its composition, being one of the few well-educated pastors in the movement at the time. A note to Article XLVIII, contained the following comment about religious liberty.

> So it is the magistrate's duty to tender the liberty of men's consciences, Eccl. vii. 8, (which is the tenderest thing unto all conscientious men, and most dear unto them, and without which all other liberties will not be worth the naming, much less enjoying) and to protect all under them from all wrong, injury, oppression, and molestation.[186]

Such a statement stood in clear contrast with not only episcopacy in the 1630s, but also with Presbyterianism in the 1640s. Clearly, the Particular Baptists believed that the government's responsibility was to ensure "liberty of men's consciences". Such a call took a radical stand. With this statement in mind, as one reads John Saltmarsh's *The Smoke In the Temple, Wherein is a Designe for Peace and Reconciliation of Believers of the Several Opinions of these Times about Ordinances, to a Forbearance of each other in Love, and Meeknesse, and Humility* (London: 1646), one might think that Hanserd Knollys would have welcomed this work. In the opening preface, Saltmarsh immediately established his perspective of unity in spite of diversity by addressing "the Beleevers of severall Opinions for outward Ordinances or dispensations, Scandalously called Independents, Presbyterians, Anabaptists, Seekers".[187] His assertion that "if any man think he knoweth anything, he knoweth nothing yet as he ought to know" at first glance might seem somewhat sceptical, yet his intended meaning was that all have part of the Truth, "like so

---

[185] In one final stroke of irony, the Imprimatur, J. Cranford, closed the second part of Bastwick's *Independency Not Gods Ordinance* with the following: "My request to the Independents in behalfe of the Expectants and Seekers. Lights, Lights, Gentlemen - INDEPENDENTS, hang out your Lights, your New-lights there; hang out your New-born-lights there, That the poore Seekers may finde a Church amongst you."

[186] "1646 Confession", p. 45.

[187] Saltmarsh, *Smoke In the Temple*, preface. He then began with the salutation "Brethren", an indication of his openness to those of other groups. Although Knollys and the Baptists certainly took a rigid, exclusivist position with respect to church membership, their views regarding the separation of Church and State and liberty of conscience would certainly lead them to a similar position on religious toleration as that of Saltmarsh.

many travellers to the City of London; some travell from the North, some from the South, and from the West, some from the East, yet all thither". This position was quite the opposite of John Bastwick's. He criticised the Independents because "they pleade for a toleration of all Religions; an opinion, though pleasing to the flesh, yet so diabolicall, as I wonder any Christian truly fearing God should so much as open his mouth in defence of it... it being a thing so abominated by God himself, and so odious to all the holy Prophets and Apostles."[188] However, Saltmarsh made it clear here that his idea of liberty of conscience was limited to "the severall godly parties of believers" and that "the Magistrates sword" should not be used to enforce "things of pure Gospel mystery" and things of Christian worship.[189] In a word, Saltmarsh sought to bring about unity in the Church through humility.

An Independent who served in the Parliamentary Army as a chaplain from June 1646 to June 1647, Saltmarsh was best known for his radical views on toleration and sectarianism. In fact, his emphasis on liberty and freedom led to his being branded an Antinomian by the Presbyterians, and mistaken by many as being a Seeker. Saltmarsh showed little interest in institutional churches, feeling that the differences between the various churches mainly concerned outward physical legalities. Rather, he showed more interest in concentrating on the spiritual realities of the Christian life. His ability to present the opinions of others impartially was rare and his desire for unity was misunderstood, making him a favourite target of the conservative Presbyterian pamphleteers.[190]

Knollys approached Saltmarsh's work differently, starting on a more friendly note than was the case in his answer to Bastwick. *The Shining of a Flaming Fire* opened with a personal letter to John Saltmarsh in which he stated that he perceived "that the love of God, which hath made a glorious union betwixt Christ Jesus, and your self, constraines you, to endeavour Unity, and Peace with all the Saints, though they differ from you in Opinion". Continuing with this amenable approach, he expressed the hope that "They, that write not as Enemies, are like to prove better friends to the Truth". Even though Knollys believed Saltmarsh had written "out of a sincere desire to receive more light of Truth", he thought it important to refute the thirteen exceptions against the "Anabaptists" that Saltmarsh had expressed in his *Smoke In the Temple*.[191] By and large in agreement with the general premise of Saltmarsh's book, Knollys limited his response to the criticisms that Saltmarsh had written about Baptists, especially about their view of what Saltmarsh called "the new

---

[188] Bastwick, *Independency Not Gods Ordinance*, Part II, Preface, pp. 3-4 (unnumbered).

[189] Saltmarsh, *Smoke In the Temple*, pp. 24-26 (see note 101 above).

[190] N.T. Burns, "Saltmarsh, John (c. 1612-1647)", in *Biographical Dictionary of British Radicals in the Seventeenth Century*, ed. by R. L. Greaves and R. Zaller, (Brighton, Sussex: Harvester, 1983) : 3.136-37.

[191] Knollys, *Shining of the Flaming Fire*, The Epistle.

Baptism".[192] Some of Saltmarsh's criticisms of believer's baptism mirrored arguments raised by the Seeker William Erbury. A Puritan turned Seeker, who denied affiliation with any church, Erbury had also served as a chaplain in the Army.[193] Erbury basically believed that since the apostolic period, the Church entered a state of apostasy and the Spirit and the supernatural gifts of the Spirit had ceased.[194] Therefore, all outward structures or activities were powerless and useless. This meant, as well, that any attempt to gather and order churches, based on the New Testament model, was bound to fail. Only with the second coming of Christ would the Holy Spirit return. In light of this, Erbury himself had no connections with any visible Christian community. With respect to baptism, he held that the apostles could baptise because the Holy Spirit had made Himself known through the many supernatural gifts they possessed and exercised (baptism of the Spirit). Since the Baptists could not evidence any gifts from on high or baptism of the Spirit, their baptisms represented a meaningless denial of the Spirit of Jesus.[195]

Saltmarsh's thirteen exceptions against the "new Baptism" could be basically divided into two groups. The first set related to Christ's commissions in Matthew 28:18-19 and Mark 16:16-17 and centred around a discussion concerning water baptism, Spirit baptism, and the names (i.e. Jesus, Holy Spirit, or Trinitarian) by which one baptised. The second set related to the issue of gifts and call. The first set of arguments put forth by Saltmarsh were somewhat repetitive and convoluted in their presentation. Knollys quickly

---

[192] Saltmarsh, *Smoke In the Temple*, pp. 14-18. In a period during which Baptists were being compared to fanatical revolutionaries in sixteenth century Europe, were being accused of outlandish practices of immorality, were being branded as harmful to the state, and even charged with murder, such a rational and Scriptural approach must have been welcome to Knollys. Ivimey, *History*, I., p.197. Kingsley, "Opposition", pp. 22, 26-30. In response to this negative charge of innovation, Knollys stated that Paul's doctrine was called new (Acts 17:19), as was Christ's (Mk. 1:27). Knollys, *Shining of the Flaming Fire*, p. 1.

[193] B.R. White, "Erbery (or Erbury), William (1604-1654)", in *Biographical Dictionary of British Radicals in the Seventeenth Century*, ed. by R. L. Greaves and R. Zaller, (Brighton, Sussex: Harvester, 1983) : 1.253-54. Michael A.G. Haykin held that Saltmarsh's arguments were basically those of Erbury, but it would seem that they were not nearly so systematically arranged or presented. Thus, it may be better to hold that Saltmarsh's views of baptism were merely 'flavoured' by Erbury's teachings. "Hanserd Knollys (ca. 1599-1691) On the Gifts of the Spirit", *Westminster Theological Journal* 54 (Spring 1992)) : 106-108.

[194] From Erbury's perspective, whichever group one was speaking of – Episcopalian, Presbyterian, Independent, or Baptist – all were lacking. The entire Church, as an institution, was apostate.

[195] White, "Erbery", p. 254. Haykin, "Knollys... the Gifts of the Spirit", pp. 106-107. Interestingly enough, Erbury believed that "the outward form of the Baptist communities of his day" was closest to the apostolic church, yet even they were apostate.

discerned this and turned it to his advantage. Saltmarsh saw two types of Baptism in the New Testament: Water baptism, practised by the Apostles in Acts, after the example of John the Baptist and performed in the name of Jesus only; and Spirit baptism, which was commissioned by Christ in Matthew 28 and Mark 16. Since these passages contained no mention of water, he argued they must have referred to a baptism of Spirit and of gifts.[196] Amazingly, Saltmarsh argued that Christ nowhere commanded the Trinitarian formula, and if one performed anything in the name of Christ (as per the baptisms in Acts), it would not literally be in His name but in His power. Knollys' response to this was simply that the Trinitarian formula was in Matthew 28:18, and that in neither case was the form of any necessity. He also showed that since all three Persons are One, to baptise in the name of Christ was the same as baptising in the name of the Father, Son, and Spirit.[197]

Knollys responded to this line of argument in a devastating way.[198] First, seeing an element of inconsistency in Saltmarsh's argument, he made Saltmarsh appear to contradict himself. In his first four exceptions, Saltmarsh argued consistently for two types of baptism, water (Acts) and Spirit/gifts (Matthew). Yet in exception ten, he argued that the two types were joined and could not be separated. Since Knollys had maintained that the Scripture passages commissioned both types of baptism, in his response to the first four exceptions, he used Saltmarsh's tenth exception as a platform for subverting the earlier exceptions.[199] The second approach, which Knollys used to answer Saltmarsh's arguments, was an exegetical one, once more exhibiting his ability and competence in using the original languages. He argued that the Greek verb βαπτίζω simply meant, "to dip in water" and was so used by the Septuagint writers and by the Gospel writers when writing of John the Baptist.[200] In fact, the Gospel of John used this meaning of the word "without Exception."[201] Therefore, baptising in the gospels, particularly in Matthew 28:19, should not be understood as being "the Baptism of Guifts, nor of Afflictions, nor of any other kinde of Baptizing, but by water."[202]

---

[196] Saltmarsh, *Smoke In the Temple*, pp. 15-17.

[197] Knollys, *Shining of the Flaming Fire*, pp. 2, 5-7.

[198] In this situation, as with Bastwick, Knollys used his training to refute his opponents exegetically, using the original languages, and logically, by turning their own arguments back on themselves.

[199] Knollys, *Shining of the Flaming Fire*, p. 4. Saltmarsh went on to argue that since no man can give the Spirit, and the two types are inseparably combined, then water baptism should not be practised. In this line of argument, one can find shades of Erbury's thought. Saltmarsh, *Smoke In the Temple*, pp. 17-18.

[200] Knollys, *Shining of the Flaming Fire*, pp. 17-18.

[201] Knollys, *Shining of the Flaming Fire*, pp. 17-18.

[202] Knollys, *Shining of the Flaming Fire*, pp. 17-18. Knollys' purpose for doing this Greek word study was to respond to Saltmarsh's second exception, which stated "that

The second set of arguments made by Saltmarsh related to gifts. He argued that "common disciples" had not received supernatural, miraculous abilities as gifts, as had the Apostles, and therefore they could not baptise.[203] Ordinances could only be administered by those as "distinctly, specially, spiritually, powerfully, enabled as the first dispensers".[204] To this objection, Knollys concurred wholeheartedly, agreeing that the only Christians who should administer the ordinances were those disciples who "have received such gifts of the Spirit as fitteth or inableth him to preach the Gospel. And those guifts being first tried by, and known to the Church." But, he countered, Baptist ministers were "as powerfully inabled as the first Dispenser of Baptism: And we having received Authority from Jesus Christ."[205] He then turned Saltmarsh against himself again, using the arguments which his opponent had used against the Seekers when dealing with their overemphasis on miraculous powers: [1] Apostolic miracles were for the purpose of bringing the Gospel into the world; [2] Truth is lessened if miracles are necessary for believing and baptising; [3] miracles can be done by the ungodly; [4] though the powerful gifts are not present, believers should still practice ordinances which are made clear to them; [5] the Scriptures themselves are a miracle. Knollys went on to show that although the Scriptures mentioned many disciples (the Twelve and later the seventy), they contained no evidence that all of these had or practised miraculous gifts.[206] Saltmarsh had also argued that Baptists "have no greater gifts in their Churches then there are in those called Independent".[207] Knollys agreed with him on this point as well, but noted that the Baptists had not attempted to establish superiority with regard to the gifts of the Holy Spirit, but only wished "to honour Christ our Head with all the guifts, which we have received from him".[208] This particular discussion on gifts certainly had correlation to Knollys' testimony about his call to ministry. Before having it impressed upon his mind by the Holy Spirit to visit John Wheelwright, Knollys related how through prayer, he had been involved in the healing of a widow who was on the verge of death. Following his call, he told of a similar incident – how God prepared his mind for preaching during the night while he slept.

---

baptizing, in *Matth. 28:18*. cannot properly, nor in the *word*, and *letter*, be understood of *baptizing* by water". Knollys, *Shining of the Flaming Fire*, p. 3.

[203] It is in these arguments that Haykin finds Erbury's thought. "Knollys... the Gifts of the Spirit", pp. 108-109. Saltmarsh had given as a distinctive practice of the Baptists that "whatsoever Disciple can teach the Word, or make out Christ, may Baptize or administer other Ordinances". Saltmarsh, *Smoke In the Temple*, p. 16.

[204] Saltmarsh, *Smoke In the Temple*, pp. 17-18.

[205] Knollys, *Shining of the Flaming Fire*, p. 9.

[206] Knollys, *Shining of the Flaming Fire*, pp. 9-11. See Saltmarsh, *Smoke In the Temple*, pp. 20-21.

[207] Saltmarsh, *Smoke In the Temple*, p. 18.

[208] Knollys, *Shining of the Flaming Fire*, p. 15.

Most importantly, when asked by the government Committee who gave him authority to preach, the answer was simply "the Lord Jesus Christ".[209]

Hanserd Knollys' interaction with John Saltmarsh had a much more positive effect than did that with John Bastwick. He had desired that Saltmarsh receive "more light of Truth" and the cause of toleration and of liberty of conscience would certainly benefit from their discussion. The following year, six months before his death, John Saltmarsh published *Sparkles of Glory*, which expanded on his thoughts about baptism and the Baptists, as well as on his proposals for toleration and unity. For Saltmarsh, the True Church was a unified Church, a spiritual body, the Temple of God. All gathered churches represented "types" of this True Church.[210] In light of this, Saltmarsh claimed, the Church should not be

> divided by any outward things which are of this Creation.... Therefore, whatsoever *fellowship* in pretence of *Church-notion*, or *Baptism-notion*, or *Presbyterial-notion*, shal cast itself into any model of the *letter*, which allows not *communion* with other beleevers in *Spirit*, in whom the power of the *Spirit*, and of *Christ* cannot be denied, but to be visible and apparent, though not in the practice of some particular *ordinance*, such *fellowship* wil in the *day* of the *Lord* see how they have offended many little ones.[211]

While Knollys desired religious tolerance in which diverse churches could freely worship side by side, Saltmarsh sought an even more inclusive tolerance, a unity that put aside ecclesiastical differences so that diverse churches could freely worship together as one. Essentially, it was their opposing views of the Truth that separated these men. For Saltmarsh, toleration had become necessary because no single group monopolised the Truth. For Knollys, however, toleration made possible the seeking after Truth. He understood Truth as unified, and believed that the Particular Baptists came closest to the Truth revealed in the Scriptures. Toleration, or probably better still, Christian liberty allowed "tender consciences" to have the freedom to seek and find that Truth.[212] At the end of this, his final book, Saltmarsh wrote a letter to Knollys,

---

[209] Knollys, *Life*, pp. 5-7, 10, 14-16, 20-21.

[210] John Saltmarsh, *Sparkles of Glory, or Some Beams of the Morning-Star*, (London: 1647), pp. 15-17.

[211] Saltmarsh, *Sparkles of Glory*, pp. 19-20.

[212] A statement made in the conclusion to the "1646 Confession" clearly elaborated the Baptist position on toleration and emphasised the importance of the freedom of conscience in the quest for Truth: "we desire... to owe nothing to any man but love, to live quietly and peaceably, as it becometh saints, endeavouring in all things to keep a good conscience, and to do unto every man (of what judgment soever) as we would they should do unto us; that as our practice is, so it may prove us to be a conscionable, quiet, and harmless people." *1646 Confession* in Underhill, *Confessions of Faith*, p. 47.

stating that he was not convinced "to believe the Ordinance of Baptism by water", but rather believed that baptism in the New Testament was a "spiritual immersion". He claimed that he did not oppose water baptism, but he objected to a compulsory one.[213] He then closed with words of high praise for Knollys:

> Dear Sir, I *love* and *tender* those *true appearances* of God that are in *you*, and rejoyce with you in beholding that *glory* by which we are all changed *from glory to glory*, etc. and am Your Friend and Brother in the Lord, John Saltmarsh.[214]

Conclusion

In the Gospel of John 18:37-38, one can read the account of Jesus Christ before the Roman Prefect, Pontius Pilate. In this passage, Jesus, wrongly accused and about to be unjustly persecuted said, "for this reason I was born, and for this I came into the world, to testify to the truth. Everyone on the side of truth listens to me." Pilate responded: "What is truth?" In the turbulent, ever-changing 1640s, such a question became very pressing. In the religious context of the time, the struggle for Truth was, in some sense, foundational. As the debate raged over the structure of the future church of England, the issue of Truth surfaced time and time again. At the heart of the debate over whether church membership should be compulsory (Presbyterians) or voluntary (Independents) stood the question of the Truth revealed in the Scriptures. John Bastwick's arguments, in essence, summed up the more conservative approach – that Truth was unified. From his perspective, only the Presbyterian model of church government embodied this unified Truth. For this reason, he viewed all other groups, including the Independents, as schismatics, who sought to subvert the Truth. John Saltmarsh, on the other hand, believed that Truth, which was not confined to any particular sect but that all Christians shared a portion of the Truth and all Christians should worship together and share their various gifts.

The many groups, which sprang up during the period, each with its own agenda for the church, provided a variety of perspectives on the question of Truth. Each group appealed to Truth as revealed in Scripture for its justification. The Baptists were no different. By 1646, when the dialogue between John Saltmarsh and Hanserd Knollys took place, the desire on the part of the Independents for accommodation for gathered congregations had passed. By this point, the Independents had issued a call for toleration, not just for themselves, but for other groups as well. The Baptists of the 1640s, like Saltmarsh, desired religious toleration, an atmosphere where they could worship without harassment and persecution. However, the basis for their belief in liberty of conscience was different from that of John Saltmarsh. Hanserd

---

[213] Saltmarsh, *Sparkles of Glory*, pp. 327-33.
[214] Saltmarsh, *Sparkles of Glory*, pp. 333-34.

Knollys and the Particular Baptists saw Truth as unified, but believed the Presbyterian system did not embody it. For this reason, Knollys defended the Independents in *A Moderate Answer*; like the Baptists, they shared the principle of voluntary, not compulsory church membership.

The kind of program set forth by John Saltmarsh proposed a way of peace, where dialogue and brotherhood could overcome differences of beliefs became the goal for many Independents.[215] For Saltmarsh, God's love provided the basis for that unity, for "the more love there is in any, the more of God there is in any".[216] In the preface of *Smoke In the Temple*, he wrote:

> We that are thus contenders for Ordinances, for the Temple and the Vessels in it, let us take heed we forget not him who is greater then the Temple... It would be spiritually considered, that while we strive for the Vessels and Cups, we spill not the Wine.

Saltmarsh's view of Truth stood at the centre of his program for tolerance. Since Truth was not unified, and since all groups had a portion of the Truth, tolerance for all was mandatory.

Although Knollys strongly held to his belief in baptism and in independent, congregational church government, he was also firmly convinced of the need for tender consciences to have the freedom to obey as they were taught by the Scriptures. As the Particular Baptists sought to gain respectability, and as Hanserd Knollys stood in the front ranks leading the way, expounding and defending their beliefs and gaining respectability in the eyes of their contemporaries became important. But just as important was the task of nurturing bonds with others who were brethren from different persuasions. Like John Saltmarsh, Hanserd Knollys understood the importance of God's love and unity for the Church and society. In that sermon for which he was "stoned out of the Pulpit", he preached:

> Let Christ be all in all in your affections, words and actions. Set your affections on Christ.... Love every one and every thing that God hath put the name of Christ upon, for his sake, but chiefly set your affectionate love upon himselfe, love Christ in his Saints, love Christ in his messengers, in his ordinances. &. this will quicken your desires to enjoy more of Christ in his Saints, Ministers, Ordinances, and in your owne hearts.[217]

However, Knollys also believed very strongly in the unity of Truth and that those "who seek shall find". To his way of thinking, the ritual of baptism became important because believer's baptism restored the practice of the

---

[215] Sirluck, *John Milton*, p. 116.
[216] Saltmarsh, *Smoke In the Temple*, p. 1.
[217] Knollys, *Christ Exalted*, 2nd ed., p. 11.

Apostolic and early Church. Knollys believed that those who called themselves Particular Baptists had been guided by their consciences and by Scripture to embrace the Truth, in this instance, about the ordinance of baptism. Because of this, he firmly, but gently, defended believer's baptism. However, he also wanted to assist Saltmarsh and others in their own quests for Truth. Knollys and the Baptists did not make arrogant, omniscient claims in these matters, despite their belief that they had found the Truth. The conclusion of the "1646 Confession" emphasised not only the unity of Truth and the Particular Baptists' confidence they had come closest to the Truth, but showed a willingness to accept further enlightenment:

> Also we confess that we know but in part, and that we are ignorant of many things which we desire and seek to know; and if any shall do us that friendly part to show us from the word of God that we see not, we shall have cause to be thankful to God and them. But if any man shall impose upon us anything that we see not to be commanded by our Lord Jesus Christ, we should in his strength rather embrace all reproaches and tortures of men, to be stripped of all outward comforts, and if it were possible, to die a thousand deaths, rather than to do anything against the least tittle of the truth of God, or against the light of our consciences.[218]

---

[218] "1646 Confession" in Underhill, *Confessions of Faith*, p. 48.

CHAPTER 4

Hanserd Knollys and the Struggle for Legitimacy: Levellers, Quakers, and the Fifth Monarchy Movement

Introduction

The sectaries being now hot upon the getting of a Toleration, there were some meetings lately in the City, wherein some persons of the several sects, some Seekers, some Anabaptists, some Antinomians, some Brownists, some Independents met... the intent of which meeting was, to consider how all these might have the liberty of their way and practice in this Kingdom.[1]

By the end of the 1640s the Presbyterians dominated the Church of England and were beginning to attack those of differing religious beliefs in an effort to force uniformity. A common tactic used by the Presbyterians against dissenters was to portray the various sects as being of the same association. The above-cited passage grouped the Baptists and Independents indiscriminately with the Seekers and Antinomians. Edwards went on to catalogue other groups on the following page, including Independents, Brownists, Chiliasts/Millenaries, Antinomians, Anabaptists, Arminians, Libertines, Familists, Enthusiasts, Seekers, Perfectists, Socinians, Arians, Antitrinitarians, Antiscripturists, and Sceptics. He proceeded to qualify this list by stating that in England, there existed hardly "any sect that's simple and pure, and not mixt and compounded, that is... which holds only the opinions and principles of its own way, without enterfering and mingling with the errours of other sects".[2]

By the late 1640s and into the 1650s, the proliferation of new religious groups, many far more radical than either the Baptists or the Independents, created a new dilemma for Hanserd Knollys and his fellow Baptists. They had

---

[1] Thomas Edwards, *Gangraena: Or a Catalogue and Discovery of many of the Errours, Heresies, Blasphemies and pernicious Practices of the Sectaries of this time...*, (London: 1646), Part I, p. 12, hereafter designated *Gangraena*.
[2] *Gangraena*, Part I, p. 13.

willingly associated with the Independents in the mid-1640s, having sprung from same theological tradition. As well, through this association had lain a path to legitimacy and toleration. Knollys in his pamphlets and the Baptists in general in their Confessions and debates attempted to show their fellow Englishmen that they were not really as utterly radical as alleged by their critics. Theologically, most of their Reformed beliefs mirrored those of even the Presbyterian Puritans. Apart from the ordinance of believer's baptism, their gathered churches were not drastically different than those of the Independents. In their public debates and published treatises, they had shown themselves not as ignorant, uneducated fools but as thinking intellectuals and theologians, schooled in the proper conventions of debate. However, the Baptists' path to legitimacy was twofold. They had to establish a positive association, by gaining the respect of the orthodox Christians; they also had to invalidate a negative association by distancing themselves from the more radical religious groups.[3]

With the establishment of a republic dominated by Puritans and a Church dominated by Presbyterians, the late 1640s and the 1650s brought new challenges to those within the Particular Baptist fold. Other, more politically charged groups were challenging the government, seeking after even more radical changes to society and government. One of these groups, the Levellers, desired a more widely-based representative approach to governance and religion. They clearly enveloped their demands in religious ideas.[4] They believed that Parliament and the Westminster Assembly had failed to bring about "a godly reformation" and fought for greater political and religious liberty.[5]

Another group, the Fifth Monarchists, also had political aims, again with very clear religious connections. Their extreme apocalyptic, millenarian interpretation of the Scripture and current events led them to desire a theocratic society with King Jesus at the head. They sought "an imminent kingdom of heaven on earth to be established with supernatural help".[6] Many of those who called themselves Levellers and Fifth Monarchists had, during the earlier years of the 1640s, been loyal and willing followers of Cromwell. Many Baptists filled their ranks and many other Baptists gave some support to these groups, sympathetic to some of their causes without embracing them wholeheartedly. In

---

[3] A similar position is taken by Mark R. Bell in *Apocalypse How? Baptist Movements During the English Revolution*, (Macon, GA: Mercer University Press, 2000), Part II.

[4] D.B. Robertson, *The Religious Foundations of Leveller Democracy*, (New York: King's Crown Press, 1951); see also Murray Tolmie, *The Triumph of the Saints*, (London: Cambridge University Press, 1977), ch. 7; Brian Manning, "The Levellers and Religion", in *Radical Religion in the English Revolution*, ed. B. Reay and J.F. McGregor, (New York: Oxford University Press, 1984).

[5] Barry Coward, *The Stuart Age*, 2nd ed., (New York: Longman, 1994), pp. 228-33.

[6] Bernard Capp, "The Fifth Monarchists and Popular Millenarianism", in *Radical Religion in the English Revolution*, ed. B. Reay and J.F. McGregor (New York: Oxford University Press, 1984), p. 165.

the late 1640s, the 1650s and the early 1660s, when these groups came into open conflict with the government, suddenly the Baptists were faced with yet another issue in their quest for legitimacy.

In the 1650s, with an increased openness in English society with respect to religion, a new sect appeared that was even more radical than the Baptists – the Quakers. In 1652, George Fox began bringing together scattered groups of separatists under his leadership. Beginning in northern England and making his way southward, Fox gathered many ordinary men and women into his movement. Many of these had moved through Puritanism, seeking even further distance from the past religious and social order. By the mid-1650s, the Quakers had begun to make an impact in the south of England.[7] The Quakers were an ecstatic religious movement, who believed in the practice of healing and performing miracles and who allowed women to prophesy freely. Like the Baptists, they tended to appeal to the lower social orders and they relied upon and encouraged lay preaching. However, they rejected predestination and embraced mystical ideas of union with God and illumination through an "inner light" that superseded even the Scriptures.[8] Many sectaries, including Baptists, converted to Quakerism, sometimes in large numbers.[9] The practice by the Quakers of adult baptism, along with the mass conversions of General Baptists to their ranks, caused many to consider them to be one and the same with the Baptists. This particularly alarmed the Particular Baptists who were in the midst of their struggle for legitimacy. In the 1660s and 1670s, full-scale persecution broke out against dissenters, especially the Quakers and Baptists. In this context, the Particular Baptists sought to distance themselves from the Quakers and to downplay the radical aspects of their own position.

The most immediate and pertinent question facing Knollys and the Baptists, of course, had to do with their relationship with these more radical groups. Were there areas of similarity and if so, did this necessarily indicate a connection? During the 1650s, many Baptists were openly sympathetic with the agenda and philosophy of the Levellers and Fifth Monarchists. But how far did that sympathy lead them? What about more mystical approaches to Christianity, which seemed quite foreign to the more systematic and rationalistic approach of Calvinistic Puritanism? How open was Hanserd Knollys to these groups and their ideas? What limits, if any should be placed on toleration? Should groups such as the Quakers, whose doctrine strayed beyond the limits of Puritan doctrine, be accorded toleration? Or what about those groups whose antagonistic behaviour threatened the stability and order of society?

---

[7] Barry Reay, "Quakerism and Society", in *Radical Religion in the English Revolution*, ed. B. Reay and J.F. McGregor (New York: Oxford University Press, 1984), p. 141.

[8] Reay, "Quakerism and Society", pp. 145-49.

[9] Reay, "Quakerism and Society", p. 143. Barry Reay, *The Quakers and the English Revolution*, (London: Temple Smith, 1985), pp. 10, 11, 13, 17.

This chapter will attempt to examine some the relationships of the Baptists with the Levellers, Quakers, and Fifth Monarchists. More specifically, it will centre upon the relationship of Knollys to these more radical sects. While these groups held beliefs which Knollys and many other Baptists found palatable, pragmatic considerations made it far too dangerous and costly for the Particular Baptists to nurture a continuing relationship with the radicals. It subverted their ongoing struggle to gain legitimacy in seventeenth-century England.[10]

The Levellers

By the late 1640s and into the 1650s, the atmosphere of freedom of expression had enabled the Particular Baptists to become more vocal in the public arena, through petitions and in other ways. A small number became M.P.s. The Long Parliament and the Rump Parliament each contained at least one Baptist M.P. With the calling of the Barebones Parliament, the number of Baptists increased to six (out of 144), with four more M.P.s being possible Baptists. Throughout the 1650s, then, each parliament had Baptist M.P.s, the majority of whom were members of the gentry.[11] For others, wider political involvement meant participation in more politically radical religious groups, such as the Levellers.

In the late 1640s, those Levellers who had actively served in the Parliamentary Armies became more and more disillusioned with the victory over the Royalists. Many felt betrayed, sensing that the senior officers of the Army had abandoned the cause for which the troops had fought. Toleration, the standard of the Independents and of Cromwell, in the opinion of the Levellers, was becoming more constricted.[12] The conservative threat orchestrated in London in 1647 by the Presbyterian party in Parliament gave further concern.[13] This animosity by the Presbyterians was not new for the Levellers. In the early 1640s, Leveller leaders such as William Walwyn, Richard Overton, and John

---

[10] This is not to make a case that Baptist opposition or distancing from the Levellers, Quakers, and Fifth Monarchists was entirely based on expediency. There were beliefs and issues, which the Baptists and Knollys rejected outright due to theological disagreement. Yet, in some instances, Knollys and many other Particular Baptists kept to the fringe of these groups, maintaining contacts in some instances, until the eleventh hour, particularly with respect to the Levellers and Fifth Monarchists.

[11] D.W. Bebbington, "Baptist M.P.s in the Seventeenth and Eighteenth Centuries", *The Baptist Quarterly*, XXVIII, (April 1980) : 247-49, 252. See also Austin Woolrych, *Commonwealth to Protectorate*, (Oxford: Clarendon Press, 1982), pp. 194-233, 403-33. These included both General and Particular Baptists, as well as Baptists who embraced Fifth Monarchist beliefs. Knollys' good friend William Kiffin served as an M.P. in one parliament (1656). Barrie R. White, "William Kiffin – Baptist Pioneer and Citizen of London", *Baptist History and Heritage* II, (July 1967) : 98.

[12] Manning, "Levellers and Religion", p. 65.

[13] Murray Tolmie, *Triumph of the Saints*, (Cambridge: Cambridge University Press, 1977), p. 144.

Lilburne had, like the Baptists, taken advantage of the unsupervised press to publish their defence of religious toleration and to attack the conservative powers. As a result, in 1646, John Lilburne ended up in prison again.[14]

John Lilburne was no stranger to prison, nor to radical religion. In the early 1630s, Lilburne had been a young apprentice of Thomas Hewson, a clothier in London and a friend of the Winthrop family. Henry Jessey, and Edmund Rosier, another clothier, had likely been Lilburne's links to separatist churches and radical Puritanism. In 1636, Lilburne had accompanied Rosier to Gatehouse prison to visit Dr. Bastwick; within a year Lilburne was arrested for publishing and importing one of Bastwick's treatises attacking the bishops. While in prison, Lilburne officially separated from the Church of England and began writing and publishing pamphlets advocating separation. Upon his release from prison in 1641, Lilburne joined a separatist church.[15] During this time, Lilburne established a friendship with William Kiffin, also a separatist, who helped Lilburne in publishing his pamphlets in 1641.[16] He had "received the support of the Baptists led by his old friend William Kiffin."[17] In fact, William Kiffin, a fellow apprentice of Lilburne in earlier days, had written the epistle to the reader in Lilburne's *The Christian Mans Triall* and in it portrayed Lilburne as a advocate for their cause.[18] In the mid-1640s, as the Particular Baptists were in formation, they found in the Levellers ready allies, and vice versa. Although sceptical of dogmatism, Walwyn defended the Baptists in his writings in 1644. This sympathy for separatists eventually led him into a relationship with Lilburne. By 1646, Lilburne himself had gained the support of the sectarians of London due to the failure of attempts at accommodation and the perception that the Independents had not upheld the common cause.[19]

Such was the situation on 10 August 1646 when the Hanserd Knollys at his church in Great St. Helens prayed publicly, "Lord, bring thy servant Lilburn out

---

[14] Tolmie, *Triumph*, p. 144. According to Tolmie, there is no doubt that the Levellers "had a deep sectarian taproot that shaped their aspirations and their polemic in a distinct way". Manning would concur to some degree, believing that they "sprang from the radical religious groups of the period". However, for Manning, the questions of which religious groups and if and when they abandoned their religious convictions are not as easily defined. Manning, "Levellers and Religion", p. 65.

[15] The church he joined was likely that of Edmund Rosier. Tolmie, *Triumph*, pp. 66, 147.

[16] Tolmie, *Triumph*, pp. 36-37. Apprenticed about a year apart, Lilburne to a clothier and Kiffin to a glover, they probably travelled in the same circles and hence became friends. White, "William Kiffin", p. 94.

[17] William Haller, ed., *The Leveller Tracts 1647-1653*, (New York: Columbia University Press, 1944), p. 6.

[18] William Kiffin, "To the Reader," in *The Christian Mans Triall*, (London: 1641), no page number.

[19] Tolmie, *Triumph*, pp. 145-47.

of prison, and honour him Lord, for he hath honoured thee."[20] These words, judged to be contemptible by the high Presbyterian, Thomas Edwards, certainly exhibited strong support. This portrayal of Lilburne as God's "servant" who deserved freedom for the honour he had brought God certainly evidenced a close bond between the Baptists and the Levellers, indeed, between Knollys and the Levellers. The Levellers, from this point onward became more intent on secular politics and on attacking social privileges. In hindsight, Lilburne's popularity among the London sects peaked in 1646. By 1647, the main supporters of the Leveller agenda in London were the General Baptists, with the Independents and Particular Baptists beginning to stand somewhat aloof. However, the conservative surge of 1647 would forge a continuing, if uneasy alliance between the Levellers and the Independents for a brief time.[21] Mark Bell argued that "common goals, mutual enemies, and shared experiences in the army" had brought the Particular Baptists and Levellers together in the early and mid 1640s, but that theirs was always an "unstable" alliance.[22]

From 1647 to 1649, many Particular Baptists and separatists had become involved significantly in the New Model Army. This went back to the earlier years of the Civil War, but the resignation of many Presbyterian officers from the New Model following the Army's refusal to disband in 1647 allowed for radicals to advance more quickly.[23] On 7 August 1647, the Army marched on London and the loose coalition between the Levellers and London radicals began to unravel. The failure or refusal of the commanders of the Army to free Lilburne and other imprisoned Levellers caused the Levellers to begin to turn against Cromwell. The further attempt of the City Independents to secure control of London following the march alienated them from the Levellers and further separated the Levellers from the Army grandees. Finally, the persistent attempts of Fairfax and Cromwell, and of some of the sectarian leaders as well, to bring about a settlement with the King produced further whittling away of Leveller support.[24]

The publication of *The Case of the Army Truly Stated* showed a resurgence of Leveller influence in the lower ranks of the Army. This was further revised and abridged in the more concise *Agreement of the People* of 27 October 1647, a Leveller document that emphasised the freedom of the individual, both in religion and politics:

---

[20] *Gangraena*, Part I, p. 35.
[21] Tolmie, *Triumph*, pp. 151-55.
[22] Bell, *Apocalypse How?*, p. 99. According to Bell, the Levellers "offered the Baptists the best possibility of realizing their goal of religious liberty." P. 103.
[23] Tolmie, *Triumph*, pp. 156-59. Tolmie pointed out that the Particular Baptists "played a leading role in the spontaneous organization that sprang up to give expression to the grievances of officers and men".
[24] Tolmie, *Triumph*, pp. 162-65.

> Having by our late labours and hazards made it appear to the world at how high a rate we value our just freedom, and God having so far owned our case as to deliver the enemies thereof into our hands, we do now hold ourselves bound in mutual duty to each other to take the best care we can for the future to avoid... the danger of returning into a slavish condition... In order whereunto we declare... that the power of this an all future representatives of this nation is inferior only to theirs who choose them... that matters of religion and the ways of God's worship are not at all entrusted by us to any human power, because therein we cannot remit or exceed a tittle of what our consciences dictate to be the mind of God without wilful sin.[25]

This document claimed that with the Civil War, the old state had reached its demise and a new constitution was needed. In the debates that followed at Putney to discuss the form that the constitution of England ought to take, the stalemate continued between the grandees and the Levellers.[26] The flight of the King, however, on 11 November allowed Cromwell and the grandees to break off discussions. Mutinous attempts by the Levellers followed at Ware on 15 November but were immobilized by the Army commanders and discipline was restored with little bloodshed or conflict.[27] Although there would continue to be isolated outbreaks of Leveller activity in the Army, these were controlled with the full support of the sectarian officers. In fact, as Tolmie pointed out, in several cases it was Particular Baptist captains who put down Leveller agitation. He argued that one of the primary reasons for the collapse of the Leveller organization in the Army was the advance of sectarians, especially of Particular Baptists, in the officer corps in the initial stages of the formation of the New Model. This advance was furthered in 1647 when the Presbyterian officers withdrew and yet again, finally, at the outbreak of the second Civil War. These men gradually gravitated more toward the positions taken by their senior officers and abandoned the Levellers who claimed to trumpet the cause of the soldiers.[28]

Leveller support crumbled not only in the Army, however. On 9 November, the House of Commons rejected the *Agreement* and the Levellers responded on 23 November with a petition in defence of their constitutional scheme. The day before the petition was presented, however, an anonymous pamphlet appeared

---

[25] Cited in J.P. Kenyon, *The Stuart Constitution*, 2nd ed., (Cambridge: Cambridge University Press, 1986), pp.274-5.

[26] Ian Gentles, *The New Model Army in England, Ireland, and Scotland, 1645-1653*, (Cambridge, MA: Blackwell, 1992), pp. 202-19. For a detailed treatment of this see Austin Woolrych, *Soldiers and Statesmen: The General Council of the Army and its Debates, 1647-1648*, (Oxford: Clarendon Press, 1987), especially chapters VIII-X. Manning, "Levellers and Religion", p. 86.

[27] Howard Shaw, *The Levellers*, (London: Longmans, 1968), p. 65.

[28] Tolmie, *Triumph*, pp. 167-69; Anne Laurence, *Parliamentary Army Chaplains, 1642-1651*, (Suffolk: Boydell Press, 1990), p. 81.

in the bookstalls of London entitled *A Declaration by Congregational societies in and about the City of London, as well of those commonly called Anabaptists, as others*. This pamphlet condemned the levelling of society, implying that anarchy would result.[29] This document contained very strong statements on the separation of Church and State, the proper sphere of the State's authority, and the importance of individual liberty:

> The truth is, wee have been, and resolve to bee as faithfull assertors, and zealous maintainers, to our power, both of Magistracy, and government, and of the Liberty of mens persons, and propriety of their estates, (to speake without vanity) as any other men whosoever.[30]

The authors clearly feared the accusation that they "were advocates of all licentious liberty, disorder and confusion".[31] Following this, several pages stressed the importance of benevolence, but never to the abolition of private property: "If therefore God hath built up a wall of separation between the estates of men and men, the affirmative whereof sufficiently appears by many acts of his will, then farre be it from us who professe our selves to be his servants, that we should indevour to throw it downe."[32] In fact, in addressing the passages in Acts 2 and 4, the pamphlet interpreted the church of Jerusalem's having "all things common" as a voluntary activity of benevolence.[33]

This was a significant blow to the Leveller cause. Although anonymous, the group that wrote it published another declaration in 1651, claiming that they had authored the declaration of 1647.[34] Sixteen influential Particular Baptist and separatist leaders had signed this second declaration, including William Kiffin, Hanserd Knollys, and Richard Wollaston, a member of Knollys' church who had earlier, at a meeting at Cromwell's house, accused Walwyn of being an anti-scripturist.[35] As a result of the *Declaration by Congregational societies*

---

[29] Although the Levellers did not, in fact, support social levelling, the fears of such a position are evident in this work.

[30] *A Declaration by Congregational Societies in, and about the City of London; as well as those commonly called Anabaptists, as others. In a way of Vindication of themselves*, (London: 1647), pp. 5-7.

[31] *A Declaration by Congregational Societies*, p. 4.

[32] *A Declaration by Congregational Societies*, p. 10.

[33] *A Declaration by Congregational Societies*, pp. 7-10.

[34] *A Declaration Of divers Elders and Brethren of Congregational Societies, in and about the City of LONDON. Decrying and Disclaiming two Bookes; the one called A CRY; and the other Book called A MODEL OF A NEW REPRESENTATIVE*, (London: 1651).

[35] *A Declaration Of divers Elders and Brethren of Congregational Societies*, p. 8; Tolmie, *Triumph*, pp. 150, 171.

in and about the City of London, Lilburne and other Leveller leaders were imprisoned.

As the second Civil War unfolded, Lilburne and the Levellers saw it as a chance to gain ground. On 1 August 1648, a petition successfully called for Lilburne's release. Immediately, he began to attempt to negotiate a new constitution with Cromwell, who was by now duly exasperated with Charles I. At this point, the Levellers presented a more moderate constitutional proposal than the first *Agreement of the People*. Aware that Parliament and the Presbyterians wished to negotiate a more conservative settlement with the king, the commanding officers of the Army threw their lot in with the Levellers for the time. Resentment over having to fight a second civil war after God had already rendered judgment turned many army officers against King Charles. At the Putney debates, Ireton had stated: "If God will destroy King or Lords he can do it without our or your wrong-doing."[36] Following the king's second declaration of war, Ireton presented to the Council of the Army a *Remonstrance* that demanded that the king be punished for his actions and subordinated the interests of the King to those of the people.[37] At this point, Cromwell vacillated over the state of the constitution. The alliance with the Levellers bought the senior officers time and strength, allowing a purge of Parliament and the trial and execution of the king. When a new *Agreement of the People* was drafted, however, it stalled again in debate in the Council of Officers, this time over the issue of religious toleration. Once again, the Levellers had failed to persuade the Army to champion their cause.[38] At this point, the Baptists also renewed their "uneasy" alliance with the Levellers. According to Bell, "Eschatology lay at the heart of the Baptist-Leveller alliance against the Presbyterians."[39]

Following the execution of Charles I, Lilburne became an even more vocal critic of the Army.[40] In the winter of 1649, discontent and Leveller agitation again began to spread through the Army.[41] In that same year, Hanserd Knollys had once again taken up the cause of the Army by serving as chaplain in the regiment of Colonel Whalley, who later became known for holding radical religious views.[42] In April, new Leveller agitation broke out in the ranks of Whalley's regiment. Part of the regiment, at the time at Bishopsgate in London,

---

[36] A.S.P. Woodhouse, ed., *Puritanism and Liberty*, selections from the Putney Debates, (Chicago: University of Chicago Press, 1951), p. 123.

[37] Woodhouse, ed., *Puritanism and Liberty*, selections from *A Remonstrance of the Army*, pp. 456-65.

[38] Gentles, *New Model Army*, pp. 272-94. Gentles claimed that "nothing else in the Agreement provoked as much debate as religion". (p. 290).

[39] Bell, *Apocalypse How?*, p. 110.

[40] At this point, ironically, Lilburne, who had earlier demanded the execution of the king, now, fearing a military dictatorship, contended against it and disputed the legality of the proceedings, as did the Royalists. Shaw, *Levellers*, p. 72.

[41] Shaw, *Levellers*, pp. 69-79.

[42] Laurence, *Chaplains*, pp. 58, 143.

mutinied. The demands of the soldiers were not constitutional but economic: the troops merely wanted their back pay. In due course, they surrendered and six were sentenced to death. Eventually, only Robert Lockyer was executed.[43] Knollys and the rest of the regiment were in Essex at the time and quickly published a declaration, which Knollys signed, clearly stating that they did not support Leveller principles.[44]

In the years between 1645 and 1647 through 1649, the allegiance of Hanserd Knollys and the Particular Baptists with respect to John Lilburne and his followers took a significant shift of direction. Why was it that Knollys went from praying publicly for Lilburne, God's servant, to publicly disclaiming and denouncing the Levellers? Tolmie argued that "the saints" who had travelled in the company of the Levellers for a time, had eventually changed their loyalty to the commanders of the Army.

> Up to the climax of the revolution, the religious radicals of the separate churches had remained clients of larger political forces and members of larger political coalitions.... In December 1648 the religious radicals had become a force in their own right as saints; they cooperated with the saints in the Army to seize the initiative in the revolution, and the execution of the King became the symbol of their triumph as saints.[45]

While this could be true of some of the more radical separatists, was it indeed the case for the Particular Baptists?

In a petition signed by Knollys and others, written in response to Lilburne's *New Chains discovered* and presented by William Kiffin to Parliament on 2 April 1649, the Baptists sought to distance themselves from the revolutionary activities that had taken place during the previous months. They once again denounced the old, recurring accusations of their opponents who compared them to "some unruly men formerly in Germany, called anabaptists".[46] The Particular Baptists wished to be perceived by the government as good citizens, not "the fountain and source of all disobedience, presumption, self-will, contempt of rulers, dignities and civil government whatsoever".[47] In an attempt to distance themselves from the Levellers and Lilburne, the petitioners claimed they

---

[43] Gentles, *New Model Army*, pp. 326-29; G.E. Aylmer, ed., *The Levellers in the English Revolution*, (London: Thames and Hudson, 1975), pp. 43-44; Shaw, *Levellers*, p. 85; Laurence, *Chaplains*, p. 143.

[44] *The Declaration and Unanimous resolution of Colonel Whalley*, (London: 1649).

[45] Tolmie, *Triumph*, p. 189.

[46] *The humble Petition and Representation of Several Churches of God in London, commonly (though falsly) called Anabaptists*, (London, 1649) in E.B. Underhill, ed., *Confessions of Faith*, (London: Hanserd Knollys Society, 1854), p. 289.

[47] *The humble Petition and Representation of Several Churches of God in London,* p. 289.

neither had nor have heart, nor hand, in the framing, contriving, abetting, or promoting of the said paper [*New Chains discovered*], which, though read in several of our public meetings, we do solemnly profess it was without our consent or approbation, being there openly opposed by us.[48]

They went on to assure Parliament: "our meetings are not at all to intermeddle with the ordering or altering civil government (which we humbly and submissively leave to the supreme power), but solely for the advancement of the gospel."[49] Upon the reading of the petition in Parliament by Kiffin, the Speaker responded:

The House doth take notice of the good affection to the parliament and public, you have expressed both in this petition and other ways; that they have received satisfaction thereby, concerning your disclaiming of that pamphlet, which gave such just offence to the parliament, and also concerning your disposition to live peaceably, and in submission to the civil magistracy; your expressions whereof they account very Christian and seasonable; that for yourselves and other Christians walking answerable to such professions as in this petition you make, they do assure you of liberty and protection, so far as God shall enable them, in all things consistent with godliness, honesty, and civil peace; and the House doth give you leave to print your petition.[50]

In these closing years of the 1640s, the Particular Baptists, desiring to hold on to the legitimacy they had worked so hard to obtain in the eyes of many of their contemporaries, clearly distanced themselves from the Levellers, who had become too radical for even the Baptists. Perhaps it was not an issue of the Baptists taking a shift of direction. Rather, it was Lilburne and his followers who had shifted. The Baptists could agree with Lilburne's view of religious toleration, but his political ideals, although they coincided nicely with Baptist congregationalism, did not find willing ears among the Particular Baptists of London.[51]

---

[48] *The humble Petition and Representation of Several Churches of God in London*, p. 289.

[49] *The humble Petition and Representation of Several Churches of God in London*, pp. 289-90.

[50] *The humble Petition and Representation of Several Churches of God in London*, pp. 291-92.

[51] Mark Bell argued that eschatology lay at the center of the schism. He claimed that the eschatology of the Baptists had shifted from "criticizing the establishment to endorsing it" whereas by this point the Levellers had shifted in the opposite direction. In 1641, Kiffin saw the Antichrist evident in those who used "authority to enforce obedience" but by 1649, he was evident through those who "tried to stir up contention." As well, by this point, the Particular Baptist leaders had become confident that they could "pursue their goals without the Levellers." Bell, *Apocalypse How?*, pp. 110-113, 117.

Knollys' Activities during the Commonwealth Period

On 6 January 1649, the House of Commons passed an ordinance for the trial of Charles Stuart in Whitehall. During his appearance before the special court erected for this purpose, Charles insisted that the assembled notables had no constitutional jurisdiction to try him and did not constitute a legitimate court. However, radical elements in the Army had purged the House of Commons and moved far beyond the moderate, constitutional aims of the majority of Parliamentarians during the 1640s. In less than a month, on 30 January, King Charles I was executed by beheading and in the following week, the House of Commons abolished the House of Lords and the Monarchy and established a republican Commonwealth.[52]

In the midst of these incredible events, on 17 January 1649, Parliament passed an order "for Mr. Kiffin and Mr. Knolles, upon the petition of Ipswich men, to go thither to preach".[53] This so pleased the citizens of Ipswich that they wrote Oliver Cromwell a letter of gratitude:

> We cannot sufficiently express our thankfulness to the honourable house, and your honour for that great favour wch out of yr sense of our present condition you were pleased to shew unto us, that there is liberty granted to Mr. Knollys and Mr. Kiffin according to our desire to come among us, whose labours (through God's blessing) are like to bee not only very comfortable to us in particular but very profitable to the state in generall.[54]

When the execution of the king took place, Knollys and Kiffin may well have been out of the city preaching in Suffolk. In spite of this rather interesting notation from the early days of the Republic, the details regarding Knollys' life

---

[52] Bulstrode Whitelocke, *Memorials of the English Affairs from the Beginning of the Reign of Charles the First to the Happy Restoration of King Charles the Second*, vol. 1, (Oxford: At the University Press, 1853), pp. 490-516, 521-23. This edition is a reprint of the edition published in 1732. Ruth Spalding in her edition of Whitelocke's Diary emphasised his "distress" at the execution of the king, "partly from legal misgivings about the trial and scruples concerning the attack on the Lord's Anointed". *The Diary of Bulstrode Whitelocke 1605-1675*, in *Records of Social and Economic History*, New Series XIII, (New York: Oxford University Press, 1990), p. 229. Coward, *Stuart Age*, pp. 234-39. Coward's point that this 'revolution' was the result of acts "carried out by a minority drawn largely from outside the traditional ruling elite in England and against the wishes of that elite" is widely accepted among historians. See also C.V. Wedgwood, *The Trial of Charles I*, (London: The Reprint Society Ltd., 1966). For detailed study of the radicalisation of Parliament, see David Underdown, *Pride's Purge: Politics in the Puritan Revolution*, (Oxford: Clarendon Press, 1971).

[53] Whitelocke, *Memorials*, p. 497. This would have been at least Knollys' second preaching tour to Suffolk. It was in Ipswich in January 1645 that Knollys was imprisoned and near Debenham where he was stoned a month later.

[54] Lambeth Palace Library, Tenison MS679, folio 105.

remain quite sketchy for the remainder of the Commonwealth. His own autobiography summarised the time between 1647 and 1660 in a brief page.[55] However, glimpses of his life appear from time to time in the various public and church records of the day.

In Knollys' own memoirs, he chose to dwell quite simply on his ministry and his teaching during this period, referring to them in rather general terms and noting that his "chiefest means of Livelihood" during this period was teaching school.[56] Teaching and education continued to be an activity near to Knollys' heart throughout his life. This not only benefited him in terms of the payments he received for his services, but in at least one instance, he received a legacy because of his teaching duties. Thomas Taylor of Wapping, Middlesex, a shipwright, included "Master Hanserd Knowles my son Caleb's schoolmaster" in his will, proved 10 January 1658.[57] Although Knollys did not expound on his teaching activity in any significant detail, he did state that it was sufficient

> to make me serviceable in my Generation to communicate liberally to the Poor of the Church, and to Strangers that stood in need, and plentifully to provide all things necessary and convenient for my Wife and Children, through God's Blessing upon my honest Labours.[58]

Indeed, Knollys developed a variety of ways to supplement his income during these years and apparently lived quite comfortably.

Knollys' comments about his involvement in ministry during this period were also very vague, emphasising primarily the relationship he had with his flock and his diligence in performing his duties as their pastor. The relationship shared between Knollys and his congregation was one of mutual service. Knollys recorded that he received financial payment from the church "according to their Ability, most of the Members of the Church being poor but I coveted no mans Gold nor Silver, but chose rather to labour, knowing it is more

---

[55] Hanserd Knollys, *The Life and Death of That Old Disciple of Jesus Christ, and Eminent Minister of the Gospel, Mr. Hanserd Knollys*, edited by William Kiffin, (London: 1692), p. 23, hereafter cited as *Life*, pp. 23-24. In total, Knollys only devoted approximately 34 lines to this period of his life.

[56] Knollys, *Life*, p. 23. Not only did he carry out this task in the context of his schools which he established at various times and places, but he also was employed as a private tutor. As will be seen below, he served as tutor to the son of Francis, Lord Willoughby, Baron of Parham.

[57] "Genealogical Gleanings in England", in *The New England Historical and Genealogical Register*, vol. 49 (Boston: 1895), p. 126. Knollys' passion for education mirrored the fascination of many Puritans of the time with education. This will be discussed in more detail below in Chapter 7.

[58] Knollys, *Life*, p. 23.

blessed to give than to receive".[59] As their pastor, he served conscientiously, preaching two or three times a week, visiting in the homes of members, especially when they were sick.[60]

The church that he gathered in 1645 was to remain his 'flock' throughout his life. However, this did not mean that he was always present or that his ministry focused exclusively on that congregation. He indicated that he was "absent from the Church sometimes upon just Occasions and with their leave, or forced from them by violent Persecution".[61] While the latter instances occurred during the Restoration period, at least some of the absences with leave took place during the 1650s as the Calvinistic Baptists embarked upon a missionary agenda.[62] This expansionism included not only helping to establish Particular Baptist Churches in the counties beyond London, but it also involved establishing a network or web of relationships between the various churches, both those which were new and those already in existence. Certainly Knollys' earlier preaching tours to Suffolk and around London were early expressions of such endeavours. Barrington White postulated that this sort of activity became a standard pattern among the London churches from 1644 on.

> Each congregation had power and, whenever possible, the duty to set aside at least one of its members for missionary labours. Such a person, with a sense of internal calling to the work and his gifts for preaching tested by the congregation of which he was a member, was given authority to go out to convert those who had no Christian faith (or those who had a faulty one), to baptize his converts, link them into congregational fellowship and bring them under congregational discipline, and then, as happened in a number of cases, to link the individual congregations into associations.[63]

He went on to say that by the end of the 1640s, the association idea had become very closely linked to the Baptist polity, spreading throughout England, Wales, and even Ireland.[64] In some instances, this meant that the London pastors

---

[59] Knollys, *Life*, p. 24.
[60] Knollys, *Life*, p. 24.
[61] Knollys, *Life*, p. 24.
[62] Whether this arose out of a desire to establish Calvinistic Particular Baptist churches throughout England or out of a conversionist philosophy is unclear, though in Knollys' sermons and treatises, a clear conversionist theology is evident.
[63] B.R. White, "The English Particular Baptists and the Great Rebellion, 1640 – 1660", in *Baptist History and Heritage*, 9 (1) (Jan. 1974) : 20-21.
[64] White, "Baptists and the Great Rebellion", p. 22. This will be dealt with further below in Chapter 7.

visited and ministered to churches other than their home congregations in London.[65]

There are several instances of Knollys' involvement in ministry outside of his gathered congregation in London during the late 1640s and 1650s. The preaching tour of Knollys and Kiffin has already been mentioned above. B.R. White made mention of a similar type of mission to Wales in early 1650. When the act for better propagation and preaching of the Gospel in Wales was put in force in February 1650, Baptist John Miles was appointed as one of those who would approve preachers.[66] Around that time, Knollys also went to Wales to minister, perhaps even moving there with his entire family for a period. As to the effectiveness of his ministry there, no records have survived to give any indication.[67] Other evidence survives to trace his relation to the newly founded Baptist congregation in Watford. According to the churchbook, at some point prior to 1659, before it had entered into "a church state", this congregation had been a "branch of a church in London meeting at a place called Coal harbour, Mr. John Spilsbury being pastor".[68] At that early stage in its history, the church in Watford entered into covenant with the Baptist churches in London, agreeing first to "wholly disown the Church of England and the ministry of it" and secondly to embrace certain doctrinal tenets held by the London Baptists. Due to this association with the London churches, the London Baptist ministers agreed to assist the Watford church once a month, with respect to its needs in ministry, by preaching and the breaking of bread. One of the ministers from London who assisted in this way was Hanserd Knollys.[69]

Sometimes these ministry ventures did not go as planned for the London Baptists. In this period of excessive religious flexibility, sometimes members who had great zeal for the Baptist cause did not have a matching commitment. Having been sent out by a church in London to a new area, they might embrace a different doctrine. Such a situation occurred for Knollys' church in 1652. In this instance, a lectureship had been established by the London Mercers' Company to preach in Hexham, Northumberland and a young man by the name

---

[65] As mentioned in Chapter 3, Knollys and many of the Particular Baptist ministers had assistant ministers who likely would have carried on the duties of ministry when they were away.

[66] B.R. White, *Hanserd Knollys and Radical Dissent in the 17th Century*, (London: Dr. Williams's Trust, 1977.), pp. 14-15. This John Miles went on to found the first Baptist church in New England, in Swansea, Massachusetts in 1663. Thomas Armitage, *The History of the Baptists*, vol. II, (1886; reprint ed. Watertown, WI: Maranatha Baptist Press, 1980), pp. 678-81.

[67] White cited Bodleian, Walker MS e.13, pp. 116, 121 as his source for information concerning Knollys' activities in Wales. After searching, however, this author has not been able to locate this source. White, *Hanserd Knollys*, p. 15; Knollys, *Life*, p. 28.

[68] B.R. White, "Baptist Beginnings in Watford", *The Baptist Quarterly*, vol. XXVI (Jan. 1976) : 205-207.

[69] White, "Baptist Beginnings in Watford", p. 206.

of Thomas Tillam, who was a recent member of Knollys' church, received this lectureship.[70] Seeing this as an excellent opportunity to gather a church in the northern regions, the Knollys' church, which was at that point meeting at Coleman Street, London, sent Tillam out as a messenger.[71] His initial preaching and evangelism in Hexham resulted in significant conversions and baptisms.[72] On 4 December 1652, the church at Hexham wrote to Knollys,

> For your debtors verily we are; for whatsoever appearances of God are risen upon us, since that your faithful messenger, and now our dearly beloved brother in the Lord, Mr. Thomas Tillam, whom we love in truth and very highly esteem for his work's sake, hath been eminently instrumental in carrying on the Lord's work amongst us.[73]

Although certainly gifted, Tillam soon began to introduce practices contrary to those of the Particular Baptists in London, practices such as Sabbath worship – a return to the Old Testament practice of worshipping on Saturday, the Jewish Sabbath, as opposed to worshipping Sunday, the Christian Sabbath. As well, contention soon arose between the church at Hexham and the Baptist congregation in Newcastle, under the leadership of Particular Baptist Paul Hobson, formerly of London. The dispute was over the practices of the "'blessing of children' (with the laying-on of hands) and congregational singing in worship", implemented by Tillam.[74] Initially, the Coleman Street church was cautious. When, on 1 March 1653, the Hexham church expressed a desire to

---

[70] White, *Hanserd Knollys*, pp. 15; Ernest A. Payne, "Thomas Tillam", *The Baptist Quarterly*, vol. XVII (Oct. 1958) : 61. Tillam had been a Roman Catholic as a youth, but joined the Independents later at Wrexham. It seems that shortly after this Tillam embraced Baptist convictions. With regard to his activity in Northumberland, it seems that the lectureship was not the only element involved. Besides this, he had been appointed examiner by the commissioners in Parliament under the act for propagating and preaching the gospel and for the maintenance of able ministers and schoolmasters, for the four northern counties, passed in February 1650 at the same time as the aforementioned act for Wales. E.B. Underhill, *The Records of the Churches of Christ Gathered at Fenstanton, Warboys, and Hexham*, (London: Hanserd Knollys Society, 1854), p. 304.

[71] The London Baptists used this designation of 'messenger' in an almost official way. The messenger functioned as an apostle or missionary of sorts, having been sent with a commission by a local congregation to plant a church or assist a newly established church. An assessment of one's gifts played an important role in one's being appointed as 'messenger'. See J.F.V. Nicholson, "The Office of 'Messenger' amongst British Baptists in the Seventeenth and Eighteenth Centuries", *The Baptist Quarterly*, N. S. XVII, Jan. 1958 : 206-23.

[72] White, *Hanserd Knollys*, pp. 15-16; Payne, "Tillam", pp. 61-62.

[73] Underhill, *Records of the Churches of Christ*, p. 303. See the response of Knollys and his church on pp. 309-11.

[74] Payne, "Tillam", p. 62.

call Tillam formally as their pastor, the response of the Coleman Street church on 24 March was noncommittal, emphasising the fact that their knowledge of and experience with Tillam was limited:

> When our brother went out from us, we judged, from that little knowledge we had of him whilst he was with us, that the Lord had enriched him with some spiritual gifts.... But as for our approbation that he might be given up to you as your pastor, or elder, if the Lord shall call him thereunto, we conceive it more concerns you than us, you having more knowledge and understanding of his qualifications than we.[75]

Knollys did not sign this letter, though he had signed earlier correspondence. Eventually, because of differences in practice, the Coleman Street church disassociated itself from Tillam, convinced by the Newcastle church that they should "disown" him.[76] However, before cutting the ties, the Coleman Street congregation cautioned Tillam in a letter to "walk worthy of the Lord unto all well pleasing" and expressed their desire that the Lord would guide him "that you may not stumble in by-ways from the ancient paths, to walk in paths and in a way not cast up; but in the highway which is called holiness, wherein the way-faring men, though fools, yet shall not err".[77]

Though the details of disagreement are not clear, the issue of Sabbath worship and singing would continue to divide the London Baptists for the next several decades. Knollys, though he did not agree with the practice, would remain on good terms with those who held to Sabbath worship and would himself become a champion of congregational singing.[78] Regarding the issue of blessing the children, there were two potential problems. The first may have concerned the blessing itself. Perhaps such activity corresponded too closely to infant baptism for the comfort of the London Particular Baptists. Tillam was also known for the laying on of hands at the baptism of believers.[79] Of the two concerns, it would appear that the larger issue related to the laying on of hands in the ceremony, which was perceived as an abuse of the institution. The London churches would have reserved the laying on of hands for specific ceremonies such as ordination and commissioning (Acts 6:6; 1 Tim. 4:14; 2 Tim. 1:6).[80] These disagreements give evidence that differing local customs might have resulted in a variation of worship practices among the Particular Baptists. They also emphasise the independence and diversity in general which could be found within Baptist congregations and which would continue toward

---

[75] Underhill, *Records of the Churches of Christ*, pp. 313-17, 319-21.
[76] White, *Hanserd Knollys*, p. 16; Payne, "Tillam", pp. 62-63.
[77] Underhill, *Records of the Churches of Christ*, p. 337.
[78] See Chapter 7 below.
[79] Payne, "Tillam", p. 62.
[80] Payne, "Tillam", p. 62; White, *Hanserd Knollys*, p. 16.

the end of the century as the Particular Baptists attempted to form a self-identity.[81]

In the midst of this situation, another mission involving the "settlement and organisation of 'the poor scattered disciples in Cornwall'" may have presented itself to Knollys. Abraham Cheare, the pastor of the Plymouth church recommended to Robert Bennet, who was from Cornwall, that Knollys was the right person for such an undertaking and that he believed Knollys would be available that spring. Whether or not Knollys actually became involved in this is not known.[82]

Throughout his years in New England and in London, Knollys never lost his connection with his childhood home in Lincolnshire. His father, Richard, had summoned him home in 1641, just as tension was mounting between King and Parliament. Presumably, as Richard continued as the vicar in Scartho, his son had frequent contact with him. When Richard Knowles died is not known due to the haphazard keeping of records during the years of the Civil Wars. However, on 12 October 1648, Hanserd Knollys was installed in St. Giles Church in Scartho. Very little evidence has survived to show how he served this church in Lincolnshire and his gathered church in London. Equally uncertain is whether St. Giles began to be more of a de facto Independent church under his ministry. However, this affiliation with the Church in Scartho continued throughout the years of the Commonwealth, at least as late as 1656, and perhaps even longer.[83]

Although heavily involved in ministry and teaching, Knollys became engaged in a variety of other activities as well, including politics with a religious edge. In 1652, he, Richard Wollaston and forty-nine others presented a petition to the Rump Parliament asking for them to abolish tithes.[84] Gathered churches relied upon contributions from members and therefore attacked the payment of tithes by all members of society to support the ministry of the Established Church. This petition was followed by yet another petition, again signed by Knollys and others, including John Simpson, Henry Jessey, William Consett and Edward Harrison. A third petition soon followed, but Knollys did not sign this one. All three contained similar wording and likely were drawn up in concert. Written by Baptists, all three attacked tithes and strongly voiced the continued independence of gathered churches. They responded to "The Humble Proposals" of 1652, a plan of Church reform proposed by Independent John Owen. Many sectaries, especially Baptists, saw these proposals as an attempt by the Independents to pull free of the coalition they had built in the 1640s to

---

[81] See Chapter 7 below.

[82] Folger Shakespeare Library, Washington. Additional MS 667.

[83] For a detailed discussion of this, see Appendix 3.

[84] "Jottings by John Lewis of Margate, 1742", in *Transactions of the Baptist Historical Society*, IV, (Oct. 1915) : 206.

seek toleration.[85] The majority of members of the Rump Parliament, whether Independent or Presbyterian, were quite conservative. In part, this was because they feared the more radical religious ideas of the Quakers and Ranters and the more radical political ideas of the Fifth Monarchists and even the Levellers (a not so distant memory in the early 1650s).[86] Although the Rump initially abolished the Monarchy and the House of Lords, the Presbyterian system established in 1646-48 remained in place and attempts to have tithes abolished, to disestablish the Church, gained little support.[87]

On 28 August 1654, an Ordinance was established for ejecting Scandalous, Ignorant, and Insufficient Ministers and Schoolmasters. This was part of Cromwell's continuing attempt to purify and reform the Church of England. Commissioners were set in place in counties throughout England to carry out the task of examining clergy and schoolmasters. Hanserd Knollys was chosen as one of the Commissioners for the county of Lincoln.[88] Prior to that, Knollys had served as Examiner at the Custom and Excise, being paid 120 pounds salary, but had resigned "for more beneficial employment".[89] This would have been a significant position, for during the period of the Interregnum, taxes were high. However, the person chosen to follow Knollys, Edwin Hatch, "who had suffered much for Parliament" it seems was willing to work for much less (£80) and was perhaps owed a favour for his earlier service, leading to possible speculation that Knollys might have been forced from his post.[90] Following this, Knollys may have served in another civil service position as the Clerk of the Check until 1655.[91]

---

[85] Carolyn Polizzotto, "The Campaign against The Humble Proposals of 1652", *Journal of Ecclesiastical History*, vol. 38 (Oct. 1987) : 569-71. According to Polizzotto, this fear felt by the sectaries was fuelled by comparisons to the Congregational autocracy in New England, comparisons made by Roger Williams, newly returned to England.

[86] Coward, *Stuart Age*, p. 250.

[87] Coward, *Stuart Age*, p. 247.

[88] C.H. Firth and R.S. Rait, eds., *Acts and Ordinances of the Interregnum, 1642-1660*, vol. II, (London: His Majesty's Stationary Office, 1911), pp. 968, 981. For more see Appendix 3.

[89] *Calendar of State Papers Domestic*, 1652-1653, p. 240. The date for this entry is March 29, 1653.

[90] *Calendar of State Papers Domestic*, 1652-1653, p. 240; Muriel James, *Religious Liberty on Trial: Hanserd Knollys – Early Baptist Hero*, (Franklin, TN: Providence House Publishers, 1997), p. 149.

[91] *Calendar of State Papers Domestic*, 1655, p. 484. He resigned from this position over an issue of conscience, it would seem. Though the details are scanty, it had to do with some money that had been given him for the care of sick and wounded men in the Navy. From the entry, it could be assumed that this money was instead used for "the necessaries for the men" who had just landed in the vessel Truelove from Bristol. It must also be noted that this entry refers to "Mr. Knowles" and does not give a first name. Thus, it is not certain that this reference was indeed to Hanserd Knollys. Both Culross and James stated without hesitation that this was Hanserd Knollys. James

During the relative peace and stability of the Commonwealth years, Knollys may well have become a merchant, as had his very good friend and fellow Baptist William Kiffin. Pastor of one of the Particular Baptist congregations of London, Kiffin combined his ministerial duties with a career as a very successful merchant, respected in and about London.[92] Perhaps through this connection Knollys also became involved in the Dutch trade as a merchant.[93] Because of his many responsibilities, Knollys found it necessary to share pastoral duties for his London church with a co-pastor throughout his life. During the 1650s, Knollys' co-pastor was John Perry.[94]

Knollys' Writings during the Commonwealth Period

From 1647 until 1664, Knollys' pen remained rather quiet.[95] Following the publication of his polemical works of the mid 1640s, he published only one

---

Culross, *Hanserd Knollys*, (London: Alexander & Shepherd, 1895), pp. 75-76; James, *Knollys*, pp. 149-50. White said nothing related to this, while Duncan gave brief mention of the entry in the *Calendar of State Papers*. Pope A. Duncan, *Hanserd Knollys: Seventeenth-Century Baptist*, (Nashville: Broadman Press, 1965), p. 55.

[92] See John Carlile, *The Story of the English Baptists*, (London: James Clarke & Co., 1905), p. 90; B.R. White, "William Kiffin – Baptist Pioneer and Citizen of London (1616-1701)", *Baptist History and Heritage*, 2 (July, 1967) : 91-103.

[93] W.T. Whitley, *A History of the British Baptists*, (London: Charles Griffin & Co., 1923), pp. 130-31. W.T. Whitley, "London Churches in 1682", *The Baptist Quarterly*, I (1922-23) : 86; according to Louise Fargo Brown, Kiffin and Knollys were "conspicuously successful men of business". Louise Fargo Brown, *The Political Activities of the Baptists and Fifth Monarchy Men In England During the Interregnum*, (London: Oxford University Press, 1912), p. 58, n.35. Though there is nothing which pinpoints a date for Knollys' involvement in trade, it would seem that his employment as Examiner at the Custom and Excise and his later employment as the Clerk of the Cheque would indicate that he had some expertise in this field and perhaps some connections as well. Whether his work as a merchant preceded or followed his holding these positions is not clear, though the former would be most logical.

[94] From the Hexham correspondence, it appears that Knollys and Perry were considered as holding equal authority in terms of their pastoral leadership. Underhill, *Records of the Churches of Christ*, p. 313. By 1682, Knollys' church had nine pastors. Why there were so many is not certain. Certainly, Knollys' involvement in a variety of other tasks, his periodic experiences of persecution, and his advancing age may all have contributed to this situation. Whitley, "London Churches", pp. 82, 86.

[95] The works that he published in the 1660s were neither polemical nor theological works but rather were of an academic nature, in all likelihood related to his teaching. These works included grammatical works, *Grammaticae Graecae compendium*, (London: 1664), *Grammaticae Latinae compendium*, (London: 1664), *Linguae Hebricae delineatio*, (London: 1664), *Radices Hebraicae Omnes, Quae in S. Scriptura, Veteris Testamenti occurrunt*, (London: 1664), *Radices simplicium vocum, flexilium maxime, Novi Testamenti*, (London: 1664), and *Grammaticae Latinae, Graecae, & Hebricae*,

treatise throughout this period, a devotional commentary written for the family of Francis, Lord Willoughby, Baron of Parham, in Suffolk whom he had served as a private chaplain and as tutor to his children.[96] In the late 1630s and early 1640s, Willoughby became dissatisfied with the government of Charles I, complaining of the partiality involved in levying ship money in Lincolnshire. In 1640, Willoughby had signed a petition of twelve Peers to the king, asking Charles to call what became the Long Parliament. As tensions rose between the king and Parliament, Parliament appointed Willoughby to serve as lord-lieutenant of the district of Lindsay in Lincolnshire, where he defied the king's orders by executing the militia ordinance. With the outbreak of war, he was appointed lord-lieutenant and commander-in-chief of Lincolnshire. Willoughby had a less than stellar military career and eventually his troops came under the command of the Eastern Association. In 1644, he became involved in a series of quarrels with the House of Commons and began to feel uneasy about aspects of the Parliamentary cause.[97]

Willoughby continued as one of the leaders of the Presbyterian faction in Parliament through 1647 and was one of those Lords who was impeached for high treason on 8 September 1647 and imprisoned without charge until 19 January 1648. Upon his release, Willoughby fled to Holland where he joined the Royalists in whose ranks he briefly served. In 1652, Willoughby appeared to have changed sides again, as he returned to England and acknowledged the sovereignty of Parliament.[98] Throughout the 1650s however, he continued supporting Royalist causes and plots to restore the King. In June 1655 and again later, he was imprisoned in the Tower for "plotting" on behalf of Charles

---

(London: 1665), a hermeneutical work, *Miscellanae sacra; or a New Method of considering so much of the history of the Apostles as is contained in Scripture*, (London: 1665), and one other academic work, *Rhetoricae adumbratio*, (London: 1663).

[96] Perhaps this is an indication that a certain level of comfort and legitimacy had been attained by the Baptists during this period.

[97] "Willoughby, Francis, fifth Baron Willoughby of Parham", *Dictionary of National Biography*, vol. XXI, pp. 502-505; *The Complete Peerage or A History of the House of Lords and All Its Members From the Earliest Times*, vol. XII, Part II, (London: The St. Catherine Press, 1959), pp. 705-709.

[98] "Willoughby," pp. 502-505; *The Complete Peerage*, vol. XII, Part II, pp. 705-709.

Stuart.[99] At the Restoration of Charles II, he received favour from the King for his loyalty.[100]

An Exposition of the first Chapter of the Song of Solomon (London: 1656) was based on daily household devotionals from this portion of Scripture that Knollys had delivered during his time within the Willoughby household.[101] When or for how long Knollys served the Willoughby family is not certain. He had nearly finished preparing a son of Lady Willoughby for university in January 1655, so presumably his time of service there was in the early 1650s, perhaps following Willoughby's return to England.[102] *An Exposition of the first Chapter of the Song of Solomon* is a verse-by-verse elucidation of the chapter which clearly demonstrated a strongly allegorical interpretive hermeneutic. He stated as much in the Epistle Dedicatory:

> if my small and weak endevours to unveil the *Mysteries*, to open the *Metaphors*, and to explain the *Allegories* of the *Song*, in Expounding and Interpreting the *Historical*, *Prophetical* and *Spiritual* Sense thereof; may but afford your Honors, and any other precious Souls, the least measure of light and understanding therein, I shall rejoyce in the Lord.[103]

Knollys understood the Song of Solomon in the way typical of other reformers, seeing it as a spiritual reference to Christ and His Bride, the Church.[104] Following his exposition of each verse, Knollys gave a devotional meditation, which was a point of application of the verse for the Christian reader.

Without doubt, Knollys' primary focus in this pamphlet was on ecclesiology. However, he very clearly linked his ecclesiology with his

---

[99] *A Collection of the State Papers of John Thurloe, Esq.; Secretary First to the Council of State, And Afterwards to the Two Protectors Oliver and Richard Cromwell* (hereafter designated *Thurloes' Papers*), vol. III, p. 537, vol. V, pp. 362, 407. During one of these imprisonments, a letter was written to Cromwell from Capt. Butler petitioning his release to house arrest. According to the letter, Lady Willoughby, who was apparently with her husband at the Tower "lies desperately sick. She will not be persuaded to remove from her husband." Butler went on to state that Lord Willoughby was in debt and willing to settle in Antigua or Suriname. Vol. IV, p. 544.

[100] *Thurloes' Papers*, vol. III, p. 537, vol. V, pp. 362, 407. Knollys may have made the acquaintance of Willoughby through his activities in Suffolk in the 1640s. Debenham, Dallinghoo, and Ipswich, places where Knollys is known to have ministered for brief periods, were all within 20 miles of Parham. Or perhaps it was due to Willoughby's family connections to Lincolnshire or through their mutual service in the Eastern Association army in 1643.

[101] See the first page of the Epistle Dedicatory.

[102] Folger Shakespeare Library, Washington. Additional MS 667.

[103] Knollys, *An Exposition of the first Chapter of the Song of Solomon* (London: 1656), see the fourth page of the Epistle Dedicatory.

[104] Knollys, *Song of Solomon*, p. 1.

eschatology.[105] Although Knollys addressed a number of themes and issues, he was especially interested in contrasting the true church with the false church. Clearly associating the false church with Babylon of Revelation, he identified the true church as those Christians "who are not defiled with the false and superstitious worships of Babilon".[106] The true church was "the Spouse of Christ... one mystical Body, consisting of many spiritual members... which are [*conjunctim*] all the Churches of the Saints, 1 Cor. 14.33. and every individual Beleever".[107] Knollys' emphasis here was on the members being believers and on the multiplicity of gathered churches. Very clearly for Knollys, the true church was the gathering of believers, and more specifically in Baptist creed, the gathering of baptised believers. In most ecclesiastical traditions of the period, the ideal of the true church would typically be understood as the existence of the invisible Church within the existing visible church. For Knollys, however, the visible church of baptised saints came as close as earthly possible to the invisible church of true saints. Further on, in dealing with verse 17 of Songs chapter 1, Knollys compared the Church to a building, in particular the Temple in Jerusalem, the House of God. Here he stated that "the spiritual Materials of this spiritual House **are Beleevers, sanctified in Christ Jesus, called Saints**".[108] Thus, the church was not a material building in a physical parish nor was it inclusive of each individual in society in the Constantinian sense. Rather, the spiritual Temple of Christ consisted of believers.

The false church, on the other hand, was characterised by forced uniformity and formalism devoid of faith experience. In fact, the "false Ministers and formal Professors" in the false church had "stirred up persecution against the Churches and sincere servants of Christ".[109] Knollys undoubtedly recognized a correlation between the Established church in England, whether Episcopal or Presbyterian, and this image of the false church. Both of these expressions of a National Church sought forced uniformity and persecuted dissenters.[110]

He went on to give three very specific examples of the false church. First, there were those of Israel who worshipped at Dan and Bethel (1 Kgs. 12:25ff; Hos. 13:2-3). Second, came the Scribes and Pharisees in Jerusalem during the ministry of Jesus who "worship God in vain, teaching for Doctrine the Commandments of men" (Matt. 15:9). Third was the Church of Rome, whose daughters were "all Antichristian Assemblies of false Ministers, and formal professors". This Antichristian, hypocritical, and superstitious formal worship Knollys equated to the mark of the Beast (Rev. 14:9-10). Knollys stated unequivocally: "it is a sin, and will be a snare to leave Christ, and his holy

---

[105] For more on Knollys' eschatology and ecclesiology, see Chapters 6 and 7 below.
[106] Knollys, *Song of Solomon*, p. 11.
[107] Knollys, *Song of Solomon*, p. 17.
[108] Knollys, *Song of Solomon*, p. 80 (emphasis added).
[109] Knollys, *Song of Solomon*, pp. 24.
[110] See Chapter 3 above.

Ordinances, and pure worship, and true Ministry; and turn aside unto false Ministers, superstitious worships, and traditions of men".[111]

In light of these teachings regarding the true and false church, Knollys urged his readers to forsake formalism and false worship. "The first step towards the true worship of God, is to forsake the Assemblies of false worship and to separate from them. When God chose a people for himself, to worship him, he severed them from all other people."[112] Of course, Knollys had separated himself from the Established Church long before and viewed separation as God's will for believers within a "False Church".[113] Not only was formalism a mark of the false church, but uniformity also pointed to such a church. This applied as much to the new Westminster Confession and Westminster Order of Worship as to the old Book of Common Prayer and Thirty-nine Articles. Obviously, in the 1630s and early 1640s when the Church of England was being accused of its Romish practices and seeking to enforce uniformity, it would have been considered a 'false church' by Knollys and the Baptists. As well, the more recent attempts to impose Presbyterianism might even be included in this scathing rebuke against 'false churches'. In this light, Knollys sharply warned those who were truly God's people against submitting "to any impulsive or coercive power of the supreme Magistrate imposing or prescribing a false worship".[114] Although the Church of Rome served as his main explicit target in this work, the principles he expounded clearly applied to the imposition of false religion in general.[115]

The Calvinist, Puritan leanings of Knollys also became very evident in this work.[116] He wrote about the effectual and powerful work of the Spirit of God in drawing the souls of men to God, "not onely unto Christ in Conversion, but after Christ in Conversation". Saving grace was of vital importance because people have "no Active power of themselves to come to Christ" and "no Subjective power of themselves to submit unto Christ". In fact, their natural inclinations worked in the opposite direction; they "have a resisting power in their will to refuse the offers of Grace". Thus, only "Christs powerful Drawing maketh the Saints willing to follow him in all his wayes... The Will being thus efficaciously and sweetly drawn by Christ".[117] According to Knollys, the Divine work of God effectually drew people to Christ, making His grace irresistible. The providential power of God ensured the perseverance of His

---

[111] Knollys, *Song of Solomon*, pp. 32-34.

[112] Knollys, *Song of Solomon*, p. 36.

[113] See Chapters 6 and 7 below.

[114] Knollys, *Song of Solomon*, p. 25. Earlier, Knollys had made the statement, "Saints must not be the servants of Men in the things of Christ.... They ought to obey God, rather then Men... and not worship God after the Commandments, Traditions, and Doctrines of Men." p. 15.

[115] See Polizzotto, "The Humble Proposals".

[116] For more on Knollys' reformed, Puritan theology, see below in Chapter 7.

[117] Knollys, *Song of Solomon*, pp. 12-14.

saints.[118] "And dothe the Spouse cool in her spiritual affections unto Christ, or fall off, and leave her first love? Nay, she is constant in her love to Christ, as appears by this continued Epithet, *My beloved*."[119] The love poetry of the Song of Solomon became an analogy for the constant empowering love of God for his saints.

The Quakers

In 1647, just as the Presbyterians were attempting to take control of Parliament in London and the New Model Army was becoming a significant political force, in the Midlands of England, a young man named George Fox began to wander from village to village. As he travelled, God "opened" to him great truths and mysteries, "great openings" such as the fact that God "did not dwell in temples which men had commanded and set up", and that "being bred at Oxford or Cambridge was not enough to fit and qualify men to be ministers of Christ".[120] In 1647, Fox came into contact with "a tender people, and a very tender[121] woman, whose name was Elizabeth Hooton".[122] Fox began to meet and teach in the home of Elizabeth Hooton in Nottinghamshire; at the time, she was about fifty years old, married and with a family.[123] He had determined to abandon institutional religion, and had begun to fashion a very individualistic and pietistic spirituality, which emphasised "charismatic phenomena" and "the coming of the 'power of the Lord'".[124] Usually trembling and shaking accompanied this ecstatic experience. 'Openings' and direct revelations from the Spirit of God were also indicative of the experience and miracles and healings were sometimes present.[125] Fox kept a very careful record of his healings, over 150 including smallpox, scrofula, dumbness, headaches, blindness, and paralysis.[126] Another influential Quaker leader, James Naylor,

---

[118] Knollys, *Song of Solomon*, p. 70.
[119] Knollys, *Song of Solomon*, p. 76. Yet another theme, which recurs, is that of the sacraments. This will be dealt with further below in chapter 7.
[120] Rufus M. Jones, ed., *The Journal of George Fox*, (Indiana: Friends United Press, 1976; reprint of 1908 edition), pp. 75-76. Hereafter *Fox – Journal*.
[121] This was Fox's word to denote spiritual sensibility and openness.
[122] *Fox – Journal*, p. 79.
[123] *Fox – Journal*, p. 79. Hooton eventually left her husband and became the first woman Quaker preacher. Rosemary Anne Moore, "The Faith of the First Quakers: The Development of their Beliefs and Practices up to the Restoration", (Unpublished Ph.D. Dissertation, University of Birmingham, 1993), pp. 26-27.
[124] *Fox – Journal*, p. 27.
[125] *Fox – Journal*, pp. 27-28, 85-86; Reay, *Quakers and the English Revolution*, pp. 36-37.
[126] Reay, " Quakerism and Society", p. 148.

was also reputed to have had the power to heal. Dorcas Erbery, daughter of Seeker William Erbery, claimed that Naylor had raised her from the dead.[127]

At the heart of Fox's teaching was his belief in the inner light, which shone in and enlightened all people so that "they that believed in it came out of condemnation to the Light of life".[128] He held that this Light and Spirit had preceded the Scriptures and had led the "holy men" of old, so that for Fox, the inner illumination and the Scriptures were of equal import.[129] This emphasis on the "inner light", though offensive to Puritans, was in some sense an extension of the Puritan emphasis on the Holy Spirit and His work in the life of a believer.[130] The "inner light" replaced other qualifications for ministry and fuelled Fox's earlier mentioned rejection of the Established Church and the requirement of education at Oxford or Cambridge for ministers. "It was the uneducated man's and woman's way of rejecting the hegemony of a learned elite."[131] Another important element of Fox's doctrine and equally offensive to the Puritans was an abandonment of the Calvinistic doctrine of predestination.[132] For the Puritans, one's own efforts or deeds could not influence one's election. This would be tantamount to justification by works. However, for the Quakers, the belief in the presence and work of the universal light within sounded much like an Arminian position emphasising free will and a more general theory of justification for people.[133]

During these early years, Fox travelled throughout the midlands, teaching and gathering groups of "Friends". He was able to move about without financial limitations due to a mysterious inheritance, which rendered him independently wealthy.[134] Those who most readily followed Fox were separatists, mainly common men and women. However, the movement was of limited consequence until 1654 when Quaker preachers moved southward.[135] Rosemary Moore pointed out that unlike the Levellers, the Diggers, and the Ranters, the Quakers "were not crushed" by the government initially. She

---

[127] Michael Watts, *The Dissenters*, vol. 1, (Oxford: Clarendon Press, 1978), p. 210.

[128] *Fox – Journal*, p. 101.

[129] *Fox – Journal*, p. 102.

[130] Reay, *Quakers and the English Revolution*, p. 34. In fact, Hugh Barbour argued that the Quakers were essentially Puritans, stating that Quaker "insights in ethics and worship" were similar to those of the Puritans and that "characteristically Quaker teachings were often puritan attitudes pushed to severe conclusions". *The Quakers in Puritan England*, (New Haven: Yale University Press, 1964), p. 2.

[131] Jones, ed., in *Fox – Journal*, p. 102.

[132] Barbour, *Quakers in Puritan England*, pp. 140-42.

[133] Moore, "Faith of the First Quakers", pp. 103-104.

[134] H. Larry Ingle, *First Among Friends: George Fox and the Creation of Quakerism*, (Oxford: Oxford University Press, 1994), p. 21.

[135] Reay, "Quakerism and Society", p. 141.

argued that because they operated further from the capital, they did not seem initially to pose as serious a threat to the social system.[136]

Fox resolutely took his message to "the Dissenting people", since he sensed in them a certain amount of "tenderness".[137] Since separatists had already left the Established Church, the step to a Quaker fellowship was shorter for them than for most Puritans. The Quakers rejected all churches but their own as invalid and preached disobedience of any 'ungodly' laws. This blatant nonconformity, while perceived by the Puritans as a hostile threat, was received with enthusiasm by some of the more radical separatists.[138] From the earliest days of Fox's itinerant ministry, the Baptists provided many of his converts, particularly in central and later in southern England.[139] When the Hexham church desired to call Thomas Tillam as pastor, one reason given was the need for leadership in light of the danger presented by the Quakers

> whose pernicious ways many do follow; a generation whose main design is to shatter the churches of the saints, by stealing away the tender lambs out of the folds of the Lord Jesus; crying down the scriptures, those sacred oracles of truth, as a dead letter, and crying up the lights within, as they call it; making great shows of self-denial in voluntary humility, and neglecting of the body, which are very taking with weak ones; all for a Christ within, nothing for a Christ without. With such smooth words and fair spiritual speeches, the hearts of simple ones are deceived from the simplicity of the gospel. Never more need of watchmen than at this day. All Sion's towers should be planted with sentinels to warn the inhabitants thereof of their enemy's approaches; to excite them to a holy watchfulness, and an earnest looking for the return of the Captain of our salvation.[140]

When Fox first left home, he had Baptist connections. As a young apprenticed cobbler, he lived with an uncle in London who was a Baptist.[141] Fox found his most ready converts among the General Baptists, due in large part to their rejection of predestination and their stress on a less structured,

---

[136] Moore, "Faith of the First Quakers", p. 28.

[137] *Fox – Journal*, pp. 81-82.

[138] Barbour, *Quakers in Puritan England*, p. 15.

[139] Barbour, *Quakers in Puritan England*, pp. 86, 93-94. He referred to a "company of shattered Baptists" whom he gathered in Nottinghamshire. Watts, *Dissenters*, vol. 1, p. 204. Even the one time Baptist Leveller, John Lilburne, eventually embraced Quakerism. Reay, *Quakers and the English Revolution*, p. 41. This was not only typical of the early years of Quakerism. H. Wheeler Robinson related the account of Richard Claridge, an Anglican priest from 1673-1691 who became a Baptist in 1692. However, he found even the Baptists to be wanting and in 1697 became a Quaker. "The Value of Denominational History", in *The Baptist Quarterly*, II, (1924-25) : 108-109.

[140] Underhill, *Records of the Churches of Christ*, pp. 315-16.

[141] Barbour, *Quakers in Puritan England*, p. 34.

formal worship service with a more charismatic emphasis. This was in seeming conflict with the General Baptist literalism prevalent at the time. Watts argued that it was this literalism and the resulting conflict between the Spirit and the Letter of Scripture that "was the chief cause of Baptist losses to the Quakers". According to Watts, earlier in the seventeenth century, John Smythe, the forefather of the English General Baptists, had himself emphasised "the supremacy of the Spirit over the letter".[142] Finding it difficult to reconcile a strict literalism and an emphasis upon the inward urges of the Spirit, many General Baptists forfeited the former for the latter. General Baptists may also have been attracted to the Quakers' spiritual emphasis on the realised Kingdom of God within the believer, a comfort after their hopes for the establishment of God's kingdom on earth had been disappointed.[143]

Of course, for the Calvinistic Particular Baptists, who had already sought to emphasise the differences between the General Baptists and themselves in the 1640s, this advance of the Quakers in the Baptist ranks was quite disconcerting, especially since they confirmed some of the accusations made by their opponents. But what of these comparisons and accusations equating them with the Quakers? Were they groundless slander or were there enough elements of similarity to warrant them? And more specifically, were there more parallels than differences between the practices and beliefs of the Quakers and those of Hanserd Knollys?

Barbour made the case that Puritanism was, in fact, an incubator of sorts to Quakerism. Like the Levellers, the Quakers emphasised social equality and religious toleration, ideas that had found some reception by Cromwell and the Independents. As well, the Puritan stress on the work of the Holy Spirit and His overt dealings in the lives of the Elect certainly shared some likeness with the Quaker ideas enlightenment and openings. So too did the Puritan idea of experiential conversion find parallel expression in Quakerism. Beyond mainstream Puritanism, Barbour argued, a radical Puritanism existed which took these parallels even further. These radical puritans expressed an even more mystical understanding, particularly with respect to the conversion experience. They laid more stress on "leadings" of the Spirit – impulses to do or speak or sudden special insight.[144] Similarly, Reay pointed out that Quaker anticlericalism certainly had precedent in more radical Puritanism.[145] One could certainly make the case that the Particular Baptists constituted a more radical wing of Puritanism. The separatist tendencies, ecclesiology, views regarding baptism, and millenarianism of some Baptists would lend credence to this.[146]

---

[142] Watt, *Dissenters*, vol. 1, p. 205.

[143] Watt, *Dissenters*, vol. 1, p. 207.

[144] Barbour, *Quakers in Puritan England*, pp. 25-28.

[145] Reay, "Quakerism and Society", p. 149.

[146] See J.F. McGregor, "The Baptists: Fount of All Heresy", in *Radical Religion in the English Revolution*, ed. B. Reay and J.F. McGregor (New York: Oxford University

Although ordained originally in the Church of England, Hanserd Knollys had also questioned the validity of the institution and had opposed its formalism.[147] Much later, as a Baptist, Knollys had protested against tithes.[148] In addition, he had a very experiential faith, which included some mystical elements, particularly his understanding and experience of spiritual illumination and his understanding of and experience with supernatural healing.

Throughout his writings, Knollys made mention of or alluded to the illumination of the believer by the Spirit of God. While not a major focus of his work, it was an element of his theology and an important element of his religious experience. In his *Exposition of the First Chapter of the Song of Solomon*, when examining the beauty of the Church and Saints, Knollys referred to the eyes of "spiritual knowledge, and divine illumination" with which God gifted the believer. He went on to explain that "the spiritual understanding and experimental knowledge, which the Ministers and Saints have in Mysteries of God and Godlinesse, accompanied with a chast, holy, and harmlesse conversation (as becomes the Gospel) renders Sion to be very beautiful. Faith can see far into the mysteries of Christ."[149] For Knollys, the illumination of the believer through the Spirit had the effect of establishing the believer in holiness and purity of living.[150] Fox's account of his own illumination one day while walking alone expressed a similar focus on holy living. He claimed he was "taken up in the love of God" and during this experience, God not only opened to him all that Christ had done, but also caused him to see his "troubles, trials, and temptations" more clearly than ever before. "As the light appeared all appeared that is out of the light; darkness, death, temptations, the unrighteous, the ungodly; all was manifest and seen in the light."[151] After this powerful experience, Fox began teaching "perfection, and of a holy and sinless life".[152] According to Moore, for Fox, "right

---

Press, 1984), pp. 23-63. In the conclusion of his article, McGregor argued that eventually the Quakers sought to replace the Baptists "as the vanguard of popular evangelism".

[147] Knollys, *Life*, p. 9.

[148] "Jottings by John Lewis of Margate", p. 206. C.f. Barry Reay, "Quaker Opposition to Tithes 1652-1660", in *Past and Present*, 86 (1980) : 100-104.

[149] Knollys, *Song of Solomon*, pp. 72-73.

[150] There is another rather intriguing reference in Knollys' writings related to the issue of public worship which might indicate yet another level of "inspiration" for Knollys: "I have also **through the riches of Free Grace**, received the holy Spirit, and have learned in some measure, what it is to pray in the Spirit, and to pray with understanding: Also to sing in the Spirit, and and [sic] to Sing with understanding" (emphasis in original). Hanserd Knollys, *The World That Now Is and the World That Is to Come*, (London: 1681), p. 79. For more on this see Chapter 7 below.

[151] *Fox – Journal*, pp. 84-85.

[152] *Fox – Journal*, p. 85.

conduct... was understood to be a necessary consequence of the experience of the teaching light of Christ".[153]

For Fox, however, this spiritual enlightenment through the inner light was not merely for the purpose of teaching God's truth to the believer or bringing one to salvation, but also served as a means by which God guided and directed the believer in the affairs of life. Through these "openings", Fox and his later followers received guidance in decisions relating to their daily lives or insight into events of the time.[154] One such occasion occurred in 1652 at a place called Pendle Hill. This was a sort of commissioning experience for Fox. He related, "From the top of this hill the Lord let me see in what places he had a great people to be gathered."[155] Similarly, Knollys' own conversion experience also had an element of commissioning. Having renounced his ordination and silenced himself, Knollys was searching to know God's desire for his life. After several weeks in prayer, one evening at sunset, while walking and meditating in the woods, "an answer of my Prayers was given to me in these words, 'Go to Mr. Wheelwright, and he shall tell thee, and shew thee how to glorifie God in the Ministry'." He went on to state that "I heard no voice, nor did I see any Vision; only those words were plainly and articulately spoken into my Ears and Understanding."[156] Following this experience, Knollys visited Wheelwright, and after much more prayer and searching, received a commission to minister from God in a similar way. For several nights afterward while sleeping, God taught him and even showed him the passages he was to preach upon.[157]

In his work examining the lives of the early Baptist leaders Kiffin, Knollys, and Keach, Michael Haykin argued that Knollys "did not believe in the continuation of the extraordinary [spiritual] gifts given to the first century church, nor look for their restoration".[158] At the same time, however, he acknowledged the inconsistency in this position with reference to the issue of physical healing. Shortly after his ordination, while still ministering in the Established Church in Humberstone, Knollys had an experience that involved the physical healing of a widow in his charge. This woman's sickness had reached such a stage that "the Doctor of Physick had given her over, some godly Ministers, Friends and Relations did take leave of her as a Dying

---

[153] Moore, "Faith of the First Quakers", p. 97. See also pp. 107-109.

[154] Fox and other Quakers claimed to have predicted such things as Pride's Purge, Cromwell's death, the Restoration, and the Plague and Fire of London. W.C. Braithewaite, *The Beginnings of Quakerism*, (Cambridge: Cambridge University Press, 1970 ed.), p. 147. Keith Thomas, *Religion and the Decline of Magic*, (London: Weidenfeld and Nicolson, 1971), p. 140.

[155] *Fox – Journal*, p. 59.

[156] Knollys, *Life*, p. 10.

[157] Knollys, *Life*, pp. 13-16. According to Knollys' autobiography, this continued to be the pattern for the next several years.

[158] Michael Haykin, *Kiffin, Knollys, and Keach – Rediscovering Our English Baptist Heritage*, (Leeds: Reformation Today Trust, 1996), pp. 54-61.

Woman".[159] After two or three days of eating nothing and of her family mourning in expectation of her death, according to Knollys, something quite extraordinary happened. Knollys had come to her house as requested, bringing his books with him, that he might prepare for her funeral sermon. In the midst of this preparation, it was impressed upon him to pray for her. Going into her room, he prayed aloud over her for more than a half hour. Suddenly, after four days of motionless silence, "she began to stir, toss, and struggled so much, that I was constrained to stand up, and holding her in her Bed, still prayed over her".[160] After another half hour of prayer, while he was still praying, she spoke out, "The Lord hath healed me, I am restored to Health."[161]

Several similar incidents took place at other times during Knollys' life. In his *Gangraena*, Thomas Edwards related an account of several "sectaries" meeting together, including Jessey and Knollys, for the purpose of restoring sight to a blind woman through the anointing with oil. After much prayer by the woman and "all the company", Knollys himself prayed for her healing "for some space of time".[162] Edwards did not relate the effects of the prayer, but since he was recounting the story in an effort to discredit Knollys, one might safely assume that her sight was not restored. According to sources cited by Keith Thomas, William Kiffin and Knollys on several occasions attempted to restore sight to the blind through the anointing with oil.[163] In 1689, toward the end of his life, Knollys' good friend and fellow Baptist minister Benjamin Keach became so seriously ill that he was expected to die. According to Keach's son-in-law, Thomas Crosby, Knollys began to pray for Keach's healing and "in an earnest and extraordinary manner begged, that God would spare him, and add unto his days, the time granted to his servant Hezekiah". Knollys was referring in this prayer to the account of King Hezekiah in Isaiah 38. In this Biblical story, because of Isaiah's intercession, Hezekiah, who was on his deathbed, was granted a further fifteen years. Immediately following his prayer, Knollys said to his friend, "Brother Keach I shall be in heaven before you." Knollys would die two years later, while Keach would live until 1704, another fifteen years.[164]

According to his autobiography, Knollys himself experienced supernatural healing through the prayers of his fellow Baptist ministers and friends. In mid-1670, he became very ill. After receiving treatment from two well-reputed doctors, Knollys resolved to "take no more Physick, but would apply to that holy Ordnance of God appointed by Jesus Christ, the great Physician" as found

---

[159] Knollys, *Life*, p. 5.
[160] Knollys, *Life*, pp. 6-7.
[161] Knollys, *Life*, p. 7.
[162] *Gangraena*, Part III, p. 19.
[163] Thomas, *Decline of Magic*, p. 127.
[164] Thomas Crosby, *The History of the English Baptists*, vol. IV, (London: 1740), pp. 307-308.

in James 5.[165] He asked William Kiffin and Vavasor Powell to anoint him and pray over him for healing, which they did. As well, many others prayed in like manner and "as an Answer of their prayers, I was perfectly healed, but remained weak long after".[166]

Only a handful of incidents like these appear in the sources. Although unusual incidents for Knollys, he gave them central importance in his autobiography, claiming them as a confirmation of his call to ministry, particularly healings in which he took part in London during the time of Plague in 1665.[167] This opinion certainly coincided with what he wrote in 1646 in response to the Independent, John Saltmarsh regarding spiritual gifts. At that time Knollys wrote that Baptists did not feel it to be proper "for any Brother to baptize, or to administer other Ordinances; unless he have received such gifts of the Spirit as fitteth or inableth him to preach the Gospel".[168] Though Knollys did not elaborate upon these particular gifts, perhaps not wanting to be too specific, he did state that these gifts were to be tried by and known to the church prior to the appointment of the "Brother" to ministry.[169]

In light of those beliefs and experiences regarding spiritual illumination and supernatural healing held by one of the most educated Baptists ministers, contemporaries might well have confused the Baptists with the Quakers.[170] Certainly, both left ample room for supernatural expressions of the Holy Spirit, especially with respect to physical healing. However, Knollys differed from the Quakers in several ways. First and foremost for Knollys, the difference in their views on regeneration could not be reconciled. Though Knollys, like the Quakers, held to an understanding of the supernatural intervention of the Holy Spirit in leading the believer to salvation, this was clearly within a Puritan understanding of particular atonement. For Knollys, the Spirit enlightened those whom He sought and chose, not those who sought and chose Him.[171] The elect came to God through being drawn by Christ, "without which powerfull

---

[165] Knollys, *Life*, p. 35.
[166] Knollys, *Life*, pp. 35-36. See more below in Chapter 5.
[167] Knollys, *Life*, p. 31.
[168] Knollys, *Shining of a Flaming Fire in Zion*, (London: 1646), p. 9. Knollys did go on to state that the main miracle which accompanied Baptist preaching of the Gospel was the miracle of regeneration, thus playing down other supernatural manifestations, such as healing; p. 10.
[169] Knollys, *Shining of the Flaming Fire*, p. 10.
[170] Whether or not Knollys' position on these was typical for the Baptists is not known for certain. However, given that he was one of the most highly regarded Baptist leaders in London in the mid-seventeenth century, it would not be unreasonable to assume that his position was at least acceptable in Particular Baptist circles.
[171] Hanserd Knollys, *Christ Exalted: A Lost Sinner Sought, and Saved by Christ: Gods People are an Holy people... the summe of divers Sermons Preached in Suffolk*, 2nd ed., (London: 1646), pp. 2-3, 15-16, 30.

drawing, no sinner can come to Christ".[172] Therefore, the elect could experience a certain assurance, for

> when God by his holy spirit shall bring home this generall truth, particularly to thy soul with divine light, life, and power of manifestation, He will so cleerly witnesse, that Christ came to seek and to save thee, who wast a lost sinner, that thou shalt have a spirituall understanding given to know it, and to believe it, yea and thou shalt be filled with joy and peace in believing.[173]

On the other hand, George Fox held a far more universal understanding of atonement. For Fox and the Quakers, "the universal light within" brought believers not only to salvation, but into a state of near unity with Christ.[174] Richard Bailey described this as "christopresent" theology, which stressed a "celestial inhabitation" resulting in a oneness between Christ and the believer.[175] The "heavenly flesh" or "heavenly body of the pre-existent Christ" inhabited the believer. In this way, the saints assumed their glorified bodies while remaining in their "human, earthly vessels".[176] This position was tightly related to Fox's understanding of the Kingdom of God and an eschatological understanding of the Lord's words at the Last Supper: "God's Christ is not distinct from his saints, for their spirits witness him... he is in the saints, and they eat his flesh and sit with him in heavenly places."[177]

Second, Knollys and the Quakers had very different understandings of the place and importance of the Scriptures. Although George Fox claimed that he "had no slight esteem of the holy Scriptures", he was extremely glad when he was "commanded to turn people to that inward Light, Spirit, and Grace, by which all might know their salvation and their way to God".[178] While some of his statements would indicate that both the Scriptures and the inner light moved and guided the believer, Fox's denial of the authority of the Scripture would land him in prison for the first time. According to his journal, while listening to a preacher proclaiming that all doctrines and opinions were to be tested according to the Scriptures, Fox cried out, "'Oh, no; it is not the Scriptures!' and I told them what it was, namely, the Holy Spirit, by which the holy men of

---

[172] Knollys, *Christ Exalted*, 2nd ed., p. 17.
[173] Knollys, *Christ Exalted*, 2nd ed., p. 29.
[174] Moore, "Faith of the First Quakers", pp. 106-107.
[175] Richard Bailey, *New Light on George Fox and Early Quakerism: The Making and Unmaking of a God*, (San Francisco, CA: Mellen Research University Press, 1992), pp. v, 23-40, 75-90.
[176] Bailey, *New Light*, pp. 84-85.
[177] George Fox, *Great Mystery of the Great Whore* cited in Bailey, *New Light*, p. 39.
[178] *Fox – Journal*, p. 103.

God gave forth the Scriptures, whereby opinions, religions, and judgments were to be tried; for it led into all truth."[179]

For Knollys and the Particular Baptists, however, the authority of the Scriptures could not be compromised. Their central importance to Knollys clearly emerged in his autobiography. In the account of the healing of the woman in Humberstone, Knollys related that it was the temptation of Satan: "That the Scriptures are not the Word of God" which prompted him to pray for her healing, in order to prove that: "The Holy Scriptures are the Word of God, and the Scriptures of Truth."[180] In *Christ Exalted*, Knollys most plainly stated his position regarding the Spirit and the Scriptures, by noting that "the powerful conviction of the Spirit and Word of God" together bring the sinner "to a sensible apprehension of his naturall condition". As well, "God doth by his Spirit and word, Enlighten the soule to know, what is the hope of his calling."[181] Knollys held that the Spirit worked in and through the Scriptures. Ultimately, "the Spirit of God in the Word, and by the Word, convinceth the sinner."[182]

Third, Knollys differed from the Quakers in matters of social attitude as well as in belief and practice. Many early Quakers, exhibited what Knollys perceived as a real attitude of pride, which accompanied their perfectionism and their desire for supernatural gifts. In the words of Barry Reay, "extravagant behaviour and perfectionist claims became the badge of divine approbation".[183] The ability to perform miracles provided them with a badge of God's favour.[184] On the other hand, Knollys downplayed his role in healings. Following the healing of the woman in Humberstone, Knollys told those who were curious about the event that "it was not any thing in me, but it was the Lord that had done it for His own Glory".[185] In each recorded instance, Knollys made it clear healing came through the "power of God" and prayer.[186] He summed up his attitude concerning spiritual gifts in the following words:

---

[179] *Fox – Journal*, pp. 109-10.

[180] Knollys, *Life*, pp. 5-6.

[181] Knollys, *Christ Exalted*, 2nd ed., p. 19.

[182] Knollys, *Christ Exalted*, 2nd ed., p. 17. Knollys further united the Spirit and Scripture in terms of the process of sanctification, stating that "God hath given to every one of his the holy spirit to sanctifie them, Rom. 15.16.... God affords them his holy word, which is a means of Sanctification, John 17.17." *Christ Exalted*, 2nd ed., p. 31.

[183] Reay, *Quakers and the English Revolution*, pp. 35-36.

[184] Reay, *Quakers and the English Revolution*, p. 36. According to Christopher Hill, however, the more eccentric elements of Quakerism which had served as such important badges in the early period were dropped as "Quaker consensus came down on the side of discipline, organization, common sense" and "as the inner light adapted itself to the standards of this commercial world where yea and nay helped one to prosper". *The World Turned Upside Down*, (London: Maurice Temple Smith, 1972; reprint ed., Penguin Books, 1991), p. 256.

[185] Knollys, *Life*, p. 9.

[186] Knollys, *Life*, pp. 31, 35-6.

Christ is not onely the Authour and finisher of our Faith. Heb. 12.2. He is the *Alpha* and *Omega*, the beginning and the ending, of all those graces, gifts, and fruits of the Spirit, which are in the New man.... Let Christ be all, in all the gifts of the Spirit, and the graces of sactification.... But you ought to prize Christ far above all his owne gifts and graces in us, for he is the life of them all, the marrow and substance of them all, what is all knowledge, unlesse ye know God in Christ?[187]

This distanced the believer from the transcendent Saviour. For Knollys, the importance placed upon gifts should be significantly subordinated to the one who gave the gifts. Although Knollys wrote this even before Fox and his ideas had gained public notice, the issue remained relevant a decade and more later when the Quakers and their emphasis on the "inner light", miraculous gifts, and participation in the spirit of Christ began to gain popularity.

Throughout the Interregnum and into the Restoration, the Particular Baptists increasingly viewed the Quakers with suspicion and eventually with a degree of intolerance. They were not alone in this. Puritan divines, whether Presbyterian, Independent, or Baptist, all became embroiled in controversy with the Quakers. Initially, due to similarities between the Quakers and Puritans, the Puritans thought of them as mistaken and naïve. They readily engaged them in open discussion. However, these debates quickly made it apparent that the differences between the Quakers and their opponents were much greater. The Quakers met the challenge with great anticipation and regularly debated with Puritans. Out of this battle of words emerged a print war as each side attempted to carry the debates into an even broader field. Anti-Quaker tracts averaged about twenty a year until the Restoration.[188] With the Restoration of Charles II, harsh persecution broke out against the sects, but in particular against the Quakers. This persecution was both official and unofficial, the latter by local militias and mobs. The Quaker Act of 1662 and the Conventicle Act of 1664 targeted them specifically. In the words of Barry Reay, "the Quakers were under a state of siege during the Restoration period".[189] This provided even more reason for the Baptists, who themselves experienced persecution during the Restoration, to show the differences between themselves and the Quakers. Between 1648 and 1717, at least 37 disputations took place between Quakers

---

[187] Knollys, *Christ Exalted*, pp. 4, 10.
[188] Barbour, *Quakers in Puritan England*, pp. 135-37.
[189] Reay, *Quakers and the English Revolution*, pp. 105-06. Reay cited one Oxfordshire deputy-lieutenant who stated, "If... the King would authorize me to do it, I would not leave a Quaker alive in England.... I would make no more... to set my Pistol to their Ears, and shoot them through the Head, than I would to kill a Dog." Such was the hostility against the Quakers.

and Baptists. George Fox himself held sixteen of these. They took place throughout England and involved a number of Baptists, both lay and clergy.[190]

One disputation, which involved Hanserd Knollys, took place at the Barbican on 28 August 1674. The chief disputants were a Baptist named Thomas Hicks and the well-known Quaker leader, William Penn. Prior to this public affair, however, the debate had been ongoing for a time in print. Hicks had published several works in the format of a dispute between a "Christian and a Quaker" which had caused great offence among the Quakers. George Whitehead, a prominent Quaker, had called the writings "a malitious Forgery, and Fiction, stuft with manifest slanders against persons and principles".[191] William Penn responded to Hicks in print, which evoked a reciprocal response. The exchange eventually led Penn to charge Hicks with "vile Forgeries, and black slanders".[192] Penn also appealed to the Particular Baptist churches throughout London, challenging them to restrain Hicks:

> Now if you the Teachers and Elders &c. among the Baptized people, do not publickly clear your selves of Tho. Hicks, and these his unjust proceedings against us, and hereafter he further persists therein, we may take it for granted, that you own his work, and may justly deal with hime, and pursue him, not onely as Tho. Hicks, but as the Baptists great Champion, peculiar Agent, or Representative; But if you ingenuously clear your selves of him, and his corrupt perverse work, then his future miscarriages will be chargeable onely upon Tho. Hicks himself, and you shall appear to the world so far clear thereof, and approve your selves the more honest and sincere towards God, Truth, and Religion.[193]

Thus, the disputation resulting from this brief print war was more than just another debate between Baptists and Quakers. It provided a public opportunity to judge as to whether or not Thomas Hicks had wrongly libelled the Quakers.[194] While the Quakers wanted the Baptists to embrace their teachings in a public forum, the dispute instead became a very public opportunity for the

---

[190] Arthur S. Langley, "Seventeenth Century Disputations", in *Transactions of the Baptist Historical Society*, VI, (July 1919) : 216-43.

[191] *The Quakers Appeal Answer'd or a Full Relation Of the Occasion, Progress, and Issue of a Meeting held in Barbican, the 28th of August last past. Wherein the Allegations of William Pen, against Thomas Hicks: were Answered and Disproved. And Tho. Hicks, his Quotations out of the Quakers own Books, Attested, by several, as being appeal'd unto,* (London: 1674), p. i (original unnumbered).

[192] *The Quakers Appeal Answer'd*, p. i.

[193] *The Quakers Appeal Answer'd*, pp ii-iii.

[194] From the summation in the opening statements to the reader, it would seem that the Baptists were sincere in that they desired to determine if Hicks had misquoted or unjustly slandered them in his work and if he had "to bring him to acknowledge his evil as Publickly as he had wronged them, or to have disowned him as a person unworthy of countenance amongst us". *The Quakers Appeal Answer'd*, pp. iii-iv.

Baptists to distance themselves from the Quakers and their teachings. In response to the challenge, William Kiffin, Hanserd Knollys, and three other Baptist leaders sent a letter to William Penn calling for the public dispute to take place at "Mr. Gosnel's meeting-place in Barbican at 2 of the Clock in the Afternoon".[195] Similar letters were sent to George Whitehead and John Osgood and other leading Quakers. However, they were allegedly out of the city at the time, though contradictory reports claimed otherwise.[196] Thus, the dispute became a forum for a public examination of Thomas Hicks' charges against the Quakers and William Penn's responses to those charges.[197] Those present, basically Baptists as the Quakers chose not to attend, then claimed to determine if Thomas Hicks had indeed slandered or libelled the Quakers.

Hicks' accusations against the Quakers examined both their opinions and their practice, listing the following specific errors:

(1.) That the Light in every man, Or the Light where-with every man is Inlightened, is God. Dial.1.pag.3.Dial. 3.pag.2.

(2.) That the Soul is part of God, and of Gods Being; without Beginning, and Infinite. Dial.1.pag.16.Dial.3.pag.2.

(3.) That Jesus Christ is not a Distinct Person without us, Dial.1.pag.1. Dial.3.pag.2.

(4.) That Christ Redeems himself. Dial.1.pag.47. Dial.3.pag.2.

(5.) That the Scripture is no Rule of Faith, and Practise unto Christians. Dial.1.pag.1. Dial.3.pag.2.

(6.) That the Speaking of the Spirit in any, is of greater Authority than the Scriptures. Dial.1.p.48.

(7.) That's no Command from God to me, which he Commands to another. Dial.2.pag.59.

(8.) That Justification by that Righteousness which Christ fulfilled for us, wholly without us, is a Doctrine of Devils. Dial.1.pag.48.

(9.) That Justification is by Works. Dial.2.pag.31.51.

(10.) That Christ fulfilled the Law, only as our Pattern or Example. Dial.2.pag, 52.

(11.) That the Doctrine of Christs Satisfaction is Irreligious and Irrational. Dial.3. pag.3.

---

[195] *The Quakers Appeal Answer'd*, p. v.

[196] *The Quakers Appeal Answer'd*, pp. v-x.

[197] *The Quakers Appeal Answer'd*, p. 2.

(12.) That this Body which Dies, shall not rise again. Dial.3.pag.3.[198]

The first four claims addressed concerns raised by the Quaker idea of "celestial inhabitation" and addressed what the Particular Baptists perceived as mistaken Christology – [1] that the Light which enlightened and inhabited every man was God; [2] that the human soul was part the Deity and, therefore eternal; [3] that Jesus Christ was not a distinct person apart from the believer; [4] and that Christ redeemed himself. Hicks' next three charges dealt with the issue of authority in relation to the Scriptures – [5] that the Scripture was no absolute rule of faith and practice for Christians; [6] that the revelation of the Spirit held greater authority than the Scriptures; [7] and that a command of God to one person was not binding upon another. The next four charges focussed on the Quakers' doctrine of justification – [8] that justification by grace through faith in Christ was a "Doctrine of Devils" and [9] that justification was by works; [10] that Christ fulfilled the law only as our example [11] and that the doctrine of Christ's satisfaction of the wrath of God is "Irreligious and Irrational". Hicks' final accusation related to Quaker eschatology – [12] that there would be no literal resurrection of the body following death.

In his work *Reason against Rayling and Truth against Fiction*, Penn had responded that these were not Quaker doctrines or sayings.[199] Hicks then proceeded to show in detail that indeed they were Quaker beliefs and sayings, drawing the majority of his proofs from the writings of the Quaker founder, George Fox, as well as from many other "noted" and "eminent" Quakers including William Penn himself.[200]

Having satisfied themselves of his accuracy, Hanserd Knollys, William Kiffin and twenty other prominent Baptists publicly supported Hicks' assertions and denounced the Quakers.[201] This condemnation of the Quakers was further strengthened by the publication of the proceedings of the dispute or hearing. The great irony of this event, of course, was that what stemmed from a cry of foul play on the part of the Quakers and was intended to be a sort of vindication for them, in the end provided a ready public platform for the London Particular Baptists to disown and distance themselves from the Quakers. Though by no means the final word on the matter, the resulting statement provided a definitive answer to Quaker doctrines and practices for the Particular Baptist Churches in and about London.

---

[198] *The Quakers Appeal Answer'd*, pp. 2-4.
[199] *The Quakers Appeal Answer'd*, p. 3.
[200] *The Quakers Appeal Answer'd*, pp. 4-31.
[201] *The Quakers Appeal Answer'd*, p. 32.

The Fifth Monarchy Movement

On 3 September 1658, Oliver Cromwell died and following the death of the Protector, the Protectorate collapsed. Within a year, public opinion had come to favour the restoration of Charles Stuart to the throne. The failure of Richard Cromwell to fill his father's boots effectively, the failure of the army grandees to establish a successful interim government, the reassembly of the Rump government and the ensuing fragmentation of the Army all contributed to the political malaise, which led to the revival of the Long Parliament. The Protectorate and then the revived republic collapsed and, in May 1660, Charles II returned as monarch.[202]

The majority of Englishmen, like the majority of members of the unpurged Parliament, favoured this return of the monarchy.[203] Most Englishmen had not supported the execution of Charles I. However, many who had preferred the Parliamentary cause due to either political or religious sentiments or both, did not favour restoration. Some desired a republican government.[204] Others, out of religious and theological convictions held that no king should rule, save King Jesus. This group, the Fifth Monarchists, were millenarians who based their interpretation of current events on the Biblical books of Daniel and Revelation. Numbered in their ranks were several influential Baptists, men such as the regicide, Major General Thomas Harrison, Hugh Peter, and Welsh evangelist, Vavasor Powell. The Fifth Monarchists believed that the cataclysmic events of the 1640s fulfilled prophecies of the end and that Christ would soon return to establish His kingdom on earth.[205] In fact, many sectaries, as well as many Presbyterians and Independents, commonly held millenarian views.[206] The Independents believed that the setting up of "gathered churches" made the first step of preparation for the coming millennium and that the execution of Charles I inaugurated of the reign of King Jesus.[207] In fact, Murray Tolmie argued, "it

---

[202] Coward, *Stuart Age*, pp. 275-77.

[203] I.M. Green recounted the widespread pomp and celebration, which accompanied the restoration of the Monarchy. *The Re-establishment of the Church of England, 1660-1663*, (Oxford: Oxford University Press, 1978), pp. 3-5.

[204] For the relationship between dissenters and Republicanism, see J. Walker, "Dissent and Republicanism after the Restoration", in *The Baptist Quarterly*, VIII (1936-37) : 263-80.

[205] B.S. Capp, *The Fifth Monarchy Men*, (London: Faber and Faber, 1972), pp. 50-55. Millenarianism will be addressed in more detail in Chapter 6 below.

[206] Mark Bell pointed out that the Fifth Monarchists beliefs were a "natural extension of the Baptists' biblicism and eschatological concern." He went on to indicate that the "Fifth Monarchists both affected and were influenced by the other Baptist movements" and while they did not "appear as their own coherent movement" one can best understand them as "pockets" existing among Baptist and Independent congregations. Bell, *Apocalypse How?*, pp. 166-69.

[207] Capp, *Fifth Monarchy Men*, pp. 50-51; Watts, *Dissenters*, pp. 132-33. See also Tolmie, *Triumph*, pp. 85-90.

was in the Independent congregations that these (millenarian) ideas were most strongly developed".[208] What set the Fifth Monarchists apart from other religious groups of the time was the fact "millenarianism formed the basic core of their doctrines, and was indeed the *raison d'être*, for the movement".[209] For them, the failure of the "Good Old Cause" and the restoration of the Stuarts marked a devastating setback to God's plan for England.[210] Prior to the Restoration, to speak of a Fifth Monarchist movement represents something of a misnomer, for the movement surfaced as "a reaction to fading, not rising expectations" and attempted to re-ignite "millenarian impulses of the sixteen-forties".[211] Indeed, prior to the restoration of Charles II, many expectant Fifth Monarchists began to fear a waning of zeal in Cromwell and the Army. The "Good Old Cause" was perceived as giving way to a new form of absolutism, particularly with the establishment of the Protectorate in 1653. The final disappointment came with the collapse of the republic and the restoration of the monarchy. Thus, one can fairly state that the movement enjoyed its greatest success and following from the early 1650s to the mid-1660s.[212]

The Fifth Monarchy movement was not unified, but rather a "loosely co-ordinated movement" which "never possessed a common programme".[213] Millenarianism crossed denominational and sectarian lines, finding adherents among Presbyterians, Independents, Baptists, and even the more radical groups such as the Diggers. Even though Capp argued that the Fifth Monarchists claimed "the right and indeed the duty of taking arms to overthrow existing regimes and establish the millennium",[214] others have pointed to "gradations in motivation... ranging from intellectual convincement, millenarian hopes or reliance on divine justice to emotional excitement, a political policy or outright plotting".[215] As to their religious affiliation, Capp admitted that they were not "easy to classify" since their belief and worship practices drew mostly from those of the Baptist or Congregational churches from whence many of them came. Although they shared mainly in eschatological ideas and political attitudes, the Fifth Monarchists, Capp argued, perhaps too emphatically, "were a sect, albeit an amorphous one".[216] Because the Fifth Monarchists drew the

---

[208] Tolmie, *Triumph*, p. 87.
[209] Capp, *Fifth Monarchy Men*, p. 14.
[210] Capp, *Fifth Monarchy Men*, p. 198.
[211] Capp, *Fifth Monarchy Men*, p. 58.
[212] Capp, *Fifth Monarchy Men*, ch. 3.
[213] Capp, *Fifth Monarchy Men*, p. 131.
[214] Capp, *Fifth Monarchy Men*, p. 14.
[215] Geoffrey F. Nuttall, "Abingdon Revisited, 1656-1675", in *The Baptist Quarterly*, XXXVI (Apr. 1995) : 101.
[216] Capp, *Fifth Monarchy Men*, p. 172. Capp did moderate this position later, stating "the movement was a pressure group rather than a new denomination or party. Its supporters came from a variety of Congregationalist and Baptist churches, and included Calvinists

hatred and fear of their contemporaries as a threat to the social and political order, the tag "Fifth Monarchy Man" was used rather indiscriminately as a pejorative category for any who held millenarian beliefs. In light of the nebulous nature of the movement, P.G. Rogers has probably correctly suggested that many could be best described as "Fifth Monarchist sympathizers or 'part Fifth Monarchy Men'".[217]

One radical Fifth Monarchist leader, Thomas Venner, who had participated in an uprising against Cromwell and the Protectorate in 1657,[218] inveighed against Charles II following the Restoration. On 6 January 1661, Venner and a band of his followers marched from their meeting place in Coleman Street[219] to St. Paul's where they defeated an armed troop sent against them. They escaped and returned on 9 January when they encountered the Life Guards and another regiment, whom they fought with great resolve. This uprising threw London into turmoil and led to the arrest of sectarians all over the city. Captured following the tumult, Venner was tried and executed for murder and treason on 19 January 1661.[220] One of those arrested following the uprisings was Hanserd Knollys. He recounted in his autobiography that he "and many other godly and peaceable persons, were taken out of their own dwelling houses, and brought to Woodstreet Counter, and many to Newgate, and other Prisons".[221] Knollys remained in prison for eighteen weeks, after refusing to take the oath of

---

and free-willers, soldiers and civilians, in a loose and sometimes acrimonious alliance." "Popular Millenarianism", p. 170.

[217] P.G. Rogers, *The Fifth Monarchy Men*, (London: Oxford University Press, 1966), p. 134.

[218] Rogers, *Fifth Monarchy Men*, pp. 81-87. It is quite interesting to note that in 1657, most Fifth Monarchists had refused to join with Venner. Again, this would seem to indicate that the majority of supposed Fifth Monarchists were of less violent tenor. B.R. White certainly held this perspective, stating "most Fifth Monarchy men, whatever their *theories* about revolution, believed that those who like Thomas Venner, resorted in practice to violence had 'jumped the gun'." "Henry Jessey: A Pastor in Politics", *The Baptist Quarterly*, XXV, (Jan. 1973) : 103.

[219] Venner, a cooper, had been in New England for a significant time, but had returned to England in a deliberate effort to help facilitate the establishment of Christ's kingdom, which he believed, was imminent in light of the events there. He was affiliated with a dissenting church in Coleman Street, Swan Alley where he met and promoted his ideas. Capp, *Fifth Monarchy Men*, pp. 114-15. W.T. Whitley, "The English Career of John Clarke, Rhode Island", *The Baptist Quarterly*, I, (1922-23) : 369. Brown, *Baptists and Fifth Monarchy*, p. 108.

[220] Capp, *Fifth Monarchy Men*, pp. 199-200. Watts, *Dissenters*, pp. 222-23. For a very good, detailed description of the uprising, see Richard L. Greaves, *Deliver Us From Evil: The Radical Underground In Britain, 1660-1663*, (New York: Oxford University Press, 1986), pp. 49-57.

[221] Knollys, *Life*, p. 24. According to Culross, Venner denied the involvement of the sectaries, yet they were held anyway. *Knollys*, p. 82.

supremacy, but was eventually released by an Act of Pardon at the King's Coronation.[222]

Exactly what was Knollys' relationship with the Fifth Monarchy Movement? According to Culross, "he held it no part of his duty as a minister of the Gospel to preach politics or to intermeddle in the political disputes of the day".[223] Whitley, on the other hand stated "Knollys imparted a Fifth-monarchy tinge, so that the church was embroiled with the State from 1657 onwards."[224] The arrest of Knollys following Venner's uprising might point either to his involvement with the Fifth Monarchists or the worries of the authorities in the aftermath of the uprising. Although Knollys' use and interpretation of apocalyptic ideas and literature will be explored in Chapter 6, his relationship to Fifth Monarchists seems to fit better into the context of the Particular Baptists' ongoing struggle for legitimacy.

From the time of his return from New England in 1641, Knollys established a relationship with Henry Jessey, the pastor of the Independent church founded by Henry Jacob in London. Their relationship deepened when Knollys became a member of that church. Later, Knollys convinced Jessey of the veracity of believer's baptism and baptised him. Although Knollys left Jessey's congregation to establish his own Baptist church in London, the two men remained friends and during the 1640s, as the Baptists struggled to gain legitimacy, maintained a loose association. The Jessey Church continued to have a mixed membership, some receiving adult baptism and others not. In most every other way, however, Jessey and Knollys remained similar with respect to doctrine. In the 1640s, Jessey became increasingly enamoured with millenarianism. His first known writing was entitled *A calculation for this present year, 1645*. This work ended with an explanation of Daniel 2, surveying the four monarchies, already manifested in world history, and claiming the Fifth monarchy would appear shortly and would exceed the others. This Fifth Monarchy would be constituted by no earthly king, but by Christ with his saints.[225]

Like other sectarians, Jessey benefited from the atmosphere of toleration provided by the Civil Wars and Republic. However, with the establishment of the Protectorate, Jessey became an outspoken critic of Cromwell, opposing, among other things, tithes. Despite this, when the "Ordinance appointing commissioners for the approbation of public preachers" was passed in March 1654, Henry Jessey's name stood as one of the Triers.[226] Although openly

---

[222] Knollys, *Life*, pp. 24-25.
[223] Culross, *Knollys*, p. 32.
[224] Whitley, *The Baptists of London, 1612-1928*, (London: Kingsgate Press, n.d.), p. 107.
[225] White, "Pastor in Politics", pp. 99-100.
[226] White, "Pastor in Politics", p. 104. White, pp. 105-106 speculated that Cromwell had promised Jessey that he would see tithes abolished by 1654, which never did happen, and with this promise, Jessey proceeded to accept the position of Trier..

hostile to many of Cromwell's policies, Jessey accepted a position on a committee of the Council of State to examine a proposal that would allow the re-entry of Jews to England.[227] His discontentment with the Protectorate brought him into close contact with more outspoken and militant Fifth Monarchists such as Christopher Feake, yet he still refused their more radical stances. On 3 April 1657, Jessey, along with other leading Independent and Baptist ministers including Hanserd Knollys, signed a petition urging Cromwell not to accept the crown offered to him with the Humble Petition and Advice.[228] With the death of Oliver Cromwell and the succession of his son Richard, Jessey became a sharp opponent of the Protectorate. In 1659, Richard stepped down and retired to private life. Following this, Jessey and some twenty Fifth Monarchists signed a broadsheet against "the setting up or introducing any person whatsoever as King or chief magistrate, or a house of Lords".[229] Clearly, Jessey favoured a republic and perhaps held moderate Fifth Monarchist views.[230]

Another signature on the petition to Cromwell of 3 April 1657 was that of John Clarke. Clarke, born in 1609 in Suffolk, arrived in Massachusetts in November 1637. Like Knollys, he found himself embroiled in the Antinomian controversy and so in 1639, he moved to Rhode Island. By 1644, he had become a Baptist and was leading a Baptist church in Newport. In 1651, Clarke was sent, along with Roger Williams, to London to defend the interests of the colony and to attempt to secure a charter.[231] Upon arriving in London, Clarke published his version of the oppressive actions of the Massachusetts

---

[227] White, "Pastor in Politics", p. 106. This openness to Jews may well have been related to eschatological beliefs. See below Chapter 6.

[228] *Address of the Anabaptist Ministers in London to the Lord Protector* (London: 1657) cited in Underhill, *Confessions of Faith*, (London: 1854), pp. 335-38. Bell pointed out that this is the only major Baptist document from the period without William Kiffin's signature, indicating perhaps, that he wished to distance himself from the Fifth Monarchy movement, but that for the time he had "momentarily lost control of the London Particular Baptists". Bell, *Apocalypse How?*, p. 191. This lines up with one of Bell's key arguments that the Particular Baptists, specifically the London congregations tended to be dominated by Kiffin's agenda during their early years. While Kiffin was clearly a significant leader in the London churches, it would seem to this author to be placing far too much influence in his 'corner' at the exclusion of other important leaders such as Knollys.

[229] White, "Pastor in Politics", pp. 108.

[230] According to Louise Fargo Brown, following the release of Thomas Harrison from imprisonment in 1656, the main headquarters for the most faithful, militant Fifth Monarchists was in Swan Alley, Coleman Street, where both private and public meetings were held. Significantly, Henry Jessey's church was located at Swan Alley on Coleman Street. *Baptists and Fifth Monarchy*, pp. 106-107.

[231] B.R. White, "Early Baptist Letters", *The Baptist Quarterly*, XXVII, (Oct. 1977) : 142.

authorities.²³² This work contained a letter from Obadiah Holmes, Clarke's fellow Baptist in Rhode Island addressed to John Spilsbury and William Kiffin, which made it clear that ties had already been established between the Baptist church in Rhode Island and the London Calvinistic Baptists.²³³ Although still in London after 1652, Clarke remained illusive. According to W.T. Whitley, the Baptist John Clarke became involved with the Fifth Monarchists in London in the 1650s.²³⁴ In 1654, the Fifth Monarchists published a manifesto to clear up any misunderstandings that prevailed concerning their beliefs and agenda. It was signed by 150 people from ten congregations of Baptist and Independent churches, including John Clarke "of the Church that walks with Mr. Jesse".²³⁵ Clarke also signed the petition to Cromwell in 1657, and on 1 April 1658, was arrested with several other Fifth Monarchists, including John Canne, Cornet Wentworth Day, and the Seventh-Day Baptist John Belcher at a meeting at Coleman Street in Swan Alley.²³⁶ On 22 April, Day and Clarke were tried for sedition at Old Bailey. Both refused to plead, citing the illegality of a government under one person based on the Act of 1649, which outlawed monarchy. Henry Jessey appeared on Clarke's behalf. In spite of Clarke's arguing his case very ably, he was sentenced to six months in prison.²³⁷

John Clarke was named by Thomas Tillam as pastor of a Baptist church at Worcester house in London about 1658.²³⁸ By this point, his close ties with the Baptists in London was evidenced by two letters, which he wrote to Robert Bennett of Cornwall. In the first of these, written in 1655, Clarke mentioned that he had conveyed greetings from Bennett to several London Baptists, including Hanserd Knollys and his co-pastor, John Perry.²³⁹ Clearly, Clarke had

---

²³² John Clarke, *Ill newes from New-England*, (London, 1652).

²³³ White, "Baptist Letters", p. 142.

²³⁴ Whitley, "English Career of John Clarke", pp. 368-72. He argued that this was the same John Clarke.

²³⁵ *A declaration of several churches of Christ and godly people in and about the citie of London; concerning the Kingly interest of Christ, and the present sufferings of his cause and saints in England*, (London: 1654), pp. 21-23; Capp, *Fifth Monarchy Men*, p. 105.

²³⁶ This was an area of London which was littered with dissenters' meeting-houses. It is no coincidence that this was Venner's 'territory'. It is also of note that Hanserd Knollys himself pastored a church located in this area during the 1650s, as did Henry Jessey. White, *Hanserd Knollys*, pp. 15; Underhill, *Records of the Churches of Christ*, pp. 303-306, 309-11, 313-17, 319-21, 334-40, 345-50.

²³⁷ Capp, *Fifth Monarchy Men*, p. 121; Whitley, "English Career of John Clarke", p. 370.

²³⁸ White, "Baptist Letters", p. 142.

²³⁹ White, "Baptist Letters", pp. 144, 148. It is of note that Richard Bennett was himself a moderate republican. Whitley stated rather unhesitatingly that Clarke was a friend of Knollys. "English Career of John Clarke", p. 370.

contacts with Knollys and his church.[240] These letters, particularly the second written in 1658, revealed a Fifth Monarchist and republican bias. Following the death of Oliver Cromwell, Clarke wrote

> I am fully satisfied that there are two special designs which the Lord of Hosts hath very much on his heart to prosecute and to appear glorious in, in and about the days and times in which we live. The one is to bring in and set up that great and glorious kingdom of Christ. The other is to cast out and throw down the kingdom of Antichrist. And how well will it become the servants of the Lord to make it their business to wait upon him for wisdom and light whereby they may be directed to know their work, even that which doth most suit with the designs of their Lord, that so they may be at it, yea abounding therein, and that continually.[241]

In the uncertainty of the times, he hoped that the Lord would "move upon the hearts of the good people" of England for "the recovery of the good old cause and good old spirit by which it was managed".[242]

Despite this Fifth Monarchist and republican leaning, Clarke had either changed his position by the Restoration or he had never held a strongly militant position in the first place. Three days after Venner's defeat in January 1661, a pamphlet appeared under the name of John Clarke entitled *The plotters unmasked, murderers no saints, or a word in season to all those that were concerned in the late rebellion against the peace of their king and country on the sixth of January last at night and the ninth of January*. On 29 January, John Clarke of Rhode Island applied for a royal charter to the colony, which was eventually granted. Thenceforth, his correspondence reflected ardent support for the restored monarchy.[243]

Another radical spirit with whom Knollys had some relationship was Thomas Tillam, a one-time member of Knollys' Coleman Street church. With the restoration of the monarchy, Tillam became a particularly outspoken opponent, not only of the government, but of the Anglican Church as well.[244] From 1660 onwards, Tillam was at the centre of plots against the government, many of which involved rebels from the Palatinate. In August 1661, spies reported to the government much celebration at a Fifth Monarchist meeting over the landing of Tillam in Essex with Whalley.[245] Several days later, reports

---

[240] Tillam was no longer closely associated with the Knollys' church, having been sent out in 1652 as a missionary to the northern region.

[241] White, "Baptist Letters", p. 145.

[242] White, "Baptist Letters", p. 145. At the end of the letter he indicated his approval of the election of several republicans to Parliament.

[243] Whitley, "English Career of John Clarke", p. 371.

[244] Capp, *Fifth Monarchy Men*, p. 206.

[245] This likely referred to Edward Whalley a moderate Officer under Cromwell whose regiment contained a significant radical presence. Following the Restoration, Parliament

circulated that Tillam and two other Baptists, Paul Hobson[246] and Christopher Pooley, were involved in a plan assisting many to escape to the Palatine and were in contact with the leading regicides.[247] In the ensuing years, several similar plots came to light involving Baptists and in part, the panic from these caused Parliament to pass the Conventicle Act in 1663.[248] By this point, Tillam, it was reported, had undertaken "a dubious errand" on the Continent.[249] Even more alarming to the authorities was an alliance between the leading regicides and the Dutch, who, in 1665 were engaged in a war with England. Fortunately for Charles II, the Dutch fleet was defeated. However, another plot involving Tillam came to light in Ireland.[250] In 1666, the Dutch still presented the English with a threat and in the midst of this, Tillam and Pooley again promoted an emigration scheme to the Palatinate. According to government spies, this activity was of concern.[251] In 1664, Tillam was in Rotterdam for a time, and according to Payne, "his behaviour was adversely commented on".[252] While Tillam's activities during this period posed less of a threat than believed by the authorities, his ties with the Fifth Monarchists, his involvement in Continental emigration schemes, and his interest in apocalypticism caused him to be perceived as a danger.

Knollys' association with Tillam dated to the early 1650s when Tillam had come to Baptist convictions under the ministry of Knollys and his church in London. Sent out by Knollys' Coleman Street church as a messenger, Tillam's embracing of Seventh day beliefs and other innovations had cooled his relationship with the London congregation.[253] However, the tone of the letters exchanged between Knollys' Coleman Street church and the Hexham church, though mildly critical, still contained evidence of a continuing association. They continued to write: "To our dear and well-beloved brother Tillam, with the the [sic] church of Christ at Hexham, grace mercy, and peace, be ever

---

declared Whalley a Regicide and he fled England, eventually ending up in New England. W.T. Whitley, "Militant Baptists, 1660-1672", *Transactions of the Baptist Historical Society*, I, (Oct. 1909) : 150.

[246] In the early 1650s, Tillam and Hobson sharply disagreed over a number of issues. Knollys and his London church attempted to mediate. By 1660, they had overcome their differences and were working together to further their common Fifth Monarchist interests. Payne, "Tillam", pp. 62-63; Underhill, *Records of the Churches of Christ*, pp. 336-40.

[247] Capp, *Fifth Monarchy Men*, p. 201. This emigration plan was hatched by Tillam while in prison in 1660.

[248] Whitley, "Militant Baptists", p. 150.

[249] Whitley, "Militant Baptists", p. 152.

[250] Whitley, "Militant Baptists", p. 152.

[251] Capp, *Fifth Monarchy Men*, p. 202; Whitley, "Militant Baptists", p. 153; Payne, "Tillam", p. 66.

[252] Payne, "Tillam", p. 66.

[253] White, *Hanserd Knollys*, p. 15; Payne, "Tillam", pp. 61-63.

renewed and multiplied in you all." [254] Knollys probably remained on fairly good terms with Tillam.

On 23 April 1661, Charles II celebrated his coronation and to commemorate it, issued a general Act of Pardon. After eighteen weeks in prison, Hanserd Knollys was released.[255] With persecution of dissenters spreading, Knollys, along with his wife Anne and two of their children, made a hasty departure to Holland.[256] According to an entry in the *Calendar of State Papers Domestic* for Sept. 26, 1661,

> The people are transported with jealousy, will not believe in the King's goodness, and spread seducing pamphlets everywhere.... They have bought a small ship to convey each other abroad. Mr. Knowles and others, who were in Newgate, are sent into Holland, where they are in good condition, but act their business more secretly than here; they only wait an opportunity.[257]

Significantly, Knollys' departure coincided with the emigration plans of Tillam. According to Knollys' autobiography, he and his family remained abroad, first in Holland and then in Germany for two to three years.[258] He likely supported himself and his family during this time through merchant activities and when he prepared to return to England, he sold all his "Goods".[259] During this time, Knollys also may have begun work on his Hebrew, Latin, and Greek grammars and lexicons and other academic works, which were published after his return to England in 1663 through 1665.[260]

Three other Fifth Monarchists with relations to the Baptist community with whom Knollys had some association were Thomas Harrison[261], Vavasor Powell, and John Simpson. One of the few Baptists who became highly prominent in the New Model Army, Harrison was a close comrade of Cromwell. Rising to the rank of Major-General in the Army, Harrison

---

[254] Underhill, *Records of the Churches of Christ*, p. 336.

[255] Knollys, *Life*, p. 25; Blair Worden, ed., *Stuart England*, (Oxford: Phaidon Press, 1986), p. 148.

[256] Knollys, *Life*, p. 25.

[257] *Calendar of State Papers Domestic, Charles II*, 1661-1662, p. 98.

[258] Knollys, *Life*, p. 25. There are two references in the *Calendar of State Papers Domestic* to "English fugitives" in Rotterdam on 28 August and 4 September of 1663, one of whom is named Knowles. While this is inconclusive, based on Knollys' own account, he may have been preparing to return to England. According to his autobiography, a dishonest ferryman waylaid them for several days. After that experience, Knollys sent Anne and his children on to England while he remained for a time to sell the house he had purchased in Germany. See more in Chapter 5 below. *Charles II*, 1663-1664, pp. 257-58, 266; Knollys, *Life*, pp. 26-27.

[259] Knollys, *Life*, p. 26.

[260] See note 89 in this chapter.

[261] Harrison was baptized in 1658. *Public Intelligencer 8 February 1658*.

eventually became Cromwell's deputy commander and served as a member of his Council of State.[262] During the years of the Rump Parliament, Harrison found opportunities to gather around himself a small group of Fifth Monarchists in London and Wales who, through him, had the ear of Cromwell. In 1649, he was made commander-in-chief of the Commonwealth forces in Wales. After the passage of the Act for better propagation of the Gospel in Wales in 1650, Harrison took a leading role in working with the saints there.[263] Following the establishment of the Protectorate, however, Harrison became disillusioned, forfeited his commission and after vocally opposing the Protectorate, was asked by Cromwell to retire to his father's house in Staffordshire.[264] After the Restoration, Harrison was one of several known Baptists executed as a regicide.[265] One of those who signed the Fifth Monarchist document *A declaration of several Churches of Christ and godly people in and about the citie of London* in 1654, Harrison noted his membership as one "of the Church that walks with M. Knowls".[266] The depth of their relationship, however, remains unknown.

Vavasor Powell was a Welsh Baptist who, like Jessey, maintained an open or mixed church.[267] Although never involved in an attempt to overthrow the government, he became a harsh vocal opponent of Cromwell after the establishment of the Protectorate and of the restored monarchy after that. On 18 December 1653, Powell, while preaching at Christ Church, Newgate Street, accused Cromwell of being "the dissemblingest perjured villain in the world". The following day, he prophesied that Cromwell's "raigne was but short" and his government would fall, faring "worse than that great tirant, the last lord protector" Charles I had.[268] He was arrested the following day.[269] Soon released,

---

[262] Watts, *Dissenters*, vol. 1, p. 135. For more detail on Harrison, see Rogers, *Fifth Monarchy Men*, ch. 1.

[263] Tai Liu, *Discord in Zion: The Puritan Divines and the Puritan Revolution 1640-1660*, (The Hague: Martinus Nijhoff, 1973), p. 68.

[264] Brown, *Baptists and Fifth Monarchy*, pp. 47-48.

[265] B.R. White, *The English Baptists of the Seventeenth Century*, rev. ed., (Oxford: The Baptist Historical Society, 1996), p. 102.

[266] *A declaration of several Churches of Christ and godly people in and about the citie of London* , (London, 1654), p. 10.

[267] Watts, *Dissenters*, vol. 1, p. 160.

[268] *Thurloe Papers*, vol. I, (London: 1742), p. 161. This entry is dated 22 December 1653, differing from the *Clarke Papers*, which gave the date 22 December 1655. However, since by late 1655 Simpson had moderated in his views, it would seem that the earlier date is the correct one (more below); *The Clarke Papers*, vol. 3, ed. by C.H. Firth, (The Camden Society, 1899), p. 62, entry for December 22, 1655 which stated that several pastors, including John Simpson read this statement from the pulpit at Allhallows church. Rogers, *Fifth Monarchy Men*, p. 41. At this same incident, Powell apparently publicly prayed "Lord, wilt Thou have Oliver Cromwell or Jesus Christ to reign over us?" Capp, *Fifth Monarchy Men*, p. 101.

Powell continued to speak out against the government. Warrants were once again issued for his arrest and he fled to his native Wales, where he continued to preach against Cromwell and the Protectorate and promote Fifth Monarchy ideas.[270] With the restoration of Charles II, Powell continued to express his Fifth Monarchist views. He condemned the new Book of Common Prayer,[271] and preached Baptist and Fifth Monarchist doctrines, resulting in frequent imprisonment.[272] He died in Fleet prison in October 1670, at age 52.[273]

As with Harrison, Powell's associations with Knollys have remained largely obscure. However, it was not likely coincidental that Knollys, when he was deathly ill in mid-1670, called for Powell and Kiffin to pray for his recovery. Whether he had become acquainted with Powell during his earlier preaching tours to Wales, or during Powell's time in London is not known. However, the intimate request for Powell's prayers in 1670 would indicate more than a passing friendship.[274]

Like Vavasor Powell and Henry Jessey, John Simpson was an Independent who eventually accepted believer's baptism and yet maintained a mixed fellowship church. Sometime after 1647, he became the pastor of the gathered church at Allhallows in London.[275] In the earliest years of the Fifth Monarchy movement, Simpson took a prominent leadership role, along with Christopher Feake.[276] As early as 1651, Simpson had stated publicly with other Independent and Baptist leaders,

> that all People in Every Nation as well, Members of Churches, as others, ought for Conscience sake, to Honor such, as by the wise Disposing Providence of God, are their Present Rulers; and are to submit to the Civill Commands, not onely of such Rulers as are faithfull, but even to Infidels.[277]

With the establishment of Cromwell as Lord Protector, however, Simpson, like other Fifth Monarchists decried it as a return to Monarchy. Simpson

---

[269] Capp, *Fifth Monarchy Men*, p. 101.

[270] Brown, *Baptists and Fifth Monarchy*, pp. 46, 63.

[271] Capp, *Fifth Monarchy Men*, p. 206.

[272] Rogers, *Fifth Monarchy Men*, p. 130.

[273] Geoffrey Nuttall, *The Welsh Saints, 1640-1660: Walter Cradock, Vavasor Powell, Morgan Llwyd*, (Cardiff: University of Wales Press, 1957), p. 51; Rogers, *Fifth Monarchy Men*, p. 130. This was only a few months after being summoned by Knollys to pray over him for healing. Obviously, even as late as 1670, Knollys still maintained some connection with or was sympathetic to those holding more radical millenarian ideas.

[274] See more below in Chapter 5.

[275] Tolmie, *Triumph*, p. 109. Simpson also held an official lectureship in another parish at St. Botolph Aldgate.

[276] Capp, *Fifth Monarchy Men*, p. 60.

[277] *A Declaration Of divers Elders and Brethren of Congregational Societies*, p. 3.

proclaimed that it had been revealed to him in a vision that Cromwell would fall within six months. On 28 January 1654, he was ordered to be imprisoned.[278] Another infamous visionary who prophesied against Cromwell was Anna Trapnell, a member of Simpson's congregation. Trapnell went so far as to proclaim that the Little Horn mentioned in Daniel's vision was none other than Cromwell.[279] In 1654, members of Simpson's church signed the Fifth Monarchist document *A Declaration of several churches of Christ and godly people in and about the citie of London; concerning the Kingly interest of Christ*.[280] However, between 1656 and 1658, Simpson's congregation was strongly divided over interpretations of the Fifth Monarchy.[281] In 1657, Simpson's own views moderated as he began to preach against Fifth Monarchists' plots and advocate passive obedience to the government.[282] In spite of this, the authorities continued to suspect Simpson of holding Fifth Monarchist views into the next decade.

No doubt a relationship existed between John Simpson and Hanserd Knollys. Simpson came to embrace believer's baptism sometime in the early 1650s and his close relationship with Henry Jessey may indicate the source of his conversion.[283] Perhaps Jessey also served as a link of sorts between Simpson and Knollys. In a letter of encouragement written to the newly founded church in Hexham, where Thomas Tillam was the pastor, Jessey clearly associated his own congregation with those of "our brother H. Knollys and... Mr. John Simpson, and others meeting at Blackfriars".[284] Apparently this group of churches had previously written a letter to the church at Hexham addressing issues of "nearer communion and provoking to pray for the pouring forth of the Spirit, for furnishing ministry and magistracy, &c".[285] Capp noted that "Baptists such as Kiffin, Jessey, and Highland as well as the Fifth Monarchists" frequently attended large services at Allhallows the Great in London during the

---

[278] *Thurloe's Papers*, vol. II, p. 67. Capp, *Fifth Monarchy Men*, p. 101.

[279] Anna Trapnel, *Cry of a Stone*, (London: 1654), p. 3; Rogers, *Fifth Monarchy Men*, p. 47. At the same time, Trapnell prayed for Cromwell and exhorted God's people not to revile Cromwell, but rather to urge him to good works. Brown, *Baptists and Fifth Monarchy*, p. 49.

[280] *A Declaration of several churches of Christ and godly people in and about the citie of London; concerning the Kingly interest of Christ*, p. 22.

[281] See Capp, *Fifth Monarchy Men*, Appendix III.

[282] Brown, *Baptists and Fifth Monarchy*, p. 104; Capp, *Fifth Monarchy Men*, p. 113.

[283] Further support for this theory is the fact that Simpson, like Jessey, continued to pastor a mixed gathered congregation, as well as to hold an official lectureship in London.

[284] Underhill, *Records of the Churches of Christ*, pp. 341-46. The congregation at Blackfriars was under the leadership of another prominent Fifth Monarchist, Christopher Feake. Capp, *Fifth Monarchy Men*, p. 271.

[285] Underhill, *Records of the Churches of Christ*, p. 346.

1650s.[286] In fact, at one such meeting on 5 January 1657, Simpson and Kiffin, a strong opponent of Fifth Monarchy ideas, debated against Christopher Feake, opposed in particular to "his fastning the terms Antichristian and Babylon upon Civil government".[287] This loose association between the churches and their pastors only tightened with the restoration of the monarchy and the Church of England. Persecution served to draw them more closely together.[288] According to the *Calendar of State Papers Domestic*, informants closely observed this cooperation:

> Information by Hodgkinson, the printer, that Knowles, Jesse, and John Simpson are the persons who preached at Great All Hallows, Mr. Bragg's church, at a Fast on August 24, and that they preach there every Monday and Thursday, where they may best be apprehended.[289]

Anna Trapnell, the aforementioned prophetess, provides another link between Simpson and Knollys. In her writings, she claimed to be "well-known... to Mr. Henry Jesse and most of his society,... [and] to Mr. Knollis and most of his society".[290] According to Trapnell, Knollys visited her in November 1652 while she was in the midst of a vision, which kept her in bed for seven days and eight nights.[291]

Perhaps the strongest evidence of a significant relationship between Hanserd Knollys and John Simpson appears in the context of the schism that took place in Simpson's congregation from 1656 to 1658. Following the establishment of the Protectorate, many Fifth Monarchists, including Simpson and his congregation, became strong vocal opponents of Cromwell. In 1654 and again in early 1656, Simpson found himself in prison because of this stand.[292] Several letters written in 1654 by Simpson from prison contain strong denunciations of Cromwell and predictions of his fall from power.[293] However, after his release in 1654 and again in 1656, Simpson created division in his congregation by praying for Cromwell's government and preaching against the teachings being

---

[286] Capp, *Fifth Monarchy Men*, p. 182.

[287] *Thurloe's Papers*, vol. V, pp. 755-59.

[288] Capp, *Fifth Monarchy Men*, p. 203. Even in the previously mentioned "Fifth Monarchist Manifesto" the members of the churches of "M. Knowls", "Mr. Simson", and "Mr. Jesse" were grouped together, listed in that order, although none of these three themselves signed it. *A Declaration of several churches of Christ*, p. 22.

[289] *Calendar of State Papers Domestic, Charles II*, 1661-1662, dated 11 Sept. 1661, p. 87.

[290] Trapnell, *Cry of a Stone*, p. 3. It is interesting to note, once again, in that paragraph, Simpson, Jessey, and Knollys are named.

[291] Trapnell, *Cry of a Stone*, p. 7.

[292] Capp, *Fifth Monarchy Men*, pp. 101-103, 276.

[293] Capp, *Fifth Monarchy Men*, p. 276; Humphrey Hathorn, *Old Leaven Purged Out, or, The apostacy of this day further opened*, (London: 1658).

put forth by the Fifth Monarchists. According to Thurloe in a letter dated 19 February 1656: "Of late, the discontented partye are fallen out with one another. John Sympson's worke now is to preach against the opinion of the fifth monarchy."[294] A schism resulted and a debate was scheduled. The debate never took place and instead, Simpson called upon several respected pastors and members of London churches for advice. These pastors included Jessey and Knollys.[295] Although the dissidents persuaded Knollys and the others not to get involved until the church could debate the issue, the fact that the moderating John Simpson would call upon Knollys and Jessey for advice and support indicates a strong level of intimacy.

While Hanserd Knollys had significant relationships and associations with other possible Fifth Monarchists, his relationship to the movement remained problematic and ambiguous. Several things must be considered here. Firstly, the Fifth Monarchy movement itself did not really begin to radicalise until the establishment of the Protectorate by Cromwell. Initially it was bound together in essence by attraction to apocalyptic theology and ideas. Indeed, Knollys had relationships with people who ranged from mild Fifth Monarchists or sympathisers, such as Jessey and Clarke, to more radical and militant advocates, such as Harrison, Simpson, and Tillam. Those individuals with whom Knollys had the strongest relationships, Jessey and Simpson, although initially more vocal in their opposition to the government, they eventually moderated. Secondly, Knollys himself never signed the "Fifth Monarchist Manifesto". In fact, in comparing the names of those who signed who were "of the Church that walks with M. Knowls" and those leaders of Knollys' church who signed the letters to the church in Hexham, no names appeared on both lists. This would lead one to believe that the leadership of Knollys' church, including Knollys himself, were not Fifth Monarchists.[296] Thirdly, the one document which Knollys signed, which might be construed as somewhat incriminating was the petition urging Cromwell not to accept the Crown.[297]

---

[294] *Thurloe Papers*, vol. IV, p. 545; Capp, *Fifth Monarchy Men*, p. 276.

[295] Hathorn, *Old Leaven*, pp. 21-23.

[296] See *A Declaration of several churches of Christ*, p. 22; Underhill, *Records of the Churches of Christ*, pp. 310-11, 321, 340. The first name on the list of those from Knollys' church is John More, a militant Fifth Monarchist. According to Louise Fargo Brown, based on church records in the Bodleian Library, More had left Peter Chamberlen's church in April 1654, five months prior to the issuing of the *Declaration* and joined Knollys' church. She postulated that he himself may have been the one who influenced those from Knollys' church to sign the document. *Baptists and Fifth Monarchy*, pp. 59-60, n. 38. Mark Bell indicated that although there was a fair bit of overlap between the those in Baptist congregations and those in the Fifth Monarchist movement, leaders of the Particular Baptists kept the movement at arm's length. Bell, *Apocalypse How?*, pp. 177, 180-82.

[297] *Address of the Anabaptist Ministers in London to the Lord Protector* (London: 1657) cited in Underhill, *Confessions of Faith*, (London: 1854), pp. 335-38.

However, many Baptist ministers and indeed members of Cromwell's army had reservations about this. Clearly, Knollys associated with and even had close relationships with some Fifth Monarchists. As well, he shared some of their apocalyptic ideas. However, at best, Knollys qualified as a mild Fifth Monarchist sympathiser.

Conclusion

The cover of an early eighteenth century German pamphlet contains an illustration of Thomas Venner in his armour, along with a picture of a trial of "Anabaptists and Quakers". Even as late as 1701 when this pamphlet appeared, the message was clear. Critics continued to link Baptists with the more radical Quakers and Fifth Monarchists.[298] The Levellers, Quakers, and Fifth Monarchists presented a dilemma to Hanserd Knollys and the Baptists. In their dealings with these groups, they faced a serious inconsistency in their position. In the struggle to gain acceptance and achieve legitimacy for themselves during the 1640s, they had championed the cause of toleration. However, with the appearance of more radical sects, and, in some cases, with the close connections between Baptists and a variety of more radical groups, the Baptists faced difficult decisions on how to represent themselves to people outside of their confession. Their own legitimacy rested in the balance. To hold to a position that appeared to give support to such groups would place their own movement in jeopardy. On the other hand, the lines connecting the Baptists with these groups were not always imagined. By abandoning their fellow radicals, and even more importantly, by abandoning the cause of toleration, the Baptists would abandon a part of their own legacy. J.F. McGregor argued that "the Baptists' fundamental weakness was their inability to attract leaders of the quality necessary to resolve the ambiguities in their relations both with the world and with their fellow radicals".[299]

However, was this seeming inconsistency primarily due to issues of pragmatism? For Hanserd Knollys and his fellow Particular Baptists, there was still great value in maintaining a significant measure of order in English society, and indeed within the church. While their belief in and practice of believer's baptism staked out a radical religious position in seventeenth-century England, their theology of salvation displayed little difference from that of other Puritans. Even in terms of church polity, again believer's baptism aside, they followed the traditions established by the Independents. They did trumpet the cause of religious toleration, a cause for which Hanserd Knollys had suffered greatly, both in New and Old England. In fact, Oliver Cromwell himself had crusaded for toleration. However, like Cromwell, Knollys and most

---

[298] This illustration appears on the cover of *Radical Religion in the English Revolution*, edited by J.F. McGregor and B. Reay (Oxford: Oxford University Press, 1984).
[299] McGregor, "The Baptists", p. 63.

of his fellow Particular Baptists realised the necessity of limitations on freedom, for the sake of order, both in terms of politics and society, and in terms of religion and theology. Though toleration of Protestant worship was highly desired by Knollys and the Particular Baptist churches, as demonstrated in the previous chapter, open unlimited toleration was not. The Levellers, Quakers, and Fifth Monarchists, as shown in this chapter, and the Roman Catholics, as will be illustrated in the subsequent chapters, confirmed for the Particular Baptists that toleration without limitations posed a serious threat to political, social, and religious order within society, a threat that Knollys and many Particular Baptists strongly resisted.

CHAPTER 5

Testing, Trials, and Tribulations: Knollys' Life during the Restoration

Introduction

Apocalyptic literature had its origins in Judaism, springing out of the period of the Babylonian exile of the tribe of Judah. According to Biblical scholar D.S. Russell, in his classic work *The Method and Message of Jewish Apocalyptic*, apocalyptic literature is at once a "literature of despair" and a "literature of hope".[1] In another work, he described apocalyptic writings as "tracts for the times", indicating that they were written not only to give record of historical events, but also to elicit the proper response of faith to those historical events.[2] In the Jewish context, apocalyptic reflected much of the heroism and tragedy, which had transpired during the Maccabean era of Jewish history. During the years in which Christianity was born and matured, apocalyptic was adopted and applied to the Church under the oppressive rule of Rome.[3] Thus, Russell is correct to assert that apocalyptic works

> cannot be understood apart from the religious, political, and economic circumstances of the times, nor can the times themselves be understood apart from these books whose hopes and fears echo and re-echo the faith of God's chosen people.[4]

Hope for the present was dependent entirely upon deliverance and justice in the future. All of life was viewed as a cosmic battle between the forces of good and the forces of evil, between God and the Devil. Ultimately, God, and His people with Him, would be victorious.

---

[1] D.S. Russell, *The Method and Message of Jewish Apocalyptic*, (London: SCM Press Ltd., 1964), p. 18.
[2] D.S. Russell, *Divine Disclosure: An Introduction to Jewish Apocalyptic*, (Minneapolis: Fortress Press, 1992), p. 14.
[3] D.S. Russell, *Divine Disclosure*, pp. 15-19, 32-34; Russell, *Method and Message*, pp. 15-20, 33-35.
[4] Russell, *Method and Message*, p. 16.

Although the apocalyptic genre fascinated a wide range of people throughout the Middle Ages and into the seventeenth century, those outside of the *status quo*, who were persecuted for their beliefs or suffering certainly had reason to be fascinated with apocalyptic. Hanserd Knollys, like many of his day, believed that culmination was near and signs of its imminence could be found in the current events of the time. The period from 1660 until 1688 was a most difficult one for Knollys and his family. During this time, Knollys experienced repeated persecution for his faith, as well as many personal trials and tragedies. His interest in eschatology grew keener through this phase of his life, for he believed that the trials and tribulations of his life and society at large provided clear and unmistakeable indicators that the end was quickly approaching. This chapter will examine the events and experiences of Hanserd Knollys' life during the period of the Restoration until the Glorious Revolution, examining them in conjunction with his eschatological worldview. His eschatological writings will be analysed in the following chapter.

Restoration and Renewed Persecution

The collapse of the "Good Old Cause" and the restoration of the House of Stuart to the Throne of England caused great concern for Hanserd Knollys and the Particular Baptists. Although King Charles II had promised "liberty to tender consciences... for differences in opinion in matters of religion which do not disturb the general peace of the kingdom",[5] the extent of that liberty and the legality of those differences would be determined by a parliament filled with members who reacted strongly against the religious changes of the past two decades.[6] In 1660 the restored Long Parliament rescinded all legislation of the

---

[5] "The Declaration of Breda, 4 April 1660", in J.P. Kenyon, *The Stuart Constitution: Documents and Commentary*, 2nd ed., (Cambridge: Cambridge University Press, 1986), pp. 331-32.

[6] Michael Watts, *The Dissenters*, vol. 1, (Oxford: Oxford University Press, 1978), pp. 221-24; I.M. Green emphasised that Charles himself seemed eager to reach a position of compromise, but his Councillors, particularly Chancellor Hyde, Earl of Clarendon, and the Cavalier gentry were zealous in their desire to purge the kingdom of Puritanism and to re-establish episcopacy. However, in the early stages of the Restoration, they were not yet in a safe position to do so. *The Re-establishment of the Church of England, 1660-1663*, (Oxford: Oxford University Press, 1978), pp. 9-11, 17. John Spurr has argued that even when the so-called Cavalier Parliament was in power, "the Cavalier Parliament was far from an homogeneous assembly of reactionary, backwoods squires; it was a divided and anxious body ready to be guided by those who knew how to play upon its fears. So although only a very few MPs were fervent for the Church of England, a small clique was able to exploit the larger body's anxiety about security and stability." *The Restoration Church of England, 1646-1689*, (New Haven: Yale U. Press, 1991), pp. 49-50.

Commonwealth that promoted toleration.[7] In the midst of the celebrations for Charles II and the return of monarchy,[8] there was also an obvious shift in the popular attitude toward recent religious reformers. Congregationalists, Quakers, and Baptists, indeed Puritans in general, experienced the abrupt swing from toleration to mockery, harassment, and discrimination. Henry Jessey, Hanserd Knollys' friend and fellow pastor, gave a clear account of such events, mentioning in particular a tumult at the Baptist meeting-place of William Kiffin and the arrest and imprisonment in 1660 of Vavasor Powell, another Baptist.[9] In the same work, Jessey warned of apocalyptic judgments that had reportedly fallen upon those who were mistreating the saints, such as the untimely sickness and death of some people who had acted in a play mocking Puritans. He also reported apocalyptic signs, such as plagues of toads, whirlwinds and earthquakes.[10] The eschatological significance of the changes in popular attitudes was not lost on contemporaries.

Venner's uprising in 1661 merely provided fuel for the fire of the more conservative element in the government. Following it, a royal proclamation issued on 10 January 1661 forbade the meeting of Anabaptists, Quakers, and Fifth Monarchy men.[11] Although Baptists and Quakers had immediately published declarations of loyalty to the king, many, including Knollys, were rounded up and imprisoned.[12] Thus began a period of persecution during which the Lord Chancellor, Edward Hyde, Earl of Clarendon and the Cavalier Parliament passed a series of oppressive acts, which would come to be known as the Clarendon Code.[13] The growing popular hysteria was evident in a letter in the *State Papers* dated 1 April 1661:

---

[7] Watts, *Dissenters*, vol. 1, p. 224.

[8] Green, *Re-establishment*, pp. 4-5.

[9] Henry Jessey, *The Lords Loud Call to England: Being a True Relation of some Late, Various, and Wonderful Judgments, or Handy-works of God, by Earthquake, Lightening, Whirlwind, great multitudes of Toads and Flyes; and also the striking of divers persons with Sudden Death, in several places; for what Causes let the man of wisdome judge, upon his serious perusal of the Book it self*, (London: 1660), pp. 8-10 (pp. 9-10 wrongly numbered 13-14). There are also many entries in the *Calendar of State Papers Domestic*, which illustrate the negative attitudes. For an example, see *Calendar of State Papers Domestic, Charles II, 1660-61*, p. 363. Although from 1656-60, there were only nine references to "Anabaptists" in the *State Papers Domestic*, in 1660-61 and 1661-62, there were twenty-two for each year and in 1663-64 there were thirty-nine, many of them negative.

[10] Henry Jessey, *The Lords Loud Call to England*, pp. 1-7.

[11] Watts, *Dissenters*, vol. 1, p. 223.

[12] W.T. Whitley, *A History of the British Baptists*, (London: Charles Griffin & Co., 1923), p. 109; Hanserd Knollys, *The Life and Death of That Old Disciple of Jesus Christ, and Eminent Minister of the Gospel, Mr. Hanserd Knollys*, edited by William Kiffin, (London: 1692), pp. 24-25, hereafter cited as *Life*.

[13] Watts, *Dissenters*, vol. 1, p. 223.

Yesterday there were great congregations of Presbyterians, Anabaptists, and Fifth-Monarchy men, so that the major part of London were there. Details of the sermons, exhorting the people to suffer rather than pollute their consciences. The meetings of sectaries cannot be particularized, for they are everywhere. They have collections at church, and from house to house, on pretence of supporting poor ministers, and are resolved to stand against episcopacy, though by resisting unto blood.[14]

While imprisoned, Knollys, like many others, refused to take the Oaths of Allegiance and Supremacy.[15] Rumours linked him to further unrest from within the prison walls. On 14 April, the authorities uncovered another plot that was to take place on the following day.[16]

While this was not Knollys' first experience as a prisoner, it was particularly trying for him, perhaps because of his age or because of concern for his family's well being. However, it did not silence him. Sometime in mid-May, soon after Charles' coronation, Knollys was released. From that time until September, it was reported that he was preaching at All Hallows the Great fairly regularly – every Monday, Wednesday, and Thursday.[17] All Hallows the Great was home to "one of the most notorious conventicles in the City" and proved a ready pulpit for any number of Independent, Baptist, or even Fifth Monarchist preachers.[18] However, by 26 September 1661, Knollys had

---

[14] *Calendar of State Papers Domestic, Charles II, 1660-61*, p. 561.

[15] Knollys, *Life*, p. 25; an entry on 19 March in the *State Papers* states that "There are abundance of Quakers in prison, and many Anabaptists too, who refuse to swear." *Calendar of State Papers Domestic, Charles II, 1660-61*, p. 542.

[16] *The Traytors Unvailed, Or A Brief and true account of that horrrid (sic) and bloody designe intended by those Rebellious People, known by the names of Anabaptists and Fifth Monarchy Being upon Sunday the 14th of April 1661, in Newgate on purpose to oppose his Majesties person and Laws*, (London: 1661), pp. 5-7; See also *A true discovery of a bloody plot contrived by the phanaticks against the proceedings of the city of London, in order to the coronation of the high and mighty King, Charles the Second, with the manner how it should have been acted on Sunday last, the number taken who should have been actors, and a true account of the late insurrections of the phanaticks in Newgate. Also the miraculous appearance of seven stars in the East on Wednesday at 11 of the clock at noon, with the branches darting from them like blazing comets, being environed round with several circles of various colours like the rain-bow, and a large white crosse betwixt them, which continued an hour and a half, with the events that hapned [sic] during the time and the manner how all vanished. As it was sent in a letter to a gentleman of quality living at Lime-street London*, (London: 1661), pp. 1-2. Bernard Capp believed that the rumours were without any merit. B.S. Capp, *The Fifth Monarchy Men*, (London: Faber and Faber, 1972), p. 200.

[17] Knollys, *Life*, p. 25; *Calendar of State Papers Domestic, Charles II, 1661-62*, dated 11 Sept. 1661, p. 87.

[18] Richard L. Greaves, *Deliver Us From Evil: The Radical Underground in Britain, 1660-1663*, (New York: Oxford University Press, 1986), pp. 61-62.

removed to Holland with his wife, a son and a daughter.[19] At the same time, his eldest son, Cheney, was installed as the Vicar of Scartho, the church where his ancestors had served before him.[20] Shortly after arriving in Holland, the Knollys family continued on to Germany, where Knollys built a house and they "sojourned about two or three years". According to his autobiography, during the time they were in the Continent, they spent another £150, perhaps savings which he had brought with him or money he had earned while there.[21]

As part of the backlash against nonconformists, Colonel Legge, "a Bedchamber Man, and Lieutenant of the Ordnance", seized Knollys' house and property in London on charges that Knollys had withheld it from the King. Although still on the Continent, Knollys proceeded to take legal action through his attorney.[22] The case seemed fairly straightforward. In January 1659, Thomas Taylor, a wealthy shipwright whose son had been a student of Knollys, had made him a beneficiary in his will. Knollys had probably used the legacy to purchase land from the Artillery Company where he built a house, "and quietly enjoyed it till the restoration".[23] According to the autobiography, Knollys had purchased the land for £300 and spent another £400 or more, some of which he had borrowed, in building a house and repairing an existing building for use as a schoolhouse.[24] While it seems as though Knollys won the court decision, he still lost the property, for

> when Col. Legge could not get my House from me by Law, he and some others brought several Red Coat-Souldiers, and took it by force, thrust out those persons I had left in Possession, and kept Possession by Souldiers, both of my House, Garden, and my Goods.[25]

---

[19] Knollys, *Life*, p. 25; *Calendar of State Papers Domestic, Charles II, 1661-62*, dated 11 Sept. 1661, p. 98.

[20] Muriel James, *Religious Liberty on Trial: Hanserd Knollys – Early Baptist Hero*, (Franklin, TN: Providence House Publishers, 1997), pp. 53, 63-64, 106, 136. Though James made this claim at several points, she nowhere gave reference or documentation for Cheney's installation at Scartho. For more on Cheney, see Appendix 4.

[21] Knollys, *Life*, pp. 26-27.

[22] Knollys, *Life*, p. 25.

[23] *Calendar of State Papers Domestic, Charles II, 1673-75*, dated 21 Dec. 1673, p. 66. According to the entry, Knollys purchased the land "about 1658". However, if he purchased the land following his receipt of the monies from this will, this would mean 1658 according to the old calendar.

[24] Knollys, *Life*, p. 25. This amount is corroborated in the above record in the *State Papers* where it is claimed that Knollys "bought for £300 the old Armory house in the Artillery Ground near Spitalfields from the Artillery Company and spent £460 more in repairs and building there and fitting the premises for his school-house and dwellinghouse". *Calendar of State Papers Domestic, Charles II, 1673-75*, dated 21 Dec. 1673, p. 66.

[25] Knollys, *Life*, p. 25.

As well, Legge confiscated £200, which Knollys had deposited at Weavers' Hall, and gave it to the King.[26] Although Knollys failed in this initial bid to regain his property, he would renew his fight over ten years later.

During the time Knollys was living in Germany, he wrote his Hebrew, Greek, and Latin grammars and lexicons as well as other academic texts. Education had always been a central aspect of Knollys' life. Although he had tutored students or had run a school during his years of ministry, he published his first academic text in 1648; it clearly reflected his interest in learning, languages, and Biblical scholarship. His purpose for writing the grammar was "for the benefit of some friends, who being ignorant of the Latine, are desirous to understand the Bible in the Originall Tongue".[27] During the three years in Germany, it seems that Knollys returned to this task, writing his grammars for Hebrew, Greek, and Latin, which he likely published after his return to England.[28] At the same time, he compiled both Hebrew and Greek lexicons.[29] All of these works were written in Latin, the scholarly language of his time, except for the Latin grammar, which targeted a less educated audience. During the same period, he also wrote an elementary outline of rhetoric[30] and another work examining the history of the early church, which was perhaps a hermeneutical one.[31] In 1665, Knollys combined all three of the grammars along with the two lexicons and his work on rhetoric into a compact "pocket Companion for his "Scholars" who were "now Apprentices in London".[32] He hoped it would serve to "excite" them "to a Review of those Rudiments of the Latine, Greek, and Hebrew Tongues" which they had learned under his

---

[26] Knollys, *Life*, p. 25. These were considerable sums of money and indicate that Knollys was of comfortable financial standing.

[27] Hanserd Knollys, *The Rudiments of the Hebrew Grammar in English*, (London: 1648), frontspiece.

[28] Hanserd Knollys, *Grammaticae Graecae compendium*, (London: 1664); Hanserd Knollys, *Grammaticae Latinae compendium*, (London: 1664); Hanserd Knollys, *Linguae Hebricae delineatio*, (London: 1664).

[29] Hanserd Knollys, *Radices Hebraicae Omnes, Quae in S. Scriptura, Veteris Testamenti occurrunt*, (London: 1664) and Hanserd Knollys, *Radices simplicium vocum, flexilium maxime, Novi Testamenti*, (London: 1664).

[30] Hanserd Knollys, *Rhetoricae adumbratio*, (London: 1663). This is a very basic, simple work, obviously intended as a rudimentary introduction or summary for reviewing the fundamentals.

[31] Hanserd Knollys, *Miscellanae sacra; or a New Method of considering so much of the history of the Apostles as is contained in Scripture*, (London: 1665). This author was unable to locate this work. Duncan cited it in his appendix "Sources of Information on Hanserd Knollys" but did not say anything further as to its location. No other author has mentioned the treatise.

[32] Hanserd Knollys, *Grammaticae Latinae, Graecae, & Hebricae Compendium. Rhetorica Adumbratio. Item Radices Graecae & Hebraicae Omnes quae in Sacra Scriptura Beteris & Novi Testamenti occurrunt*, (London: 1665), preface, i-ii.

tutelage, in order that they might "make a further progress in the study of those Tongues".[33] More important than the knowledge gained, however, was the character and qualities of leadership developed by such study, which helped to increase "both for Piety and Learning" and "may serve [their] Generation to the glory of God, the honour of the City and the comfort of [their] Relations".[34] Knollys saw his own life and work as a living example and addressed his former students as: "Your loving and studious Master, Hanserd Knollys."[35]

Although never explicitly expressing a philosophy of education, Hanserd Knollys seemed to understand that education was not only for the elite, but also for people from other social spheres. Although he tutored children of aristocrats, preparing them for university, he also ran and financed his own grammar schools, offering a basic education to young men who became apprentices to tradesmen and merchants. As well, he strongly advocated a rigorous education for the young men who entered the ministry of Particular Baptist churches.[36] All of these students needed a strong classical education, grounded in classical languages and rhetoric. Knollys wrote his academic works and ran his grammar schools not only to supplement his income, but also to further this goal. It was also part of his programme to bring respectability to the Particular Baptists.

During his time on the Continent, Knollys also wrote prefaces to some rather controversial works by friends and acquaintances, including one written by a woman, certainly not the norm in the seventeenth century.[37] In the preface to Katherine Sutton's book, *A Christian Womans Experiences of the glorious working of Gods free grace*, Knollys spoke highly both of the author and of her writings. [38] He also wrote a preface for an educational work by a fellow Particular Baptist, Benjamin Keach, *Instructions for Children Or the Child's and Youth's Delight, Teaching an Easie Way to Spell and Read True English*, published in 1664. In this preface, Knollys highly praised the book and its author.[39] In the uneasy times of the early 1660s, Keach's work met with open hostility. Not only had it failed to receive official approval, but it also contained a Baptist catechism. Although Keach originally published this book anonymously, the authorities discovered his authorship and had him and all known copies of the book seized. Later at trial, he admitted to writing the work.

---

[33] Knollys, *Grammaticae Latinae, Graecae, & Hebricae Compendium*, preface, i-ii.
[34] Knollys, *Grammaticae Latinae, Graecae, & Hebricae Compendium*, preface, iii.
[35] Knollys, *Grammaticae Latinae, Graecae, & Hebricae Compendium*, preface, iii.
[36] For more on this aspect, see Chapter 7.
[37] Katherine Sutton, *A Christian Womans Experiences of the glorious working of Gods free grace*, (Rotterdam: 1663).
[38] For more, see Chapter 7 below.
[39] Hanserd Knollys, "Recommended to the Use of All Parents and Schoolmasters", in Benjamin Keach, *Instructions for Children Or the Child's and Youth's Delight, Teaching an Easie Way to Spell and Read True English*, (London: 1664). For more, see Chapter 7 below.

Initially, the jury could not come to consensus, but eventually it ruled that he was guilty. He was fined and sentenced to time in jail and in the pillory and all copies of his book were burnt.[40] Keach later rewrote the book from memory and it went on to be published numerous times into the eighteenth century.[41]

After living in Germany for two or three years, Knollys ran out of money, sold his home and property, and returned to England with his family.[42] After being cheated by a Skipper who was to bring them from Cullen to Rotterdam, he recovered his money through the help of a "Gentleman" whom he met en route.[43] Upon arriving in Rotterdam, Knollys sent his wife and children ahead of him to England, where they stayed with a friend until his return.[44] Meanwhile, Knollys remained in Rotterdam to complete his business. Two Catholics back in Cullen assisted him so that he was able to sell the house he had built there for 160 Rix-dollars and return to England. This is a rather curious entry in his autobiography, for Knollys' vehement feelings about the Church of Rome are clearly evident throughout his apocalyptic writings, yet his words for these two Roman Catholics are surprisingly warm, proclaiming them to be instruments of God.[45]

Throughout the period of the Protectorate, Knollys had managed to attain a fairly comfortable financial standing.[46] His financial stability had also enabled him to provide for his children. In the mid-1650s, Knollys had granted his

---

[40] Keach's indictment read as follows: "that thou being a seditious, heretical, and schismatical person, evilly and maliciously disposed, and disaffected to his Majesty's government, and the government of the Church of England; didst maliciously and wickedly, on the first day of May, in the sixteenth year of the reign of our sovereign Lord the King, write, print, and publish… one seditious and venomous book *The Child's Instructor; or, a new and easy Primer;* wherein are contain'd by way of question and answer, these damnable positions, contrary to the book of Common Prayer, and the Liturgy of the Church of England." For the full account of Keach's trial and punishment, see Thomas Crosby, *History of the English Baptists*, vol. II, (London: 1739), pp. 185-209.

[41] Michael Haykin, *Kiffin, Knollys, and Keach – Rediscovering our English Baptist heritage*, (Leeds: Reformation Today Trust, 1996), pp. 84-85.

[42] The date of his return is uncertain. A spy in Rotterdam reported: "Knowles is come to London and is in Wapping." Although the first name was not given, this would have been about the right timeframe for Knollys' return and Wapping was the area where Knollys' church was located for much of this period. *Calendar of State Papers Domestic, Charles II, 1663-64*, dated 29 August 1663, pp. 257-58.

[43] Knollys, *Life*, pp. 26-27.

[44] This was in all likelihood due to the fact that Col. Legge had taken possession of their house and they had no place in which to live.

[45] Knollys, *Life*, pp. 26-27.

[46] As mentioned above, he had continued to minister and teach, but he had also become involved in trade with his friend William Kiffin, among other things. He had purchased land and built a house and school (£700) and had £200 invested at Weavers' Hall. As well, he had funds enough to go to live on the Continent for about three years (£150).

oldest son, Cheney, a pension of £60, which he enjoyed until his death in 1670.[47] Having lost his house, property, and his savings in London during his time in Germany, Knollys and his family were no longer affluent. Upon his return, Knollys began gathering students and teaching again.[48] By his own account, in the final years of the decade his "honest Labours... provided things Honest, Necessary, and Convenient, for my Family".[49]

While Knollys had been on the Continent, persecution of dissenters had escalated, culminating in the passage of the First Conventicle Act in May 1664. Except for an initial surge of persecutions following the passage of the act, the situation for dissent began to ease. However, this was perhaps due to other factors, events that turned the attention of the authorities away from nonconformists.[50] Knollys had barely settled back in London, when two events of great calamity fell upon London. Writing a generation later, Thomas Crosby saw these events as judgments for "the persecution against the professing people of God".[51] An outbreak of the Plague in London in 1665 resulted in high mortality, though primarily among the poorest people.[52] The King, parliament, and most of the citizens of substantial social standing fled to Oxford and the countryside. Many clergy left as well.[53] Numerous dissenting ministers, however, chose to remain and care for the people, including Knollys, who noted in his autobiography that many were healed of the Plague through his prayers and care.[54] The second catastrophic event was the outbreak of the Great Fire of London, which raged from 3-6 September 1666 and destroyed a large part of the older section of the city.[55] Knollys viewed both the outbreak of

---

[47] Knollys, *Life*, pp. 27-28. Since Knollys took only a son and a daughter with him to the Continent, yet he had at least five other children, one might assume the two children who accompanied him were still dependents. As far as the others, perhaps they were old enough to be in school or apprenticed, another expense for Knollys. See Appendix 4.
[48] Knollys, *Life*, p. 27.
[49] Knollys, *Life*, p. 27.
[50] B.R. White, *The English Baptists of the 17th Century*, rev. ed., (London: The Baptist Historical Society, 1997), p. 109.
[51] Crosby, *History*, vol. II, pp. 209, 213.
[52] Estimates are about 70,000 of London's 500,000 citizens died from this outbreak. Barry Coward, *The Stuart Age*, 2nd ed., (New York: Longman, 1994), p. 301; Watts, *Dissenters*, vol. 1, p. 225.
[53] Watts, *Dissenters*, vol. 1, p. 225.
[54] Knollys, *Life*, p. 31; White, *English Baptists of the Seventeenth Century*, p. 109.
[55] Over thirteen thousand houses and eighty-nine churches were destroyed along with schools, libraries and public buildings. It was widely rumoured that Papists started the fire. Although fewer lives were lost, in the end, it could be argued that the fire was more devastating than the plague due to the economic ramifications. Coward, *Stuart Age*, pp. 301, 314, 316; Crosby, *History*, vol. II, pp. 213-14. A few weeks prior to this, on 28 June 1666, Knollys participated in the setting apart of an elder and two deacons in William Kiffin's congregation. When the elder, Thomas Patient, died Knollys

plague and of fire in apocalyptic terms, interpreting them as precursors to the final judgments that would befall the world.[56] Indeed, his first eschatological treatise, *Apocalyptical Mysteries*, was published in 1667, the year following the fire, which he understood as "the latter Times" prophesied in the Scripture.[57]

Following the plague and fire, the authorities continued to pass legislation aimed at persecuting dissenters. However, with the fall of Clarendon in December 1667, the enforcement of these laws was less stringent.[58] In March 1669, the First Conventicle Act expired and immediately the conservative Parliament set about pressuring Charles to extend the penalties, which he passed it into law in February 1670.[59]

Personal Tragedy

Throughout this period, scepticism increased about the religious orientation of Charles II's brother and heir, James, Duke of York. In the words of Richard Greaves,

> no issue aroused more concern in British politics in the period 1673-88 than James' Catholicism, particularly as it was a convenient symbol of court policies deemed by many to threaten traditional liberties and Protestant convictions.[60]

Certainly, this suspicion played a role in the conservative approach of Parliament toward dissenters. In spite of the persecution of dissenters after 1664, it appears that Hanserd Knollys enjoyed a measure of peace until 1670.[61]

---

participated in a similar ceremony on 17 February 1668. B.R. White, *Hanserd Knollys and Radical Dissent in the 17th Century*, (London: Dr. Williams's Trust, 1977.), p. 19.

[56] Knollys, *The World That Now Is and the World That Is to Come*, (London: 1681), Book II, p. 48.

[57] Knollys, *Apocalyptical Mysteries*, (London: 1667), "To the Reader", pp. 1-2.

[58] In October 1665, Parliament passed the Five Mile Act, which banned nonconforming clergy from coming within five miles of towns, cities, or parishes where they had ministered or held conventicles. Watts, *Dissenters*, vol. 1, p. 226.

[59] Watts, *Dissenters*, vol. 1, p. 226. Charles had been in negotiation with the French prior to this, in an attempt to sign a treaty, which would gain him financial aid from Louis XIV of France. This was being brokered through his sister, Henrietta, wife of Louis' brother. An agreement was eventually reached in the Treaty of Dover on 22 May 1670, which declared that Charles was convinced of the veracity of Catholicism and was "resolved to declare it, and to reconcile himself with the Church of Rome as soon as his country's affairs permit". Coward, *Stuart Age*, p. 306.

[60] Richard L. Greaves, *Secrets of the Kingdom: British Radicals from the Popish Plot to the Revolution of 1688-1689*, (Stanford, CA: Stanford University Press, 1992), p. 1.

[61] B.R. White speculated that the easing of persecution against dissent in the last half of the decade was due in part to the "government's unwillingness to stir the Calvinists at

In the preface to his first eschatological work, Knollys made obvious mention of persecution, both in the past and yet to come and signed the preface: "This done, I remain your Brother in the best Bonds." These words presented Knollys' understanding of the clear threat of imprisonment as well as the honour of such suffering for Christ.[62]

The years 1670/71 would prove to be difficult ones for Knollys. With the passage of the Second Conventicle Act in May 1670, Knollys once again experienced imprisonment. The Lord Mayor of London arrested him for preaching in George-Yard, near Broken-Wharf and committed him to the Compter in Bishopsgate.[63] In spite of his incarceration, Knollys continued to preach in prison, for he had found favour with the wardens and "had liberty to preach to the Prisoners there, twice everyday of the Week, in the common Hall, where most of the Prisoners" came to hear his sermons. In this circumstance, Knollys' saw God's providence, for through his preaching, many were blessed.[64]

Shortly thereafter, Knollys was released, only to encounter further tribulations of a more personal nature. In his own words, "God made me his Prisoner, by a sharp and painful Distemper in my Bowels, called the griping of the Guts, and he brought me near to the Grave."[65] This painful sickness also led to spiritual self-examination:

> I saw the Sin of my sinful Nature, which was not so Crucified, as that it was destroyed, but I found some motions of it of late stirring in my sinful heart. The Sence of this was a very sore burden and trouble to my Soul in this day of my Calamity, for which I mourned in secret before the Lord, and lay at the Throne of Grace loathing my self, and begging, that God would kill that Sin, and destroy it, and all the rest of my Sins.[66]

Knollys did not divulge the particular sin with which he struggled, but hardships of the past decade brought forward some doubts, for in the midst of his illness he confessed "Satan was sometimes very busy... and tempted me in the Night season, sometimes suggesting to me, that I was but an Hypocrite, at

---

home... when [England was] engaged in war with their close friends in Holland". White, *English Baptists of the Seventeenth Century*, p. 109.

[62] Knollys, *Apocalyptical Mysteries*, "To the Reader", pp. 4, 6.

[63] Knollys, *Life*, p. 32. Knollys would later have a meeting-house in this very area. At this particular time, however, it seems that his church may have been meeting at Booby Lane, Wapping. W.T. Whitley, "London Churches in 1682", *The Baptist Quarterly*, I, 1922-23 : 86.

[64] Knollys, *Life*, p. 32.

[65] Knollys, *Life*, p. 32.

[66] Knollys, *Life*, p. 33.

other times that my Evidences for Heaven were not good."[67] When "two learned, well practised, and judicious Doctors of Physick", after earnest efforts, failed to affect a cure, Knollys purposed to take no further medical treatment and called upon his friends and fellow ministers, William Kiffin and Vavasor Powell to anoint him and pray over him according to New Testament practice. This was followed by recovery, an occurrence that he attributed to God's healing through "very many godly Ministers and gracious Saints that prayed day and night for me".[68]

During this dark period, other members of his family also experienced illness, misfortune, and death. One of his grandchildren died, while another contracted a nearly fatal case of smallpox.[69] During Knollys' own sickness, two of his sons died including his eldest son, Cheney, who was still serving as vicar of the church in Scartho.[70] As well, the wife of another son had delivered a stillborn child after hard labour and had nearly died herself.[71] On 30 April 1671, Knollys experienced his most heartbreaking affliction. Anne, his "dear loving wife" of thirty-nine years, died after more than six months of painful suffering and intense endurance:

> the Lord gave her a great measure of Faith and Patience even to the end; She enjoyed the Light of Gods Countenance, had full Assurance of Gods Love, the Pardon of her Sins, and of eternal Life.[72]

On the day of her death, Knollys was concluding his sermon, and felt "a strong impulse upon [his] Spirit" that Anne "was departing". In his closing prayer, he commended her to God and blessed God for the gift of her life.[73]

---

[67] Knollys, *Life*, p. 33. Note the puritan emphasis on election here with the use of the word "evidences".
[68] Knollys, *Life*, pp. 35-36.
[69] Knollys, *Life*, p. 34.
[70] Knollys, *Life*, p. 34; Will of Cheney Knowles probated 1670, Lincolnshire Archives, document LCC Wills 1670/ii/728r.
[71] Knollys, *Life*, p. 34; see Appendix 4.
[72] Knollys, *Life*, p. 36; see pp. 34-36.
[73] Knollys, *Life*, pp. 36-37. According to James Culross, she was buried in Bunhill Fields. The inscription upon her tombstone was a touching tribute to her and included a poem, probably composed by Knollys. It read: "Here lyeth the body of Mrs. Anne Knollys, Daughter of John Cheney, Esq., and wife of Hanserd Knollys (Minister of the Gospel), by whom he had issue 7 sons and 3 daughters; who dyed April 30th, 1671, and in the 63rd year of her age.

> My only wife, that in her life
> > Lived forty years with me,
> Lyes now in rest, for ever blest
> > With immorality.
> My dear is gone – left me alone
> > For Christ to do and dye,

Finally, after all of this tragedy, Knollys faced yet another. His son Isaac, his "most loving and beloved son"[74] also fell ill, overcome by "Grief for his dearly loving and beloved Mother, for he drooped ever since she first was taken ill".[75] Enveloped by a "deep Consumption", which worsened with each passing day, Isaac also experienced severe pain and fever. On 15 November 1671, he died, but not before he encountered "a manifest and powerful Work of Conversion, Repentance and Faith upon his soul", which brought a measure of joy to his father. In June and October, Knollys fell ill again "by a sudden and sore Fit of the Wind-Cholick and Vomiting" and came near to death on both occasions.[76]

In the span of one and a half years, Knollys had experienced imprisonment, three near-fatal illnesses, and the loss of two grandchildren, three sons, and his wife. In all of these instances, Knollys' puritan ideals and his apocalyptic worldview remained very evident. Whatever the hardship faced, through agonizing soul-searching and a tender conscience, God's sufficient grace could overcome the sin and evil.[77] Like Job in the Old Testament, Knollys understood these personal circumstances as playing an even larger role in the wider picture of God's plan:

> It was the Tryal of my Faith, and the exercise of my Patience, and that I might be to his praise and an example unto weak Believers, whose Eyes were upon me, and were observing and hearkening how I did behave my self, under all the great Rebukes and Chastisements of the Lord upon me.[78]

Financial Troubles

During this time of trial, Knollys revisited another unpleasant incident – the unlawful seizing of his property and holdings by Col. Legge nearly a decade before. The tragic circumstances and his desperate financial situation may have prompted him once again to pursue this case. Following the death of his wife,

> having had great Expences and a great Charge of dear Relations, and owing some considerable debts, I was necessitated to teach School again

---

> Who dyed for me, and dyed to be
> My Saviour – God Most High."

This elegy is preserved at Herald's College, London. James Culross, *Hanserd Knollys*, (London: Alexander & Shepherd, 1895), pp. 94-5

[74] Knollys, *Life*, p. 38. As Knollys recounted this event, he twice referred to Isaac as his "then only living son". When one examines the chronology of Knollys' life and children, this assertion causes some difficulty. See Appendix 4.

[75] Knollys, *Life*, p. 37.

[76] Knollys, *Life*, p. 38. Likely, both Knollys and his son Isaac suffered from an influenza virus or pneumonia.

[77] Knollys, *Life*, pp. 32-35.

[78] Knollys, *Life*, p. 34.

in my Old Age; That I might pay my Debts, succour my dear Relations, and not be too great a burden to the Church of God.[79]

In addition, he had to borrow £200 to pay the debts of his son Isaac.[80] The will of Thomas Bell, a wealthy London merchant, proved 3 May 1672, left a sum of money "to be distributed among poor necessitous men late ministers of the Gospel", including Knollys.[81] In another will, Anne Grave a widow in St. Buttolph without Algate, London, provided "for the maintenance of eight poor, aged decayed ministers…during their natural lives". Hanserd Knollys was the first name of those listed.[82] Clearly, godly lay people saw his financial state as being considerably deteriorated.

Between 1 January and 24 March 1671, Hanserd Knollys submitted a petition to King Charles II

> for confirmation of his purchase under the late usurped authority of the old artillery ground, Spitalfields, and the armoury room, which was obstructed on a former petition by a caveat put in by Col. Legge, late Master of the Ordnance.[83]

In December 1673, Knollys submitted a new, more detailed petition, explaining where the land was, how much he had spent on it, and outlining the circumstances under which he lost it. He punctuated his petition by stating "the poor and aged petitioner has for above ten years been kept out of his right to the impoverishing of himself and his poor family".[84] He requested that "his Majesty… appoint some one to examine and report" on his petition and if that person were to find in his favour, that he would cause those who had unlawfully seized his holdings to repay him for their value or give him lease of them for 99 years at a small rent.[85] This time his petition did not fall on deaf ears. Upon its review, a recommendation was made that indeed, Legge had taken the land illegally and Knollys should be reimbursed or given a low-rent lease. However, a second report, filed on 22 June 1674, claimed that leasing the property to Knollys was not possible because the property was being used for

> airing the stuff in the Tower, but chiefly because it is already granted to David Walter [the Lieutenant who took over the premises following the

---

[79] Knollys, *Life*, p. 37.
[80] Knollys, *Life*, p. 42.
[81] *New England Historical and Genealogical Register*, vol. 38, (Boston, 1884), p. 63.
[82] *New England Historical and Genealogical Register*, vol. 50, (Boston, 1896), p. 424.
[83] *Calendar of State Papers Domestic, Charles II, 1671*, dated Jan. 1 – March 24 1670-1, p. 143.
[84] *Calendar of State Papers Domestic, Charles II, 1673-75*, dated 21 Dec. 1673, p. 66.
[85] *Calendar of State Papers Domestic, Charles II, 1673-75*, dated 21 Dec. 1673, p. 66.

death of Col. Legge] and after him to George Legge in reversion and so in a manner annexed to the Ordnance Office.[86]

The second report recommended that the only way "of preserving Knollys, whose whole estate is laid out there, from ruin" was for him to be reimbursed the money "as it may best suit with his Majesty's occasions".[87]

Although no evidence from the *Calendar of State Papers* confirms that Knollys was actually reimbursed, his finances seemed less strained toward the end of the 1670s, especially after his nineteen-year old granddaughter "did take Charge of my Houshold affairs, and of my Boarders, who managed all things with so much discretion, that my life was very comfortable, and I had great Content".[88]

Pastoral Ministry, Peace, and Popish Plots

Throughout this difficult period, Knollys continued his pastoral ministry. Since he always had assistant pastors, the congregation continued even in his absence on the Continent. After 1660, the congregation moved to "Wapping (in Shakespear's Walk), Tower Street, Artichoke lane" and then at Booby Lane, Wapping.[89] Following Charles' Declaration of Indulgence of March 1672, dissenters experienced a brief period of toleration. They were offered licenses to preach, but many, including Baptists, declined for fear that the information supplied about preachers and meeting-places would later be used to persecute them.[90] Even though they had experienced ill-treatment from Parliament, most Particular Baptists were unwilling to concede that the king possessed "extra-parliamentary" powers and, like many dissenters, shared with the Anglicans the fear and suspicion of Catholicism.[91] From 1672 to 1682, the Particular Baptists in London seem to have enjoyed relative freedom from active persecution, even though the Act of Indulgence was withdrawn a year later and occasional persecutions ensued.[92] On 22 April 1672, Knollys assisted his close friend and fellow pastor, Benjamin Keach, by marrying him to his second wife, Susannah Partridge.[93]

During this period of calm, Knollys and other Particular Baptist leaders involved themselves in public disputes, supporting the Baptist cause and countering positions more radical than their own. Several Baptists, including

---

[86] Ibid.
[87] Ibid., pp. 66-7.
[88] Knollys, *Life*, p. 42.
[89] W.T. Whitley, *The Baptists of London, 1612-1928*, (London: Kingsgate Press, n.d.), p. 107; Whitley, "London Churches in 1682", p. 86.
[90] Watts, *Dissenters*, vol. 1, pp. 247-8.
[91] White, *English Baptists of the Seventeenth Century*, p. 111.
[92] Ibid., pp. 112-13.
[93] White, *Hanserd Knollys*, p. 20.

Knollys, engaged some notable Quakers in debate in 1674.[94] As well, between 1673 and 1675, a pamphlet war about baptism erupted between Henry Danvers, a Baptist, and Obediah Wills, a paedo-baptist.[95] After exchanging several published attacks against one another, Wills, satisfied by the integrity with which the Particular Baptists had dealt with the Quakers the year prior, appealed to them to mediate. Their response, by and large in Danvers' favour, was published as *The Baptists answer to Mr. Obed. Wills his appeal against Mr. Danvers*, (London: 1675).[96] At around the same time, Andrew Gifford and the members of the Pithay Baptist Church in Bristol asked Knollys and other Particular Baptist leaders to help solve a dispute within their church over whether believers could pray with unbelievers. The response of Knollys and the London Particular Baptists was very clear and cogent. All people, whether regenerate or unregenerate, should pray and be encouraged to pray, for prayer is "a duty belonging to natural, and not only instituted religion".[97]

The peace of the late 1670s also afforded the Particular Baptists in London and in the countryside the opportunity to publish a new Confession in 1677.[98] A revision of the Savoy Confession of the Congregationalists and closely based on the Westminster Confession, it would later form the basis of the Particular Baptist Confession of 1689.[99] It brought the Particular Baptists alongside of the Presbyterians and Congregationalists as fellow dissenters against the Church of England and at times, partakers in persecution.[100] During this period, Knollys

---

[94] *The Quakers Appeal Answer'd or a Full Relation Of the Occasion, Progress, and Issue of a Meeting held in Barbican, the 28th of August last past. Wherein the Allegations of William Pen, against Thomas Hicks: were Answered and Disproved. And Tho. Hicks, his Quotations out of the Quakers own Books, Attested, by several, as being appeal'd unto*, (London: 1674). See Chapter 4 above.

[95] Henry Danvers, *A Treatise of Infant-Baptism asserted & vindicated* (London: 1673/74); Obediah Wills, *Infant-Baptism asserted & vindicated... in answer to a treatise on baptism lately published by Mr. Henry D'Anvers* (London: 1674); Henry Danvers, *Innocency and Truth Vindicated: or, A Sober reply to Mr. Will's...* (London: 1675); Obediah Wills, *Vindiciae Vindiciarum*, (London: 1675); Henry Danvers, *A Rejoynder to Mr. Wills in his Vindiciae* (London: 1675).

[96] See Crosby, *History*, vol. III, pp. 90-96.

[97] Joseph Ivimey, *A History of the English Baptists*, vol. 1, (London: 1811), pp. 417-20.

[98] Interestingly, this Confession was anonymous, perhaps a sign that, as peaceful as things were, the Particular Baptist Leaders of London still had some reservations about becoming too visible. Prior to this, on 2 October 1675, some of the London Particular Baptists had sent a circular letter to Particular Baptist Churches in England and Wales inviting them to a meeting in London the following May. There is no indication of whether or not the meeting took place. Ivimey, *English Baptists*, vol. 1, p. 417.

[99] White, *English Baptists of the Seventeenth Century*, pp. 119-20; Haykin, *Kiffin, Knollys, and Keach*, chs. 6-7.

[100] Haykin, *Kiffin, Knollys, and Keach*, pp. 62-63; Greaves, *Deliver Us From Evil*, pp. 62-63.

also had a renewed opportunity to publish unhindered. Four of his six apocalyptic treatises were published between 1672 and 1682.[101]

The pro-French foreign policy of Charles II and his court gave critics pause to rally under the "twin dangers of 'popery and tyranny.'" In this climate of popish paranoia, memories of the Marian persecutions, the Gunpowder Plot, and the charges of "popery" of the 1640s lurked in the minds of many. The Declaration of Indulgence, James' public stand for Catholicism and marriage to a new Catholic bride, and the refusal of Charles II to annul his own marriage to a Roman Catholic all combined to increase concerns about the succession and led to an anti-Catholic backlash.[102] Some English Protestants continued to place limited hope in the wedding of Mary, the daughter of James from his first marriage, to William, Duke of Orange in October 1677.[103] Many, however, feared the ascension of the Catholic brother of Charles II to the throne. This led to the disclosure of the so-called "Popish Plot" in June 1678, and the Exclusion crisis of the following years.[104] During this short time of panic and anti-Catholic hysteria, Knollys published two apocalyptic works, clearly targeting Rome.[105]

In 1680, Knollys and a group of London pastors wrote the foreword to John Russell's book *A brief narrative of some considerable passages concerning the first gathering and further progress of a church of Christ in Gospel-order in Boston in New England*, (Boston: 1680). They urged the people of Boston to extend toleration to the Baptists there. Having suffered so much in recent years themselves, they could readily trumpet the cause of religious toleration.[106] The

---

[101] Hanserd Knollys, *The Parable of the Kingdom of Heaven Expounded*, (London: 1674); Hanserd Knollys, *Mystical Babylon Unvailed*, (London: 1679); Hanserd Knollys, *An Exposition of the Eleventh Chapter of the Revelation*, (London: 1679); Hanserd Knollys, *The World That Now Is and the World That Is to Come*, (London: 1681).

[102] Greaves, *Secrets of the Kingdom*, pp. 2-4.

[103] Greaves, *Secrets of the Kingdom*, pp. 2-4.

[104] For the "Popish Plot", see Greaves, *Secrets of the Kingdom*, pp. 5-25; see also John P. Kenyon, *The Popish Plot*, (London: William Heinemann Ltd., 1972). For the Exclusion Crisis, see J.R. Jones, *The First Whigs: The Politics of the Exclusion Crisis, 1678-83*, (London: Oxford University Press, 1961); Tim Harris, *Politics Under the Later Stuarts: Party Conflict in a Divided Society, 1660-1715*, (London: Longman, 1993), ch. 4.

[105] Hanserd Knollys, *Mystical Babylon Unvailed*, (London: 1679); Hanserd Knollys, *An Exposition of the Eleventh Chapter of the Revelation*, (London: 1679). For a more detailed look at Knollys' response to the Popish Plot, see Dennis Bustin, "*Papacy, Parish Churches, and Prophecy: The Popish Plot and the London Particular Baptists – A Case Study,*" *Canadian Journal of History*, XXXVIII, (December 2003): 69-81.

[106] This work by John Russell, with the preface was republished later in Nathan Wood, *The history of the First Baptist church of Boston, 1665-1899*, (Philadelphia: American Baptist Publication Society, 1899), pp. 149-72.

final four years of rule by Charles II were characterised by authoritarian government and a renewed hostility against dissenters.[107]

Renewed Persecution and the Glorious Revolution

After nearly four and a half years of freedom from strife, Knollys and his fellow Particular Baptists once again suffered persecution. From 1680 until the death of Charles II, many came under attack, particularly ministers.[108] By 1683, Hanserd Knollys' congregation was meeting at Broken Wharf, George Yard on the Thames. In the previous year, many dissenting meeting places had come under the close surveillance of spies. One report listed ten Presbyterian congregations and twenty-two Baptist congregations. For each Baptist congregation it included the name of the primary minister, the number of assisting ministers, the number of houses in which they met, the number of members in the congregation, and the type of Baptist church it was. According to the list, the church of "Mr. Knoleses" was meeting in two houses and was comprised of "about 200 pirtikler paptises [sic]". His church had the most assistants with nine.[109] In spite of the close scrutiny and renewed harassment, Knollys remained steadfast in his preaching. A letter written from James Warner in London to Mrs. Jane Harvey shortly after the failed Rye House Plot noted that "meetings here are suppressed generally, though when I am with Mr. Knowles, we keep our public meetings, which I determine to do to the end, while God gives me life and ability".[110]

It was during this period of renewed persecution that Knollys was imprisoned for the last time. In the spring of 1684, a lord approached Knollys on behalf of the king, asking him "and his friends of persuasion" to offer support for a new act of toleration. Seeking a show of public support from leading dissenters, the king was also attempting to provide relief for English Catholics. Knollys' response was guarded at first, stating simply "I am old, and

---

[107] John Miller, *Popery and Politics in England, 1660-1688*, (Cambridge: At the University Press, 1973), pp. 191-94.

[108] White, *English Baptists of the Seventeenth Century*, p. 113.

[109] Whitley, "London Churches in 1682", pp. 82, 86. Whitley claimed that this large number of assistants was due to the fact that even at this point, "he was often away trading in Holland", though by this point, Knollys would have been 73 years old, making it quite unlikely that he would still be involved in merchant activities. Whitley gave no documentation to support this thesis.

[110] *Calendar of State Papers Domestic, Charles II, 1683*, dated 24 July 1683, pp. 196-97. The reference to "Mr. Knowles" in this context probably meant Hanserd Knollys. The allusions to current events (ie. the death of Shaftsbury and the suicide of Essex) and the apocalyptic overtones ("I suppose you may not be wholly estranged to God's works now on foot in the world, the Turk at Vienna, the Emperor foiled and the Popish interest in danger of a fatal fall, if he proceed") in this letter betray similar eschatological expectation.

know but few men's minds." However, when pressured further, the reason he gave for rejecting the request was more political than religious: "I am of opinion that no liberty but what came by Act of Parliament would be acceptable, because that would be stable, firm, and certain."[111] As a result of this refusal, Knollys, at the age of 75, spent the next six months in Newgate Prison.[112]

When Charles II died on 6 February 1685, for the first time in over a century England had a Roman Catholic Monarch in James II. For Baptists and other dissenters, what had already seemed like a bleak situation now became desperate. When the illegitimate son of Charles and pretender to the throne, the Duke of Monmouth, attempted to seize power, among the ranks of the rebels were found a number of Baptists. Several prominent Particular Baptist pastors were involved, as well as William and Benjamin Hewling, two of William Kiffin's grandsons.[113] After James' army ruthlessly crushed the rebellion, Kiffin's grandsons were captured and brought to trial. Kiffin, whose wealth had proven extremely advantageous on numerous occasions prior to this,[114] offered £3000 for their acquittal. It was refused and at their sentencing, the prosecutor actually claimed that their grandfather "did as well deserve the death" they were to suffer.[115] Perhaps his own death would have been a more merciful punishment, for two years later, when approached by King James II for a favour, Kiffin painfully, with tears remarked, "the death of my grandsons gave a wound to my heart which is still bleeding, and never will close but in the grave".[116] Surely Hanserd Knollys shared in the deep pain of his close friend.

---

[111] Ivimey, *English Baptists*, vol. 1, p. 420.

[112] Ivimey, *English Baptists*, vol. 1, p. 420. The record is not totally clear on this point. Knollys' autobiography abruptly ends following his entries around 1672, and Kiffin completed it after Knollys' death. Thus, there is no mention of this imprisonment in his work. The earliest historian of the English Baptists, Thomas Crosby, made no reference to it either. It seems that the only two historians who recorded this event were Joseph Ivimey (1811) and James Culross (1895), both of whom tended to romanticise the history. According to Ivimey, Knollys was imprisoned in the spring for six months. Culross, on the other hand, claimed his imprisonment lasted sixteen months, during which time Knollys preached to the prisoners "the things that concern the Kingdom of God" and many "were greatly strengthened and comforted". These passages were quoted by Culross, but he gave no indication as to their source. *Knollys*, p. 100.

[113] White, *English Baptists of the Seventeenth Century*, p. 159.

[114] In 1664, Kiffin had used his wealth & position to save twelve General Baptists who had been sentenced to death. He gained an audience with King Charles II, an impressive achievement in and of itself, and gained grace for every one of them. Haykin, *Kiffin, Knollys, and Keach*, p. 47.

[115] Haykin, *Kiffin, Knollys, and Keach*, p. 48; B.R. White, "William Kiffin – Baptist Pioneer and Citizen of London (1616-1701)", *Baptist History and Heritage*, 2 (July, 1967) : 102.

[116] Ivimey, *English Baptists*, vol. 1, p. 474.

Just when the situation must have appeared quite hopeless for the London dissenters, they received help from a very unlikely source – James II. On 10 March 1686, James issued a general pardon to all subjects who had been imprisoned on religious grounds.[117] He even went so far as to ask Kiffin to be an Alderman of the City of London.[118] In defiance of Parliament, the king announced "that the army raised to fight Monmouth would not be disbanded, and that he had promoted Catholic officers despite the Test Acts".[119] His Declaration of Indulgence on 4 April 1687 was a clear attempt to provide respite for Catholics and to alienate the Anglican Establishment from dissenters.[120] A second Declaration of Indulgence a year later on 27 April 1688 moved England a step closer to Toleration, something for which Knollys and his fellow Particular Baptists had striven for years. Ironically, when the court sought expressions of gratitude from dissenting churches, many Particular Baptist pastors refused. Instead, some raised questions about the king's claim to have the power "to dispense any of his subjects from the effects of the laws of the land" and articulated a hope that eventually the declaration would find parliamentary support.[121]

James' fate would be sealed when Queen Mary gave birth to a son, a Roman Catholic heir, giving all Protestants a powerful reason to unite.[122] The birth of a Catholic heir accomplished much more than the efforts of Shaftesbury and other Whigs in the early 1680s to foment panic and bring about James' exclusion from the Throne, and more than the Rye House plotters or the rebels of the Argyle and Monmouth uprisings had hoped. The birth of this son prompted an aggressive campaign by the radical press in England. It was even rumoured that the baby born to James had been a girl, but that she had been switched at birth with a baby boy:

And now Thou'rt prompted by that cursed Faction, / To cheat us with a Brat of base extraction, / T'exclude thine Heir, our greatest consolation, / That Thou to Rome may'st Sacrifice the Nation.[123]

The birth of a male heir gave new life to the radicals and Whigs, many of whom had maintained contact with William, Prince of Orange for some time, and it encouraged many Tories to shift their allegiance from James to William.[124] James' flight to the Continent was the final stroke and the Glorious

---

[117] White, *English Baptists of the Seventeenth Century*, p. 160.

[118] White, "William Kiffin", p. 102. Most Particular Baptists, Kiffin included, were extremely suspicious and reluctant to "play along" with James' plan.

[119] Coward, *Stuart Age*, pp. 336-37.

[120] Greaves, *Secrets of the Kingdom*, p. 317.

[121] White, *English Baptists of the Seventeenth Century*, pp. 160-61.

[122] Coward, *Stuart Age*, p. 341.

[123] Anonymous, cited in Greaves, *Secrets of the Kingdom*, pp. 318-19.

[124] Greaves, *Secrets of the Kingdom*, pp. 319-29; Coward, *Stuart Age*, pp. 341, 344.

Revolution followed. In February 1689, William III and Mary II were crowned King and Queen of Britain. For Hanserd Knollys, like many of his contemporaries, these days were perceived as a time of eschatological fulfilment.

Conclusion

The years between the Restoration of Charles II and the Glorious Revolution of 1688 were difficult ones for Hanserd Knollys. Suffering through imprisonment, persecution, exile, illness, the loss of loved ones, and financial duress, his eschatological perspective most certainly sharpened. The political circumstances of the day, which accentuated the already smouldering anti-Catholic sentiments of the radical community, contributed to rising eschatological expectations as well. It is no coincidence that in the midst of Knollys' personal trials and tribulations and of the nation's political turmoil, he published primarily works focused on eschatology. Although no stranger to suffering throughout his life, the intensity of his struggles during this period and the circumstances of his times indicated to him that important eschatological events were unfolding around him.

Above all, in times such as these, Knollys believed that one's faith must not waver. Therefore, regardless of the difficulties he faced, Knollys maintained a strong faith. Evidence of this faith could be found in his service to others in his ministry or teaching activities, his assistance to those in London who suffered during the Great Plague and Great Fire, and in his submission to a King and parliament who carried out harsh persecutions against dissenters. His faith provided him with the hope necessary to trust in God's providence and the strength to forgive his persecutors and stand firm in the face of trials and tribulations. Like the children of Israel in Babylon or the early Christians living in the Roman Empire, Knollys and the Particular Baptists drew strength and courage from the Biblical apocalyptic books to withstand their current circumstances and to hold fast for future deliverance.

CHAPTER 6

"The World That Now Is And the World That Is To Come"[1]: Knollys' Use and Interpretation of Apocalyptic Literature

Introduction

Before the restored monarchy of Charles II had reached its first anniversary, a violent insurrection rocked London. What would later be known as Venner's uprising, a militant Fifth Monarchist rebellion, resulted in the arrest and imprisonment of many sectarians including Hanserd Knollys. The list of persecuted nonconformists continued to grow with the establishment of the Conventicles Act of 1664, forbidding the meeting of non-parochial conventicles. Knollys' arrest was related to suspicions that he was a Fifth Monarchist. Chapter 4 explored his relationships with those of the Fifth Monarchist movement which might have made his contemporaries suspect that he was a Fifth Monarchy man himself. However, in terms of thought, one might ask the question as to the similarity between Knollys and the Fifth Monarchists.

Although Fifth Monarchists often differed in religious opinions and affiliations, millenarianism bound the movement together; in contemporary events, they saw signs of the imminent return of Jesus to usher in his millennial kingdom on earth. However, seventeenth-century millenarianism was not exclusive to the Fifth Monarchists, but formed a component of mainstream Puritanism and became more significant in the 1630s and 1640s.[2] Indeed, apocalypticism existed from the earliest days of reformation in England and

---

[1] This was the title of one of Knollys' eschatological treatises.
[2] Tai Liu, *Discord In Zion: The Puritan Divines and the Puritan Revolution, 1640-1660*, (The Hague: Martinus Nijhoff, 1973), xiv; William M. Lamont, *Godly Rule: Politics and Religion, 1603-1660*, (New York: St. Martin's Press, 1969), pp. 24-26; Paul Christianson, *Reformers and Babylon: English apocalyptic visions from the reformation to the eve of the civil war*, (Toronto: University of Toronto Press, 1978), chs. 4-5; Christopher Hill, *Antichrist in Seventeenth-Century England*, rev. ed., (London: Verso, 1990), pp. 77, 85-88.

millenarianism was gaining respectability in the early years of the seventeenth century.³

Richard Bauckham in his work *Tudor Apocalypse*, argued that the period during which the Reformation in England occurred was one of "widespread apocalypticism throughout Western Christendom".⁴ All over Europe, an air of expectancy flourished, as a vivid sense of "historical crisis" loomed. Belief in the pending conflict between the forces of good and evil, of Christ and Antichrist, characterised the period.⁵ England was no different than the continent in this respect, and writers from the two regions often influenced one another.⁶ According to William Lamont, millenarianism "has been too often dismissed as a creed for cranks" and Bryan Ball made a similar observation when he stated that it has been too easy to "associate eschatological expectation with the fanatical fringe".⁷ Such expectations did not seem abnormal during the early Stuart period, as Christianson and Katherine Firth have shown. Visions of millenarian glory played a role in the hopes of all Puritan groups, not merely those of the sects, in the early stages of the revolution.⁸

The apocalyptic idea of the struggle between Christ and Antichrist was well developed during the medieval period. Thus, the "Antichrist legend" had a rich and full medieval tradition upon which the post-Reformation English church built.⁹ In fact, according to Katharine Firth, interest in prophecy and applying apocalyptic texts to contemporary society was as prevalent among Catholics as it was Protestants during the Middle Ages and the Renaissance.¹⁰ It was during this period that an historicist exegetical approach was adopted. It became the accepted view that the book of Revelation was dealing with three distinct eras

---

³ Christianson, *Reformers and Babylon*, chs. 1-3; Hill, *Antichrist*, chs. 1-2; R.G. Clouse, "The Rebirth of Millenarianism", in *Puritans, the Millennium and the Future of Israel: Puritan Eschatology 1600 to 1660*, Peter Toon, ed., (Cambridge: James Clarke, 1970), pp. 42-65.
⁴ Richard Bauckham, *Tudor Apocalypse. Sixteenth century apocalypticism, millenarianism and the English Reformation: from John Bale to John Foxe and Thomas Brightman*, Courtenay Library of Reformation Classics, vol. 8 (Oxford: The Sutton Courtney Press, 1978), p. 11.
⁵ Bauckham, *Tudor Apocalypse*, p. 11.
⁶ Bauckham, *Tudor Apocalypse*, p. 14.
⁷ Lamont, *Godly Rule*, p. 13; Bryan W. Ball, *A Great Expectation: Eschatological Thought in English Protestantism to 1660*, (Leiden: E. J. Brill, 1975), pp. 2-3. Ball went on to clarify this, claiming, "that not all who believed in the second coming were millenarians, and that not all millenarians were Fifth Monarchy Men".
⁸ Ball, *Great Expectation*, pp. 2-3.
⁹ Bauckham, *Tudor Apocalypse*, pp. 17-21; Hill, *Antichrist*, pp. 3-8. Hill made the point that the most consistent identification of Antichrist with the Pope/Papacy occurred among the so-called heretics, like Wyclif and Hus.
¹⁰ Katherine Firth, *The Apocalyptic Tradition in Reformation Britain, 1530-1645*, (Oxford: Oxford University Press, 1979), pp. 1-3.

of time: the Roman empire from the time of Christ through to the rule of Constantine, the Millennium during which Satan would be bound, and the final forty-two months of the world's history when God would judge evil and usher in Christ's second coming.[11] During the English Reformation and the struggles that followed, authors such as John Bale and John Foxe would build on these ideas, but would clearly identify the Pope and Church of Rome as the Antichrist and the suffering of the Marian martyrs with persecution of the saints by the Antichrist.[12]

Bauckham differentiated between the purpose of apocalyptic in the sixteenth and seventeenth centuries. While apocalyptic during the reformation of the sixteenth century was "primarily a theology of persecution and a theology of history" related to the experience of the Marian martyrs, apocalyptic in the seventeenth century was "a theology of revolution and a theology of hope" related to the experience of those Puritans alienated or persecuted by Laud.[13] For nonconformists such as Hanserd Knollys, who wrote later in the seventeenth century, the apocalyptic was a theology of persecution and history as well as of hope and revolution.[14] Paul Christianson has argued that the widely accepted interpretive tradition of John Bale and John Foxe, which

---

[11] Bauckham, *Tudor Apocalypse*, p. 19; Firth, *Apocalyptic Tradition*, p. 3. Though this interpretation would be revised, it would continue to serve as somewhat of a template for other later interpreters.

[12] Firth, *Apocalyptic Tradition*, pp. 38-68; 69-110; Christianson, *Reformers and Babylon*, pp. 13-46; Bauckham, *Tudor Apocalypse*, pp. 21-30. Most Tudor apocalyticists held a medieval interpretation of the Millennium based on Augustinian presuppositions that it was not a future age, but coincided with the Church Age (amillennialism). Francis Lambert had interpreted Revelation 20 as referring to a future age of peace and although Bale relied heavily on Lambert, he did not embrace his millennial views. Bauckham, *Tudor Apocalypse*, pp. 27-28. Peter Lake maintained that although there was broad consensus within the Elizabethan Protestant Church with respect to the identification of the Pope as the Antichrist, there remained subtle differences in that interpretation, which were related to differing "visions of the community of the godly". While the more "formal, conformist" position was chiefly a doctrinal one, the "evangelical Protestant or 'puritan'" position was a more strongly polemical one, for the purity of "the community of the godly" was at stake. Thus, for those embracing the latter position, a "hatred of popery" vindicated them as loyal Protestants. This polarisation would continue to grow into the seventeenth century, contributing to the divisions that would eventually lead to the radicalisation of the Puritan cause. See Peter Lake, "The Significance of the Elizabethan Identification of the Pope as Antichrist", *Journal of Ecclesiastical History*, 31, April 1980 : 161-78; Peter Lake, "William Bradshaw, Antichrist and the Community of the Godly", *Journal of Ecclesiastical History*, 36, October 1985 : 570-89.

[13] Bauckham, *Tudor Apocalypse*, p. 13.

[14] However, as will be argued, for Knollys and the majority of Particular Baptists, the "revolution" aspect is more spiritual and ideological than physical. Though they often disagreed with the political and religious policies of Parliament, the Church, and the King, their dissent did not take the form of armed rebellion.

clearly believed that the Church of Rome was the Antichrist, became the basis for attacks against the Established Church of England by reformers during the rule of Charles I and Archbishop Laud. This "parting of the stream" began during the later Elizabethan period among the earliest separatists, with people like Henry Barrow, a tradition from which the Independents and Baptists themselves arose.[15] In a sense, persecuted people such as Prynne, Bastwick, Burton, and Lilburne, shared in the 'inheritance' of the Marian tradition.[16] Certainly for individuals like Hanserd Knollys, who separated early in the seventeenth century and became nonconformists later, a similar fellowship existed.[17]

In the early seventeenth century, English millenarianism emerged in the writings of men such as Thomas Brightman and Joseph Mede, who would build upon the ideas of Bale and Foxe.[18] Brightman, whose life barely extended into the seventeenth century, was the first Englishman to dismiss the widely accepted Augustinian view of the Millennium as a non-literal spiritual period consisting of the Church age. Though Brightman still did not understand the Millennium as an entirely future period, he did see it as more than a religious reformation, especially during what he perceived as the second Millennium (Rev. 20:5-7), which he understood as following the resurrection of the preached word, leading to mass conversions of both Gentiles and Jews to the true church.[19] This second Millennium would last from 1300, the time of Wyclif, until 2300. Throughout this period the final battle would take place,

---

[15] Christianson, *Reformers and Babylon*, pp. 47-92.

[16] Christianson, *Reformers and Babylon*, pp. 132-78.

[17] See B.R. White, *The English Separatist Tradition: From Marian Martyrs to the Pilgrim Fathers*, (London: Oxford University Press, 1971) and B.R. White, *The English Baptists of the 17th Century*, rev. ed., (London: The Baptist Historical Society, 1997), pp. 95-133.

[18] Alfred Cohen, "The Kingdom of God in Puritan Thought: A Study of the English Puritan Quest for the Fifth Monarchy", (unpublished Ph.D. dissertation, Indiana University, 1961), pp. 51-60; 66-9; Clouse, "Rebirth of Millenarianism", pp. 56-61. The "rebirth" of millenarianism referred to was the re-emergence of the ancient idea, which was prevalent in the early Church, of a future literal Millennium, a concept that had been replaced in the early Middle Ages by Augustine's non-literal spiritual interpretation of the Millennium as being 'the Church age'. Bauckham, *Tudor Apocalypse*, pp. 17-19. Clouse has argued that the German scholar, Johann Alsted, who had been a teacher of John Amos Comenius, also had a significant influence on Mede. Clouse, "Rebirth of Millenarianism", pp.42-56.

[19] Brightman believed that the first Millennium (Rev. 20:3) took place from the time of Constantine until 1300. The second Millennium was to follow the first resurrection, which was not understood as a literal resurrection.

Satan, the Antichrist and the Turks would be conquered[20] and the saints would come to reign, ushering in the second coming of Christ (postmillenialism).[21]

The mild mannered Cambridge scholar, Joseph Mede, an academic of broad interests, introduced the idea of a purely future Millennium following a period of tribulation for the saints.[22] In his scheme, the Papal power of Rome was a continuation of the Antichrist first manifest in imperial Rome. Mede believed that his contemporaries lived in the final days of the cataclysmic events preceding the Millennium. The Saints would soon overthrow Turk and Pope and converted Jews would return to the Holy Land. However, difficulties and tribulation were in store for the saints. They were to await patiently the return of Christ, which would happen at the Battle of Armageddon, at which time Christ would conquer his foes and establish his earthly millennial Kingdom, over which the saints would rule. Although not specific, Mede believed that the Millennium would begin some time between 1625 and 1716.[23] The writings and ideas of Brightman and Mede continued to play a significant role in the persistent spread of millenarianism and apocalypticism in the seventeenth century, as later interpreters took up, developed, and applied their insights.

Hanserd Knollys displayed a considerable fascination for apocalyptic literature. Over half of his treatises dealt with the subject of eschatology,[24]

---

[20] He understood this as being accomplished by the converted Jews, whom he believed would be resettled in the region of Israel, by 1695 or 1696. Christianson, *Reformers and Babylon*, pp. 104-105.

[21] Peter Toon, "The Latter-Day Glory", in *Puritans, the Millennium and the Future of Israel: Puritan Eschatology 1600 to 1660*, Peter Toon, ed., (Cambridge: James Clarke, 1970), pp. 26-31. Obviously, for Brightman, the English Reformation played a crucial role in the decline and destruction of the Antichrist, with Elizabeth (the first blast of the seventh trumpet) initiating the final fall of the Antichrist. England would play a unique role in this as the elect nation. Christianson, *Reformers and Babylon*, pp. 102-104.

[22] Alfred Cohen referred to him as an "Armchair theorist" in "Kingdom of God in Puritan Thought", p. 57. See also Christianson, *Reformers and Babylon*, p. 124.

[23] In terms of details about the Millennium, Mede remained vague, purposefully perhaps. See Brian G. Cooper, "The Academic Re-discovery of Apocalyptic Ideas in the Seventeenth Century: Joseph Mede", *The Baptist Quarterly*, XIX, (1961-62) : 29-34; Christianson, *Reformers and Babylon*, pp. 124-31; Cohen, "Kingdom of God in Puritan Thought", pp. 57-60; Clouse, "Rebirth of Millenarianism", pp. 56-61; Firth, *Apocalyptic Tradition*, pp. 213-29.

[24] Of Knollys' eleven treatises, six concentrated on eschatology: *Apocalyptical Mysteries*, (London: 1667); *The Parable of the Kingdom of Heaven Expounded. Or, An Exposition of the first thirteen Verses of the twenty fifth Chapter of Matthew*, (London: 1674); *Mystical Babylon Unvailed*, (London: 1679); *An Exposition of the Eleventh Chapter of the Revelation*, (London: 1679); *The World That Now Is and the World That Is to Come*, (London: 1681); *An Exposition of the Whole Book of the Revelation Wherein the Visions and Prophecies of Christ are Opened and Expounded*, (London: 1688). Although in the past Knollys has been credited with authorship of the apocalyptic pamphlet *A Glimpse of Zion's Glory*, he was not the author. Pope A. Duncan, *Hanserd*

including some of his longest and most exegetically detailed works. All of these were published from 1667 onwards, well past the supposed peak of the Fifth Monarchy movement and of apocalyptic interest in seventeenth-century England. Eschewing a militant eschatology, these treatises proclaimed hope to those oppressed ones who remained in the true church and promised that God would establish Christ's Kingdom and overthrow the Antichristian Kingdom that currently prevailed in England.

Although Knollys foresaw the imminent overturning of the religious and political order by God, and believed that the Saints would play a role in this event, he also emphasised that the true church and her members were to ready themselves by pursuing a life of righteousness, holiness, and separation from the Antichristian institutions of the day, not by preparing for militant political action.[25] Even at his most radical, Knollys continued to honour the established order, while at the same time waiting for God to bring about judgment and establish his Kingdom.[26]

Despite the rich historiography on apocalypticism and millenarianism in Tudor and early Stuart England, very little research and writing has been done on the topic in the period after 1660.[27] For Hanserd Knollys and fellow Particular Baptist Benjamin Keach, it was not until after this time that they began to publish their eschatological writings. The following study of Knollys' eschatology both builds upon and extends previous research on the topic.

Knollys: Seventeenth-Century Baptist, (Nashville: Broadman Press, 1965), 52-55; Christianson, *Reformers and Babylon*, pp.251-52.

[25] See Knollys, *Parable of the Kingdom of Heaven*.

[26] Knollys, *Apocalyptical Mysteries*, Part II, pp. 19, 28-29.

[27] Robert Clouse has written an article, which traces millenarianism into the eighteenth century. "The Millennium that Survived the Fifth Monarchy Men", in *Regnum, Religio et Ratio: Essays Presented to Robert M. Kingdon*, Vol. VIII of *Sixteenth Century Essays and Studies*, Jerome Friedman, ed, (Kirksville, MO: Sixteenth Century Journal Publishers, 1987), pp. 19-29. Christopher Hill, in fact, argued a decline in millenarianism post-1660 claiming "radical Protestants, disenchanted by the constant postponement of the date of the end, abandoned the physical concept of Antichrist". Hill, *Antichrist*, pp. 158-59; Dennis C. Bustin, "Papacy, Parish Churches, and Prophecy: The Popish Plot and the London Particular Baptists – A Case Study", in the *Canadian Journal of History*, XXXVIII, 3 (Dec. 2003) : 497-98. Mark Bell basically accepts Hill's position, stating "As these dreams turned to memories for the majority of sectaries, there was one last significant manifestation of Baptist eschatology in the seventeenth century." This "godly remnant" was the Seventh-Day Baptists. Thus, Bell failed to realise the importance eschatology held for the Particular Baptists through the remainder of the century, a clear weakness in his work. As well, in light of this, Bell fails to give Knollys adequate treatment, ironic since Knollys is one of the Particular Baptists most prolific publishers in terms of eschatological works. Mark R. Bell, *Apocalypse How? Baptist Movements During the English Revolution*, (Macon, GA: Mercer University Press, 2000), p. 205.

Overview of Knollys' Eschatological Works

A close examination of Knollys' eschatological works reveals both continuity and variety. The variety appeared in themes and style. Some of his works tend to be exegetical, such as *An Exposition of the Eleventh Chapter of the Revelation* and *An Exposition of the Whole Book of the Revelation*. In these exegetical works, Knollys endeavoured a verse-by-verse elucidation and analysis of the Biblical text, in some instances dealing with an entire Biblical book and in others with a selection of verses or a chapter. Other works, such as *The World That Now Is and the World That Is to Come* and *Mystical Babylon Unvailed* took a more thematic and general approach, examining such topics as the second coming of Christ and the identity of the Antichrist. A clear continuity was evident in the apocalyptic vision put forward in these treatises. These works sometimes built upon one another, including the insertion of text from earlier works into later ones.[28] In other instances Knollys restated more fully or paraphrased and summarised something he had published in an earlier work.[29] The overall message appeared to have changed little.

Three observations should be made concerning Knollys' hermeneutical method in these works. First, he often approached the apocalyptic or eschatological passages in Scripture allegorically or metaphorically.[30] Second, he identified certain passages with corresponding stages of sacred or secular history. Third, he often interpreted the Book of Revelation thematically rather than strictly chronologically. Each of these will be examined in turn below.

An allegorical hermeneutic is one which is quite often used when deciphering the meaning to stories, such as the parables of Christ. In an allegorical hermeneutic, each element of the story represents a precise thing. An example of Knollys' use of this hermeneutic came in his exegesis of the parable of the Ten Virgins, an eschatological story told by Christ about his return. According to Knollys, the five foolish Virgins signified "all sorts of Gospel Professors, who having a form of Godliness, want the power thereof". The wise Virgins represented "Worshippers of God" who not only made "a Profession of Christ", but also had a "Possession of Christ dwelling in their hearts".[31] He went on to further allegorise the passage by interpreting the "Lamps" of the Virgins as being "Divine knowledge and spiritual Gifts". In this

---

[28] In his *An Exposition of the Whole Book of the Revelation*, Knollys' exegesis of Revelation 11 is the insertion of his earlier published *An Exposition of the Eleventh Chapter of the Revelation*.

[29] For an example of this, compare Knollys, *An Exposition of the Eleventh Chapter of the Revelation*, pp. 9-39 and Knollys, *Apocalyptical Mysteries*, Part I, pp. 1-35.

[30] This is not to say that he interpreted in only these two ways. On occasion, he employed a literal hermeneutic. For instance, he clearly understood the Millennium as a literal 1000-year period (see more below). Knollys, *An Exposition of the Whole Book of the Revelation*, p. 222.

[31] Knollys, *Parable of the Kingdom of Heaven*, pp. 20-21.

way, both the foolish and wise Virgins had a form of godliness. The "Oyle" was "The Light of the knowledge of Christ and of the Prophecies and of the Mysteries of the Kingdom and Coming" of Christ. Even more specifically, the oil was "Jesus Christ, and the spirit of Christ and the sanctifying knowledge of Christ". Thus, though they had lamps, the outward appearance of religion, "the form of godliness", the foolish Virgins lacked a vital and intimate relationship with Jesus Christ, the "power of godliness".[32]

A metaphorical hermeneutic differs from an allegorical one in that it does not systematically attempt to place a one for one value upon different elements in the text. It merely interprets in a more loosely symbolic manner. This was often seen in Knollys' interpretations of numbers in apocalyptic passages.[33] He saw the number seven, for instance, as signifying "both variety of Instruments, and perfection of the Judgements of God" in the prophecy of the seven Vials.[34] As well, he understood of the power of the Witnesses of Revelation 11 to "smite the Earth with all Plagues" as signifying spiritual judgment as opposed to "material Plagues, and temporal Judgments".[35] Finally, Knollys' metaphorical hermeneutic appeared in his designation of the Whore of Babylon as Rome.[36]

His practice of assigning certain elements or passages to certain stages of Church or world history appeared most clearly in his *Exposition of the Whole Book of Revelation*. He divided the book into sections: the first pertaining to the "present state and condition" of the churches in the New Testament era, the second to things which had yet to happen during the "Roman Pagan State", and the third to things which were to take place under the "Roman Papal State". The last, he believed, extended into his own day. Following these categories, Knollys held that Revelation 1-3 dealt with the New Testament period, that of the Seven Churches of Asia, Revelation 4-6 dealt with the era of the "Roman

---

[32] Knollys, *Parable of the Kingdom of Heaven*, pp. 22-23. Further allegorical interpretations can also be found on pp. 60-61 of the same treatise. Allegorical interpretation is also found in Knollys, *Exposition of the Eleventh Chapter of the Revelation*, pp. 3-4, where the Temple is equated with the true church, and the Altar in the Temple with true worship.

[33] Knollys, *Exposition of the Eleventh Chapter of the Revelation*, pp.12-13; *Apocalyptical Mysteries*, Part I, pp. 8-11. In these pages, Knollys gave his interpretation of the 1260 days of the prophesying of the two Witnesses, which will be dealt with in more detail below.

[34] Knollys, *Apocalyptical Mysteries*, Part II, p. 4; see also Knollys, *An Exposition of the Whole Book of the Revelation*, p. 3.

[35] Knollys, *Apocalyptical Mysteries*, Part I, p. 8. The Earth here, was understood by Knollys not as being the planet, but metaphorically as "the Foundation, Doctrines, and Principles of all false Religions", which he went on to detail as doctrines of the Roman Catholic Church such as Mass, Purgatory, Justification by works, etc. Part II, p. 11.

[36] See Knollys, *Mystical Babylon Unvailed* and Knollys, *Apocalyptical Mysteries*, Part II. More on this below.

Pagan State", and the remainder of the book with the "Roman Papal State", especially the recent past and the present.[37] This framework was a variation on the medieval scheme, which divided history into three different eras.[38]

Knollys did not interpret the book of Revelation in a strictly chronological manner. In other words, he did not always understand that passages or chapters, which preceded or followed one another in the text, necessarily elucidated events, which would precede or follow one another chronologically. A clear example of this can be seen in the *Exposition of the Whole Book of Revelation*, in his commentary on chapters 11 and 12 where he tended to interpret these chapters in a recapitulative sense. In other words, he interpreted the account of the Two Witnesses and that of the Woman in the Wilderness as signifying the same events, not as two different sets of chronologically connected events:

> The time of Christ's Two Witnesses, prophesying in sackcloth, and the time of the Womans being in the Wilderness, is the same, [a thousand two hundred and three score Prophetical days;] each day for a year.... So by the Wilderness here, we may understand the persecuted condition of the Church of God, and his Ministers, under the Roman Papal Powers, the Beast, the Whore, and the false Prophet, unto the day of the Resurrection of the Two Witnesses.[39]

Hanserd Knollys drew two conclusions in his eschatological writings that remained certain and constant: first, that the end was imminent and second, in order to prepare for the end, one had to stand on the side of Christ, as a "true professor". Knollys clearly saw himself as participating in the last Act of human history, and was determined to ally himself on the side of Good and not of Evil.

The first eschatological treatise, *Apocalyptical Mysteries*, was published in London in 1667, during the lull in persecutions between the first and second Conventicles Act, and following the outbreak of the Great plague and fire. All of these circumstances played well for creating an apocalyptic atmosphere. *Apocalyptical Mysteries* focused on three eschatological themes or "mysteries", each accorded its own section and pagination. First, Knollys examined the "mystery" of the two Witnesses of Revelation 11 – who they were, the nature of their task and when they were to appear – as well as the identity of the Beast. The two Witnesses represented God's true ministers and prophets and all the saints of "Congregational Churches of Jesus Christ".[40] The Beast, he identified as "the whole complex Body of the Roman Antichristian Politick &

---

[37] Knollys, *An Exposition of the Whole Book of the Revelation*, pp. 15-16.
[38] Bauckham, *Tudor Apocalypse*, p. 19; Firth, *Apocalyptic Tradition*, p. 3. This will be dealt with below in the discussion of Knollys' interpretation of the Millennium.
[39] Knollys, *An Exposition of the Whole Book of the Revelation*, p. 162.
[40] Knollys, *Apocalyptical Mysteries*, Part I, pp. 1-5.

Ecclesiastick State and Government".[41] The Apostle John had described the Beast as a two-fold creature, which Knollys saw as meaning the "Roman-Antichristian-Politick-and-Ecclesiastick-State and Government exercised coercively over mens Consciences in any Place or Case whatsoever". This definition combined pagan Rome with Papal Rome.[42]

The seven vials of wrath mentioned in Revelation 16 constituted the second "mystery". These vials contained the judgment of God's wrath against not only the Beast, but also against "every one that worshippeth the Beast and his Image, and receiveth his Mark".[43] This judgment would be administered by the Saints, the true Worshippers of God, just as the prophets of the Old Testament proclaimed God's judgment in that dispensation.[44] These vials represented "the Cup of God's Indignation, and the Cup of the Wine of the fiercenesse of his wrath" and would bring about the "utter destruction" of the Beast.[45] The third "mystery" Knollys examined in this work was how the Kingdoms of this world had become the Kingdom of Antichrist and how the Kingdom of Antichrist would fall to the Kingdom of Christ. A significant focus of this work was on the spiritual nature of the Kingdom of Christ and its conquest.[46]

With renewed persecution in 1670 and the overwhelming personal tragedy suffered by Knollys in 1671 and 1672, belief in the immanency of the latter days may have seemed even more pressing. When circumstances seemed to settle down in 1674, Knollys once again picked up his pen. For those who had just come through a period of persecution, and for Knollys personally, having just experienced a time of intense trial, the focus of this particular work was very appropriate. *The Parable of the Kingdom of Heaven Expounded*, at 135 pages, was one of Knollys' longest works. It contained a verse-by-verse exegesis of the first thirteen verses of Matthew 25, the parable of the ten virgins awaiting the coming of the bridegroom. While this passage certainly dealt with an eschatological theme – the second coming of Christ – it clearly addressed a present concern as well – the readiness of the believer. Like the Donatists of the fourth century, Knollys and many other dissenters were concerned about the purity of faith and commitment to Christ in the face of persecution and difficulty.[47] *The Parable of the Kingdom of Heaven Expounded* dealt with the theme of the true versus the false professors of Christianity.

---

[41] Knollys, *Apocalyptical Mysteries*, Part I, p.13.
[42] Knollys, *Apocalyptical Mysteries*, Part I, pp. 13-16. This will be discussed in further detail below.
[43] Knollys, *Apocalyptical Mysteries*, Part II, p. 1.
[44] Knollys, *Apocalyptical Mysteries*, Part II, pp. 6-10.
[45] Knollys, *Apocalyptical Mysteries*, Part II, p. 19.
[46] Knollys, *Apocalyptical Mysteries*, Part III, pp. 9-18.
[47] Henry Chadwick, *The Early Church*, (Markham, ON: Penguin Books, 1967), pp. 123-24; William H.C. Frend, *The Rise of Christianity*, (Philadelphia: Fortress Press, 1984), pp. 488-92.

The first sentence of the preface went right to this point: "Art thou a Professour? I intreat thee do not rest in the form of Godliness without the power thereof; that undid the foolish Virgins to Eternity. It's a vain thing for any person to seem to be Religious, and be not so in truth."[48] Further on, he asked another question: "Art thou a Believer? Ponder then what is propounded in this little Treatise, and search the Scriptures, whether what is therein affirmed be so or not."[49] In this work, Knollys sought to deal with two issues: hypocrisy and assurance, both in the context of preparation for Christ's return.

Knollys warned his readers directly, and English society indirectly, of the danger of being a false professor.[50] Interpreting the parable from a presentist perspective, he cautioned the readers that just prior to Christ's return, there would be a great Tribulation, and many would fall away or experience a cooling of their faith.[51] Knollys believed that this was happening in his own day and that this particular parable spoke directly to the situation. The ten virgins represented the contemporary visible Church. Many "professors" in various churches, like the five foolish virgins, did not have the oil of God's spirit within them and, therefore, were unprepared for the coming of the Bridegroom.[52] The presence of God's Spirit infused all true believers, making them "willing to sell all, lose all, and forsake all".[53] The wise virgins represented the "true visible Constituted Church of Christ under the Gospel... a Congregation of Saints... Called out of the World... Separated from Idolaters and Idol Temples".[54] The grave danger for the false professors, who may seem like believers and hold communion and fellowship with believers, was that

> when Christ comes, yea when death comes, and they are awakened by that midnight dispensation, then they see themselves lost and undone to Eternity, then they know not what to do, nor how to dye without Christ and without Grace.[55]

Much of the treatise was dedicated to expounding upon marks of false professors and true professors, explaining signs of Christ's return, and encouraging true professors to stand firm in the face of persecution and trial.

The threat of Catholicism resurfaced in the late 1670s, as did a strong anti-Catholic backlash. For a brief season, it seemed, the radicals from the 1640s re-

---

[48] Knollys, *Parable of the Kingdom of Heaven*, "To The Reader", p. 1.
[49] Knollys, *Parable of the Kingdom of Heaven*, "To The Reader", p. 1.
[50] Knollys, *Parable of the Kingdom of Heaven*, pp. 8, 11, 25-28, 33-41, 54-55.
[51] Knollys, *Parable of the Kingdom of Heaven*, pp. 2-3; 53-55. See more on this below.
[52] Knollys, *Parable of the Kingdom of Heaven*, pp. 12-18.
[53] Knollys, *Parable of the Kingdom of Heaven*, p. 18.
[54] Knollys, *Parable of the Kingdom of Heaven*, p. 5.
[55] Knollys, *Parable of the Kingdom of Heaven*, p. 100.

emerged to revive the godly reformation.⁵⁶ The revelation of the "Popish Plot" fanned the flames of radicalism and provided a new platform from which to stir up support. Therefore, it should not be startling that the treatises published by Knollys in 1679 drew upon and contributed to this radical spirit. *Mystical Babylon Unvailed* and the appended *Call to the People of God to Come Out of Babylon* very aggressively attacked Roman Catholicism. Knollys, normally a conciliatory and gracious writer, was uncharacteristically harsh in these particular works. In the "Epistle to the Reader" of *Mystical Babylon Unvailed*, Knollys made clear that he was responding to the "Popish Plot". He made no effort to conceal his revulsion:

> It is an Astonishment... that the Papists (especially the Priests and Jesuits of the Church of Rome) so odious in their bloody Tenents so Prodigious in their Hellish Plots... should be suffered to increase, and indulged to Multiply in a Protestant Nation as of late years they have done in this Kingdom.⁵⁷

He went on to explain that it had only happened in England because God "in his just Indignation" allowed it as punishment for its "Sins of Atheism, Idolatry, Profaneness, Adultery, and other heinous wickedness" and that the continued presence of Catholics and of their plotting was a source of grave danger to national security.⁵⁸ Knollys then proceeded to argue against Rome by making four main points: That Rome Papal was the Mystical Babylon mentioned in the Revelation of John;⁵⁹ that the Pope of Rome represented the Beast of the latter days;⁶⁰ that the Church of Rome was the great Whore of Revelation;⁶¹ that the Roman Catholic priests were the false Prophet of Revelation.⁶² Throughout the treatise Knollys made use of numerous Scripture references and citations from a variety of classical, medieval, and contemporary authors along with examples from Church history.⁶³

In building his arguments against Rome and the Papacy, Knollys claimed that a major reason for the Pope's illegitimacy was that he had usurped his

---

[56] Richard L. Greaves, *Secrets of the Kingdom: British Radicals from the Popish Plot to the Revolution of 1688-1689*, (Stanford, CA: Stanford University Press, 1992), pp. 6-7, 50-51; John Miller, *Popery and Politics in England, 1660-1688*, (Cambridge: At the University Press, 1973), 148-53.
[57] Knollys, *Mystical Babylon Unvailed*, "An Epistle to the Reader", p. 1. See also Bustin, "Papacy, Parish Churches, and Prophecy", 493-504.
[58] Knollys, *Mystical Babylon Unvailed*, "An Epistle to the Reader", pp. 1-2.
[59] Knollys, *Mystical Babylon Unvailed*, "An Epistle to the Reader", pp. 1-4.
[60] Knollys, *Mystical Babylon Unvailed*, pp. 5-13.
[61] Knollys, *Mystical Babylon Unvailed*, pp. 13-21
[62] Knollys, *Mystical Babylon Unvailed*, pp. 22-25.
[63] He cited authors such as Virgil, Ovid, Aquinas, Celsus and Bellarmine.

authority.[64] The Whoredom of the Roman Church was linked to its idolatry and "barbarous and bloody Persecutions" of God's people, the Protestants.[65] Taking his accusations a step further and without mincing any words, Knollys claimed that this Whore of Babylon "hath begotten, born, and nourished all those National and Parochial Churches,... which National Churches are harlots".[66] Giving France, Italy, Spain, and Germany as examples of National Churches, Knollys stopped just short of naming the Church of England as a harlot, though such was implied since it was itself a national and parochial church.[67] Following his exposition on the Roman Church as the Whore of Babylon, Knollys called upon his readers to separate from this false and idolatrous church. Failure to do so was to risk God's disfavour and judgment.[68] To the kings of Europe, and to the King and Parliament of Britain in particular, Knollys issued an additional call to abandon the Whore and "make her Desolate".[69]

In Knollys' second major work of 1679, *An Exposition of the Eleventh Chapter of the Revelation*, he returned his attention once more to the identity and role of the two Witnesses. In his exegesis of this chapter, Knollys' treatment of the subject was much more detailed than his treatment of the same subject in *Apocalyptical Mysteries*. Not only did he level a scathing criticism against the false church, Rome, but he also clearly understood that the two witnesses represented the true church.[70] Knollys believed that the very events prophesied in this chapter of the Bible were approaching fulfilment. Based on several Ecclesiastical histories, including the *Magdeburg Centuries* and those written by Socrates, Helvicus, and Sympson, he reckoned that the period of the testimony and martyrdom of the two witnesses was to end in 1688.[71] Taking his contemporary application of the passage a step further, Knollys stated that he believed the fulfilment of the events in Revelation 11 would happen in London, a city not unlike Jerusalem of the first century "where our Lord was Crucified, and wherein his two prophets must be killed".[72] Knollys did not understand the killing of the witnesses as signifying primarily literal, physical death. Rather his

---

[64] Knollys, *Mystical Babylon Unvailed*, p. 8.
[65] Knollys, *Mystical Babylon Unvailed*, pp. 16, 20-21.
[66] Knollys, *Mystical Babylon Unvailed*, p. 17.
[67] Knollys, *Mystical Babylon Unvailed*, pp. 17, 20.
[68] Knollys, *Mystical Babylon Unvailed*, pp. 25-29.
[69] Knollys, *Mystical Babylon Unvailed*, pp. 30-31.
[70] Knollys, *Exposition of the Eleventh Chapter of the Revelation*, pp. 4-8.
[71] Knollys, *Exposition of the Eleventh Chapter of the Revelation*, pp. 13, 29. This is quite fascinating, considering the events which would occur in 1688 and the fact that this was written a decade prior. Certainly, this understanding of eschatology must have impacted Knollys even more during the last years of his life as the Glorious Revolution took place.
[72] Knollys, *Exposition of the Eleventh Chapter of the Revelation*, p. 25.

was a broader interpretation and involved the persecution of the true church and its members. However, this persecution did include the saints being

> deprived of all their Civil Rights, Priviledges, and Liberties: their Estates will be Confiscated, Proscribed, or Decimated, etc. Their Persons confined, imprisoned, or banished etc. and in fine, all their Livings and Livelihood taken from them by the Beast, and his Instruments of Cruelty.[73]

Certainly Knollys' own experiences – numerous imprisonments, having his house and property unlawfully taken from him, being forced into exile – these contributed to his interpretation of the passage. As well, in his application of this passage to the situation in England he pointed to a connection between the Established Church and the church of Papal-Rome. Following the period of the two Witnesses, Babylon would fall, ushering in the Kingdom of Christ and the rule of the saints.[74]

Knollys published his longest and most comprehensive eschatological works in the 1680s. *The World that Now is and the World that is to Come* was published in the summer of 1681 at the height of the Exclusion Crisis and the Tory backlash.[75] It took a more tempered approach than the two treatises published in the previous year and tended to be more didactical than polemical in nature. Divided into two separate but related books, it dealt with "the First and Second Coming of Jesus Christ". The first book contained elements of Knollys' soteriology and ecclesiology, while the second book detailed his eschatology.

In the first section, Knollys examined issues relating to the work of Christ in the provision of salvation. The soteriology expressed here, typically Puritan, emphasised the significant tenets of Calvinist theology such as election, limited atonement, total depravity, and irresistible grace. He also gave significant attention to issues related to worship and ecclesiology.[76] In spite of this emphasis in the first section, it also related to eschatology. Only those who responded properly to Christ's first coming would count as his true followers at his second coming, for those who were not "true Converts", who were "stony-hearted Hearers", would fall away during "the time of the Tryal of their Faith".[77] Knollys emphasised the importance of separating from the false Church and joining with the true Church, though not as forcefully as he had in

---

[73] Knollys, *Exposition of the Eleventh Chapter of the Revelation*, pp. 22-23.
[74] Knollys, *Exposition of the Eleventh Chapter of the Revelation*, pp. 38-46. Knollys' understanding of the Kingdom of Christ and the rule of his saints will be addressed below in the next section.
[75] At this point, Knollys' congregation was meeting at Bartholomew Lane. Knollys, *The World that Now Is*, "To the Reader", p. v.
[76] See below, Chapter 7.
[77] Knollys, *The World that Now Is*, Book I, p. 23.

his two treatises published in 1679.[78] The final two chapters of the first section dealt specifically with eschatology. In Chapter IV, Knollys examined the second coming of Christ and the signs that would precede it,[79] placing a major emphasis on the apostasy of believers who would fall away from the faith in the latter days.[80] Chapter V reiterated the importance of separating from "Idolaters" and "Unbelievers", just as Noah had done when he was building the Ark, "for the Ending Time of this world draws near".[81]

The second section, *The World to Come*, focused strictly on eschatology, expounding upon Knollys' eschatological position and understanding of Scripture. It examined such topics as the recreation, the return of Christ and its signs, the apostasy of some of the saints, the Antichrist, the millennial rule of Christ and his saints, and the final judgment and resurrection.[82] Finally, Knollys proceeded to present the application of his theological position, calling upon his readers to repent and abandon false religion and a profane lifestyle.[83] At the heart of this call was a strong evangelistic appeal.[84] Knollys gave special instructions to the Kings and governments of Earth, entreating vigilance lest they "set themselves" against Christ's kingdom or "counsel together against the LORD, and against his Anointed".[85] He concluded with a special word to the "Magistrates and inhabitants" of London, warning that God had already judged them with plague (the Great Plague of 1665) and fire (the Great Fire of 1666) and would soon visit "a Famine of Bread" upon them and a "Famine of the Word" if the Papists should prevail.[86]

On 12 September 1688, three months following the birth of a Catholic heir to James II and two months before James II fled London intending to go to France, Hanserd Knollys published his final eschatological work.[87] At 244 pages, this would be Knollys' most voluminous work. It was both his *magnum opus*, the culmination of years of study and experience and the summation and combination of several earlier works. While some sections recapitulated themes

---

[78] Knollys, *The World that Now Is*, Book I, pp. 44-47.
[79] Knollys, *The World that Now Is*, Book I, pp. 81-95.
[80] Knollys, *The World that Now Is*, Book I, pp. 86-91.
[81] Knollys, *The World that Now Is*, Book I, pp. 95-104.
[82] Knollys, *The World that Now Is*, Book II, pp. 1-30. These themes will be examined in detail below in the next section.
[83] Knollys, *The World that Now Is*, Book II, pp. 31-48.
[84] Knollys, *The World that Now Is*, Book II, pp.33-37.
[85] Knollys, *The World that Now Is*, Book II, pp. 45-48.
[86] Knollys, *The World that Now Is*, Book II, p. 48.
[87] Barry Coward, *The Stuart Age*, 2nd ed., (New York: Longman, 1994), pp. 341, 344; Knollys, *An Exposition of the Whole Book of the Revelation*, Frontspiece. Christopher Hill in a rather cursory passing comment stated that in this work, Hanserd Knollys "applied the prophecies of the Apocalypse to William's invasion". However, that could not actually be the case since the book was written and published prior to William's invasion of England. *Antichrist*, p. 151.

or directly quoted from earlier publications,[88] a large part of this book was original. The only commentary on an entire Biblical book by Knollys, it underscored his interest eschatology. Knollys claimed to have written this commentary for two reasons: First, "I dare not hide my Talent, knowing that my Lord and Master will shortly call me to give an account of my Stewardship."[89] Second, he wrote his exposition "for the benefit of them that shall read it, that they also may be partakers of that blessing" promised in Revelation 1:3.[90]

Knollys interpreted the prophecies of Revelation in three ways: those passages that had been fulfilled, those that were being fulfilled in his own day, and those that were yet to be fulfilled.[91] He wanted his readers to understand better which passages should be interpreted in which way. This resulted in a verse-by-verse commentary on the Revelation of John, giving an exegesis of the Biblical text using other passages of Scripture as well as extra-biblical sources, especially theologians and Church Fathers. Knollys' exposition dealt meticulously with each verse and covered every major theological theme related to eschatology. Periodically, Knollys applied the text to contemporary circumstances and, as in his other eschatological writings, paid particular attention to the Roman Catholic Church, the Papacy, the Jews and the Turks.[92] Knollys clearly believed that his last days were indeed the last days of the history of the world, that the return of Jesus was imminent. Indeed, this commentary represented much more than an academic or theological exercise. The words on these pages contained an air of urgency. Certainly, as the events continued to unfold in England through the remainder of 1688 and into the early years of 1689, Knollys must have continued to interpret the circumstances about him in increasingly apocalyptic ways.

Themes in Knollys' Eschatological Works

Apart from his *Exposition of the Whole Book of Revelation*, Knollys nowhere presented an exhaustive or systematic overview of his eschatology. Even in the above-mentioned work, his presentation was only systematic in its exegesis of the text. In attempting to understand Knollys' eschatology and his application of the apocalyptic texts of the Bible, one must examine various central

---

[88] His commentary in this treatise on Revelation 11, for instance, is a verbatim reproduction of his *An Exposition of the Eleventh Chapter of the Revelation*, pp. 9-39

[89] Knollys, *An Exposition of the Whole Book of the Revelation*, "An Epistle to the Reader", p. 2, quoting from Matthew 25, Christ's parable of the talents.

[90] Knollys, *An Exposition of the Whole Book of the Revelation*, "An Epistle to the Reader", p. 2.

[91] Knollys, *An Exposition of the Whole Book of the Revelation*, "An Epistle to the Reader", p. 2.

[92] Knollys, *An Exposition of the Whole Book of the Revelation*, pp. 194, 196-99; see also Knollys, *Apocalyptical Mysteries*, Part II, pp. 22-29.

eschatological themes throughout his works. However, Knollys was not always clear about his position on some themes and sometimes seemed self-contradictory. Perhaps his thought was in transition or had changed between the publication of one treatise and another. However, in other cases, Knollys treated themes in great depth and detail, leaving the reader with a clear sense of his position.

Antichrist

> And I saw a Beast coming out of the sea. He had ten horns and seven heads, with ten crowns on his horns, and on each head a blasphemous name. The Beast I saw resembled a leopard, but had feet like those of a bear and a mouth like that of a lion. The Dragon gave the Beast his power and his throne and great authority. (Revelation 13:1-2)

Perhaps no other theological idea has caused as much speculation throughout the history of Christianity as has the theme of the Antichrist or the Beast. Though it was a concept of relative obscurity in the period of the Old Testament, during the Intertestamental and New Testament eras, it became a central eschatological doctrine. The heightened emphasis on cosmic dualism in the apocalyptic tradition and perhaps on the personification of God in the person of Jesus Christ contributed to this new understanding of the personification of evil in the Latter days. In the Biblical book of the Revelation of John, the Antichrist or the Beast played a central role in the cosmic clash between the Son of Man and his followers and Satan and his followers. Throughout Christian history, attempts have been made at discovering the identity of this cosmic villain. The seventeenth century was no exception. In fact, the subject was of extreme importance to sixteenth and seventeenth century intellectuals.[93] This obsession with the Beast resulted in a multiplicity of interpretations, ranging from the Roman Pope to Archbishop Laud to Oliver Cromwell. For some, the personification took on a plural meaning and was applied to the persons of the antichristian bishops. And still others, such as William Erbury or the Quakers, interpreted the Antichrist as an internal spirit of evil.[94]

---

[93] Hill, *Antichrist*, pp. 1-2, 29-31. Speculation about the person of the Beast was not only the fare of crackpots but intellectuals such as Francis Bacon, John Milton, Isaac Newton, Henry Vane, William Waller, John Dury, and Samuel Hartlib were equally as concerned and intrigued with his identity.

[94] Hill, *Antichrist*, chs. 2-3. The Biblical portrayal of the Antichrist is itself varied. The actual word only appears four times in Scripture, all within the Johannine letters. These occurrences refer to both an individual Antichrist, to a plurality of antichrists, and to a general "spirit of antichrist". In Matthew 24 and Mark 13, Jesus spoke of false prophets and "false Christs" coming in the last days. In the Pauline letters, 2 Thessalonians 2

During the sixteenth century in England, Protestants came to equate the Antichrist with the Papacy. The English Reformation in the early part of the century and the experiences of the Marian martyrs later created an environment in England that was highly antagonistic toward the Roman Church. However, even John Bale did not limit his interpretation of Antichrist to the Pope alone, though he concentrated the Antichrist into two institutions primarily – the Church of Rome, headed by the Pope and the Turks, headed by Mohammed.[95] In the writings of Thomas Brightman and Joseph Mede at the end of the sixteenth century and beginning of the seventeenth century, respectively, the person of the Antichrist was exclusively designated as being the Papacy.[96] Through the early years of the seventeenth century, this gradually shifted so that by 1640, the Established Church and its leader, Archbishop Laud, who were perceived as moving the Church of England back toward Rome, were equated with the Antichrist.[97] Even with this shift, there was an obvious link to the Papacy.

Hanserd Knollys and the Particular Baptists, like many of their contemporaries, were very concerned regarding the identity of the Beast. The Baptist ecclesiology, which placed great emphasis on the believing church, certainly intersected well with an eschatology that stressed such apocalyptic dualism. Although Knollys touched on the theme of Antichrist in each of his eschatological treatises, in certain ones, he treated the subject in greater detail.[98] In these treatises, Knollys' intent was not merely to identify the Antichrist, but also to give very clear evidence of his kingdom and followers and his downfall and destruction.

In *Mystical Babylon Unvailed* in particular, Knollys went to great lengths to identify the Beast and Babylon with the Pope and the Church of Rome. In this work, Knollys used the Hebrew and Greek Scriptures, as well as the works of numerous others, Protestant and Catholic alike, to build his argument. He compared the ancient city of Babylon to the city of Rome, concluding that "Mysterie Babylon" in Revelation 17 represented "Rome Pagan and Papal" and "that the Pope of Rome is the Beast".[99] The similarities between ancient Babylon and Rome (both the Roman empire and the Roman Catholic Church) were found in five main areas: Idolatry, persecution, violence, oppression, and

---

details the coming of "the Man of Lawlessness" and the theme of the individual Antichrist is given its fullest treatment in the Beast of the Revelation 13ff.

[95] Christianson, *Reformers and Babylon*, pp. 9-21; Bauckham, *Tudor Apocalypse*, pp. 94-99.

[96] Toon, "The Latter-Day Glory", p. 28; Clouse, "Rebirth of Millenarianism", p. 59.

[97] Obviously, in this context, the Roman Catholic Church still had a role in the interpretation of Antichrist. See Christianson, *Reformers and Babylon*, ch. 4.

[98] Those treatises, which offer a very detailed interpretation of the Beast, include *Exposition of the Whole Book of Revelation*, *Mystical Babylon Unvailed*, and *Apocalyptical Mysteries*.

[99] Knollys, *Mystical Babylon Unvailed*, pp. 2-3.

pride.[100] It was in the charge of idolatry and adultery that Knollys made his second attack against the Roman Church. By falling away into false doctrine and idolatry, the Roman Church became a False church. In essence, argued Knollys, the Church of Rome committed "the spiritual Adultery, whoredom, and fornication of Judah and Jerusalem (Ezek. 4:11, 37)". In this, the Roman Church was revealed as the Whore of Babylon (Rev. 17).[101] The evidence of this idolatry came in the Church's emphasis on prayer to the saints, images, crucifixes, and relics, but it was seen especially in the mass:

> The Church of Rome is guilty of gross Idolatry and spiritual Adultery in Adoring and worshipping the Host, for at the Priest's Elevation of the Host (the Papists breaden God) they all fall down upon their Knees, and worship it with very great Devotion.[102]

However, for Knollys, "Mystery Babylon" included not only Rome, "the Mother of Harlots", but her daughters as well, "all National Churches", specifically "the National Churches of the Papists, of the Lord Bishops, and of the Presbyterians".[103] Although Knollys had made a similar interpretation earlier in 1679 in *Mystical Babylon Unvailed*, the forceful and straightforward nature of his comments in this work on the eve of the Glorious Revolution gave an indication of his heightened expectations:

> BABYLON THE GREAT, that is, the great Whore, the Roman Papal Church, and THE MOTHER OF HARLOTS. All National Churches, Parish Churches, Cathedral Churches, Provincial Churches, etc. who own, acknowledge, and subject themselves to the Ecclesiastical headship of the Roman Hierarchy, Pope, and Papal Prelacy, Episcopacy, or Presbytery.[104]

Knollys not only argued that the Pope was the Antichrist, and that the Roman Church was the False church and the Whore of Babylon, but also that the priests of the Roman Catholic Church, "the Cardinals, the Jesuits, and all those Priests that do receive Orders of Priesthood from the Church of Rome", collectively represented the False Prophet, who taught false doctrines reaffirmed by the Council of Trent. There were three doctrines in particular, which Knollys believed to be "pernicious": Papal supremacy over secular rulers, justification by works, and the false worship of God.[105]

The Antichrist, according to Knollys, had past, present, and future states in the apocalyptic visions of the seven-headed Beast of Daniel 7 and Revelation

---

[100] Knollys, *Mystical Babylon Unvailed*, p. 2.
[101] Knollys, *Mystical Babylon Unvailed*, p. 14.
[102] Knollys, *Mystical Babylon Unvailed*, pp. 15-17.
[103] Knollys, *An Exposition of the Whole Book of the Revelation*, p. 200.
[104] Knollys, *An Exposition of the Whole Book of the Revelation*, p. 203.
[105] Knollys, *Mystical Babylon Unvailed*, pp. 22-24.

17. In his past state, the Beast who "was and is not" (Rev. 17:8) represented the Roman Empire and its rulers (the first six heads) who persecuted Christ and the Church. In his present state, the Beast, who "yet is" (Rev. 17:8) was symbolised by the seventh head, the Papacy, particularly in its attempts to usurp secular power from governments. The final state, also symbolised by the seventh head, was the Beast who "is not yet come" (Rev. 17:10), the Papacy with "Supreme Power ... Political and Ecclesiastical" over the magistrates and kings of the Earth.[106] The Beast, with its seven heads then, represented "the whole complex Body of the Roman Antichristian Politick & Ecclesiastick State and Government".[107] This union of political and ecclesiastical power in the Beast encompassed both "the Roman-Antichristian-Pollitick-and-Ecclesiastick-Power, Dominion, and Government" and "the Antichristian-POWERS, Potentates, Kings, and Governours who exercise that Antichristian-power and dominion coercively over the Bodies, Estates, and Consciences of men".[108] Both church and state institutions and officials shared the guilt in allowing themselves to become the tools of the Beast.

Knollys was hardly unique in linking the Antichrist with Rome, or even his inclusion of National churches in the guilt of the Beast, for many of his contemporaries held to similar positions.[109] His understanding of the future state of the Antichrist had more originality. The Antichrist would receive his power from the secular rulers of the Earth, represented by the ten horns of the Beast,

---

[106] Knollys, *Mystical Babylon Unvailed*, pp. 6-11; Knollys, *An Exposition of the Whole Book of the Revelation*, pp. 200-207.

[107] Knollys, *Apocalyptical Mysteries*, Part I, p. 13. Knollys realised that the Beast was also described in association with the false Prophet (Rev. 19:20) and the Woman (Rev. 17:3), this showing/emphasising more clearly the "two-fold Power mixed and exercised together".

[108] Knollys, *Apocalyptical Mysteries*, Part I, p. 17.

[109] It should be noted that Christopher Hill's assessment of the interpretation of Antichrist was that Antichrist was less personified following the Restoration and that the debacle of the Popish Plot sounded the death knell for such interpretations. However, there continued to be many publications following 1660, the authors of which, like Knollys, clearly held to a personified interpretation of Antichrist. For some examples, see Thomas Manton, *XVIII sermons on the second chapter of the 2d Epistle to the Thessalonians containing the description, rise, growth, and fall of Antichrist : with divers cautions and arguments to establish Christians against the apostacy of the Church of Rome : very necessary for these times*, (London: 1679); William Ramsay, *Mirmah, Maroumah, Maroum: a discourse consisting of three sermons : a New-years gift of love to the Protestant Church...*, (London: 1680); Thomas Tenison, *A friendly debate between a Roman Catholick and a Protestant concerning the doctrine of transubstantiation wherein the said doctrine is utterly confuted, and Antichrist is clearly and fully described, and his inevitable destruction predicted...* (London: 1688); Benjamin Keach, *Antichrist stormed, or, Mystery Babylon the great whore, and great city, proved to be the present Church of Rome*, (London: 1689). See Bustin, "Papacy, Parish Churches, and Prophecy", 493-504.

and together they would wage war against Christ and his elect, the Saints. Eventually, however, "Christ and his Army" would overcome and destroy the Beast and his allies.[110] Knollys gave further attention to this future state of the Antichrist in his exegesis concerning the two Witnesses of Revelation 11 and concerning the seven vials of Revelation 16.

In his interpretation of the two Witnesses, Knollys dealt with the period during which the Beast, in his future power, would wage war against the Church. Knollys focused on identifying the Witnesses, their activities, and the time of their activities. The two Witnesses, according to Revelation 11, would prophesy for 1260 days, after which, the Beast would rise up, make war on them, and kill them. Three and a half days later, the Witnesses would be resurrected, thus ushering in the end of the Kingdom of the world, which was to be overtaken by the Kingdom of Christ (Rev. 11:3-15). Knollys interpreted the two Witnesses metaphorically, not as "any two individual persons", but rather as "the Lords Ministers and Prophets, who are called Sons of Oyl,... all the Saints who are a Royal Priesthood".[111] He believed, then, that the two Witnesses were the "Ministers of Christ in the Churches of the Saints... who ought to bear their Testimony for Christ and against Anti-christ, both Pagan and Papal".[112] They would bear testimony not merely against the Beast, but against all the Kings of the Earth who had received their power from the Beast.[113]

In contrast, the Witnesses did not wield an earthly, magisterial power, but rather a spiritual one – the power of the Word and of the gifts of prophecy given by Christ, "the Power of the Word, not the Power of the Sword".[114] The Witnesses would bear spiritual judgment against the Beast and Kings, and this would result in their oppression and persecution.[115] The Beast would overcome them with "fear", "flattery", "alurements", and "threats and confinements" temporarily silencing the Witnesses.[116] While the Witnesses would experience steady persecution from the beginning of their testimony, toward the end, that persecution would become more open until the Beast finally killed the Witnesses. Knollys did not interpret this death as necessarily a literal death, but rather the death of their civil and religious liberties, confiscation of Estates, imprisonment, or banishment, but for some it could mean literal death.[117]

In his handling of this passage, Knollys clearly saw a very contemporary significance to it. On the title page of *Apocalyptical Mysteries*, Knollys stated

---

[110] Knollys, *An Exposition of the Whole Book of the Revelation*, pp. 207-209.
[111] Knollys, *Apocalyptical Mysteries*, Part I, pp. 2-3.
[112] Knollys, *Exposition of the Eleventh Chapter of the Revelation*, p. 10.
[113] Knollys, *Apocalyptical Mysteries*, Part I, pp. 4-5.
[114] Knollys, *Exposition of the Eleventh Chapter of the Revelation*, pp. 11-12; Knollys, *Apocalyptical Mysteries*, Part I, p. 7.
[115] Knollys, *Apocalyptical Mysteries*, Part I, p. 8.
[116] Knollys, *Apocalyptical Mysteries*, Part I, pp. 18-19.
[117] Knollys, *Apocalyptical Mysteries*, Part I, p. 20.

that the book "contained some things necessary for the Saints in this present Generation to know. And therein is also shewed, what the Israel of God ought to do in this Day." A bit further on he claimed that the testimony of the Witnesses "is properly the Truth of this present Age and Generation... to be preached in all the World for a Witness... and then the END of the WORLD will come".[118] In deciphering the 1260 days mentioned in chapter 11 of Revelation, Knollys understood them as "Prophetical Daies", each representing a year. Following the lead of other commentators, Knollys believed that this 1260-year period began around 428 and postulated that it would therefore come to an end "about 1688... or sooner".[119] The persecution of the Two Witnesses had begun during the Roman-Pagan era and continued through "the time of Charles the fifth, in Germany, France, Scotland, &c. and in Queen Maries dayes in England, &c".[120] The earlier persecutions had also included the attacks of Rome against the Waldensians, the Hussites, and the Lollards.[121] Later ones included the massacres of Protestants by Irish Catholics, the attempt by the Spanish Armada against England in 1588, the Gunpowder Plot of 1605, and "that damnable, and Hellish-Plot", the Popish Plot.[122] Yet the final fury of the Beast was about to break forth in the final days of the 1260 days of the prophecy. At this point, the testimony of the Witnesses would become "more manifest" and would "make a more open and Visible Opposition" against the Beast. In response, the Antichrist would begin "to rage" and make "a greater and more cruel Opposition" against the godly.[123] In this light, Knollys gave a very apocalyptic interpretation to such contemporary events as the Popish Plot: "And at this very Time the Papists... have a Hellish Plot and a bloody Design to destroy the Protestants, and the Protestant Religion in England, and to Reestablish Popery, and Reinforce that bloody Religion by Fire and Sword."[124] The increased opposition would lead to the death of the Witnesses, a metaphorical death whereby the saints were deprived of property and civil liberties, and a spiritual death, depriving the saints of "that Zeal, Vigor, and

---

[118] Knollys, *Apocalyptical Mysteries*, frontspiece, Part I, p. 7.

[119] Knollys, *Exposition of the Eleventh Chapter of the Revelation*, pp. 13, 29. Knollys made this prediction in 1679. He had refrained from being so precise in his earlier work dealing with this topic (*Apocalyptical Mysteries*, 1667). In his *Exposition of the Whole Book of Revelation*, published in September 1688, on the eve of the Glorious Revolution, Knollys made a subtle adjustment. The exposition of chapter 11, was by and large verbatim from his earlier publication, *Exposition of the Eleventh Chapter of the Revelation*, but Knollys changed the words "or sooner" to "or soon after" indicating perhaps that Knollys was rethinking his timeline of the end. p. 144.

[120] Knollys, *Apocalyptical Mysteries*, Part I, pp. 18-19.

[121] Knollys, *Exposition of the Eleventh Chapter of the Revelation*, p. 22.

[122] Knollys, *Mystical Babylon Unvailed*, p. 21.

[123] Knollys, *Apocalyptical Mysteries*, Part I, pp. 18-19.

[124] Knollys, *Apocalyptical Mysteries*, Part I, pp. 18-19.

Courage" and leading them to experience a "cooling in their Spiritual affections unto Christ" and a short period of Apostasy.[125]

According to John's prophecy in Revelation 11, the killing of the Witnesses would take place in the street of the great city. Knollys claimed that this referred to London, England, where "the highest and most eminent Testimony for Christ his Kingdom, his Worship, and his Government and against the Kingdom, Worship, and Government of Anti-Christ hath been, yet is, and will be born by Christ's faithful Ministers".[126] This "death" would be short-lived, "three days and a half", and would end the 1260 days. According to Knollys, the slaying of the Witnesses would be the "last Act of the Beast's tyrannical-Power", for "as soon as the Witnesses rise, Babylon begins to fall".[127] This meant that the end time was "near at hand"[128] but "not yet come".[129]

In order to fulfil this prophecy, a number of important events still needed to take place. First, the Saints would experience intense tribulation, which would result in the greatest Apostasy ever experienced in the Church. Knollys warned his fellow believers to take care, lest they lose their future glory by present failure and he called on them to "come out of Babylon" before it was too late.[130] Another significant event was the resurrection of the Witnesses. There would follow "a very glorious Reformation in the Worship of God, by the Spirit of Life from God".[131] These imminent events would signify the end of history and would precede the return of Christ, the defeat and judgment of Antichrist, the establishment of Christ's millennial kingdom, and the final judgment and reward.

The Second Coming of Christ

One of the more significant apocalyptic problems with which Knollys grappled was that of the return of Christ to earth. In several of his works, Knollys examined specifically the signs, the timing, and the nature of Christ's return, as well as the benefits that it would bring. *The World that Now is and the World that is to Come* contained his most extensive treatment of the topic. Knollys paid significant attention to the signs of Christ's return, not to pinpoint an exact date or time, but rather to encourage his readers to faithfulness, "that when the ending-time is come and begun, before it be expired, there shall be such

---

[125] Knollys, *Apocalyptical Mysteries*, Part I, pp. 20-21.
[126] Knollys, *Exposition of the Eleventh Chapter of the Revelation*, pp. 24-25.
[127] Knollys, *Apocalyptical Mysteries*, Part I, pp. 26-27.
[128] Knollys, *Apocalyptical Mysteries*, Part I, p. 28.
[129] Knollys, *Exposition of the Eleventh Chapter of the Revelation*, p. 29.
[130] See Knollys, *Parable of the Kingdom of Heaven* and Knollys, *Mystical Babylon Unvailed*, pp. 25-30.
[131] Knollys, *Apocalyptical Mysteries*, Part I, pp. 28-29. The Apostasy and the eschatological Reformation will be examined further below.

remarkable and wonderful things come to pass… whereby the wise shall understand, and certainly know that it is the time of the END".[132] Many of these signs were beginning to be observed or were imminent, and they were closely linked to the work, persecution, and victory of the Two Witnesses.[133] The first sign of Christ's return would be increased wickedness. "Iniquity shall abound, a little before his Second Coming", as in the days of Noah and of the cities of Sodom and Gomorrah, places that God punished because the people there were overwhelmingly immoral.[134]

The second sign would be the proclamation or preaching of the Gospel, represented in Revelation by the testimony of the Two Witnesses. Prior to the coming of Christ, there would be an open proclamation of that coming, an announcing of "the Gospel of the Kingdom" throughout the world.[135] This would be accompanied by an "anointing of the Spirit… poured out upon them", which would bestow on them boldness and "the Gifts and powerful operations of the Spirit".[136] This "finishing testimony" would represent the culmination of the work and words of Christ's saints and would consist of a proclamation of the Kingship of Christ – that "the Lord Jesus Christ is King of the Nations, King of Kings, and all the kingdoms of this world shall be the Kingdom of Christ".[137] Although temporarily silenced during the period of Apostasy (the death of the Witnesses), it will be revived with renewed fervour immediately prior to the coming of the Bridegroom (the resurrection of the Witnesses).[138] The "resurrection" following the period of silence would result in "a very glorious Reformation in the Worship of God by the Spirit of Life".[139]

A third sign of Christ's return would be "that great *Tribulation*, which our Saviour foretold his Disciples would be *immediately* before his Second Coming, and Appearance".[140] This Tribulation would be unlike any the world had ever experienced and "the People of God (*especially his two Prophetical Witnesses, to wit, the separated Churches, and their faithful Ministers*) shall not be exempted… for they shall suffer Persecution."[141] A general persecution would accompany the proclamation of the Witnesses, and would lead to the death of the Two Witnesses, the persecution of the "separated Churches of Saints" their dispersing congregations, destroying their meeting places, with many saints imprisoned, banished, and even put to death.[142] Persecution would

---

[132] Knollys, *Apocalyptical Mysteries*, Part I, p. 28.
[133] Knollys, *The World that Now Is*, Book II, p. 13.
[134] Knollys, *The World that Now Is*, Book II, pp. 13-14.
[135] Knollys, *Parable of the Kingdom of Heaven*, pp. 65-66, 130.
[136] Knollys, *Parable of the Kingdom of Heaven*, pp. 18-19.
[137] Knollys, *Exposition of the Eleventh Chapter of the Revelation*, pp. 19-20.
[138] Knollys, *Parable of the Kingdom of Heaven*, pp. 92-93.
[139] Knollys, *Apocalyptical Mysteries*, Part I, p. 29.
[140] Knollys, *The World that Now Is*, Book II, p. 18 (emphasis in the original).
[141] Knollys, *The World that Now Is*, Book II, pp. 18-19 (emphasis in the original)
[142] Knollys, *The World that Now Is*, Book II, pp. 19-20.

lead to apostasy; indeed, this Tribulation would lead many to become silent and cooled in their affections toward Christ.[143]

The fourth and final sign of the Second Coming would be an increase in sinfulness in the world and in the Church. During the final "three and a half days" of the period of the Two Witnesses, the Beast would unleash his rage with unprecedented fury leading to the death of the Witnesses. This would result in a period of cooled faith, a temporary silence of the Testimony of the Church, and a falling away of many saints – a great Apostasy. This "very great formality, lukewarmness, and Worldliness &c. among Church-Members" would constitute "the last and greatest Apostasie among Gospel-Professors".[144]

This apostasy would have a dual nature – false doctrine, "especially in Faith and Love", and false affections.[145] Knollys believed that many would be seduced into "teaching justification by works, and salvation by works, holding Free-will, and falling away".[146] A temporary silencing of the testimony of the true Gospel would follow and many would "begin to be Sinfully silent, and dare not bear their Testimony boldly and publickly for Christ against Antichrist".[147] This "slumber of sinful-silence"[148] would infect not only the people, but also their clergy,[149] who would "cease to teach, and preach the Doctrine of Christs Second Coming, and of the glorious Majesty of his Davidical Kingdom".[150]

During this time, many would also fall prey to false affections:

> Many Professors will fall from their first Love… many depart from the Faith, and many cool in their Spiritual Affections to Christ; there are great decaies of Grace, and many flourishing Professors experience great withering, fading, and decaying in their spiritual gifts and graces; their backslidings are increased.[151]

As a result of this cooling of spiritual affections, many would "begin to grow carnal, worldly, careless, and secure, formal and lukewarm".[152] This would also lead to apostasy in worship, which Knollys equated to Laodicean lukewarmness,[153] so that some professors "having the form of Godliness will

---

[143] Knollys, *Exposition of the Eleventh Chapter of the Revelation*, pp. 22-23.
[144] Knollys, *Exposition of the Eleventh Chapter of the Revelation*, p. 30.
[145] Knollys, *The World that Now Is*, Book II, p. 14.
[146] Knollys, *The World that Now Is*, Book II, p. 15.
[147] Knollys, *The World that Now Is*, Book II, p.17.
[148] Knollys, *Parable of the Kingdom of Heaven*, p. 55.
[149] Knollys, *Apocalyptical Mysteries*, Part II, p. 9.
[150] Knollys, *The World that Now Is*, Book II, pp. 17-18.
[151] Knollys, *The World that Now Is*, Book II, pp. 15-16.
[152] Knollys, *The World that Now Is*, Book II, p. 18.
[153] Knollys, *The World that Now Is*, Book II, p. 16. In this passage, Knollys bluntly applied this to the National and Papal churches. However, in his *Parable of the Kingdom*

deny the power thereof".[154] Formality would impact the "External religious performance of... Evangelical duties".[155] Protestants would follow a self-centred, self-serving religion grounded in custom, tradition, superstition, and legalism, much like that of the Scribes and Pharisees of Jesus' day and of Paul before his conversion.[156]

This coming apostasy was cause of great concern for Knollys. He had given much attention in his writings to the formality and lukewarmness of the Roman church and the state churches, the so-called false churches. However, Knollys believed that this last-days apostasy would affect those in "the Churches of the Saints" as well as others. This belief instilled within him a great sense of urgency in calling upon believers to prepare for the last days. In *Mystical Babylon Unvailed*, Knollys concluded with an appeal for separation, warning of the dangers of continued communion with the "false church".[157] This warning echoed through his exposition of Jesus' parable of the ten virgins awaiting the bridegroom in Matthew 25. Knollys likened the five wise virgins, to the "True Professors" who remain faithful until the second coming of Christ.[158] On the other hand, those who would "grow secure, careless, invigilant, and all slumber and sleep",[159] would fall into apostasy, unfaithful and unprepared for Christ's return like the five foolish virgins.[160] This

> form of Godliness will comport with a spirit of Worldliness, Earthlymindedness, Covetousness, Pride, Uncleanness, Drunkenness; so that these Lusts be but secretly committed. A Professor and Church-member may be a self-lover and a lover of pleasures, a Covenant or Promise-breaker, and yet have and hold up a form of Godliness without the power thereof.[161]

Thus, they "like Christ as Saviour but refuse him as Soveraign".[162] In this way, they "may avoid troubles and persecutions".[163] For "the inward power of Godliness is cross to their outward and worldly Interests" and so rather than "hazard the loss of Life, Liberty or Estate, and expose himself to poverty, prison, banishment or death for his Religion, he will deny Christ, deny God and

---

of Heaven, p. 25, Knollys applied this to "Professors in the Churches of the Saints" as well.

[154] Knollys, *Parable of the Kingdom of Heaven*, p. 25.
[155] Knollys, *Parable of the Kingdom of Heaven*, pp. 25-26.
[156] Knollys, *Parable of the Kingdom of Heaven*, pp. 26-28.
[157] Knollys, *Mystical Babylon Unvailed*, pp. 25-29.
[158] Knollys, *Parable of the Kingdom of Heaven*, pp. 29-32.
[159] Knollys, *The World that Now Is*, Book II, p. 17.
[160] Knollys, *Parable of the Kingdom of Heaven*, pp. 24-28.
[161] Knollys, *Parable of the Kingdom of Heaven*, p. 36.
[162] Knollys, *Parable of the Kingdom of Heaven*, p. 38.
[163] Knollys, *Parable of the Kingdom of Heaven*, p. 36.

the power of Godliness".[164] Ultimately, the true believer would embrace suffering whereas "Professors... may avoid troubles and persecutions".[165]

The coming apostasy, although it would silence and tarnish the testimony of Christ's followers, would not defeat them utterly. After a short time, the Two Witnesses would come back to life so that "some of the Virgin-professors shall be recovered out of their Security, Backsliding, and Apostasie, and shall rise and shine at the coming of Jesus Christ as the Bridegroom of his Church". Even those saints who had fallen had hope, for "God hath promised to heal the Backslidings of his People upon their repentance and returning to the Lord".[166]

A year to the day from the publication of Knollys' *Exposition of the Whole Book of Revelation*, his most comprehensive eschatological work, Particular Baptists from London and other areas of England and Wales, met for what was their first General Assembly. The octogenarian Hanserd Knollys attended and appeared to exert significant influence, even in his old age. One of the issues that came under scrutiny was the condition of their churches and in particular, of their ministry.[167]

In the wake of the recent Glorious Revolution, the eschatological interpretation of events, as recorded in the *Narrative of the Proceedings of the General Assembly*, displayed unmistakeable evidence of Knollys' vision. The years immediately prior to the coming of William and Mary were interpreted as "so dismal an Hour of Sorrow and Persecution, in which the Enemy doubtless designed to break our Churches to pieces".[168] Although the Particular Baptist Churches survived this tribulation, they had nevertheless experienced some "decay... for want of holy Zeal for God" so that "the Power of Godliness being greatly decayed, and but little more than the Form thereof remaining amongst us". The *Narrative* continued: "The Spirit of this World we clearly discern is got too too (sic) much into the Hearts of most Christians and Members of our Churches."[169] In reply, the Assembly proclaimed "a Solemn Day to Fast and Mourn before the Lord" for "those many grievous Backslidings, Sins, and Provocations, not only of the whole Nation, but also of the Lord's own

---

[164] Knollys, *Parable of the Kingdom of Heaven*, p. 40.
[165] Knollys, *Parable of the Kingdom of Heaven*, p. 36.
[166] Knollys, *Parable of the Kingdom of Heaven*, pp. 94-95.
[167] For more detail, see Chapter 7 below.
[168] *A Narrative of the Proceedings of the General Assembly Of divers Pastors, Messengers, and Ministering Brethren of the Baptized Churches, met together in London from Septemb. 3. to 12. 1689 from divers parts of England and Wales : Owning the Doctrine of Personal Election, and final Perseverance*, (London: 1689), p. 4. The language used and the themes expressed in this *Narrative*, certainly echo many of Knollys' own writings.
[169] *A Narrative of the Proceedings of the General Assembly*, (1689), pp. 4-5. The Narrative in this context cites Revelation 2:5, the charge against the Church of Ephesus for having lost its first love.

People".¹⁷⁰ These backslidings also related to "a strange Death of late come upon the Lord's faithful Witnesses" and "storms of Persecution having been raised upon us, a new War commenc'd by the Beast, (through the Divine Permission of God, and Hand of his Justice) to a total overcoming to appearance the Witnesses of Christ in these Isles".¹⁷¹

Knollys wrote very little about the details of the timing of Christ's return. The most explicit statement he made merely highlighted the lack of specificity. "Though of that Day, and that Hour (when Christ shall come) knoweth no man, no not the Angels of Heaven, nor the Son of Man, but the Father only."¹⁷² Still, this coming would be sudden, and to some extent, unexpected.¹⁷³ However, even though God the Father had "reserved the knowledge" of that time, Knollys believed that the presence of detailed signs provided clear evidence of Christ's imminent return.¹⁷⁴ "HE is upon his March... HE hath been coming a great while... and now He is very near even at the Door ready to enter the Bride-chamber; Only HE stands and stayes at the Door till the Bride have made herself ready."¹⁷⁵ The most evident indicator of the imminence of Christ's return was the "death" of the Two Witnesses, characterised by the Great Tribulation and the accompanying apostasy and silence of the saints. These things were to occur "immediately before his Second Coming, and Appearance".¹⁷⁶

Since the most certain characteristic of Christ's return was its uncertain and unexpected nature, and since the signs were somewhat vague, Knollys tended to focus on the importance of preparation. Time and again, he entreated his readers, both saint and sinner, to remain vigilant and prepared. This was the essence of *The Parable of the Kingdom of Heaven Expounded*. Knollys called upon those outside of the true church to repent or face exclusion from the divine kingdom:

> Sinners, you must get Jesus Christ, if you will not receive and entertain Christ into your hearts, by faith, a true penitent and lively faith, he will

---

¹⁷⁰ *A Narrative of the Proceedings of the General Assembly*, (1689), p. 7.

¹⁷¹ *A Narrative of the Proceedings of the General Assembly*, (1689), p. 7.

¹⁷² Knollys, *The World that Now Is*, Book II, p. 13; Knollys, *Parable of the Kingdom of Heaven*, p. 129.

¹⁷³ Knollys, *Apocalyptical Mysteries*, Part II, pp. 28-29; Knollys, *An Exposition of the Whole Book of the Revelation*, p. 198.

¹⁷⁴ Knollys, *The World that Now Is*, Book I, p. 81; Book II, p. 13; Knollys, *Parable of the Kingdom of Heaven*, p. 130.

¹⁷⁵ Knollys, *Parable of the Kingdom of Heaven*, p. 67.

¹⁷⁶ Knollys, *The World that Now Is*, Book I, p. 94; Book II, p. 18; Knollys, *An Exposition of the Whole Book of the Revelation*, pp. 186-87.

not receive and admit you into the Marriage Chamber of his Kingdom when he comes.[177]

His stress upon the necessity of an intimate relationship with Christ was evident in Knollys' use of imagery. When Christ returned, those without an intimate faith would not enter the Marriage Chamber, the place where the most intimate consummation of the marriage relationship occurred. Knollys linked this to Revelation 3:20, "Behold I stand at the door and knock. If any man hear my voice and open the door, I will come into him and sup with him", telling sinners to "open the door" of their hearts, so that Christ could enter and "set up the Kingdom of Grace".[178]

Likewise Knollys warned the "saints" to prepare for the second coming by attending worship and communion services; "it is their Duty to attend diligently and conscionably upon the Ministry of the Gospel and means of Grace".[179] They were required to "put on their beautiful Garments" and be "cloathed with fine Linnen, white and clean (which is the Righteousness of the Saints, Rev. 19.8.) as a Bride adorned for her husband, Rev. 21.2".[180] This meant putting off one's own righteousness and putting on "the Robes of Christs Righteousness",[181] accepting salvation by faith alone, since there was still "much cleaning, purging, sanctifying work" to be done by the Spirit and word of God.[182] As well, Christians had a duty to watch "at all times", watching in prayer, watching their "hearts, thoughts, and affections", setting "a watch before the doors of their Lips". But most importantly the saints "ought to watch for the glorious appearance of the Bridegroom, our Lord Jesus Christ".[183]

In examining the nature of Christ's Second Coming, Knollys appears to have embraced two quite different positions. His first position was set forth in his *Parable of the Kingdom of Heaven Expounded*, which analysed the Second Coming very closely and concluded that it had a dual nature. Christ's second coming would occur in two stages. First, he would return spiritually and would later and finally return personally. Immediately following the completion of those signs, which Jesus gave to his disciples, Knollys argued "then shall appear (*not the person but*) the sign of the Son of Man in Heaven (Matt.24:30)".[184] In other words, upon the completion of the signs of Christ's coming, He would return spiritually. He explained this position later in the treatise:

---

[177] Knollys, *Parable of the Kingdom of Heaven*, p. 120.
[178] Knollys, *Parable of the Kingdom of Heaven*, p. 120.
[179] Knollys, *Parable of the Kingdom of Heaven*, p. 113.
[180] Knollys, *Parable of the Kingdom of Heaven*, pp. 96-97.
[181] Knollys, *Parable of the Kingdom of Heaven*, pp. 114-15.
[182] Knollys, *Parable of the Kingdom of Heaven*, pp. 122-23.
[183] Knollys, *Parable of the Kingdom of Heaven*, p. 132.
[184] Knollys, *Parable of the Kingdom of Heaven*, p. 3 (emphasis mine).

I do believe and am perswaded that the coming of Christ (spoken of in this Parable, ver. 6. 10.) is not the coming of Christ in his own person upon the Earth (though I do believe Christ will come the second time in his own person upon the Earth, Heb. 9. 28. Zach. 3. 4, 5.) but this is his virtual, spiritual, powerful and glorious coming in his Saints and Sanction as the Bridegroom of his Church, the new Jerusalem.[185]

The first stage of his return then, took the form of the triumph of the separatist churches over the Antichristian Papal, Episcopal, and national churches. Knollys gave several reasons in support of his theory of the two stages of Christ's return. The Scriptures show that at the personal coming of Christ, he would be attended by "all his Saints".[186] For this to happen, a general resurrection of all the dead would have to occur, which pointed to a later time. It seemed more likely that those "living Saints only will enter into the Bride-Chamber" at this first stage of his coming.[187] When Christ came "virtually and spiritually" he would begin the restoration and recreation process, renewing the Earth. However, at his personal coming, he will bring "the final Consumption and Conflagration of all things... a great Desolation of all things".[188] This cannot happen prior to the Millennium. Knollys stipulated that there were "three special kinds and times of Christ's coming. The first was "in the form of a servant" when he came as Saviour. When he comes "as a Judge at the last day" it will be "called his appearance the second time".[189] The general resurrection of all the dead would take place for this event.[190] Between his arrival as a servant and that as a judge, Christ would appear in a "virtual, spiritual, powerful and glorious coming in his Saints and Sanction".[191] In an earlier writing, *Apocalyptical Mysteries* (1667), Knollys gave a chronology of last events. In this chronology, the establishment of Christ's millennial kingdom and rule of his saints would pave the way for the final judgment: "Then Will Christ come again, and all the Saints with HIM."[192] In this interpretation, Christ would return spiritually in the persons of the saints to set up his millennial rule and only later would return physically after the Millennium to bring judgment and to usher in the new Heavens and Earth.

In his last two treatises, *The World that Now Is and the World that Is to Come* (1681) and *An Exposition of the Whole Book of the Revelation* (1688), Knollys abandoned his two-stage interpretation and understood the Second

---

[185] Knollys, *Parable of the Kingdom of Heaven*, p. 68.
[186] Knollys, *Parable of the Kingdom of Heaven*, p. 69.
[187] Knollys, *Parable of the Kingdom of Heaven*, p. 70.
[188] Knollys, *Parable of the Kingdom of Heaven*, pp. 71-72.
[189] Knollys described both of these as personal comings.
[190] Knollys, *Parable of the Kingdom of Heaven*, p. 71.
[191] Knollys, *Parable of the Kingdom of Heaven*, pp. 85-86; also p. 78.
[192] Knollys, *Apocalyptical Mysteries*, Part III, pp. 18.

Coming solely as a physical reappearance of Jesus.[193] In the *Exposition of the Whole Book of the Revelation*, Knollys stated explicitly "Christ's second coming will be visible, Act. 1. 11. and Matth. 24. 27" and "his second coming, called his appearing the second time Heb. 9. 27, 28... will be personal, Act. 1. 11. visible, Matth. 24. 30. and Rev. 1. 7. and all his Saints with him, I Thess. 3. 13".[194] In *The World that Now Is and the World that Is to Come*, Knollys laid down the following clear timeline: [1] "the LORD Jesus Christ will come again from Heaven" (Phil. 3:20; Heb. 9:28; I Thes. 3:13); [2] "then there will be a New Heavens, and a New Earth" (Isa. 65:17; 2 Pet. 3:13; Rev. 21:1, 2; Heb. 12:22-24); [3] "then the LORD Jesus Christ and his Saints shall have a Kingdom, and shall Reign on Earth" (Dan. 7:13-14, 27; Zech. 14:9; Rev. 5:9-10; 11:15; 20:4); [4] "then there shall be a Resurrection from the Dead" (I Thes. 4:16; Rev. 20:5-6; I Cor. 15:21-23, 51-52); [5] "then shall be the last and Eternal Judgment" (Rom. 14:10; 2 Cor. 5:10; Acts 17:31; I Pet. 4:5).[195] Later in the treatise, Knollys emphatically stated "That our LORD Jesus Christ will certainly, suddenly, and visibly appear the Second Time, and come from Heaven upon the Earth in his own Person" (Acts 1:11; Matt. 24:27; Rev. 1:7).[196] Thus, it would appear that Christ would return personally and with the saints establish his millennial kingdom on Earth.

The second book of *The World that Now Is and the World that Is to Come* provides a very comprehensive treatment of the Second Coming of Christ and *An Exposition of the Whole Book of the Revelation* contains a detailed exegetical treatment of eschatology and of the book of Revelation. Both treatises are deafening in their silence on the virtual, spiritual return of Christ set forth by Knollys in his earlier works.

More explicit evidence of a shift in interpretation appears within the texts. In dealing with the question of "the Time of Christ's Second Personal Coming from Heaven" in *The World that Now Is*, Knollys linked the *personal* coming to the "signs" listed in Scripture.[197] In his earlier treatise, *The Parable of the Kingdom of Heaven Expounded*, he had linked the "signs" to the "spiritual, virtual" return of Christ.[198] When discussing the "spiritual, virtual" return of Christ, Knollys cited Matthew 24:27-30, emphasising the appearance of the "sign of the Son of Man in Heaven" as opposed to the person.[199] However, in the later treatises, this very Scripture passage was explicitly used to support the

---

[193] Nowhere in these writings did he mention a spiritual or virtual appearance, but rather, he was very deliberate in emphasising the physical nature of Christ's return.
[194] Knollys, *An Exposition of the Whole Book of the Revelation*, pp. 5, 239.
[195] Knollys, *The World that Now Is*, Book II, pp. 1-4.
[196] Knollys, *The World that Now Is*, Book II, p. 10.
[197] Knollys, *The World that Now Is*, Book II, p. 13.
[198] Knollys, *Parable of the Kingdom of Heaven*, pp. 2-3.
[199] Knollys, *Parable of the Kingdom of Heaven*, pp. 2-3.

"visible" and "personal" coming of Christ.[200] An example of this is found in *The World that Now Is and the World that Is to Come*, where Knollys examined the question of the "Manner of Christ's Second Personal Coming".[201] Knollys claimed that Christ would come in the "Excellent Glory of the Father... Attended with all his holy Angels, and glorified Saints from Heaven, and met in the Air by all the changed Saints then living on Earth". In support of this he cited Matthew 24:30.[202] Clearly, at some point between 1674 and 1681, Knollys had shifted his position on the manner or nature of Christ's return. This had major implications for his interpretation of the Millennium as well.

The Millennium

And I saw an angel coming down from heaven, having the key of the abyss and a great chain in his hand. And he laid hold of the dragon, the serpent of old, who is the devil and Satan, and bound him for a thousand years, and threw him into the abyss, and shut it and sealed it over him so that he should not deceive the nations any longer, until the thousand years were completed; after these things he must be released for a short time. And I saw thrones, and they sat upon them, and judgment was given to them. And I saw the souls of those who had been beheaded because of the testimony of Jesus and because of the word of God, and those who had not worshipped the beast or his image, and had not received the mark upon their forehead and upon their hand; and they came to life and reigned with Christ for a thousand years. (Revelation 20:1-4)

The interpretation of these powerful verses has provided fuel for speculative fires throughout the history of the Christian church. From the time of Augustine through the medieval and Reformation periods, the thousand-year binding of Satan had been interpreted a symbolic period. This position, known as amillennialism, held that the Millennium was not literally a thousand-years, but symbolically represented the period between the first and second comings of Christ. At the beginning of the seventeenth century, a shift began to take place and the Millennium began to be viewed as a literal, future period when Satan would be bound and the saints would rule with Christ. Within this futurist mindset, two positions developed: premillennialism and postmillennialism. For the premillennialist, the Millennium would be inaugurated by the physical

---

[200] Knollys, *An Exposition of the Whole Book of the Revelation*, pp. 5, 239; Knollys, *The World that Now Is*, Book II, pp. 10, 13.

[201] Knollys, *The World that Now Is*, Book II, p. 11.

[202] Knollys, *The World that Now Is*, Book II, pp. 11-13. In this work, Knollys pinpointed this glorious coming with the saints as happening immediately following the "signs" while in *The Parable of the Kingdom of Heaven Expounded*, this "powerful and glorious coming... with all his Saints" was specifically understood as following the period of the millennial kingdom but the "virtual, spiritual" coming was to follow the "signs" and precede the personal coming.

return of Christ. The postmillennialist, on the other hand, emphasised that the Millennium would be culminated by the physical return of Christ. What separated these interpretations was the timing of the literal return of Christ. In the seventeenth century, "a clear majority" of millenarians were premillennialists. However, they divided over whether the kingdom would be a spiritual one with Christ reigning through his saints or whether it would be a physical one with Christ reigning in person on Earth.[203]

In his work focussing on Knollys' various theological positions, Barry Howson stated unequivocally that "in all of his eschatological works except for one [Knollys'] position appears unclear. It is only when we read his work entitled, *The Parable of the Kingdom of Heaven Expounded* written in 1674 that we clearly see that he was a postmillennialist."[204] He went on to qualify this in a footnote by claiming that at times "he sounds like a premillennialist".[205] Was Knollys' position regarding the Millennium that straightforward? Can one state with such certainty that he was a postmillennialist? Exactly what were Hanserd Knollys' beliefs about the Millennium?

In Revelation 16, the apostle John wrote of the pouring out of the seven Vials of judgment upon the Beast and those who followed the Beast. In the futurist interpretation, the pouring out of these Vials would precede and usher in the Millennium. In *Apocalyptical Mysteries*, Knollys wrote at length about the seven Vials and the coming of the Kingdom of Christ. These Vials expressed judgment against the Roman Church, its daughter churches, and the kings of Earth who embraced the false teachings of the Church of Rome.[206] In the midst of the pouring out of these Vials, the Kingdom of the Turks would join forces with the Papists against the saints and the Jews. At Armageddon, the forces would come against one another and the "Enemies against Christ and his Kingdom shall be destroyed by the pouring out of this seventh Vial".[207]

Although in references such as this one, Knollys appeared to attribute a very literal, military character to the Battle of Armageddon, other passages interpreted this battle and the victory won by Christ's saints in a metaphorical sense, in which "Kings, Captains, and great Men and their Armies, Souldiers, both small and great" would be "slain with the sword, that is the Word of God, and Commands of Christ, written in the holy Scripture".[208] Victory would come by "The sword of the Spirit... in the hand of his Saints".[209] Thus, for Knollys,

---

[203] Ball, *Great Expectation*, pp. 160-67.

[204] Howson, "The Question of Orthodoxy in the theology of Hanserd Knollys (c. 1599-1691): a Seventeenth Century English Calvinistic Baptist", (Unpublished Ph.D. Dissertation, McGill University, 1999), p. 311.

[205] Howson, "Question of Orthodoxy", p. 347, n. 218.

[206] Knollys, *Apocalyptical Mysteries*, Part II, pp. 14-19.

[207] Knollys, *Apocalyptical Mysteries*, Part II, pp.24-31; Knollys, *An Exposition of the Whole Book of the Revelation*, pp. 196-97.

[208] Knollys, *An Exposition of the Whole Book of the Revelation*, pp. 218-21.

[209] Knollys, *An Exposition of the Whole Book of the Revelation*, p.188.

the conquest of Babylon represented a spiritual defeat by "the Doctrine, Worship, and Discipline of the Church of God in some measure restored to their primitive Purity".[210] A renewal of "Spiritual-Gifts" would accompany this victory of the separatist churches.[211] In this manner, the "Kingdoms of this World do become the Kingdom of Christ and of his Anointed".[212]

In *An Exposition of the Whole Book of Revelation*, Knollys understood the Millennium as a literal thousand years "that is, a certain definite time... They are not any mystical or prophetical number, but literal."[213] The rule of Christ and his saints over the New Earth, which Christ himself will constitute, would characterise this Millennium. With the defeat of the Beast and its followers, the kingdom of Christ would replace the kingdom of Antichrist. "And then the Whole CREATION shall be delivered from the BONDAGE of Corruption, and Restored into the Glorious LIBERTY of the Children of God."[214] The "same Rule, Authority, Dominion, and Power" which Christ had received from God, he would also bestow upon the saints over the nations of the world "at his second coming".[215] This kingdom of Christ on Earth would not take the form "of a Worldly Constitution; but it is a spiritual and heavenly Kingdom".[216] It would not be "that eternal State of God's Kingdom of GLORY in Heaven" but rather "the glorious and spiritual State of the KINGDOM of Christ on EARTH".[217] According to the vision of Daniel, Knollys argued "the Saints of the Most High shall take the KINGDOM [of the World], and possess the Kingdom for ever, even for ever and ever".[218] Further to this, "Christ and his Saints shall have the DOMINION in all the EARTH".[219]

This kingdom would become "enlarged" through a massive spiritual regeneration of the people of the Earth and a gathering of the Elect, both Jew and Gentile.[220] This would include a mass conversion of Jewish people, in fulfilment of Biblical prophecy, and Judah and Israel would be "Reunited into one Nation".[221] The Jewish people would return spiritually to God and

---

[210] Knollys, *Apocalyptical Mysteries*, Part II, p. 10; Knollys, *An Exposition of the Whole Book of the Revelation*, p. 190.
[211] Knollys, *Exposition of the Eleventh Chapter of the Revelation*, p. 37.
[212] Knollys, *Apocalyptical Mysteries*, Part II, p. 38.
[213] Knollys, *An Exposition of the Whole Book of the Revelation*, p. 222.
[214] Knollys, *Apocalyptical Mysteries*, Part III, p. 12.
[215] Knollys, *An Exposition of the Whole Book of the Revelation*, pp. 40-41.
[216] Knollys, *Apocalyptical Mysteries*, Part III, pp. 12-13; Knollys, *The World that Now Is*, Book II, pp. 26.
[217] Knollys, *Apocalyptical Mysteries*, Part III, p. 15.
[218] Knollys, *Apocalyptical Mysteries*, Part III, p. 10.
[219] Knollys, *Apocalyptical Mysteries*, Part III, p. 11.
[220] Knollys, *The World that Now Is*, Book II, pp. 20, 22, 26; Knollys, *An Exposition of the Whole Book of the Revelation*, p. 229.
[221] Knollys, *The World that Now Is*, Book II, p. 21; Knollys, *Parable of the Kingdom of Heaven*, p. 72.

physically to their land.[222] Following the Jewish renewal, "then shall also the fulness of the Gentiles be converted".[223] Jew and Gentile together would worship Christ as the fulfilment of God's elect.[224]

This massive regeneration of the people of Earth would happen through two means – the preaching of the Gospel of Christ's kingdom to all Nations and an extraordinary pouring out of the Spirit.

> And therefore the Kingdom of Christ cannot be set up in any Nation until the GOSPEL of the Kingdom be first preached in that Nation; And then that NATION, Kingdom, or PEOPLE, which do believe the GOSPEL of the Kingdom preached unto them, and are made WILLING (in the DAY of God's POWER, Psal. 110. 3.) to Admit the Saints to RULE and GOVERN that Nation according to the LAWS of our LORD and KING Jesus, shall become the Kingdom of Christ.[225]

This represented a spiritual conquest carried out through ordinary means, although with extraordinary success. Those who "will not receive the TESTIMONY of the Kingdom of Christ", but reject and kill Christ's witnesses "shall be utterly Wasted and Destroyed".[226] Knollys did not expand on this destruction, however, other than to state that "our LORD Jesus Christ will put down" his enemies who refuse to submit to his authority.[227] The success of this preaching depended upon the people being "made WILLING" to receive the message.[228] An extraordinary "pouring out of the Spirit upon all Flesh" would result in many conversions.[229] In addition, the saints would receive gifts from the Holy Spirit to enable their ruling with Christ in his Kingdom.[230] According to Knollys, "the Saints will be rarely qualified and spirited for Government" and "embued with courage, clad in Zeal, and girded with strength to bind Kings in Chains, and Nobles in fetters of Iron, and execute upon them the Judgment

---

[222] Knollys, *Apocalyptical Mysteries*, Part II, pp. 26-27, 33. Knollys held that both the "Papists" presented "a very great Stumbling-block unto the Conversion of the Jews" and the "Turks" were "a great impediment unto their return unto their own Land". Thus, with the defeat of the kingdom of Antichrist (Rome) and of the kingdom of the Turk at Armageddon, the way is cleared not only for their conversion, but for their resettlement as well.

[223] Knollys, *The World that Now Is*, Book II, p. 22; Knollys, *Apocalyptical Mysteries*, Part I, p. 32.

[224] Knollys, *An Exposition of the Whole Book of the Revelation*, pp. 214, 236.

[225] Knollys, *Apocalyptical Mysteries*, Part III, p. 17.

[226] Knollys, *Apocalyptical Mysteries*, Part III, pp. 17-18.

[227] Knollys, *Apocalyptical Mysteries*, Part III, p. 18.

[228] Knollys, *Apocalyptical Mysteries*, Part III, p. 17.

[229] Knollys, *The World that Now Is*, Book II, p. 26.

[230] Knollys, *Exposition of the Eleventh Chapter of the Revelation*, p. 37.

written (Luk, 19. 27.)".²³¹ The saints would be "rarely qualified" to rule because of their righteous character – "they shall be all righteous,... shall do no iniquity,... shall be without fault".²³² Beyond this, they would "be SPIRITED for Government", again, a reference to spiritual gifting for a specific task.²³³ Finally, they would "be cloathed with Humility", exalting Christ alone, in distinction from the current world order.²³⁴

Knollys understood this as being a spiritual kingdom on Earth lasting for a thousand years, and saw it as the fulfilment of Old Testament prophecy regarding the Davidic kingdom. Christ's kingdom will be a continuation of "the THRONE of his Father David, Isa. 9. 7. and Luke 1. 32, 33. which Throne Solomon his Son (who was a Type of Christ) sat upon, when he reigned".²³⁵ The establishment of this kingdom represented the specific goal of Christ's return, not merely a consequence.²³⁶ During this period, not only would the saints rule in righteousness, all things would be restored to "their original purity and perfection".²³⁷ It would usher in a Heaven on Earth, a Paradise restored, a return to Eden, so that "all those things that occasioned sorrows and sufferings, tears and temptations, lamentations and weeping to the Church and People of God are come to an end".²³⁸ Finally, God's saints would experience "rest, peace, and glory".²³⁹

Only the question of when Christ's personal return would occur in relation to the Millennium was not addressed in these works. In his earlier works, Knollys took a postmillennialist position by claiming that Christ would return "virtually and spiritually" prior to the Millennium, but would not return "personally and physically" until after the thousand-year spiritual triumph of the saints.²⁴⁰ Although Knollys shifted to a premillennial position in his later works, he did so with a high degree of ambiguity.²⁴¹ His earlier treatises took a minority position and very laboriously defended it, spelling out arguments for it

---

[231] Knollys, *The World that Now Is*, Book II, pp. 27-8; Knollys, *Apocalyptical Mysteries*, Part III, p. 16.
[232] Knollys, *Apocalyptical Mysteries*, Part III, p. 16.
[233] Knollys, *Apocalyptical Mysteries*, Part III, p. 16.
[234] Knollys, *Apocalyptical Mysteries*, Part III, p. 16.
[235] Knollys, *Apocalyptical Mysteries*, Part III, p. 13.
[236] Knollys, *The World that Now Is*, Book II, p. 24.
[237] Knollys, *An Exposition of the Whole Book of the Revelation*, p. 230.
[238] Knollys, *An Exposition of the Whole Book of the Revelation*, p. 230.
[239] Knollys, *An Exposition of the Whole Book of the Revelation*, p. 230.
[240] Knollys, *Apocalyptical Mysteries*, Part III, p. 18; Knollys, *Parable of the Kingdom of Heaven*, pp. 72-78; 85-86.
[241] His *Exposition of the Whole Book of Revelation*, contained only one passage, which vaguely implied Knollys' earlier position of a postmillennial return of Christ. What makes this whole issue especially confusing is Knollys' use of the phrase "second coming" in his earlier works interchangeably for both the virtual and the personal comings of Christ.

and against contending views.[242] The later works did not clearly state a position on this issue. In the earlier treatises, the spiritual coming would begin the Millennium and the physical coming would culminate it. In the later treatises, he had a very different set of bookends, the resurrection of the Two Witnesses ushered in the Millennium and the resurrection of the "rest of the dead" ushered in the final judgment and the end.[243]

The Eschaton

Upon the completion of the Millennium the finale of Earthly history would occur. This *Eschaton* would result in the righting of all wrong. The Greek word ἔσχατος (*eschatos*) literally means last or last things. This concept has a rich and vast tradition in both the New Testament and in the Old Testament. The Jews in the Old Testament era expressed it in the phrase "Day of Yahweh" or Day of the LORD, when Yahweh, the God of Israel, would visit his judgment upon the wicked and pour out his reward upon his people.[244] Thus, the Old Testament prophets described the day of the LORD as a day of wrath and destruction and as a day of hope and renewal. In the book of Isaiah, for example, both themes existed:

Behold, the day of the LORD comes,

    cruel, with wrath and fierce anger,

to make the earth a desolation

    and to destroy its sinners from it (Isa. 13:9).

For behold, I create a new heavens and a new earth;

    and the former things shall not be remembered

    or come into mind (Isa. 65:17; cf. Isa. 32 & 35).

By the later Old Testament period, this judgment and restoration theme also began to emphasise an element of resurrection (Dan. 12:2; Ezek. 37), and this became a dominant theme in the New Testament era.

Knollys treatment of the Eschaton remained very much within this tradition. Knollys emphasised all of these elements – resurrection, judgment, re-creation, although he tended to incorporate the re-creation into his understanding of the Millennium. In terms of simple chronology, Knollys believed that the resurrection of the dead would precede the final judgment, following which "Christ shall deliver up the Kingdom unto God the Father, that GOD may be

---

[242] Knollys, *Parable of the Kingdom of Heaven*, pp. 67-75.
[243] Knollys, *An Exposition of the Whole Book of the Revelation*, p. 77.
[244] Anthony Hoekema, *The Bible and the Future*, (Grand Rapids, Michigan: William. B. Eerdmans Publishing Co., 1979), pp. 3-12.

ALL in ALL".²⁴⁵ However, Knollys' explanation of the eschatological resurrection was not entirely clear.

In Revelation 20:4-5, the apostle John wrote of the coming to life of those who had suffered for the cause of Christ, which he described as the first resurrection. He went on to assert that the rest of the dead would not return to life until after the thousand-year reign of Christ and his saints. According to Knollys' earlier writings, this first resurrection was not a literal, physical resurrection, but a metaphorical resurrection of the Two Witnesses of Revelation 11, who represented living saints.²⁴⁶ In *Parable of the Kingdom of Heaven Expounded*, his post-millennial scheme viewed the spiritual coming as preceding the physical coming. No physical resurrection of the dead would take place until after the Millennium. Then, at the personal coming of Christ, there "will be the Universal Physical Resurrection of all that are dead".²⁴⁷ However, in the later works, Knollys seemed to take a pre-millennial position. When dealing with the resurrection, Knollys laid out an "order" to the resurrection of the dead. Christ's physical resurrection came first, then "they that are Christ's at his coming. But the rest of the Dead lived not again until the thousand years were finished."²⁴⁸ This meant a resurrection of the saints was "the first Resurrection. They shall Reign with Christ a thousand years, and that on Earth."²⁴⁹ What differed between the earlier and later apocalyptic works was not the sequence of events, but the fact that the first resurrection was of dead saints rather than the revival of the faith and power of living saints. In his earlier writings, he clearly saw the first resurrection as a spiritual or metaphorical event. In his later works, however, he envisaged the first resurrection as a physical event, "After the Saints deceased are raised, and have lived and reigned with Christ a thousand years, shall be the general Resurrection."²⁵⁰

The purpose for the resurrection of the dead was for God to administer final judgment upon all people. Although other "dayes of Judgment" had existed in the Old Testament era, and in that era immediately preceding the Millennium, this one ushered in "the Eternal Judgment... that last Sentence which our LORD Jesus Christ shall pronounce upon, and unto the Righteous, and the Wicked".²⁵¹ For the saints, this judgement would result in the reward of eternal

---

²⁴⁵ Knollys, *Apocalyptical Mysteries*, Part III, p. 18. Knollys, *The World that Now Is*, Book II, pp. 3-4.
²⁴⁶ Knollys, *An Exposition of the Whole Book of the Revelation*, pp. 223-24;
²⁴⁷ Knollys, *Parable of the Kingdom of Heaven*, pp. 69-70.
²⁴⁸ Knollys, *The World that Now Is*, Book II, p. 29.
²⁴⁹ Knollys, *The World that Now Is*, Book II, p. 29.
²⁵⁰ Knollys, *The World that Now Is*, Book II, p. 30.
²⁵¹ Knollys, *The World that Now Is*, Book II, p. 30; Knollys, *Parable of the Kingdom of Heaven*, pp. 13-15; Knollys, *An Exposition of the Whole Book of the Revelation*, p. 240.

life,[252] while the wicked would receive the wrath of God[253] with an emphasis on "the Extremity, and the Eternity of their Torments in Hell Fire".[254] The most vital aspect of this judgment was as the precursor to the final end, which included God's people dwelling with him in Heaven. Knollys remained extremely vague on this aspect, stating merely that following the resurrection and judgment "Christ shall deliver up the Kingdom unto God the Father".[255] At this point, "Time shall pass into Eternity of Glory, and Beatifical Vision, and eternal life."[256]

Conclusion

By 1688, it was obvious to Knollys that unique events were afoot in England. His acute awareness of the apocalyptic and eschatological potential of recent events had consumed much of his energy during the last thirty years of his life. Between 1667 and his death in 1692, Knollys focussed his theological and academic attentions primarily on issues regarding the end of the world and the establishment of the Kingdom of Christ on Earth. This intense interest in eschatology brought forward repeated accusations of Knollys' Fifth Monarchism from his contemporaries. Given the partisanship of the times, such accusations do not seem startling. However, that label has remained, well into the twentieth century. In the early twentieth century, renowned Baptist Historian, W.T. Whitley characterised Knollys as being "influenced gravely" by Fifth Monarchism.[257] More recently, Baptist historians A.C. Underwood and Leon MacBeth identified Knollys as a Fifth Monarchist.[258] According to Underwood, Knollys' fascination with apocalyptic writings "infected his mind with Fifth Monarchy views".[259]

Certainly Knollys was a millenarian with a strong interest in eschatology, but was his position indeed parallel to that of the radical Fifth Monarchy movement, openly espousing an active overthrow of the order and authorities of his day? According to B.S. Capp, the Fifth Monarchy movement "more than any other movement of the period... represented the total fusion of millenarian

---

[252] Knollys, *The World that Now Is*, Book II, p. 30; Knollys, *An Exposition of the Whole Book of the Revelation*, p. 231.
[253] Knollys, *Exposition of the Eleventh Chapter of the Revelation*, pp. 44-46.
[254] Knollys, *An Exposition of the Whole Book of the Revelation*, p. 185; Knollys, *Apocalyptical Mysteries*, Part II, p. 2.
[255] Knollys, *Apocalyptical Mysteries*, Part III, p. 18.
[256] Knollys, *The World that Now Is*, Book II, p. 40.
[257] W.T. Whitley, *A History of the British Baptists*, (London: Charles Griffin & Co., 1923), pp. 85-86.
[258] A.C. Underwood, *A History of the English Baptists*, (London: Carey Kingsgate Press, 1947), pp. 61, 110; H. Leon McBeth, *The Baptist Heritage*, (Nashville: Broadman Press, 1987), p. 94.
[259] Underwood, *English Baptists*, p. 110.

theology and political extremism".²⁶⁰ Capp went on to indicate that their vision included a "professed readiness to use violence" and that they remained so focused on the end that they were "neither interested in, nor capable of, large-scale Biblical commentaries", but were interested only in those particular passages "which they believed to relate to the political affairs of the day".²⁶¹ Of course, Knollys' *Exposition of the Whole Book of Revelation* was a "large-scale Biblical commentary" on the prophecies of Revelation and his other apocalyptic works did not centre exclusively on political events.

Capp outlined three major distinctive features of Fifth Monarchist eschatology. First, they believed that it was the task of the saints to "clear the way for the millennium and not leave this to God alone".²⁶² When the signs so indicated, the saints must be prepared to use military force, if necessary, to implement Christ's Kingdom. In the words of one anonymous Fifth Monarchist treatise, one might as well "go into harvest without his Sickle as to this work without... his Sword".²⁶³ This aggressive worldview set them apart from other millenarians, like Knollys, who readily called on the saints to prepare for Christ's coming through personal purification and patient waiting.²⁶⁴ The Fifth Monarchist call for violent action was not occasional, but appeared "in nearly all their pamphlets, and even face to face with the Protector".²⁶⁵ For their part, Fifth Monarchists believed that the process of establishing Christ's Kingdom had begun with the execution of Charles I. Any government that did not carry it through to completion was ungodly, treasonous against Christ, and should be rooted out by force.²⁶⁶ Most Fifth Monarchists were hesitant to create anarchy and desired a very clear sign before they would move against the government. Therefore, for many Fifth Monarchy men, the violence "was strictly verbal".²⁶⁷ However, their violent language was not merely symbolic, for they believed in the use of violence when it became appropriate.

A second characteristic of Fifth Monarchy eschatology was the tendency to apply specific prophecies to specific current events and people. Much of their focus was on such images as the little horn in the Daniel 7 and Revelation 17, which they interpreted at various times as Charles I and Oliver Cromwell, while Charles II was understood as being the Beast.²⁶⁸ They also set dates for the

---

²⁶⁰ B.S. Capp, "Extreme Millenarianism", in *Puritans, the Millennium and the Future of Israel: Puritan Eschatology 1600 to 1660*, Peter Toon, ed., (Cambridge: James Clarke, 1970), p. 66.
²⁶¹ Capp, "Extreme Millenarianism", p. 66.
²⁶² Capp, "Extreme Millenarianism", p. 68.
²⁶³ Anonymous, *A Witness To the Saints*, (London: 1657), p. 6, cited in Capp, "Extreme Millenarianism", p. 69.
²⁶⁴ B.S. Capp, *The Fifth Monarchy Men*, (London: Faber and Faber, 1972), p. 131.
²⁶⁵ Capp, *The Fifth Monarchy Men*, p. 132.
²⁶⁶ Capp, *The Fifth Monarchy Men*, pp. 132-33.
²⁶⁷ Capp, *The Fifth Monarchy Men*, pp. 134-35.
²⁶⁸ Capp, *The Fifth Monarchy Men*, p. 202; Capp, "Extreme Millenarianism", pp. 70-71.

completion of the prophecies of Revelation, the most common of which was 1666. At the end, a mass conversion of the Jews and their return to Israel would usher in the final battle. Although Knollys placed eschatological and apocalyptic importance on current events, he exercised great caution in applying specific prophecies to specific events. Although he held a similar understanding on the Jews, so did many others who were not Fifth Monarchists.

The last characteristic of Fifth Monarchy eschatology related to their elaboration of the millennium.[269] They put forth a very detailed description of the "political, social, and economic nature of the kingdom of God, and went far beyond the words of Scripture."[270] Politically, the millennium would be monarchic, with Christ as King, and hierarchic, ruled by a new hierarchy of the saints, similar to the Jewish Sanhedrin. Only the godly would have a political voice. The laws governing this new state would be the laws of God as found in Scripture. The legal code developed for this Kingdom called for an abolition of all existing laws and Courts and a reinstitution of Mosaic Law with its laws and penalties. Socially, they proposed inversion of the current system with the saints replacing the aristocracy as rulers, a clear expression of social vengeance. Only in this way might social inequality disappear. Along with this social revolution were proposed economic reforms, which clearly echoed ideals of the artisans, merchants, and the middling ranks.[271] Finally, a new voluntary church would sweep away the national church. This church of saints would abolish tithes and prescribed services and would centre upon preaching, prayer, and hymn-singing.[272] Knollys never elaborated a scheme with such detail on the political, social, and economic structure of the millennium. His treatment of the eschaton was even more vague. For him, it represented a time when Christ with his saints would rule the Earth in righteousness.

Scattered throughout Knollys' eschatological writings were references to the Fourth Monarchy and the Fifth Monarchy and to Christ's Earthly Kingdom and the reign of the Saints.[273] At points, Knollys used very forceful and militant language in connection with the coming Kingdom. However, he interpreted even the most militant images and descriptions in spiritual and metaphorical ways. Christ's spiritual Kingdom would overtake the world, not through an armed uprising but through the preaching of the Word and the work of the Holy Spirit. The plans of the radical Fifth Monarchists seemed like disorder and chaos to Knollys. For him, the coming of Christ's Kingdom would be an

---

[269] Capp, *Fifth Monarchy Men*, p. 136.
[270] Capp, "Extreme Millenarianism", p. 72.
[271] Capp, "Extreme Millenarianism", pp. 72-75; Capp, *Fifth Monarchy Men*, pp. 136-50; see also chapter 7 on law reform.
[272] Capp, "Extreme Millenarianism", pp. 76-77.
[273] Examples of this include: Knollys, *Apocalyptical Mysteries*, Part I, pp. 5, 14; Part II, pp. 7-8; Part III; Knollys, *Exposition of the Eleventh Chapter of the Revelation*, pp. 40-41; Knollys, *Parable of the Kingdom of Heaven*, pp. 86-88.

orderly affair, which would bring an end to chaos.[274] Though Knollys called upon his readers to separate from the false church and extolled them "not to Obey, nor to submit themselves unto the Roman-Antichristian-Politick and Ecclesiastick-Power, Rule, Authority, Dominion, and Government of the BEAST", he never advocated taking arms against either the Established Church or the State.[275] As well, he warned "the King, the Nobles, the Judges, and all the Magistrates in this Island, and in this City" of God's judgment, that Christ, not the saints, would "break them... and dash them in pieces".[276] He also stated: "That God will set his King (namely King Jesus) opon his holy Hill of Zion", not the Saints.[277] In fact, when dealing with the question of the reign of the Saints, at no point did he describe the situation as one in which the Saints would seize the Kingdom for Christ, but rather as one of Christ establishing his Kingdom and giving it to the Saints.[278]

Pope A. Duncan wrote: "Without doubt, [Knollys] shared many of the [Fifth Monarchists'] ideas. Certainly, he held millennial views which were in essential accord with those of that party."[279] For the most part, however, Knollys' position on the Antichrist, the Second Coming, the Millennium, and the Eschaton was neither radical nor new. His identification of the Pope with the Antichrist and the Roman Church as the Beast was hardly novel. Many English contemporaries believed in an imminent return of Christ to establish his Kingdom on Earth, accompanied by an overthrow of Popish institutions and the Turks and a return of the Jewish people to God.[280] Though his earlier postmillennialism and his understanding of Christ's virtual return represented an unusual approach, his later premillennial position was not.

Certainly, the events of his time and experiences of Knollys and his fellow Particular Baptists informed his opinion and position. His interpretation of the signs of the second coming of Christ rarely pinpointed specific contemporary events, but in a general manner depicted circumstances (tribulation, apostasy) which were given fuller meaning by his belief in a gathered believers' church. Knollys' depiction of the Beast cast a wider net than an abhorrence of the Church of Rome, taking in all national churches as well. The Particular Baptist ecclesiology – an understanding of the gathered church, a belief in the congregational manner of government, and an emphasis on believer's baptism – perhaps sharpened his eschatology.[281] Knollys' understanding of the "True

---

[274] Knollys, *An Exposition of the Whole Book of the Revelation*, pp. 123-24 Knollys, *The World that Now Is*, Book II, pp. 5-6.

[275] Knollys, *Apocalyptical Mysteries*, Part III, p. 9. At best, he advocated passive resistance.

[276] Knollys, *The World that Now Is*, Book II, pp. 45-46.

[277] Knollys, *The World that Now Is*, Book II, p. 46.

[278] Knollys, *The World that Now Is*, Book II, p. 27.

[279] Duncan, *Hanserd Knollys*, p. 47.

[280] Ball, *Great Expectation*.

[281] More below on Knollys and the developing ecclesiology of the Particular Baptists.

Church" and of "False Professors", his interpretation of the Two Witnesses, and his call to preparation for Christ's return unquestionably received deeper meaning from his ecclesiology. His understanding of Christ's Kingdom and its inception also linked very nicely with his conviction of the believers' Church and with his Calvinistic understanding of God's people and election. The early practice of Knollys and many other Particular Baptists of preaching tours with an emphasis on the conversion of the listeners had a direct relation to his emphasis on the preaching of the Gospel and the conquest of Christ and his Saints through the Spirit and the Word. Knollys' most impassioned published passages entreating his readers to confess and turn from their sin appeared in his eschatological works.[282] Although Knollys and the Particular Baptists often promoted beliefs and ideas, which challenged the traditional position of society and the Church of England, they also emphasised the importance of order. Regardless of how they were perceived or mistreated for their beliefs, patience in the face of persecution, rather than armed insurrection, remained the solution advocated by Knollys:

> And let the Churches, Ministers, and all the Saints know and Consider *seriously*, That though they ought to pray for Kings, and all that are in Authority,... to obey Magistrates, and be subject to Principalities, and Powers, being God's Ordinance,... *For so is the Will of God*.... Yet in Case the Powers of this World shall command them to do any thing, which God hath forbidden, or shall forbid them to do any thing, which God hath Commanded, they ought to obey God rather then Men, as they [Apostles] did... and patiently Suffer for Righteousness sake,... as the Saints and Servants of Christ have done.[283]

---

[282] Knollys, *Parable of the Kingdom of Heaven* and Knollys, *The World that Now Is,* Part II, pp. 31-37.
[283] Knollys, *Exposition of the Eleventh Chapter of the Revelation*, p. 43.

CHAPTER 7

A Sect No More: Hanserd Knollys' Role in Particular Baptist Formalisation

Introduction

In late 1689, Hanserd Knollys turned eighty years old, a ripe old age for one to reach in the seventeenth century. During those eighty years, Knollys had experienced intolerance and persecution under Laud and the Massachusetts Bay Puritans in the 1630s, limited freedom and toleration in the 1640s and 1650s, and renewed intolerance and persecution during the Restoration. However, a far more significant occurrence took place in 1689, the legal toleration of religious dissent. The prior year had witnessed the flight of the King of England from invading forces led by his son-in-law, William of Orange. With the meeting of a newly elected Parliament in January 1689, came limited, yet significant constitutional and religious changes, including the Toleration Act.[1] Within a month after Knollys' eightieth birthday, both the Declaration of Rights and the Declaration of Toleration became law. While the Bill of Rights brought little fundamental change to the constitution, the Toleration Bill, though limited, did legally allow dissenters to worship according to their consciences for the first time since the Interregnum.[2]

The original Toleration Bill represented one-half of an attempt on the part of Parliament finally to bring about a measure of unity and uniformity to the Protestant church in England. In early March 1689, a Comprehension Bill was introduced into the House of Lords; it sought to provide enough flexibility to

---

[1] Barry Coward and Ernest Payne both stated clearly that these political/constitutional and religious shifts were in reality quite restricted. The flight of James II meant that the more conservative Lords and many Bishops supported William, lest they face again the uncertainty and potential radicalisation that had taken over in the 1640s. However, they did use their position and power to limit the restrictions on royal power intended by the Declaration of Rights passed by Parliament. The Declaration of Toleration was very limited, applying only to Protestants. Barry Coward, *The Stuart Age*, 2nd ed., (New York: Longman, 1994), pp. 342-44, 351-65. Ernest Payne, "Toleration and Establishment: I. A Historical Outline", in *From Uniformity to Unity 1662-1962*, Geoffrey F. Nuttall and Owen Chadwick, eds., (London: S.P.C.K., 1962), pp. 257-61.

[2] Coward, *Stuart Age*, pp. 361-63; Payne, "Toleration and Establishment", p. 259.

allow most Protestant dissenters to enter the Anglican Church, leaving only a minority to fall under the protection of the Toleration Bill. In reality, the two bills attempted to keep Anglican hegemony intact, while offering some concessions to Protestant dissenters. William III had himself proposed a much more liberal alternative within a few weeks of his accession, when he suggested the repeal of the Test and Corporation Acts.[3] Whigs such as John Locke, had also proposed more freedom of thought and expression. However, the conservative Anglican element of Parliament, already struggling with the constitutional difficulties of abandoning James II, resisted the suggestions to allow more freedom in the area of religion. The Comprehension Bill, "widely regarded as the natural, if not essential, complement" of the Toleration Bill failed to garner sufficient support and only the latter became law in May 1689.[4] Under it, dissenters still had to take the oath of allegiance and to subscribe to most of the Thirty-nine Articles.[5] Those omitted related to church traditions, the homilies, the consecration of bishops and ministers, and rites and ceremonies. As well, all subjects would continue to pay tithes and parochial taxes and dissenting houses of worship still needed to be licensed by the diocesan bishop, arch-deacon or Justice of the Peace.[6] Public office continued to be restricted to those who conformed to the Church of England, and the legal situation of the dissenting academies remained unclear.[7]

In effect, the Toleration Act brought an end to persecution, but little else. However, dissenters had suffered degrees of persecution since the late sixteenth century and Hanserd Knollys and the Particular Baptists had experienced more than their share of persecution since the 1630s. Not only did the Toleration Act end the arrest and fining of Protestants, it also guaranteed freedom of worship for Protestants outside of the forms and ceremonies of the Established Church.[8]

---

[3] Coward, *Stuart Age*, p. 362.

[4] Payne held that had the Comprehension Bill passed, it would have dealt a severe blow to the Baptists, since it would likely have allowed the Presbyterians and most Independents to become part of the new National Church, thereby breaking the strength of English Protestant dissent and isolating the Baptists. Payne, "Toleration and Establishment", pp. 259-260; Coward, *Stuart Age*, pp. 362-63.

[5] The exceptions were Articles Thirty-four through Thirty-six and part of Article Twenty.

[6] The penalties for failure to swear or subscribe were still based on the Act of Uniformity of 1662 and the Conventicle and Five Mile Acts. Peter Naylor, *Picking Up a Pin for the Lord: English Particular Baptists from 1688 to the Early Nineteenth Century*, (London: Grace, 1992), p. 34; Nicholas Tyacke, "The 'Rise of Puritanism' and the Legalizing of Dissent", in *From Persecution to Toleration: The Glorious Revolution and Religion in England*, Ole Peter Grell, Jonathan I. Israel, and Nicholas Tyacke, eds., (Oxford: Clarendon Press, 1991), pp. 18-19.

[7] Naylor, *Picking Up a Pin*, p. 34.

[8] Payne, "Toleration and Establishment", pp. 259.

A half-century had passed since the Particular Baptist had gathered their first churches in London. Those few scattered congregations had grown in number and in size. Most Englishmen in the 1630s and 1640s had viewed the Baptists as a radical sect; many believed that they had transgressed orthodoxy or at best had stretched its limits. However, by the 1680s the Particular Baptists had achieved a measure of legitimacy and toleration, thanks in no small part to the efforts of leaders such as Hanserd Knollys. The London Particular Baptists had sprung from the so-called separatist or dissenting tradition.[9] They had renounced the Church of England as impure and set about forming an alternative, pure church.[10] Like the Elizabethan Puritan movement from which the separatist tradition evolved, the desire of the dissenters was for further godly reformation of the Church in England.[11] Hanserd Knollys and the Particular Baptists shared this goal of forming a "new church" to replace the corrupt "old church". The peace and stability afforded by the new Toleration Act gave them greater opportunity and freedom to carry out this task.

In his work on the history of the Christian religion, Ernst Troeltsch outlined three major types, which embodied the "sociological structuring of the Christian religious idea".[12] The first he called the "church-type", the view that "Christianity is the institution of salvation and grace – the church that receives redemption from Christ and mediates this salvation to the individual".[13] Thus, the church became "the objective institution of grace" entrusted with the means of salvation; it demanded the devotion of the believer. Often, the pragmatic reality of this is that the church-type has existed in relationship with other structures, even secular ones, often to the point of compromise for the sake of order. The church-type typically took the form of a parochial or national church.[14]

The second type Troeltsch called the "sect-type", characterised by its "rigoristic demand for an unconditional application of the evangelical ethic". Whereas the church-type often compromised and abandoned or downplayed the ideal of Christian perfection, the sect-type refused to "give in to the general

---

[9] See B.R. White, *The English Separatist Tradition: From Marian Martyrs to the Pilgrim Fathers*, (London: Oxford University Press, 1971) and Michael R. Watts, *The Dissenters: From the Reformation to the French Revolution*, vol. I, (Oxford: Clarendon Press, 1978).

[10] Patrick Collinson, "Towards a Broader Understanding of the Early Dissenting Tradition", *The Dissenting Tradition: Essays for Leland H. Carlson*, C. Robert Cole and Michael E. Moody, eds., (Athens: Ohio University Press, 1975), p. 3.

[11] Collinson, "Towards a Broader Understanding of the Early Dissenting Tradition", p. 4; Watts, *The Dissenters*, pp. 14-34; White, *English Separatist Tradition*, chs. 1-2.

[12] Ernst Troeltsch, "Stoic-Christian Natural Law and Modern Secular Natural Law", (originally published in 1911) in *Religion in History*, James Luther Adams and Walter F. Bense, eds., (Edinburgh: T & T Clark, 1991), p. 324.

[13] Troeltsch, "Stoic-Christian Natural Law and Modern Secular Natural Law", p. 324.

[14] Troeltsch, "Stoic-Christian Natural Law and Modern Secular Natural Law", p. 325.

state of sinfulness" and demanded "the actual overcoming of sin". Instead of seeing the Christian community as "an all-inclusive institution into which one is born", the sect-type desired to bring together confessing Christians into "a holy community" of professed believers. Sects placed an emphasis on the role of lay people and stressed the relationship of the individual with God.[15] The third type Troeltsch characterised by enthusiasm and mysticism. With an emphasis on inward religious experience, enthusiasts reacted against "the objective character of cult, dogma, and institution".[16] Mysticism took religion even further than the sect-type in that it emphasised a "radical, non-communal form of individualism" putting the Christian into immediate communion with Christ without an external institution or dogma.[17]

Troeltsche's classification of Christianity still provides many insights into the religious situation in seventeenth-century England. The Established Church (Episcopalian to Presbyterian back to Episcopalian) provided an obvious example of the church-type. The most radical groups such as the Ranters and Quakers fit into the mystical or enthusiastic type. The Independents and Baptists, especially the latter, more clearly represented the sect-type.[18] The accusation that had been levelled against the Baptists from the beginning in the 1640s was that they embraced principles from which all heresies flowed, principles such as the rejection of the national church, an emphasis on lay involvement, democratic church government, religious toleration and liberty of conscience. Their opponents called them Anabaptists in an effort to link them with sixteenth century continental radicals who were perceived as a "menace to authority and social order".[19] In some sense, from the days of the 1640s, when Knollys and the Baptists attempted to gain a form of legitimacy, the move had begun from the more fluid sect-type to the more institutionalised and ordered church-type.

---

[15] Troeltsch, "Stoic-Christian Natural Law and Modern Secular Natural Law", p. 325.
[16] Troeltsch, "Stoic-Christian Natural Law and Modern Secular Natural Law", p. 326.
[17] Troeltsch, "Stoic-Christian Natural Law and Modern Secular Natural Law", p. 327.
[18] While some Independents might not have been comfortable with such a designation, "by transferring the headship or kingly office of Christ from the mystical body of the universal church to the immediate local congregation of saints on earth, the Independents eliminated all intermediaries – whether royal supremacy or the papal, Episcopal, or presbyterian hierarchies – between Christ as head of the church and the individual saint." Murray Tolmie, *Triumph of the Saints*, (Cambridge: Cambridge University Press, 1977), p. 85.
[19] J.F. McGregor, "The Baptists: Fount of All Heresy", in *Radical Religion in the English Revolution*, ed. B. Reay and J.F. McGregor (New York: Oxford University Press, 1984), pp. 24-25; Robert Baillie, *Anabaptism, the trve fovntaine of independency, Brownisme, Antinomy, Familisome, and the most of the other errours, which for the time due trouble the Church of England, vnsealed: also the questions of pædobaptisme and dipping handled from scripture : in a second part of the disswasive from the errors of the time*, (London: 1647).

The publication of the London Confessions (1644, 1646, 1677/88) and the move to plant Baptist churches outside of London and gather them into associations provided clear evidence of this institutionalisation of the Particular Baptists. The establishment of toleration in 1689 certainly provided a more favourable atmosphere for such a move. The Toleration Act enabled the calling of a General Assembly of Particular Baptist Churches in London in September 1689, another obvious step toward institutionalisation.[20] In light of these issues, several questions present themselves: In what sense did the move toward institutionalisation derive from the desires and intentions of the pastors or members and in what sense were the Particular Baptists merely being moved along by their circumstances and society? How important for Knollys and the Particular Baptists was order and the perception of order among and within their churches? In what ways did they become more formalised with clearer institutional qualities and in what ways did they retain a more sectarian identity? And what role did Hanserd Knollys play in this move from sect to a more formalised institution?

This chapter will examine five specific areas in an attempt to answer these questions: Particular Baptist understanding of polity, doctrine, ministry, sacraments, and worship. A definitive portrait of the early Particular Baptists will not necessarily emerge from this endeavour. In many instances the evidence will reveal a continuing debate and lack of consensus in these areas. That institutionalisation was only in progress at the end of Knollys' life clearly emerged in the debates over these issues that would carry on for some time following his death. In fact, Benjamin Keach would write and publish extensively on many of these same issues into the early eighteenth century. The perspective, position, and role of Knollys on many of these issues remained in development throughout much of his life. However, in one of his last major works, *The World That Now Is and the World That Is to Come*, Knollys provided a very clear declaration of his beliefs in many of these areas. [21] Divided into three parts, this treatise dealt with his soteriology, ecclesiology, and eschatology. The first two sections of this work related especially to the move from sect to a more formal institution.

Polity – Independence and Interdependence

Hanserd Knollys arrived at his ecclesiology or doctrine of the church as part of a lifelong journey. At an early date, Knollys and his fellow Particular Baptists

---

[20] *A Narrative of the Proceedings of the General Assembly Of divers Pastors, Messengers, and Ministering Brethren of the Baptized Churches, met together in London from Septemb. 3. to 12. 1689 from divers parts of England and Wales : Owning the Doctrine of Personal Election, and final Perseverance*, (London: 1689).

[21] Hanserd Knollys, *The World That Now Is and the World That Is to Come*, (London: 1681).

were first and foremost Separatists.[22] At some time after 1633, Knollys "was convinced of some things about the Worship of God (which I had conformed unto) to be sinful, to wit the Surplice, the Cross in Baptism, and admitting wicked persons to the Lord's Supper".[23] These scruples did not set him off from other puritans but Knollys took the unusual step of separating himself from the Church of England and these sinful practices. Separation would not only characterise Knollys' actions throughout his life, but it would become central to his theology of the church.[24] The confusion presented by the practices of the Established Church caused the drift toward or plunge into separatism. Separatists recognised godly elements and people present within the Church of England and other "corrupted" churches, but as Patrick Collinson aptly put it: "The question on the side of the Separatists was whether the godly, by adhering to a Church which was a confused heap of good and bad, and by submitting themselves to the corrupt power of the bishops, had put themselves beyond public communion and even private fellowship."[25] For Knollys and the Particular Baptists as for the separatists of the Jacob Church in the early seventeenth century, the true Church, as revealed in Scripture, was a pure fellowship of believers "which must be separated from the ungodly and the uncommitted".[26]

Although Knollys' own separation in the early 1630s was initiated by stirrings and doubts within his own conscience, it would give way to a theology of separation which would become central to the Particular Baptist ideal of independent congregationalism. The ideal of a pure or true church, found throughout Knollys' writings, expressed and realised both the acts of separating and of gathering together. However: "The first step towards the true worship of God, is to forsake the Assemblies of false worship and to separate from them. When God chose a people for himself, to worship him, he severed them from all other people."[27] In his apocalyptic works, Knollys kept the true church and

---

[22] The Separatist background for their ecclesiology is very clearly presented in Stephen Brachlow, *The Communion of the Saints: Radical Puritan and Separatist Ecclesiology, 1570-1625*, (Oxford: Oxford University Press, 1988), pp. 150-229. See also Geoffrey F. Nuttall, *Visible Saints: The Congregational Way, 1640-1660*, (Oxford: Basil Blackwell, 1957), pp. 43-69.

[23] Hanserd Knollys, *The Life and Death of That Old Disciple of Jesus Christ, and Eminent Minister of the Gospel, Mr. Hanserd Knollys*, edited by William Kiffin, (London: 1692), p. 9, hereafter cited as *Life*.

[24] Knollys experienced similar 'scruples of conscience' during his brief stay in Dover, New England. See Chapter 2.

[25] Collinson, "Towards a Broader Understanding", p. 19.

[26] White, *English Separatist Tradition*, p. 166.

[27] Hanserd Knollys, *An Exposition of the first Chapter of the Song of Solomon* (London: 1656), p. 36.

the false church in constant juxtaposition.[28] In fact, for Knollys, the appearance of congregational churches had a clear eschatological function.[29] He did this not only to contrast the two, but also to entreat the reader to separate from the false church. *Mystical Babylon Unvailed* ended with a section entitled "A Call to all the People of God to come out of Babylon" where he argued that failure to separate from the papal church was a dangerous sin. For proof he quoted Revelation 18:4, "And I heard another voice from Heaven, saying, Come out of HER my People, That ye be not Partakers of her Sins, And that ye receive not of her Plagues."[30] The true worshipper had no option but separation: "You cannot enjoy Communion with God, whilst you hold a Communion with Idols, and Image-worshipers."[31]

In chapter five of *The World That Now Is and The World That Is To Come*, Knollys fleshed out his theology of separation by building upon the Old Testament principle of God separating the people of Israel from the Gentiles "to be the peculiar People to worship him according to his Institutions and Commandments".[32] This received confirmation in the New Testament, where God commanded "Believing Gentiles to be separated from Idolaters, and Unbelievers, or Infidels, and to have no Communion or Fellowship with them in any false Worship".[33] From the Particular Baptists' earliest days, one of the accusations they consistently faced related to the schismatic nature of their separation, which, it was claimed, destroyed the unity of the Church.[34] Knollys took such accusations very seriously. He himself argued that: "Separation from a true Church is Schism, and Schism is a Sin, 1 Cor. 12.25, which causeth Division."[35] As seen in his interaction with John Saltmarsh[36] and his involvement and interaction with the Quakers, Levellers, and Fifth Monarchists,[37] Knollys was a very tolerant and gracious person who desired unity. In keeping with that spirit, his theology of separation left no room for

---

[28] For examples see Hanserd Knollys, *An Exposition of the Whole Book of the Revelation Wherein the Visions and Prophecies of Christ are Opened and Expounded*, (London: 1688), pp. 24, 61, 106; *An Exposition of the Eleventh Chapter of the Revelation*, (London: 1679), pp. 4-8.

[29] Knollys, *Exposition of the Eleventh Chapter of the Revelation*, pp. 14-15.

[30] Hanserd Knollys, *Mystical Babylon Unvailed*, (London: 1679), pp. 25-27.

[31] Knollys, *Mystical Babylon Unvailed*, p. 28. See also Knollys, *Exposition of the Whole Book of Revelation*, p. 125.

[32] Knollys, *The World that Now Is*, Book I, p. 95.

[33] According to the New Testament scriptures, this separation was from unbelieving Jews in their synagogues, worship and worshippers of the Beast or his Image, and assemblies of all false worshippers and false worship (Acts 19:8-9; Rev. 14:9-10; 20:4; 2 Cor. 6:16-17). Knollys, *The World that Now Is*, Book I, pp. 95-96.

[34] Nuttall, *Visible Saints*, pp. 61-64.

[35] Knollys, *Exposition of the Whole Book of Revelation*, p. 62.

[36] See Chapter 3.

[37] See Chapter 4.

separation from "true Churches of God".[38] Rather, the believer was to attempt to bring about restoration or correction and thus "to imitate Christ in this matter" with "each one endeavouring to keep the Unity of the Spirit in the Bond of Peace".[39] This same spirit of forbearance also appeared in the Confession of 1646, which Knollys probably helped to compile. Section XLVI stated that a church "being rightly gathered, and continuing in the obedience of the gospel of Christ, none are to separate for faults and corruptions... until they have, in due order and tenderness, sought redress thereof".[40] The Confession itself said little about separation though, limiting it to the brief but crucial statement that "the church is a company of visible saints... called and separated from the world by the word and... Spirit of God".[41]

The London Confession of 1646 also required that a pure or true church be "gathered". Since many of the Particular Baptists in the early days of the movement had themselves come out of the Independent church tradition, this position was quite familiar to them.[42] Although it drew them closer to the Independents in London, it brought forth constant criticism from their opponents. Knollys had clearly stated the case for Independent gathered churches in his debate in print with John Bastwick in 1645.[43] *A Moderate Answer Unto Dr. Bastwicks Book called Independency not God's Ordinance*, dealt specifically with Bastwick's previous attacks against independent, gathered churches. In this work, Knollys also stated the Particular Baptist practice for gathering churches. The conditions for admission were simple: faith, repentance, and baptism.[44]

The idea of the pure, gathered, believers' church remained central in many of Knollys' later writings. In his allegorical interpretation of the Song of Solomon of 1656, he gave the following comparison of a false, coercive church and a true, believer's church:

---

[38] However, Knollys, like other separatists, did not view a national church as a "True Church" but in fact as a "daughter" of the Harlot and Antichrist, Rome. Thus, to separate from it was not, in fact, schism at all. See above Chapter 6 on the eschatological ramifications. Nuttall, *Visible Saints*, pp. 63-65.

[39] Knollys, *The World That Now Is*, Book I, pp. 50-51, 96-99.

[40] "A Confession of Faith of Seven Congregations or Churches of Christ in London, Which are Commonly (But Unjustly) called Anabaptists", (London: 1646), in *Confessions of Faith and Other Public Documents, Illustrative of the History of the Baptist Churches of England in the 17th Century*, edited by Edward Bean Underhill, (London: Hanserd Knollys Society, 1854), pp. 43-44; hereafter designated "Confession of 1646".

[41] "Confession of 1646", (Section XXXIII), p. 39.

[42] See Tolmie, *Triumph*, chapter 3.

[43] See Chapter 3 above.

[44] Hanserd Knollys, *A Moderate Answer Unto Dr. Bastwicks Book called Independecy not God's Ordinance,* (London: 1645), pp. 18-19.

> Antichrist opposeth Christ, and exalteth himself above all that is called God, or that is worshipped, shewing himself that he is God, by imposing Laws, Commandements, and Traditions of men upon the saints and Churches of God contrary unto Christ,... using a Coercive power to force their obedience unto, and observance of such Antichristian Inventions, and Superstitious Traditions of men [False Church]... Christ bringeth Beleevers into his Churches, and giveth them Spiritual Communion with himself in his holy ordinances... The Spouse of Christ is but one mystical Body, consisting of many spiritual members, compacted and fitly joined together [True Church].[45]

He went on to compare the Church to a house. The spiritual materials for building this house were believers.[46] He used a similar analogy in *World That Now Is*.[47] As well, Knollys repeatedly stated in his writings that the true churches were not national, but congregational churches, "a particular visible true Constituted Gospel Church of God". The visible church consisted of believers "engaging themselves to come together in ONE Congregation... to worship God publickly in all his holy Ordinances".[48] *An Exposition of the Whole Book of Revelation* most succinctly stated this congregational, gathered principle: "The essential form of a true visible Church of God is the right joining and orderly compacting of those Sanctified Believers together into one mystical body, by the Ministers of Christ, according to the constitution of the Gospel."[49] A primary example that he gave of such a church was the Ephesian church, which was

> a particular Congregation consisting of a few baptized Believers, who were separated from the profane Idolatrous Gentiles and their Idol Temples; also from the formal superstitious Jews and their Synagogues... and congregated together to worship God in Spirit and in Truth visibly, walking in all the Commandments and Ordinances of God blamelessly, according to the Order of the Gospel.[50]

---

[45] Knollys, *Song of Solomon*, pp.15-16. It is interesting to note that even in this exposition, which was intended as devotional, the obvious apocalyptic, eschatological implications of Knollys' ecclesiology. For a treatment of "The Apocalyptic Significance of the Song of Solomon", see Bryan W. Ball, *A Great Expectation: Eschatological Thought in English Protestantism to 1660*, (Leiden: E. J. Brill, 1975), Appendix I.

[46] Ball, *Great Expectation*, pp. 80-81.

[47] Knollys, *The World that Now Is*, Book I, pp. 42-46.

[48] Knollys, *The World That Now Is*, Book I, pp. 45-49. See also Knollys, *Exposition of the Eleventh Chapter of the Revelation*, pp. 10, 15; Knollys, *Exposition of the Whole Book of Revelation*, pp. 9, 17.

[49] Knollys, *Exposition of the Whole Book of Revelation*, p. 61.

[50] Knollys, *Exposition of the Whole Book of Revelation*, p. 18.

In this one example, Knollys brought together the principles of separation and the gathered church of believers.

The ideal of the gathered congregation guarded the purity of the church in other ways, even beyond the issue of membership. Congregationalism also involved self-government and self-determination, and these provided the proper means of insuring continued purity. The right for a church to choose and evaluate its own leaders and pastors was key, for the leadership of the church could often determine the orthodoxy and spiritual temperature of the church. According to Knollys, individual gathered churches had "Power and Authority from Christ to try the Calling, Gifts, Doctrine, and Conversion of their Teachers".[51] This statement coincided with the London Confession of 1646, Section XXXVI: "Being thus joined, every church... hath power given them from Christ, for their well-being, to choose among themselves meet persons for... elders and deacons, being qualified according to the word".[52] This self-government and self-determination had firm roots in the doctrine of the priesthood of all believers, an issue that, surprisingly, received relatively little attention from Knollys.[53] Knollys understood the spiritual work accomplished by God in the life of the believer as being central in the concept of self-determination. Through the "spiritual senses" God empowered and equipped each individual believer.[54] Through Christ, all believers received spiritual gifts and enlightenment in wisdom and understanding of God's word.[55] In times of persecution, when a congregation could no longer meet as a whole, those "Brethren who have received a Spiritual Gift, may minister the same to one another".[56] Self-government prepared the way for individual initiative, when needed.

A further benefit of self-government was the maintenance of purity within the church through church discipline. Schism within the True church was not permitted; instead, repentance should lead to reconciliation. However, in cases where reconciliation seemed impossible, each congregation had the authority to suspend or withdraw from a member who acted in a "disorderly" manner and to excommunicate a member who lived "in gross and scandalous sins".[57] Such sinners not only threatened the purity of the congregation, but their actions led

---

[51] Knollys, *Exposition of the Whole Book of Revelation*, p. 22.

[52] *1646 Confession* in Underhill, *Confessions of Faith*, p. 41.

[53] However, Knollys did have very definite opinions about ministers and a hierarchy of authority. This will be dealt with below pp. 257-71.

[54] Knollys, *Song of Solomon*, pp. 10-11.

[55] Hanserd Knollys, *Christ Exalted: A Lost Sinner Sought, and Saved by Christ: Gods People are an Holy people... the summe of divers Sermons Preached in Suffolk*, 2nd ed., (London: 1646), pp. 2-9.

[56] Knollys, *Exposition of the Whole Book of Revelation*, p. 63.

[57] Knollys, *World That Now Is*, Book I, pp. 52-54. Note Knollys' use of the word disorderly.

"to the dishonour of God and scandal of the Church".[58] Knollys used the church in Ephesus as a clear example of the evils that could occur where some "were corrupted by evil Manners, or wicked Opinions" and through them "others might be leavened and corrupted by their false Doctrines or sinful Practices". Christ gave this church the authority to admonish, withdraw from, or excommunicate the offending members.[59] The so-called Second London Confession, originally published in 1677, and officially endorsed and accepted by English Particular Baptists in 1688, made similar provisions for the calling and ordaining of Officers and church discipline.[60]

Another important aspect of developing Baptist polity was that of interdependence. While congregational autonomy stood at the heart of the congregational form of church government, at the same time, congregationalists had a desire for fellowship and association with others of like mind, though never to the detriment of independence. Again, this was something common to mid-seventeenth century congregational churches in England, not something special to the Particular Baptists. Many of the London congregations remained in a continued relationship with the Jessey church and other separatist Independent churches.[61] For the Particular Baptists, however, the impetus for fellowship also took formal shape through printed confessions. As early as 1644, the Particular Baptist congregations in London joined together to publish a Confession of Faith, which clearly delineated an understanding of interdependence:

> And although the particular Congregations be distinct and severall Bodies, every one a compact and knit Citie in it selfe; yet are they all to walk by one and the same Rule, and by all meanes convenient to have the counsell and help one of another in all needfull affaires of the Church as members of one body in the common faith under Christ their onely head.[62]

A very similar statement appeared in the Confession of 1646, which revised the Scripture references to include ones mentioning financial assistance between churches. An even fuller statement appeared in the Confession of 1648, which

---

[58] Knollys, *Exposition of the Eleventh Chapter of the Revelation*, p. 6.
[59] Knollys, *Exposition of the Whole Book of the Revelation*, p. 21.
[60] *A Confession of Faith Put Forth by the Elders and Brethren of many Congregations of Christians, (baptized upon Profession of their Faith) in London and the Country*, (London: 1688), Chapter XXVI, sections 7-9, 12, pp. 88-91; hereafter called the *Second London Confession*.
[61] See Chapters 3 and 4 above. Also, see Tolmie, *Triumph*, chapters 3 and 6.
[62] "The Confession of Faith, Of those Churches which are commonly (though falsly) called Anabaptists", Section XLVII, (London: 1644), in *Baptist Confessions of Faith*, ed. William L. Lumpkin, (Philadelphia: The Judson Press, 1959), pp. 168-69; hereafter designated *1644 Confession*.

included a very detailed plan for churches to assist other churches if difficulties arose related to doctrine or administration. This "intervention" had very clear limits, however: "These Messengers assembled are not entrusted with any Church power properly so called; or with any Jurisdiction over the Churches themselves, to exercise any Censures either over any churches or Persons; or to impose their determination on the Churches, or Officers."[63] In other words, they could persuade, not command.

The efforts made by London Baptists such as Knollys to plant and support new fellowships outside of London during the 1640s and 1650s provided another example of the principle of interdependence.[64] This early collaboration among the Particular Baptists formed the seedbed for the idea of associations.[65] However, during the periods of persecution, which followed the Restoration, these associations became both more difficult and more important to maintain.[66] In part, the association principle developed as a tool of necessary support against a hostile world. However, it also developed out of the early connections with the Jessey church and other Independent congregations.

In *The World That Now Is* Hanserd Knollys dealt with the subject of association among the congregations. Upon the gathering of a new congregation, he argued, "the Ministers and Brethren of other Churches being also present, ought to own and acknowledge them to be a Sister Church, by giving them the Right hand of Fellowship; and so commend them by Prayer unto God."[67] This principle of association was reflected in the involvement of Knollys in the activities of sister Baptist churches in London. On 28 June 1666, he joined with Edward Harrison of the Petty France congregation in setting apart elder Thomas Patient as co-pastor with William Kiffin. On the same occasion, he also took part in the ordaining of two deacons for Kiffin's church at Devonshire Square. Less than a month later, Patient suddenly died and a shortly thereafter, Knollys came again, this time to ordain Daniel Dyke on 17 February 1668. In October 1690, he joined with William Collins of Petty France and Hercules Collins of Wapping in appointing Richard Adams as co-pastor with William Kiffin.[68] In *The World That Now Is*, Knollys argued that

---

[63] *1644 Confession*, Chapter XXVI, Section 15, p. 93.

[64] See Chapter 4.

[65] B.R. White, *The English Baptists of the Seventeenth Century*, rev. ed., (Oxford: The Baptist Historical Society, 1996), pp. 65-66. W.T. Whitley proposed that the concept for Baptist associations had its origins in the division of the Parliamentary army into Associations. W.T. Whitley, *A History of the British Baptists*, (London: Charles Griffin & Co., 1923), pp. 90-91. White very adeptly disputed that theory in his *English Baptists of the Seventeenth Century*, pp. 66-68.

[66] White, *English Baptists of the Seventeenth Century*, pp. 97, 128-31. Whitley, *British Baptists*, pp. 91-92.

[67] Knollys, *World That Now Is*, Book I, p. 50.

[68] B.R. White, *Hanserd Knollys and Radical Dissent in the 17th Century*, (London: Dr. Williams's Trust, 1977.), pp. 21, 23.

even when more than one congregation existed in a particular city, there should be only one church in that city. All the congregations should bear the same name, that is, the church of God in London or some other particular city, as in the days of the New Testament Church. This practice was not followed, however, and Particular Baptist congregations were usually known either by the building or street where they met or by the pastor who led them.[69]

On 22 July 1689, a letter was sent from the leadership of the London churches to Particular Baptist congregations throughout England. Hanserd Knollys, William Kiffin, Benjamin Keach, and several other prominent London Particular Baptists, proposed an Assembly of Particular Baptist Churches from across the land to discuss the general situation and "the great neglect of the present ministry" within the Particular Baptist Churches throughout England.[70] They encouraged the participation "of two principle brethren, of every Church of the same faith with us, in every county respectively".[71] They were to send their response to one of the two elder statesmen of the Particular Baptists – Hanserd Knollys or William Kiffin.[72] The Assembly did take place in September 1689 with 107 churches sending representatives.[73] The Assembly published a narrative of its proceedings and Hanserd Knollys, as the most senior leader of the Particular Baptists became the first signatory.[74] From the outset, those assembled unanimously declared that the Assembly did not claim any "superiority, superintendency" or "Authority or Power" over any church in attendance, but rather that they came together to give assistance to one another. Thus, any determinations of the Assembly would in no way be "binding to any one Church, till the Consent of that Church be first had, and they conclude the same among themselves".[75] Clearly, the congregational principle took precedence.

---

[69] Knollys, *World That Now Is*, Book I, p. 50. In a limited way, the London churches did that type of thing, by coming together under the London Confessions.

[70] White, *Hanserd Knollys*, p. 22; Pope A. Duncan, *Hanserd Knollys: Seventeenth-Century Baptist*, (Nashville: Broadman Press, 1965), p. 35.

[71] Thomas Armitage, *A History of the Baptists*, vol. II, (Watertown, WI: Maranatha Baptist Press, 1980 reprint; original published in 1890), p. 558. This letter followed on the heels of the publication of the *Second London Confession* in 1688. Whitley linked the two events in his *British Baptists*, p. 175.

[72] White, *English Baptists of the Seventeenth Century*, p. 163. By this point, Kiffin and Knollys were the only leaders left who had lived during the seminal days of the 1640s.

[73] This was encouraging as was the spirit of unity, despite the differences, which had surfaced during recent debates. *A Narrative of the Proceedings of the General Assembly*, (1689), pp. 4, 19-25.

[74] By this point the church he had gathered in 1645 was meeting in George Yard near Broken Wharf. Knollys signed this document with his co-pastor Robert Steed, who upon Knollys' death in 1691 moved the congregation to Bagnio Court off Newgate Street. W.T. Whitley, *Baptists in London, 1612-1928*, (London: Kingsgate Press, n.d.), p. 107.

[75] *A Narrative of the Proceedings of the General Assembly*, (1689), p. 10.

The narrative of the proceedings of the Assembly made it clear that all felt a general concern regarding the "Spiritual Decay, and loss of Strength, Beauty and Glory in our Churches" and sought to find some means to return them to a "more prosperous State and Condition".[76] Those assembled outlined two principal causes of decay. First, a general laxity of commitment, a "want of holy Zeal for God, and the House of our God".[77] Either the persecution of recent years or the disappearance of some of the earlier Particular Baptist congregations had caused a waning of the churches' first love.[78] The decline of fervour greatly concerned Knollys, since his eschatological interpretation postulated a great Tribulation, which would bring "a very great formality, lukewarmness, and Worldliness, &c. among Church-members".[79] The second principle cause of this malaise was a neglect of the ministry in many churches.[80] As an expression of their concern over the decay of the churches, those assembled appointed a general fast to be held on 10 October 1689.[81] They also initiated an annual "Free-Will Offering"[82] to establish a Public fund to help economically less fortunate churches.[83] Issues of church discipline also arose and produced practical recommendations.[84] One final significant document to come out of this assembly was *Innocency Vindicated; or Reproach wip'd off*, a statement by the assembly addressing many slanderous statements or opinions previously made or held against the Particular Baptists. Again, William Kiffin's and Hanserd Knollys' names headed the list of signatories.

The success of the Assembly of 1689 was evident in the fact that those present planned and called for a further assembly in 1690. However, the next assembly could not be held until June 2-8, 1691. Again, Knollys attended and was the first signatory of the proceedings.[85] By the time the next General

---

[76] *A Narrative of the Proceedings of the General Assembly*, (1689), p. 3.

[77] *A Narrative of the Proceedings of the General Assembly*, (1689), p. 4.

[78] Knollys had stated, almost prophetically, in his *Exposition of the first Chapter of the Song of Solomon*, p. 62, that "Souls ought not to coole in their spiritual affections unto Christ Jesus; Christ doth take it unkindly that any believers should leave their first love, Rev. 2.4. And this they do first, when they neglect to live by Faith."

[79] Knollys, *Exposition of the Eleventh Chapter of the Revelation*, p. 30. See Chapter 6 above.

[80] *A Narrative of the Proceedings of the General Assembly*, (1689), p. 5. This will be dealt with further below.

[81] *A Narrative of the Proceedings of the General Assembly*, (1689), pp. 7-8.

[82] This is a bit of an anomaly for a group of Calvinistic Baptists.

[83] *A Narrative of the Proceedings of the General Assembly*, (1689), pp. 10-12. What is especially impressive about this is that this donation would be above and beyond the tithes and parochial taxes still required of the dissenters.

[84] *A Narrative of the Proceedings of the General Assembly*, (1689), pp. 14-15. Other aspects of this Assembly will be examined below as they pertain to the discussion.

[85] *A Narrative of the Proceedings of the General Assembly Of the Elders and Messengers of the Baptized Churches sent from divers parts of England and Wales*,

Assembly was held in 1692, Hanserd Knollys had died. By then, however, he had made a significant contribution to the formation of a national Particular Baptist fellowship. The commitment of Hanserd Knollys and other first generation Particular Baptists to independent, congregational government and to interdependence through associations had not merely been established, but the English Particular Baptists were well on their way to becoming institutionalised by the time the third General Assembly met in 1692. Without question, the uncompromising commitment to the ideals of independence and interdependence gave evidence of the desire of the Particular Baptists have a representative church which maintained order and accountability.

Theology – Puritan and Orthodox?

In his recent Ph.D. dissertation Barry Howson has raised the question of the orthodoxy of Hanserd Knollys' theology within the context of the seventeenth century.[86] For Knollys and other Particular Baptists in the seventeenth century, such a question constantly arose. In their ongoing struggle for recognition as legitimate, this question was raised and answered repeatedly. The earliest confessions of the Particular Baptists sought to lay to rest any doubts.[87] So too did the many debates with opponents, both within the Established Church and without.[88] Knollys himself, when taken before the authorities during the chaotic days of the 1640s, took the opportunity to preach before them in order to dispel their concerns.[89] At the heart of these concerns was a desire to avoid a reputation of disorder. The *Second London Confession*, any pertinent issues arising from the General Assembly of 1689, and Knollys' own theology continued to address this question in the late seventeenth century.

As has been shown, the theological persuasion of Hanserd Knollys and the Particular Baptists could be described as a moderate form of High-Calvinism, balancing election with an emphasis on evangelism. They emphasised an

---

which began in London the 2d of June and ended the 8th of the same, 1691 (Owning the Doctrine of Personal Election, and Final Perseverance), (London: 1691). B.R. White mistakenly stated that the next assemblies took place in 1690 and 1691 and implied that Knollys attended both. White, *Hanserd Knollys*, p. 23. However, the records indicate that the next two assemblies took place in 1691 and 1692 and that Knollys only attended the first assembly. Because of his reliance on White, Howson made the same mistake, "The Question of Orthodoxy in the theology of Hanserd Knollys (c. 1599-1691): a Seventeenth Century English Calvinistic Baptist", (Unpublished Ph.D. Dissertation, McGill University, 1999), pp. 74, 91, n.97. Thomas Crosby corroborated this fact in his *History of the English Baptists*, vol. III, (London: 1740), pp. 259, 264.

[86] "The Question of Orthodoxy in the theology of Hanserd Knollys (c. 1599-1691): a Seventeenth Century English Calvinistic Baptist".

[87] See Chapter 3 above.

[88] See Chapters 3 and 4 above.

[89] Knollys, *Life*, p. 21.

unquestionably Calvinist and Puritan theology of election with strong importance placed on God's sovereignty, in part to dispel any perception that they were unorthodox.[90] During the 1640s through the 1650s, a strong Calvinist theology predominated as the Presbyterians formed the Church of England, while the Independents and "Puritan Episcopalians", although stressing different polities, held to a similar theology of justification and sanctification.[91] During the Restoration, the reestablishment of episcopacy also brought a backlash aimed at Puritanism and its perceived excesses, and the Presbyterians now joined the ranks of the dissenters.[92] With the accession of William and Mary, and the Toleration Act, the climate once again became more favourable to a Calvinistic theology. In order to identify themselves with the theology of the Elizabethan Church, the Particular Baptists continued to display their orthodox, Puritan theology beyond the end of the Protectorate through to the Glorious Revolution.

However, the stress on evangelism and on the responsibility of the individual to embrace God's truth and requirements was equally evident. The most obvious reason for this two-fold thrust due to the fact that the Particular Baptists gathered their churches. People joined their congregations; they were not born into them as in the parishes of the Established Church. They endeavoured to attract people to their churches in order to advance their cause and they founded new Particular Baptist churches, or in the case of the period of persecution during the Restoration, preserved the churches already in existence. A second reason for the evangelistic thrust of their theology related

---

[90] In terms of the more general issues of orthodoxy, such as pertaining to the doctrines of the Trinity, the nature, person, and work of Christ, and the majesty and attributes of God, the Particular Baptists clearly lined up with orthodox, historical Christianity. See *Second London Confession*, pp. 9-12, 17-18, 27-34. This is clearly evident in "The Epistle to the Reader", written by Knollys in Thomas Collier's *The Exaltation of Christ in the days of the Gospel*, (London: 1647). See also Knollys, *World That Now Is*, Book I, pp. 4-5, 9-10; Knollys, *Exposition of the Whole Book of the Revelation*, pp. 11, 73. Perhaps the greatest assault on Knollys' orthodoxy was the accusation of his being antinomian. In *An Exposition of the Whole Book of the Revelation*, p. 93, he stated that the Elect receive salvation "From the Law, not from Evangelical obedience unto the moral part of the Law... but from the Ceremonial part of the Law... and from the curse of the Law". See above Chapter 2. For a detailed treatment of Knollys' antinomianism see, Howson, "Question of Orthodoxy", pp. 93-156.

[91] Robert S. Paul, *The Assembly of the Lord: Politics and Religion in the Westminster Assembly and the 'Grand Debate'*, (Edinburgh: T & T Clark, 1985), pp. 101-27.

[92] For the members of the Cavalier Parliament, this was due primarily to avoid chaos, for they saw an Episcopal Church of England as the bulwark against the spread of schism and disorder. Ironically, Charles II himself was less antagonistic to the Puritans and Presbyterians than the Parliament. I.M. Green, *The Re-establishment of the Church of England 1660-1663*, (Oxford: Oxford University Press, 1978), chapters IV and IX. Watts, *The Dissenters*, pp. 228-29.

to the first. Not only were the Particular Baptist congregations gathered churches, but they were also believers' churches. They limited membership to believers only. Thus, it was vital for the Particular Baptists to seek the conversion of others. It would be too callous to state that this evangelistic drive merely served the purpose of expanding their congregations. Rather, the desire for the conversion of others joined a concern for the spiritual well being of those they sought to convert.

Reformed Doctrine

The Calvinist theology of the Puritans was built upon a soteriology, which expressed a distinct understanding of the sovereignty of God and the fallen state of humanity.[93] The main elements of this soteriology included the total depravity of all human beings and their inability to do good works or acquire salvation; the unconditional election by God of those upon whom He bestowed salvation; the irresistible nature of this salvation through the inward work of Holy Spirit; the limited or particular nature of this salvation (arguing that the death of Jesus did not atone for all but only for the elect); and the eternal perseverance of those elect in their faith due to God's sovereign guardianship.[94] Closely related to these major points was a belief in the overarching providence of God controlling and guiding every aspect of life. While most people in seventeenth-century English society embraced an understanding of providence, the Puritans tended to hold to a "hotter sort" of providence.[95] The majority of society embraced the concept of providence from an often-mixed perspective, which included superstition as well as theological ideals, while the Puritan understanding of providence was firmly rooted in the Calvinistic doctrine of the sovereignty of God.[96] Finally the Particular Baptists emphasised the centrality of God's word, the Bible. In one of Knollys' earliest works, *Christ Exalted: A Lost Sinner Sought, and Saved by Christ*, he clearly expounded a reformed soteriology that fit this pattern. Throughout his works, his soteriology did not

---

[93] John Spurr has made a case for the fluidity of Calvinism. He argued that Puritan theology "never stood still. It was constantly being defined in religious controversy, in intellectual speculation, and in pastoral practice." *English Puritanism: 1603-1689*, (New York: St. Martin's Press, 1998), pp. 166-70.

[94] For a detailed treatment of Puritan soteriology and its evolution, see Dewey D. Wallace, Jr., *Puritans and Predestination: Grace in English Protestant Theology, 1525-1695*, (Chapel Hill: University of North Carolina Press, 1982).

[95] Alexandra Walsham, *Providence in Early Modern England*, (Oxford: Oxford University Press, 1999), pp. 2-3.

[96] Walsham, *Providence*, pp. 8-15. See also Keith Thomas, *Religion and the Decline of Magic*, (London: Weidenfeld and Nicolson, 1971). Both of these works emphasised the purging of Roman Catholic "superstition" by the Reformers. The resulting void was filled in part by this Reformed view of providence.

change greatly and in one of his final works, *The World That Now Is*, he again gave a clear exposition of it.

The *Second London Confession* clearly expressed the Particular Baptists' understanding of humanity's sinful condition and inability to do good works or obtain salvation. Because of the sin of Adam and Eve, human beings were "utterly indisposed, disabled and made opposite to all good, and wholly inclined to all evil". All of humanity was "dead in Sin, and wholly defiled, in all the faculties, and parts of soul, and body".[97]

In terms of the sinful state of humanity and its inability to do good or to gain God's salvation, Knollys also painted a despairing picture. Using the biblical imagery of Christ as the shepherd and people as the sheep, Knollys claimed that Christ in "seeking his lost sheep findes them in their blood, polluted, corrupted, filthy, naked, and loathsome", something the sinner was unaware of until convinced by the Holy Spirit and word of God.[98] Instead of the typical picture of a lamb as being pure, cuddly, and innocent, Knollys portrayed the lost sheep as utterly ugly, emphasising their corruption and dissipation. The reference to finding them in their blood and nakedness alluded to the guilt of the human race, perhaps referring back to the fall of humanity. In the book of Genesis, the feeling of guilt or spiritual nakedness by Adam and Eve came in their realisation of their physical nakedness (Genesis 3:6-11). And again, in the story of their sons, Cain and Abel, after Cain had murdered his brother, the blood of Abel proclaimed Cain's guilt (Genesis 4:8-12).[99] According to Knollys, sin made the human race "loathsome;" "both sins of Omission, and sins of Commission" – failure by doing what God has forbidden and by not doing what He has commanded.[100]

The natural state of humanity made the sinner unable to attain God's favour. This inability necessitated that God "drawes" the sinner by his loving kindness, "without which powerfull drawing, no sinner can come to Christ".[101] Knollys referred to this process as conviction of conscience and he held that it took place through the work and power of Holy Spirit and the word of God. Early in the process of conviction, having begun to become aware of "the vileness of his Nature and the sinfulness of his sins to be such, so many, and so great", the sinner attempted to reform himself. However, this only led him to further despair as he realised that his attempts at good were "as menstruous Raggs". In

---

[97] *Second London Confession*, pp. 24-25.
[98] Knollys, *Christ Exalted*, p. 17.
[99] He explained this phrase to be in one's blood as being in one's "naturall estate of sinful corruption". Again, this would be in an unregenerate state, guilty before God. Knollys, *Christ Exalted*, pp. 15, 17. See also Knollys, *Song of Solomon*, p. 70 where he stated "when we lay in our blood, our time was the time of love, and Christ tooke us out of our blood, and spread his skirt over us (put his righteousnesse upon us)."
[100] Knollys, *World That Now Is*, Book I, p. 12.
[101] Knollys, *Christ Exalted*, p. 17.

utter helplessness, the sinner cried out: "But this is my impotency, and here is my misery, I cannot believe in Christ of my selfe."[102] Having come to this place, God awakened the elect through "Spiritual Illumination, in the Saving Knowledge of the LORD Jesus Christ, whereby the Eyes of his Understanding is enlightened" leading the sinner to Conversion.[103] For Knollys, faith and repentance, both necessary for conversion, came as gifts from God.[104] Knollys expressed his view of total depravity and inability in the following statement:

> Sinners are often called upon to turn unto God, and to turn from their sins, Ezek. 14.6, 18, 30, 32. 33.11. that they may know it is their duty so to do; and that finding by experience it is not in their power, being faln in Adam, they should pray to God to turn them from their sins unto himself by his Spirit and Grace.[105]

The process of conviction, which Knollys portrayed in *World That Now Is* as one of a struggle against despair, appeared in a slightly different manner elsewhere, where he highlighted the irresistible nature of God's salvation to the sinner. In his exposition of the Song of Solomon, interpreted allegorically as expressing the relationship between Christ and his bride, the Church, the process of coming to awareness of election became one of a lover wooing his beloved in language filled with intimacy and affection. The drawing work of Christ caused the Saints follow him willingly, being "sweetly drawn".[106] Knollys described it as a situation in which the woman's heart was won over by her lover: "Thus, Christ gets into the hearts of his poor Saints, & doth win upon them, and gain their affections... by his sweet insinuations."[107] While one's natural will had "a resisting power... to refuse the offers of Grace", the sweetness of his drawing caused the sinner to respond positively:

> Draw me not onely from the World, from Satan, from Sin, from Self; but allure me, and incline my will and affections, my resolutions, desires and loves after thee my beloved Lord Jesus Christ.[108]

Another term used to describe this irresistible grace was effectual calling. This term appeared in the *Second London Confession*, which stated that those called "come most freely, being made willing by his Grace".[109]

---

[102] Knollys, *World That Now Is*, Book I, pp. 11-19.
[103] Knollys, *World That Now Is*, Book I, pp. 26-31.
[104] Knollys, *World That Now Is*, Book I, pp. 37, 103. See also Knollys, *Christ Exalted*, p. 2; "I say Christ is the foundation of all that faith, repentance, love, and other graces, gifts, and fruits of the Spirit."
[105] Knollys, *World That Now Is*, Book I, p. 31.
[106] Knollys, *Song of Solomon*, p. 14.
[107] Knollys, *Song of Solomon*, p. 71.
[108] Knollys, *Song of Solomon*, p. 12.
[109] *Second London Confession*, p. 37.

When the Particular Baptists published the proceedings of their first General Assembly in 1689, the title page stated unequivocally that they were churches "Owning the Doctrine of Personal Election and final Perseverance". This distinguished them from the General Baptists who held to general atonement and freedom of the will. Not long before this assembly, this distinction also appeared in the *Second London Confession*, Chapter III, which addressed the topic of predestination in the following terms:

> By the Decree of God, for the manifestation of his glory, some Men and Angels are pre-destinated, or fore-ordained to Eternal Life through Jesus Christ, to the praise of his glorious grace; others being left to act in their sin to their just condemnation, to the praise of his glorious justice.

> Those of Mankind that are pre-destined to life, God before the foundation of the world was laid, according to his eternal and immutable Purpose, and the secret councel and good pleasure of his Will, hath chosen in Christ unto everlasting glory, out of his meer free grace and love; without any other thing in the creature as a condition or cause moving him thereunto.[110]

This statement on predestination was based on those in Westminster Confession of the Presbyterians and the Savoy Declaration of the Independents. When the *Second London Confession* was originally published (1677), all three groups were part of the community of persecuted dissenters and represented the bulwark of reformed Puritan doctrine in England.[111] This statement on election or predestination clearly aligned the Particular Baptists with the Independents and Presbyterians and set them apart from the more Arminian theologians of the Church of England, the General Baptists, and the Quakers. This reformed doctrine of predestination addressed three important issues: the election of the saints to salvation, the limited nature of Christ's atonement, and the eternal perseverance of the elect.

Knollys' writings contained many references to "the Elect".[112] As well, his various works make many statements and references based upon Calvinist assumptions. However, at no point in his writings did Knollys set forth a

---

[110] *Second London Confession*, Sections 3 and 5, pp. 14-15.

[111] Haykin, *Kiffin, Knollys, and Keach*, pp. 63, 69-70. They differed slightly on the doctrine of double predestination, that God not only predestined some people for salvation, but others for damnation as well. While both the Westminster Confession and the Savoy Declaration made such a statement, the *Second London Confession* remained more ambiguous, simply stating that the unregenerate are "left to act in their sin to their just condemnation".

[112] Knollys, *Christ Exalted*, pp. 5, 17; Knollys, *Exposition of the Whole Book of the Revelation*, pp. 60, 90; Knollys, *World That Now Is*, Book I, p. 35; Knollys, *Song of Solomon*, p. 70 (in this work, the usual word he used was "the saints").

detailed or systematic treatment of the doctrine of election. In one sermon on Ephesians 1:4, he simply stated, "First, that there is an Election. Secondly, That the Elect are chosen in Christ. Thirdly, That Election was before the Wor[l]d. And fourthly, that the Elect of God should be holy, and without blame in his presence, in love."[113] The most systematic treatment of the topic in his works appeared in the context of the relationship between Christ and his bride, the Church, in his exegesis of the Song of Solomon. He began by stating that although Christ loved all men, "Yet he loveth his Spouse, his Churches, his Saints with a peculiar love".[114] The "peculiar" nature of this love was rooted, not in anything done by the Church, but in God's choice: "Before we be actually his, he loved us with a *love of goodwill*, as beholding us in his Fathers choice, and given to himself in Election, Jer. 31.3. and therefore gave himself for us, Ephes. 5.2."[115] Here, Knollys clearly embedded the doctrine of election in the love of Christ. Although this passage made a claim regarding the unconditional election of believers, it also dealt with the extent of the atonement. Those whom God elected for salvation were those for whom Christ died and provided salvation.[116] For Knollys and the Particular Baptists, the two ideas were explicitly joined. "God did from all eternity decree to justifie all the Elect, and Christ did in the fullness of time die for their Sins and rise again for their Justification."[117] Some might see in this passage a "corporate" understanding of election, i.e. that it was the corporate group, the Church, which God elected. However, Knollys saw it as personal election, as well, understanding this passage as combining the corporate with the individual:

> when Christ hath called, justified, and sanctified his elected ones, made them partakers of his divine Nature, given them his Holy Spirit, changed them into his own Image... then Christ loveth them, with a love of most intimate friendship.[118]

---

[113] Knollys, *Christ Exalted*, p. 30.
[114] Knollys, *Song of Solomon*, p. 70.
[115] Knollys, *Song of Solomon*, p. 70.
[116] See also Knollys, *World That Now Is*, Book I, pp. 6-7.
[117] *Second London Confession*, Chapter XI, section 4, p. 42. See also Chapter VIII, sections 5 and 8, pp. 31-33. Knollys' hearty recommendation in the Epistle Dedicatory of Robert Garner's work on particular redemption, certainly gave evidence of his support for the doctrine of limited atonement. Hanserd Knollys, "To the Churches of God in London and elsewhere in all places with the Bishops and Deacons", in *Mysteries Unvailed. Wherein The Doctrine of Redemption by Jesus Christ, flowing from the glorious Grace, and everlasting Love of God, the very fountain of Life and Salvation unto lost Sinners is handled, The most usual Scriptures explained, and Reasons answered, which are urged for the universality of the death of Christ for all Persons*, (London: 1946).
[118] Knollys, *Song of Solomon*, p. 70.

In his eschatological works, Knollys perceived the doctrine of election as the unifying factor of history, that which tied the beginning to the end of human history. In this context, Knollys did not merely refer to the election of people by God for salvation, but also included the election of Jesus for the accomplishment of that salvation.

> This Jesus was the Lamb slain before the foundation of the World, see Chap. 5 vers. 9. in God's Purpose and Decree of the Salvation of his Elect, chosen in Christ, before the foundation of the World, Ephs 1.4, 5, 6.[119]

The election of the saints clearly related to their perseverance.[120] Knollys not only considered election in relation to the creation of the world, but also in relation to the process of being "sealed" and "marked" in the book of Revelation. There, St. John represented the elect as having "the seal of the Living God" on their foreheads and contrasted them to those having the seal and mark of the Beast.[121] Knollys understood that the seal was reserved "for all Gods Elect... chosen in him, Eph. 1.4. and given him of the Father, John 17.6-10. and Christ must loose none of them, John 6. 37, 38, 39".[122] Likewise, he interpreted the Lamb's Book of Life as "the Record or Decree of Election".[123] The same position was taken in the *Second London Confession*, in Chapter XVII, "Of Perseverance of the Saints":

> and they shall be sure to be kept by the Power of God unto Salvation, where they shall enjoy their purchase Possession, they being graven upon the Palm of his Hands, and their Names having been written in the Book of Life from all Eternity.[124]

These sealed ones are the 144,000 mentioned in the book of Revelation, the fullness of "Christ's redeemed ones", both from among the Jews and the Gentiles and the sealing was done "so that our Lord Jesus Christ had lost none of all them that the Father had given him".[125] Knollys identified the perseverance of the saints as a vital aspect of the work of Christ. As "the Alpha and Omega, the beginning and the ending... the Authour, Preserver and Finisher of all; He purchased all, He is the Donour of all, He is the beauty of

---

[119] Knollys, *Exposition of the Whole Book of the Revelation*, p. 93.

[120] Again, this was not unusual for the Particular Baptists. See the title page of the *A Narrative of the Proceedings of the General Assembly*, (1689), which clearly states that they were of the "Baptized Churches... Owning the Doctrine of Personal Election, and final Perseverance".

[121] Knollys, *Exposition of the Whole Book of the Revelation*, p. 179.

[122] Knollys, *Exposition of the Whole Book of the Revelation*, pp. 90, 180-81.

[123] Knollys, *Exposition of the Whole Book of the Revelation*, p. 49.

[124] Knollys, *Exposition of the Whole Book of the Revelation*, p. 57.

[125] Knollys, *Exposition of the Whole Book of the Revelation*, pp., 91-92, 180, 182.

all, the summe of all, the perfection of all in the New man."[126] He even went so far as to state that Christ would be held accountable by God the Father, that "all, which he hath given him; he must keepe them, and preserve to himselfe, when he gives up the Kingdom to God the Father".[127]

Perseverance for Knollys, however, went beyond the issue of eternal security of salvation. It also included sanctification, perseverance in a life of holiness. Christ's work of election included his calling, justification, and sanctification of sinners so that they became "partakers of his divine Nature".[128] Basing his belief here on Ephesians 2:8-9, Knollys claimed that the workmanship of God's election involved the death of sin in our persons and freedom from its power, only to be realised in totality in eternity.[129] Thus, the believer must work with the help of the Holy Spirit to avail him or herself of this holiness.[130] For Knollys, a life of holiness separated true believers from false professors.[131]

The *Second London Confession* has a separate chapter for God's general providence and the centrality of Scripture.[132] Again, the Particular Baptists took a typically Puritan approach to these doctrines. In terms of God's providence in general, Knollys clearly interpreted events in his own life in this context, seeing God's providential hand at work at various points from his childhood to his older years.[133] In fact, William Kiffin, who finished the work for Knollys after his death, stated as much in the preface. He also saw it as a testimony "of the gracious goodness and Providences of God" towards Knollys. This "anthropomorphic emphasis on the intimate link" between the sovereign God and the finite human was central to the Puritan ideal of providence. God's chosen method of communication with his Saints, "the predestined elite" was through "particular providences".[134] Providence also evidenced itself through the perseverance of the saints, an ideal which often left the saints vacillating between assurance and "self-scrutiny, even morbid self-absorption" that often led to "self-loathing, melancholy, and deliberating despair".[135] Certainly, Hanserd Knollys shared in this experience.[136] Interestingly, in his writings, with

---

[126] Knollys, *Christ Exalted*, p. 4.
[127] Knollys, *Christ Exalted*, p. 26.
[128] Knollys, *Song of Solomon*, p. 70. See also Knollys, *Christ Exalted*, p. 30.
[129] Knollys, *World That Now Is*, Book I, pp. 37-42.
[130] Ibid. pp. 41-2; Knollys, *Christ Exalted*, pp. 30-32, 36-37.
[131] Knollys, *Christ Exalted*, pp. 33-34.
[132] *Second London Confession*, "Of the Holy Scriptures", Chapter I, pp. 1-9 and "Of Divine Providence", Chapter V, pp. 19-23.
[133] Knollys, *Life*, pp. 1, 5-8, 10,18-19, 23, 27, 34-36.
[134] Walsham, *Providence*, p. 15.
[135] Walsham, *Providence*, pp. 17-20.
[136] Knollys, *Life*, pp. 32-42.

the exception of his apocalyptic works, Knollys wrote very little about providence.[137]

Throughout his writings, Knollys made it clear that Scripture had a role of vital importance. In his autobiography, he related a story of how he struggled with Satan over the issue of the truth and power of God's word. Eventually, this struggle with Satan led to his first healing experience.[138] For Knollys, the word of God served as the ultimate guide to Truth, both for the individual and for the Church.[139] Knollys frequently emphasised the function of the Bible in the spiritual enlightenment of the sinner to conversion and sanctification.[140] To sum it up, he said, "This Faith God worketh in us *ordinarily*, by his holy Spirit and Word in the Ministry, and administrations of the Gospel of his Grace."[141] For Knollys, this meant that the preaching of the word of God was central for the conversion of souls.[142] In *The World That Now Is*, Knollys outlined how to conduct a typical service of worship. At the heart of this service stood the reading of Scripture, followed by an exposition and interpretation of its meaning, for "Reading the holy Scripture, is an Ordinance of God, unto which Christ hath promised a Gospel-blessing". Following the reading came the preaching of the Gospel and a call to repentance.[143] Scripture served not only for repentance, but also as a guide and rule for the Church.[144] In his exposition of Revelation 11:1, where John was commanded to take a rod and measure the Temple, Knollys interpreted the rod as the word of God, by which ministers measured or assessed the Church, as well as its ordinances and worship.[145] He went on to state unequivocally that "All things in the Church and Worship of God ought to be done according to the Rule of the written Word of God."[146] The centrality of Scripture for Hanserd Knollys stood out clearly in the many scriptural references made in his writings, often to such an extent that they interrupted the flow of the text.

---

[137] See Chapter 6. It is no surprise that Knollys' apocalyptic works dealt with the subject of providence, for it was often linked with calamities and judgment upon the wicked and God's mercies and blessings upon the godly, a central theme in apocalyptic writings. Walsham, *Providence*, pp. 15-17. Walsham gave significant attention to this theme throughout her work.

[138] Knollys, *Life*, p. 6.

[139] Knollys, *Mystical Babylon Unvailed*, p. 29.

[140] Knollys, *Christ Exalted*, pp. 17, 19, 21, 33; Knollys, *World That Now Is*, Book I, pp. 16, 22.

[141] Knollys, *World That Now Is*, Book I, p. 36.

[142] Knollys, *Christ Exalted*, p. 12. See also Hanserd Knollys, *The Parable of the Kingdom of Heaven Expounded. Or, An Exposition of the first thirteen Verses of the twenty fifth Chapter of Matthew*, (London: 1674), p. 51.

[143] Knollys, *World That Now Is*, Book I, p. 71.

[144] Ibid., p. 51.

[145] Knollys, *Exposition of the Eleventh Chapter of the Revelation*, pp. 2-3.

[146] Knollys, *Exposition of the Eleventh Chapter of the Revelation*, pp. 4-5.

Evangelical Emphasis

In the midst of the very strict and uncompromising Calvinism of the Particular Baptists, came an almost paradoxical stress on evangelism. In the preaching tours of the early Particular Baptists, the main thrust undoubtedly was evangelism. Knollys presented no exception to this rule. The Greek New Testament used two words associated with the task of evangelism, translated by the Authorised Bible in Ephesians 4:11 as apostle and evangelist. Rather than using either of these terms, the London Particular Baptists preferred another – Messenger.[147] Inspired by the evangelistic activities of the New Testament church, when specially commissioned men such as Silas, Barnabas, and Paul, were sent out on special journeys, the London churches did likewise. Initially, each journey represented a separate commission, but eventually the Messenger apparently evolved into a specific office, albeit an unofficial one.[148] Though the main purpose and function of the Messenger was evangelisation through the preaching of the word of God, his duties also included the organisation of new Particular Baptist congregations and associations. Usually, the Messenger received the support of a group of churches since such support was often more than a single congregation could carry.[149]

This emphasis on evangelism appeared in the 1644 Confession and the 1646 Confession in Sections XXIV and XXV, which state "Faith is ordinarily begotten by the preaching of the gospel, or word of Christ" and "The Preaching of the gospel to the conversion of sinners is absolutely free".[150] The *Second London Confession* however, focused more on the Calvinist theology of election and gave considerably less attention to the work of evangelism.[151] The proceedings of the General Assembly of 1689 made it a special point to encourage the churches "to send Ministers that are ordained (or at least solemnly called) to preach, both in City and Country, where the Gospel hath or hath not yet been preached".[152] This restored the earlier emphasis on evangelism. The emphasis upon evangelism often carried with it an urgent eschatological thrust, having a sort of post-millennial accent. As individual people became perfected from within (converted), the entire world would be reformed. The Kingdom of God would advance internally and externally.

---

[147] J.F.V. Nicholson, "The Office of 'Messenger' amongst British Baptists in the Seventeenth and Eighteenth Centuries", *Baptist Quarterly*, XVII, (Jan. 1958) : 208.

[148] The General Baptists insisted that it was an official office like the Bishop, Elder, and Deacon, listed in the New Testament as the office of Apostle. The Particular Baptists denied this but still held that the Messenger or apostle was a functional office. Nicholson, "The Office of 'Messenger'", pp. 208-13.

[149] Whitley, *British Baptists*, pp. 87-88.

[150] *1646 Confession* in Underhill, *Confessions of Faith*, pp. 36-37.

[151] *Second London Confession*, p. 46.

[152] *Narrative of the Proceedings of the General Assembly*, (1689), p. 12.

Thomas Collier, a Particular Baptist in the Western Association, was an extremely influential evangelist who held to such a belief.[153]

Evangelism played an important role in the ministry of Hanserd Knollys. As a young minister in the Church of England, he resigned his living due to scruples over some aspects of the worship in the Church of England. However, beyond that, he renounced his ordination and silenced himself shortly after because he sensed that his ordination was invalid, not because it came through the Church of England, but because it lacked "any Seal from Christ of my Ministry".[154] He sought the blessing of Christ on his preaching, which would lead to the conversion of his hearers, for "tho many had been reformed and moralized, yet I knew not that I had been Instrumental to convert any Souls to God".[155] This same conviction led him toward the end of his life to make the despairing statement that the reason for the conversion of so few was that "Ministers of the Gospel do not labour in the Word and Doctrine of a thorow Gospel-Conviction".[156] Only those ministers who "labour most in the Word and Doctrine of Gospel-Conviction of Sinners" were "most instrumental in converting Souls unto God".[157] Knollys went on to state rather bluntly that "those Ministers have most Converts; those are workers together with God".[158] In fact, he evaluated the success of his own ministry on this basis.[159]

The sermons that he preached while on a tour in 1645 provide evidence of the importance to Knollys of preaching of the "Gospel-Conviction". These sermons emphasised three things in particular: the seeking and saving of a lost sinner by Christ, the work of Christ on behalf of the believer, and the call to holy living by God's people.[160] A clear evangelistic thrust appeared in the theme that Jesus Christ came to save sinners.[161]

> Now the Lord seeing the poore sinner polluted in his own blood, that is in his naturall estate of sinfull corruption, and looking upon him with an eye of compassion (for his time is the time of love) he drawes him with his

---

[153] Mark R. Bell, *Apocalypse How? Baptist Movements During the English Revolution*, (Macon, GA: Mercer University Press, 2000), pp. 139-41; Thomas Collier, *A Vindication of the Army-Remonstrance*, (London: 1648), "Epistle Dedicatorie", p. a.2-a.5.
[154] Knollys, *Life*, p. 9.
[155] Knollys, *Life*, p. 9.
[156] Knollys, *World That Now Is*, Book I, p. 23.
[157] Knollys, *World That Now Is*, Book I, p. 24.
[158] Knollys, *World That Now Is*, Book I, p. 24.
[159] Knollys, *Life*, p. 31.
[160] Knollys, *Christ Exalted*.
[161] Knollys, *Christ Exalted*, p. 15.

everlasting loving kindnesse... without which powerfull drawing, no sinner can come to Christ.[162]

Although Knollys presented this mission of Christ in reformed terms, making clear the necessity of the illumination of the Holy Spirit through the word of God, he also made an unmistakeable "Gospel-Conviction" appeal:

> But albeit some of you see it is that which you ought to do, and that you had neede to do, to wit, to seeke the Lord; assenting to what you heard in the first use of the doctrine, that there is much worth, beauty and excellency in Christ, and that poor lost undone sinners stand in neede of him: Notwithstanding how to obtaine Christ, you know not as yet. Let me tell you, God offers you Christ upon Gospel-termes, which are these three.... First, God in the dispensation of the Gospell propounds Christ to lost sinners, as the only necessary, and and [sic] all sufficient meanes of Salvation.... Secondly, God doth offer Christ to lost sinners without respect to price or person. And any one, that will, are invited to take Christ freely.... Thirdly, God requires, that those, who do receive him, shall depart from iniquity,... Live soberly, righteously, and Godly in this present world... And that they shall sell all, lose all, and hate all for the sake of Christ, and take up the Crosse and follow him.[163]

Knollys expanded upon the same theme nearly forty years later in much greater detail and with the same Calvinist emphasis. For over thirty pages, in *The World That Now Is*, Knollys tediously delineated the message of "Gospel-Conviction" starting with sinful human nature and the need for Christ for salvation and ending with the conviction and conversion of the sinner, at every point emphasising the work of God in bringing the sinner to that place.[164] Once again, as in the sermons preached in 1645[165], he stressed the importance of conversion leading to a life of sanctified holiness, as "the Spirit of God by Faith works out sin and corruption, both out of the heart, and out of the life gradually, killing and crucifying our Old Man".[166] Once again, following this and a detailed examination of the signs of Christ's second coming, Knollys presented a passionate plea to the unconverted.

---

[162] Knollys, *Christ Exalted*, p. 17.

[163] Knollys, *Christ Exalted*, p. 13.

[164] Knollys, *World That Now Is*, Book I, pp. 4-37.

[165] According to the title page of the original publication, these were preached in February 1645. Hanserd Knollys, *Christ Exalted: in a Sermon Begun to be preached at Debenham in Suffolk, upon the 14. day of Febr. last*, (London: 1645). Thomason noted that he had purchased it on May 16, indicating that it may have been published near that date. The revised edition from which the citations for this work were taken, was noted by Thomason as being purchased on Feb. 18, 1645/46.

[166] Knollys, *Christ Exalted*, pp. 38-42.

> Any one, every one that is willing may come to Christ, and receive Christ, and have Christ freely; for HE is the free Gift of God to Sinners, who are without Christ in the World... Be but willing to take Christ, and the work is done. Christ complained of them that would not come to him, that they might have life... suffer the LORD Jesus Christ to come by his Spirit and Word into your hearts, and set up the Kingdom of his Grace in your souls... Open your hearts to Christ when he knocks at the Door of your Souls, and calls you to come to him, to receive him, and let him come into your hearts, and dwell in your hearts by his holy Spirit, and sanctifying Grace... Let the LORD Jesus Christ have the Throne, and be exalted above ALL in your Souls, that every Thought may be brought into Captivity to the Obedience of Christ.[167]

This sounded more like a wider appeal rather than an address to the elected saints, but having petitioned so earnestly, Knollys immediately reasserted his reformed position:

> not that you can do those things of your selves; I have told you, without Christ you can do nothing... But it is your duty to do them, and it is the Free Grace of God, to work in you to will and to do, according to his good pleasure... that he so working in you, you may work out your own salvation with fear and trembling.[168]

Was the conversionist, evangelistic inclination of Knollys and the Particular Baptists at odds with typical Puritan theology? According to Norman Pettit, a central element to Puritan theology was an understanding of "heart preparation" whereby the sinner experienced contrition and humiliation. While such feelings did not necessarily guarantee salvation, they certainly went a long way to promote sound conversion. The rise of this doctrine of preparation came in response to a dilemma or tension in which the rather rigorous theology of Theodore Beza had placed Calvinists. How could preachers encourage sinners to seek assurance of salvation within the rather constricting parameters of a double predestinarian doctrine?[169] So-called Antinomians, such as John Wheelwright and Anne Hutchinson, opposed such teaching on the basis that it embraced a "Covenant of Works" instead of a "Covenant of Grace". The doctrine of preparation stood at the heart of the Antinomian debate.[170]

Sidney H. Rooy followed a similar theme, claiming that the conversionist doctrine of "moderate Puritans" who emphasised human responsibility along with divine sovereignty was the forerunner of a theology of missions. He understood that the "fundamental principles of mission... are found in Sibbes

---

[167] Knollys, *World That Now Is*, Book II, pp. 34-36.
[168] Knollys, *World That Now Is*, Book II, p. 36.
[169] Norman Pettit, *The Heart Prepared: Grace and Conversion in Puritan Spiritual Life*, (New Haven: Yale University Press, 1966), pp. 16-19. See Chapter 2 above.
[170] Pettit, *The Heart Prepared*, pp. 19, 125-57.

[and] reach through the whole Puritan period".[171] Although the work of the Spirit was necessary in opening the heart of sinners, the Christian "could, out of concern for man's need, teach him the gospel and encourage him to use the divinely appointed means". Since depravity was rooted in a corrupt will, every means must be used to convince men "to choose the right way".[172] Certainly this attempt by the Puritans to interject responsibility and experience into an otherwise sterile and one-sided approach to soteriology appealed especially to those adopting ideas of "the gathering of the saints" or "believing churches".

Knollys and the Particular Baptists undoubtedly placed great stress on human inability and depravity and the necessity of God's grace for conversion.[173] At the same time, they clearly embraced the concepts of individual responsibility and experiential religion, and they firmly believed that although "God hath appointed the Elect unto glory, so he hath by the eternal and most free purpose of his Will, fore-ordained all the means thereunto wherefore they who are elected... are redeemed by Christ",[174] the most ordinary means of "which God hath in his infinite wisedome appointed to convert sinners... is the Word preached". [175]

Of Ministers and the Ministry

In the 1640s, when Hanserd Knollys became a Baptist, he joined congregations made up largely of the "middling sort" – craftsmen, tradesmen, weavers, tailors, glovers, and merchants – and which emphasised the role of the laity.[176] Except for a handful of professional clergy who had abandoned the Established Church (including Knollys), the ministers consisted largely of lay elders, chosen because of their abilities to preach and teach.[177] Due to his own experience as a clergyman in the Church of England and his education, Knollys promptly became one of the leading pastors in the London fellowship of Particular Baptist congregations and one of their more popular preachers.[178] The

---

[171] Sidney H. Rooy, *The Theology of Missions in the Puritan Tradition – A Study of Representative Puritans: Richard Sibbes, Richard Baxter, John Eliot, Cotton Mather, and Jonathan Edwards*, (Grand Rapids: William B. Eerdmans Publishing Co., 1965), p. 13.

[172] Rooy, *The Theology of Missions in the Puritan Tradition*, pp. 315-16.

[173] *Second London Confession*, Chapters III, X, XIV.

[174] *Second London Confession*, p. 15.

[175] Knollys, *Christ Exalted*, p. 12.

[176] McGregor, "Baptists", pp. 36, 40.

[177] McGregor, "Baptists", pp. 38-40.

[178] As mentioned above, Thomas Edwards reported that as many as a thousand people came on Sundays to hear Knollys preach. Though that number may have been an exaggeration, Tolmie speculated that indeed many more would likely have come to hear Knollys rather than other Baptist preachers since they would be more comfortable listening to former clergyman than to a lay preacher. Tolmie, *Triumph*, p. 60.

lowly status of Baptist preachers made them a ready target for critics. Many of these so-called "mechanic preachers", who laboured all week and preached on Sunday, were elected by their congregations and often received little or no pay for their pastoral labours.[179] The 'democratisation' of religion, where any believer with the Spirit's leading could preach and be better accepted than an educated divine, gave extreme discomfort to the religious establishment. To many, the order of the religious sector of society was in severe jeopardy, with comparisons often being made between the Baptists and the more radical Anabaptists of the Continental reformation. As well, stories abounded of immorality.[180]

Hanserd Knollys became quite aware of the unusual nature of the ministry in the newly developing Baptist denomination. Although the Particular Baptists embraced a more open attitude toward lay clergy than the Episcopalians and Presbyterians, Knollys certainly did not want the ministry to devolve to a position where its integrity was compromised or under question. And he certainly did not want Particular Baptist congregations to degenerate to the point of disorder that he perceived in some of the more radical sects, such as the Quakers and Ranters.[181] This concern for the ministry led Knollys to give significant attention to the subject in his writings. Although he certainly supported the priesthood of believers, he also held the office of the minister in high esteem, as a specially appointed office under Christ, and strongly desired the ordination of godly Particular Baptist ministers. As well, Knollys wanted an educated, professional ministry. Finally, he believed that ministers held authority within their congregations, while at the same time, acted as servants of the church.

Particularly in his apocalyptic writings, Knollys devoted significant attention to the topic of the true church and the false church. As part of his examination of this topic, Knollys addressed the issues of true and false worship and teaching, and of true and false ministers, teachers, and prophets. Evidence of a false minister, from Knollys' perspective, came across in the teaching and doctrine that minister expounded, as well as the lifestyle, conduct, and integrity of the minister. Knollys often coupled the phrase "false ministers" with "formal professors", those daughters of Babylon "who commit spiritual whordoms".[182] Finally, a minister should also exhibit gifts, which would testify to God's call of that minister. Knollys often compared "formal professors" with the Scribes

---

[179] Christopher Hill, *The World Turned Upside Down*, (London: Maurice Temple Smith, 1972; reprint ed., Penguin Books, 1991), pp. 28-30.

[180] McGregor, "Baptists", pp. 25-26, 41-42.

[181] In one instance, when addressing the question of mode of baptism, he actually drew the connection between paedobaptists and the Ranters. Playing on the Greek word meaning 'to sprinkle' (ραντίζο - rantizo), Knollys stated "to Sprinkle with Water is to Rantize". Knollys, *World That Now Is*, Book I, p. 74.

[182] Knollys, *Song of Solomon*, p. 33.

and Pharisees of Jesus' day, having a "form of Godliness" but "no Power of Godliness".[183] He described these "formal professors" as "proud, covetous, carnal, covenant-breakers, false accusers, incontinent, fierce, heady, high-minded, Lovers of pleasures more than Lovers of God, &c.".[184] They "like Christ as a Saviour but refuse him as a Soveraign".[185] They were "formal" in their "External form of publick Worship", yet "with a spirit of Wor[l]dliness".[186] According to Knollys, these false ministers had "defiled the Garments of their profession", that is the "inward purity of heart and that Spiritual power of Godliness in their life".[187] On the other hand, the "Garments" of true ministers should be "kept undefiled, unspotted, uncorrupted, unpolluted", exhibiting the "Power of Godliness" which provided the evidence of the "Growth and perfection of Grace".[188] This meant "living soberly, righteously and Godly" in love and humility, with clear evidence of the fruit of righteousness and a life of holiness.[189] The most apparent fruit of righteousness for the godly minister came in the conversion of souls. The true minister involved himself in a "Soul-feeding Ministry", the work of which was "to convert Souls,... to feed Souls,... to comfort Souls,... To strengthen and confirm Souls,... to establish Souls,... to save Souls".[190]

Another evidence of a godly minister came in the confirmation of his being called and set apart by God through spiritual gifts.[191] "Able Ministers, who are found in the faith, and experienced Beleevers, who are eminent in Spiritual gifts and graces, are needful both for use and ornament in the Churches of Christ."[192] According to the *Second London Confession*, congregations should choose their pastors based on their being "fitted and gifted by the Holy Spirit".[193] Knollys further emphasised the attributes of the clergy by claiming that "Pastors and Teachers... that Rule well... ought to be Learned and holy Men, taught of God by his holy Spirit, qualified with Spiritual and Ministerial Gifts and Graces".[194] Spiritual gifts provided evidence of Divine favour and equipped pastors for their calling as preachers and leader in their congregations.

---

[183] Knollys, *Parable of the Kingdom of Heaven*, pp. 28-40. Although the designation "formal professors" is not limited to clergy in Knollys' writings, there are clear instances when he has the clergy particularly in mind. Knollys, *Parable of the Kingdom of Heaven*, p. 39; Knollys, *World That Now Is*, Book I, pp. 86-87.

[184] Knollys, *Parable of the Kingdom of Heaven*, p. 33.

[185] Knollys, *Parable of the Kingdom of Heaven*, p. 38.

[186] Knollys, *Parable of the Kingdom of Heaven*, p. 36.

[187] Knollys, *Exposition of the Whole Book of the Revelation*, p. 47.

[188] Ibid.; Knollys, *Parable of the Kingdom of Heaven*, p. 31.

[189] Knollys, *Parable of the Kingdom of Heaven*, pp. 29-32.

[190] Knollys, *Song of Solomon*, pp. 29-30.

[191] Knollys, *Exposition of the Whole Book of the Revelation*, p. 44.

[192] Knollys, *Exposition of the Whole Book of the Revelation*, p. 81.

[193] *Second London Confession*, Chapter XXVI, section 9, p. 89.

[194] Knollys, *Exposition of the Eleventh Chapter of the Revelation*, p. 5.

In addition to the spiritual gifts, however, Knollys believed that pastors should be "Learned and holy Men". A few sentences prior to this, he called for able ministers "both of the letter, and also of the Spirit".[195] While both of these phrases clearly emphasised spiritual qualifications, they also stressed the importance of education. From the earliest days of their existence, English Particular Baptists had been derided and criticised for being "unlearned".[196] Few of their leaders had possessed a formal university education.

Education had always placed highly in Knollys' scheme of priorities. Like his father before him, he had matriculated at Cambridge and his son Cheney would follow in their footsteps as well.[197] Knollys also attempted to provide an education for another son, John, at Charterhouse.[198] Two other sons very likely pursued education as well: Samuel, like Cheney, eventually followed in Knollys' footsteps, becoming a minister and Hanserd Jr. may have become a teacher like his father.[199]

Knollys had always displayed a strong commitment to education. Beginning with his teaching position in Gainsborough prior to the renunciation of his ordination, and throughout his life, Knollys found opportunities to teach students. At several points, he served as a private tutor and, at other times, he taught in existing schools or founded his own boarding or day schools. According to W.T. Whitley, Knollys ran a fashionable and profitable school in the late 1650s and early 1660s in Spitalfields at the old Artillery Ground. Many wealthy London merchants sent their sons to study under Knollys.[200] Although he was preparing boys primarily for commercial life, the curriculum of his school included mathematics and classical studies as well.[201] However, the

---

[195] Knollys, *Exposition of the Eleventh Chapter of the Revelation*, p. 5.

[196] *Tub-Preachers Overturn'd or Independency to be Abandon'd and Abhor'd as destructive to the Magistracy and Ministery, of the Church and Common-wealth of England*, (London: 1647). This particular treatise rails against "Lay illiterate men and women" who "usurpe the Ministery, and Audaciously vent their own Hereticall opinions" and cites one "Kiffin, a glover" as an example.

[197] John Venn and J.A. Venn, *Alumni Cantabrigienses*, Part I to 1751, vol. III Kaile to Ryves, (Cambridge: University Press, 1924), pp. 31-32. See Chapter 2 above and Appendix 4 below.

[198] See Appendix 4 below.

[199] "Genealogical Gleanings in England", in *The New England Historical and Genealogical Register*, vol. 38 (Boston: 1884), p. 63. James dealt with some of the questions surrounding Knollys' sons in her book, though not conclusively. See Appendix 4 below.

[200] W.T. Whitley, "The Contribution of Nonconformity to Education Until the Victorian Era", *The Educational Record With the Proceedings of the British and Foreign School Society*, XIX, (June 1915) : 207 cited in Thomas P. Dixon, "The Contribution of the English Baptists to Education, 1660-1820", (Vanderbilt University, unpublished Ph.D. dissertation, 1975), p.101.

[201] Dixon, "English Baptists... Education", p. 101.

Clarendon Code of the Restoration, excluded dissenters from the schools and universities. Rather than abandoning education altogether, many nonconformists founded their own schools and, in some cases, these academies came to rival the existing schools.[202] Upon his return from Holland and Germany in 1663 or 1664, Knollys once again opened a school.[203] While the location and longevity of this school remain obscure, some sources indicate that Knollys taught in Bishopsgate, London prior to 1672.[204] Knollys mentioned in his autobiography that following Anne's death in 1671, debts and financial strains forced him to return to teaching.[205] He also mentioned having given 50 students to one of his sons and 50 additional students to his son-in-law for their dissenting school.[206] During this period, Knollys also compiled and published a number of academic works, including grammars and lexicons of the classical languages (Hebrew, Greek, and Latin).[207] When Benjamin Keach published his own primer for the education of children, he asked Knollys to write the preface.[208] In it, Knollys proclaimed that all parents and schoolmasters ought to purchase and use Keach's primer for educating children. The value of the book was not only that it would "Catechise their Children, and teach them to know the H[oly] Scripture", but it would also open their minds to learn basic arithmetic and grammar.[209] The value of a sound education clearly emerged in some of the stanzas of a poem printed in this primer:

---

[202] Helen M. Jewell, *Education in Early Modern England*, (New York: St. Martin's Press, 1998), pp. 115-16. Irene Parker, *Dissenting Academies in England*, (Cambridge: At the University Press, 1914), pp. 45-50.

[203] Knollys, *Life*, p. 27.

[204] "Dissenters' Schools, 1660-1820", *Transactions of the Baptist Historical Society*, IV, (Oct. 1915) : 221.

[205] Knollys, *Life*, p. 37. See also p. 42.

[206] Knollys, *Life*, pp. 27-28. It appears that at this point, Knollys turned his own school over to his son and son-in-law to run jointly. He was not specific as to when this exchange took place. James was fairly insistent that it took place prior to 1664. However, she cited no evidence to support this theory. James, *Knollys*, p. 158.

[207] See Chapter 5 above. For a list of Knollys' language grammars and lexicons and other academic writings, see Chapter 4 above, note 89.

[208] Hanserd Knollys, "Recommended to the Use of All Parents and Schoolmasters", in Benjamin Keach, *Instructions for Children Or the Child's and Youth's Delight, Teaching an Easie Way to Spell and Read True English. Containing "The Father's Godly Advice, And directing Parents in a Right and Spiritual manner to Educate their Children. With A Scripture Catechism, Wherein all the Chief Principles of True Christianity Are clearly Open'd Together with many other Things, both Pleasing and Useful for the Education of CHILDREN*, 15th ed. (London: 1723). Keach originally published this book in 1664, but because it was not approved by the authorities, and contained a Baptist catechism, he was arrested and punished, and all copies of the book were burnt. He later rewrote it from memory. Haykin, *Kiffin, Knollys, and Keach*, pp. 84-85.

[209] Knollys, "Recommended to the Use".

> To learn to Read, good Child, give heed,
> For 'tis a precious thing:
> What may compare with Learning rare:
> From hence doth Virtue spring.
>
> Take therefore Care, Learning is rare,
> Like Chains of purest Gold;
> Look, look about, and find it out,
> Its Worth cannot be told.
>
> Consonants know, and Vowels too,
> Nay, learn rightly to spell;
> Be not a Fool, but go to School
> Till thou read English well.
>
> Yet rest not here, but learn to fear
> The blessed GOD of Truth;
> O! understand, 'tis GOD's Command
> Thou serve Him in thy Youth.[210]

Many radical sectaries who challenged several of the conventions of society at the time displayed strong reaction against formal education. Part of this was a form of anti-professionalism and anticlericalism.[211] The Particular Baptists, however, did not necessarily share this position. Not only did Knollys give significant emphasis to the education of young men, but he played a leading role in converting to the Particular Baptist position, Charles Marie de Veil, a Huguenot who was a renowned scholar and expositor of Scripture and who was intimate with several Bishops in the Established Church. De Veil would in turn also emphasise the importance of education among the Particular Baptists.[212] During the Commonwealth period, a rise in interest concerning education resulted in an educational revolution.[213] In spite of the fact that many of their number had limited education, the Particular Baptists shared in this interest in education. Hanserd Knollys was not the only Particular Baptist publishing academic books. Sometime between 1677 and 1681, Francis Bampfield, a Particular Baptist Minister, published several works on the benefits of education. Bampfield claimed, "all useful sciences and profitable arts were

---

[210] Keach, *Instructions for Children*, pp. 6-8.

[211] Richard L. Greaves, *The Puritan Revolution and Educational Thought*, (New Jersey: Rutgers University Press, 1969), pp. 137-46.

[212] Wilfred S. Samuel, "Charles-Marie de Veil", *The Baptist Quarterly* V (1930-31) : 74-81, 118-29, 177-89. Armitage, *History of the Baptists*, vol. I, pp. 470-71; Whitley, *British Baptists*, p. 142.

[213] Jewel, *Education*, pp. 33-36; Foster Watson, "The State and Education During the Commonwealth", *English Historical Review*, XV, Jan. 1900 : 58-72.

taught in one book, the Bible".[214] Although the Particular Baptists denied that the right to preach and expound the word of God was tied to an office, an ecclesiastical hierarchy, or a form of education, this was not due primarily to a suspicion of education, but rather to a desire not to impede the Holy Spirit by forms and ordinances, plus the fear that higher education might inculcate pride. In fact, the obsession of the Particular Baptists with the word of God often led them, like many Puritans, to a desire to get behind the words of the translation to the original languages themselves.[215] For them and the other dissenters of the Restoration period, the training of ministers became a central focus in the founding of academies. They placed a great emphasis on the learning of Latin, Greek, and Hebrew for the purpose of scriptural study and theological studies.[216] Bampfield upon his death left his library to the Baptists in order to "promote a Design of Training up Young Men in Scripture-Learning".[217]

Knollys and other leaders within the Particular Baptist community paid strong attention to the training of young men for the ministry.[218] In September 1689, when the Particular Baptists came together in London for their first General Assembly, one of their greatest concerns was the state of the ministry. Just prior to this gathering, Knollys and several others published a treatise, that raised the problem of the death of many ministers and the fact that others had grown "Ancient, and almost become unserviceable, and not like to continue long".[219] The answer to this problem was to give encouragement to gifted young men to "endeavour after the Knowledg of the Tongues, &c. which we all confess is very good and serviceable, though not of absolute necessity in a Minister".[220] This recommendation stressed the importance of education while not claiming an absolute necessity of knowledge of the Biblical languages for potential ministers. The General Assembly made these same points when it agreed that "the Graces and Gifts of the Holy Spirit" were "sufficient to the making and continuing of an Honourable Ministry" while at the same time stressing it was "advantageous" for both those in ministry and those beginning

---

[214] "Bampfield's Plan for an Educated Ministry", *Transactions of the Baptist Historical Society*, III, 1, (May 1912) : 9.

[215] D. Mervyn Himbury, "Training Baptist Ministers", *The Baptist Quarterly*, XXI, (Oct. 1966) : 338-39.

[216] Jewel, *Education*, p. 115.

[217] "Bampfield's Plan", p. 10.

[218] This concern was first raised in 1675 at a convention of Particular Baptists, where it was proposed that a fund be established to assist in the training and education of young ministers. Dixon, "English Baptists... Education", pp. 116-17.

[219] Hanserd Knollys, et. al., *The Gospel Minister's Maintenance Vindicated. Wherein A Regular Ministry in the Churches, is first Asserted, and the Objections against a Gospel Maintenance for Ministers, Answered*, (London: 1689), p. 55.

[220] The context of this comment had to do with financial issues, which will be addressed further below. Knollys, et. al., *The Gospel Minister's Maintenance Vindicated*, pp. 52-53.

ministry "to attain to a competent knowledge of the Hebrew, Greek, and Latin Tongues".[221] The influence Hanserd Knollys was likely at play here. Although less important than spiritual gifts, formal education still had great value. An educated ministry would help the Particular Baptists not only to gain social respect, but also to maintain doctrinal purity and help in the proper expounding of the Scriptures.[222]

Related to this desire for education for pastors was the aim to create a more professional ministry. Many Particular Baptists, Knollys included, had, in the early years of the movement, reacted against the ministry of the Church of England. They saw the established clergy as corrupt and their calling as merely a vocation that could be bought, sold, and passed on. While they sought to avoid that sort of professional ministry, the Particular Baptists wished to institutionalise the call and training of pastors by the end of the seventeenth century, including a move toward a paid ministry. As early as November 1650, the Associations of Wales had made a move in this direction.

> Further, consideringe the present condition of such brethren as are nowe to bee imployed in the worke of the ministry, and the duty that lyes upon each member to provide for them, it is judged necessary, and therefore it is desired, that the sume of £30 per annum be raysed by the churches in equall portions, (viz.) £10 in every church, towards the maintenance of the ministry.[223]

In the Midlands during the 1650s, the support for a paid ministry was not as strong, some approving of this move and others opposing it.[224]

Three primary reasons under girded this move toward institutionalisation: the quest for a measure of respectability in society, quality control (maintaining and even increasing the quality of leadership), and fairness (the treatment of all ministers as equally as possible). At the heart of this professionalisation of the ministry stood two major concerns – the issue of monetary payment for ministers and the issue of ordination of ministers.

When *The Gospel Minister's Maintenance Vindicated* appeared in 1689, Knollys and other Particular Baptists leaders made clear recommendations regarding the payment of ministers for their work. They held that it was "very dishonourable to God, and a reproach to our Sacred Religion" for churches to fail to provide "a due maintenance" for their pastors. In fact, they boldly

---

[221] *Narrative of the Proceedings of the General Assembly*, (1689), p. 18.
[222] Knollys, *Song of Solomon*, pp. 38-39; Knollys, *Exposition of the Eleventh Chapter of the Revelation*, p. 5; Knollys, et. al., *The Gospel Minister's Maintenance Vindicated*, pp. 27-30.
[223] B.R. White, ed., *The Association Records of the Particular Baptists of England, Wales and Ireland to 1660*, (London: The Baptist Historical Society, 1971), p. 3.
[224] White, ed., *The Association Records of the Particular Baptists*, pp. 22-23.

proclaimed that it was "a great and crying Sin".[225] As churches were able, ministers should receive "a Comfortable Livelyhood" so that "they may be delivered from the Incumbrance of this Life, and so not be hindered or obstructed in their Holy and most Sacred Imployment, with secular Affairs".[226] As well, they displayed concern that ministers would be discouraged by financial debt.[227]

In the early years, the fluidity of the movement had not necessitated a professional ministry. According to the *1646 Confession*, congregations chose their ministers according to the qualifications laid out in the New Testament and supplied their needs. During this time, ministers often attended to the needs of the church while at the same time practicing a trade or working in another capacity. Indeed, Knollys spent most of his life as a teacher and at various times served as a civil servant or engaged in trade abroad in addition to his pastoral duties. However, with the gradual decline of first generation Particular Baptists and the growth into a more formalised institution, the need for a more "regularly and orderly" ministry became evident.[228] The move toward a more educated ministry was part of that change. In addition, the concern also emerged that unless fair payment for service was instituted among the Particular Baptist congregations, they would decline in the numbers and the quality of pastors would diminish. Partly for this reason, the General Assembly determined to start a fund of money to assist those churches too poor to pay a pastor on their own.[229]

The years of persecution following the Restoration had taken their toll on members and pastors of the Particular Baptist congregations, particularly in relation to financial matters. Hanserd Knollys related how a lack of funds had forced him back to teaching school in the early 1670s. In fact, Knollys had received money from the will of a Thomas Bell, a London merchant, proven in May 1672, as one of the "poor necessitous men late ministers of the Gospel".[230] The will of Anne Grave of St. Butolph, London, proven March 1676, stipulated that "provision" was to be made "for the maintenance of eight poor, aged, decayed ministers... during their natural lives". [231] The name of Hanserd Knollys also appeared in this group. None knew any better than he the reality of financial insecurity in ministry. In his treatment of ministry in *The World That*

---

[225] Knollys, et. al., *The Gospel Minister's Maintenance Vindicated*, pp., 13-15.
[226] Knollys, et. al., *The Gospel Minister's Maintenance Vindicated*, pp. 22, 26-29.
[227] Knollys, et. al., *The Gospel Minister's Maintenance Vindicated*, pp. 31-32. There was also concern that capable young men might be discouraged from entering the ministry due to the financial constraints of such a prospect. See pp. 52-53.
[228] Knollys, et. al., *The Gospel Minister's Maintenance Vindicated*, p. 2.
[229] Knollys, et. al., *The Gospel Minister's Maintenance Vindicated*, p. 5; *Narrative of the Proceedings of the General Assembly*, (1689), pp. 5, 10-12.
[230] "Genealogical Gleanings in England", in *The New England Historical and Genealogical Register*, vol. 38 (Boston: 1884), p. 63.
[231] "Genealogical Gleanings in England", vol. 50, (Boston: 1896), pp. 423-24.

Now Is, Knollys did not give much attention to the subject of paid ministry, simply stating that "Elders are indeed fixed Officers for Rule and Government, who are to be counted worthy of double Honour", the same phrase used by himself and the other London pastors in *The Gospel Minister's Maintenance Vindicated* to refer to payment for Pastors.[232]

One of the major concerns raised by the authors of *The Gospel Minister's Maintenance Vindicated* was that the quality of the pastors and elders was being or would be affected by the failure of churches to pay them for their work. Distracted or dismayed by their financial needs or by the trade or employ they had taken up in order to supplement that need, they would not give enough attention to shepherding the congregation.[233] Failure to provide financially for elders, thereby forcing them to find other employment, brought scandal upon the Particular Baptist churches.[234] To Knollys and the other authors of this treatise, the payment of ministers was not merely a pragmatic issue. It had ethical implications, as well. When God set apart the Levites as ministers in the Old Testament, they argued, he also "Ordained and appointed a Comfortable Livelyhood to them". A similar provision should apply to ministers of the Gospel.[235] In essence, they concluded,

> It is very dishonourable to God, and a reproach to our Sacred Religion for the Churches when they have called forth such Pastors and Ministers, who are competently qualified according to the Rule of the Gospel, to let them lye under those unsupportable burdens, of worldly Snares and Incumbrances, without providing a due maintenance for them, according to the Ordaination of our Lord Jesus Christ in the New Testament.[236]

In fact, to pay pastors was not an act of charity, but instead a due portion for the work they had done.[237] Even independently wealthy pastors should receive payment, because they had earned it. Part of the elder's office was providing hospitality, and those with independent wealth, could more easily share of their goods with others, including less fortunate pastors, if rightfully paid for their work.[238]

---

[232] Knollys, *World That Now Is*, Book I, p. 56; Knollys, et. al., *The Gospel Minister's Maintenance Vindicated*, p. 16. Perhaps he wrote little about it in the former treatise since it had been dealt with at great length in the latter one, of which he had shared in writing.

[233] Knollys, et. al., *The Gospel Minister's Maintenance Vindicated*, pp. 20, 25-27, 424-3, 59.

[234] Knollys, et. al., *The Gospel Minister's Maintenance Vindicated*, pp. 28-29.

[235] Knollys, et. al., *The Gospel Minister's Maintenance Vindicated*, pp. 21-22.

[236] Knollys, et. al., *The Gospel Minister's Maintenance Vindicated*, p. 13.

[237] Knollys, et. al., *The Gospel Minister's Maintenance Vindicated*, p. 89.

[238] Knollys, et. al., *The Gospel Minister's Maintenance Vindicated*, pp. 40-42, 47-48, 90-91.

Apparently, some Particular Baptists had asserted that payment of ministers was "Unlawful, if not Anti-Christian", perhaps because they saw the payment of pastors as reopening the possibility of a ministry infected by worldliness. Knollys and his colleagues, however, saw the opposite as true: "to with-hold it from them by a Church, who is able comfortably to provide for them, is a great and crying Sin, and will be attended... with severe Judgment from the Holy God".[239] Those who withheld payment, while spending "needlessly on [their] own ceiled Houses, on costly Attire and Dresses and delicious Diet, when God's House lies almost waste" displayed considerable worldliness.[240] Others objected to paying ministers who were "Idle and Negligent in their Business". However, Knollys and the others did not support payment of such ministers, but rather payment was "to encourage the Faithful and Labourous Person, who is willing to give himself up to the Lord".[241]

The other issue raised in relation to the establishment of a professional ministry was ordination. The members of the General Assembly expressed distress that some churches had neglected to ordain, "Brethren competently qualified" for office. This impeded their effectiveness as ministers of the Gospel.[242] According to Knollys and the other Particular Baptist leaders, when a particular congregation had ascertained the "meetness and Abilities of any Person, or Persons" for ministry, they should, after congregational election, set him or them apart by ordination. Other elders or pastors would participate through prayer and the laying on of hands, creating a new relationship between the church and the pastor. More than just an official way to establish someone in an office, the ordination ceremony had a spiritual significance and involved spiritual empowerment (1 Tim. 4:14).[243] Mutually voluntary acts of the elder and the congregation established a morally binding contract with each party having particular duties and responsibilities. The pastor was to "Watch, Feed, and Govern the Flock" while the congregational members were to "submit themselves to Him in the Lord, to Love, Reverence, and Administer freely to him".[244] Thus, the failure to ordain officials stood in the way of establishing such a contract and negated the authority of the elder.[245]

---

[239] Knollys, et. al., *The Gospel Minister's Maintenance Vindicated*, pp. 14-15.

[240] *Narrative of the Proceedings of the General Assembly*, (1689), p. 6.

[241] Knollys, et. al., *The Gospel Minister's Maintenance Vindicated*, p. 94.

[242] *Narrative of the Proceedings of the General Assembly*, (1689), p. 5. It is not totally clear why these churches were not ordaining their leaders. Perhaps, once again, it went back to scruples that had developed over the issue of ordination in the Established Church.

[243] *Narrative of the Proceedings of the General Assembly*, (1689), p. 13; *Second London Confession*, Ch. XXVI, sect., 9, pp. 89-90; Knollys, et. al., *The Gospel Minister's Maintenance Vindicated*, p. 8;

[244] Knollys, et. al., *The Gospel Minister's Maintenance Vindicated*, p. 8.

[245] *Narrative of the Proceedings of the General Assembly*, (1689), p. 5.

For Hanserd Knollys, a former clergyman in the Church of England who renounced his ordination, taking such a firm stand on the ordinance of ordination may seem somewhat ironic. And for the Particular Baptists who held to the priesthood of believers, that God had given all believers "all that Power and Authority, which is any way needful, for their carrying on that Order in Worship, and Discipline"[246] this emphasis on a pastor's authority seems contradictory. For Knollys, however, a strong stress on ordination was neither ironic nor contradictory. Without question, he stood for an authoritative, educated ministry. Although the congregational approach certainly embraced some democratic principles, the need for order necessitated an hierarchical approach to church government as well. Thus, God "gave Authority and Power to his Ministers and Churches to rule, govern, and order the Saints, who are the Members of the Churches.... The Saints ought to be subject to their Elders, and one to another in the Church.... And the Church ought to be subject unto Christ."[247] Under Christ, the Elders had a duty "to take the Charge, Oversight and Care" of church members, "to Rule, Guide, and Govern them (by virtue of their Commission, and Authority received from Christ)".[248] Knollys held that "there was... a Priority and Pre-eminence among the Ministers of Christ, approved of God" and appointed by God.[249] He drew upon the New Testament, the Church Fathers, and the Reformers to support this claim for a hierarchy among believers.[250]

> Gospel-Order is a great Beauty and Ornament to the Church, and Order makes very much for the Well-Being of the Church. And Gospel-Order consisteth in these things; First, That the Bishop and Presbyters set in Order the things which are wanting in the Church, Secondly, That all things in the Church are done decently, and in Order.... And God hath committed the Government of his Gospel-Church and Kingdom unto Christ, to Order it, &c. God is not the Author of Confusion.[251]

Having made this argument for order, Knollys proceeded to put an almost Lockean spin on it. First, he qualified ecclesiastical hierarchy by stating: "That this Priority, Presidence, and Pre-eminence of any on Bishop above other Bishops, Pastors, Teachers, Presbyters, or Elders, and Ministers of Christ, is not any Lordly Prelacy, with coercive Power over the Conscience, or Dominion over the Faith of God's Clergy." In other words, it did not mirror the episcopacy of the Roman Catholics or Anglicans, but was a representative, consensual relationship, whereby elders, etc. "are, or shall by the Consent,

---

[246] *Second London Confession*, p. 88.
[247] Knollys, *Song of Solomon*, p. 38.
[248] Knollys, *World That Now Is*, Book I, pp. 56-57.
[249] Knollys, *World That Now Is*, Book I, p. 58.
[250] Knollys, *World That Now Is*, Book I, pp. 58-68.
[251] Knollys, *World That Now Is*, Book I, pp. 52-53.

Approbation and Choice of the rest be appointed, ordained, and set over them" and so, "for Order sake in Gospel-Government, hath Priority, Pre-eminence, and Authority above the rest of the Presbyters or Bishops of the same Church".[252] This is clearly stated in the 1646 Confession, Article XLIV:

> Christ, for the keeping of this church in holy and orderly communion, placeth some special men over the church, who by their office are to govern, oversee, visit, watch; so likewise for the better keeping thereof, in all places by the members, he hath given authority, and laid duty upon all to watch over one another.[253]

Second, he emphasised that it was not a matter of seeking pre-eminence or loving power. Rather, this authority came from service.

> The Shepherds are the Lords, Pastors, the Ministers of Christ... who are Shepherds under the chief Shepherd, Christ Jesus, I Pet. 5.1, 2, 3, 4. Whoever hath the care and charge of Souls, ought to bring them to the Congregations of the Lords people, where his faithful Ministers dispense his holy Ordinances that they may be fed and nourished, converted and comforted, sanctified and saved by the Spirit of grace of God in Jesus Christ.[254]

True ministry must be done "in sincerity", "with zeal to God's glory", and "with affection to the Souls of the people by improving all their Ministerial Gifts, Graces and Abilities to the utmost, making full proof of their Ministry for the Conversion of Sinners unto Christ".[255] For the sake of order, Knollys recognised a hierarchy within the churches, a line of authority, but he understood it to function within the model of submission and servitude established by Christ. Hanserd Knollys and the Particular Baptists were concerned that the ministry should be "intelligent and responsible, as well as committed and Spirit-filled".[256]

The Sacraments/Ordinances

The area of greatest debate that emerged from the Continental Reformation had to do with the sacraments – baptism and the Lord's Supper or Communion. Differing views of the Lord's Supper kept Luther from joining with Zwingli, and differing views on baptism separated the Radical reformers, the so-called Anabaptists, from other Protestants. Although the sacraments did not initially

---

[252] Knollys, *World That Now Is*, Book I, pp. 68-69.
[253] *1646 Confession* in Underhill, *Confessions of Faith*, p. 43.
[254] Knollys, *Song of Solomon*, p. 39.
[255] Knollys, *Exposition of the Whole Book of the Revelation*, p. 44.
[256] Duncan, *Knollys*, p. 29.

raise similar divisions among English Protestants, during the seventeenth century, baptism became the primary source of difference between the Baptists and Anglicans, Presbyterians, and Independents. Indeed, baptism stood at the centre of the debates between Baptists and other English Protestants. However, the Particular Baptists did not reach their position on baptism instantaneously. In fact, they arrived in stages. During the late 1630s and early 1640s, a variety of issues emerged. Who should be baptised? How should one baptise? Who had the authority to baptise? What determined the legitimacy of one's baptism? What was the purpose and meaning of baptism? As Baptist theologians began to address these issues, a doctrine of baptism slowly emerged. Hanserd Knollys had an instrumental role in formulating the fairly settled understanding about baptism that had become widespread by his latter years.

The Lord's Supper, on the other hand, did not elicit nearly as much open controversy among English Protestants. Puritans strongly opposed "Popish" doctrine of transubstantiation, or the real presence of Christ in the elements, but paid little attention to the theological debates that divided the Continental reformers. Prior to the Civil War, the debate tended to focus on the ritual of communion more than its meaning – the placement of the communion table and whether or not one knelt when receiving the elements.[257] Contemporaries saw these as implying doctrines about the nature of the sacrament. Following the Civil War, the focus shifted to the issue of efficacy. For whom was Communion effective? The Puritans tended to embrace the concept that only the godly benefited from participation and thus, only the godly should participate.[258] The debate within the Westminster Assembly tended to focus on the practice of communion more than on its theology – who could administer the sacrament, who could exclude members of the congregation from participating, and who could participate. Generally speaking, English Protestants embraced a Calvinistic position that recognised the value of the "spiritual nourishment" of the sacrament.[259] While the "communication" of Christ to the communicant was "a spiritual transaction", beyond the strictly spiritual benefits of communion, one became a partaker of Christ's substance through "the secret and mysterious working of the Holy Spirit".[260] The Westminster Confession sought to combine "hints of Zwingli, Calvin, and Luther" so that "'The sign and the thing signified' are so mutually independent

---

[257] Spurr, *Puritanism*, pp. 87, 90, 95.

[258] Spurr, *Puritanism*, p. 180; James E. White, *The Sacraments in Protestant Practice and Faith*, (Nashville: Abingdon Press, 1999), p. 22.

[259] Stephen Mayor, *The Lord's Supper in Early English Dissent*, (London: Epworth Press, 1972), pp. 74-84.

[260] E. Brooks Holifield, *The Covenant Sealed: The Development of Puritan Sacramental Theology in Old and New England, 1570-1720*, (New Haven: Yale University Press, 1974), pp. 20-21.

as to be inseparable."²⁶¹ However, though it "avoided explicitly instrumental language and omitted specific mention of the Holy Spirit's activity", in essence it remained primarily Calvinistic.²⁶² The Particular Baptists developed their position from that of the Puritans and saw the efficacy extending only to the godly, a view that reflected their polity as gathered churches of believers. Debates involving the Particular Baptist position on the Lord's Supper, often centred on resolving who could participate and officiate, with less attention paid to the meaning of the sacrament itself. For Knollys, the "Ordinances" included not only baptism and the Lord's Supper, but the reading and preaching of the Scriptures, and the singing of praises to God in public worship as well.²⁶³

Baptism

In the mid-1630s, when Knollys renounced his ordination, he had not yet embraced the doctrine of adult baptism. While in New England in the late 1630s, it seems he began to struggle with some of the theological issues related to infant baptism.²⁶⁴ Upon his return to England, he joined fellowship with Henry Jessey's church, a congregation that had already begun debating and exploring the issue of adult baptism. In 1633, Samuel Eaton and others had left that congregation because they rejected their first baptism by the clergy of the Church of England, which they now saw as a false church, and they felt that rebaptism was necessary.²⁶⁵ A further split took place five years later, when six members left and joined John Spilsbury's congregation. In this instance, the debate appeared to revolve around the issue of believer's baptism.²⁶⁶ With the death of Samuel Eaton in 1639, several of his congregation returned to the Jessey church, including one Richard Blunt. The baptism controversy once again arose and in 1640, those opposed to the readmission of the Eaton group separated under Praise-God Barbone, a staunch opponent of rebaptism. The Jessey church continued as an "open" congregation with the rebaptised worshipping alongside of other members. Rebaptised most likely by Eaton, Blunt now introduced the issue of baptism by immersion, representing the death, burial, and resurrection of Christ, into the discussion. Apparently,

---

²⁶¹ White, *Sacraments*, p. 22. It might be argued that Calvin's 'spiritual' understanding of the ceremony was itself an attempt to blend the Zwinglian and Lutheran positions into a middle ground.
²⁶² Holifield, *Covenant Sealed*, pp. 131-33.
²⁶³ Knollys, *World That Now Is*, Book I, pp. 71-76.
²⁶⁴ Thomas Leckford, *Plaine Dealing or News From New England*, (London, 1642), p. 98.
²⁶⁵ Tolmie, *Triumph*, p. 192. William Kiffin joined this group later, but returned to the Jessey church following Eaton's death.
²⁶⁶ Tolmie, *Triumph*, p. 24; "Kiffin Manuscript", as transcribed in "Rise of the Particular Baptists in London, 1633-1644", *Transactions of the Baptist Historical Society*, I, (Jan. 1910) : 231.

Spilsbury still practiced sprinkling. The issue of who had the authority to baptise also arose. Following a trip to Holland to meet with a group of Anabaptists there, Blunt determined that any members considered fit to teach and evangelise were also fit to baptise.[267] In January 1642, Blunt was baptised yet again and out of this, two more Particular Baptist churches were formed.[268] In 1642, William Kiffin embraced adult believer's baptism by immersion, yet he remained in the Jessey church for a time.[269] A short time later, Jessey himself became convinced of baptism by immersion, even for infants.[270]

Such was the situation in the Jessey church when Hanserd Knollys and his family joined in late 1643, upon his return from being chaplain in the Parliamentary Army. By early 1644, Knollys entered the baptism discussion. Eaton had raised the question of the validity of baptism from a false church and Blunt had introduced the subject of mode. Kiffin had raised the issue of adult believer's baptism. What Knollys reintroduced to the discussion was the final issue – the question the validity of infant baptism.[271]

Jessey and some others had been attempting to persuade Hanserd and Anne Knollys to have their newborn son baptised, but they had become uncertain about the Scriptural validity of this practice. Informal discussions arose within the church, "that they might satisfye him, or he rectify them if amiss herein".[272] The discussions occurred weekly from January until March 1644, with William Kiffin siding with Knollys. The congregation had earlier argued the position of most reformed theologians that baptism had replaced circumcision as the sign of the covenant. Knollys countered by arguing that the Lord's Supper was the sign of the New Covenant and reminded his colleagues that all the saints prior to Abraham had never received circumcision and yet remained in covenant with God.[273] However, the real breakthrough came when Kiffin argued that they should interpret the new ordinances primarily according to the New Testament and not the Old.[274] Many were won over by this simple argument, and following the meeting on 17 March 1644, Kiffin and a group withdrew to form their own church.[275] Hanserd and Anne Knollys remained in the Jessey church,

---

[267] Tolmie stated that at issue here for Blunt was also the matter of believer's baptism (*Triumph*, p. 26), but the "Kiffin Manuscript" only mentioned that the focus of his concerns had to do with the "diping the Body into the Water, resembling Burial & riseing again". See pp. 232-33.

[268] "Kiffin Manuscript", pp. 232-33; Tolmie, *Triumph*, pp. 26-27.

[269] Tolmie, *Triumph*, p. 27.

[270] "Knollys Memorandum", as transcribed in W.T. Whitley, "Debate on Infant Baptism, 1643" in *Transactions of the Baptist Historical Society*, I (Jan. 1910) : 238.

[271] Those who joined Spilsbury's congregation had raised this issue in 1638, but it appears that discussion on the issue ended following their exit.

[272] Whitley, "Debate on Infant Baptism, 1643", p. 240.

[273] Whitley, "Debate on Infant Baptism, 1643", pp. 241-42.

[274] Whitley, "Debate on Infant Baptism, 1643", p. 242.

[275] Whitley, "Debate on Infant Baptism, 1643", p. 243.

however, because she still had uncertainties and doubts as to who could validly administer baptism. Finally, Anne's conscience was satisfied that: "Such Disciples as are gifted to teach & Evangelize may also baptize &c." and she and several others were baptised, withdrew from the Jessey congregation, and formed a new church with Hanserd Knollys as pastor.[276] Neither this source nor any other has pinpointed Knollys' own adult baptism. By June 1645, Jessey became convinced of believer's baptism and, after receiving baptism from Hanserd Knollys, Jessey proceeded to baptise many others in his church.[277] Although the Jessey church would continue as a "mixt fellowship" it maintained close relations with the Particular Baptists.[278]

Even though Knollys mentioned nothing in his autobiography about this debate and his role in it, it was clearly an important event in the rise of the Particular Baptists. Following the "Knollys debate", in 1644, the three Particular Baptist churches in London increased to seven and this number would continue to grow. By this point, all of the basic elements of the Particular Baptists' doctrine of baptism were in place and would not change greatly thereafter. Knollys would continue to sound a strong voice in the debate of believer's versus infant baptism. In 1673, Henry Danvers published a treatise tracing the history of the practice of baptism, arguing for believer's baptism.[279] This publication received a flurry of answers from paedobaptists. In reply, Knollys and the leaders in the Particular Baptist community examined the disputed works and sources, and published in support of Danvers' position.[280] The analysis and interaction with the Greek and Latin sources in their response provides evidence of Knollys' involvement.

Each of the Confessions that the Particular Baptists subsequently published, very clearly and carefully outlined their position with relation to the doctrine of baptism. In each case, they emphasised not any benefit incurred by this ordinance, but stressed baptism as a sign of the redemption that the believer had already received.[281] None of the Confessions made baptism an initiatory ordinance or rite of membership to a specific congregation or church. In fact, Hanserd Knollys, Benjamin Cox and Henry Jessey in writing to John Tombes, claimed "we do not baptize any into this or that particular congregation: but

---

[276] Whitley, "Debate on Infant Baptism, 1643", p. 244.

[277] Whitley, "Debate on Infant Baptism, 1643", p. 245. Jessey embraced believer's baptism after "many conferences" with such noted Independents as Philip Nye, Thomas Goodwin, and Jeremiah Burroughs.

[278] Tolmie, *Triumph*, pp. 59-60.

[279] Henry Danvers, *A Treatise of Baptism: wherein that of believers and that of infants is examined by the Scriptures, with the history of both out of antiquity*, (London: 1673).

[280] Hanserd Knollys, et. al., *The Baptists Answer to Mr. Obed Wills, His Appeal Against Mr. H. Danvers*, (London: 1675).

[281] *Second London Confession*, Ch. XXIX, p. 97.

only into that one body in general spoken of I Cor. 12.13."[282] Rather, they usually portrayed baptism as a highly important duty.[283] The consistent use of the word "ordinance" here was significant, for they associated the word sacrament with those groups holding to the more traditional doctrine that grace leading to salvation was "transmitted and received through" the elements of the sacraments. The word ordinance, however, more clearly emphasised the duty of the believer in carrying out the command ordained by Christ, which did not "produce any spiritual change" in the individual nor convey any "direct spiritual benefit or blessing". It emphasised the "testimony" which brought the believer "into membership or participation in the local church".[284] The fact that the Scriptures actually used the word ordinance gave further support for the Baptists' use of the same word.

Knollys' own treatment of baptism in *The World That Now Is*, was very brief, stating simply that it was intended for believers, both men and women but not infants.[285] Administered by dipping, according to the Greek term, baptism involved immersion with both the candidate and the person baptising entering the water. Symbolically, the person being baptised was buried in the water and raised up again "in the Name of the Father, Son, and holy Spirit".[286] Knollys did not state who was to perform the baptism in this treatise. However, in 1646, when debating John Saltmarsh, Knollys revealed that Baptists did not believe "that every common Disciple may Baptize" or "for any Brother to baptize, or to administer other Ordinances; unless he have received such gifts of the Spirit as fitteth or inableth him to preach the Gospel".[287] However, he also noted "We do not affirme that the Administrator of Baptisme must be an Officer."[288] In other words, they did not confine baptism to the elected elders of congregations. The Particular Baptist Confessions were equally ambiguous. The *1644 Confession*, written shortly after the debate over baptism, claimed that administration of the

---

[282] John Tombes, *An Addition to the Apology For the two Treatises concerning Infant-Baptisme*, (London: 1652), p. 21.

[283] J.M. Ross, "The Theology of Baptism in Baptist History", *The Baptist Quarterly*, XV, (1953) : 105.

[284] Millard J. Erickson, *Christian Theology*, (Grand Rapids, MI: Baker Book House, 1986), pp. 1007-11, 1096-97; Holifield, *Covenant Sealed*, pp. 76-87.

[285] Knollys, *World that Now Is*, Book I, pp. 72-73.

[286] Knollys, *World That Now Is*, Book I, pp. 72-74. The Trinitarian emphasis was clearly significant for Knollys. See above, p. 114. Hanserd Knollys, *The Shining of a Flaming Fire In Zion Or, A clear Answer unto 13 Exceptions, against the Grounds of New Baptism; (so called) in Mr. Saltmarsh his Book; Intituled, "The Smoke in the Temple"*, (London: 1645), pp. 5-7.

[287] Knollys, *The Shining of a Flaming Fire in Zion*, p. 9. This treatise written in response to John Saltmarsh was Knollys' most extensive treatment of the doctrine of baptism, yet ironically, it was not even dealing with the issue of believer's baptism versus infant's baptism. See Chapter 3 above.

[288] Knollys, *The Shining of a Flaming Fire in Zion*, p. 13.

ordinance extended to any whom "the Scriptures hold forth to be a preaching Disciple, it being no where tyed to a particular Church, Officer, or person extraordinarily sent".[289] The *Second London Confession*, simply stated that it was to be administered "by those only, who are qualified and thereunto called according to the Commission of Christ".[290] Perhaps the ambiguity of these statements derived from the expansive nature of the Particular Baptists, who sought to establish congregations where an ordained pastor or elder might not be readily available. Or perhaps it reflected the position taken as early as 1644 by Anne Knollys and the others who agreed that "Such Disciples as are gifted to teach & Evangelize may also baptize." This reflected the desire of Knollys and his wife to maintain a sense of order, while at the same time allowing a measure of freedom.

One of the most significant questions raised about the doctrine of believer's baptism had to do with the place of children within the soteriology of the Particular Baptists. Since Knollys' initial involvement in the debate arose from the baptism of his child, he must have considered this question carefully. Whereas some doctrinal positions held that infant baptism actually brought salvation to the child and others that it protected the child until the child reached an age of assent, believer's baptism did not provide any assurance for a child's salvation. Although Knollys did not address the issue of children's salvation directly, he did offer assurances to godly parents. He challenged them to take care to raise their children "in the nurture and instruction of the Lord... That they may continue in the doctrine of truth and faith which they have learned in their youth".[291] Several examples from the Scriptures illustrated how children had become godly leaders because they had learned to follow God while young.[292] Knollys expounded on this further in *The World That Now Is*, stating that not only did he know this to be true from Scriptural accounts, but from his "Experience".[293] He claimed that "some sinners, who have had Religious Education under godly Parents or Governours; and have lived (from their youth up) under a godly Soul-saving Ministry, and have thereby been restrained (by the Common Grace of God) from all gross sins." Eventually, this

---

[289] *1644 Confession*, p. 167. The statement in the "Confession of 1646" is virtually identical. See p. 42.

[290] *Second London Confession*, Ch. XXVIII, sect. 2, p. 96. The Association of Particular Baptists in South Wales was more direct. As early as the General Meeting in August 1654, it was declared unequivocally that it is the "pastor's office" to "administer all ordinances in the church". The Western Association, however, followed more the line put forth in the London confessions stating that it was "not clear in scripture, ye we conclude it not unlawfull in all cases". White, *Association Records*, pp. 11, 58.

[291] Knollys, *Song of Solomon*, p. 39. See also White, *Association Records*, p. 26.

[292] Knollys, *Song of Solomon*, p. 39.

[293] Knollys, *World That Now Is*, Book I, p. 25. Was he here perhaps referring to his own experience or that of his children? See Knollys, *Life*, pp. 1-2.

led to a conviction of their sinfulness and ultimately to their salvation.[294] However, he also clearly stated that a parent could not impart salvation to a child:

> Godly Parents and Relations may and ought to pray that God will give pardoning Grace, sanctifying Grace, saving Grace to their children, or any other Relations but they cannot give any, nor can they impart any Grace to them.[295]

Another way the Particular Baptists attempted to provide security for children was to stipulate that a believer should only marry a believer.[296] In fact, failure to abide by this rule in some Particular Baptist congregations could result in church discipline.[297] The most obvious security available to parents had nothing to do with their actions or the minister's actions (i.e. in baptising the child), but with the sovereignty of God.[298] The *Second London Confession* stated very clearly that "Elect Infants dying in infancy are regenerated and saved by Christ through the Spirit; who worketh when and where, and how he pleaseth."[299] This position in some ways showed a consistent devotion by the Particular Baptists to the soteriology of Reformed theology. By recognising the election of children, they probably felt more consistent than the Presbyterians, who seemed to be reneging on their belief in God's sovereignty by initiating their children into the covenant community through baptism.[300]

The Lord's Supper

The Particular Baptists' doctrine of baptism was formulated and settled, for the most part, quite early in their existence, largely because this doctrine clearly set them apart from other Puritans. The same could not be said, however, for the doctrine of communion. Apart from a very definite denial of transubstantiation, Particular Baptists held differing points of view on both the method and meaning of communion. This aspect of Particular Baptist thought continued to be discussed and developed beyond the seventeenth century.

---

[294] Knollys, *World That Now Is*, Book I, pp. 25-26.
[295] Knollys, *Parable of the Kingdom of Heaven*, p. 110.
[296] *Second London Confession*, Ch. XXV, p. 83-84.
[297] This 'requirement' was often stipulated within a specific church's covenant. E.P. Winter, "The Lord's Supper: Admission and Exclusion Among the Baptists of the Seventeenth Century", *The Baptist Quarterly*, XVII, (Apr. 1958) : 277.
[298] Katherine Sutton, a friend of Knollys, wrote of her despair following the loss of her child. In the end, it was in the love and sovereignty of God that she found her solace. *A Christian Womans Experiences of the glorious working of Gods free grace*, (Rotterdam: 1663), pp. 5-6.
[299] *Second London Confession*, Ch. X, sect. 3, p. 38.
[300] See Holifield, *Covenant Sealed*, pp. 81-83.

The administration of the Lord's Supper raised several questions. Some, such as Benjamin Keach, felt that only the pastor, duly called and ordained, could administer communion in a specific congregation.[301] However, not all Particular Baptist congregations held such a restrictive position. One of the criticisms raised by Robert Baillie was that the Baptists had given authority "to others besides ministers to celebrate... even the Lord's Supper, without so much as the presence of any Ministers".[302] As with baptism, many Particular Baptist congregations struggled with a shortage of pastors and ordained elders, due to a variety of circumstances including imprisonment (especially after the Restoration). Smaller congregations did not necessarily have pastors nor could they financially support a full-time pastor.

The leadership of the Particular Baptist churches recognised this difficulty. In the earliest Confessions (1644, 1646), the Lord's Supper received barely a mention.[303] The *Second London Confession* paid more attention to the Lord's Supper (Chapter XXX). However, it remained ambiguous on who could administer the ordinance. In the introduction to the section on ordinances, it merely stated that they should be "administered by those only who are qualified and thereunto called according to the Commission of Christ".[304] In the chapter dealing with the Lord's Supper, it became a bit more specific, though not much more emphatic: "The Lord Jesus hath in this Ordinance, appointed his Ministers to Pray, and Bless the elements of Bread and Wine."[305] The administrator had to be a minister, though not exclusively an ordained minister and not necessarily the minister of that particular congregation. Taken together, these statements indicated only that a minister should administer communion. A similar position was also recommended by the General Assembly of 1689.[306]

Knollys was equally as specific and elusive in his treatment of the subject. Clearly he felt that a minister should preside over communion, but he did not demand that the minister must come from that particular fellowship. The use of ministers from other congregations seemed a normative situation and Knollys discussed the issue within the context of the typical worship of a church.[307] His

---

[301] Benjamin Keach, *The glory of a true church and its discipline display'd: Wherein a true Gospel-Church is described together with the power of the keys, and who are to be let in, and who to be shut out*, (London: 1697), pp. 16-18; E.P. Winter, "Who may administer The Lord's Supper?" *The Baptist Quarterly*, XVI (July, 1955) : 130.

[302] Robert Baillie, *The disswasive from the errors of the time, vindicated from the exceptions of Mr. Cotton and Mr. Tombes*, (London: 1655), p. 83.

[303] No mention is made in the *1644 Confession* and a passing mention is made in relation to baptism is made in the "Confession of 1646".

[304] *Second London Confession*, Ch. XXVIII, sect. 2, p. 96.

[305] *Second London Confession*, Ch. XXX, sect. 3, p. 100.

[306] *Narrative of the Proceedings of the General Assembly*, (1689), p. 18.

[307] Knollys, *World That Now Is*, Book I, pp. 75-76. Where Knollys was quite specific and adamant was with regard to when it was to be celebrated, which was on Sunday evening.

desire for order tempered his desire for flexibility, for Knollys held that the ministers had the responsibility to act as caretakers of "all the Sacred Ordinances", making certain that they did not become contaminated by the "Rudiments of the world" or the "Commandments of Men".[308]

Participation in communion became another topic of debate among the early Particular Baptists. Although all would permit only believers, the difficulty arose when determining which believers. Ernest Payne correctly judged that the terms of communion "occupied far more attention in Baptist circles than have theological questions regarding the meaning and significance of the Lord's Supper itself".[309] Two major issues arose. Firstly, should the Lord's Table only be open to baptised believers or to all believers? Secondly, what role did exclusion from the Lord's Supper play in church discipline? These same issues arose in other Puritan churches in seventeenth-century Britain.[310]

General Baptists usually followed the practice known as "Strict" communion, meaning that only Baptists could participate in the communion service.[311] Particular Baptists embraced a more open stance. Many, if not most, of the first generation of Particular Baptists came from the Independent churches and often maintained ties and fellowship with believers in these congregations. Knollys himself maintained close relations with a number of Independent churches and believers throughout his life and ministry. Thus, the earlier Particular Baptist congregations tended to embrace the practice of "open" communion, even though they clearly sustained a "closed" membership, dependent on believer's baptism. In time, this began to change, however, and "strict" churches favouring "closed" communion appeared.[312] Although most of the earliest Particular Baptists practiced "open" communion, the only comment in the *1646 Confession* about the Lord's Supper sounded more "strict" by stating that a person professing faith "ought to be baptized, and after to partake of the Lord's supper".[313] One Particular Baptist who was quite adamant about "closed" communion was Benjamin Keach.[314] This fit with his other views. Keach unwaveringly held that only the pastor of a particular congregation could

---

[308] Knollys, *Exposition of the Eleventh Chapter of the Revelation*, pp. 5-6. The administering minister played a key role in the 'purity' of the Lord's table. As a young minister, Knollys had begun to question his role in the Church of England in part because of the "admitting wicked persons to the Lords Supper". Knollys, *Life*, p. 9. He also encountered difficulty in New England a few years later over the same issue. See Chapter 2 above.

[309] Ernest Payne, *The Fellowship of Believers: Baptist Thought and Practice Yesterday and Today*, (London: Kingsgate Press, 1944), p. 54.

[310] For an examination of the Erastian Controversy, which revolved around similar issues of participation, see Holifield, *Covenant Sealed*, pp. 110-26.

[311] Winter, "The Lord's Supper: Admission and Exclusion", p. 267.

[312] Winter, "The Lord's Supper: Admission and Exclusion", p. 272.

[313] *1646 Confession* in Underhill, *Confessions of Faith*, p. 41.

[314] Winter, "The Lord's Supper: Admission and Exclusion", p. 273.

administer baptism in that church, which meant that he took a "strict" position in relation to the ordinances in general. In addition, Keach was a second generation Particular Baptist who converted from the General Baptists.[315] Rather than having had the ties to the Independents, he had grown up under the General Baptist "strict" position.

Although *The World That Now Is*, provides the most definitive statement about the practice of the Lord's Supper made by Knollys, he remained silent about this aspect of the subject. In the post-script of his response to John Saltmarsh published in 1646, Knollys appealed to the seemingly "strict" position of the *1646 Confession*.[316] However, Knollys' open fellowship with the Independents in London would seem to indicate a more "open" approach to communion. The only definitive statement Knollys made regarding the openness of communion appeared in the letter of Cox, Jessey, and Knollys cited by John Tombes:

> as touching joining in communion, we in this case require no more, than a manifest readinesse to hold communion with all the Churches of Christ in the things of Christ, and accordingly to shew a real willingnesse to have communion with any particular Church of Christ according as the hand of God shall give opportunity.[317]

Although this spoke more generally about having fellowship with others, it followed immediately after the statement on baptism: only "a persons manifestation of himselfe to be a believer in Jesus Christ" was required for baptism and that baptism was not "into this or that particular congregation: but only into that one body in general spoken of in 1 Cor. 12.13."[318] This clearly indicates that they were referring to the ordinances, while maintaining a rather ecumenical focus. The *Second London Confession*, which Knollys signed, also remained silent on the issue, except to exclude "all ignorant and ungodly Persons". As so often was the case, Knollys strove for a certain level of toleration and unity, particularly in areas that the Scriptures did not address clearly.[319] The Scriptures appeared clear on two things related to this subject and Knollys and the majority of Particular Baptists held firmly to these. First

---

[315] Haykin, *Kiffin, Knollys, and Keach*, p. 86.

[316] Knollys, *The Shining of a Flaming Fire*, p. 16.

[317] Tombes, *Addition*, p. 21.

[318] Tombes, *Addition*, p. 21. It is intriguing that Knollys wrote this letter with his fellow Particular Baptist, Benjamin Cox, and long-time Independent fellow pastor, Henry Jessey.

[319] Knollys, *World That Now Is*, Book I, pp. 50-51, 96; Knollys certainly understood that there were true believers outside of the Particular Baptist congregations. Thus, his desire was that they "be one in Christ" even though they might "think differently", keeping a "Brotherly Amity, Unity, and Peace amongst the Saints". Knollys, *The Shining of a Flaming Fire*, Epistle.

was the duty of the believer to partake of the Lord's Table. In fact, Knollys found it "a grievous sin to be negligent in the keeping of the Ordinances of God".[320] Second, participation in communion was forbidden of unbelievers.[321] Beyond these two requirements, they remained uncommitted for the sake of unity and accommodation.[322]

The *Second London Confession* stated that "The denyal of the Cup to the People" was "contrary to the Nature of this Ordinance", highlighting the importance of participation. However, the Particular Baptists believed that participation was not only a duty of the believer. It was also a privilege. Without question, they understood that the "ungodly" were "unfit" to partake in communion.[323] This was certainly the position held by Knollys. He himself had renounced his ordination and the Church of England in the 1630s because, among other things, he disagreed with "admitting wicked persons to the Lords Supper".[324] Indeed, exclusion from the Lord's Supper and church discipline often went hand in hand.[325] In his exegesis of the book of Revelation, Knollys argued that Christ had commended the church at Ephesus, in part, because of its care in the practice of church discipline. He proceeded to outline the three stages of discipline of sinners: "First, In admonishing them; Secondly, In withdrawing from them; and Thirdly, In Excommunicating of them, according to the Laws of Christ."[326] This process emphasised restoration over separation, attempting to encourage the erring member to repent and reform.[327] However, failing that, separation of sinners from the congregation was necessary, lest "others might be leavened and corrupted by their false Doctrines or sinful

---

[320] Knollys, *Song of Solomon*, p. 25; Knollys, *World That Now Is*, Book I, p. 74; *Second London Confession*, Ch. XXX, sect. 1, pp. 98-99; Winter, "The Lord's Supper: Admission and Exclusion", p. 274.

[321] *Second London Confession*, Ch. XXX, sect. 8, p. 102; Winter, "The Lord's Supper: Admission and Exclusion", p. 274.

[322] The ambiguities within the Particular Baptists in this aspect of the doctrine of communion in many ways reflected the ambiguities present in Reformed Puritan theology.

[323] *Second London Confession*, Ch. XXX, sect. 4, 8, p. 100. Like other Puritans, the Particular Baptists placed great emphasis upon the importance of preparation so that one might not be impure when taking communion. Spurr, *Puritanism*, p. 31.

[324] Knollys, *Life*, p. 9.

[325] Winter, "The Lord's Supper: Admission and Exclusion", pp. 276-77; Knollys connected the Lord's Table and Matthew 16:18-20, the passage in which Peter/the church is given the "keys of the Kingdom" that "whatever you bind on earth will be bound in heaven, and whatever you loose on earth will be loosed in heaven", a passage which has been interpreted by some as referring to church discipline. Knollys, *Song of Solomon*, p. 56.

[326] Knollys, *Exposition of the Whole Book of the Revelation*, p. 21.

[327] Knollys, *World That Now Is*, Book I, pp. 97-98.

Practices".[328] The church at Pergamon, unlike the Ephesian church, did not exercise a diligent discipline. This was no small matter, for: "It is a sinful fault in any Church to suffer those Ministers or Members to continue in their Society, and to have Communion with them who teach such Doctrines, or practice such deeds as Christ hateth."[329] Once again, the communion spoken of here appeared in the context of fellowship as well as sacrament. For Knollys and the Particular Baptists, the communion of fellowship and the Communion of the Lord's Table were inseparable: "Christ and his Saints, do enjoy mutual communion and spiritual fellowship one with another, at the Lord's Supper, and in all other his holy Ordinances."[330]

The issue of the meaning of the Lord's Supper received little intentional treatment from the Particular Baptists. According to Ernest Payne, Baptists embraced no one interpretation of the presence of Christ in the bread and wine.[331] They agreed that transubstantiation did not provide a correct interpretation of the Scriptures. This view held that upon the consecration by a priest, through miraculous intervention, the bread and wine became the actual body and blood of Christ. The "accidences" or sense perceptions of the bread and wine remained, but their unseen "substance" changed into that of the body and blood of Jesus. Thus, through this real presence and renewed sacrifice of Christ, the communicant received the grace that led to salvation.[332] The Particular Baptists clearly denied this interpretation as being superstitious, "repugnant to Scripture alone, but even to common sense and reason".[333] Knollys wrote very harshly against the "papal principle Idol-work" calling transubstantiation a "Breaden-God" worshipped in "their Superstitious, and blasphemous Invention of Transubstantiation of the Bread and Wine into the very true and real Body and Blood of Christ by vertue of the Priests Consecration".[334] Like the later *Second London Confession*, Knollys attacked the "irrational and sensless" nature of the doctrine.[335] Even more stinging was his characterisation of transubstantiation as drinking "of the Cup of Devils" and partaking of the "Table of Devils".[336]

The other views, which emerged from the Continental Reformation, included the Lutheran (real presence), Zwinglian (memorial), and Calvinist (spiritual presence). From a Reformed point of view, Luther's doctrine of real presence did not differ greatly from transubstantiation. Rather than the elements

---

[328] Knollys, *Exposition of the Whole Book of the Revelation*, p. 21.
[329] Knollys, *Exposition of the Whole Book of the Revelation*, p. 33.
[330] Knollys, *Song of Solomon*, p. 57.
[331] Payne, *Fellowship of Believers*, p. 51.
[332] Erickson, *Christian Theology*, pp. 1115-16.
[333] *Second London Confession*, Ch. XXX, sect. 2, 6, pp. 99, 101.
[334] Knollys, *Exposition of the Eleventh Chapter of the Revelation*, p. 20; Knollys, *Mystical Babylon Unvailed*, p. 18.
[335] Knollys, *Mystical Babylon Unvailed*, pp. 18-19.
[336] Knollys, *Exposition of the Whole Book of the Revelation*, p. 113.

becoming the actual blood and body of Christ, they merely contained the actual blood and body through a miraculous work of the Spirit, independent of the priest. The "body and bread are concurrently present" and the "blood and wine coexist".[337] At the other extreme, Zwingli held that the elements merely represented the blood and body of Christ and therefore participation commemorated Christ's sacrifice, serving as a memorial with no miraculous content.[338] Calvin sought the middle ground between the two positions. He claimed that in the partaking of communion, Christ was present spiritually and miraculously bestowed special grace upon the participant, even though the elements remained bread and wine.[339]

While the General Baptists tended to embrace a Zwinglian memorial view, the Particular Baptists tended to embrace either a Calvinist approach, a Zwinglian approach or a combination of the two.[340] The *Second London Confession*, described the Lord's Supper as "the perpetual remembrance" and "only a Memorial of that one offering up of himself", noting that the elements "represent... the Body and Blood of Christ". However, it also stressed that this ordinance provided "confirmation of the Faith of Believers in all the benefits thereof, their spiritual nourishment, and growth in him" which participants received not only outwardly, but "also inwardly by Faith, really and indeed... spiritually receive, and feed upon Christ crucified" so that "all the benefits of his Death" are "spiritually present to the Faith of Believers".[341] On the whole, this closely resembled the Calvinist doctrine.

In his brief biography of Hanserd Knollys, B.R. White argued that Knollys seemed to hold to a "rather 'high' doctrine of the Lord's Supper".[342] In another article, he stated more emphatically that Knollys "in no sense intended to point to a belief in the 'real absence' of Christ from the Supper".[343] The writings of Knollys show that he did not hold to the simple symbolic understanding of the Lord's Supper. However, by the same token, Knollys rejected the doctrine of transubstantiation, and did not express it when claiming that "His flesh is our meat indeed, His blood our drink indeed."[344] Knollys "quite obviously recognized a disjunction between the elements and the Presence which a Catholic Christian would not".[345]

---

[337] Erickson, *Christian Theology*, pp. 1117-18.

[338] Erickson, *Christian Theology*, 1120-21.

[339] Erickson, *Christian Theology*, pp. 1118-20; White, *Sacraments*, pp. 75-80; Mayor, *Lord's Supper*, pp. ix-xix.

[340] E.P. Winter, "Calvinist and Zwinglian Views of the Lord's Supper among the Baptists of the Seventeenth Century", *The Baptist Quarterly*, XV, (1954) : 329.

[341] *Second London Confession*, Ch. XXX, sect. 1, 2, 5, 7, pp. 98-102.

[342] White, *Hanserd Knollys*, p. 18.

[343] B.R. White, "Echoes of Medieval Christendom in Puritan Spirituality", *One In Christ*, (1980) : 88.

[344] Knollys, *Christ Exalted*, p. 7.

[345] White, "Echoes of Medieval Christendom", p. 89.

White was quite correct here in discerning a complexity in Knollys' thought on the Eucharist. Along with his Particular Baptist contemporaries, Knollys combined Zwingli's symbolic approach with Calvin's spiritual approach. Knollys stated clearly that Christ instituted his supper to be celebrated "in *Remembrance* of him... and as a *Memorial* of his Death" (emphasis in original).[346] In another work, he stressed that statements Christ made about being the "Bread" and "Drink" of believers emphasised his role as the means through which God communicated his love and grace to Christians.[347] However, Knollys quite explicitly claimed that the ceremony went well beyond a mere symbolic remembrance. He viewed it as having special significance, to the point that he implored believers to give both of the ordinances high priority:

> O dear Friends! be not wanting to your precious souls, either in sleighting or neglecting the Ordinances of God, why should you cry, O my leanness, my barrenness, &c? Seeing Christ in the great day of the Feast, stands & cryes *If any man thirst, let him come to me and drink.* Joh. 7.37.38.39. How unkindly do ye deal with Christ, to sleight and neglect or refuse his gracious Invitations, to heavenly banquets at his Table?[348]

The importance of the celebration was not just in the act of remembering what Christ had done on the behalf of sinners, but also in the significant blessing it imparted to the believer. "Christ giveth his saints spiritual Bread, hidden Manna, New-wine and water of life at his Supper, and in his Ordinances."[349] The blessing, the "Feast of fat things full of marrow... and wine" consisted of spiritual refreshment and comfort in the graces of Christ so that those who "sup with Christ, have meat and drink, which others know not of".[350] The ordinances of baptism and communion came as a gift from Christ to the Church "for the feeding, nourishing, strengthening, and establishing of the Saints".[351] In some special sense, the ordinances for Knollys were an aid to spiritual survival.

> O how are the hunger-thirsty Soules of the poor Saints revived, refreshed, comforted, and satiated with the Communications of the Spirit and grace of Christ, in his holy Ordinances? when the Lord meets them, manifesteth himself to them, speaketh gracious words unto their hearts, and witnesseth his love and sealeth it by his Spirit in the promises of the new Covenant.[352]

---

[346] Knollys, *World That Now Is*, Book I, p. 74.
[347] Knollys, *Christ Exalted*, pp. 2-3, 6-7.
[348] Knollys, *Song of Solomon*, pp. 57-58.
[349] Knollys, *Song of Solomon*, p. 57.
[350] Knollys, *Song of Solomon*, p. 57.
[351] Knollys, *Song of Solomon*, p. 38.
[352] Knollys, *Song of Solomon*, p. 67.

Knollys even went so far as to say that the ordinances acted as a "means of Grace".[353] However, he took great care to emphasise that "Beleevers live above Ordinances upon Christ in the use of Ordinances, neither resting in them, nor sleighting of them", thus emphasising that salvation did not depend upon these vessels of grace.[354]

A part of the blessing implicit in the partaking of the ordinances came in the strengthening of the relationship between the believer and Christ. In participating in the ordinances "by the hand of faith", the believer received not only "Spiritual gifts and fruits from Christ", but "abundance of sweet Communion with Christ" as well.[355] This mutual fellowship between the Father and Son and the believer was likened by Knollys to a "Marriage-communion", which was "mutually enjoyed in the holy Ordinances of God, wherein Christ and his Spouse, his Churches, his Saints do sup together".[356] The intimacy of this relationship in the reception of the Lord's Supper and baptism "are fitly resembled by a Bed", for the wedding bed marked the highest point of intimacy and oneness for a husband and wife.[357] Continuing this analogy, the ordinances provided opportunity for procreation, for grace to grow through the winning of "many converts". Hence the Church, through a proper use of the ordinances, could prove "fruitful" and "hath many children and much spiritual fruit".[358]

While much of this discussion has centred on the communion service, Knollys was not always so specific in his writings. In many of the passages cited, he referred generally to the "Ordinances". While White has interpreted many of the passages from *Exposition of the first Chapter of the Song of Solomon* as portraying a "rather 'high' doctrine of the Lord's Supper", a truer interpretation would stress that Knollys held a "high" view of all the elements of worship as "means of grace". For Knollys, Christ not only met with his saints in a special way through baptism and the Lord's Supper, but through corporate reading and exposition of the Scriptures and public singing and worship as well.

Corporate Worship

In his definition of a true church, Knollys often used the expression churches that "worship God in Spirit and in Truth". In *The World That Now Is*, Knollys attempted to clarify this. He claimed that one of the main reasons Christ came into the world "was to institute those Gospel-Ordinances, in which his

---

[353] Knollys, *Song of Solomon*, p. 78.
[354] Knollys, *Song of Solomon*, p. 17.
[355] Knollys, *Song of Solomon*, p. 66.
[356] Knollys, *Song of Solomon*, p. 78.
[357] Knollys, *Song of Solomon*, p. 78.
[358] Knollys, *Song of Solomon*, p. 79.

Churches of Saints must worship God in Spirit and in Truth".[359] Though he made it clear elsewhere in his writings that the most important aspect of worship related to the believer's inward condition and attitude, outward activity played a significant role as well. Many Puritans, including Knollys and the Particular Baptists, found the formalism and ritual in the Church of England as too "Romish" and, therefore, disturbing. The set prayers of the Prayer Book, kneeling to receive communion, a formal funeral liturgy, vestments, excessive laying on of hands – all of these were anathema to the Puritan mind.[360] While Knollys wrote many pages rebuking false Professors,[361] he was every bit as adamant about false religion, decrying its idolatry, with its "Images, Crucifixes, Ave Maria's, Masses", and ordinances "corrupted by men's Inventions, and superstitions", "worship... after the Traditions and Customs... as the Scribes and Pharisees" and legalism.[362] Knollys supported a simple service of worship that followed an orderly pattern.[363] At the heart of the service, in true Puritan style, was the reading and preaching of the word of God, but it included prayer,[364] prophesying,[365] baptism, the Lord's Supper, and congregational singing.[366]

Seventh-Day Sabbath

One of the growing issues of debate among the Particular Baptists by the end of the seventeenth century had to do with the question of the proper day for Christian worship. In the 1650s a new group emerged among the Particular Baptists who held to the belief that worship should take place on Saturday, according to the teachings of the Old Testament Scriptures. The earliest and most prominent Seventh-day Particular Baptist Church was located in London at Pinner's Hall. As the movement grew in the 1650s, several prominent leaders emerged, such as Dr. Peter Chamberlen, John Spittlehouse, Edward Stennet,

---

[359] Knollys, *World That Now Is*, Book I, p. 70.
[360] Spurr, *Puritanism*, pp. 29-36; *Second London Confession*, Ch. XXX, sect. 4, p. 100; Knollys, *Life*, p. 9.
[361] Knollys, *Parable of the Kingdom of Heaven*.
[362] Knollys, *Song of Solomon*, p. 24; Knollys, *Exposition of the Eleventh Chapter of the Revelation*, p. 20; Knollys, *Parable of the Kingdom of Heaven*, pp. 13, 26-28.
[363] Knollys, *Parable of the Kingdom of Heaven*, pp. 43-44.
[364] The *Second London Confession* stipulated that audible prayer in the presence of others was to be "in a Known Tongue", an obvious attempt to avoid the excesses of other more ecstatic radical groups such as the Ranters and Quakers. Ch. XXII, sect. 3, 6, pp. 74, 76.
[365] Knollys did not elaborate on this activity. Suffice it to say that it was to be orderly and judged by others present.
[366] Knollys, *World That Now Is*, Book I, pp. 70-80. Except for the emphasis on congregational singing (more below) this is not dissimilar to the description given in the *Second London Confession*. See Ch. XXII, pp. 73-77.

Thomas Tillam, Christopher Pooley, and Francis Bampfield.[367] W.T. Whitley hypothesised that the Fifth Monarchy movement, as it lost steam, evolved into Seventh-day Particular Baptist movement.[368] Capp, on the other hand, held that despite the connections between the two groups, not all "Fifth Monarchy men" became "Seventh-day men". Seventh-day beliefs did not replace Fifth Monarchy ideas, but became an addition by some Fifth Monarchists.[369] By December 1690, the year after the gathering of over one hundred Particular Baptist Churches in London for the General Assembly, some twenty Seventh-day Particular Baptist Churches existed in England, three of them in London.[370]

Seventh-day Sabbath worship was not entirely new in England, having antecedents going back to the early part of the century.[371] For the Particular Baptists, though, it provided a major issue of internal disagreement. In the 1650s, the newly evolving Particular Baptist Churches and Associations had begun to debate the issue. Generally speaking, they believed that Seventh-day observance was instituted for Israel under the Law and was no longer binding in the time of the Gospel.[372] The *Second London Confession* claimed that God ordained that His people keep one day a week as holy. From the time of creation until the resurrection of Christ, that day was the seventh day. At the resurrection of Christ, though, it "was changed into the first day of the Week, which is called the Lord's Day; and is to be continued until the end of the World, as the Christian Sabbath; the observation of the last day of the Week being abolished".[373] An extensive explanation of this position was endorsed by the General Assembly of 1689, most of the eight arguments hinging on the resurrection of Christ.[374] Although the Particular Baptists held a firm position about Sunday as the proper day of worship, they did not end relations with the Seventh-day Baptists.[375]

---

[367] Oscar Burdick, "Sleuthing the Origins of English Seventh Day Baptists in the 1650's: A Bibliography", *Summary of the Proceedings of the American Theological Library Association*, vol. 38 (1984) : 135.

[368] Whitley, *History of the British Baptists*, p. 86; W.T. Whitley, "Seventh Day Baptists in England", *The Baptist Quarterly*, VII, (1946-48) : 253.

[369] B.S. Capp, *The Fifth Monarchy Men*, (London: Faber and Faber, 1972), p. 124.

[370] From a list in the church-book of Llanwenarth Baptist Church, Monmouthshire, published in Ernest Payne, "More About the Sabbatarian Baptists", *The Baptist Quarterly*, XIV, (1951) : 165.

[371] Bryan W. Ball, *The Seventh-day Men: Sabbatarians and Sabbatarianism in England and Wales, 1600-1800*, (Oxford: Clarendon Press, 1994), chs. 1-3.

[372] White, *Association Records*, pp. 32-33.

[373] *Second London Confession*, Ch. XXII, sect. 7, pp. 76-77.

[374] *Narrative of the Proceedings of the General Assembly*, (1689), pp. 16-17.

[375] Ball, *Seventh-day Men*, ch. 4.

Hanserd Knollys made clear arguments against the observing of the Seventh-day Sabbath,[376] but still maintained personal and professional relationships with Seventh-day Baptists. In the section where he dealt with proper worship in *The World That Now Is*, he emphasised that worship should take place "when the Church is Assembled on the *first* day of the week, in some convenient place to worship God...."[377] Although he held this belief very strongly, he graciously maintained fellowship with some who held Seventh-day beliefs. At some point in the 1650s, Henry Jessey embraced such a position, though like believer's baptism, he did not press it upon his congregation.[378] In spite of this shift, Knollys continued his relationship with his old friend and they continued preaching together into the early 1660s.[379] In 1689, Knollys was one of several Particular Baptist leaders who became involved as mediators in a dispute between two Seventh-day churches. The following year, according to the Pinners' Hall Church Book, he officiated at the ordination of Seventh-day Baptist Joseph Stennet.[380] In the seventeenth century, this doctrine strained but did not break relations among the Particular Baptists.

Singing in Public Worship

Perhaps the 'hottest' internal debate the Particular Baptists experienced surfaced toward the end of Hanserd Knollys' life – that over singing during corporate worship. The Particular Baptists introduced something of an innovation into religious life in England for according to W.T. Whitley, the London Particular Baptists were the "first to popularise the singing of English hymns by the congregation".[381] Although the singing of vernacular hymns was very widespread in Germany in the sixteenth and seventeenth centuries, among the English, Presbyterians and Independents favoured only the singing of Psalms during corporate worship.[382]

Although the majority of Particular Baptists enthusiastically embraced the practice of congregational singing, a small group of dissenters did not hesitate to voice their disapproval. In 1690, Isaac Marlow, a prosperous London "button-maker" (jeweller) and merchant, published a book that would ignite a

---

[376] Knollys, *World That Now Is*, Book I, p. 49; Knollys, *Exposition of the Whole Book of the Revelation*, p. 7; Knollys, *Parable of the Kingdom of Heaven*, p. 5.

[377] Knollys, *World That Now Is*, Book I, p. 70 (emphasis in original).

[378] Ball, *Seventh-day Men*, pp. 128-30. Ball speculated that Jessey actually began to embrace Seventh-day beliefs in the late 1640s.

[379] *Calendar of State Papers Domestic, Charles II*, 1661-1662, dated Sept. 11, 1661, p. 87.

[380] Cited in Ball, *Seventh-day Men*, pp. 111-12, 120.

[381] Whitley, *British Baptists*, p. 184.

[382] Haykin, *Kiffin, Knollys, Keach*, p. 91.

bitter debate within the circle of London Particular Baptist churches.[383] Marlow objected to vocal singing in the churches for a number of reasons. First, such behaviour was equivalent to saying "Forms of Prayers" which would cause many to backslide, perhaps leading them to return to the Established Church.[384] Second, the singing mentioned in Ephesians 5:19 was not vocal but in the heart, prayers offered only for the ears of God.[385] Third, although the primitive church sang Psalms of David, nowhere did they prescribe that it should be done thereafter.[386] Fourth, women should not "teach or pray vocally" in the service and singing would violate that principle.[387] Finally, vocal singing would introduce disorder into the service.[388]

As early as 1654, the Association of South Wales raised the question of singing, as had the Western Association in 1655.[389] However, the discussion moved into the public forum through publications during the debate at the end of the century. Several books appeared, most written by Marlow and the spirited Benjamin Keach, and the debate stretched from 1690 until 1696. By 1692 the debate had become so bitter that the major statement ensuing from the General Assembly of that year centred on addressing grievances and bringing an end to the strife. This statement included a stern rebuke emphasising "how far short" the participants had come "in answering that Character which the Spirit of God gives of true Charity". Instead, their actions "tended rather to beget greater Offences and Stumblings, than Convincing, Healing, and Recovering" and gave "our Enemies occasion to rejoice over our Failings".[390]

Although this debate erupted, near the end of Hanserd Knollys' life, he did play a significant role in the rise of congregational singing in Particular Baptist Churches. Typically, Benjamin Keach has received pre-eminence as the "father of Particular Baptist hymnody".[391] As the most vocal opponent of those against

---

[383] Isaac Marlow, *A Brief Discourse Concerning Singing in the Publick Worship of God in the Gospel-Church*, (London: 1690); Haykin, *Kiffin, Knollys, and Keach*, p. 92; W.T. Whitley, *British Baptists*, pp. 152, 177.

[384] Marlow, *A Brief Discourse*, p. 4 (should be 2; improperly numbered), 6-7, 18-20.

[385] Marlow, *A Brief Discourse*, pp. 5-6 (should be 3-4), 7-9.

[386] Certainly, non-scriptural compositions were unacceptable. Marlow, *A Brief Discourse*, p. 5, 9-15.

[387] Marlow, *A Brief Discourse*, pp. 21-22.

[388] Marlow, *A Brief Discourse*, pp. 22-23.

[389] White, *Association Records*, pp. 9, 58.

[390] *A Narrative of the Proceedings of the General Assembly Consisting Of Elders, Ministers, and Messengers, met together in London, from several Parts of England and Wales, on the 17th Day of the 3d Month, 1692, and continued unto the 24th of the same. Asserting the Doctrine of Personal Election and Final Perseverance)*, (London: 1692), pp. 9-13.

[391] Hugh Martin, *Benjamin Keach, Pioneer of Congregational Hymn Singing*, (London: Independent Press, 1961); Hugh Martin, "The Baptist Contribution to Early English

singing, he gained some prominence. In addition, he published a compilation of his hymns on the eve of that controversy and another work containing "Spiritual Songs" in 1700.[392] However, Knollys had long advocated the use of singing in public worship. In books written well before the singing controversy, Knollys expressed the importance of hymns and singing in the worship of God. In fact, he claimed to have the "gift of singing", a gift of musical composition inspired by the Spirit.[393] Long before the outbreak of the debate and before Keach published a single hymn, Knollys' friend Vavasor Powell had also written hymns.[394] In 1663, Katherine Sutton published a work containing some hymns that she had penned and Knollys recommended their singing in worship "in private" or "more publickly".[395] Another acquaintance of Knollys, Abraham Cheare, published a collection of hymns for children in 1673, the same year

---

Hymnody", *The Baptist Quarterly*, XIX, (Jan. 1962) : 198-99; Carey Bonner, "Some Baptist Hymnists", *The Baptist Quarterly*, VIII, (1936-7) : 259-60.

[392] Benjamin Keach, *Spiritual Melody Containing near Three Hundred Sacred Hymns*, (London: 1691); Benjamin Keach, *Spiritual Songs Being the Marrow of the Scripture, In Songs of Praise to Almighty God; From the Old and New Testament. With A Hundred Divine Hymns on Several Occasions: As now Practised in several Congregations in and about London*, (London: 1700).

[393] Hanserd Knollys, "Courteous Reader" in *A Christian Womans Experiences of the glorious working of Gods free grace*, (Rotterdam: 1663), p. i. Pope A. Duncan claimed that Knollys penned the hymns in Sutton's work. However, he is mistaken, for they were clearly written by a woman, Sutton herself. Sutton, *A Christian Womans Experiences*, p. 40; Duncan, *Knollys*, p. 55.

[394] W.T. Whitley held that hymn singing experienced its "first impulse" in Fifth Monarchism. For the Fifth Monarchists, songs possessed a value as propaganda, using familiar tunes to promote their cause. Anna Trapnel printed some of her hymns in *The Cry of the Stone*, and according to Whitley, Powell was one of the earliest hymn writers. Thomas Tillam, the one-time messenger from Knollys' Coleman St. congregation was also a hymn-writer. This theory is quite interesting, in light of Knollys' connections with this group. *British Baptists*, pp. 185-86; Ian Mallard, "The Hymns of Katherine Sutton", *The Baptist Quarterly*, XX (1963-64) : 24; For an example of an hymn by Powell, see Louise Fargo Brown, *The Political Activities of the Baptists and Fifth Monarchy Men In England During the Interregnum*, (London: Oxford University Press, 1912), p. 51, n. 20.

[395] Knollys, "Courteous Reader" in *A Christian Womans Experiences*, pp. ii-iii. From 1661 to 1663, Knollys and his family were on the Continent and spent some time in Rotterdam where this work was published. According to Sutton, she was also living in Holland at that time. Though Mallard stated that "it is almost certain that Katherine Sutton was a member of his [Knollys] church and went over to Holland with him", this is highly unlikely since in her own work, Sutton clearly said that she departed for Holland in 1658. However, Knollys could have known her before she went over or perhaps he made her acquaintance there. Mallard, *Hymns*, p. 24; Sutton, *A Christian Womans Experiences*, pp. 22, 30.

Powell published a hymnal for adults.[396] Shortly after being given a copy of Marlow's work by the author, and probably before Keach had entered the fray, Knollys penned a brief and, as always, gracious response.[397] His *An Answer to A Brief Discourse Concerning Singing in the publick Worship of God in the Gospel-church*, (London: 1691) very briefly responded to some of Marlow's criticisms against public singing.[398] For Knollys, this debate must have been particularly difficult and disturbing. Although few Baptists leaders opposed public singing, two of the leaders in London, his close friend, William Kiffin, and his co-pastor, Robert Steed took that position.[399]

For Hanserd Knollys, the public singing in worship of hymns and psalms was a spiritual exercise on the same level as prayer. He referred to both as "distinct Ordinances under the Gospel... two distinct parts of the Worship of God, both which are to be perfomed by the anointing of the Spirit".[400] These exercises served to strengthen the communion between Christ and His Church.[401] Knollys saw eschatological foreshadowing in the songs of the believers, which differed from other singing in that "all other Songs will end in sorrows, and all carnal rejoicing will at the last be turned into mourning" when saints returned singing to Zion.[402]

---

[396] Whitley, *British Baptists*, p. 186; John C. Foster, "Early Baptist Writers of Verse", *Transactions of the Baptist Historical Society*, III (Oct. 1912) : 95-96.

[397] In the Preface of his work, Knollys addressed his response with his typical grace – "Beloved Brother, ... I have read your Little Book (which you gave me) concerning Singing. And now after Prayers to GOD, and Serious Consideration of what you have said therein; I return to you this Brief Answer, which I do intreat you to Consider: So I remain, Your Brother in our Lord JESUS CHRIST, H. K." Hanserd Knollys, *An Answer to A Brief Discourse Concerning Singing in the publick Worship of God in the Gospel-church*, (London: 1691), pp. i-ii.

[398] According to both Duncan and White, a treatise was written regarding public singing but was lost and is no longer extant. Duncan listed it, as well as *A small piece in defence of Singing ye Praises of God*, (London: 1691), claiming both to be lost. This is based on Whitley's entry in his *Baptist Bibliography* (23-691). Howson claimed *An Answer to a Brief Discourse Concerning Singing in the Publick Worship of God in the Gospel-church* was in existence but *A small piece in defence of Singing ye Praises of God* was not. It would seem that a better explanation is that they were one and the same treatise, since the publication date for both was 1691, but that at the time Whitley, Duncan, and White were writing, the piece had been lost. However, since that time, *An Answer* has re-surfaced. Thus, it would seem that Howson is mistaken in his assessment that they are two different treatises. Duncan, *Knollys*, p. 55; White, *Hanserd Knollys*, p. 23; Howson, "Question of Orthodoxy", pp. 74, 91 n. 94.

[399] Haykin, *Kiffin, Knollys, and Keach*, pp. 92-93; H. Wheeler Robinson, "Baptist Church Discipline 1689-1699", *The Baptist Quarterly*, I, (1922-23) : 112.

[400] Knollys, *Exposition of the Whole Book of the Revelation*, p. 76.

[401] Knollys, *Song of Solomon*, p. 2.

[402] Knollys, *Song of Solomon*, "Epistle Dedicatory", p. iii.

While Knollys certainly believed that singing "ought to be performed by the Church as a part of God's Publick Worship", he also felt that it should be proceed in an orderly manner with the proper attitude.[403] Psalms, hymns, and spiritual songs should derive primarily from the Scriptures, and should be sung "in Meeter and Measure, with audible Voice, as our English manner is".[404] This did not mean that people could not compose songs or hymns. Believers should approach non-Scriptural songs with caution, and the composers of such songs should make sure that they used clear texts. All spiritual songs were to be sung for the purpose of edification, "to instruct and exhort one another". And one should never claim that his or her hymn was as "materially the Inspiration of the holy Spirit as the Book of Psalms were".[405] Such songs were not devoid of the Holy Spirit's activity, for songs "ought to be performed by a gift, and the assistance of the Spirit".[406] In his discussion of the "gift of Singing", Knollys pointed out that he had "some experience of this kind of Anoynting of the Spirit of praise". He compared the inspiration of songs to that present in prayers: "The holy Spirit can dictate the Matter, yea and words of praise and singing as well as the matter and words of prayer."[407] Haykin has argued that Knollys believed that only individuals should sing, but did not permit congregational singing.[408] However, the verse that Knollys cited to support his contention that singing ought to be part of public worship was Isaiah 52:8, "With the Voice together shall they sing."[409] While receptive to solo singing for the purposes of edification, Knollys probably did not rule out congregational singing. For him, the ultimate "end of singing" was not the noise made, but the heart of the singer: "Singing with a tunable Voice makes Melody in our Ears... but Singing with Grace in our Hearts doth make melody to the Lord." [410] The "melody (which the Lord loveth) is in the heart, rather then in the voice".[411]

Isaac Marlow's initial effort to build a case against singing, while it attempted to advance an organised argument, relied on poor exegesis, careless proof-texting, and self-contradictory statements. His argument consisted of five major points. First, singing during public worship was tantamount to "precomposed Forms of Prayers".[412] Second, the singing mentioned in the Bible did not refer to vocal singing.[413] The "Essence of Singing is in the Heart" and

---

[403] Knollys, *World That Now Is*, Book I, p. 76.
[404] Knollys, *World That Now Is*, Book I, pp. 76, 80.
[405] Knollys, *World That Now Is*, Book I, p. 78.
[406] Knollys, "Courteous Reader" in *A Christian Womans Experiences*, p. ii.
[407] Knollys, "Courteous Reader" in *A Christian Womans Experiences*, p. iii.
[408] *Kiffin, Knollys, and Keach*, p. 92.
[409] Knollys, *World That Now Is*, Book I, p. 76.
[410] Knollys, *World That Now Is*, Book I, p. 77.
[411] Knollys, "Courteous Reader" in *A Christian Womans Experiences*, p. iii.
[412] Marlow, *Brief Discourse*, p. 2 (wrongly numbered as 4).
[413] Although, at several points he admitted it was vocal singing. Marlow, *Brief Discourse*, pp. 3, 5, 8.

should proceed silently.[414] Third, the Psalms did not apply to the Gospel era for a number of reasons. Their expressions of joy did not apply to the Christian Church, since, eschatologically speaking, it existed in a "Wilderness State".[415] As well, they arose in a particular period for use by a particular group of people – the Levites.[416] This made them inappropriate for Christian congregations. Fourth, since women should remain silent in the church, they certainly should not sing publicly.[417] Fifth, in his first letter to the Corinthian church, the Apostle Paul, commanded that spiritual gifts should be publicly expressed one at a time so as to be orderly. Accordingly, Marlow argued, congregational singing, which involved a plural use of the gift of singing, transgressed "the Rule" of "Order in the Gift".[418] In dealing with some possible objections to his position, Marlow claimed that the verb "to sing" was not in the Greek, but rather the word was "to hymn", which, he argued, was not confined to singing. In addition, he warned that public singing would lead to apostasy. As people returned to such forms, what he labelled "Crutches for Lame Men", they would backslide, "as a Dog [returning] to his Vomit" (2 Pet. 2:22) to worship at a false church.[419]

Knollys' reply to Marlow's treatise was reminiscent of his publications written in response to Bastwick and Saltmarsh nearly a half century before. Although over eighty years old, his scholarly edge had dulled little. Like those treatises published in the 1640s, his answer in this case was brief, yet cut directly to the point. The preface, addressed to his "Beloved Brother", took a gracious, yet firm, line. Knollys may have realised the divisive potential of this issue and he was not a divisive person.[420] However, Knollys was firmly committed to continuing in the Apostles' doctrine and held that because singing "was used in the Primitive and Apostolical Church", it should continue.[421] He obviously believed this to be an important issue, since he implied that for one to hold Marlow's position was sin. Citing James 5:19-20, "Brethren, if any of you do err from the Truth, and one Convert him; Let him know, that he which Converteth a Sinner from the Errour of his Way, shall Save a Soul from Death, and shall hide a multitude of Sins", Knollys implored Marlow to consider his position on singing.[422]

In his *Answer*, Knollys did not simply address Marlow point for point, but employed a variety of approaches to show the weaknesses and flaws of

---

[414] Marlow, *Brief Discourse*, pp. 3 (wrongly numbered as 5), 5-9.
[415] Marlow, *Brief Discourse*, p. 12.
[416] Marlow, *Brief Discourse*, pp. 12-15.
[417] Marlow, *Brief Discourse*, pp. 21-22.
[418] Marlow, *Brief Discourse*, pp. 22-23.
[419] Marlow, *Brief Discourse*, pp. 37, 48.
[420] Knollys, *Life*, p. 24.
[421] Knollys, *Answer Concerning Singing*, p. 1.
[422] Knollys, *Answer Concerning Singing*, preface.

Marlow's arguments. Within the first few sentences, he began to point out the contradictions and inconsistencies in Marlow's *Brief Discourse*.[423] He added force and urgency by claiming that singing was not merely part of worship in the days of the Apostles, but it was commanded of Christ's followers. Proof of this came in the Apostle Paul's use of the imperative, "Let" – the same word that Marlow emphasised to prove women's silence.[424] He questioned Marlow's logic of the interpretation of apostolic singing as inward and claimed that Marlow had "neither Scripture nor sound Reason for [his] Opinion about Singing without the Voice".[425] In addition, he compared Marlow's position to that of the Seekers and Quakers:

> O my Brother! I know you are not one of them that approve of silent Meetings, who supposing that they have a Light within them, whereby they are capable to worship God acceptably without his Gospel-Ordinances of Baptism, the Lord's Supper, and Singing without verbal and vocal Instruments in their Silent Meetings. In a word, This unsound Opinion of yours, will lead you, and others of the same mind, into some Erroneous Principles of them called Seekers, Quakers and such as are for Non-Churches.[426]

This reference to the Quaker and Seeker tendency to internalise their religion and rely upon the Inner light implied that to deny the importance of vocal singing in worship was tantamount to denying the importance of the public exposition of the Scriptures and the participation of believers in the ordinances of baptism and communion.

In dealing with Marlow's claim that God's people could not be joyful while in a "Wilderness State", Knollys showed several instances in Scripture when in this "Wilderness-state… under the Gospel" joyous singing was considered very appropriate.[427] Knollys also brought his training in Biblical languages to bear. He challenged Marlow's understanding of the Greek word ὑμνέω (*humneo*), arguing that Beza and Owen both translated it as "to sing", adding that "neither you, nor all the Learned Men and Books in Sion College can prove that the word signifies the Essence of Singing (without the Voice) in Heart and Mind only".[428] Finally, Knollys challenged Marlow's contention that women should always remain completely silent during worship.[429] Time and again in this small treatise, Knollys displayed his scholarship and academic prowess. Isaac Marlow, the button maker appeared to be outmanoeuvred. By the time Marlow

---

[423] Knollys, *Answer Concerning Singing*, p. 1.
[424] Knollys, *Answer Concerning Singing*, p. 2.
[425] Knollys, *Answer Concerning Singing*, p. 3.
[426] Knollys, *Answer Concerning Singing*, pp. 4-5.
[427] Knollys, *Answer Concerning Singing*, pp. 6-7.
[428] Knollys, *Answer Concerning Singing*, pp 8-9.
[429] Knollys, *Answer Concerning Singing*, p. 11.

published a rebuttal to Knollys' response, Knollys' life had come to an end. In this response, Marlow tended to focus on bringing doubt upon Knollys' position through personal criticism, rather than on strengthening his previous arguments. He emphasised that Knollys' "failure of his Intellects" exposed "the Weakness of his great Age".[430] Unable to provide scholarly refutations of the points raised by the scholarly Knollys, Marlow responded with bitter, personal attacks.

Only a small number of Particular Baptist leaders actually embraced Marlow's position. The *Second London Confession*, originally published in 1677 and republished in 1688, recognised singing as a vital part of worship along with prayer, the ministry of the word, baptism, and the Lord's Supper.[431] The debate would rage on for several years with Benjamin Keach championing the cause of those who favoured singing. At times the argument would get petty, tedious, and even nasty. In spite of the controversy, however, singing and music would remain an integral part of worship for the Particular Baptists and Hanserd Knollys certainly played a key role in establishing this pattern.

Women and their Role

As the structures of the English world came under attack at a dizzying pace in the 1640s, the issue of gender and gender roles became open to debate. According to Keith Thomas, one of the main attractions for women to the various radical sects that appeared during the period came from their emphasis on "spiritual equality". In some instances they provided educational opportunities for women, in others, opportunities to preach or participate in leadership. Some women found appeal in the freedom for self-expression in the sects.[432] Patricia Crawford provided further support for this position. In a day when relatively little changed for women in terms of sexuality and work, and in some instances the gender roles became more restrictive, "the main effect of the English Revolution on women was in providing greater opportunities for them to express their ideas individually and collectively."[433] Crawford argued, "the greatest single force influencing women's social situation in the revolutionary decades was their religious beliefs."[434] The appearance of women as

---

[430] Isaac Marlow, *Truth Soberly Defended In A Serious Reply to Mr. Benjamin Keach's Book intituled, The Breach Repaired in God's Worship; or Singing of Psalms, Hymns, and spiritual Songs, proved to be an Holy Ordinance of Jesus Christ*, (London: 1692), pp. 142-45.

[431] *Second London Confession*, Ch. XXII, sect. 5, p. 71.

[432] Keith Thomas, "Women and the Civil War Sects", in *Crisis in Europe, 1560-1660*, ed. T. Aston, (London: Routledge, 1965), p. 330.

[433] Patricia Crawford, "The Challenges to Patriarchalism: How did the Revolution affect Women?" in *Revolution and Restoration: England in the 1650s*, ed. John Morrill, (London: Collins & Brown, 1992), pp. 113-19.

[434] Crawford, "Challenges to Patriarchalism", p. 119.

prophetesses caused alarm for the more conservative element of society.[435] These sorts of opportunities became available in some of the more radical groups such as the Fifth Monarchists and the Quakers.[436] Women were vital to the survival of dissent for two reasons. First, their presence swelled the ranks of dissenting congregations – they outnumbered the men two to one. Second, they produced children. During the years of persecution following the Restoration, few conversions to independent churches took place. Thus, expansion of the congregations through natural means became even more vital. Women produced the needed children, and also played an important role in household religion and piety.[437]

However, Baptists tended to remain the most conservative of all the radical groups springing from the revolutionary years.[438] B.R. White pointed out "while there is every indication that they [women] formed a majority of the membership, comparatively little was recorded specifically about them."[439] This may have related to the close ties between the Particular Baptists and the Puritans, who also exalted in the family and specific gender roles. While the Puritans did much to alleviate such abuses as wife beating and the double standard regarding sexual morality, they still upheld the commitments of the social order of the day, including gender roles.[440] Another reason for the conservative approach of the Particular Baptists came from their emphasis on Biblical authority and their literalist interpretive hermeneutic. In an effort to re-institute the New Testament church, they approached Scripture from a "plain sense" perspective that took the strictures of St. Paul as normative.[441] Finally, the desire of the Particular Baptists to distance themselves from the more radical sects, such as the Quakers, also probably caused them to take a more restrictive position on women's role in the church and ministry.[442]

The Baptist Confessions remained significantly silent on this issue. As well, the General Assembly of 1689 only addressed the issue of men and women dressing in ways that were "inconsistent with Modesty, Gravity, Sobriety, and a Scandal to Religion".[443] Though both men and women are addressed in this statement, the women clearly received much more attention and analysis than

---

[435] Crawford, "Challenges to Patriarchalism", p. 119-20; Phyllis Mack, "Women as prophets during the English Civil War", *Feminist Studies*, 8 (1982) : 19-45.

[436] Barry Reay, "Quakerism and Society", in *Radical Religion in the English Revolution*, ed. B. Reay and J.F. McGregor (New York: Oxford University Press, 1984), pp. 144-46; Mack, "Women as prophets", pp. 24-34;

[437] Crawford, "Challenges to Patriarchalism", p. 123.

[438] McGregor, "Baptists", p. 47.

[439] White, *English Baptists of the Seventeenth Century*, p. 134.

[440] White, *English Baptists of the Seventeenth Century*, pp. 134-35; Thomas, "Women and the Civil War Sects", p. 318; White, *Association Records*, p. 69.

[441] White, *English Baptists of the Seventeenth Century*, pp. 135-36.

[442] White, *English Baptists of the Seventeenth Century*, p. 136.

[443] *Narrative of the Proceedings of the General Assembly*, (1689), pp. 14-15.

did men. The leaders within the Particular Baptist congregations were the male elders and pastors, though some churches instituted the office of deaconess for women.[444] Particular Baptist statements on education focused on boys and men, as well. One issue, which consistently provided a problem for the sects and for the Baptists, was that of prophecy, particularly in congregations with a more millenarian focus. One of the signs of the end times, which many believed were upon them, was the increase in activity of prophets and prophetesses. How to be open and inclusive to this activity, while at the same time maintaining order and obedience to the Scriptures, created a dilemma for many Particular Baptists.[445]

The Association records of the early decades of the Particular Baptists provided a few guidelines regarding the place and role of women. In the Western Association, women were not "to speak at all in the church, neither by way of praying, prophesying, nor enquiring" in public services. However, they could exercise such appropriate gifts "in private".[446] In the Midlands Association, a fuller discussion on the topic took place in 1656. The central issue here became not whether a woman should remain silent, but whether she should usurp authority from a man. In this instance, it was determined that there were five situations when women could speak in public without usurping authority. However, none of these included teaching.[447] The South Wales Association did allow a narrow scope for female participation in ministry by permitting widows to assist deacons in caring for the needs of the congregation, primarily in caring for the poor and sick.[448] Women also could vote on church matters as members.[449] However, even this could change from congregation to congregation. For Baptists, as with the other sects, the place of women very often presented an awkward situation. While they preached no distinction between clergy and laity and claimed equality for all believers, both male and female, in practice, distinctions existed and these distinctions heightened with the passage of time as they moved from a sectarian existence to a more institutionalised one.[450]

---

[444] Patricia Crawford, *Women and Religion in England 1500-1720*, (London: Routledge, 1993), pp. 144-45.

[445] Crawford, *Women and Religion in England*, pp. 146-47.

[446] White, *Association Records*, p. 55.

[447] She might publicly give her testimony when seeking baptism or church membership, she could give a public report if she had been sent by the congregation to rebuke a wayward female church member, she might be asked to relay a message sent through her from another congregation, she might appeal to the congregation for help, and if she had been excommunicated due to sin, she could make public repentance. White, *Association Records*, p. 28.

[448] White, *Association Records*, p. 11.

[449] John Briggs, "She-preachers, Widows and Other Women: The Feminine Dimension in Baptist Life since 1600", *The Baptist Quarterly*, XXXI, (July 1986) : 342.

[450] Crawford, *Women and Religion*, pp. 140-44.

Although Hanserd Knollys did not present an ordered theology of women's place and roles, his writings contained scattered references to the topic and his own life provided numerous examples of his dealings with women. In April 1671, Hanserd Knollys experienced a challenging trial – the loss of Anne, his wife of 40 years.[451] Knollys' assessment of women and their role in the church emerged concretely in his own relationship with his wife. Throughout all the changes in his life, all the trials and hardships, she remained at his side. The esteem in which he held her and the role she played as his partner received the following short summary in his autobiography: she "was a Holy, Discreet Woman, and a meet Help for me, in the ways of her Houshold, and also in the way of Holiness; who was my companion in all my Sufferings, Travels, and Hardships that we endured for the Gospel."[452] Knollys clearly understood Anne as his equal, as his partner. She was not merely one who bore and raised his children and tended to the household, though she certainly fulfilled this role with great capability. His "companion" in difficulties, she embraced his causes as they ministered together. He claimed, "we endured [them] for the Gospel". He considered her his ministry partner, his "meet Help... in the way of Holiness". One of the clearest evidences of this appeared when they struggled over the issue of baptism. Although Knollys became convinced of the validity of believer's baptism, he remained a member at the Jessey church for another six months until Anne had overcome her doubts on the issue.[453] Although Knollys embraced traditional Puritan roles for men and women, with husbands as the head of the household and women as the household managers, he certainly understood their relationship as mutually respectful.[454] He chastised fathers and husbands who often harshly misused their role as head of the household by dealing with their wives and children abusively. Instead of abusing their power, he contended, they "should especially shew forth the power of godliness" in their leadership.[455]

In his response to John Saltmarsh in 1646, Knollys addressed a claim that Saltmarsh had made that according to the Particular Baptists, "every common disciple" could baptise. Not so, claimed Knollys, "For though believing Women being baptized are Disciples... we do not hold, that a woman may preach, baptize, nor administer other Ordinances."[456] Although eligible for the privileges of membership conferred by baptism, women still could not hold

---

[451] Knollys, *Life*, pp. 36-37
[452] Knollys, *Life*, pp. 8-9.
[453] "Knollys Memorandum", pp. 243-44.
[454] Edmund S. Morgan, *The Puritan Family: Religion and Domestic Relations in Seventeenth-Century New England*, rev. and enlarged ed., (New York: Harper and Row, 1966), pp. 44-45.
[455] Knollys, *Christ Exalted*, p. 35.
[456] Knollys, *The Shining of a Flaming Fire*, p. 9.

positions of leadership.[457] Knollys reinforced this position in his *Exposition on the Whole Book of Revelation* by denying that the false prophetess, Jezebel, the church of Thyatira, could be a literal person, "who taught or spake publickly in the Church, for that was against the Law of Christ and command of the Apostle".[458] Isaac Marlow had criticised public singing of women on the grounds that "all Orthodox Christians" agreed that women should neither teach nor pray "vocally" in church. Marlow had extended this by arguing that it was wrong for women to "presume to sing vocally".[459] In his answer to Marlow, though, Knollys took the same position as that expressed by the Midlands Association in the 1650s. Although women ought not to teach, they could speak in church, specifically to testify of their conversion or to bring to the attention of the church the activities of a sinful member. This opened the door for their singing, as well.[460]

Although Knollys, considered his wife a partner in his ministry, he also expressed the generally accepted position of the Particular Baptists with regard to women. However, other ambiguities on the role of women in the church arose during the course of his life. For example, Knollys was present on at least one occasion when Anna Trapnell, the Fifth Monarchist prophetess, was in a trance and prophesying.[461] Although not necessarily signifying his agreement, his presence certainly showed a level of tolerance. In addition, Knollys wrote a preface for Katherine Sutton's book of reflections on her spiritual journey. He certainly had known godly women who acted as instruments of God to teach both men and women, outside of the bounds of corporate worship.[462] Knollys spoke highly of Katherine Sutton, claiming that:

> when God was pleased to poure out of his Spirit upon some of his faithful Servants in our Generation, he had also some of his Handmaides, who gathered up the Crumes of that spiritual Bread, which the Lord blessed and distributed among his Disciples: Of which Number this holy Matron was one.[463]

---

[457] Knollys, *World That Now Is*, Book I, p. 73.
[458] Knollys, *Exposition on the Whole Book of Revelation*, pp., 36-37.
[459] Marlow, *Brief Discourse*, p. 21.
[460] Knollys, *Answer Concerning Singing*, pp. 11-12.
[461] Anna Trapnel, *Cry of a Stone*, (London: 1654), p. 7.
[462] Knollys, *Life*, pp. 4-5.
[463] Knollys, "Courteous Reader" in *A Christian Womans Experiences*, p. i. It is likely no accident that this statement makes reference to Matthew 15:21-28 which records the incident when Jesus was approached by a Gentile woman, asking Him to deliver her daughter from demon-possession. Wishing to benefit from an 'overflow' of Jesus' grace, the woman stated that even the dogs benefit from the meal of their master. The Canaanite woman understood that for the Jews, Gentiles, women, and dogs were often accorded the same level of appreciation. So too in seventeenth-century English society,

While she fulfilled the traditional duties of teaching "her children and Maidens", she probably went beyond these duties. Having received "an Unction from the holy Spirit" and as one "taught of God", she compiled her spiritual experiences and published them.[464] Although this represented her testimony, "fragments" of her experiences, she felt "pressed in Spirit to Communicate them more publikely" and these "extraordinary Teachings of God by his holy Spirit and Word" poured forth, according to Knollys, "fresh Anoyntings of the Lords Spirit... promised... in the last days".[465] More than merely simple testimony, these writings voiced teachings of a prophetess in a very public forum.

While Knollys wished to preserve the order of the worship service[466] and the "letter of the law" with respect to the Apostles' teachings about women, he clearly recognised the importance of women to the ministry of the church. Therefore, he could welcome his wife as a partner in his ministry and appreciate the witness of other godly women, prophetesses through whom the Holy Spirit taught.

Conclusion

Despite the claims of their detractors, the Particular Baptists did not come from social groups that could really be classified as "mean rogues" or rabble. Very few sprang from the ranks of the upper gentry or the aristocracy, but most were middling sort – artisans, tradesmen, and merchants. In the boisterous days of the 1640s, some Particular Baptists sought to take advantage of the new measure of liberty. Many joined their congregations in the midst of a search after truth. The 1640s and 1650s allowed the Particular Baptists the relative freedom and opportunity to establish themselves. In the late 1680s and early 1690s, after the fires of persecution during the Restoration, the Act of Toleration allowed new freedom and new opportunities.

In the atmosphere of freedom established by toleration, the task of the Particular Baptists was to regroup and reiterate the doctrines and practices that constituted their identity. The old 'founders of the faith' were quickly

---

those outside the Established Protestant church (sects such as the Baptists) and women in general usually received the respect given to dogs. One might assume by this statement that Knollys was placing Sutton and the "Handmaides" with the dogs. However, it seems more likely that he was, to an extent, mocking the lack of value society placed upon spiritually gifted women. One should not lose sight of the other passages Knollys was alluding to (Joel 2:28-32; Acts 2:18), which emphasised the role of men *and* women prophesying who had been filled with the Holy Spirit.

[464] Knollys, "Courteous Reader" in *A Christian Womans Experiences*, pp. i-ii.
[465] Knollys, "Courteous Reader" in *A Christian Womans Experiences*, p. i.
[466] In his *World That Now Is*, Knollys emphasised propriety in worship by stating that women at prayer must wear veils and should "adorn themselves in modest apparel" when they come to worship. Book I, p. 88.

disappearing and a new generation of leaders was emerging. Numerous churches now sprang up, both in London and throughout the countryside, yet many of them had inadequate leadership and needed assistance. As Hanserd Knollys and the few remaining first generation Particular Baptists called together leaders throughout England, they hoped to solidify their identity as a distinct community of faith. Realising the need for change, they had taken some radical positions, but had ultimately held to the need for order and institutional boundaries. The process had begun in the earliest days of the 1640s and, by 1688, had progressed significantly along the path toward institutionalisation.

Although Hanserd Knollys and the Particular Baptists embraced a separatist position and sought to gather independent congregations of believers, they did not see their position as one of disunity or schism. Believing that they were establishing congregations of the true church, their desire for independence went hand in hand with their belief in the priesthood of all believers. In their desire for independence, the Particular Baptists displayed an intense aspiration to guard the purity of the church and this led to a need for interdependence and fellowship with those congregations of like faith. At the simplest level, this interdependence occurred as congregations assisted one another and shared together in ministry. On a broader level, regional associations of churches and general assemblies of Particular Baptist congregations from around the nation served to establish a developing identity and furthered the process of institutionalisation.

By 1688, the Particular Baptists had achieved a measure of legitimacy with respect to their theology, especially with the Presbyterians and the Independents with whom they had shared a bond of suffering during the Restoration. Their soteriology was unquestionably Calvinistic, with a strong emphasis on the depravity of human beings and their inability to procure salvation through works, and on God's unconditional election of some to salvation and the perseverance of the elect through God's providence. Knollys' understanding of the centrality of the Scriptures was also typically Puritan. Like other Puritans, the Particular Baptists embraced a preparationist theology, which allowed for the evangelistic emphasis central to their movement. The stress on evangelism was instrumental for the spread of the movement from its humble beginnings. Beyond that, however, a genuine concern for conversion propelled their evangelistic fervour, particularly in the context of eschatological expectancy of the 1680s. This evangelistic urgency made itself known in Hanserd Knollys' activities, sermons, and published treatises. His strongly Puritan theology always intertwined with his desire that people experience a true conversion.[467]

During the process of institutionalisation, one of the chief concerns of Hanserd Knollys and the Particular Baptists was to establish an educated, professional ministry. By providing ministers with a sound education and

---

[467] Knollys, *World That Now Is*, Book I, pp. 4-37.

financial security, the Particular Baptists not only sought to bring about the improvement of their clergy, but also to quell the criticisms of their opponents. In *The Gospel Minister's Maintenance Vindicated*, Hanserd Knollys and his colleagues clearly argued for this position. Knollys was one of the few educated, professional clergymen among the Particular Baptists, and during his years as a Baptist, he had become involved in multiple vocations, at times out of necessity. Therefore, many of his concerns arose out of his own experience. A paid, educated ministry meant that churches no longer needed to depend upon lay preachers who themselves relied upon a trade for financial security. The value, which the Particular Baptists placed upon this issue, gave evidence of their desire to maintain an orderly church. Beyond that, however, Knollys believed that churches had an ethical obligation to care for the material needs of their ministers. Above all, he desired that Particular Baptist ministers be godly ministers in contrast to the "false ministers" found in the churches that were "daughters of Babylon".

Probably the area that reflected the greatest tension with other English Protestants for the Particular Baptists was their interpretation of the Sacraments. Believer's baptism had distinguished them since their inception in the 1640s. Certainly their position was radical both in terms of means and method. The Particular Baptists had gradually come to accept adult believer's baptism as true baptism for two reasons primarily: it separated them from the false church, but more importantly, it was instrumental in establishing a true, believing church. Certainly, in terms of their ecclesiology (gathered believers' churches), believer's baptism coincided very well. The means of baptism (immersion), understood as a re-enactment of the death, burial, and resurrection of Christ, served as a visual testimony of the individual believer's faith experience.

The Particular Baptists never came to an explicit and unambiguous understanding of the Lord's Supper. While they clearly rejected the more sacramentarian view, most churches held to either a Zwinglian memorial or a Calvinist spiritual view of this ordinance, with some combining the two. Hanserd Knollys seemed to adopt such a compromise position himself, understanding the ordinances as having a special role of grace, though not to the extent of imparting salvation. Initially, the administration of the ordinances, remained in the hands of "disciples" with proper gifts and calling, ambiguous language that left the way open to lay as well as clerical administration. By 1688, however, the recommendation was that ministers should administer the ordinances, clear evidence of movement toward a more orderly position. Knollys reflected this ambiguity in his own position. Both Knollys and the Particular Baptists held that only believers could take part. Indeed, they had a duty to participate in baptism and the Lord's Supper as confirmations of their faith and election. While Knollys appeared to hold to "open" communion – that any believer could participate in the Lord's Supper – communion could and should be withheld, in his opinion, for disciplinary purposes, but always with the hope of the restoration of the believer to fellowship.

As the Particular Baptists moved toward becoming more formalised, they faced various questions regarding corporate worship. In their attempt to separate from the formalism and ritual found in the Established Church, and to form a pure church, three issues came to the forefront: seventh-day Sabbath worship, congregational singing, and the role of women. The questions over singing and seventh-day Sabbath observance came under strong debate in the late seventeenth century. While some Particular Baptist churches embraced the seventh-day Sabbath, the majority did not, clearly endorsing this position in their Confessions and in their General Assembly in 1689. Their arguments for Sunday as the Sabbath hinged upon the resurrection of Christ. Knollys also held this opinion, yet continued to maintain personal and professional relations with Seventh-day Baptists.

The subject of public singing in worship created significant dissension among the Particular Baptists as the century drew to a close. Knollys, a long-time proponent of congregational hymn-singing, found himself caught up in the debate. Though in his eighth decade, Knollys rose to the occasion, defending the practice with characteristic competence and grace. Knollys considered singing in worship an important spiritual exercise, referring to it as a "gift", an "ordinance", and a "command". The Particular Baptists would continue the debate after Knollys' death. Eventually the majority of their churches embraced the stance advocated by Knollys.

The position of the Particular Baptists on the role of women developed through the last half of the seventeenth century, becoming more stringent over time. Even in the changeable context of seventeenth-century England, the Particular Baptist point of view was quite conservative. Though they accepted women as members within their gathered congregations, allowing them some voice, encouraging them to use their gifts in private, and permitting them to assist the deacons in caring for needs in the congregation, their Confessions were quite silent regarding women's roles. Hanserd Knollys was also quiet regarding this issue. However, he certainly afforded women high regard, particularly women whom he perceived as having obvious spiritual gifts. Though preserving a conservative position on the role of women in worship, Knollys clearly recognised the important ministry women had within the church, particularly in teaching children and younger women. As well, he undoubtedly considered Anne, his wife, a partner in his life and ministry.

Perhaps in these three issues could be found the greatest measure of ambiguity and disagreement. For some Particular Baptists, these proved to be extremely divisive. Hanserd Knollys tended to remain somewhat ambiguous, taking a stance, yet maintaining a gracious attitude with those of different points of view, and even continuing fellowship with them.

Without question, as the seventeenth century drew to a close, the Particular Baptists of London had reached a new stage in their development.

Characterised by their opponents in the 1640s as a radical sect, by 1689 they had clearly begun moving toward institutionalisation. Though as Watts emphasised, the process would continue into the next century, as dissent became an ever-increasing force in English society, clearly, under the leadership of men such as Hanserd Knollys, the process of institutionalisation was well underway. Although the Particular Baptists would continue to be regarded as radical in several matters, such as the ordinances, church government, and singing in worship, the first generation leaders such as Hanserd Knollys made every effort to maintain order and orthodoxy within Scriptural limits.

EPILOGUE

The Twilight Years: "An Inheritance among them which are Sanctified"[1]

The years 1688 to 1691 marked a turning point in English history, according to B.R. White, "when Puritanism entered into a twilight period and began to take on the shape and colour which were to mark eighteenth-century Dissent".[2] Puritanism had emerged in the late sixteenth century in hopes of bringing about "the reformation of the structures of the Church... according to the apostolic model provided in the New Testament".[3] All attempts to do so throughout the seventeenth century, however, had not met with lasting success. In reaction to the Laudian formalism and oppression of the 1630s, the drive for reformation reached a new intensity in the 1640s, leading to unprecedented political, social, and religious changes. An inability to overcome diversity, however, had crippled the Puritans' efforts to effect that reformation in the 1640s and 1650s. The years between 1662 and 1688 saw the great reform impetus of those outside of the Established Church wither under the intensity of persecution so that in 1688, when toleration made it possible for dissenters to worship openly again, their hope for a godly reformation of the whole society had become a distant dream. As Puritanism gave way, in part, to dissent, the Particular Baptists found themselves on more or less equal footing with the Presbyterians and Congregationalists.

The year 1688 saw the death of the Independent and Baptist pastor, John Bunyan. Three years later, in 1691, George Fox, the founder of the Quakers, Richard Baxter, the Presbyterian pastor and scholar, and Hanserd Knollys all

---

[1] Hanserd Knollys, "Mr. Knollys's last Legacy to the Church, written a little before his Death", in *The Life and Death of That Old Disciple of Jesus Christ, and Eminent Minister of the Gospel, Mr. Hanserd Knollys*, edited by William Kiffin, (London: 1692), p. 50.
[2] B.R. White, "The Twilight of Puritanism in the Years Before and After 1688", in *From Persecution to Toleration: The Glorious Revolution and Religion in England*, ed. Ole Peter Grell, Jonathan I. Israel, and Nicholas Tyacke, (Oxford: Clarendon Press, 1991), pp. 307-308.
[3] White, "The Twilight of Puritanism", p. 308.

died.⁴ The passing of these significant leaders punctuated the end of the era. Hanserd Knollys had ministered inside and outside of the Church of England for about 60 years and had pastored his gathered church in London for nearly 50 of those years.⁵ Throughout that time, he had also served as a teacher and in other employments as well. The years between 1681 and 1687 left little record of Knollys in public or published documents. While his age may have had a part in this silence, the intensified persecution during the period probably played a larger role.

In 1688, as William of Orange prepared to become the King of England, Hanserd Knollys published his final major treatise, *An Exposition of the Whole Book of Revelation*.⁶ Knollys claimed to have written and published this work for two reasons. First, because of his insights into the book of Revelation, revealed in his four prior works on eschatology. Publishing the work was also a matter of good stewardship since he knew he would not live long.⁷ This work also represented the fruit of a series of sermons he had preached throughout his ministry. By publishing this work, those who had not heard him could profit.⁸ His sense of living in the last days made the task even more urgent and thus, he entreated the reader to "observe what is already past and fulfilled and what is now fulfilling in our days, and what is thereafter to be fulfilled".⁹ This last major work was also his most considerable work, both in terms of length (244 pages) and in terms of content. As an exegetical work, rather than a polemical or sermonic one, it displayed his skills as a Biblical scholar and exegete. *An Exposition of the Whole Book of Revelation* examined St. John's prophecy through a verse-by-verse exposition, taking into account the original Greek and relevant passages in the Hebrew Old Testament, as well as displaying a broad understanding of the whole of Scripture. Although Knollys did not interact with nor integrate classical or contemporary authors or Church Fathers, as he did in many of his other works, this was in order to make the his commentary more accessible to ordinary people.¹⁰ In spite of the fact that he was 79 years old, this treatise provided evidence of the continued sharpness of his mind.¹¹

---

⁴ White, "The Twilight of Puritanism", p. 310. Fox died on 13 January, while Knollys died on 19 September and Baxter on 8 December.

⁵ William Kiffin, "To the Reader", in Knollys, *Life*, pp. ii-iii.

⁶ Hanserd Knollys, *An Exposition of the Whole Book of the Revelation Wherein the Visions and Prophecies of Christ are Opened and Expounded*, (London: 1688).

⁷ Knollys, *An Exposition of the Whole Book of the Revelation*, "To the Reader", p. ii.

⁸ Knollys, *An Exposition of the Whole Book of the Revelation*, "To the Reader", p. ii.

⁹ Knollys, *An Exposition of the Whole Book of the Revelation*, "To the Reader", p. ii.

¹⁰ Knollys, *An Exposition of the Whole Book of the Revelation*, "To the Reader", p. iii. The sole exception to this is his exposition of chapter 11, which is merely the insertion of his *Exposition of the Eleventh Chapter of Revelation* verbatim.

¹¹ In his response to Knollys' work *An Answer to A Brief Discourse Concerning Singing in the publick Worship of God in the Gospel-church*, written in 1691, Isaac Marlow made the claim that Knollys was 'slipping' due to his age. This work certainly does not

Within a year of publishing *An Exposition of the Whole Book of Revelation*, Knollys' name headed the list of signatories of the preface of a work to addressing the subject of payment for Particular Baptist ministers.[12] On 22 July 1689, Knollys and his good friend and fellow pastor, William Kiffin, and four other Particular Baptist leaders, sent a letter to the Particular Baptist Churches throughout England and Wales, inviting them to an assembly in London to be held in September 1689. The churches were to reply to either Kiffin or Knollys.[13] Despite his age, Knollys apparently played an active role in this assembly.

Not long after the General Assembly of Particular Baptists took place in London, Knollys faced a situation involving his good friend, Benjamin Keach, who, according to Crosby, his son-in-law, had become seriously ill and expected to die. According to Crosby, through Knollys' prayers, Keach was healed.[14] The old patriarch could still pray with authority. Even as late as 1690, Knollys continued to play an active role among the Particular Baptists. On 4 March, Knollys was one of three Particular Baptist elders to officiate at the ordination of Joseph Stennett at the Seventh-day congregation meeting at Pinner's Hall.[15] And in October, he took part in the ordination of Richard Adams, who was to serve as co-pastor with William Kiffin at Devonshire Square church, the third time he had assisted in the ordination of a co-pastor for

---

support such a conclusion. Isaac Marlow, *Truth Soberly Defended In A Serious Reply to Mr. Benjamin Keach's Book intituled, The Breach Repaired in God's Worship; or Singing of Psalms, Hymns, and spiritual Songs, proved to be an Holy Ordinance of Jesus Christ*, (London: 1692), pp. 142-45.

[12] Hanserd Knollys, et. al., *The Gospel Minister's Maintenance Vindicated. Wherein A Regular Ministry in the Churches, is first Asserted, and the Objections against a Gospel Maintenance for Ministers, Answered*, (London: 1689). Although this work has been ascribed to Benjamin Keach, the document made no such claim. The letter, which makes up the preface, was actually written and signed in July 1681, even though the document itself was not published until 1689. Some have speculated that Knollys' name came first in the preface was due to the fact that he was the Particular Baptist elder statesman. B.R. White, *Hanserd Knollys and Radical Dissent in the 17th Century*, (London: Dr. Williams's Trust, 1977.), p. 22; Pope A. Duncan, *Hanserd Knollys: Seventeenth-Century Baptist*, (Nashville: Broadman Press, 1965), p. 29; Barry Howson, "The Question of Orthodoxy in the theology of Hanserd Knollys (c. 1599-1691): a Seventeenth Century English Calvinistic Baptist", (Unpublished Ph.D. Dissertation, McGill University, 1999), p. 91.

[13] Joseph Ivimey, *A History of the English Baptists*, vol. I, (London: 1811), pp. 478-80.

[14] Thomas Crosby, *The History of the English Baptists*, vol. IV, (London: 1740), pp. 307-308. See Chapter 4 above.

[15] *Pinner's Hall Churchbook*, cited in Bryan W. Ball, *The Seventh-day Men: Sabbatarians and Sabbatarianism in England and Wales, 1600-1800*, (Oxford: Clarendon Press, 1994), 120; Ivimey, *History*, II, p. 485.

that congregation.[16]

In 1691, Knollys became involved in the hymn-singing controversy that dominated and divided the Particular Baptists for most of the next decade.[17] On opposite sides in this debate were Knollys and his co-pastor, Robert Steed. Since Steed supposedly urged Marlow to write his treatise against singing in the first place, one might assume that their difference of opinion made for a difficult relationship.[18] Shortly before his death, Knollys wrote his "last Legacy to the Church".[19] This letter to the church he had founded and pastored for nearly 50 years also contained some evidence of a strain:

> I do humbly beseech my Reverend and Beloved Brother Steed for Christs sake, that the fervent Love to the Church, and the watchful Care over the particular Members of it, Expressed and Published in his little Epistle touching Singing, may be revived.[20]

If Steed had written and published a treatise on singing, it has not survived. However, the call for a pastor to express "fervent Love" and exercise "watchful Care" over his flock reflected Knollys' sense of mission and it was characteristic of him to attempt to use his colleague's own words as a means of correction and reconciliation. The final words of the letter appealed to the congregation

> to look out a Minister of Jesus Christ, whom he hath in some competent measure, qualified with such Ministerial Gifts and Graces as may make him worthy of so great honour, as is due a Pastor, and Elder of the Church of God.[21]

Knollys' 'dying wish' was that his church should appoint a second pastor to take his own place. Knollys may well have felt concern about the lack of graciousness evident in the leadership of Robert Steed – concern for the church that he had led for so long.[22] The church book of this congregation, which

---

[16] White, *Hanserd Knollys*, p. 23, citing from the *Devonshire Square Churchbook B*, October 1690. It was also in 1690 that Knollys along with eleven other pastors signed the preface of an edition of Tobias Crisp's sermons being published by his son Samuel Crisp, commending them to the reader. Knollys was the only Baptist minister to sign the preface. Crisp, like Knollys earlier in his life, had been accused of being an antinomian. White, *Hanserd Knollys*, pp. 7, 23-24.

[17] See Chapter 6.

[18] Michael Haykin, *Kiffin, Knollys, and Keach – Rediscovering our English Baptist heritage*, (Leeds: Reformation Today Trust, 1996), pp. 92-93.

[19] Knollys "Last Legacy" in *Life*, pp. 44-52.

[20] Knollys "Last Legacy" in *Life*, p. 45.

[21] Knollys "Last Legacy" in *Life*, pp. 49-50.

[22] H. Wheeler Robinson interpreted in this instruction that Knollys "commended Steed to the Church as his successor". However, nowhere in this statement is the language of

began to be kept from the time of Robert Steed's leadership, following Knollys' death, did not mention the appointment of a new co-pastor. Instead, it reads like an oppressive catalogue of church discipline. Knollys' fear of a lack of graciousness may not have been misplaced.[23]

Knollys' concern in his last letter was not only about leadership, but also about the spiritual condition and commitment of the members of the congregation. He commended them for their faithfulness "especially not only in this time of Liberty, but when it was a time of violent Persecution" and for their charity and selflessness with the goods that God had given them.[24] However, he found it very disturbing that some had "fallen in some degree from [their] first love, and cooled in [their] Spiritual Affections to Jesus Christ, and to the Saints".[25] For Knollys, this dampening of zeal and love had clear eschatological significance. In the last days, he believed some "Gospel-Professors" would fall away.[26] In order to remedy this serious situation, Knollys implored his wayward parishioners to repent in earnest prayer and fasting. "Alas, where are our Tears of Godly Sorrow, our broken Hearts, and our afflicted Souls? Reformation after Humiliation?"[27] He encouraged them to be zealous in their faith, not as 'legal professors' but as sincere followers of God.[28] Until the very end, Knollys retained his clarity of mind and his concern for his church.

Although this last letter of Knollys to his church does not contain a date, it probably was written very near to the end of his life. According to the opening paragraph, at the time of its writing, Knollys was no longer "able to Preach any more"[29] to his congregation, evidence that he may have remained at home due to illness. At some point in early August of 1691, Knollys was taken sick. According to William Kiffin, who wrote the final pages of Knollys' autobiography, "He was not very long sick, not keeping to his Chamber above five weeks, nor his Bed above ten days."[30] According to Kiffin, Knollys approached this final illness and his final days with as much grace and patience

---

commendation used. Rather, it is more of an instruction. H. Wheeler Robinson, "Baptist Church Discipline 1689-1699", *The Baptist Quarterly*, I (1922-23) : 112.

[23] Robinson, "Baptist Church Discipline", pp. 112-28. The Church book is at the Angus Library at Regent's Park College, Oxford.

[24] Knollys "Last Legacy" in *Life*, pp. 45-46.

[25] Knollys "Last Legacy" in *Life*, p. 47.

[26] Hanserd Knollys, *An Exposition of the Eleventh Chapter of the Revelation*, (London: 1679), p. 30; Hanserd Knollys, *The World That Now is; and the World that is to Come; Or the First and Second Coming of Jesus Christ. Wherein several Prophesies not yet fulfilled are Expounded*, (London: 1681), pp. 15-16.

[27] Knollys "Last Legacy" in *Life*, p. 48.

[28] Knollys "Last Legacy" in *Life*, pp. 49-50.

[29] Knollys "Last Legacy" in *Life*, p. 44.

[30] Hanserd Knollys, *The Life and Death of That Old Disciple of Jesus Christ, and Eminent Minister of the Gospel, Mr. Hanserd Knollys*, edited by William Kiffin, (London: 1692), hereafter cited as *Life*, p. 43.

as he had faced the other experiences of his life: "this holy Man's Life was all of a piece, and that he maintained his Zeal, Fidelity, and Integrity in the latter part of it, as well as in the former, even to the end of it."[31] On 19 September 1691, at about age 82, Hanserd Knollys died.[32]

The funeral service was held at his church congregation. While it might seem logical that Robert Steed should have preached the funeral sermon, Thomas Harrison indicated that someone of significant position or reputation in the Particular Baptist community did instead.[33] James Culross postulated that Benjamin Keach may have preached at his funeral since Keach published a funeral sermon that same year.[34] Two weeks later, on 4 October, Thomas Harrison of the Petty-France congregation, "voluntarily" preached a memorial sermon at the morning lecture at Pinner's Hall, a lecture that Knollys apparently had established. After a lengthy discourse on death and its role in bringing relief to God's prophets and ministers after their labours and troubles in persecutions, Harrison acknowledged the impact of Knollys as a minister, even in his final years:

> That Reverend Minister, whose *Decease* occasion'd this Discourse, had a *great deal of work to do for God in his declining Age,* which is evident from the many *Seals which God gave to his Ministry, even towards the close of it.* When he had, as it were, *one foot in the Grave,* he was *Instrumental to the Resurrection of many Dead Souls to a Spiritual Life.* God put an end to his *Ministerial Work* but a very little time before he *call'd him to receive his Crown,* which was a singular favour granted to this *Venerable Old Man.*[35]

As he reflected upon the life of Hanserd Knollys, that "Reverend Old Man",[36] Harrison first emphasised his "accurate and circumspect walking", making it clear that Knollys was not perfect, but that in his life he was "one who carefully endeavour'd" to avoid sin. Because of the life he led, even his enemies gave reverence to the doctrine he preached. Harrison characterised him as "a Preacher out of the Pulpit as well as in it", which would have no doubt pleased Knollys who so ardently wrote against those who had a "form of godliness" without the "power of godliness".[37] Secondly, Harrison highlighted Knollys' gracious, loving spirit.

---

[31] Knollys, *Life*, p. 43.
[32] Knollys, *Life*, "To the Reader", p. iv.
[33] Thomas Harrison, *A Sermon On the Decease of Mr. Hanserd Knollis, Minister of the Gospel. Preached at Pinners Hall, Octob. 4. 1691*, (London: 1694), p. 2.
[34] James Culross, *Hanserd Knollys*, (London: Alexander & Shepherd, 1895), p. 107. After searching however, this author was not able to locate the said sermon of Keach.
[35] Harrison, *A Sermon*, p. 39.
[36] Harrison, *A Sermon*, p. 56.
[37] Harrison, *A Sermon*, pp. 56-57.

He had a great respect to Christ's New Commandment which he gave to his Disciples, to love one another. He loved the Image of God wheresoever he saw it. He was not a man of a narro and private, but of a large and publick spirit. The difference of his fellow Christians Opinions from his did not alienate his affections from them. He lov'd all his fellow Travellers, tho they did not walk in the same particular path with himself. He embrac'd those in the Arms of his Love upon Earth with whom he thought he should joyn in singing the Song of the Lamb in Heaven.[38]

This attitude of love for fellow believers, evident even in debate, certainly characterised Knollys' life. Related to that attitude was the third characteristic emphasised by Harrison – his meekness and humility. Not "of proud and lofty Temper" Knollys, like the Christ whom he served, was "meek and lowly... willing to bear with and forbear others. To stoop and condescend to others, and to pass by those injuries which he received from them".[39] Endowed with a strong work ethic, "He was not a loyterer, but a labourer. He was willing to spend and to be spent in the service of his Lord and for the good of poor souls." He worked with every ounce of strength he had, even to his old age.[40] Finally, Knollys cheerfully suffered and courageously accepted the "Thorny Road of Tribulation" in his ministry for Christ. Not only a faithful servant, he provided a shining example for others to follow, as well.[41] Fittingly, this sermon closed with a hymn specifically composed for and sung in commemoration of the ministry of Hanserd Knollys.[42]

Following his death, Knollys was buried near his wife at the dissenters' burial ground, Bunhill Fields.[43] This area to the north of the part of the city where Knollys had ministered for most of his life, had become a favourite burial site of nonconformists by the mid-seventeenth century since their ministers could not officiate in parish church-yards.[44] Due to changes related to leases and insecure tenure, many of the burial sights of the early Baptists became lost in the future, that of Knollys being one of them.[45] For nearly fifty years, Hanserd Knollys had been associated with the Particular Baptists. Only he and William Kiffin had remained actively involved in the life of the group

---

[38] Harrison, *A Sermon*, pp. 57-58.

[39] Harrison, *A Sermon*, p. 58.

[40] Harrison, *A Sermon*, p. 59.

[41] Harrison, *A Sermon*, pp. 59-60.

[42] Harrison, *A Sermon*, pp. 69-70.

[43] "The Tombs in Bunhill Fields", *Transactions of the Baptist Historical Society*, II, (Oct. 1910) : 128.

[44] W.T. Whitley, "Bunhill Fields: The Place and the Records", *The Baptist Quarterly*, V, (Jan. 1931) : 220-22. As early as the time of Edward VI, the area was known as Bonehill Fields, so called because of the cartloads of bones deposited there when the charnel-house of St. Paul's was emptied.

[45] Whitley, "Bunhill Fields: The Place and the Records", p. 220-22; Culross, *Knollys*, p. 107.

from its inception in the 1640s through the persecutions of the Restoration until the dawn of Toleration in 1689. The continuity and stability, which he provided, played an instrumental role in leading the Particular Baptists from the status of a radical sect to that of a more settled and ordered institution. One of the last pieces of advice he wrote to his congregation was "The Aim and End of our Zeal must always be the Glory of God, and guided, as I said, by Discretion."[46] Certainly, this was a hallmark of Hanserd Knollys' life. Throughout his days, Hanserd Knollys remained a minister of God, who saw his commission and calling as coming not from men or institutions, but from Christ. The evidence of that commission and calling, in his mind, could be seen in the fruits of his labour, the lives of his flock. Appropriately, the last words to come from the pen of this pastor and teacher reflected continued stress upon the grace of God working through the Word to build up the faith and lives of believers:

> And now my dearly beloved Brethren and Sisters, I commit you all to the Word of his Grace, which is able to build you up, and to give you an Inheritance among them which are Sanctified. So I remain, while in this Tabernacle,
>
> Your Brother in the Lord, Hanserd Knollys.[47]

---

[46] Knollys "Last Legacy" in *Life*, p. 50.
[47] Knollys "Last Legacy" in *Life*, p. 52 (wrongly numbered 50).

CONCLUSION

In May 1689, as Hanserd Knollys neared the end of his life, the passing of the Bill of Rights and the Toleration Act by William III and Mary II and Parliament created a new political and religious landscape in England. Although the Toleration Act provided only a limited toleration for dissenters, it certainly created an atmosphere free from persecution.[1] Without a doubt, the situation in England in 1691 was very different from the situation in 1609. People in the seventeenth century had witnessed both subtle shifts and radical changes. They had seen traditional institutions such as the Established Church and the monarchy challenged and yet revived. Even though significant upheaval had occurred during the middle decades of the century, with the Restoration, something like the status quo was re-established. This paradoxical reality created within English society a tension as people sought to live within and come to grips with this ambiguity. Hanserd Knollys, who lived through much of the century, himself reflected many of the tensions and ambiguities of the age, embracing many positions seen by contemporaries as radical, and yet very deliberately striving for order in the midst of what often seemed like chaotic circumstances.

During the early years of his life, Knollys encountered a variety of people who would play significant roles in shaping his life. Throughout this period, he struggled between his desire to follow his conscience, even to the point of separation from the Church of England, and his desire to be acceptable within conventional societal norms. Knollys' father, a clergyman in the Church of England, influenced him in a variety of ways. Richard Knowles stressed the worth of a pious Christian commitment within a tradition that could be called Puritan. As well, he emphasised to his son the importance of education. Many of these values would have been reinforced during Hanserd Knollys' time as a student at Cambridge University. Knollys proceeded to ordination as a minister in the Church of England, coming under the influence of the John Williams, Bishop of Lincoln and rival of Archbishop Laud. During this time, Knollys began to have doubts about certain practices within the Church of England and about his own call to ministry. Simultaneous to this time of internal turmoil, he encountered separatist and nonconformist influences. One of these was a woman who had Brownist leanings and another was John Wheelwright, a silenced Puritan preacher who would eventually migrate to New England. In the midst of his uncertainty, Knollys resigned his living, for a time abandoned

---

[1] See Jonathan I. Israel, "William III and Toleration" in *From Persecution to Toleration: The Glorious Revolution and Religion in England*, Ole Peter Grell, Jonathan I. Israel, and Nicholas Tyacke, eds., (Oxford: Clarendon Press, 1991.

the ministry, and eventually took up itinerate preaching. Pressure from Laudian efforts to enforce conformity eventually compelled Knollys to flee with his family to New England in 1638. His experiences there had a further impact on him as he encountered not only a working congregational polity, but also persecution and intolerance from many, including the governor of the colony, John Winthrop.

Throughout these first three decades of his life, Knollys began to formulate his own beliefs, turning his back on the Established Church and embracing more nonconformist and separatist leanings. At the same time, he endured ridicule and persecution. Yet he strove to demonstrate that he was neither disorderly in his activities nor unorthodox in his beliefs. Although one might view this period as one of disenchantment and perhaps even failure for Knollys, it was formative and brought forward the ambiguities with which he would grapple his whole life, the struggle to combine his interpretation of apostolic Christianity with social respectability.

Returning to England on the eve of the breakdown of Charles I's government, Hanserd Knollys immediately encountered the restlessness which had come to characterise English society during the three years since he had left. Ironically, the turbulent 1640s would provide Knollys with a relatively settled life and career as a teacher and preacher. During that decade, his separation from the Church of England found a fruitful resolution in his acceptance of the congregational or Independent ecclesiastical tradition. His theology, already well formed by Puritan influences, would also shift ever so slightly, as he embraced the position of believer's baptism, but otherwise remained thoroughly Calvinistic. As the nation drifted into Civil War, Knollys threw his lot in with the Parliamentary cause. This may have reflected some of his more radical political tendencies, which would also raise suspicions of his involvement with the Leveller and Fifth Monarchist movements during the 1640s and 1650s. However, Knollys never took up arms in a political cause and the closest he came to serving in the Parliamentary armies was as a chaplain, which he soon abandoned because he felt the commanders were more dedicated to self-serving purposes than to godly causes.

In the 1640s, Knollys preached itinerantly, promoting both a conversionist and a Baptist message. In 1645, he gathered his own Particular Baptist congregation, which he would pastor for the remainder of his life. He also entered the visible area of publishing, promoting the cause of toleration for the Particular Baptists by emphasising their legitimacy and orthodoxy. Through an often cordial relationship with the Independents and their reformed Confessional statements, Knollys and his fellow Particular Baptists hoped to illustrate to their contemporaries that they held orthodox Puritan positions on most issues, rather than the radical ones claimed by their opponents. In his public debates and publications, however, Knollys never shrank from emphasising and elucidating those doctrines of the Particular Baptists that seemed radical to their opponents – especially believer's baptism and congregationalism. These distinctive doctrines, contended Knollys, were not heretical but Biblical.

As the 1640s drew to a close, Charles I was executed, and a minority of Parliamentarians established a republic, which would eventually give way to a Protectorate under Oliver Cromwell. During these years, Knollys prospered, pastoring his gathered church in London and the church in Scartho, Lincolnshire where members of his family had ministered for generations. As well, he planted and established new churches outside of London, tutored pupils, established his own school, worked in government posts, and became involved in foreign trade. Though he published little during this period, he still took an active role in the continued attempts to establish the legitimacy of the Particular Baptists.

Due to the relative religious freedom of the Civil War years and the Interregnum, newer, more radical religious sects and political groups arose, including the Levellers, Diggers, Quakers, and Fifth Monarchists, who attacked the religious, social, and political order in new aggressive ways and seemed to challenge the hierarchical nature of Stuart society. For Knollys and the Particular Baptists, the road to acceptance and legitimacy suddenly lay not only in allying themselves with the Independents and in showing the Presbyterians that they were orthodox, but also in distancing themselves from more radical groups. Even though they shared some of the goals of the radicals, Knollys and the Particular Baptists quickly to identified the differences and minimised the similarities. When their membership overlapped with radical movements, the Particular Baptists tended to downplay those relationships and, in some instances, to terminate them altogether. During the Republic and Protectorate, Knollys and the Particular Baptists carefully affirmed publicly their support for government officials as rulers ordained by God. Such activity was more than a pragmatic survival strategy for the leaders of the Particular Baptists; within their Confessions, it was plainly linked to a theological ideal, which held that God had established the world to exist within a hierarchical order that clearly involved secular rulers.[2]

After a decade and a half of relative freedom from persecution, the restoration of the Stuart monarchy and a conservative, reactionary Parliament meant that Hanserd Knollys suddenly found himself in prison again. For the next quarter century, the Particular Baptists would face sporadic persecution. During these years, Knollys felt forced to emigrate to the Continent for a time. After his return to England, he faced numerous difficulties, including

---

[2] This was the prevailing position of Knollys and the Particular Baptists. However, that is not to say that there were not those within their ranks who disagreed with it. In fact, it has been clearly shown that numerous Baptists joined the ranks of both the Levellers and the Fifth Monarchists. Murray Tolmie, *The Triumph of the Saints*, (London: Cambridge University Press, 1977); B.S. Capp, *The Fifth Monarchy Men*, (London: Faber and Faber, 1972).

persecution by the authorities and sickness and death of various members of his family, including Anne, his wife. These were extremely testing years for Knollys. In this period of his life, as he struggled to make sense of his circumstances and those of his society, Knollys began to express particular interest in the apocalyptic Scriptures. Sensing very strongly that he was living in the final days of earthly history, Knollys published several works, which focused on eschatology and sought to interpret the Scripture regarding the return of Jesus and the end times. Understanding his suffering and the persecution facing the Saints, as well as the apostasy he perceived in the Church, as signs of Christ's imminent return, he was certain that 1688 would mark the beginning of the events that would lead to the Millennium.

Throughout these eschatological writings, Knollys' interpretations never deviated sharply from accepted opinions of his day. The fears of Popery, which resurfaced in England toward the end of the reign of Charles II and grew during that of his successor, James II, made themselves very evident in these eschatological writings. His interpretation of the Papacy as the Antichrist and the Church of Rome as the Whore of Babylon was neither new nor uncommon. What was somewhat more radical was his claim that all national churches, such as the Church of England and the Presbyterian Church, were the harlot's daughters. Knollys' eschatological writings also gave evidence of his continued hope for a fuller reformation of the Church in England. Certainly his vision of the Millennium as an era when the Saints would rule with Christ in preparation for the end of history coincided with the thought of many Puritans of his day. So too did his understanding that the conquest of Christ and His Saints would be a spiritual one. At no point did he espouse an armed conquest, as did the Fifth Monarchists. Rather, he believed the victory would come through a mass conversion of people to God's truth, including the conversion of the Jews. Once again, this was not an especially radical position, except, perhaps, for the considerable emphasis he placed upon the importance of one not being found unprepared, and thus being revealed as a false professor. If anything, this stress on conversion and the true church as opposed to the false professors in the Established Church meshed nicely with his Baptist ecclesiology, and though radical in some measure, it was a far cry from the disorderly approach of the Fifth Monarchists.

In 1688, James II fled his realm and William and Mary were crowned the new rulers of England. Within the year, an Act of Toleration had created a less hostile environment for the Particular Baptists. Through all the years of persecution and times of peace, the Particular Baptists of London had grown from a small group of seven dissenting congregations, considered a radical sect by most members of English society, to a much larger and more widespread movement. Due to their Confessions and the publications of Baptist leaders, such as Knollys, the Particular Baptists not only began slowly to gain an identity and legitimacy in society at large, but also to build a self-identity. Gradually they became better organised, particularly during those periods when persecution waned. Knollys and most other Particular Baptists did not want to be perceived as extreme. By the 1680s, the Particular Baptists had moved from their identity as a separatist sect and had begun to move toward more of an institutional model. The move from sect toward formalisation took place gradually from the 1640s to the 1680s through the publication of Confessions, the planting of Particular Baptist congregations outside of London, the formation of associations of Particular Baptist congregations in different regions, and finally the calling of a General Assembly of Particular Baptist Churches in London in September 1689.

As the Particular Baptists advanced toward institutionalisation, they addressed a variety of issues related to polity, doctrine, ministry, sacraments, and worship. Through his writings and leadership Hanserd Knollys usually stood at the heart of the discussions and debates surrounding these issues. For Knollys, it was of utmost importance that the Particular Baptists develop in an orderly fashion so that even when they embraced a position that might seem radical or unorthodox, such as believer's baptism, they did so on Apostolic principles and in an orderly manner. Certainly, their stance on church government embraced the newer, more radical views of congregational independence and evangelism. At the same time they maintained the orthodox Reformed doctrine of election and the orderly goals of unity within the local church and interdependence among separate congregations. They championed the principle of lay involvement in ministry, which sprang from their understanding of the priesthood of all believers and of ministry as a calling from God. In its application, this was quite a radical position in the seventeenth century. However, their growing insistence on an educated, professional ministry and their understanding of the limited role of women in church life clearly emphasised more conventional attitudes. In their stance on the sacraments and worship, Knollys and the Particular Baptists reflected some of the ambiguities of their Puritan roots. For example, some interpreted the Lord's Supper in the Zwinglian representative way, others embraced a more spiritual Calvinistic interpretation, and some, like Knollys, tried to combine these interpretations. While all Particular Baptists favoured non-liturgical forms of worship, they disagreed on such issues as corporate singing and seventh day Sabbath worship. All agreed that their churches consisted only of consenting baptised believers. Despite some tensions and ambiguities, the Particular Baptists had moved toward a fairly clear formation of their own identity by the end of Hanserd Knollys' life.

Without dispute, Hanserd Knollys played a significant role in the rise and development of the Particular Baptists in London. However, his importance far exceeded that distinction. An Englishman of middling social status during a very turbulent century in early modern England, he reflected the realities of the age in his own life – the uncertainty, the change, the tension, the ambiguity, and the paradox. In many ways, Knollys was a radical, questioning religious and social convention in his pursuit of truth. In other ways, he was very conventional, desiring order and orthodoxy, a product of a past era, and yet a prophet of a new one. While he sought change and toleration, both were limited and when he disagreed and debated, a gracious spirit tempered his treatment of opponents. Perhaps Knollys was not a radical anomaly, but rather, a more typical representative of a moderate, early modern worldview, which sought to navigate the tensions and ambiguities of a shifting and changing society.

APPENDIX 1

Hanserd Knollys' Date of Birth

In 1692, William Kiffin, a close friend and associate of Hanserd Knollys throughout most of his adult life, wrote the finishing touches on a biography of his friend who had recently died. Knollys had begun this autobiography as a sort of memoir of his life, probably in 1672, shortly after the death of his wife and son and his own near passing.[1] For some reason, he either did not complete the memoir or else the remainder was lost. On the title page and in the preface of the biography, Kiffin wrote that Knollys died "in the ninety third year of his age".[2] From that point onward, historians have concluded that Knollys' year of birth was 1598/99. In reality, no conclusive evidence exists suggesting this date as valid.[3]

Actually, Hanserd Knollys was most probably born in 1609, ten years later than the traditionally held date. This conclusion has been reached based on the testimony of parish records stating the date of Knollys' baptism, the date of Richard Knowles' installation at Cawkwell, and the date of his marriage to Rachell Pagett, as well as the will of Knollys' grandmother, Christobel Lacon, the entry in *Alumni Cantabrigienses*[4] and other records of Knollys'

---

[1] Although this is merely postulation on the part of the author, it seems to hold for a few reasons. First, it abruptly ends in 1672. Knollys went on to live until 1691. Though William Kiffin claimed in the preface that the remainder was lost, it is just as likely or possibly even more likely that it was never written. Second, it is not written as a journal or a diary, which is kept regularly to chronicle something or someone. Rather, it is much more like a memoir, like a work looking back trying to briefly and succinctly recount past events, etc. Third, the fact that Knollys had just gone through a rather traumatic experience when even his own mortality became quite evident, and because he was an elderly man, particularly in that context, it would not be unusual for one to begin to contemplate his legacy and to take a time to summarize that legacy to date.

[2] Hanserd Knollys, *The Life and Death of That Old Disciple of Jesus Christ, and Eminent Minister of the Gospel, Mr. Hanserd Knollys*, edited by William Kiffin, (London: 1692), "Epistle to the Reader", p. ii.

[3] Without exception, every secondary source unhesitatingly claims his date of birth to be 1598/99.

[4] John Venn and J.A. Venn, *Alumni Cantabrigienses*, Part I to 1751, vol. III Kaile to Ryves, (Cambridge: University Press, 1924), p. 31.

Appendix 1: Hanserd Knollys' Date of Birth 325

matriculation to Cambridge, and a rather obscure reference in the opening pages of a work Knollys published in 1674, *The Parable of the Kingdom of Heaven Expounded*.

In her will, which was written on December 12, 1611 and proved on January 12, 1612, Christobel Lacon gave detailed statements regarding the members of her family, including what she left to each individual grandchild.[5] This will provides one of the earliest mentions of Hanserd Knollys, who, along with many of her other grandchildren, was to receive 2s. 6d.:

> To Edward Skipwith, sonne of the said Edward, one Frenche crowne. To Mary Skipwith, his sister, my best gowne, my best kirtle, and the bodies belonging unto it. To Elizabeth, her sister, my best petticoate. To Gibert, Rikhard, Elizabeth and Marie Hansard, my grandchildren, ijs. vjd. apiece. To William Pagett, Hanserd Knowles and Zacharie Knowles, my grandchildren, ijs. vjd. apiece. To William Hanserd, my grandchild, xls.[6]

One of Christobel Lacon's daughters was married to Edward Skipwith. The Skipwith grandchildren are mentioned first.[7] Not included in the list of grandchildren receiving money, with the exception of Edward, they received clothing.[8] Christobel Lacon's only son and principle heir, William, had five children. Four were named first, Gibert, Rikhard, Elizabeth, and Marie and each of these was to receive a monetary inheritance (2s. 6d.). Christobel named William's fifth child, his son William, last of all the grandchildren and he received the largest inheritance of the grandchildren (15s.). This may have been due to the fact that he was the eldest son of the heir.

Christobel's other daughter and son-in-law were also mentioned as "dawghter Knowles" and "sonne Knowles", that is Richard and Rachell Knowles.[9] She was probably the eldest daughter, for she and her husband inherited part of the landed estate.[10] Their children comprised the third group of grandchildren, Hanserd and Zacharie Knowles. But what of William Pagett? Who were his parents? No other Pagett was named in the will. Clearly, he was a grandson, for Christobel included him with the other grandchildren. Later, the will made additional mention of him:

---

[5] See Appendix 2.
[6] A.R. Maddison, *Lincolnshire Wills 1500-1617*, vol. 2 (Lincoln: James Williamson, 1891), p. 59. See also A.R. Maddison, *Lincolnshire Pedigrees*, vol. 2 in *Publications of the Harleian Society*, vol. 51 (London: 1903), pp. 451-52. In her identification of the grandchildren, Lacon listed them according to family groups.
[7] Maddison, *Lincolnshire Wills 1500-1617*, vol. 2, p. 58.
[8] Perhaps these grandchildren were older, thus these items would be of use to them.
[9] Maddison, *Lincolnshire Wills 1500-1617*, vol. 2, p. 59.
[10] Maddison, *Lincolnshire Wills 1500-1617*, vol. 2, p. 59. William Hanserd received the manor at Gayton-Le-Wold and Richard and Rachell Knowles received the manor at Gayton-Le-Marsh.

> Whereas I bought certaine thinges of my grandchilde William Pagett which are yet unpaid for viz. iiij silver spoons, one plate cupboard, one chest, one blankett, one coverlet, one paire of bellowes, and one fyre shovell, my will and desire is that he have them all againe in full satisfaction and payment for them.[11]

These were expensive items, typically used by adults, purchased for him by Christobel Lacon but not yet paid for.

Muriel James suggested that Christobel in her marriage to Richard Hanserd Jr. had three daughters. One daughter married Richard Knowles, another Edward Skipwith, and the last married Richard Pagett.[12] However, if this was the case, why then did the will make no mention of this last daughter or her husband (Pagett)?[13] The answer appears in a Cawkwell parish record claiming that on 26 January 1609, Richard Knowles married Rachell Pagett, a widow.[14] Richard Knowles had been installed as minister at Cawkwell parish about four months earlier on 5 August 1608.[15] Rachell very likely brought to the marriage a son from a previous marriage – William.[16] Soon after their marriage, Rachell and Richard conceived Hanserd who would have been born in late 1609, and soon after that, Zacharie.[17] This would account for why William Pagett, Hanserd Knowles and Zacharie Knowles are listed in the will together. All three were the sons of Christobel Lacon's daughter Rachell (Pagett) Knowles.

This may appear to be rather weak evidence, based for the most part on conjecture. However, three further pieces of evidence give strong support for the birth of Hanserd Knollys in 1609. First, a baptismal record, from Cawkwell parish states that Hanserd Knowles was baptised on 13 November 1609.[18] This tells strongly against the traditional date of Knollys' birth. According to the traditionally accepted birth date of Knollys, Hanserd would by this time be

---

[11] Maddison, *Lincolnshire Wills 1500-1617*, vol. 2, p. 59.

[12] Muriel James, *Religious Liberty on Trial: Hanserd Knollys – Early Baptist Hero*, (Franklin, TN: Providence House Publishers, 1997), pp. 37-38. Her reasoning here is confusing and contradictory.

[13] Interestingly enough, there is mention of a "daughter Patchett" but no daughter Knowles in the will of Harbert Lacon, Christobel's second husband, which was written in March 1602 and probated in March 1607. Maddison, *Lincolnshire Wills 1500-1617*, vol. 2, p. 25.

[14] Lincolnshire Archives, document Calkwell BT, 1608/9.

[15] Lincolnshire Archives, document PD 1608/3.

[16] How long she had been married the first time or how old William was is not known.

[17] It must be remembered that Richard Knowles was not a young man at this point. According to *Alumni Cantabrigienses*, Richard matriculated at Cambridge in 1581. Assuming that he was of the usual age for University, sixteen to eighteen, he would have been at least forty-four when he married Rachell Pagett. Assuming she was ten years his junior, it is possible that her first marriage could have taken place ten to fifteen years prior, making William Pagett a young man when his grandmother Lacon died.

[18] Lincolnshire Archives, document Calkwell BT, 1609/10.

about eleven. The usual practice in the Church of England in the early seventeenth century was for a child to be baptised soon after birth. The attempt by James to explain this away as a deliberate delay by Hanserd's parents is highly speculative, especially her claim that "at the time of his birth (she assumed the early date of 1598), baptism issues were extremely controversial. In Lincolnshire a growing number were agreeing that baptism should be delayed until the person was old enough to understand its meaning".[19] She went on to hypothesise that Hanserd's father, Richard, was of that mindset, being "a well-educated vicar of two churches and a bit of a nonconformist".[20] This seems to be making a huge intellectual jump. Although he might have had Puritan leanings, there is no evidence that Richard Knowles had nonconformist leanings.

The second piece of evidence, the date of Knollys' matriculation at Cambridge University, also confirms the later date of birth. According to *Alumni Cantabrigienses*, Knollys matriculated at St. Catherine's Hall at Easter, 1629.[21] Muriel James stated that another record at Cambridge placed Knollys matriculation at Michaelmas of 1627.[22] The age of eighteen or even twenty for matriculation makes much more sense than one of twenty-eight or thirty. As well, in Knollys' autobiography the progression from Great Grimsby Grammar School to Cambridge University seems immediate. Given the importance that Richard Knowles placed upon education, one would expect his son to have matriculated immediately following his initial education. If Knollys were born

---

[19] James, *Knollys*, p. 27. James gave no documentary support for these statements. In reality, infant baptism was not so great an issue of debate at this time. In fact, those known as 'Anabaptists' by the English authorities were mostly foreigners who had come from the continent, primarily Holland. J.W. Martin, *Religious Radicals in Tudor England*, (London: The Hambledon Press, 1989), pp. 20-21. Although there was a small presence of Anabaptists in England throughout the sixteenth century, they undoubtedly comprised a small, radical minority, not likely to have an Anglican vicar in their following. See Michael Watts, *The Dissenters*, vol. 1, (Oxford: At the Clarendon Press, 1978), pp. 7-14. As far as Baptist influence in the region, the first Baptists arrived in England in 1612, following Thomas Helwys from Amsterdam. Otherwise, there were no Baptist churches established until the mid-1620s. While the earliest founders of what would become the General Baptist denomination, John Smythe and Thomas Helwys, both hailed from that region, they were not actively Baptists in 1598. This direction in their thinking emerged while exiled in Holland. B.R. White, *The English Baptists of the Seventeenth Century*, rev. ed. (London: The Baptist Historical Society, 1996), pp. 22-23.
[20] James, *Knollys*, p. 27.
[21] Venn and Venn, *Alumni Cantabrigienses*, p. 31.
[22] James, *Knollys*, p. 55. Unfortunately, James again did not cite her source for this information. However, in light of the fact that university matriculation typically occurred between the ages of sixteen or eighteen, it is likely that Venn & Venn's reference to 1629 was perhaps an error and 1627 was the correct year of matriculation, particularly since Venn & Venn went on to state that in June of 1629, Knollys was ordained a deacon and priest.

in 1609, then in 1627 he would have been eighteen years of age, quite typical for entry into University at that time.[23]

There is one last minor piece of evidence, which is rather intriguing and comes perhaps from the hand of Knollys himself. The frontispiece of Knollys' work *The Parable of the Kingdom of Heaven Expounded* contains a portrait of Hanserd Knollys. No other published work of his has such a frontispiece. The description beneath the portrait states that he is 67 years old. This particular work was published in 1674. If the publication took place between January and March, then it would have in actuality been published in 1675.[24] By making the calculation, if Hanserd Knollys was born in 1609, by early 1675, he was in his 67th year. Perhaps Knollys or the publisher chose to include with the publication of his work a recently completed portrait. In any case, it lends support to the hypothesis that Knollys was born in 1609.

Thus, in summary, it would appear that Richard Knowles, cleric and vicar at Cawkwell, Lincolnshire, married Rachell Pagett (Hanserd), a widow, in January 1609. Later that year, sometime between September and November, they had a son whom they named Hanserd after Rachell's maiden name, something not uncommon in that period. Hanserd Knollys was then baptised in November 1609 in Cawkwell parish. In 1627, at age eighteen, Hanserd Knollys matriculated at St. Catherine's Hall, Cambridge University. Therefore, the earlier date for Hanserd Knollys' birth of 1598/99, based purely upon a written comment of a friend and associate after Knollys' death, and many years after his birth, appears to have been mistaken by approximately ten years. Hanserd Knollys was born in 1609.

---

[23] Helen M. Jewell, *Education in Early Modern England*, (New York: St. Martin's Press, 1998), pp. 109-19. See also Barry Coward, *The Stuart Age*, 2nd ed., (New York: Longman, 1994), pp. 68-9.

[24] At this point, England continued to follow the Julian calendar and the new year began on 25 March.

APPENDIX 2

The Will of Christobel Lacon, Grandmother of Hanserd Knollys[1]

The 12th Dec. 1611. I Christobell Lacon of Biskerthorp within the Countie of Lincolne, wydowe, late wife of Herbert Lacon late of Humberston in the Countie of aforesaid, gent., deceased, sick in bodie but whole in mynde etc. First and principallie I commend

To Edward Skipwith, sonne of the said Edward, one Frenche crowne. To Mary Skipwith, his sister, my best gowne, my best kirtle, and the bodies belonging unto it. To Elizabeth, her sister, my best petticoate. To Gibert, Rikhard, Elizabeth and Marie Hansard, my grandchildren, ijs. vjd. apiece. To William Pagett, Hanserd Knowles and Zacharie Knowles, my grandchildren, ijs. vjd. apiece. To William Hanserd, my grandchild, xls.

To my dawghter Knowles my cloth gowne, my burrato kirtle, my pillyon seate, and pillion clothe, my truncke, and some of my lynnen which I used to weare. My will is that my sonne Knowles shall have all my arable land and leas belonging to my farme at Gayton this yeare, to sowe or otherwyse to dispose of as he shall thinke best.

Whereas I bought certaine thinges of my grandchilde William Pagett which are yet unpaid for viz. iiij silver spoons, one plate cupboard, one chest, one blankett, one coverlet, one paire of bellowes, and one fyre shovell, my will and desire is that he have them all againe in full satisfaction and payment for them.

---

[1] A.R. Maddison, *Lincolnshire Wills 1500-1617*, vol. 2 (Lincoln: James Williamson, 1891), pp. 58-9. See also A.R. Maddison, *Lincolnshire Pedigrees*, vol. 2 in *Publications of the Harleian Society*, vol. 51 (London: 1903), pp. 451-52.

APPENDIX 3

Hanserd Knollys' Continuing Ministry in Lincolnshire

Muriel James in her work on Hanserd Knollys stated several times that Hanserd Knollys had been installed as the rector in 1648 at St. Giles Church in Scartho, Lincolnshire.[1] Her claim drew harsh rebuke from Stephen Copson in his review of her work:

> It is asserted as a matter of fact, and without supporting reference, that Hanserd took the living of Scartho, Lincolnshire, in 1648. If this were true, historians would look in a very different light at the man who had to all intents renounced his orders and steadfastly held to his Baptist convictions, setting himself beyond the pale of the established church that had been home to so many of his forefathers, and indeed his son.[2]

Having already encountered a few references that implied what James was openly proclaiming, this writer was intrigued enough to search further on this point. Though it was annoying, as Copson pointed out, that James did not provide any references, there are several other sources, which support her claim.

From March to October of 1648, the Second Civil War took place. Charles I, in an attempt to regain the control of his realm, allied himself with the Scots. The Army and Parliament had already experienced distraction from the Levellers and their conflicting efforts to reach a settlement with the King. In the midst of this turmoil, the Westminster Assembly of Divines, established by Parliament in 1643, had yet to settle on an acceptable solution to the question of the form English religion should take. The majority party, the Presbyterians, desired to make England a Presbyterian nation, but a vocal minority fought for a congregational alternative.[3] After several years of Civil War and political jockeying in Parliament, the political scenario remained uncertain. Religious

---

[1] Muriel James, *Religious Liberty on Trial: Hanserd Knollys – Early Baptist Hero*, (Franklin, TN: Providence House Publishers, 1997), pp. 63-64, 135-36.
[2] Stephen Copson, "Reviews: Muriel James", *The Baptist Quarterly*, XXXVII, 5, (Jan. 1998) : 259.
[3] See Chapter 3 above.

Appendix 3: Hanserd Knollys' Continuing Ministry in Lincolnshire

indecision in the Westminster Assembly and radical religious expressions had created an atmosphere of opportunity for Particular Baptist Ministers like Hanserd Knollys.[4]

According to the Bishop's Certificates of Institutions, on 12 October 1648, Hanserd Knollys was installed in St. Giles Church in Scartho.[5] Knollys, even during his sojourn in New England, never lost touch with his home region of Lincolnshire. A request from his father Richard had caused him to return to England in 1641.[6] In 1648, Knollys' father, who had ministered in the church in Scartho since December 1613, either through death or incapacity had left the pulpit vacant.[7] The vicarage of Scartho had been under the patronage of Hanserd's great-grandfather, Richard Hanserd during the reign of Elizabeth I.[8] Prior to the tenure of Richard Knowles in Scartho, the charge had been held by his wife's uncle, Sir Hammond Hanserd.[9] Thus, there existed a clear family connection with St. Giles Church in Scartho. Therefore, with the vacancy of 1648, the patron naturally asked the son of the previous incumbent to fill the

---

[4] During the unconventional years of the 1640s, A Committee for Preaching Ministers was appointed in December 1640 and eventually it was made "lawful for the parishioners of any parish to set up a lecture and maintain an orthodox minister at their own expense, to preach every Sunday when there was no other preaching". This privilege began to be stretched during the Civil War years. If an incumbent was a Royalist, preached against Parliament, or refused the Solemn League and Covenant, his living would be sequestered. "Under the Lecture system, parishioners were free to arrange for themselves" but still needed Parliament's approval. "The Use of Parish Churches, 1641-1662", *Transactions of the Baptist Historical Society*, III, 2, (Oct. 1912) : 121-22.

[5] Public Record Office, KEW, IND: 1, 17002, E331, Vol. 3, p. 95.

[6] Hanserd Knollys, *The Life and Death of That Old Disciple of Jesus Christ, and Eminent Minister of the Gospel, Mr. Hanserd Knollys*, edited by William Kiffin, (London: 1692), pp. 18-19.

[7] Richard Knollys' installation is recorded in Lambeth Palace Library, Abbot Register, part 1, f. 310. There is no record of his death in this case, perhaps due to the haphazard record keeping of the Civil war period.

[8] Liber Cleri, A.D. 1576 in C.W. Foster, ed., *Lincoln Episcopal Records in the Time of Thomas Cooper, A.D. 1571 to A.D. 1584*, in *The Publications of the Lincoln Record Society*, vol. 2, (Lincoln: W. K. Morton & Sons Ltd., 1912), pp. 177-78.

[9] Hammond Hanserd was installed in September 1580 and served until his death in March 1595. Ibid., p. 27; A.R. Maddison, ed., *Lincolnshire Pedigrees*, vol. 2 in *Publications of the Harleian Society*, vol. 51, (London: 1903), p. 452; C.W. Foster, ed., *The State of the Church in the Reigns of Elizabeth I and James I*, vol. 1, in *The Publications of the Lincoln Record Society*, vol. 23, (Horncastle: W. K. Morton & Sons Ltd., 1926), p. 89. The vicar before Hammond Hanserd, also presented by Richard Hanserd was Francis Tompson, installed in 1576. Between Tompson and Richard Knowles, Maurice Gulson served. Muriel James suggested that these two men were perhaps husbands of women in the Hanserd family. James, *Knollys*, pp. 62-64; Foster, *Lincoln Episcopal Records in the time of Thomas Cooper*, pp. 177-78.

pulpit. Indeed, the patronage may well have been given to Hanserd Knollys as well, who was mentioned as having this position in a petition from the parish in 1656.[10]

There were some Particular Baptists who would have been uncomfortable with their ministers accepting state pay.[11] Knollys, however, showed fewer scruples in accepting religious positions with established incomes. In the aftermath of the second Civil War, Hanserd Knollys once again became an army chaplain, this time for the New Model Army.[12] As well, in 1649/50, the act "for the better propagation and preaching of the Gospel in Wales" resulted in the appointment of preachers, paid by the state, to serve as evangelists, and Knollys accepted one of these positions.[13] In 1654, in an attempt to purify and reform the church in England, Cromwell introduced an Ordinance for ejecting Scandalous, Ignorant, and Insufficient Ministers and Schoolmasters.

> Whereas by the continuance of divers scandalous and insufficient Ministers and Schoolmasters in many Churches, Chappels and Publique Schools within this Nation, the more effectual Propagation of the Gospel, and settlement of a godly and painful Ministery is much obstructed, and no Authority now in force for removing such Ministers and Schoolmasters.[14]

In August, the state appointed Commissioners in the various counties throughout England to enforce this Ordinance. Their task involved examining clergymen and schoolmasters to determine if they had adequate qualifications. Parliament appointed Hanserd Knollys as one of the Commissioners for the county of Lincoln, likely due to the fact that he was the incumbent of a church in that county.[15] This Ordinance followed one passed in March, which had resulted in Knollys' close friend Henry Jessey being appointed a Trier, a

---

[10] In *Calendar of State Papers Domestic*, 1655-1656, p. 319, Knollys was referred to as the "patron" of the Church in Scartho. More on this entry below.

[11] "May a Minister take State Pay?" *Transactions of the Baptist Historical Society*, I, (Apr. 1909) : 65-68. In the mid-1650s, the Midlands Association of Particular Baptist Churches debated the issue of ministers taking pay. They differed in opinion. However, those who favoured it determined that it was acceptable only if the "maintenance be freely given, except tythes". Cited in B.R. White, "The English Particular Baptists and the Great Rebellion", *Baptist History and Heritage*, 9, 1, (Jan. 1974) : 23.

[12] Anne Laurence, *Parliamentary Army Chaplains, 1642-1651*, (Suffolk: Boydell Press, 1990), pp. 58, 143.

[13] White cited Bodleian, Walker MS e.13, pp. 116, 121 as his source for information concerning Knollys' activities in Wales. After searching, however, this author has not been able to locate this reference. White, *Hanserd Knollys*, p. 15.

[14] C.H. Firth and R.S. Rait, eds., *Acts and Ordinances of the Interregnum, 1642-1660*, vol. II, (London: His Majesty's Stationary Office, 1911), p. 968.

[15] Firth and Rait, eds., *Acts and Ordinances of the Interregnum, 1642-1660*, vol. II, pp. 968, 981.

Appendix 3: Hanserd Knollys' Continuing Ministry in Lincolnshire

position with a similar purpose to that of the Commissioners of the later Ordinance.[16]

Whatever the explanation for Knollys' service at St. Giles Church at Scartho, he probably served there for some time. Though he never wrote of it explicitly in his autobiography, he did provide evidence of an ongoing connection with Lincolnshire:

> In the space of 40 years that I and my dear faithful Wife Lived together; we removed several times with our whole Family, whereof once from Lincolnshire to London [1635], and from London to New-England [1637]: Once from England into Wales; *twice from London into Lincolnshire*, once from London to Holland, and from thence into Germany, and thence into Rotterdam, and thence to London again [1661-64?].[17]

This list of moves follows a roughly chronological sequence. Therefore, the moves to Wales and Lincolnshire probably took place during the 1640s or 1650s.[18]

On 12 May 1656, "Hanserd Knollys (patron of the church)" submitted a petition "for the inhabitants of Scartho, co. Lincoln" to Cromwell and his Council. The petitioners desired assistance in repairing their building: "Our parish church is much decayed, and the spire ready to fall. We beg your order to Thos. Clayton and 5 other inhabitants to take down the spire, and in 3 years time to repair the south aisle and other parts of the church."[19] It is clear from this reference that Knollys held the post as patron for this church, as well as serving in a clerical role. Thus, when Knollys fled to Holland with his family in 1662, he probably appointed his eldest son, Cheney, as the minister of Scartho in his stead. The son must have conformed during the 1660s, because he held

---

[16] Knollys did protest against tithes in 1652 during Cromwell's rule. "Jottings by John Lewis of Margate, 1742", in *Transactions of the Baptist Historical Society*, IV, (Oct. 1915) : 206. However, so did his friend Henry Jessey, but this did not stop him from accepting state pay as a Tryer. B.R. White, "Henry Jessey: A Pastor in Politics", The *Baptist Quarterly*, XXV, (Jan. 1973) : 105-6. White postulated that Cromwell had promised to Jessey that he would abolish tithes by September, which helped to convince Jessey to participate. Perhaps Jessey persuaded his good friend Hanserd Knollys to serve as a Commissioner in August with this same information.

[17] Knollys, *Life*, p. 28, emphasis mine. This contradicts James Culross, who readily admitted that Knollys "was appointed Rector of Scartho" in 1648, but claimed with assurance that "it is certain that he did not reside in the parish". *Hanserd Knollys*, p. 66.

[18] According to B.R. White, Knollys "worked in Radnor and Breconshire" Wales sometime during 1650-2. Bodleian, Walker MS e.13, pp. 116, 121 cited in White (this author could not locate the above MS), *Hanserd Knollys*, p. 15.

[19] *Calendar of State Papers Domestic*, 1655-1656, p. 319.

the call until his death in 1670.[20] On 3 March 1670, when the new vicar was installed, Hanserd Knollys name was transcribed as the patron.[21] The property rights as advowson outweighed his status as a non-conforming clergyman!

Although this research may cause some Baptist historians to "look in a very different light"[22] at Hanserd Knollys, it sheds additional illumination upon the nature and degree of his separation from the Established Church. He certainly took issue with some of the practices of the Church of England in the 1630s and 1640s, whether Episcopalian or Presbyterian, he viewed National Churches as antichristian,[23] and he vocally opposed tithes.[24] However, at the same time he maintained a close relationship with Independents such as Henry Jessey and members the Jacob Church.[25] Perhaps St. Giles embraced an Independent polity during the 1640s and 1650s. Perhaps Hanserd Knollys was closer to Bunyan in terms of the mixed church ideal than previously supposed. Or perhaps his scruples did not extend to include receiving state pay, at least during the fluid years of the Interregnum. This underlines the ambiguities of his position during this time of great change. Although the details remain somewhat unclear, it would appear that Muriel James was correct in her assertions that Hanserd Knollys was installed as the rector in 1648 at St. Giles Church in Scartho, Lincolnshire.

---

[20] James, *Knollys*, pp. 53, 63-64, 106, 136. See also Will of Cheney Knowles probated January 1670, Lincolnshire Archives, document LCC Wills 1670/ii/728r

[21] Bishop's Certificates of Institutions, Public Record Office, KEW, IND: 1, 17005, E331, Vol. 6, p. 182.

[22] Copson, "Reviews: Muriel James", p. 259.

[23] See Chapter 6 above.

[24] "Jottings by John Lewis of Margate, 1742", in *Transactions of the Baptist Historical Society*, IV, (Oct. 1915) : 206.

[25] See Chapters 3 and 4 above.

APPENDIX 4

Children of Hanserd and Anne (Cheney) Knollys

Although this book has focused on Hanserd Knollys and his work, mention of his children occurred periodically in the primary sources. Muriel James devoted significant attention to these children, especially in her genealogical research on a John Knowles of Hampton, New Hampshire, whom she postulated was a son of Hanserd Knollys.[1] In his autobiography, Knollys recorded his marriage to Anne Cheney and mentioned that they had seven sons and three daughters.[2] However, further references to his children in his autobiography were vague and sporadic. He mentioned the death of one child on his family's passage to New England and, upon their return from New England, noted that they had a child about three years old and that his wife was "great with another child".[3] These references pertain to the period from 1637 to 1641. Around 1661, he wrote of his flight to the Continent with his wife, son, and daughter.[4] On the same page, Knollys detailed how he provided for his children:

> To my Eldest Son, I had given 60 l. per Annum during his Life, which he enjoyed above 21 Years ere he Died. To my next Son, that lived to be Married, I gave the full value of 250 l. in Money, House, School, and Household Goods, and left him 50 Scholars in his School-House. To my only Daughter then Living, I gave upon her Marriage above 300 l. in Money, Annuity, Plate, Linnen, and Houshold-stuff, and left her Husband 50 Scholars in the said School-House, in Partnership with my said Son. To my youngest Son, that lived to be Married, I gave more than 300 l.

---

[1] Muriel James, *Religious Liberty on Trial: Hanserd Knollys – Early Baptist Hero*, (Franklin, TN: Providence House Publishers, 1997), pp. xi-xiii, 104-109.

[2] Hanserd Knollys, *The Life and Death of That Old Disciple of Jesus Christ, and Eminent Minister of the Gospel, Mr. Hanserd Knollys*, edited by William Kiffin, (London: 1692), p. 3. This was also engraved on Anne's gravestone. James Culross, *Hanserd Knollys*, (London: Alexander & Shepherd, 1895), pp. 94-95.

[3] Knollys, *Life*, pp. 17-18.

[4] Knollys, *Life*, p. 27.

Sterling besides it cost me above 60 pounds in his Apprenticeship, and 40 l. afterwards.[5]

Finally, writing of the period in the early 1670s when his family experienced severe sickness, he shared the account of one son, who died while Knollys was himself very ill, as well as of the death of his eldest son who was "Buried in the Country".[6] Shortly thereafter, Knollys' wife became very ill and died, leading to their "only Son then living" being overcome by depression. Eventually this son, Isaac, took ill and died.[7] The final reference is found near the end of his autobiography, where he related how his only living daughter's husband left her.[8]

Other sources that refer to Hanserd Knollys' children include wills, baptismal records, parish and church records, and school and university records. While these provide limited information, they supplement the evidence from the autobiography to support the following account of the children of Hanserd and Anne (Cheney) Knollys.[9]

Sons

Cheney (b. 1633):
According to church records from the church at Humberstone, Lincolnshire, where Hanserd Knollys served in his first pastorate, "Cheyney the sonne of Hanserd Knollys was baptized March the 13th, 1632[3]."[10] It seems that it was

---

[5] Knollys, *Life*, pp. 27-28. It is likely that much of this dividing of his estate took place after his self-exile to the Continent, perhaps in the late 1660s, just prior to his imprisonment. To suggest that he did it earlier than this (in the 1650s) would not be supported by the fact that most of his children would have been too young. This is supported by James Culross, who held that when he returned from abroad, "he prospered so greatly in his profession, that he was able handsomely to portion off his surviving sons and daughter." Culross, *Knollys*, p. 92.

[6] Knollys, *Life*, p. 34.

[7] Knollys, *Life*, p. 36-39. Muriel James gave considerable attention to this passage from Knollys' autobiography due to Knollys' assertion that Isaac was his "only Son then living". If John Knowles of Hampton, NH was the son of Hanserd Knollys, it was problematic since John Knowles of Hampton lived well past that to 1705. She speculated that John had lost contact with his family, perhaps during their sojourn on the Continent or that Knollys' reference in his autobiography meant his last son living in England. James, *Knollys*, p. 106.

[8] Knollys, *Life*, p. 42. The circumstances of their separation are not given. Knollys only wrote that he "went by her consent into the Country, and left her".

[9] The sons have been listed in what would seem to be proper chronological order with birth years. In some cases, the birth order or year are possible but hypothetical due to lack of documentation.

[10] Lincolnshire Archives, document Humberstone BT, 1632/3. According to the new calendar, this would be in 1633.

the custom in Knollys' family for the name of the firstborn son to be the mother's maiden name. Such was the case for Hanserd Knollys himself, whose mother was Rachel Hanserd.[11] On 21 July 1647, Cheney matriculated at Cambridge University, the same university attended by his father Hanserd and his grandfather Richard. Like them, he eventually became a minister. Cheney received his B.A. in 1651/2 and his M.A. in 1655.[12] In 1662, when Hanserd Knollys fled to the Continent, Cheney was installed as vicar in Scartho, Lincolnshire, the church where his father and grandfather had served before him.[13] He continued to serve this church until his death in December 1670 or January 1671, after which he was buried in Lincolnshire.[14]

Cheney's will, probated in January 1671, gives some significant information about the Knollys family. In the will, written in 1670,[15] Cheney named "Mr. Hanserd Knollis and my three Brothers" and "my Mother and three sisters" as beneficiaries. Earlier in the will, he mentioned that he left his daughter, Mary Knollis some property near Grimsby, asking that she "lett her uncle John Knollis my second brother to have the first reasonable refusal of it provided that he will come and live of it himselfe".[16] What is so fascinating about this information is that to Cheney's knowledge, who had this will transcribed in 1670, he had four brothers still living (John and three unnamed) and three unnamed sisters.[17] This differs from his father's account that by the late 1660s he had only one daughter left and by 1672, Isaac had been his last living son.[18]

---

[11] See Chapter 2 above.

[12] John Venn and J.A. Venn, *Alumni Cantabrigienses*, Part I to 1751, vol. III Kaile to Ryves, (Cambridge: University Press, 1924), p. 31.

[13] James, *Knollys*, pp. 53, 63-64, 106, 136. Though James made this claim at several points, she nowhere gave reference or documentation for Cheney's installation at Scartho. This author was unable to locate the record. Not only had Richard Knowles and Hanserd Knollys served this church, but before them, relatives in Hanserd Knollys' mother's family had served as vicars of that church (see Appendix 3).

[14] Knollys, *Life*, p. 34.

[15] Cheney's signature at the end of the will is very shaky. Since he was a well-educated man, it would not be unreasonable to assume that his penmanship would have been good. Thus, one could deduce that the shakiness at this time was likely due to sickness and weakness, since he died a short time afterward.

[16] Will of Cheney Knowles probated January 1670, Lincolnshire Archives, document LCC Wills 1670/ii/728r.

[17] This reference to "sisters" could also refer to sisters-in-law. Perhaps two were sisters-in-law and one his sister, the daughter mentioned by Knollys as still living.

[18] Why there is this discrepancy, is not clear. James put forth her theories, but in the end, they are purely speculative. James, *Knollys*, pp. 172-73.

John 1 (b. 1634):
Hanserd Knollys' second-born son was John, perhaps named after Anne's father John Cheney. The only record extant of John is a baptismal record from 1634, which states "John the Sonne of Hanserd Knollys was baptized March 11th day."[19] Shortly thereafter, Hanserd Knollys probably resigned his living and separated from the Church of England.[20] Therefore, in 1638, when Hanserd and Anne Knollys fled to New England from Laudian persecution, they had at least two children – Cheney, aged five and John, aged four, whom they took with them. However, the voyage over was rough and the conditions appalling, and John became ill and died.[21] Since they only had one child on their return, they likely only had the two boys when they left for New England.

John 2 (b. 1642):
After a brief but tumultuous stay in New England, Hanserd Knollys returned to England with his wife and their son Cheney. Anne by this point was pregnant and due to give birth. They landed in December 1641 and in early 1642, a baby was born. Though no official record has survived, the child could well have been "John my second brother" mentioned by Cheney in his will.[22] Cheney's reference to "John my second brother" is curious. Muriel James understood this to mean his second brother to be named John, on the understanding that the first John died enroute to New England. It was not unusual for parents in that era having lost a child, to give the same name to another child born later, especially if the name had family significance.[23]

---

[19] Lincolnshire Archives, document BT Goulceby, 1633/4.

[20] Alan Betteridge argued that Knollys resigned his living in 1631 and afterward preached itinerantly. He went on to claim that Knollys baptised his son at Goulceby as an itinerant. Alan Betteridge, "Asterby and Donington-on-Bain Lincolnshire", *The Baptist Quarterly*, XXIV, 1, (Jan. 1971) : 22. This is unlikely, since Knollys was married in 1632 and claimed that it was after that when he began to question some practices in the Church of England. Thus, he would have left the Church of England sometime after 1632. Knollys, *Life*, p. 9. Knollys did not give the exact year of his separation from the Church of England. According to Benjamin Stinton, writing shortly after Knollys' death, Knollys left the Church of England in 1636. *An Account of Some of the Most Eminent & Leading Men among the English Antipaedobaptists*, p. 43. The Stinton Manuscripts are housed at the Angus Library, Regent's Park College, Oxford University.

[21] Knollys, *Life*, p. 17.

[22] Will of Cheney Knowles probated January 1670, Lincolnshire Archives, document LCC Wills 1670/ii/728r.

[23] Lawrence Stone, *The Family, Sex, and Marriage In England: 1500-1800*, abridged edition, (New York: Harper and Row, 1977), p. 257. Stone indicated that this practice declined and disappeared in the eighteenth century.

Appendix 4: Children of Hanserd and Anne (Cheney) Knollys 339

In 1653, Knollys convinced Bulstrode Whitelocke, who was on the board of governors of Charterhouse, to sponsor John.[24] On 12 January 1652, Bulstrode Whitelocke presented John Knowles as a scholar at Charterhouse: "It was ordered 1 July 1653, that as John Knollis, son of Hanserd Knollis, clerk, presented by Bulstrode Whitelock, was too blind to be admitted, 3s be allowed him weekly while being cured."[25] Since there was also a hospital at Charterhouse, John likely stayed there while they treated his eyes. Within six months, John's sight showed no improvement and an entry on 20 December 1653 stated that the Standing Committee of Charterhouse ordered that John Norris "be admitted for Lord Whitelock in the place of John Knollis".[26] A later Charterhouse record mentioned a "John Knollis for the Mr of the Hosp. apprentice 23 May 1661".[27] It would seem that Cheney had a special affection for his brother John, perhaps because of his visual handicap and left a special bequest for him in his will.[28]

Hanserd Jr. (b. 1643):
In the preface to his last language handbook, Hanserd Knollys dedicated the work "To my Son Hanserd Knollys" who was listed among his father's scholars who were apprenticed in London.[29] It is quite possible that Hanserd Jr. was Hanserd's and Anne's next son, hence his being named after his father.

In 1643, after returning from his brief service as a Parliamentary Army chaplain, Hanserd Knollys joined Henry Jessey's Independent congregation. They became involved in a discussion there about baptism. At the end of 1643, Anne Knollys had another son and Jessey pressured the Knollys to have their infant son baptised. Anne had reservations about this, which were shared by her husband as well. This son was probably Hanserd Jr.[30]

---

[24] What Knollys' relationship was to Whitelocke is not known. Whitelocke's second wife, Frances, was a sister of Lord Willoughby, whom Knollys served at this time as household chaplain and tutor for his son. Perhaps it was through this connection. "Whitelock, Bulstrode", *Dictionary of National Biography*, XXI, p. 115.
[25] Bower Marsh and Frederic A. Crisp, *Alumni Carthusiani: A Record of the Foundation Scholars of Charterhouse, 1614-1872*, (1913), p. 22.
[26] Marsh and Crisp, *Alumni Carthusiani*, p. 23.
[27] James, *Knollys*, p. 108-109. James received this information through correspondence with Charterhouse. James assumed this was the son mentioned in Knollys autobiography who received an apprenticeship endowment from his father. However, the son mentioned was his "youngest Son, that lived to be Married" and therefore not likely to be John.
[28] See above.
[29] Hanserd Knollys, *Grammaticae Latinae, Graecae, & Hebricae Compendium. Rhetorica Adumbratio. Item Radices Graecae & Hebraicae Omnes quae in Sacra Scriptura Beteris & Novi Testamenti occurrunt*, (London: 1665), preface.
[30] "Knollys Memorandum", as transcribed in W.T. Whitley, "Debate on Infant Baptism, 1643", *Transactions of the Baptist Historical Society*, I (Jan. 1910) : 240.

According to the International Genealogical Index, a Hanserd Knolles married Elisebeth Trapson on 15 December 1669 in Saint James, London.[31] This was not a common name and he was probably the "next Son that lived to be Married" who, according to Knollys' autobiography, received his father's property, school, and fifty students.[32] Based on the brief comments in the preface to the language handbook, Hanserd Jr. seems to have followed in his father's scholarly footsteps and was probably about 27 years old by this point. He was likely one of the unnamed brothers listed in Cheney's will.[33] As well, Hanserd Jr. was perhaps the son who died and was buried during Knollys' sickness.[34]

Samuel (b. 1644/45?):
There is only one mention of Samuel Knollys. In the will of Mr. Thomas Bell, Sr., a merchant from London but settled in Roxbury, Massachusetts, proven 3 May 1672, the following entry is found:

> The sum of one hundred pounds to be distributed among poor necessitous men late ministers of the Gospel, of which number I will that that [sic] Mr Knoles and Mr John Colling, both late of New England be accounted. Legacies to the said Mr Knoles and Mr Samuel Knolls his son, Mr John Colling and one Mr Ball.[35]

It appears that Samuel, like his father, was a minister since he was mentioned in the context of money to be divided among "poor necessitous men late ministers of the Gospel". Samuel was likely one of the unnamed brothers in Cheney's will as well.[36]

Isaac (b. 1647/48?):
Isaac was the only son mentioned in Knollys' autobiography by name. From the reference, it appears that Isaac held a place of special affection to Knollys, perhaps due to his position as the youngest son. It could be that he was the son who accompanied Knollys to the Continent in 1661.[37] He was also likely the "youngest Son, that lived to be Married" to whom Knollys gave more than

---

[31] This would make Hanserd Jr. 26 years old when he married. International Genealogical Index, Family Search, "Hanserd Knolles", (www.familysearch.org)
[32] Knollys, *Life*, pp. 27-28.
[33] Will of Cheney Knowles probated January 1670, Lincolnshire Archives, document LCC Wills 1670/ii/728r.
[34] Knollys, *Life*, p. 34.
[35] *New England Historical and Genealogical Register*, vol. 38, (Boston, 1884), p. 63.
[36] Will of Cheney Knowles probated January 1670, Lincolnshire Archives, document LCC Wills 1670/ii/728r.
[37] Knollys, *Life*, p. 27.

£300 sterling and paid £60 for his Apprenticeship and a further £40.[38] He may have received his endowment for his apprenticeship in late 1660s when the family returned from the Continent. He was probably one of the unnamed sons in Cheney's will.[39] It may have been his wife who nearly died after having a stillborn child in 1670.[40] Isaac died in 1671, after suffering through depression and a brief illness.[41] Following his death, his widow remarried a gentleman worth £300 per annum.[42]

Unaccounted unnamed brother:
There is no mention made of this brother in any source. Perhaps he, like John 1, died in childhood, and for that reason was not mentioned in Cheney's will.[43]

Daughters

According to Knollys' autobiography, he had three daughters.[44] Very little evidence survives about Knollys' daughters – not even their names. Between 1660 and 1670, the autobiography indicated only one as still living. However, the will of Cheney Knollys, written in 1670, mentioned three sisters.[45] One of the daughters may have accompanied Knollys when he fled to Rotterdam in 1661.[46] One certainly married a teacher, who inherited fifty students and a share in the Knollys' school.[47] In September 1672, the husband of one of Knollys' daughters left her and went "into the Country".[48] From these meagre scraps of evidence, it is not possible to patch together even a short biography for any of the daughters.

---

[38] Knollys, *Life*, p. 28. What the further £40 was for is not stated, though it is clear in Knollys' autobiography that Isaac had financial difficulties and debt. Knollys, *Life*, p. 42.
[39] Will of Cheney Knowles probated January 1670, Lincolnshire Archives, document LCC Wills 1670/ii/728r.
[40] Knollys, *Life*, p. 34.
[41] Knollys, *Life*, p. 38.
[42] Knollys, *Life*, p. 42.
[43] Will of Cheney Knowles probated January 1670, Lincolnshire Archives, document LCC Wills 1670/ii/728r.
[44] Knollys, *Life*, p. 8.
[45] Will of Cheney Knowles probated January 1670, Lincolnshire Archives, document LCC Wills 1670/ii/728r. See note 17 above. Perhaps two of these daughters were born in the 1640s and the youngest in the 1650s.
[46] Knollys, *Life*, p. 27
[47] Knollys, *Life*, pp. 27-28.
[48] Knollys, *Life*, p. 42.

APPENDIX 5 - MAPS

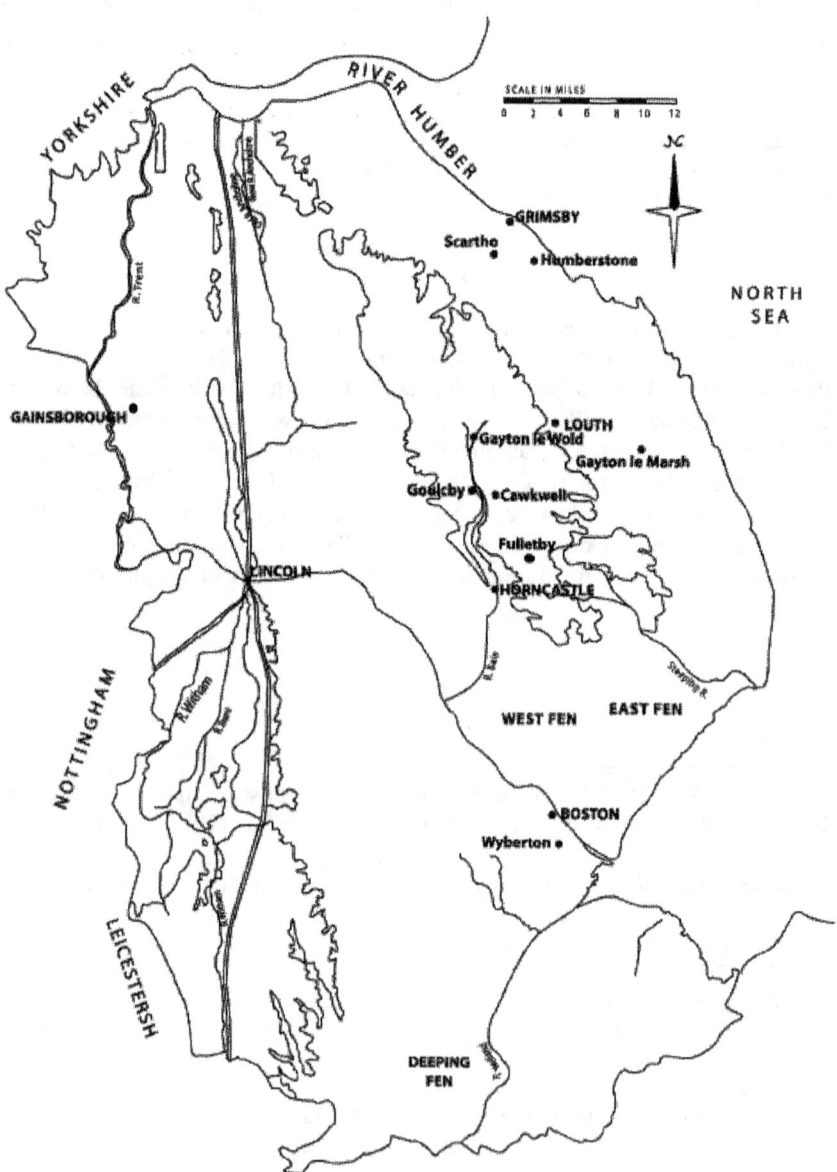

Figure 1. Lincolnshire - Places Mentioned

Appendix 5 – Maps

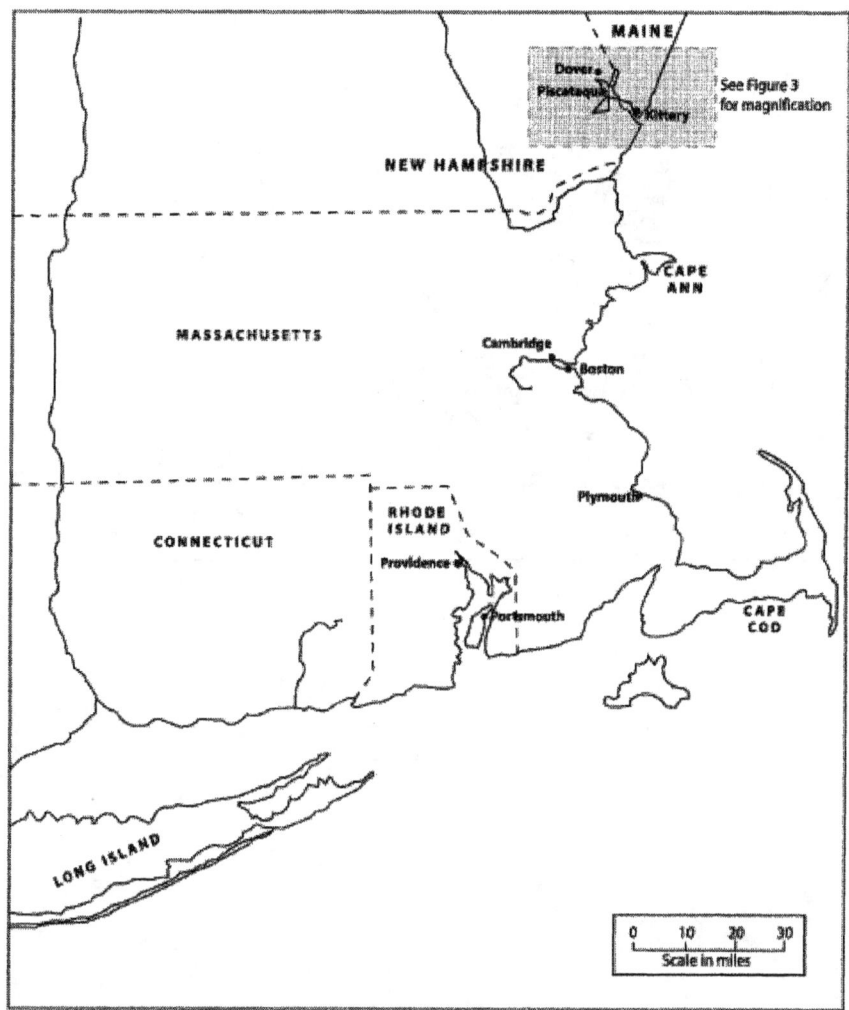

Figure 2. New England in the 1630s

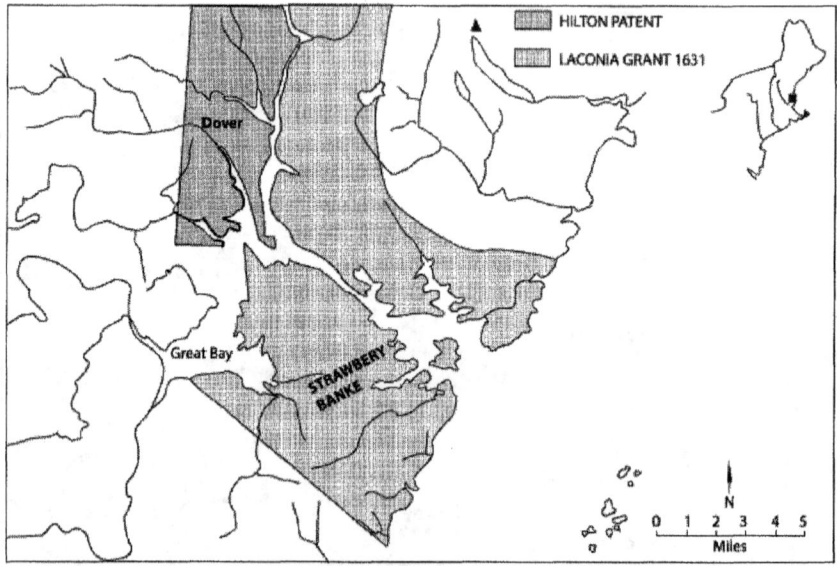

Figure 3. New Hampshire in the 1630s

Bibliography

Works by Hanserd Knollys

Publications and Treatises

Knollys, Hanserd. *A Moderate Answer unto Dr. Bastwicks Book Called "Independency not God's Ordinance".* London: 1645.

Knollys, Hanserd. *An Exposition of the Eleventh Chapter of the Revelation.* London: 1679.

Knollys, Hanserd. *An Exposition of the first Chapter of the Song of Solomon* London: 1656.

Knollys, Hanserd. *An Exposition of the Whole Book of the Revelation Wherein the Visions and Prophecies of Christ are Opened and Expounded.* London: 1688.

Knollys, Hanserd. *Apocalyptical Mysteries.* London: 1667.

Knollys, Hanserd. *Christ Exalted: A Lost Sinner Sought, and Saved by Christ: Gods People are an Holy people... the summe of divers Sermons Preached in Suffolk.* 2nd ed. London: 1646.

Knollys, Hanserd. *Christ Exalted: in a Sermon Begun to be preached at Debenham in Suffolk, upon the 14. day of Febr. last.* London: 1645.

Knollys, Hanserd. *Grammaticae Graecae compendium.* London: 1664.

Knollys, Hanserd. *Grammaticae Latinae compendium.* London: 1664.

Knollys, Hanserd. *Grammaticae Latinae, Graecae, & Hebricae Compendium. Rhetorica Adumbratio. Item Radices Graecae & Hebraicae Omnes quae in Sacra Scriptura Beteris & Novi Testamenti occurrunt.* London: 1665.

Knollys, Hanserd. *Grammaticae Latinae, Graecae, & Hebricae.* London: 1665.

Knollys, Hanserd. *Linguae Hebricae delineatio.* London: 1664.

Knollys, Hanserd. *Miscellanae sacra; or a New Method of considering so much of the history of the Apostles as is contained in Scripture.* London: 1665.

Knollys, Hanserd. *Mystical Babylon Unvailed.* London: 1679.

Knollys, Hanserd. *Radices Hebraicae Omnes, Quae in S. Scriptura, Veteris Testamenti occurrunt.* London: 1664.

Knollys, Hanserd. *Radices simplicium vocum, flexilium maxime, Novi Testamenti.* London: 1664.

Knollys, Hanserd. *Rhetoricae adumbratio.* London: 1663.

Knollys, Hanserd. *The Life and Death of That Old Disciple of Jesus Christ, and Eminent Minister of the Gospel, Mr. Hanserd Knollys*, edited by William Kiffin. London: 1692.

Knollys, Hanserd. *The Parable of the Kingdom of Heaven Expounded. Or, An Exposition of the first thirteen Verses of the twenty fifth Chapter of Matthew.* London: 1674.

Knollys, Hanserd. *The Rudiments of the Hebrew Grammar in English.* London: 1648.

Knollys, Hanserd. *The Shining of a Flaming Fire In Zion Or, A clear Answer unto 13 Exceptions, against the Grounds of New Baptism; (so called) in Mr. Saltmarsh his Book; Intituled, "The Smoke in the Temple".* London: 1645.

Knollys, Hanserd. *The World That Now Is and the World That Is to Come.* London: 1681.

Prefaces in Works of Others

Knollys, Hanserd. "Recommended to the Use of All Parents and Schoolmasters". In Benjamin Keach. *Instructions for Children Or the Child's and Youth's Delight, Teaching an Easie Way to Spell and Read True English.* London: 1664.

Knollys, Hanserd. "The Epistle to the Reader". In Thomas Collier. *The Exaltation of Christ in the days of the Gospel.* London: 1647.

Knollys, Hanserd. "To the Churches of God in London and elsewhere in all places with the Bishops and Deacons". In Robert Garner. *Mysteries Unvailed. Wherein The Doctrine of Redemption by Jesus Christ, flowing from the glorious Grace, and everlasting Love of God, the very fountain of Life and Salvation unto lost Sinners is handled, The most usual Scriptures explained, and Reasons answered, which are urged for the universality of the death of Christ for all Persons.* London: 1946.

Knollys, Hanserd. "To the Reader". In Katherine Sutton. *A Christian Womans Experiences of the glorious working of Gods free grace.* Rotterdam: 1663.

Written with Others

A Confession of Faith of Seven Congregations or Churches of Christ in London, Which are Commonly (But Unjustly) called Anabaptists. London: 1646. In *Confessions of Faith and Other Public Documents, Illustrative of the History of the Baptist Churches of England in the 17th Century.* Edited by Edward Bean Underhill. London: Hanserd Knollys Society, 1854.

A Letter of the Ministers of the City of London... Against Toleration. London: 1645.

A Narrative of the Proceedings of the General Assembly Of divers Pastors, Messengers, and Ministering Brethren of the Baptized Churches, met together in London from Septemb. 3. to 12. 1689 from divers parts of England and Wales : Owning the Doctrine of Personal Election, and final Perseverance. London: 1689.

Address of the Anabaptist Ministers in London to the Lord Protector. London: 1657. In *Confessions of Faith.* Edited by E.B. Underhill. London: Hanserd Knollys Society. 1854.

Cox, Benjamin; Knollys, Hanserd; Kiffin, William. *A Declaration Concerning the Publike Dispute Which Should have been in the Publike Meeting-House of Alderman-Bury, the 3d of this instant Moneth of December; Concerning Infants-Baptisme. Together, with some of the Arguments which should then have been propounded and urged by some of those that are falsly called Anabaptists, which should then have disputed.* London: 1645.

Innocency Vindicated; or, Reproach Wip'd off. London: 1689.

Knollys, Hanserd, et. al. *The Baptists Answer to Mr. Obed Wills, His Appeal Against Mr. H. Danvers.* London: 1675.

Knollys, Hanserd, et. al. *The Gospel Minister's Maintenance Vindicated. Wherein A Regular Ministry in the Churches, is first Asserted, and the Objections against a Gospel Maintenance for Ministers, Answered.* London: 1689.

Knollys, Hanserd, et. al. The Quakers Appeal Answer'd or a Full Relation Of the Occasion, Progress, and Issue of a Meeting held in Barbican, the 28th of August last past. Wherein the Allegations of William Pen, against Thomas Hicks: were

Answered and Disproved. And Tho. Hicks, his Quotations out of the Quakers own Books, Attested, by several, as being appeal'd unto. London: 1674.

Primary Sources

Publications and Treatises

A Confession of Faith Put Forth by the Elders and Brethren of many Congregations of Christians, (baptized upon Profession of their Faith) in London and the Country. London: 1688.

A Delaration Against Anabaptists: To stop the Prosecution so their Errours, falsly pretended to be a Vindication of the Royall Commission of King Jesus, as they call it. London: 1644.

A Declaration by Congregational Societies in, and about the City of London; as well as those commonly called Anabaptists, as others. In a way of Vindication of themselves. London: 1647.

A Declaration Of divers Elders and Brethren of Congregational Societies, in and about the City of LONDON. Decrying and Disclaiming two Bookes; the one called A CRY; and the other Book called A MODEL OF A NEW REPRESENTATIVE. London: 1651.

A declaration of several churches of Christ and godly people in and about the citie of London; concerning the Kingly interest of Christ, and the present sufferings of his cause and saints in England. London: 1654.

A Letter of the Ministers of the City of London Presented the first of Jan. 1645. to the Reverend Assembly of Divines Sitting at Westminster by the Authority of Parliament Against Toleration. London: 1645.

A Narrative of the Proceedings of the General Assembly Consisting Of Elders, Ministers, and Messengers, met together in London, from several Parts of England and Wales, on the 17th Day of the 3d Month, 1692, and continued unto the 24th of the same. Asserting the Doctrine of Personal Election and Final Perseverance). London: 1692.

A Narrative of the Proceedings of the General Assembly Of the Elders and Messengers of the Baptized Churches sent from divers parts of England and Wales, which began in London the 2d of June and ended the 8th of the same, 1691 (Owning the Doctrine of Personal Election, and Final Perseverance). London: 1691.

A Short Story of the Rise, reign, and ruine of the Antinomians, Familists, and Libertines that Infected the Churches of New England. London: 1644.

A true discovery of a bloody plot contrived by the phanaticks against the proceedings of the city of London, in order to the coronation of the high and mighty King, Charles the Second, with the manner how it should have been acted on Sunday last, the number taken who should have been actors, and a true account of the late insurrections of the phanaticks in Newgate. Also the miraculous appearance of seven stars in the East on Wednesday at 11 of the clock at noon, with the branches darting from them like blazing comets, being environed round with several circles of various colours like the rain-bow, and a large white crosse betwixt them, which continued an hour and a half, with the events that hapned [sic] during the time and the manner how all vanished. As it was sent in a letter to a gentleman of quality living at Lime-street London. London: 1661.

Anonymous. *A Witness To the Saints*. London: 1657.

Anonymous. *Tub-Preachers Overturn'd or Independency to be Abandon'd and Abhor'd as destructive to the Magistracy and Ministery, of the Church and Common-wealth of England*. London: 1647.

Baillie, Robert. *Anabaptism, the trve fovntaine of independency, Brownisme, Antinomy, Familisome, and the most of the other errours, which for the time due trouble the Church of England, vnsealed: also the questions of pædobaptisme and dipping handled from scripture : in a second part of the disswasive from the errors of the time*. London: 1647.

Baillie, Robert. *The disswasive from the errors of the time, vindicated from the exceptions of Mr. Cotton and Mr. Tombes*. London: 1655.

Bastwick, John. *Independency Not Gods Ordinance Or a Treatise concerning Church Government, occasioned by the Distractions of these times*. London: 1645.

Baxter, Richard. *The Practical Works of Richard Baxter: Select Treatises*. Grand Rapids: Baker Book House, 1981.

Brown, David. *Two Conferences Between Some of Those That Are Called Separatists and Independents*. London: 1650.

Burton, Henry. *A Vindication of Churches Commonly Called Independent*. London: 1644.

Clarke, John. *Ill newes from New-England*. London, 1652.

Claxton, Lawrence. *The Lost Sheep Found or The Prodigal returned to his Fathers house, after many sad and weary Journey through many Religious Countreys*. London: 1660.

Crosby, Thomas. *The History of the English Baptists*. 4 vols. London: 1738-40.

Danvers, Henry. *A Rejoynder to Mr. Wills in his Vindiciae*. London: 1675.

Danvers, Henry. *A Treatise of Baptism: wherein that of believers and that of infants is examined by the Scriptures, with the history of both out of antiquity*. London: 1673.

Danvers, Henry. *A Treatise of Infant-Baptism asserted & vindicated*. London: 1673/74.

Danvers, Henry. *Innocency and Truth Vindicated: or, A Sober reply to Mr. Will's...* London: 1675.

Edwards, Thomas. *Gangraena: Or a Catalogue and Discovery of many of the Errours, Heresies, Blasphemies and pernicious Practices of the Sectaries of this time...*, London: 1646.

Edwards, Thomas. *Reasons Against the Independent Government of Particular Congregations: As Also Against the Toleration of Such Churches to be Erected in this Kingdom*. London: 1641.

Featley, Daniel. *The Dippers Dipt. Or, The Anabaptists Duck'd and Plung'd Over Head and Eares*. London, 1645.

Freeman, Samuel, *A Plain and Familiar Discourse*. London: 1687.

Hall, Bishop Joseph, *The Old Religion*. London: 1628.

Harrison, Thomas. *A SERMON On the Decease of Mr. Hanserd Knollis, Minister of the Gospel. Preached at Pinners Hall, Octob. 4. 1691*. London: 1694.

Hathorn, Humphrey. *Old Leaven Purged Out, or, The apostacy of this day further opened*. London: 1658.

Jessey, Henry. *The Lords Loud Call to England: Being a True Relation of some Late, Various, and Wonderful Judgments, or Handy-works of God, by Earthquake, Lightening, Whirlewind, great multitudes of Toads and Flyes; and also the striking of* divers persons with Sudden Death, in several places; for what Causes let the man of wisdome judge, upon his serious perusal of the Book it self. London: 1660.

Keach, Benjamin. *Antichrist stormed, or, Mystery Babylon the great whore, and great city, proved to be the present Church of Rome.* London: 1689.

Keach, Benjamin. *Spiritual Melody Containing near Three Hundred Sacred Hymns.* London: 1691.

Keach, Benjamin. *Spiritual Songs Being the Marrow of the Scripture, In Songs of Praise to Almighty God; From the Old and New Testament. With A Hundred Divine Hymns on Several Occasions: As now Practised in several Congregations in and about London.* London: 1700.

Keach, Benjamin. *The Breach Repaired in God's Worship or, Singing of Psalms, Hymns, and Spiritual Songs, proved to be an Holy Ordinance of Jesus Christ.* London: 1691.

Keach, Benjamin. *The glory of a true church and its discipline display'd: Wherein a true Gospel-Church is described together with the power of the keys, and who are to be let in, and who to be shut out.* London: 1697.

Kiffin, William. "To the Reader." In John Lilburne, *The Christian Mans Triall.* London: 1641.

Knutton, Immanuel. *Seven Questions about the Controversie betweene the Church of England and the Separatists and Anabaptists, briefely discussed.* London: 1644.

Leckford, Thomas. *Plaine Dealing or News From New England.* London, 1642.

Manton, Thomas. *XVIII sermons on the second chapter of the 2d Epistle to the Thessalonians containing the description, rise, growth, and fall of Antichrist : with divers cautions and arguments to establish Christians against the apostacy of the Church of Rome : very necessary for these times.* London: 1679.

Marlow, Isaac. *A Brief Discourse Concerning Singing in the Publick Worship of God in the Gospel-Church.* London: 1690.

Marlow, Isaac. *The Controversie of Singing Brought to an End.* London: 1696.

Marlow, Isaac. *Truth Soberly Defended In A Serious Reply to Mr. Benjamin Keach's Book intituled, The Breach Repaired in God's Worship; or Singing of Psalms, Hymns, and spiritual Songs, proved to be an Holy Ordinance of Jesus Christ.* London: 1692.

Marshall, Stephen. *A Sermon of the Baptizing of Infants. Preached In the Abbey-Church at Westminster, at the Morning Lecture, appointed by the Honorable House of Commons.* London: 1644.

Mather, Cotton. *Magnalia Christi Americana.* Vol. 2. London: 1702.

Pagett, Ephraim. *Heresiography: Or, A Description of the Heretickes and Sectaries of These Latter Times.* London: 1645.

Paye, Edward. *Antichrist in Spirit unmasked: or, Quakerism a great Delusion.* London: 1692.

Ramsay, William. *Mirmah, Maroumah, Maroum: a discourse consisting of three sermons : a New-years gift of love to the Protestant Church....* London: 1680.

Salmon, Joseph, a member of the Army. *Antichrist in Man: or A Discovery of the great Whore that sits upon many waters.* London: 1647.

Saltmarsh, John. *An End of One Controversie: Being an Answer or Letter To Master Ley's Large Last Book, called Light for Smoke.* London: 1646.

Saltmarsh, John. *Sparkles of Glory, or Some Beams of the Morning-Star.* London: 1647.

Saltmarsh, John. *The Smoke In the Temple, Wherein is a Designe for Peace and Reconciliation of Believers of the Several Opinions of these Times about Ordinances, to a Forbearance of each other in Love, and Meeknesse, and Humility.* London: 1646.

Sutton, Katherine. *A Christian Womans Experiences of the glorious working of Gods free grace.* Rotterdam: 1663

Tenison, Thomas. *A friendly debate between a Roman Catholick and a Protestant concerning the doctrine of transubstantiation wherein the said doctrine is utterly confuted, and Antichrist is clearly and fully described, and his inevitable destruction predicted...* London: 1688.

The Clergyes Bill of Complaint. Oxford: 1643.

The Confession of Faith, Of those Churches which are commonly (though falsly) called Anabaptists. London: 1644. In *Baptist Confessions of Faith.* Edited by William L. Lumpkin. Philadelphia: The Judson Press, 1959.

The Declaration and Unanimous resolution of Colonel Whalley. London: 1649.

The humble Petition and Representation of Several Churches of God in London, commonly (though falsly) called Anabaptists. London, 1649. In *Confessions of Faith.* Edited by E.B. Underhill. London: Hanserd Knollys Society. 1854.

The Papers and Answers of the Dissenting Brethren and Committee of the Assembly of Divines... for Accomodation 1645. London: 1648.

The Petition for the Prelates Briefly Examined. London: 1641.

The Traytors Unvailed, Or A Brief and true account of that horrrid (sic) and bloody designe intended by those Rebellious People, known by the names of Anabaptists and Fifth Monarchy Being upon Sunday the 14th of April 1661, in Newgate on purpose to oppose his Majesties person and Laws. London: 1661.

Tombes, John. *An Addition to the Apology For the two Treatises concerning Infant-Baptisme Published December 15. 1645.* London: 1652.

Trapnel, Anna. *Cry of a Stone.* London: 1654.

Williams, G., L. Bishop of Ossory. *The Great Antichrist Revealed, Before this time, never discovered. And, Proved to be neither Pope, nor Turk; nor any Single Person, nor the Succession of any one Monarch, or Tyrant in any Policie; But A collected pack, or multitude of Hypocritical, Heretical, Blasphemous, and most scandalous wicked men... the Assembly of Presbyterians consulting at Westminster, Together with the Independents, Anabaptists, and Lay-Preachers.* London: 1660.

Wills, Obediah. *Infant-Baptism asserted & vindicated... in answer to a treatise on baptism lately published by Mr. Henry D'Anvers.* London: 1674.

Wills, Obediah. *Vindiciae Vindiciarum.* London: 1675.

Whitelock, Bulstrode. *Memorials of the English Affairs from the Beginning of the Reign of Charles the First to the Happy Restoration of King Charles the Second.* Vol. 1. Oxford: At the University Press, 1853. This edition is a reprint of the edition published in 1732. The original work was published in 1682.

Manuscripts

Anderson, Philip J. "A Fifth Monarchist Appeal and the Response of an Independent Church at Canterbury, 1653". *The Baptist Quarterly* XXXIII (Apr. 1989) : 72-80.

Anderson, Philip J. "Letters of Henry Jessey and John Tombes to the Churches of New England, 1645". *The Baptist Quarterly* XXVIII (Jan. 1979) : 30-40.

Folger Shakespeare Library, Washington. Additional MS 667.
"Jottings by John Lewis of Margate, 1742". *Transactions of the Baptist Historical Society* IV (Oct. 1915) : 206.
Lambeth Palace Library, Tenison MS679, folio 105.
"May a Minister take State Pay?" *Transactions of the Baptist Historical Society* I (Apr. 1909) : 65-68.
"Rise of the Particular Baptists in London, 1633-1644". *Transactions of the Baptist Historical Society* I (Jan. 1910) : 226-36.
Stinton, Benjamin. *An Account of Some of the Most Eminent & Leading Men among the English Antipaedobaptists*. The Stinton Manuscripts are housed at the Angus Library, Regent's Park College, Oxford University.
White, B.R. "Early Baptist Letters". *The Baptist Quarterly* XXVII (Oct. 1977) : 142-49.

Records

A Collection of the State Papers of John Thurloe, Esq.; Secretary First to the Council of State, And Afterwards to the Two Protectors Oliver and Richard Cromwell. Vol. III to V.
Bishop's Certificates of Institutions, Public Record Office, KEW, IND: 1, 17005, E331, Vol. 6, p. 182.
Boulton, Nathaniel. *Documents and Records of the Province of New Hampshire: 1623-1686*. Vol. 1. Concord: George Jenks, State Printer, 1867.
Boulton, Nathaniel. *New Hampshire Papers*. Vol. 27. Concord, NH: Edward Jenks, Printer, 1877.*Calendar of State Papers Domestic, Charles I*, 1635-36.
Boulton, Nathaniel. *New Hampshire Provincial Papers*. Vol. 10. Concord, NH: Edward Jenkes, 1877.
Calendar of State Papers Domestic, 1652-1653.
Calendar of State Papers Domestic, 1655.
Calendar of State Papers Domestic, 1655-1656
Calendar of State Papers Domestic, Charles I, 1638-39.
Calendar of State Papers Domestic, Charles II, 1660-61.
Calendar of State Papers Domestic, Charles II, 1661-1662.
Calendar of State Papers Domestic, Charles II, 1663-1664.
Calendar of State Papers Domestic, Charles II, 1673-75.
Calendar of State Papers Domestic, Charles II, 1683.
Firth, C.H. and Rait, R.S., eds. *Acts and Ordinances of the Interregnum, 1642-1660*. Vol. II. London: His Majesty's Stationary Office, 1911.
Firth, C.H., ed. *The Clarke Papers*. Vol. 1. The Camden Society, 1891.
Foster, C.W., ed. *Lincoln Episcopal Records in the Time of Thomas Cooper, A.D. 1571 to A.D. 1584*. In *The Publications of the Lincoln Record Society*. Vol. 2. Lincoln: W. K. Morton & Sons Ltd., 1912.
Foster, C.W., ed. *The State of the Church in the Reigns of Elizabeth I and James I*. Vol. 1. In *The Publications of the Lincoln Record Society*. Vol. 23. Horncastle: W. K. Morton & Sons Ltd., 1926.
Holmes, Clive, ed. *The Suffolk Committee for Scandalous Ministers 1644-46*. Suffolk: Suffolk Records Society, 1970.
Lambeth Palace Library, Abbot Register, part 1, f. 310.
Lincolnshire Archives, document Benington in Holland Parish 1/2, 1608.

Lincolnshire Archives, document BT Goulceby, 1633/4.
Lincolnshire Archives, document Calkwell BT, 1608/9.
Lincolnshire Archives, document Calkwell BT, 1609/10.
Lincolnshire Archives, document Humberstone BT, 1632/3.
Lincolnshire Archives, document LCC Wills 1670/ii/728r.
Lincolnshire Archives, document PD, 1608/3.
Lincolnshire Archives, document Wyberton Parish 1/1, 1632.
Maddison, A.R. *Lincolnshire Wills, 1500-1600.* Vol. 1. Lincoln: James Williamson, 1888.
Maddison, A.R. *Lincolnshire Wills, 1500-1617.* Vols. 1 and 2. Lincoln: James Williamson, 1888, 1891.
Mitchell, Alex F. and Struthers, John, eds. *Minutes of the Sessions of the Assembly of Divines.* London: William Blackwood and Sons, 1874.
New England Historical and Genealogical Register. Vol. 38. Boston, 1884.
New England Historical and Genealogical Register. Vol. 49. Boston: 1895.
New England Historical and Genealogical Register. Vol. 50. Boston, 1896.
Province and Court Records of Maine. Vol. 1. Portland: Maine Historical Society, 1928.
Public Record Office, KEW, IND: 1, 17002, E331, Vol. 3, p. 95.
Savage, John, ed. *Winthrop's History.* Vol. I. Boston: Little & Brown, 1853.
Suffolk Deeds, Liber I. Boston: 1880.
The Winthrop Papers. Vol. IV, 1638-1644. Boston: Massachusetts Historical Society, 1944.
Underhill, E.B., ed. *The Records of the Churches of Christ Gathered at Fenstanton, Warboys, and Hexham.* London: Hanserd Knollys Society, 1854.
Webster, W.F., ed. *Protestation Returns of 1640/41 for Lincolnshire*, Nottingham: 1984.
White, B.R., ed. *The Association Records of the Particular Baptists of England, Wales and Ireland to 1660.* London: The Baptist Historical Society, 1971.
Whiteman, E.A.O., ed. *The Compton Census of 1676.* 1986.
Whitley, W.T. "Debate on Infant Baptism, 1643". *Transactions of the Baptist Historical Society* I (January 1910) : 237-45.
Whitley, W.T. "The Jacob-Jessey Church, 1616-1678". *Transactions of the Baptist Historical Society* I (4 Jan. 1910) : 246-56.

Diaries and Journals

Bradford, William. *Of Plimouth Plantation 1620-1647.* Edited by Samuel Eliot Morison. New York: Knopf, 1953.
Hosmer, James Kendall, ed. *Winthrop's Journal.* New York: Scribner's, 1908.
Hutchinson, Thomas. *The Hutchinson Papers.* Vol. 1. Boston: The Prince Society, 1865, reprinted 1967.
Lightfoot, John. *The Whole Works of the Rev. John Lightfoot, D.D. Master of Catherine Hall, Cambridge.* Vol. XIII: *The Journal of the Proceedings of the Assembly of Divines.* Edited by J.R. Putnam. London: J.F. Dove, 1825.
MacFarlane, Alan, ed. *The Diary of Ralph Josselin.* London: Oxford University Press, 1976.
Spalding, Ruth, ed. *The Diary of Bulstrode Whitelocke 1605-1675.* In *Records of Social and Economic History.* New Series XIII. New York: Oxford University Press, 1990.

Published Collections

Hall, David. *The Antinomian Controversy, 1636-38: A Documentary History*. Connecticut: Wesleyan University Press, 1968.

Haller, William, ed., *The Leveller Tracts 1647-1653*, New York: Columbia University Press, 1944.

Kenyon, J.P., ed. *The Stuart Constitution*. 2nd ed. Cambridge: Cambridge University Press, 1986.

Lumpkin, William L., ed. *Baptist Confessions of Faith*. Philadelphia: The Judson Press, 1959.

Woodhouse, A.S.P., ed. *Puritanism and Liberty, Being the Army Debates, 1647-9*. 2nd edition. Chicago: University of Chicago Press, 1951.

Secondary Sources

Adair, John. *The Founding Fathers*. Grand Rapids, MI: Baker Book House, 1982.

Allen, Thomas. *History of the County of Lincoln*. London: John Saunders, 1834.

Anderson, Virginia DeJohn. *New England's Generation: The Great Migration and the formation of society and culture in the seventeenth century*. Cambridge: Cambridge University Press, 1991.

Armitage, Thomas. *A History of the Baptists: traced by their principles and practices from the time of our Lord and Saviour Jesus Christ to the year 1886*. New York: Bryan, Taylor, & Co., 1890.

Armitage, Thomas. *The History of the Baptists*. 2 Vols. Watertown, WI: Maranatha Baptist Press, 1980. Reprint of 1886 ed.

Ashley, Maurice. *The English Civil War: A Concise History*. London: Thames and Hudson, 1974.

Aylmer, G.E., ed. *The Levellers in the English Revolution*. London: Thames and Hudson, 1975.

Bailey, Richard. *New Light on George Fox and Early Quakerism: The Making and Unmaking of a God*. San Francisco, CA: Mellen Research University Press, 1992.

Ball, Bryan W. *A Great Expectation: Eschatological Thought in English Protestantism to 1660*. Leiden: E. J. Brill, 1975.

Ball, Bryan W. *The Seventh-day Men: Sabbatarians and Sabbatarianism in England and Wales, 1600-1800*. Oxford: Clarendon Press, 1994.

"Bampfield's Plan for an Educated Ministry". *Transactions of the Baptist Historical Society* III (May 1912) : 8-17.

Barbour, Hugh. *The Quakers in Puritan England*. New Haven: Yale University Press, 1964.

Barker-Benfield, Ben. "Anne Hutchinson and the Puritan Attitude Toward Women". *Feminist Studies* 1 (Fall, 1972) : 65-96.

Battis, Emery. "A Diagnosis of Mrs. Hutchinson's Behaviour in Terms of Menopausal Symptoms". In *Saints and Sectaries: Anne Hutchinson and the Antinomian Controversy in the Massachusetts Bay Colony*. Chapel Hill: University of North Carolina Press, 1962.

Bauckham, Richard. *Tudor Apocalypse. Sixteenth century apocalypticism, millenarianism and the English Reformation: from John Bale to John Foxe and

Thomas Brightman. Courtenay Library of Reformation Classics. Vol. 8. Oxford: The Sutton Courtney Press, 1978.

Bebbington, D.W. "Baptist M.P.s in the Seventeenth and Eighteenth Centuries". *The Baptist Quarterly* XXVIII (April 1980) : 245-62

Belknap, Jeremy. *The History of New Hampshire*. Vol. 1. 2nd ed. Boston: Bradford and Read, 1813 (originally published in 1784).

Bell, Mark R. *Apocalypse How? Baptist Movements During the English Revolution*. Macon, GA: Mercer University Press, 2000.

"Benjamin Cox". *Transactions of the Baptist Historical Society* VI (1918) : 50-59.

Betteridge, Alan "Asterby and Donington-on-Bain Lincolnshire". *The Baptist Quarterly* XXIV (Jan. 1971): 22-29.

Betteridge, Alan "Early Baptists in Leicestershire and Rutland". *The Baptist Quarterly*, XXVI (Jan. 1973): 209-23.

Bonner, Carey. "Some Baptist Hymnists". *The Baptist Quarterly* VIII (1936-7) : 256-62, 302-31.

Brachlow, Stephen. *The Communion of the Saints: Radical Puritan and Separatist Ecclesiology, 1570-1625*. Oxford: Oxford University Press, 1988.

Braithewaite, W.C. *The Beginnings of Quakerism*. Cambridge: Cambridge University Press, 1970 ed.

Brauer, J.C. "Bastwick, John (1593-1654)". In *Biographical Dictionary of British Radicals in the Seventeenth Century*. Edited by R. L. Greaves and R. Zaller. Brighton, Sussex: Harvester, 1983 : 1.47-48.

Bremer, Francis. *The Puritan Experiment: New England Society from Bradford to Edwards*. New York: St. Martin's Press, 1976.

Briggs, John. "She-preachers, Widows and Other Women: The Feminine Dimension in Baptist Life since 1600". *The Baptist Quarterly* XXXI (July 1986) : 337-52.

Brown, Louise Fargo. *The Political Activities of the Baptists and Fifth Monarchy Men In England During the Interregnum*. London: Oxford University Press, 1912.

Burdick, Oscar. "Sleuthing the Origins of English Seventh Day Baptists in the 1650's: A Bibliography". *Summary of the Proceedings of the American Theological Library Association*, 38, (1984) : 134-45.

Burns, N.T. "Saltmarsh, John (c. 1612-1647)". In *Biographical Dictionary of British Radicals in the Seventeenth Century*. Edited by R. L. Greaves and R. Zaller. Brighton, Sussex: Harvester, 1983.

Bustin, Dennis C. "Papacy, Parish Churches, and Prophecy: The Popish Plot and the London Particular Baptists – A Case Study", in the *Canadian Journal of History*, XXXVIII, 3 (Dec. 2003) : 69-81.

Cannon, John and Ralph Griffiths. *The Oxford Illustrated History of the British Monarchy*. Oxford: Oxford University Press, 1988.

Capp, B.S. "Extreme Millenarianism". In *Puritans, the Millennium and the Future of Israel: Puritan Eschatology 1600 to 1660*, pp. 66-90. Edited by Peter Toon. Cambridge: James Clarke, 1970.

Capp, B.S. *The Fifth Monarchy Men*. London: Faber and Faber, 1972,

Capp, Bernard. "The Fifth Monarchists and Popular Millenarianism". In *Radical Religion in the English Revolution*, pp. 165-89. Edited by J.F. McGregor and B. Reay. New York: Oxford University Press, 1984,.

Carlile, John. *The Story of the English Baptists*. London: James Clarke & Co., 1905.

Chadwick, Henry. *The Early Church*. Markham, ON: Penguin Books, 1967.

"Charterhouse". *The Baptist Quarterly* V (1930-31) : 101.
Christianson, Paul. *Reformers and Babylon*. Toronto: University of Toronto Press, 1978.
Clement, C.J. *Religious Radicalism in England, 1535-1565*. Edinburgh: Rutherford House, 1997.
Clifton, Robin. "Fear of Popery". In *The Origins of the English Civil War*, pp. 144-67. Edited by Conrad Russell. London: MacMillan, 1973.
Clouse, R.G. "The Rebirth of Millenarianism". In *Puritans, the Millennium and the Future of Israel: Puritan Eschatology 1600 to 1660*, pp. 42-65. Edited by Peter Toon. Cambridge: James Clarke, 1970.
Clouse, Robert. "The Millennium that Survived the Fifth Monarchy Men". In *Regnum, Religio et Ratio: Essays Presented to Robert M. Kingdon*. Vol. VIII of *Sixteenth Century Essays and Studies*, pp. 19-29. Edited by Jerome Friedman. Kirksville, MO: Sixteenth Century Journal Publishers, 1987.
Cohen, Alfred. "The Kingdom of God in Puritan Thought: A Study of the English Puritan Quest for the Fifth Monarchy". Unpublished Ph.D. dissertation: Indiana University, 1961.
Cohen, Ronald D. "Church and State In Seventeenth Century Massachusetts: Another Look at the Antinomian Controversy", pp. 475-93. In *Puritan New England: Essays on Religion, Society, and Culture*. Edited by Alden T. Vaughan and Francis J. Bremer. New York: St. Martin's Press, 1977.
Collinson, Patrick. "Towards a Broader Understanding of the Early Dissenting Tradition", pp. 3-38. In *The Dissenting Tradition: Essays for Leland H. Carlson*. Edited by C. Robert Cole and Michael E. Moody. Athens: Ohio University Press, 1975.
Collinson, Patrick. *The Elizabethan Puritan Movement*. London: Jonathan Cape, 1967.
Collinson, Patrick. *The Puritan Character*. Los Angeles: William Andrews Clark Memorial Library, 1989.
Collinson, Patrick. *The Religion of the Protestants*. New York: Oxford University Press, 1982.
Cooper, Brian G. "The Academic Re-discovery of Apocalyptic Ideas in the Seventeenth Century: Joseph Mede". *The Baptist Quarterly* XIX (1961-62) : 29-34.
Copson, Stephen. "Reviews: Muriel James". *The Baptist Quarterly* XXXVII (Jan. 1998) : 259.
Coward, Barry. *The Stuart Age – England 1603-1714*. 2nd ed. London: Longman, 1994.
Crawford, Patricia. "The Challenges to Patriarchalism: How did the Revolution affect Women?", pp. 112-28. In *Revolution and Restoration: England in the 1650s*. Edited by John Morrill, London: Collins & Brown, 1992.
Crawford, Patricia. *Women and Religion in England 1500-1720*. London: Routledge, 1993.
Cressy, David. *Coming Over: Migration and communication between England and New England in the seventeenth century*. Cambridge: Cambridge University Press, 1987.
Cressy, David. *Literacy and the Social Order*. New York: Cambridge University Press, 1980.
Culross, James. *Hanserd Knollys*. London: Alexander & Shepherd, 1895.
Davies, Julian. *The Caroline Captivity of the Church: Charles I and the Remoulding of Anglicanism, 1625-1641*. Oxford: Clarendon Press, 1992.
Dexter, Henry Martyn and Dexter, Morton. *The England and Holland of the Pilgrims*. Boston: Houghton, Mifflin and co., 1905.

Dickens, Charles. *A Tale of Two Cities*. New York: Penguin Books, 1985.
Dictionary of National Biography. "Claxton or Clarkson, Laurence". IV. 461-63.
Dictionary of National Biography. "Knollys, Hanserd". XI : 279-81.
Dictionary of National Biography. "Whitelocke, Bulstrode". XXI : 110-16.
Dictionary of National Biography. "Willoughby, Francis, fifth Baron Willoughby of Parham". Vol. XXI. Pp. 502-505.
"Dissenters' Schools, 1660-1820". *Transactions of the Baptist Historical Society* IV (Oct. 1915) : 220-27.
Dixon, Thomas P. *The Contribution of the English Baptists to Education, 1660-1820*. Unpublished Ph.D. dissertation: Vanderbilt University, 1975.
Dow, F.D. *Radicalism in the English Revolution*. Oxford: Basil Blackwell, 1985.
Dowley, T.E. "A London Congregation during the Great Persecution". *The Baptist Quarterly* XXVII (Jan. 1972) : 233-39.
Duffy, Eamon. *The Voices of Morebath: Reformation and Rebellion in an English Village*. New Haven, Connecticut: Yale University Press, 2001.
Duncan, Pope A. *Hanserd Knollys: Seventeenth-Century Baptist*. Nashville: Broadman Press, 1965.
Elton, G.R. *England Under the Tudors*. London: Methuen & Co. Ltd., 1955.
Erickson, Millard J. *Christian Theology*. Grand Rapids, MI: Baker Book House, 1986.
Estep, William R., Jr. "On the Origins of English Baptists". *Baptist History and Heritage* 22 (Apr. 1987) : 19-26.
Evans, B. *The Early English Baptists*. 2 Vols. London: J. Heaton & Son, 1864.
Finlayson, Michael. "Puritanism and Puritans: Labels or Libels?" *Canadian Journal of History* 8 (Dec. 1973) : 201-23.
Firth, C.H. *Cromwell's Army*. London: Methuen & Co. Ltd., 1902; reprint ed., University Paperbacks, 1962.
Firth, Katherine. *The Apocalyptic Tradition in Reformation Britain, 1530-1645*. Oxford: Oxford University Press, 1979.
Fletcher, Anthony. "The Coming of War". In *Reactions to the English Civil War*, pp.29-49. Edited by John Morrill. New York: St. Martins, 1982.
Fletcher, Anthony. *Reform in the Provinces: the Government of Stuart England*. New Haven, 1986.
Fletcher, Anthony. *The Outbreak of the English Civil War*. London: Edward Arnold Publishers Ltd., 1981.
Foster, John C. "Early Baptist Writers of Verse". *Transactions of the Baptist Historical Society* III (Oct. 1912) : 95-110.
Frend, William H.C. *The Rise of Christianity*. Philadelphia: Fortress Press, 1984.
Garrett, James L. "Restitution and Dissent Among Early English Baptists, 1". *Baptist History and Heritage* 12 (Oct. 1977) : 198-210, 251.
Gentles, Ian. *The New Model Army in England, Ireland, and Scotland, 1645-1653*. Cambridge, MA: Blackwell, 1992.
Gillett, Edward. *A History of Grimsby*. London: Oxford University Press, 1970.
Greaves, Richard L. "The Puritan-Nonconformist Tradition in England, 1560-1700". *Albion* 17 (Winter, 1985) : 449-86.
Greaves, Richard L. *Deliver Us From Evil: The Radical Underground in Britain, 1660-1663*. New York: Oxford University Press, 1986.
Greaves, Richard L. *Enemies Under His Feet: Radicals and Nonconformists in Britain, 1664-1677*. Stanford, California: Stanford University Press, 1990.

Greaves, Richard L. *Saints and Rebels: Seven Nonconformists in Stuart England*. Macon, GA: Mercer University Press, 1985.

Greaves, Richard L. *Secrets of the Kingdom: British Radicals from the Popish Plot to the Revolution of 1688-1689*. Stanford, California: Stanford University Press, 1992.

Greaves, Richard L. *The Puritan Revolution and Educational Thought*. New Jersey: Rutgers University Press, 1969.

Green, I.M. *The Re-establishment of the Church of England, 1660-1663*. Oxford: Oxford University Press, 1978.

Grell, Ole Peter, Israel, Jonathan I., and Tyacke, Nicholas, eds. *From Persecution to Toleration: The Glorious Revolution and Religion in England*. Oxford: Clarendon Press, 1991.

Gura, Philip F. *A Glimpse of Sion's Glory: Puritan Radicalism in New England, 1620-1660*. Connecticut: Wesleyan University Press, 1984.

Hall, Timothy L. *Separating Church and State: Roger Williams and Religious Liberty*. Urbana and Chicago: University of Illinois Press, 1998.

Haller, William. *The Rise of Puritanism*. New York: Columbia University Press, 1938, reprint ed. Philadelphia: University of Pennsylvania Press, 1984.

Harris, T., P. Seward, and M. Goldie, eds. *The Politics of Religion in Restoration England*. Oxford: Blackwell, 1990.

Harris, Tim. *Politics Under the Later Stuarts: Party Conflict in a Divided Society, 1660-1715*. London: Longman, 1993.

Haykin, Michael. "Hanserd Knollys (ca. 1599-1691) On the Gifts of the Spirit", *Westminster Theological Journal* 54 (Spring 1992) : 99-113.

Haykin, Michael. *Kiffin, Knollys, and Keach – Rediscovering our English Baptist heritage*. Leeds: Reformation Today Trust, 1996.

Hey, David. *The Oxford Guide to Family History*. Oxford: Oxford University Press, 1993.

Hill, Christopher. "Antinomianism in 17th-century England". In *The Collected Essays of Christopher Hill*. Vol. 2, pp. 162-84. Sussex: The Harvester Press, 1986.

Hill, Christopher. *A Century of Revolution, 1603-1714*. Edinburgh: Thomas Nelson and Sons Ltd., 1961.

Hill, Christopher. *Antichrist in Seventeenth-Century England*. Rev. ed. London: Verso, 1990.

Hill, Christopher. *Society and Puritanism in Pre-Revolutionary England*. London: Secker & Wartburg, 1964.

Hill, Christopher. *The World Turned Upside Down*. London: Maurice Temple Smith, 1972; reprint ed., Penguin Books, 1991.

Hill, J.F. *Tudor and Stuart Lincoln*. Cambridge: At the University Press, 1956.

Himbury, D. Mervyn. "Training Baptist Ministers". *The Baptist Quarterly* XXI (Oct. 1966) : 337-48, 363.

Hodgett, Gerald. *Tudor Lincolnshire*. Lincoln: History of Lincolnshire Commission, 1975.

Hoekema, Anthony. *The Bible and the Future*. Grand Rapids, Michigan: William. B. Eerdmans Publishing Co., 1979.

Holifield, E. Brooks. *The Covenant Sealed: The Development of Puritan Sacramental Theology in Old and New England, 1570-1720*. New Haven: Yale University Press, 1974.

Holmes, Clive. *Seventeenth-century Lincolnshire*. Lincoln: History of Lincolnshire Committee, 1980.

Horle, Craig W. "Quakers and Baptists: 1647-1660". *The Baptist Quarterly* New Series XXVI (1975/76) : 344-62.

Howson, Barry. "The Question of Orthodoxy in the theology of Hanserd Knollys (c. 1599-1691): a Seventeenth Century English Calvinistic Baptist". Unpublished Ph.D. Dissertation: McGill University, 1999.

Hubbard, William. *General History of New England: From Discovery to MDCLXXX*. In *Collections of the Massachusetts Historical Society*. Vol. V. Second Series. Boston, 1848.

Ingle, H. Larry. *First Among Friends: George Fox and the Creation of Quakerism*. Oxford: Oxford University Press, 1994.

Israel, Jonathan I. "William III and Toleration", pp. 129-70. In *From Persecution to Toleration: The Glorious Revolution and Religion in England*. Edited by Ole Peter Grell, Jonathan I. Israel, and Nicholas Tyacke. Oxford: Clarendon Press, 1991.

Ivimey, Joseph. *A History of the English Baptists*. 4 Vols. London: 1811-30.

James, Muriel. *Religious Liberty on Trial: Hanserd Knollys – Early Baptist Hero*. Franklin, TN: Providence House Publishers, 1997.

Jewell, Helen M. *Education in Early Modern England*. New York: St. Martin's Press, 1998.

Jewson, Charles B. "St. Mary's, Norwich". *The Baptist Quarterly* X (1940-41) : 168-236.

Jones, J.R. *The First Whigs: The Politics of the Exclusion Crisis, 1678-83*. London: Oxford University Press, 1961.

Jones, Rufus M., ed. *The Journal of George Fox*. Indiana: Friends United Press, 1976; reprint of 1908 edition.

Keeble, N.H. *The Literary Culture of Nonconformity in Later Seventeenth-century England*. Leicester: 1987.

Kendall, R.T. *Calvin and English Calvinism to 1649*. Oxford: Oxford University Press, 1981.

Kenyon, John P. *The Popish Plot*. London: William Heinemann Ltd., 1972.

Kerridge, Eric. *The Agricultural Revolution*. London: Allen & Unwin, 1967.

Kershaw, R.R. "Lincoln: Gentlemen, musicians, and bakers". *The Baptist Quarterly* XXXVII (Apr. 1997) : 87-95,147-48.

Kingsley, Gordon. "Opposition to Early Baptists (1638-1645)". *Baptist History and Heritage* 4 (Jan. 1969) : 18-30, 66.

Kishlansky, Mark. *The Rise of the New Model Army*. Cambridge: Cambridge University Press, 1979.

Lacey, Douglas. *Dissent and Parliamentary Politics*. New Jersey: Rutgers University Press, 1969.

Lake, P. *Anglicans and Puritans? Presbyterianism and English Conformist Thought from Whitgift to Hooker*. 1988.

Lake, Peter. "Calvinism and the English Church: 1570-1635", pp. 179-207. In *Reformation to Revolution: Politics and Early Modern England*. Edited by Margot Todd. London: Routledge, 1995.

Lake, Peter. "Defining Puritanism – again?", pp. 3-29. In *Puritanism: Transatlantic Perspectives on a Seventeenth-Century Anglo-American Faith*. Edited by Francis J. Bremer. Boston: Massachusetts Historical Society, 1993.

Lake, Peter. "The Laudian Style: Order, Uniformity, and the Pursuit of the Beauty of Holiness in the 1630s". In *The Early Stuart Church, 1603-1642*, pp.161-85. Edited by Kenneth Fincham. Stanford, CA: Stanford University Press, 1993.

Lake, P. "The Significance of the Elizabethan Identification of the Pope as Antichrist". *JEH* 31 (1980) : 161-78.

Lake, P. "William Bradshaw, Antichrist and the Community of the Godly". *JEH* 36 (1985) : 570-89.

Lake, P. and Dowling, M., eds. *Protestantism and the National Church in Sixteenth-century England.* 1987.

Lamont, William M. *Godly Rule: Politics and Religion, 1603-1660.* New York: St. Martin's Press, 1969.

Lamont, William M. *Puritanism and Historical controversy.* London: UCL Press, 1996.

Lang, Amy Schrager. *Prophetic Woman: Anne Hutchinson and the problem of dissent in the literature of New England.* Berkeley: University of California Press, 1987.

Langley, Arthur S. "Seventeenth Century Disputations". *Transactions of the Baptist Historical Society* VI (July 1919) : 216-43.

Laurence, Anne. *Parliamentary Army Chaplains 1642-1651.* A Royal Historical Society Publication, Suffolk: Boydell Press, 1990.

Lincoln, Robert. *The Rise of Grimsby.* Vol. 1. London: Farnol, Eades, Irvine and Co., 1913.

Liu, Tai. *Discord in Zion: The Puritan Divines and the Puritan Revolution 1640-1660.* The Hague: Martinus Nijhoff, 1973.

MacBeth, H. Leon. *The Baptist Heritage: Four Centuries of Baptist Witness.* Nashville, TN: Broadman Press, 1987.

Mack, Phyllis. "Women as prophets during the English Civil War". *Feminist Studies* 8 (1982) : 19-45.

Maddison, A.R. *Lincolnshire Pedigrees.* Vols. 1-3. In *Publications of the Harleian Society.* Vols. 50-51. London: 1902-1904.

Mallard, Ian. "The Hymns of Katherine Sutton". *The Baptist Quarterly* XX (1963-64) : 23-33.

Manley, Kenneth Ross. "Origins of the Baptists: the Case for Development from Puritanism – Separatism". *Baptist History and Heritage* 22 (Oct. 1987) : 19-26.

Manning, Brian. "The Levellers and Religion". In *Radical Religion in the English Revolution*, pp. 65-90. Edited by J.F. McGregor and B. Reay. London: Oxford University Press, 1984.

Marsh, Bower and Crisp, Frederic, eds. *Alumni Carthusiani: A Record of the Foundation Scholars of Charterhouse, 1614-1872.* 1913.

Martin, Hugh, *Benjamin Keach, Pioneer of Congregational Hymn Singing.* London: Independent Press, 1961.

Martin, Hugh. "The Baptist Contribution to Early English Hymnody". *The Baptist Quarterly* XIX (Jan. 1962) : 195-208.

Martin, J.W. *Religious Radicals in Tudor England.* London: The Hambledon Press, 1989.

Mayor, Stephen. *The Lord's Supper in Early English Dissent.* London: Epworth Press, 1972.

McGregor, J.F. "The Baptists: Fount of All Heresy". In *Radical Religion in the English Revolution*, pp. 23-63. Edited by J.F. McGregor and B. Reay. London: Oxford University Press, 1984.

McGregor, J.F. and Reay, B., eds. *Radical Religion in the English Revolution*. London: Oxford University Press, 1984.
Miller, John. *Popery and Politics in England, 1660-1688*. Cambridge: At the University Press, 1973.
Miller, Perry. *Orthodoxy in Massachusetts, 1630-1650*. Boston: Beacon Press, 1933.
Miller, Perry. *Roger Williams: His Contribution to the American Tradition*. New York: Athenum, 1962.
Miller, Perry. *The New England Mind: From Colony to Province*. Cambridge, MA: Harvard University Press, 1953.
Milton, A. *Catholic and Reformed : the Roman and Protestant churches in English Protestant Thought, 1600-1640*. Cambridge: University Press, 1994.
Milton, A. "The Laudians and the Church of Rome c. 1625-1640". Unpublished Cambridge University Ph.D. thesis, 1989.
Milton, Anthony. "The Church of England, Rome, and the True Church: The Demise of a Jacobean Consensus". In *The Early Stuart Church, 1603-1642*, 187-210. Edited by Kenneth Fincham. Stanford, CA: Stanford University Press, 1993.
Moore, Rosemary Anne. *The Faith of the First Quakers: The Development of their Beliefs and Practices up to the Restoration*. Unpublished Ph.D. Dissertation: University of Birmingham, 1993.
Morgan, Edmund S. *Roger Williams: The Church and the State*. New York: Harcourt, Brace, & World, Inc., 1967.
Morgan, Edmund S. *The Puritan Dilemma: The Story of John Winthrop*. Boston: Little, Brown, and Co., 1958.
Morgan, Edmund S. *The Puritan Family: Religion and Domestic Relations in Seventeenth-Century New England*. Revised and enlarged ed. New York: Harper and Row, 1966.
Morgan, Edmund S. *Visible Saints: The History of a Puritan Idea*. Ithaca, NY: Cornell University Press, 1963.
Morgan, J. *Godly Learning - Puritan Attitudes Towards Reason, Learning and Education, 1560-1640*. Cambridge: 1986.
Morison, Elizabeth Forbes and Morison, Elting E. *New Hampshire: A Bicentennial History*. New York: Norton, 1976.
Morrill, J.S. "The Religious Context of the English Civil War". *TRHS* 34 (1984) : 55-178.
Morrill, John. *The Nature of the English Revolution*. London: Longman, 1993.
Morton, A.L. *The World of the Ranters: Religious Radicalism in the English Revolution*. London: Lawrence & Wishart, 1970.
Naylor, Peter. *Picking Up a Pin for the Lord: English Particular Baptists from 1688 to the Early Nineteenth Century*. London: Grace, 1992.
Newport, Kenneth G.C. "Benjamin Keach, William of Orange, and the Book of Revelation – A Study in English Prophetical Exegesis". *The Baptist Quarterly* XXXVI (Jan. 1995) : 43-51.
Nicholson, J.F.V. "The Office of 'Messenger' amongst British Baptists in the Seventeenth and Eighteenth Centuries". *The Baptist Quarterly*, N. S. XVII (Jan. 1958) : 206-25.
Nuttall, G.F., "The First Nonconformists", pp. 151-87. In *From Uniformity to Unity, 1662-1962*. Edited by G.F. Nuttall and O. Chadwick. London: Society for the Promoting of Christian Knowledge, 1962.

Nuttall, Geoffrey F. "Abingdon Revisited, 1656-1675". *The Baptist Quarterly* XXXVI (Apr. 1995) : 96-103.
Nuttall, Geoffrey F., and Chadwick, Owen, eds. *From Uniformity to Unity, 1662-1962*. London: Society for the Promoting of Christian Knowledge, 1962.
Nuttall, Geoffrey F. *The Puritan Spirit: Essays and Addresses*. London: Epworth Press, 1967.
Nuttall, Geoffrey F. *The Welsh Saints, 1640-1660: Walter Cradock, Vavasor Powell, Morgan Llwyd*. Cardiff: University of Wales Press, 1957.
Nuttall, Geoffrey F. *Visible Saints: The Congregational Way, 1640-1660*. Oxford: Basil Blackwell, 1957.
Palfrey, John Gorham. *History of New England*. Vol. 1. Boston: Little, Brown, & Company, 1858.
Parker, Irene. *Dissenting Academies in England*. Cambridge: At the University Press, 1914.
Patrick, J. Max, "The Idea of Liberty in the Theological Writings of Sir Henry Vane the Younger". In *The Dissenting Tradition*, pp. 100-107. Edited by C. Robert Cole and Michael E. Moody. Athens: Ohio University Press, 1975.
Paul, Robert S. *The Assembly of the Lord: Politics and Religion in the Westminster Assembly and the 'Grand Debate'*. Edinburgh: T & T Clark, 1985.
Payne, Ernest. *Baptists and 1662*. London: Kingsgate Press, 1962.
Payne, Ernest. "More About the Sabbatarian Baptists". *The Baptist Quarterly* XIV (1951) : 161-66.
Payne, Ernest. *The Fellowship of Believers: Baptist Thought and Practice Yesterday and Today*. London: Kingsgate Press, 1944.
Payne, Ernest A. "Thomas Tillam". *The Baptist Quarterly* XVII (Oct. 1958) : 61-66.
Payne, Ernest A., "Toleration and Establishment: I An Historical Outline". In *From Uniformity to Unity, 1662-1962*, pp.257-87. Edited by G.F. Nuttall and O. Chadwick. London: Society for the Promoting of Christian Knowledge, 1962.
Pettit, Norman. *The Heart Prepared: Grace and Conversion in Puritan Spiritual Life*. New Haven: Yale University Press, 1966.
Polizzotto Carolyn. "The Campaign against The Humble Proposals of 1652". *Journal of Ecclesiastical History* 38 (Oct. 1987) : 569-81.
Porter, H.C. *Reformation and Reaction in Tudor Cambridge*. Cambridge: University Press, 1958.
Powicke, Fredrick T. "Richard Baxter's Relation to the Baptists". *Transactions of the Baptist Historical Society* VI (July 1919) : 193-215.
Reay, B. "Quakerism and Society", pp. 1-21. In *Radical Religion in the English Revolution*. Edited by J.F. McGregor and B. Reay. London: Oxford University Press, 1984.
Reay, B. "Radicalism and Religion in the English Revolution: An Introduction", pp. 141-64. In *Radical Religion in the English Revolution*. Edited by J.F. McGregor and B. Reay. London: Oxford University Press, 1984.
Reay, Barry. "Quaker Opposition to Tithes 1652-1660". *Past and Present* 86 (1980) : 100-104.
Reay, Barry. *The Quakers and the English Revolution*. London: Temple Smith, 1985.
Robertson, D.B. *The Religious Foundations of Leveller Democracy*. New York: King's Crown Press, 1951.

Robinson, H. Wheeler. "Baptist Church Discipline 1689-1699". *The Baptist Quarterly* I (1922-23) : 112-28.

Robinson, H. Wheeler. *Life and Faith of the Baptists*. London: Methuen and Co., 1927.

Robinson, H. Wheeler. "The Value of Denominational History". *The Baptist Quarterly* II (1924-25) : 100-12.

Rogers, P.G. *The Fifth Monarchy Men*. London: Oxford University Press, 1966.

Rooy, Sidney H. *The Theology of Missions in the Puritan Tradition – A Study of Representative Puritans: Richard Sibbes, Richard Baxter, John Eliot, Cotton Mather, and Jonathan Edwards*. Grand Rapids: William B. Eerdmans Publishing Co., 1965.

Ross, J.M. "The Theology of Baptism in Baptist History". *The Baptist Quarterly* XV (1953) : 100-12.

Russell, Conrad. *The Crisis of Parliaments: English History, 1509-1660*. Oxford: Oxford University Press, 1971.

Russell, Conrad. *The Fall of the British Monarchies, 1637-1642*. Oxford: Clarendon Press, 1991.

Russell, D.S. *Divine Disclosure: An Introduction to Jewish Apocalyptic*. Minneapolis: Fortress Press, 1992.

Russell, D.S. *The Method and Message of Jewish Apocalyptic*. London: SCM Press Ltd., 1964.

Samuel, Wilfred S. "Charles-Marie de Veil". *The Baptist Quarterly* V (1930-31) : 74-81, 118-29, 177-89.

Savage, James. *A Genealogical Dictionary of First Settlers of New England*. Vol. III. "Knollys, Hanserd". Baltimore: Genealogical Publication Co., 1965. Originally published in Boston: 1860-62.

Seaward, P. *The Cavalier Parliament and the Reconstruction of the Old Regime, 1661-1667*. Cambridge: 1989.

Shaw, Howard. *The Levellers*. London: Longmans, 1968.

Sirluck, Ernest. "Introduction", pp. 1-126. In *The Complete Prose Works of John Milton*. Vol. 2. New Haven: Yale University Press, 1959.

Slafter, Edmund. *Sir William Alexander and American Colonization*. Boston: The Prince Society, 1873, reprinted, 1966.

Spurr, John. *English Puritanism: 1603-1689*. New York: St. Martin's Press, 1998.

Spurr, John. *The Restoration Church of England, 1646-1689*. New Haven: Yale University Press, 1991.

Tanner, J.R. *English Constitutional Conflicts of the Seventeenth Century, 1603-1689*. Cambridge: University of Cambridge Press, 1928, reprinted 1961.

The Complete Peerage or A History of the House of Lords and All Its Members From the Earliest Times. Vol. XII. Part II. London: The St. Catherine Press, 1959.

The Founders: Portraits of Persons Born Abroad Who Came to the Colonies in North America Before the Year 1701. Vol. III. Boston, MA: 1926. Reprinted Baltimore Publishers, 1976.

"The Tombs in Bunhill Fields". *Transactions of the Baptist Historical Society* II (Oct. 1910) : 127-28.

"The Use of Parish Churches, 1641-1662". *Transactions of the Baptist Historical Society* III (Oct. 1912) : 121-26.

Thirsk, Joan. *English Peasant Farming – The Agrarian History of Lincolnshire from Tudor to Recent Times*. London: Routledge & Kegan Paul, 1957.

Thirsk, Joan, ed. *The Agrarian History of England and Wales.* Vol. IV 1500-1640. H. P. R. Finberg, gen. ed. Cambridge: University Press, 1967.

Thomas, Keith. *Religion and the Decline of Magic.* London: Weidenfeld and Nicolson, 1971.

Thomas, Keith. "Women and the Civil War Sects", pp. 17-40. In *Crisis in Europe, 1560-1660.* Edited by T. Aston, London: Routledge, 1965.

Thompson, Roger. *Mobility and Migration: East Anglican Founders of New England, 1629-1640.* Amherst: University of Massachusetts Press, 1994.

Tolmie, Murray. *The Triumph of the Saints: The separate churches of London 1616-1649.* London: Cambridge University Press, 1977.

Toon, Peter. "The Latter-Day Glory". In *Puritans, the Millennium and the Future of Israel: Puritan Eschatology 1600 to 1660*, pp. 23-41. Edited by Peter Toon. Cambridge: James Clarke, 1970.

Torbet, Robert G. *A History of the Baptists.* Valley Forge: Judson Press, 1950.

Trevelyan, G.M. *England in the Age of Wycliffe.* London: Longmans, Green and Co., 1948 ed.

Trevor-Roper, H.R. *Archbishop Laud*, 2nd ed. New York: MacMillan, 1965.

Troeltsch, Ernst. "Stoic-Christian Natural Law and Modern Secular Natural Law" (Originally published in 1911), pp. 321-42. In *Religion in History.* Edited by James Luther Adams and Walter F. Bense. Edinburgh: T & T Clark, 1991.

Tyacke, Nicholas. "Puritanism, Arminianism and Counter-revolution", pp. 119-43. In *The Origins of the English Civil War.* Edited by C. Russell. London: MacMillan, 1973.

Tyacke, Nicholas. "The 'Rise of Puritanism' and the Legalizing of Dissent, 1571-1719". In *From Persecution to Toleration*, pp. 3-38. Edited by O.P. Grell, J.I. Israel, and N. Tyacke. Oxford: Clarendon Press, 1991.

Underdown, David. *Pride's Purge: Politics in the Puritan Revolution.* Oxford: Clarendon Press, 1971.

Underwood, A.C. *A History of the English Baptists.* London: The Baptist Union of Great Britain and Ireland, 1947.

Van Deventer, David E.. *The Emergence of Provincial New Hampshire, 1623-1741.* Baltimore: The John's Hopkins University Press, 1976.

Venn, John and J.A. Venn. *Alumni Cantabrigienses.* Part I to 1751. Vol. III Kaile to Ryves. Cambridge: University Press, 1924.

Walker, J. "Dissent and Republicanism after the Restoration". *The Baptist Quarterly* VIII (1936-37) : 263-80.

Wallace Jr., Dewey D. *Puritans and Predestination: Grace in English Protestant Theology, 1525-1695.* Chapel Hill: University of North Carolina Press, 1982.

Walsham, Alexandra. *Providence in Early Modern England.* Oxford: Oxford University Press, 1999.

Watson, Foster. "The State and Education During the Commonwealth". *English Historical Review* XV (Jan. 1900) : 58-72.

Watson, Foster. *The English Grammar Schools to 1660.* New York: Augustus M. Kelley, 1970.

Watts, Michael. *The Dissenters: From the Reformation to the French Revolution*, vol. 1. Oxford: Clarendon Press, 1978.

Webster, Tom. *Godly Clergy in Early Stuart England: The Caroline Puritan Movement c. 1620-1643.* Cambridge: Cambridge University Press, 1997.

Wedgwood, C.V. *The Trial of Charles I*. London: The Reprint Society Ltd., 1966.
Westerkamp, Marilyn J. "Anne Hutchinson, Sectarian Mysticism, and the Puritan Order". *Church History* 59 (Dec. 1990) : 482-96.
White, B.R. "Baptist Beginnings in Watford". *The Baptist Quarterly* XXVI (Jan. 1976) : 205-208.
White, B.R. "Echoes of Medieval Christendom in Puritan Spirituality". *One In Christ* (1980) : 78-90.
White, B.R. "Erbery (or Erbury), William (1604-1654)". In *Biographical Dictionary of British Radicals in the Seventeenth Century*, pp. 253-54. Edited by R. L. Greaves and R. Zaller. Brighton, Sussex: Harvester, 1983.
White, B.R. *Hanserd Knollys and Radical Dissent in the 17th Century*. London: Dr. Williams's Trust, 1977.
White, B.R. "Henry Jessey: A Pastor in Politics". *The Baptist Quarterly* XXV (Jan. 1973) : 98-110.
White, B.R. "How did William Kiffin join the Baptists?" *The Baptist Quarterly* XXIII (Jan. 1970) : 201-7.
White, B.R. "Knollys, Hanserd (c. 1599-1691)". In *Biographical Dictionary of British Radicals in the Seventeenth Century*, pp. 160-62. Edited by R. L. Greaves and R. Zaller. Brighton, Sussex: Harvester, 1983.
White, B.R. "The Doctrine of the Church in the Particular Baptist Confession of 1644". *Journal of Theological Studies*, N. S. Vol. XIX (Oct. 1968) : 570-90.
White, B.R. *The English Baptists of the Seventeenth Century*. Rev. ed. London: The Baptist Historical Society, 1997.
White, B.R. *The English Separatist Tradition: From Marian Martyrs to the Pilgrim Fathers*. London: Oxford University Press, 1971.
White, B.R. "The London Calvinistic Baptist Leadership: 1644-1660". *The Baptist Quarterly* XXII supplement (1987) : 34-45.
White, B.R. "The Twilight of Puritanism in the Years Before and After 1688". In *From Persecution to Toleration: The Glorious Revolution and Religion in England*, pp. 307-30. Edited by Ole Peter Grell, Jonathan I. Israel, and Nicholas Tyacke. Oxford: Clarendon Press, 1991.
White, Barrie. "The English Particular Baptists and the Great Rebellion, 1640-1660". *Baptist History and Heritage* 9 (Jan. 1974) : 16-29.
White, Barrie. "The Origins and Convictions of the First Calvinistic Baptists". *Baptist History and Heritage* 25 (Oct. 1990) : 39-47.
White, Barrie R. "William Kiffin – Baptist Pioneer and Citizen of London". *Baptist History and Heritage* II July 1967 : 91-103.
White, James E. *The Sacraments in Protestant Practice and Faith*. Nashville: Abingdon Press, 1999.
Whiteman, E.A.O. "The Re-establishment of the Church of England, 1660-1663". *TRHS* 5 (1955) : 111-31.
Whiteman, E.A.O. "The Restoration of the Church of England". In *From Uniformity to Unity, 1662-1962*, pp. 21-88. Edited by G.F. Nuttall and O. Chadwick. London: Society for the Promoting of Christian Knowledge, 1962.
Whitley, W.T. *A History of the British Baptists*. London: Charles Griffin & Co., 1923; rev. 1932.
Whitley, W.T. "Baptists and Bartholomew's Day". *Transactions of the Baptist Historical Society* I (Nov. 1908) : 24-41.

Whitley, W.T. *Baptists in London, 1612-1928*. London: Kingsgate Press, 1928.
Whitley, W.T. "Baptist Meetings in the City of London". *Transactions of the Baptist Historical Society* V (June 1916) : 74-82.
Whitley, W.T. "Bunhill Fields: The Place and the Records". *The Baptist Quarterly* V (Jan. 1931) : 220-26.
Whitley, W.T. "London Churches in 1682". *The Baptist Quarterly* I (1922-23) : 82-87.
Whitley, W.T. "Militant Baptists, 1660-1672". *Transactions of the Baptist Historical Society* I (Oct. 1909) : 148-55.
Whitley, W.T. "Private Schools, 1660-1689". *Transactions of the Congregational Historical Society* 12/13 (1934) : 172-85.
Whitley, W.T. "Seventh Day Baptists in England". *The Baptist Quarterly* XII (Oct. 1947) : 252-58.
Whitley, W.T. "The Contribution of Nonconformity to Education Until the Victorian Era". *The Educational Record With the Proceedings of the British and Foreign School Society* XIX (June 1915) : 200-220.
Whitley, W.T. "The English Career of John Clarke, Rhode Island". *The Baptist Quarterly* I (1922-23) : 368-72.
Williams, Selma. *Divine Rebel: The Life of Anne Marbury Hutchinson*. New York: Holt, Rinehart and Winston, 1981.
Wilson, John F. *Studies in Puritan Millenarianism Under the Early Stuarts*. Ann Arbour, MI: University Microfilms, Inc., 1962.
Winter, E.P. "Calvinist and Zwinglian Views of the Lord's Supper among the Baptists of the Seventeenth Century". *The Baptist Quarterly* XV (1954) : 323-29.
Winter, E.P. "The Lord's Supper: Admission and Exclusion Among the Baptists of the Seventeenth Century". *The Baptist Quarterly* XVII (Apr. 1958) : 267-81.
Winter, E.P. "Who may administer The Lord's Supper?" *The Baptist Quarterly* XVI (July 1955) : 128-33.
Wood, Nathan. *The history of the First Baptist church of Boston, 1665-1899*. Philadelphia: American Baptist Publication Society, 1899.
Woolrych, Austin. "The English Revolution: an introduction", pp. 1-33. In *The English Revolution, 1600 to 1660*. Edited by E. W. Ives. London: Edward Arnold Ltd., 1968.
Woolrych, Austin. *Commonwealth to Protectorate*. Oxford: Clarendon Press, 1982.
Woolrych, Austin. *Soldiers and Statesmen: The General Council of the Army and its Debates, 1647-1648*. Oxford: Clarendon Press, 1987.
Worden, Blair, ed. *Stuart England*. Oxford: Phaidon Press, 1986,
Young, Joy Ann. *The Language of Conversion in Early America: Social Identity and the Ineffable, 1630-1850*. UMI Dissertation Services: University of California, Berkeley, 1999.

Index of Names

A

Alexander, Sir William, 64
Ames, William, 35

B

Bale, John, 193, 194, 195, 209
Bampfield, Francis, 268, 269, 292
Barbone, Praise God, 94, 99, 277
Barrow, Henry, 8, 195
Bastwick, Dr. John, 3, 47, 48, 69, 72, 74, 85, 101, 102, 103, 104, 105, 106, 107, 108, 109, 111, 112, 114, 121, 195, 242, 298
Baxter, Richard, 43, 44, 76, 263, 310, 311
Belcher, John, 160
Beza, Theodore, 104, 262, 299
Blunt, Richard, 277, 278
Bradford, John, 35
Bradstreet, Simon, 35
Brewster, William, 35, 38
Brightman, Thomas, 193, 195, 196, 209
Browne, Robert, 8, 35, 90
Bunyan, John, 20, 310, 334
Burdett, George, 55, 60, 64, 77
Burroughs, Jeremiah, 99, 279
Burton, Henry, 47, 48, 69, 71, 99, 107, 195

C

Calamy, Edmund, 99
Calvin, John, 43, 104, 276, 277, 288, 289
Canne, John, 160
Cartwright, Thomas, 35
Chamberlen, Dr. Peter, 168, 291
Charles I, 3, 11, 14, 15, 25, 36, 46, 48, 63, 64, 73, 75, 83, 88, 91, 125, 128, 137, 138, 151, 155, 157, 162, 163, 164, 167, 172, 173, 174, 175, 178, 180, 184, 185, 187, 188, 189, 191, 192, 195, 231, 250, 293, 319, 320, 321, 330
Charles II, 14, 15, 138, 151, 155, 156, 157, 162, 163, 165, 167, 172, 173, 174, 175, 178, 180, 184, 185, 187, 188, 189, 191, 192, 231, 250, 293, 321
Cheare, Abraham, 134, 295
Cheney, Frances, 39, 47
Cheney, John, 39, 47, 182, 338
Cheney, Sir John, 39
Cheney, Sir Thomas, 39
Cheney, William, 39
Clarke, John, 157, 159, 160, 161, 168
Claxton, Lawrence, 70, 80
Clyfton, Robert, 38
Cotton, John, 35, 49, 50, 54, 59, 283
Cox, Benjamin, 3, 36, 98, 99, 100, 279, 285
Cromwell, Oliver, 6, 25, 57, 87, 88, 90, 92, 118, 120, 122, 123, 124, 125, 128, 135, 138, 144, 146, 155, 156, 157, 158, 159, 161, 163, 164, 165, 166, 167, 168, 169, 208, 231, 320, 332, 333
Cromwell, Richard, 138, 155
Crosby, Thomas, 16, 17, 22, 23, 147, 178, 179, 186, 189, 249, 312

Index of Names

D

Danvers, Henry, 186, 279
Day, Coronet Wentworth, 160
de Veil, Charles Marie, 268
Dyer, Mary, 52

E

Eaton, Samuel, 93, 277, 278
Edwards, Thomas, 16, 17, 76, 77, 79, 80, 83, 86, 90, 117, 122, 147, 263
Elizabeth I, 2, 7, 29, 46, 196, 331
Erbury, William, 99, 109, 110, 111, 208

F

Feake, Christopher, 159, 165, 166, 167
Featley, Daniel, 96, 97, 98, 101, 105
Fox, George, 119, 141, 142, 143, 145, 146, 149, 150, 151, 152, 154, 310, 311
Foxe, John, 193, 194, 195

G

Goodwin, Thomas, 35, 99, 279
Gorges, Sir Fernando, 59

H

Hanserd, Richard Jr., Hanserd Knollys' grandfather, 32, 33, 326, 331
Hanserd, Richard Sr., Hanserd Knollys' great grandfather, 32, 331
Hanserd, Sir Hammond, Hanserd Knollys' great uncle, 331
Harrison, Edward, 134, 246
Harrison, Thomas, 81, 102, 155, 159, 163, 165, 168, 315, 316

Harvard, John, 35
Helwys, Thomas, 37, 93, 327
Hicks, Thomas, 152, 153, 154, 186
Hooker, Thomas, 35
Hooton, Elizabeth, 141
Hutchinson, Anne, 50, 51, 52, 53, 54, 262
Hyde, Sir Edward, Earl of Clarendon, 172, 173, 180

J

Jacob, Henry, 8, 90, 158
James I, 3, 6, 7, 14, 15, 19, 29, 32, 64, 187, 189, 190, 206, 235, 236, 321, 331
James II, 6, 14, 15, 19, 180, 187, 189, 190, 206, 235, 236, 321
Jessey, Henry, 3, 8, 20, 36, 67, 77, 79, 94, 95, 99, 121, 134, 147, 157, 158, 159, 160, 164, 165, 166, 167, 168, 173, 245, 246, 277, 278, 279, 285, 293, 303, 332, 333, 334, 339
Johnson, Francis, 8
Josselin, Ralph, 45

K

Keach, Benjamin, 4, 17, 24, 146, 147, 177, 178, 185, 186, 189, 197, 211, 239, 247, 254, 267, 268, 283, 284, 285, 293, 294, 295, 296, 297, 300, 312, 313, 315
Kiffin, William, 2, 3, 4, 21, 22, 24, 29, 73, 77, 91, 94, 99, 120, 121, 124, 126, 127, 128, 129, 131, 136, 146, 147, 148, 153, 154, 159, 160, 165, 166, 173, 178, 179, 182, 186, 189, 190, 240, 246, 247, 248, 254, 257, 266, 267, 277, 278, 285, 293, 294, 296, 297, 310, 311, 312, 313, 314, 315, 317, 324, 331, 335

Knollys, Anne (Cheney), 39, 73, 74, 182, 278, 281, 303, 308, 321, 335, 338, 339
Knollys, Hanserd Jr., 66, 266, 339, 340
Knollys, Isaac, 183, 184, 336, 337, 340, 341
Knollys, Samuel, 66, 266, 340
Knowles, Cheney, 25, 39, 73, 175, 179, 182, 333, 334, 337, 338, 340, 341
Knowles, John (1), 40, 114, 150, 256, 338, 341
Knowles, John (2), 266, 335, 336, 337, 339
Knowles, Rachel (Hanserd) Pagett, 32, 337
Knowles, Richard, 29, 32, 33, 34, 36, 134, 318, 324, 325, 326, 327, 328, 329, 331, 337
Knowles, Zacharie, 33, 34, 65, 325, 326, 329

L

Lacon, Christobel (Sutcliffe), 31, 32, 33, 34, 38, 324, 325, 326, 329
Lacon, Harbert, 32, 326, 329
Lambert, Francis, 194
Larkham, Thomas, 55, 56, 59, 62, 63, 64, 65, 66, 77
Laud, Archbishop William, 3, 36, 40, 46, 47, 60, 69, 71, 74, 83, 194, 208, 209, 235, 318
Leckford, Thomas, 51, 56, 63, 64, 277
Legge, Col., 175, 176, 178, 183, 184, 185
Lilburne, John, 121, 122, 125, 126, 127, 143, 195
Luther, Martin, 275, 276, 287

M

Marlow, Isaac, 293, 294, 296, 297, 298, 299, 300, 304, 311, 313
Marshall, Stephen, 78, 87
Mary II, 3, 6, 187, 191, 218, 250, 318, 321
Mason, Captain John, 59, 60
Mather, Cotton, 53, 56, 64, 263
Mede, Joseph, 195, 196, 209
Miles, John, 131
Milton, John, 71, 84, 85, 86, 87, 89, 90, 115, 208

N

Naylor, James, 141
Nye Philip, 99, 279

O

Osgood, John, 153
Overton, Richard, 120
Owen, John, 134, 235, 299

P

Penn, William, 152, 153, 154
Perkins, William, 35, 43
Perry, John, 80, 136, 160
Peter, Hugh, 56, 57, 63, 155
Pooley, Christopher, 162, 292
Powell, Vavasor, 20, 148, 155, 163, 164, 165, 173, 182, 295
Prynne, William, 47, 48, 69, 71, 85, 195

R

Ravis, Christian, 3
Robinson, John, 35, 38

S

Saltmarsh, John, 23, 72, 89, 99, 101, 102, 108, 109, 110, 111,

Index of Names

112, 113, 114, 115, 148, 241, 280, 285, 298, 303
Sibbes, Richard, 35, 262, 263
Simpson, John, 76, 134, 163, 164, 165, 166, 167, 168
Simpson, Sidrach, 99
Smythe, John, 8, 37, 38, 144, 327
Spittlehouse, John, 291
Starbuck, Edward, 61
Stennet, Edward, 291
Stennet, Joseph, 293, 312
Sutton, Katherine, 177, 193, 282, 295, 304, 305

T

Tillam, Thomas, 132, 133, 143, 160, 161, 162, 163, 166, 168, 292, 295
Tombes, John, 36, 279, 280, 283, 285
Tomlins, Edward, 64
Tomlins, Timothy, 64
Trapnell, Anna, 166, 167, 304
Troeltsch, Ernst, 237, 238

U

Underhill, Captain John, 56, 57, 58, 60, 61, 63

V

Vane, Sir Henry, 50, 55, 69, 208
Venner, Thomas, 14, 157, 158, 160, 161, 169, 173, 192

W

Walwyn, William, 120, 121, 124
Whalley, Col. Edward, 77, 125, 126, 161
Wheelwright, John, 2, 40, 41, 47, 48, 49, 50, 51, 52, 54, 55, 61, 66, 112, 146, 262, 318
Whitehead, George, 152, 153
Whitelocke, Bulstrode, 128, 339
Wiggan, Thomas, 60
William III, 3, 6, 15, 187, 190, 218, 235, 236, 250, 311, 318, 321
Williams, Francis, 63
Williams, John, 3, 40, 46, 318
Williams, Roger, 35, 49, 53, 135, 159
Willoughby, Lady, 5th Baroness of Parham, 3, 138
Willoughby, Lord Francis, 5th Baron of Parham, 129, 137, 138, 339
Wills, Obediah, 186, 279
Wilson, John, 50
Winthrop, John, 3, 35, 47, 48, 49, 50, 51, 52, 53, 54, 55, 56, 57, 58, 59, 60, 61, 62, 63, 64, 65, 121, 319
Wollaston, Richard, 91, 124, 134

Z

Zwingli, Ulrich, 275, 276, 288, 289

Index of Places

B

Battle of Edgehill, 75, 76
Battle of Marston Moor, 87
Battle of Naseby, 88, 89
Benington, Lincsh., 39, 47
Biscathorpe, Lincsh., 29, 32
Boston, Lincsh., 39, 47, 49
Boston, Mass., 27, 35, 48, 49, 50, 51, 54, 55, 56, 57, 58, 62, 63, 64, 66, 129, 184, 187, 266, 271, 340

C

Cawkwell, Lincsh., 22, 29, 32, 34, 324, 326, 328
Charterhouse School, 3, 66, 266, 339

D

Dover, New Hampshire, 55, 56, 57, 59, 60, 61, 62, 63, 66, 77, 180, 240

E

Exeter, New Hampshire, 32, 51, 61

F

Fulletby, Lincsh., 46

G

Gainsborough, Lincsh., 37, 38, 66, 266
Gayton le Wold, Lincsh., 33
Germany, 2, 95, 126, 163, 175, 176, 178, 179, 204, 213, 267, 293, 333
Goulceby, Lincsh., 40, 338
Grimsby, Lincsh., 22, 29, 31, 32, 33, 34, 35, 38, 327, 337

H

Holland, 2, 8, 31, 35, 38, 39, 93, 137, 163, 175, 181, 188, 267, 278, 295, 327, 333
Horncastle, Lincsh., 29, 33, 331
Humberstone, Lincsh., 32, 37, 38, 39, 40, 73, 146, 150, 336

K

Kittery, New Hampshire, 64

L

Lincoln, 2, 3, 5, 22, 27, 29, 31, 32, 33, 35, 37, 40, 46, 135, 318, 325, 329, 331, 332, 333
Lincolnshire, 5, 28, 29, 30, 31, 32, 34, 36, 39, 40, 46, 47, 49, 65, 73, 134, 137, 138, 182, 320, 325, 326, 327, 328, 329, 330, 331, 333, 334, 336, 337, 338, 340, 341
Long Island, 64, 65
Louth, Lincsh., 22, 29

M

Maine, 55, 60
Massachusetts Bay Colony, 3, 27, 47, 48, 49, 51, 53, 54, 55, 56, 57, 59, 60, 61, 62, 63, 64, 65, 82, 131, 159, 235, 340

Index of Places 371

N

New England, 2, 3, 5, 8, 25, 27, 28, 35, 38, 47, 48, 49, 51, 52, 53, 54, 55, 56, 59, 60, 62, 64, 65, 66, 73, 74, 85, 103, 129, 131, 134, 135, 157, 158, 162, 184, 187, 240, 266, 271, 276, 277, 284, 303, 318, 331, 335, 338, 340

P

Piscataqua, New Hampshire, 51, 55, 59, 60, 61, 64
Plymouth, 134
Plymouth Plantation, 35, 38

R

Rhode Island, 35, 48, 49, 52, 157, 159, 161

Rotterdam, 162, 163, 177, 178, 282, 295, 333, 341

S

Scartho, Lincsh., 22, 25, 29, 31, 32, 33, 36, 38, 65, 134, 175, 182, 320, 330, 331, 332, 333, 334, 337

W

Wainfleet, Lincsh., 46
Wales, 4, 30, 130, 131, 132, 164, 165, 186, 218, 239, 248, 270, 281, 292, 294, 302, 312, 332, 333
Wood Enderby, Lincsh., 46
Wyberton, Lincsh., 39

General Index

A

A Representation of the Army, 92
A Solemn Engagement, 92
accommodation, 71, 86, 87, 89, 92, 94, 101, 106, 114, 121, 286
Acts and Declarations of Indulgence, 15, 185, 187, 190
Agreement of the People, 122, 125
amillennialism, 194, 223
anti-Catholicism, 15, 45, 187
antichrist, 208–14
Antichrist, the Beast, 83, 127, 139, 161, 167, 192, 193, 194, 195, 196, 197, 198, 200, 201, 203, 205, 206, 208, 209, 210, 211, 212, 213, 214, 216, 219, 221, 224, 225, 226, 232, 233, 241, 242, 243, 256, 321
antinomianism, 41, 53, 55, 81, 82, 250, 313
apocalypticism, 6, 25, 42, 69, 118, 158, 162, 168, 171, 172, 173, 178, 180, 183, 187, 188, 191, 192, 193, 194, 196, 197, 198, 199, 200, 207, 208, 209, 210, 213, 214, 229, 230, 231, 232, 240, 243, 258, 264, 321
apostasy, falling away, 95, 167, 210, 211, 216
Arminianism, 16, 69, 93, 142, 254
Associations, 21, 40, 41, 42, 48, 64, 95, 117, 118, 130, 131, 158, 162, 163, 165, 167, 168, 211, 239, 245, 246, 249, 259, 306, 322
atonement, 149

B

Baptism, 283–91
baptism, adult, 3, 119, 158, 277, 279
baptism, believer's, 5, 17, 20, 23, 45, 72, 73, 77, 79, 93, 94, 95, 100, 107, 109, 115, 118, 158, 165, 166, 169, 234, 277, 278, 279, 281, 285, 293, 303, 307, 319, 322
baptism, immersion, 95, 98, 99, 101, 113, 278, 280, 307
baptism, infant, 17, 63, 66, 77, 86, 93, 95, 133, 277, 278, 279, 281, 327
Baptist Confessions of faith, 3, 21, 72, 90, 92, 94, 95, 96, 97, 98, 100, 113, 116, 118, 126, 159, 168, 239, 242, 244, 245, 247, 259, 275, 279, 281, 283, 285, 302, 308, 320, 321
Baptist Confessions of Faith, 92–100
Battle of Armageddon, 196, 224, 226
Bill of Rights, 235, 318
blessing of children, 132
Brownists, 38, 318

C

Cambridge University, 2, 3, 28, 29, 30, 34, 35, 36, 37, 45, 47, 62, 65, 66, 69, 71, 73, 74, 76, 78, 88, 118, 120, 123, 141, 142, 146, 172, 188, 193, 196, 203, 231, 238, 266, 267, 318, 320, 324, 325, 326, 327, 328, 337

chaplains in the army, 3, 76, 77, 109, 137, 278, 339
Charles I - execution, 125, 128, 129, 155, 231
church discipline, 85, 102, 130, 242, 244, 248, 282, 284, 286, 308, 313, 314
Church of England, 2, 5, 7, 14, 27, 33, 36, 37, 40, 42, 45, 46, 49, 62, 65, 66, 69, 70, 71, 72, 76, 84, 86, 87, 94, 110, 117, 121, 131, 135, 140, 145, 155, 161, 167, 172, 178, 186, 204, 209, 234, 236, 237, 238, 240, 250, 254, 260, 263, 264, 270, 274, 277, 284, 286, 291, 311, 318, 319, 321, 327, 334, 338
Clarendon Code, 173, 267
communion, 240, 276, 277, 278, 282, 283, 284, 285, 286, 287, 288, 289, 290, 291, 292, 299, 300, 307, 308, 322
communion, closed, 285
communion, open, 284, 285, 308
Confession of 1644, 94, 95, 96, 97, 245, 246, 259, 281, 283
Confession of 1646, 80, 97, 98, 100, 108, 113, 116, 242, 244, 245, 259, 271, 275, 281, 283, 285
Confession of 1677, Second London Confession, 245, 247, 249, 250, 252, 254, 255, 256, 257, 259, 263, 265, 273, 274, 280, 281, 282, 283, 286, 287, 288, 291, 292, 293, 300
Confession of 1689, 186
congregationalism, 5, 8, 35, 42, 45, 54, 67, 72, 76, 87, 95, 100, 101, 105, 106, 107, 115, 127, 130, 234, 240, 243, 245, 319, 320
Conventicles Act, 14, 192, 200
conversion, conversionist theology, 41, 42, 43, 44, 45, 66, 77, 79, 81, 130, 144, 146, 166, 217, 225, 226, 232, 234, 251, 253, 258, 259, 260, 261, 262, 263, 265, 304, 307, 319, 321
corporate worship, 294, 305, 308
Cromwell's rule, 3, 6, 49, 120, 128, 129, 134, 135, 136, 151, 155, 156, 157, 158, 164, 167, 168, 173, 178, 235, 250, 268, 296, 320, 332, 334

D

death of Christ, 95, 98, 251, 278, 307
debates, disputations, 2, 3, 24, 27, 49, 50, 51, 54, 66, 71, 72, 77, 86, 87, 90, 94, 97, 98, 99, 100, 92–100, 101, 102, 105, 107, 114, 118, 123, 125, 132, 151, 152, 154, 158, 168, 185, 211, 239, 242, 247, 249, 262, 276, 277, 279, 281, 284, 292, 293, 294, 295, 300, 308, 313, 316, 319, 322, 327
Diggers, 8, 9, 11, 142, 156, 320
dissent, dissenters, 4, 7, 10, 12, 13, 15, 24, 26, 28, 46, 52, 85, 117, 119, 139, 155, 160, 163, 179, 180, 185, 186, 188, 189, 190, 191, 194, 201, 235, 236, 237, 248, 250, 254, 267, 269, 294, 301, 309, 310, 316, 318
Dover Combination, 61, 62, 63

E

ecclesiology, 3, 5, 8, 21, 23, 25, 35, 40, 41, 42, 45, 48, 54, 64, 67, 72, 76, 79, 85, 87, 95, 100, 101, 102, 105, 106, 107, 115, 117, 118, 127, 130, 131, 133, 134, 138, 139, 144, 158, 162, 163, 165, 167, 168, 205, 209, 211, 233, 234, 238, 239, 240,

242, 243, 244, 245, 246, 248, 249, 259, 264, 274, 282, 284, 286, 306, 307, 308, 313, 314, 319, 320, 321, 322
education, 2, 5, 26, 28, 33, 35, 36, 37, 38, 53, 65, 73, 74, 76, 97, 100, 103, 129, 132, 134, 135, 136, 137, 138, 142, 163, 175, 176, 177, 178, 179, 191, 263, 266, 267, 268, 269, 270, 271, 300, 301, 302, 305, 307, 309, 318, 320, 327, 328, 332, 336, 337, 339, 340, 341
Elect, 41, 44, 148, 196, 212, 226, 251, 253, 254, 256, 306
election, predestination, 41, 43, 44, 45, 50, 82, 95, 98, 119, 142, 143, 148, 161, 182, 196, 205, 212, 226, 234, 250, 251, 253, 254, 255, 256, 257, 259, 273, 282, 306, 308, 322
English Civil War, 3, 7, 10, 11, 19, 25, 28, 45, 68, 74, 75, 78, 83, 88, 89, 122, 123, 134, 158, 276, 301, 302, 319, 320, 330, 331
English Civil War - first war, 71, 84
English Civil War - second war, 123, 125, 332
English Commonwealth, 49, 120, 128, 129, 134, 136, 164, 173, 268
English Reformation, 8, 72, 193, 194, 196, 209
English Republic, 6, 129, 158, 320
English Revolution, 5, 7, 9, 10, 11, 12, 20, 21, 68, 69, 70, 75, 83, 84, 93, 96, 118, 119, 126, 141, 142, 143, 144, 150, 151, 169, 193, 197, 238, 260, 301
eschatology, 20, 21, 25, 69, 78, 82, 83, 85, 86, 90, 95, 110, 118, 127, 139, 144, 149, 154, 155, 156, 158, 159, 161, 165, 167,
172, 173, 180, 181, 188, 191, 192, 193, 194, 195, 196, 197, 198, 199, 200, 201, 203, 204, 205, 206, 207, 208, 209, 210, 211, 212, 213, 214, 215, 216, 217, 218, 219, 220, 221, 222, 223, 224, 225, 226, 227, 228, 229, 230, 231, 232, 233, 239, 241, 242, 243, 248, 256, 260, 262, 297, 298, 302, 305, 307, 311, 314, 321
Eschaton, Last days, Day of Yahweh, 228, 233
Eschaton, Last Days, Day of Yahweh, 228–30
Established Church, 2, 4, 5, 8, 10, 42, 85, 100, 134, 140, 142, 143, 146, 195, 205, 209, 233, 236, 238, 240, 249, 250, 263, 268, 273, 294, 308, 310, 318, 319, 321, 334
European Reformation, 2, 7, 12, 17, 69, 71, 193, 223, 237, 276, 288
evangelism, 259–63
evangelism, evangelical activity, 12, 19, 43, 44, 45, 48, 81, 95, 131, 132, 145, 148, 162, 194, 215, 226, 234, 237, 250, 258, 259, 296, 307, 322, 332
Exclusion Crisis, 15, 187, 205

F

False church, 210
false worship, 42, 45, 99, 139, 140, 145, 210, 211, 217, 240, 241, 251, 264, 276, 283, 287, 288, 289, 291, 308, 310
Fifth Monarchism, 3, 5, 9, 11, 13, 19, 20, 21, 23, 25, 26, 70, 117, 118, 119, 120, 135, 136, 155, 156, 157, 158, 159, 160, 161, 162, 163, 164, 165, 166, 167,

168, 155–69, 170, 173, 174, 192, 193, 195, 197, 230, 231, 232, 233, 241, 292, 295, 301, 304, 319, 320, 321
Final judgement, 78, 180, 199, 201, 206, 212, 214, 221, 228, 229
formalism, 42, 45, 99, 139, 140, 145, 291, 308, 310

G

Gathered church, 134
General Assembly of 1689, 4, 218, 219, 239, 247, 248, 249, 256, 259, 260, 270, 271, 273, 274, 284, 292, 293, 295, 302, 312, 322
General Assembly of 1691, 248
General Assembly of 1692, 248
general atonement, 93, 254
General Baptists, 16, 17, 19, 20, 37, 92, 93, 95, 96, 119, 122, 143, 144, 189, 254, 259, 284, 288, 327
Glorious Revolution, 13, 15, 172, 188, 191, 204, 210, 213, 218, 236, 250, 310, 318
Good Old Cause, 14, 156, 172
grace, 40, 41, 43, 44, 54, 66, 82, 95, 98, 140, 154, 162, 177, 183, 189, 237, 254, 263, 275, 280, 282, 287, 288, 289, 290, 291, 295, 296, 305, 308, 315, 317
Great Fire of London of 1666, 68, 173, 179, 180, 191, 200, 206
Great Plague of 1665, 146, 148, 179, 191, 200, 206

H

healing - supernatural, 40, 112, 119, 142, 145, 146, 147, 148, 150, 165, 179, 182, 218, 258, 312

holiness, 43, 54, 82, 133, 145, 197, 257, 261, 265
Holy Spirit - His work and gifts, 24, 42, 43, 44, 45, 81, 82, 105, 107, 110, 112, 113, 140, 141, 142, 144, 145, 148, 149, 150, 151, 215, 226, 233, 242, 251, 252, 256, 257, 258, 261, 262, 263, 265, 269, 270, 277, 280, 288, 295, 297, 305
House of Commons, 75, 77, 78, 83, 87, 88, 91, 123, 128, 137
House of Lords, 73, 75, 128, 135, 137, 235
hymn singing controversy, 294–300
hymns, hymn-singing, hymn-singing controversy, 132, 133, 232, 292, 294, 295, 297, 298, 299, 300, 304, 308, 311, 313, 316

I

imprisonment, 79, 80, 102, 121, 122, 149, 159, 160, 162, 165, 167, 173, 174, 178, 181, 183, 189, 191, 192, 212, 217, 283, 336
independence of the local church, 133, 134, 245, 249, 306, 322
Independents, 3, 6, 10, 11, 13, 20, 26, 42, 67, 70, 71, 72, 76, 77, 80, 83, 84, 85, 86, 87, 88, 89, 90, 83–92, 93, 95, 98, 99, 100, 101, 103, 104, 105, 106, 107, 108, 109, 110, 112, 114, 115, 117, 120, 121, 122, 132, 134, 144, 148, 151, 155, 156, 158, 159, 160, 165, 169, 174, 195, 236, 238, 242, 245, 246, 250, 254, 266, 276, 279, 284, 285, 294, 295, 306, 310, 319, 320, 334, 339

interdependence of the local churches, 245, 246, 249, 306, 322
Interregnum, 3, 135, 136, 151, 235, 296, 320, 332, 334
irresistible grace, effectual calling, 205, 254

J

Jacob/Lathrop/Jessey church, 8, 77, 79, 95, 99, 245, 246, 277, 278, 279, 303
Jews, conversion of, 159, 195, 196, 207, 224, 225, 226, 228, 232, 233, 241, 243, 256, 305, 321
justification, 49, 54, 114, 142, 154, 210, 216, 250, 257

K

Kingdom of Christ on Earth, rule of the Saints, millennial Kingdom, 85, 86, 118, 155, 196, 201, 205, 212, 215, 223, 224, 225, 226, 227, 229, 230, 233, 321
Knollys - children, 335–41
Knollys - army chaplain, 77, 125, 278, 319, 332, 339
Knollys - Artillery property dispute, 79, 175, 176, 178, 183, 184, 185, 266
Knollys - childhood, 25, 29, 34, 38, 66, 134, 257
Knollys - date of birth, 324–28
Knollys - government employment, 135, 136, 271, 320, 332
Knollys - illness, 147, 165, 183, 336
Knollys - language grammars, 34, 103, 163, 176, 267
Knollys - marriage, 39, 40, 73, 74, 103, 163, 175, 178, 182, 183, 278, 281, 303, 304, 305, 309, 316, 321, 324, 331, 335, 338, 339, 341
Knollys - merchant, 2, 136, 163, 178, 188, 271, 320
Knollys - ministry in Lincolnshire, 330–34
Knollys - New England, 48–65
Knollys - ordination, 28, 37, 40, 66, 78, 146, 260, 266, 274, 277, 286
Knollys - pastoral ministry, churches, 2, 40, 56, 79, 129, 132, 133, 134, 136, 160, 161, 162, 175, 178, 181, 185, 188, 246, 247, 266, 279, 311, 319, 320, 330, 331, 333, 334
Knollys - personal trials, 180–85
Knollys - prison, 79, 80, 157, 163, 174, 181, 188, 320

L

Laudian church, Laudianism, 45, 46, 62, 66, 67, 69, 75, 76, 85, 102, 310, 319, 338
laying on of hands, 133, 273, 291
legalism, 42, 217, 291
Levellers, 3, 5, 8, 9, 10, 11, 12, 13, 19, 21, 23, 70, 88, 117, 118, 119, 120, 121, 122, 123, 124, 125, 126, 127, 120–27, 135, 142, 144, 169, 170, 241, 320, 330
liberty of conscience, 5, 6, 51, 55, 67, 71, 86, 97, 98, 101, 108, 112, 114, 238
limited atonement, 148, 205, 254, 255
Lord's supper, 283–91

M

messengers, 48, 115, 132, 162, 296
Militia Bill, 73

General Index 377

Millennium, millenarianism, 20, 69, 86, 118, 144, 155, 156, 158, 165, 192, 193, 194, 195, 196, 197, 198, 200, 206, 214, 221, 222, 223, 224, 225, 227, 223–28, 229, 230, 231, 233, 260, 302, 321
ministers and ministry, 263–75
ministry, 2, 5, 23, 28, 38, 39, 40, 41, 42, 46, 50, 66, 78, 79, 81, 82, 95, 100, 112, 129, 130, 131, 134, 139, 142, 143, 148, 162, 166, 176, 177, 191, 200, 218, 239, 247, 248, 260, 264, 265, 269, 270, 271, 272, 273, 275, 284, 300, 302, 303, 304, 305, 306, 309, 311, 316, 318, 322
ministry - professional, 264, 270, 271, 272, 273, 307, 322
ministry - professional, educated, 270, 271, 274, 307
monarchy, 6, 16, 100, 155, 160, 161, 164, 167, 173, 192, 318, 320

N

national church, state church, 6, 31, 85, 87, 217, 221, 232, 233, 237, 238, 242, 321
New Model Army, 71, 77, 84, 88, 89, 91, 92, 122, 123, 125, 126, 141, 163, 332
nonconformity, 2, 10, 11, 12, 13, 14, 15, 16, 28, 31, 42, 46, 66, 143, 175, 179, 192, 194, 267, 316, 318, 319, 327

O

order, 1, 4, 5, 6, 21, 24, 53, 58, 65, 68, 69, 87, 110, 119, 157, 169, 174, 187, 197, 227, 230, 234, 237, 238, 239, 242, 249, 264, 274, 275, 281, 284, 302, 305, 306, 309, 318, 320, 323, 333
ordination, 2, 5, 35, 36, 37, 40, 72, 78, 103, 133, 145, 246, 254, 259, 260, 263, 264, 270, 273, 274, 275, 280, 281, 283, 293, 312, 318, 320, 327
original sin, 95, 98
Oxford University, 7, 11, 12, 14, 27, 28, 31, 32, 40, 43, 45, 46, 68, 75, 83, 86, 87, 90, 91, 92, 93, 118, 119, 120, 123, 128, 136, 141, 142, 144, 155, 157, 163, 164, 169, 172, 174, 179, 187, 193, 195, 236, 237, 238, 240, 246, 250, 251, 293, 296, 301, 310, 312, 314, 318, 327, 338

P

Parliament, 6, 15, 45, 63, 69, 71, 72, 73, 75, 78, 80, 83, 84, 85, 86, 87, 88, 89, 90, 91, 92, 93, 94, 96, 101, 118, 120, 125, 126, 127, 128, 132, 134, 135, 137, 141, 155, 161, 162, 172, 180, 185, 189, 190, 194, 204, 235, 250, 318, 320, 330, 331, 332
Parliament, Barebones, 120
Parliament, Cavalier, 172, 173, 250
Parliament, Long, 3, 65, 69, 70, 71, 72, 78, 83, 87, 120, 137, 155, 172
Parliament, Rump, 120, 134, 164
Parliamentarians, 6, 71, 83, 88, 128, 320
Parliamentary Army, 76, 84, 109, 120, 123, 332
persecution, 2, 3, 5, 6, 7, 14, 18, 23, 26, 27, 48, 56, 58, 67, 69, 70, 71, 80, 84, 87, 97, 100, 102, 106, 114, 119, 136, 139, 151,

163, 172, 173, 179, 180, 182, 185, 186, 188, 191, 194, 201, 202, 204, 209, 212, 213, 215, 218, 234, 235, 236, 244, 246, 248, 251, 271, 301, 306, 310, 311, 318, 319, 320, 321, 338, 341
perseverance of the saints, assurance of salvation, 26, 98, 140, 251, 254, 256, 257, 306
Perseverance of the saints, assurance of salvation, 43, 44, 54, 58, 149, 202, 256, 257, 262, 281, 333
Pope, Papacy, 85, 102, 187, 193, 194, 196, 197, 203, 207, 208, 209, 210, 211, 233, 238, 241, 287, 321
Popish Plot, 15, 180, 185, 187, 197, 203, 211, 213
popishness, 14, 73, 75, 83, 187, 188, 194, 233
postmillennialism, 223, 224, 227, 229, 233, 260
prayer, 42, 112, 146, 147, 150, 182, 186, 210, 220, 232, 273, 292, 297, 300, 305, 314
preaching, itinerant, 42, 46, 80, 128, 130, 131, 143, 165, 234, 259, 260, 319, 338
preaching, lay, 71, 76, 91, 119, 307
preaching, preachers, 2, 3, 37, 38, 40, 41, 42, 44, 46, 50, 54, 55, 56, 62, 66, 76, 78, 79, 80, 81, 82, 83, 84, 85, 86, 89, 91, 96, 104, 106, 112, 115, 128, 129, 130, 131, 132, 141, 142, 143, 146, 148, 149, 158, 164, 165, 166, 167, 174, 181, 185, 188, 189, 195, 213, 216, 226, 232, 234, 249, 258, 259, 260, 261, 262, 263, 264, 266, 269, 277, 280, 291, 293, 301, 303, 304,

311, 315, 318, 319, 331, 332, 338
premillennialism, 223, 224, 227, 229, 233
preparationists, preparationism, 43, 44, 45, 54, 81, 144, 145, 263, 307
Presbyterians, 3, 10, 11, 13, 16, 69, 70, 71, 72, 74, 76, 80, 81, 83, 84, 85, 86, 87, 88, 89, 90, 91, 92, 83–92, 95, 96, 98, 99, 100, 101, 102, 103, 104, 105, 106, 108, 109, 110, 114, 117, 118, 120, 122, 123, 125, 135, 137, 139, 140, 141, 151, 155, 156, 174, 186, 188, 210, 236, 238, 250, 254, 264, 276, 282, 294, 306, 310, 320, 321, 330, 334
priesthood of believers, 244, 264, 274, 306, 322
Protectorate, 6, 120, 155, 156, 157, 158, 164, 167, 168, 178, 250, 320
providence, divine, 181, 191, 251, 257, 258, 306
Puritanism, 2, 5, 13, 26, 27, 28, 35, 36, 38, 40, 42, 43, 44, 45, 46, 49, 52, 53, 54, 55, 57, 60, 62, 64, 66, 70, 74, 78, 81, 82, 83, 85, 93, 100, 109, 119, 128, 140, 142, 143, 144, 148, 151, 164, 192, 193, 194, 195, 196, 205, 231, 237, 240, 249, 250, 251, 254, 257, 262, 263, 268, 277, 284, 286, 289, 291, 303, 304, 307, 318, 319, 322, 327

Q

Quakers, 3, 5, 9, 11, 13, 23, 70, 92, 117, 119, 120, 135, 141, 142, 143, 144, 145, 146, 148, 149, 150, 151, 152, 153, 154, 141–54, 169, 170, 173, 174, 186,

General Index 379

208, 238, 241, 254, 264, 292, 299, 301, 302, 310, 320
Quakers' inner light, 119, 142, 146, 149, 150, 151

R

Ranters, 8, 9, 11, 13, 70, 80, 135, 142, 238, 264, 292
recreation, 206, 221, 228
Reformed theology, Calvinism, 17, 25, 26, 27, 28, 36, 41, 43, 45, 46, 65, 81, 84, 86, 87, 89, 95, 118, 140, 205, 250, 251, 254, 255, 259, 261, 262, 278, 282, 286, 288, 308, 319, 322
religious liberty, 18, 23, 24, 70, 108, 118, 122
republicanism, 68, 128, 155, 160, 161
Restoration of Charles II, 6, 13, 16, 27, 91, 128, 130, 138, 141, 146, 151, 155, 156, 157, 161, 164, 171, 172, 191, 211, 235, 246, 250, 251, 267, 269, 271, 283, 301, 306, 317, 318
resurrection of Christ, 95, 98, 278, 293, 307, 308
Resurrection of the saints, 154, 195, 206, 214, 215, 221, 228, 229
Roman Catholic Church, 7, 8, 15, 24, 132, 139, 140, 170, 178, 180, 187, 188, 189, 190, 191, 193, 195, 199, 202, 203, 206, 207, 209, 210, 211, 213, 217, 224, 233, 251, 275, 289, 321
Royalists, 78, 83, 87, 89, 120, 125, 137, 331
Royalists, Royalist army, 75

S

sacraments, 141, 211, 239, 276, 280, 283, 287, 288, 289, 322
sacraments/ordinances, 276–77
salvation, children, 282
sanctification, perseverance, 26, 43, 49, 54, 82, 98, 140, 150, 250, 251, 254, 256, 257, 258, 306
sanctification, perseverance, assurance of salvation, 43, 54, 82, 133, 145, 197, 257, 261, 265
Savoy Declaration, 186, 254
Scripture, 6, 36, 38, 41, 42, 66, 85, 96, 98, 100, 101, 103, 104, 105, 107, 111, 112, 113, 114, 115, 118, 119, 137, 138, 142, 144, 149, 150, 153, 154, 176, 180, 198, 202, 203, 206, 207, 208, 209, 221, 222, 224, 232, 240, 245, 255, 257, 258, 267, 268, 270, 277, 279, 280, 281, 286, 287, 291, 292, 295, 297, 299, 300, 302, 307, 311, 321
Scrooby congregation, 38
second coming of Christ, 214–23
second coming, Christ's return, 86, 110, 192, 193, 194, 196, 198, 201, 205, 206, 207, 214, 217, 220, 222, 223, 225, 227, 233, 262, 321
sects, sectarian, 3, 6, 8, 12, 20, 22, 23, 70, 76, 87, 88, 89, 90, 114, 117, 119, 120, 121, 122, 123, 134, 135, 147, 151, 155, 156, 157, 169, 174, 193, 197, 237, 238, 239, 264, 268, 300, 302, 303, 305, 309, 317, 320, 321
Seekers, 8, 11, 13, 49, 70, 107, 108, 109, 112, 117, 142, 299
Self Denying Ordinance, 84
separation of Church and State, 124
Separatism, 7, 8, 10, 12, 28, 37, 86, 89, 93, 95, 96, 99, 195, 237, 240
Separatism, separation, 5, 8, 40, 50, 87, 93, 108, 121, 124, 140,

197, 217, 240, 241, 244, 287, 318, 319, 334, 336, 338
Seven Vials, 199, 224
seventh-day Baptists, 292–94
signs of Christ's return, 90, 215, 220, 222
Solemn League and Covenant, 84, 331
soteriology, 25, 26, 40, 41, 43, 44, 45, 49, 50, 54, 58, 66, 82, 93, 95, 98, 114, 119, 133, 140, 142, 143, 145, 146, 148, 149, 150, 154, 161, 162, 169, 177, 182, 183, 189, 196, 197, 202, 205, 210, 212, 216, 220, 226, 234, 237, 239, 250, 251, 252, 253, 254, 255, 256, 257, 258, 259, 261, 262, 263, 265, 273, 275, 278, 280, 281, 282, 287, 288, 289, 290, 291, 293, 295, 296, 305, 306, 307, 308, 315, 317, 322, 333
Spiritual illumination, 119, 142, 145, 148, 261
St. Catherine's Hall, Cambridge University, 35, 327, 328
St. Giles Church, 29, 134, 330, 331, 333, 334

T

The Heads of the Proposals, 92
The Humble Proposals, 134, 135, 140
Tithes, 91, 134, 145, 158, 232, 236, 248, 333, 334
Toleration Act, 235, 236, 237, 239, 250, 306, 318, 321
Toleration Bill, 235
toleration, religious toleration, 2, 3, 6, 15, 26, 35, 69, 71, 72, 81, 84, 85, 89, 90, 91, 100, 107, 108, 109, 112, 113, 114, 118, 119, 121, 125, 127, 135, 144, 158, 169, 173, 185, 187, 188, 235, 237, 238, 239, 286, 306, 310, 318, 319, 323
total depravity, sinful human nature, 95, 98, 205, 251, 253, 263, 306
transubstantiation, 211, 276, 283, 287, 288, 289
True church, pure church, 244
Turks, 196, 207, 209, 224, 226, 233
two witnesses of Revelation, 204

U

uniformity, 69, 84, 98, 101, 102, 117, 139, 140, 235
unity, 53, 101, 109, 235, 242, 286

W

Westminster Assembly, 72, 77, 78, 79, 84, 86, 107, 118, 250, 276, 330
Westminster Confession, 140, 186, 254, 277
Whore of Babylon, 149, 199, 200, 203, 204, 210, 321
women, 2, 11, 12, 19, 47, 50, 51, 52, 53, 55, 59, 80, 97, 119, 142, 266, 280, 294, 298, 299, 300, 301, 302, 303, 304, 305, 308, 331
women - controversy, 50, 51, 52, 53, 54, 166, 167, 262, 295, 301, 302, 304, 305
women - role and activities in Baptist churches, 167, 177, 193, 282, 295, 296, 300, 301, 302, 303, 304, 305, 308, 322
women - role in Particular Baptist churches, 300–305

Studies in Baptist History and Thought

(All titles uniform with this volume)
Dates in bold are of projected publication
Volumes in this series are not always published in sequence

David Bebbington and Anthony R. Cross (eds)
Global Baptist History
(SBHT vol. 14)

This book brings together studies from the Second International Conference on Baptist Studies which explore different facets of Baptist life and work especially during the twentieth century.

2006 / 1-84227-214-4 / approx. 350pp

David Bebbington (ed.)
The Gospel in the World
International Baptist Studies
(SBHT vol. 1)

This volume of essays from the First International Conference on Baptist Studies deals with a range of subjects spanning Britain, North America, Europe, Asia and the Antipodes. Topics include studies on religious tolerance, the communion controversy and the development of the international Baptist community, and concludes with two important essays on the future of Baptist life that pay special attention to the United States.

2002 / 1-84227-118-0 / xiv + 362pp

John H.Y. Briggs (ed.)
Pulpit and People
Studies in Eighteenth-Century English Baptist Life and Thought
(SBHT vol. 28)

The eighteenth century was a crucial time in Baptist history. The denomination had its roots in seventeenth-century English Puritanism and Separatism and the persecution of the Stuart kings with only a limited measure of freedom after 1689. Worse, however, was to follow for with toleration came doctrinal conflict, a move away from central Christian understandings and a loss of evangelistic urgency. Both spiritual and numerical decline ensued, to the extent that the denomination was virtually reborn as rather belatedly it came to benefit from the Evangelical Revival which brought new life to both Arminian and Calvinistic Baptists. The papers in this volume study a denomination in transition, and relate to theology, their views of the church and its mission, Baptist spirituality, and engagements with radical politics.

2007 / 1-84227-403-1 / approx. 350pp

July 2005

Damian Brot
Church of the Baptized or Church of Believers?
A Contribution to the Dialogue between the Catholic Church and the Free Churches with Special Reference to Baptists
(SBHT vol. 26)

The dialogue between the Catholic Church and the Free Churches in Europe has hardly taken place. This book pleads for a commencement of such a conversation. It offers, among other things, an introduction to the American and the international dialogues between Baptists and the Catholic Church and strives to allow these conversations to become fruitful in the European context as well.

2006 / 1-84227-334-5 / approx. 364pp

Dennis Bustin
Paradox and Perseverence
Hanserd Knollys, Particular Baptist Pioneer in Seventeenth-Century England
(SBHT vol. 23)

The seventeenth century was a significant period in English history during which the people of England experienced unprecedented change and tumult in all spheres of life. At the same time, the importance of order and the traditional institutions of society were being reinforced. Hanserd Knollys, born during this pivotal period, personified in his life the ambiguity, tension and paradox of it, openly seeking change while at the same time cautiously embracing order. As a founder and leader of the Particular Baptists in London and despite persecution and personal hardship, he played a pivotal role in helping shape their identity externally in society and, internally, as they moved toward becoming more formalised by the end of the century.

2006 / 1-84227-259-4 / approx. 324pp

Anthony R. Cross
Baptism and the Baptists
Theology and Practice in Twentieth-Century Britain
(SBHT vol. 3)

At a time of renewed interest in baptism, *Baptism and the Baptists* is a detailed study of twentieth-century baptismal theology and practice and the factors which have influenced its development.

2000 / 0-85364-959-6 / xx + 530pp

Anthony R. Cross and Philip E. Thompson (eds)
Baptist Sacramentalism
(SBHT vol. 5)

This collection of essays includes biblical, historical and theological studies in the theology of the sacraments from a Baptist perspective. Subjects explored include the physical side of being spiritual, baptism, the Lord's supper, the church, ordination, preaching, worship, religious liberty and the issue of disestablishment.

2003 / 1-84227-119-9 / xvi + 278pp

Anthony R. Cross and Philip E. Thompson (eds)
Baptist Sacramentalism 2
(SBHT vol. 25)

This second collection of essays exploring various dimensions of sacramental theology from a Baptist perspective includes biblical, historical and theological studies from scholars from around the world.

2006 / 1-84227-325-6 / approx. 350pp

Paul S. Fiddes
Tracks and Traces
Baptist Identity in Church and Theology
(SBHT vol. 13)

This is a comprehensive, yet unusual, book on the faith and life of Baptist Christians. It explores the understanding of the church, ministry, sacraments and mission from a thoroughly theological perspective. In a series of interlinked essays, the author relates Baptist identity consistently to a theology of covenant and to participation in the triune communion of God.

2003 / 1-84227-120-2 / xvi + 304pp

Stanley K. Fowler
More Than a Symbol
The British Baptist Recovery of Baptismal Sacramentalism
(SBHT vol. 2)

Fowler surveys the entire scope of British Baptist literature from the seventeenth-century pioneers onwards. He shows that in the twentieth century leading British Baptist pastors and theologians recovered an understanding of baptism that connected experience with soteriology and that in doing so they were recovering what many of their forebears had taught.

2002 / 1-84227-052-4 / xvi + 276pp

Steven R. Harmon
Towards Baptist Catholicity
Essays on Tradition and the Baptist Vision
(SBHT vol. 27)

This series of essays contends that the reconstruction of the Baptist vision in the wake of modernity's dissolution requires a retrieval of the ancient ecumenical tradition that forms Christian identity through rehearsal and practice. Themes explored include catholic identity as an emerging trend in Baptist theology, tradition as a theological category in Baptist perspective, Baptist confessions and the patristic tradition, worship as a principal bearer of tradition, and the role of Baptist higher education in shaping the Christian vision.

2006 / 1-84227-362-0 / approx. 210pp

Michael A.G. Haykin (ed.)
'At the Pure Fountain of Thy Word'
Andrew Fuller as an Apologist
(SBHT vol. 6)

One of the greatest Baptist theologians of the eighteenth and early nineteenth centuries, Andrew Fuller has not had justice done to him. There is little doubt that Fuller's theology lay behind the revitalization of the Baptists in the late eighteenth century and the first few decades of the nineteenth. This collection of essays fills a much needed gap by examining a major area of Fuller's thought, his work as an apologist.

2004 / 1-84227-171-7 / xxii + 276pp

Michael A.G. Haykin
Studies in Calvinistic Baptist Spirituality
(SBHT vol. 15)

In a day when spirituality is in vogue and Christian communities are looking for guidance in this whole area, there is wisdom in looking to the past to find untapped wells. The Calvinistic Baptists, heirs of the rich ecclesial experience in the Puritan era of the seventeenth century, but, by the end of the eighteenth century, also passionately engaged in the catholicity of the Evangelical Revivals, are such a well. This collection of essays, covering such things as the Lord's Supper, friendship and hymnody, seeks to draw out the spiritual riches of this community for reflection and imitation in the present day.

2006 / 1-84227-149-0 / approx. 350pp

Brian Haymes, Anthony R. Cross and Ruth Gouldbourne
On Being the Church
Revisioning Baptist Identity
(SBHT vol. 21)

The aim of the book is to re-examine Baptist theology and practice in the light of the contemporary biblical, theological, ecumenical and missiological context drawing on historical and contemporary writings and issues. It is not a study in denominationalism but rather seeks to revision historical insights from the believers' church tradition for the sake of Baptists and other Christians in the context of the modern–postmodern context.
2006 / 1-84227-121-0 / approx. 350pp

Ken R. Manley
From Woolloomooloo to 'Eternity': A History of Australian Baptists
Volume 1: Growing an Australian Church (1831–1914)
Volume 2: A National Church in a Global Community (1914–2005)
(SBHT vols 16.1 and 16.2)

From their beginnings in Australia in 1831 with the first baptisms in Woolloomoolloo Bay in 1832, this pioneering study describes the quest of Baptists in the different colonies (states) to discover their identity as Australians and Baptists. Although institutional developments are analyzed and the roles of significant individuals traced, the major focus is on the social and theological dimensions of the Baptist movement.
2 vol. set 2006 / 1-84227-405-8 / approx. 900pp

Ken R. Manley
'Redeeming Love Proclaim'
John Rippon and the Baptists
(SBHT vol. 12)

A leading exponent of the new moderate Calvinism which brought new life to many Baptists, John Rippon (1751–1836) helped unite the Baptists at this significant time. His many writings expressed the denomination's growing maturity and mutual awareness of Baptists in Britain and America, and exerted a long-lasting influence on Baptist worship and devotion. In his various activities, Rippon helped conserve the heritage of Old Dissent and promoted the evangelicalism of the New Dissent
2004 / 1-84227-193-8 / xviii + 340pp

Peter J. Morden
Offering Christ to the World
Andrew Fuller and the Revival of English Particular Baptist Life
(SBHT vol. 8)

Andrew Fuller (1754–1815) was one of the foremost English Baptist ministers of his day. His career as an Evangelical Baptist pastor, theologian, apologist and missionary statesman coincided with the profound revitalization of the Particular Baptist denomination to which he belonged. This study examines the key aspects of the life and thought of this hugely significant figure, and gives insights into the revival in which he played such a central part.

2003 / 1-84227-141-5 / xx + 202pp

Peter Naylor
Calvinism, Communion and the Baptists
A Study of English Calvinistic Baptists from the Late 1600s to the Early 1800s
(SBHT vol. 7)

Dr Naylor argues that the traditional link between 'high-Calvinism' and 'restricted communion' is in need of revision. He examines Baptist communion controversies from the late 1600s to the early 1800s and also the theologies of John Gill and Andrew Fuller.

2003 / 1-84227-142-3 / xx + 266pp

Ian M. Randall, Toivo Pilli and Anthony R. Cross (eds)
Baptist Identities
International Studies from the Seventeenth to the Twentieth Centuries
(SBHT vol. 19)

These papers represent the contributions of scholars from various parts of the world as they consider the factors that have contributed to Baptist distinctiveness in different countries and at different times. The volume includes specific case studies as well as broader examinations of Baptist life in a particular country or region. Together they represent an outstanding resource for understanding Baptist identities.

2005 / 1-84227-215-2 / approx. 350pp

James M. Renihan
Edification and Beauty
The Practical Ecclesiology of the English Particular Baptists, 1675–1705
(SBHT vol. 17)

Edification and Beauty describes the practices of the Particular Baptist churches at the end of the seventeenth century in terms of three concentric circles: at the centre is the ecclesiological material in the Second London Confession, which is then fleshed out in the various published writings of the men associated with these churches, and, finally, expressed in the church books of the era.

2005 / 1-84227-251-9 / approx. 230pp

Frank Rinaldi
'The Tribe of Dan'
A Study of the New Connexion of General Baptists 1770–1891
(SBHT vol. 10)

'The Tribe of Dan' is a thematic study which explores the theology, organizational structure, evangelistic strategy, ministry and leadership of the New Connexion of General Baptists as it experienced the process of institutionalization in the transition from a revival movement to an established denomination.

2006 / 1-84227-143-1 / approx. 350pp

Peter Shepherd
The Making of a Modern Denomination
John Howard Shakespeare and the English Baptists 1898–1924
(SBHT vol. 4)

John Howard Shakespeare introduced revolutionary change to the Baptist denomination. The Baptist Union was transformed into a strong central institution and Baptist ministers were brought under its control. Further, Shakespeare's pursuit of church unity reveals him as one of the pioneering ecumenists of the twentieth century.

2001 / 1-84227-046-X / xviii + 220pp

Karen Smith
The Community and the Believers
A Study of Calvinistic Baptist Spirituality in Some Towns and Villages of Hampshire and the Borders of Wiltshire, c.1730–1830
(SBHT vol. 22)

The period from 1730 to 1830 was one of transition for Calvinistic Baptists. Confronted by the enthusiasm of the Evangelical Revival, congregations within the denomination as a whole were challenged to find a way to take account of the revival experience. This study examines the life and devotion of Calvinistic Baptists in Hampshire and Wiltshire during this period. Among this group of Baptists was the hymn writer, Anne Steele.

2005 / 1-84227-326-4 / approx. 280pp

Martin Sutherland
Dissenters in a 'Free Land'
Baptist Thought in New Zealand 1850–2000
(SBHT vol. 24)

Baptists in New Zealand were forced to recast their identity. Conventions of communication and association, state and ecumenical relations, even historical divisions and controversies had to be revised in the face of new topographies and constraints. As Baptists formed themselves in a fluid society they drew heavily on both international movements and local dynamics. This book traces the development of ideas which shaped institutions and styles in sometimes surprising ways.

2006 / 1-84227-327-2 / approx. 230pp

Brian Talbot
The Search for a Common Identity
The Origins of the Baptist Union of Scotland 1800–1870
(SBHT vol. 9)

In the period 1800 to 1827 there were three streams of Baptists in Scotland: Scotch, Haldaneite and 'English' Baptist. A strong commitment to home evangelization brought these three bodies closer together, leading to a merger of their home missionary societies in 1827. However, the first three attempts to form a union of churches failed, but by the 1860s a common understanding of their corporate identity was attained leading to the establishment of the Baptist Union of Scotland.

2003 / 1-84227-123-7 / xviii + 402pp

Philip E. Thompson
The Freedom of God
Towards Baptist Theology in Pneumatological Perspective
(SBHT vol. 20)

This study contends that the range of theological commitments of the early Baptists are best understood in relation to their distinctive emphasis on the freedom of God. Thompson traces how this was recast anthropocentrically, leading to an emphasis upon human freedom from the nineteenth century onwards. He seeks to recover the dynamism of the early vision via a pneumatologically-oriented ecclesiology defining the church in terms of the memory of God.

2006 / 1-84227-125-3 / approx. 350pp

Philip E. Thompson and Anthony R. Cross (eds)
Recycling the Past or Researching History?
Studies in Baptist Historiography and Myths
(SBHT vol. 11)

In this volume an international group of Baptist scholars examine and re-examine areas of Baptist life and thought about which little is known or the received wisdom is in need of revision. Historiographical studies include the date Oxford Baptists joined the Abingdon Association, the death of the Fifth Monarchist John Pendarves, eighteenth-century Calvinistic Baptists and the political realm, confessional identity and denominational institutions, Baptist community, ecclesiology, the priesthood of all believers, soteriology, Baptist spirituality, Strict and Reformed Baptists, the role of women among British Baptists, while various 'myths' challenged include the nature of high-Calvinism in eighteenth-century England, baptismal anti-sacramentalism, episcopacy, and Baptists and change.

2005 / 1-84227-122-9 / approx. 330pp

Linda Wilson
Marianne Farningham
A Plain Working Woman
(SBHT vol. 18)

Marianne Farningham, of College Street Baptist Chapel, Northampton, was a household name in evangelical circles in the later nineteenth century. For over fifty years she produced comment, poetry, biography and fiction for the popular Christian press. This investigation uses her writings to explore the beliefs and behaviour of evangelical Nonconformists, including Baptists, during these years.

2006 / 1-84227-124-5 / approx. 250pp

Other Paternoster titles relating to Baptist history and thought

George R. Beasley-Murray
Baptism in the New Testament
(Paternoster Digital Library)

This is a welcome reprint of a classic text on baptism originally published in 1962 by one of the leading Baptist New Testament scholars of the twentieth century. Dr Beasley-Murray's comprehensive study begins by investigating the antecedents of Christian baptism. It then surveys the foundation of Christian baptism in the Gospels, its emergence in the Acts of the Apostles and development in the apostolic writings. Following a section relating baptism to New Testament doctrine, a substantial discussion of the origin and significance of infant baptism leads to a briefer consideration of baptismal reform and ecumenism.

2005 / 1-84227-300-0 / x + 422pp

Paul Beasley-Murray
Fearless for Truth
A Personal Portrait of the Life of George Beasley-Murray

Without a doubt George Beasley-Murray was one of the greatest Baptists of the twentieth century. A long-standing Principal of Spurgeon's College, he wrote more than twenty books and made significant contributions in the study of areas as diverse as baptism and eschatology, as well as writing highly respected commentaries on the Book of Revelation and John's Gospel.

2002 / 1-84227-134-2 / xii + 244pp

David Bebbington
Holiness in Nineteenth-Century England
(Studies in Christian History and Thought)

David Bebbington stresses the relationship of movements of spirituality to changes in their cultural setting, especially the legacies of the Enlightenment and Romanticism. He shows that these broad shifts in ideological mood had a profound effect on the ways in which piety was conceptualized and practised. Holiness was intimately bound up with the spirit of the age.

2000 / 0-85364-981-2 / viii + 98pp

July 2005

Clyde Binfield
Victorian Nonconformity in Eastern England 1840–1885
(Studies in Evangelical History and Thought)

Studies of Victorian religion and society often concentrate on cities, suburbs, and industrialisation. This study provides a contrast. Victorian Eastern England—Essex, Suffolk, Norfolk, Cambridgeshire, and Huntingdonshire—was rural, traditional, relatively unchanging. That is nonetheless a caricature which discounts the industry in Norwich and Ipswich (as well as in Haverhill, Stowmarket and Leiston) and ignores the impact of London on Essex, of railways throughout the region, and of an ancient but changing university (Cambridge) on the county town which housed it. It also entirely ignores the political implications of such changes in a region noted for the variety of its religious Dissent since the seventeenth century. This book explores Victorian Eastern England and its Nonconformity. It brings to a wider readership a pioneering thesis which has made a major contribution to a fresh evolution of English religion and society.

2006 / 1-84227-216-0 / approx. 274pp

Edward W. Burrows
'To Me To Live Is Christ'
A Biography of Peter H. Barber

This book is about a remarkably gifted and energetic man of God. Peter H. Barber was born into a Brethren family in Edinburgh in 1930. In his youth he joined Charlotte Baptist Chapel and followed the call into Baptist ministry. For eighteen years he was the pioneer minister of the new congregation in the New Town of East Kilbride, which planted two further congregations. At the age of thirty-nine he served as Centenary President of the Baptist Union of Scotland and then exercised an influential ministry for over seven years in the well-known Upton Vale Baptist Church, Torquay. From 1980 until his death in 1994 he was General Secretary of the Baptist Union of Scotland. Through his work for the European Baptist Federation and the Baptist World Alliance he became a world Baptist statesman. He was President of the EBF during the upheaval that followed the collapse of Communism.

2005 / 1-84227-324-8 / xxii + 236pp

Christopher J. Clement
Religious Radicalism in England 1535–1565
(Rutherford Studies in Historical Theology)

In this valuable study Christopher Clement draws our attention to a varied assemblage of people who sought Christian faithfulness in the underworld of mid-Tudor England. Sympathetically and yet critically he assess their place in the history of English Protestantism, and by attentive listening he gives them a voice.

1997 / 0-946068-44-5 / xxii + 426pp

July 2005

Anthony R. Cross (ed.)
Ecumenism and History
Studies in Honour of John H.Y. Briggs
(Studies in Christian History and Thought)

This collection of essays examines the inter-relationships between the two fields in which Professor Briggs has contributed so much: history—particularly Baptist and Nonconformist—and the ecumenical movement. With contributions from colleagues and former research students from Britain, Europe and North America, *Ecumenism and History* provides wide-ranging studies in important aspects of Christian history, theology and ecumenical studies.

2002 / 1-84227-135-0 / xx + 362pp

Keith E. Eitel
Paradigm Wars
*The Southern Baptist International Mission Board
Faces the Third Millennium*
(Regnum Studies in Mission)

The International Mission Board of the Southern Baptist Convention is the largest denominational mission agency in North America. This volume chronicles the historic and contemporary forces that led to the IMB's recent extensive reorganization, providing the most comprehensive case study to date of a historic mission agency restructuring to continue its mission purpose into the twenty-first century more effectively.

2000 / 1-870345-12-6 / x + 140pp

Ruth Gouldbourne
The Flesh and the Feminine
Gender and Theology in the Writings of Caspar Schwenckfeld
(Studies in Christian History and Thought)

Caspar Schwenckfeld and his movement exemplify one of the radical communities of the sixteenth century. Challenging theological and liturgical norms, they also found themselves challenging social and particularly gender assumptions. In this book, the issues of the relationship between radical theology and the understanding of gender are considered.

2005 / 1-84227-048-6 / approx. 304pp

July 2005

David Hilborn
The Words of our Lips
Language-Use in Free Church Worship
(Paternoster Theological Monographs)
Studies of liturgical language have tended to focus on the written canons of Roman Catholic and Anglican communities. By contrast, David Hilborn analyses the more extemporary approach of English Nonconformity. Drawing on recent developments in linguistic pragmatics, he explores similarities and differences between 'fixed' and 'free' worship, and argues for the interdependence of each.

2006 / 0-85364-977-4

Stephen R. Holmes
Listening to the Past
The Place of Tradition in Theology
Beginning with the question 'Why can't we just read the Bible?' Stephen Holmes considers the place of tradition in theology, showing how the doctrine of creation leads to an account of historical location and creaturely limitations as essential aspects of our existence. For we cannot claim unmediated access to the Scriptures without acknowledging the place of tradition: theology is an irreducibly communal task. *Listening to the Past* is a sustained attempt to show what listening to tradition involves, and how it can be used to aid theological work today.

2002 / 1-84227-155-5 / xiv + 168pp

Mark Hopkins
Nonconformity's Romantic Generation
Evangelical and Liberal Theologies in Victorian England
(Studies in Evangelical History and Thought)
A study of the theological development of key leaders of the Baptist and Congregational denominations at their period of greatest influence, including C.H. Spurgeon and R.W. Dale, and of the controversies in which those among them who embraced and rejected the liberal transformation of their evangelical heritage opposed each other.

2004 / 1-84227-150-4 / xvi + 284pp

Galen K. Johnson
Prisoner of Conscience
John Bunyan on Self, Community and Christian Faith
(Studies in Christian History and Thought)

This is an interdisciplinary study of John Bunyan's understanding of conscience across his autobiographical, theological and fictional writings, investigating whether conscience always deserves fidelity, and how Bunyan's view of conscience affects his relationship both to modern Western individualism and historic Christianity.

2003 / 1-84227- 151-2 / xvi + 236pp

R.T. Kendall
Calvin and English Calvinism to 1649
(Studies in Christian History and Thought)

The author's thesis is that those who formed the Westminster Confession of Faith, which is regarded as Calvinism, in fact departed from John Calvin on two points: (1) the extent of the atonement and (2) the ground of assurance of salvation.

1997 / 0-85364-827-1 / xii + 264pp

Timothy Larsen
Friends of Religious Equality
Nonconformist Politics in Mid-Victorian England

During the middle decades of the nineteenth century the English Nonconformist community developed a coherent political philosophy of its own, of which a central tenet was the principle of religious equality (in contrast to the stereotype of Evangelical Dissenters). The Dissenting community fought for the civil rights of Roman Catholics, non-Christians and even atheists, on an issue of principle which had its flowering in the enthusiastic and undivided support which Nonconformity gave to the campaign for Jewish emancipation. This reissued study examines the political efforts and ideas of English Nonconformists during the period, covering the whole range of national issues raised, from state education to the Crimean War. It offers a case study of a theologically conservative group defending religious pluralism in the civic sphere, showing that the concept of religious equality was a grand vision at the centre of the political philosophy of the Dissenters.

2007 / 1-84227-402-3 / x + 300pp

Donald M. Lewis
Lighten Their Darkness
The Evangelical Mission to Working-Class London, 1828–1860
(Studies in Evangelical History and Thought)

This is a comprehensive and compelling study of the Church and the complexities of nineteenth-century London. Challenging our understanding of the culture in working London at this time, Lewis presents a well-structured and illustrated work that contributes substantially to the study of evangelicalism and mission in nineteenth-century Britain.

2001 / 1-84227-074-5 / xviii + 372pp

Stanley E. Porter and Anthony R. Cross (eds)
Semper Reformandum
Studies in Honour of Clark H. Pinnock

Clark Pinnock has clearly been one of the most important evangelical theologians of the last forty years in North America. Always provocative, especially in the wide range of opinions he has held and considered, Pinnock, himself a Baptist, has recently retired after twenty-five years of teaching at McMaster Divinity College. His colleagues and associates honour him in this volume by responding to his important theological work which has dealt with the essential topics of evangelical theology. These include Christian apologetics, biblical inspiration, the Holy Spirit and, perhaps most importantly in recent years, openness theology.

2003 / 1-84227-206-3 / xiv + 414pp

Meic Pearse
The Great Restoration
The Religious Radicals of the 16th and 17th Centuries

Pearse charts the rise and progress of continental Anabaptism – both evangelical and heretical – through the sixteenth century. He then follows the story of those English people who became impatient with Puritanism and separated – first from the Church of England and then from one another – to form the antecedents of later Congregationalists, Baptists and Quakers.

1998 / 0-85364-800-X / xii + 320pp

Charles Price and Ian M. Randall
Transforming Keswick

Transforming Keswick is a thorough, readable and detailed history of the convention. It will be of interest to those who know and love Keswick, those who are only just discovering it, and serious scholars eager to learn more about the history of God's dealings with his people.

2000 / 1-85078-350-0 / 288pp

Jim Purves
The Triune God and the Charismatic Movement
A Critical Appraisal from a Scottish Perspective
(Paternoster Theological Monographs)

All emotion and no theology? Or a fundamental challenge to reappraise and realign our trinitarian theology in the light of Christian experience? This study of charismatic renewal as it found expression within Scotland at the end of the twentieth century evaluates the use of Patristic, Reformed and contemporary models (including those of the Baptist Union of Scotland) of the Trinity in explaining the workings of the Holy Spirit.

2004 / 1-84227-321-3 / xxiv + 246pp

Ian M. Randall
Evangelical Experiences
A Study in the Spirituality of English Evangelicalism 1918–1939
(Studies in Evangelical History and Thought)

This book makes a detailed historical examination of evangelical spirituality between the First and Second World Wars. It shows how patterns of devotion led to tensions and divisions. In a wide-ranging study, Anglican, Wesleyan, Reformed and Pentecostal-charismatic spiritualities are analysed.

1999 / 0-85364-919-7 / xii + 310pp

Ian M. Randall
One Body in Christ
The History and Significance of the Evangelical Alliance

In 1846 the Evangelical Alliance was founded with the aim of bringing together evangelicals for common action. This book uses material not previously utilized to examine the history and significance of the Evangelical Alliance, a movement which has remained a powerful force for unity. At a time when evangelicals are growing world-wide, this book offers insights into the past which are relevant to contemporary issues.

2001 / 1-84227-089-3 / xii + 394pp

Ian M. Randall
Spirituality and Social Change
The Contribution of F.B. Meyer (1847–1929)
(Studies in Evangelical History and Thought)

This is a fresh appraisal of F.B. Meyer (1847–1929), a leading Free Church minister. Having been deeply affected by holiness spirituality, Meyer became the Keswick Convention's foremost international speaker. He combined spirituality with effective evangelism and socio-political activity. This study shows Meyer's significant contribution to spiritual renewal and social change.

2003 / 1-84227-195-4 / xx + 184pp

Geoffrey Robson
Dark Satanic Mills?
Religion and Irreligion in Birmingham and the Black Country
(Studies in Evangelical History and Thought)
This book analyses and interprets the nature and extent of popular Christian belief and practice in Birmingham and the Black Country during the first half of the nineteenth century, with particular reference to the impact of cholera epidemics and evangelism on church extension programmes.
2002 / 1-84227-102-4 / xiv + 294pp

Alan P.F. Sell
Enlightenment, Ecumenism, Evangel
Theological Themes and Thinkers 1550–2000
(Studies in Christian History and Thought)
This book consists of papers in which such interlocking topics as the Enlightenment, the problem of authority, the development of doctrine, spirituality, ecumenism, theological method and the heart of the gospel are discussed. Issues of significance to the church at large are explored with special reference to writers from the Reformed and Dissenting traditions.
2005 / 1-84227330-2 / xviii + 422pp

Alan P.F. Sell
Hinterland Theology
Some Reformed and Dissenting Adjustments
(Studies in Christian History and Thought)
Many books have been written on theology's 'giants' and significant trends, but what of those lesser-known writers who adjusted to them? In this book some hinterland theologians of the British Reformed and Dissenting traditions, who followed in the wake of toleration, the Evangelical Revival, the rise of modern biblical criticism and Karl Barth, are allowed to have their say. They include Thomas Ridgley, Ralph Wardlaw, T.V. Tymms and N.H.G. Robinson.
2006 / 1-84227-331-0

Alan P.F. Sell and Anthony R. Cross (eds)
Protestant Nonconformity in the Twentieth Century
(Studies in Christian History and Thought)
In this collection of essays scholars representative of a number of Nonconformist traditions reflect thematically on Nonconformists' life and witness during the twentieth century. Among the subjects reviewed are biblical studies, theology, worship, evangelism and spirituality, and ecumenism. Over and above its immediate interest, this collection provides a marker to future scholars and others wishing to know how some of their forebears assessed Nonconformity's contribution to a variety of fields during the century leading up to Christianity's third millennium.
2003 / 1-84227-221-7 / x + 398pp

Mark Smith
Religion in Industrial Society
Oldham and Saddleworth 1740–1865
(Studies in Christian History and Thought)
This book analyses the way British churches sought to meet the challenge of industrialization and urbanization during the period 1740–1865. Working from a case-study of Oldham and Saddleworth, Mark Smith challenges the received view that the Anglican Church in the eighteenth century was characterized by complacency and inertia, and reveals Anglicanism's vigorous and creative response to the new conditions. He reassesses the significance of the centrally directed church reforms of the mid-nineteenth century, and emphasizes the importance of local energy and enthusiasm. Charting the growth of denominational pluralism in Oldham and Saddleworth, Dr Smith compares the strengths and weaknesses of the various Anglican and Nonconformist approaches to promoting church growth. He also demonstrates the extent to which all the churches participated in a common culture shaped by the influence of evangelicalism, and shows that active co-operation between the churches rather than denominational conflict dominated. This revised and updated edition of Dr Smith's challenging and original study makes an important contribution both to the social history of religion and to urban studies.
2006 / 1-84227-335-3 / approx. 300pp

David M. Thompson
Baptism, Church and Society in Britain from the Evangelical Revival to *Baptism, Eucharist and Ministry*

The theology and practice of baptism have not received the attention they deserve. How important is faith? What does baptismal regeneration mean? Is baptism a bond of unity between Christians? This book discusses the theology of baptism and popular belief and practice in England and Wales from the Evangelical Revival to the publication of the World Council of Churches' consensus statement on *Baptism, Eucharist and Ministry* (1982).

2005 / 1-84227-393-0 / approx. 224pp

Martin Sutherland
Peace, Toleration and Decay
The Ecclesiology of Later Stuart Dissent
(Studies in Christian History and Thought)

This fresh analysis brings to light the complexity and fragility of the later Stuart Nonconformist consensus. Recent findings on wider seventeenth-century thought are incorporated into a new picture of the dynamics of Dissent and the roots of evangelicalism.

2003 / 1-84227-152-0 / xxii + 216pp

Haddon Willmer
Evangelicalism 1785–1835: An Essay (1962) and Reflections (2004)
(Studies in Evangelical History and Thought)

Awarded the Hulsean Prize in the University of Cambridge in 1962, this interpretation of a classic period of English Evangelicalism, by a young church historian, is now supplemented by reflections on Evangelicalism from the vantage point of a retired Professor of Theology.

2006 / 1-84227-219-5

Linda Wilson
Constrained by Zeal
Female Spirituality amongst Nonconformists 1825–1875
(Studies in Evangelical History and Thought)

Constrained by Zeal investigates the neglected area of Nonconformist female spirituality. Against the background of separate spheres, it analyses the experience of women from four denominations, and argues that the churches provided a 'third sphere' in which they could find opportunities for participation.

2000 / 0-85364-972-3 / xvi + 294pp

July 2005

Nigel G. Wright
Disavowing Constantine
*Mission, Church and the Social Order in the Theologies of
John Howard Yoder and Jürgen Moltmann*
(Paternoster Theological Monographs)

This book is a timely restatement of a radical theology of church and state in the Anabaptist and Baptist tradition. Dr Wright constructs his argument in dialogue and debate with Yoder and Moltmann, major contributors to a free church perspective.

2000 / 0-85364-978-2 / xvi + 252pp

Nigel G. Wright
Free Church, Free State
The Positive Baptist Vision

Free Church, Free State is a textbook on baptist ways of being church and a proposal for the future of baptist churches in an ecumenical context. Nigel Wright argues that both baptist (small 'b') and catholic (small 'c') church traditions should seek to enrich and support each other as valid expressions of the body of Christ without sacrificing what they hold dear. Written for pastors, church planters, evangelists and preachers, Nigel Wright offers frameworks of thought for baptists and non-baptists in their journey together following Christ.

2005 / 1-84227-353-1 / xxviii + 292

Nigel G. Wright
New Baptists, New Agenda

New Baptists, New Agenda is a timely contribution to the growing debate about the health, shape and future of the Baptists. It considers the steady changes that have taken place among Baptists in the last decade – changes of mood, style, practice and structure – and encourages us to align these current movements and questions with God's upward and future call. He contends that the true church has yet to come: the church that currently exists is an anticipation of the joyful gathering of all who have been called by the Spirit through Christ to the Father.

2002 / 1-84227-157-1 / x + 162pp

Paternoster
9 Holdom Avenue,
Bletchley,
Milton Keynes MK1 1QR,
United Kingdom
Web: www.authenticmedia.co.uk/paternoster

July 2005

٢

www.ingramcontent.com/pod-product-compliance
Lightning Source LLC
Chambersburg PA
CBHW071141300426
44113CB00009B/1042